ROWING BLAZERS

JACK CARLSON

PHOTOGRAPHS BY

F.E CASTLEBERRY, ADRIAN KRAJEWSKI

and

URŠA MALI

Thames & Hudson

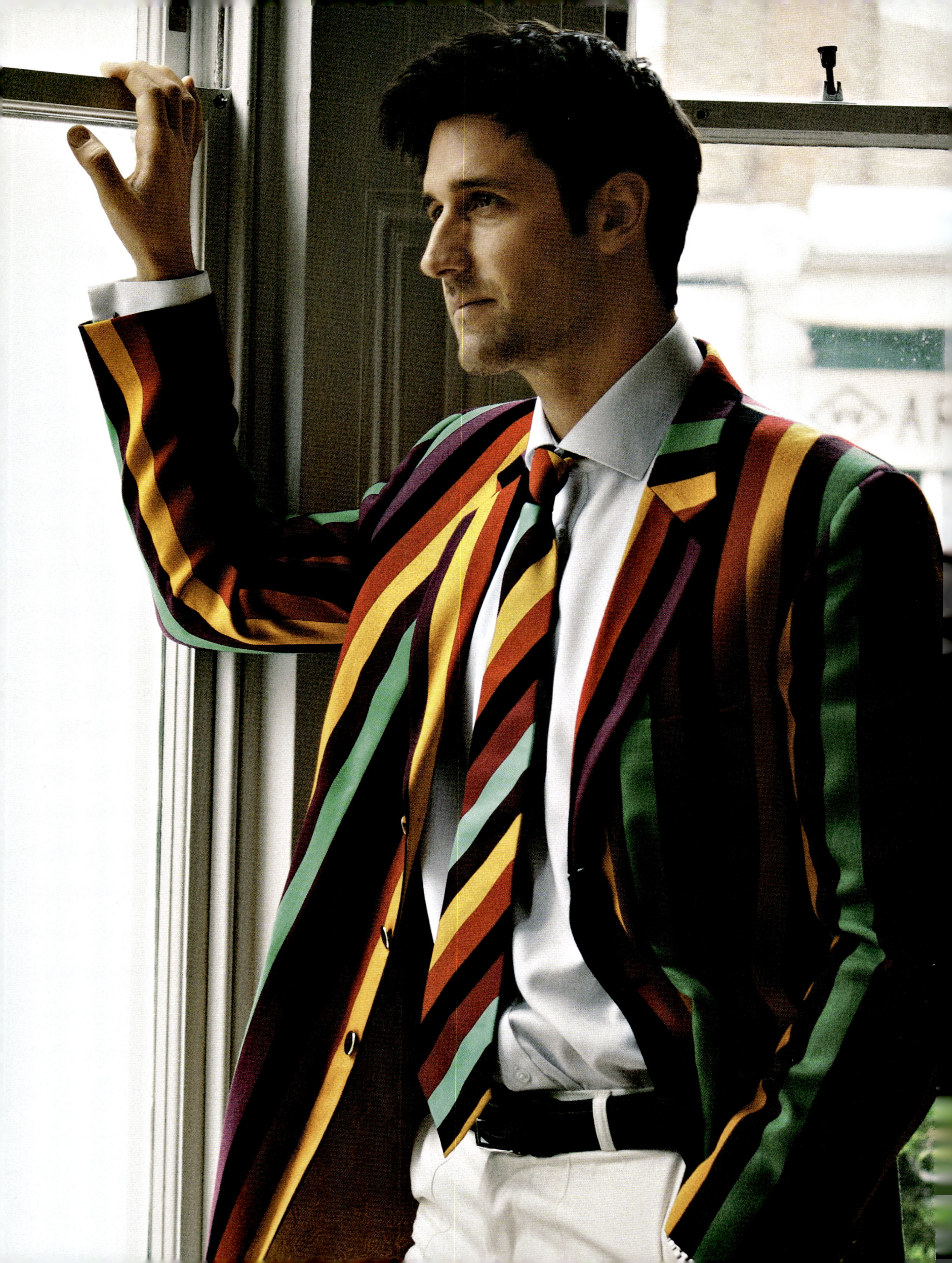

Contents

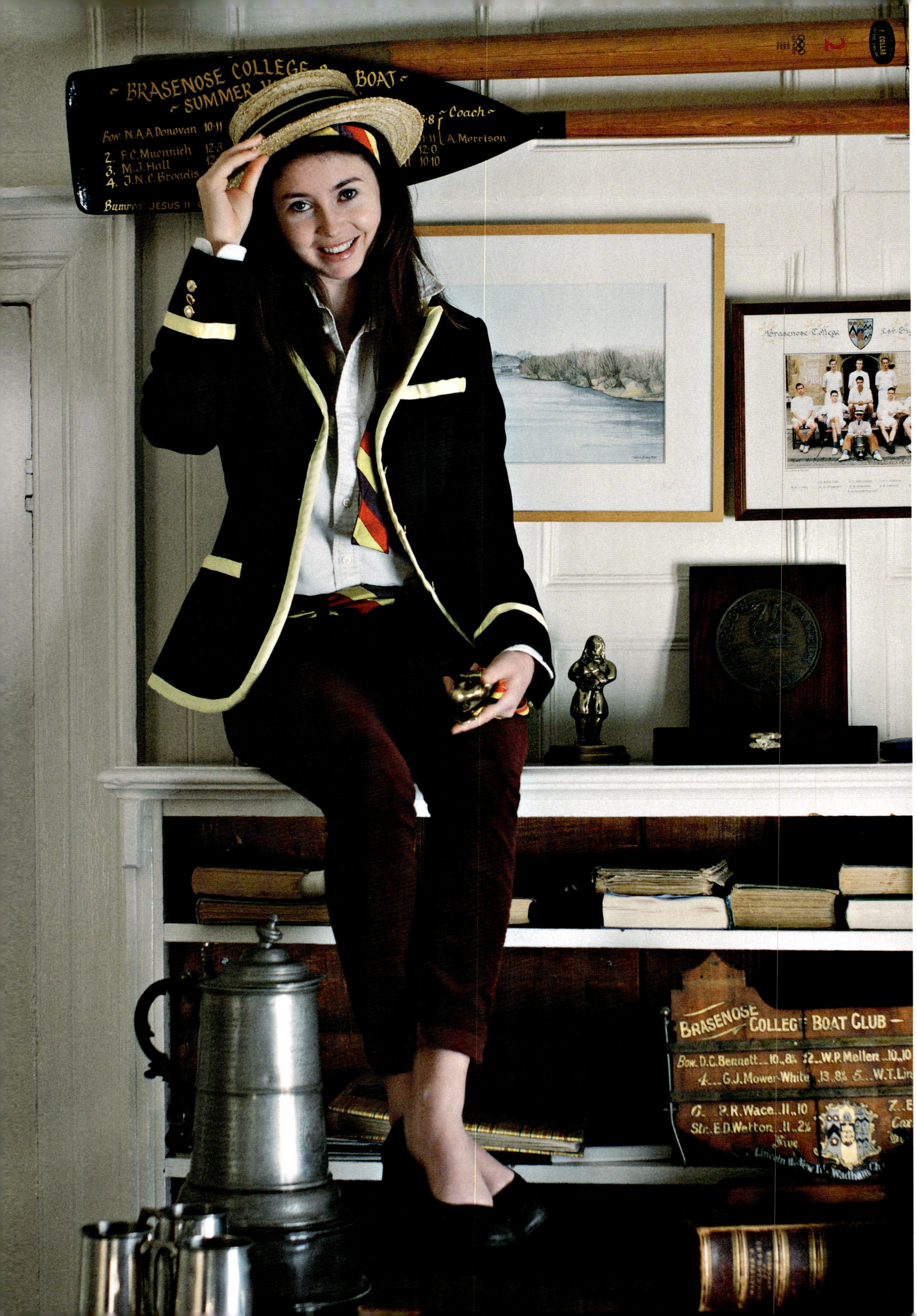
BRASENOSE COLLEGE
BOAT
SUMMER
Coach
Bow. N.A.A.Donovan 10-11
2. F.C.Muennich 12-3
3. M.J.Hall
4. J.N.C.Broadis
A.Morrison
Bumped JESUS
BRASENOSE COLLEGE BOAT CLUB
Bow. D.C.Bennett
W.P.Mellen
G.J.Mower-White
6. P.R.Wace 11..10
Str. E.D.Welton

Preface

My own blazer journey began in 2004. My crew, it was announced, would be crossing the Atlantic to race on the hallowed waters of the Thames at the world-famous Henley Royal Regatta. After a training session one sunny day in May, we all walked to the Andover Shop in Harvard Square—the most traditional of traditional New England tailors—so that we could be measured for our blazers. We were schoolboys, and we approached the occasion with disproportionate solemnity and smugness. That smugness quickly wore off at the regatta itself, when we were knocked out in the first round. The venerable competition is a series of do-or-die two-boat races, and when one loses, one is out. But our elimination did leave us with plenty of time to study and admire the bewildering array of club blazers swanning about the regatta's spectator enclosures. The gaudy stripes and absurd color combinations made our blazers—navy blue with bright white binding and a pocket badge—look positively mundane.

The experience imbued me with a ravenous determination to win Henley (a goal I finally achieved nine years later). It also left me with an intense interest in the pageantry of rowing blazers and their colorful histories and traditions. Nearly a decade after my first trip to Henley, I found myself ideally placed to investigate these bizarre vestments in depth as a doctoral student at Oxford University (spiritual home of the boating jacket and one of the few places in the world where rowing blazers are still a perfectly ordinary sight).

The rowing world is a small one. Club rivalries notwithstanding, members of the rowing community are always willing to help one another and assist in any effort that promotes the sport. So—thanks to the fraternal spirit and enthusiasm of hundreds of rowers (and coxswains)—I was able to arrange visits to rowing clubs around the world and photo shoots with some of the most prominent oarsmen and -women at these clubs. I recruited a number of excellent photographers to accompany me, including F.E. Castleberry, the celebrated photographer of "prep" culture; Adrian Krajewski; Urša Mali; Jory Cordy; and Matt Burrard-Lucas.

Nearly three years of traveling took us to the world's most historic clubs, prestigious campuses, and beautiful boathouses—from Eton to Exeter, New Haven to New Zealand. We photographed college crews and the world's most decorated Olympic rowers. We heard the secret histories and esoteric traditions behind the blazers. We jumped over burning boats in Oxford, slept on strangers' couches in Wisconsin, and witnessed beer-soaked blazer rituals in the Netherlands.

There are a great many people whom I cannot thank enough and without whose help and hospitality I could not have made this book. I have listed as many of these individuals as I can on page 254. This book does not attempt to be exhaustive (though I sincerely wish that I could have included more clubs and more blazers), but I do hope that it brings the rowing community in touch with our sport's colorful heritage and serves as an introduction for the uninitiated into an otherwise arcane world. I felt in 2004, and still feel today, that one's imagination cannot help being captured by the garish, mysterious, sporty splendor of rowing blazers.

Jack Carlson

OXFORD, ENGLAND

OPPOSITE: Victoria Stulgis wears her Brasenose College Boat Club blazer and Childe of Hale colors.

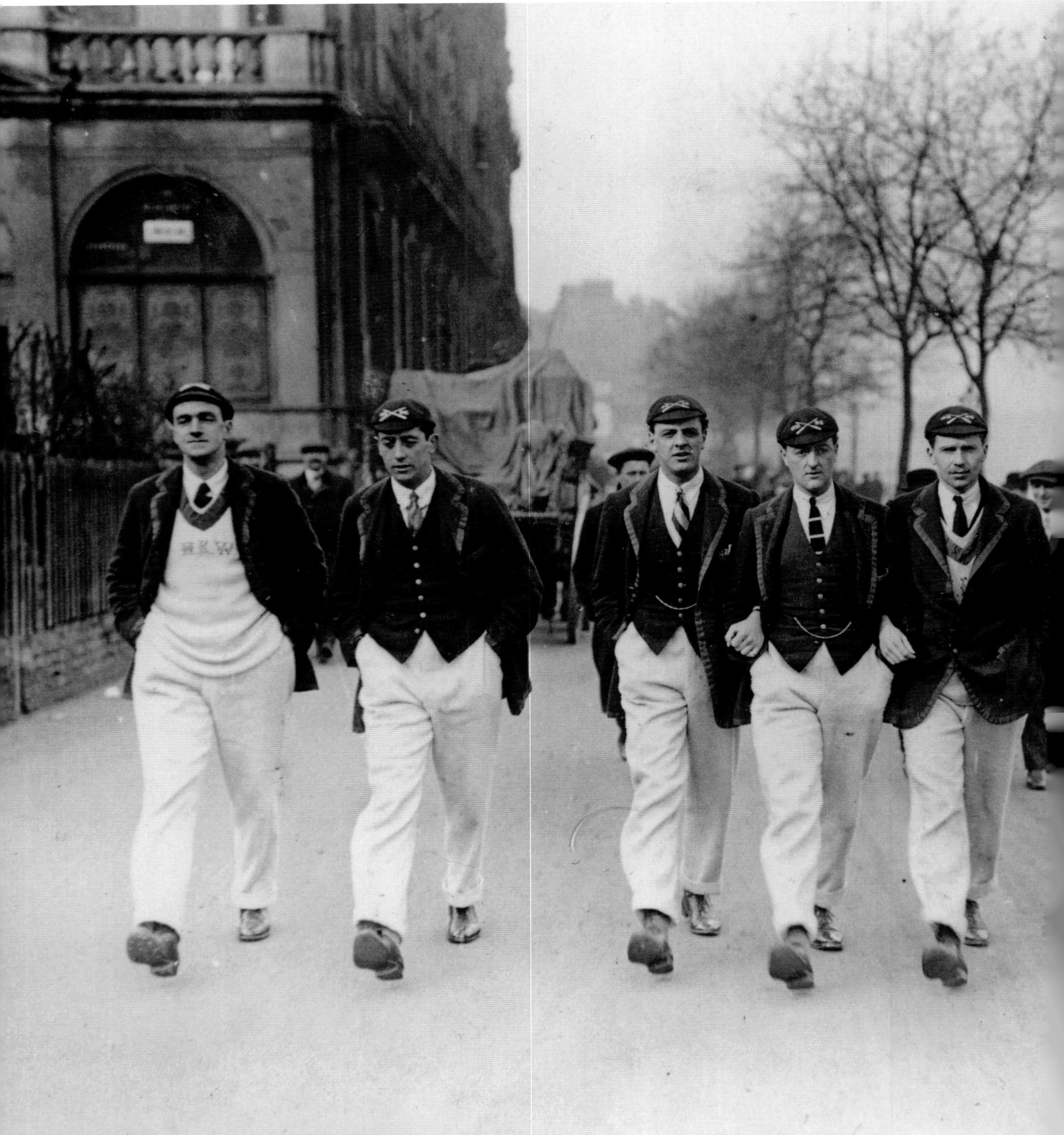

The 1913 Oxford University crew, walking along the riverbank in Putney.

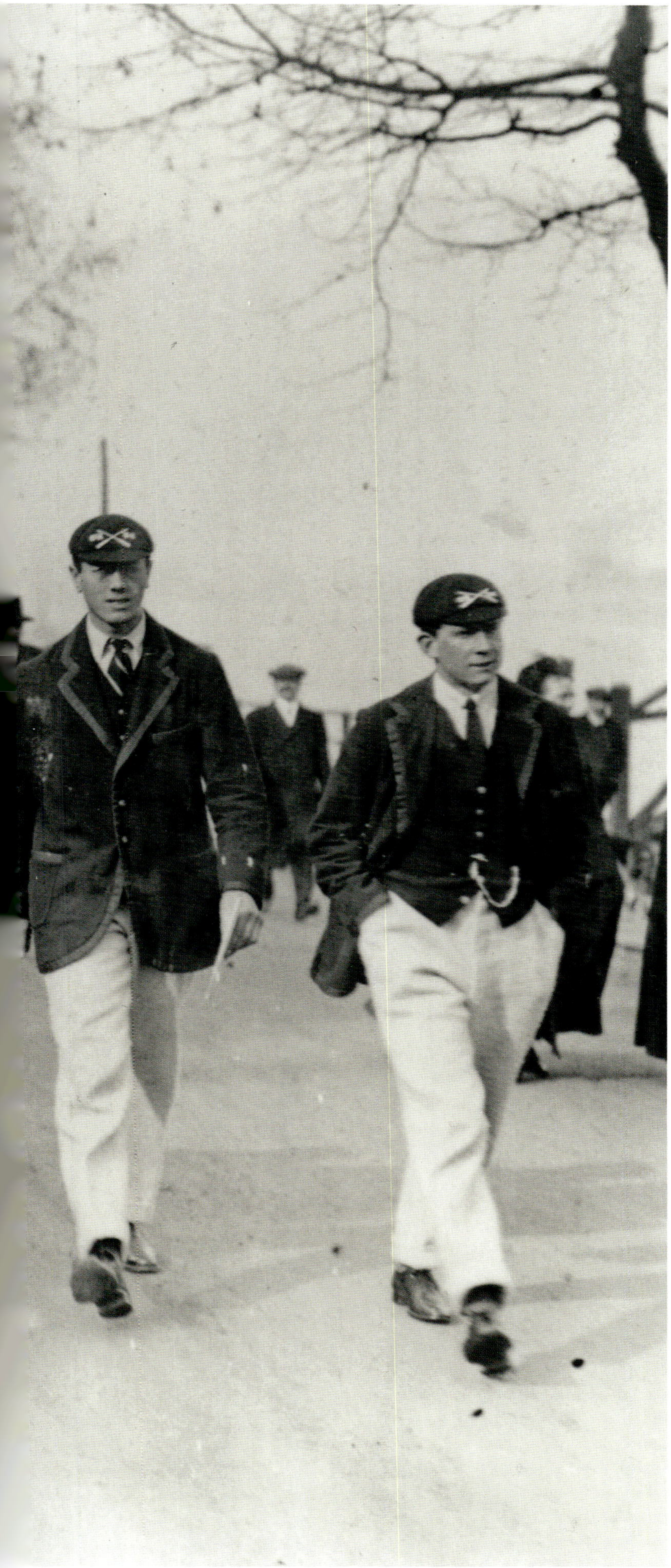

Introduction

"Blazer \'blā-zər\

(originally Cambridge: now general): –

A light jacket of bright colour. Originally applied to the bright red uniform of the Lady Margaret Boat Club of St. John's College, Cambridge."

— J. S. Farmer, *The Public School Word-Book*, 1900

THE BLAZER: A SARTORIAL ICON

There is no article of clothing that can quite match the blazer in both pedigree and street cred. The now-ubiquitous dark blue blazer is inexorably British but has become a permanent icon of American style. The blazer is both ineffably cool and deeply traditional, equally at ease on a boat or in the boardroom, in the classroom or the club. Wear it with Oxford shoes, deck shoes, or no shoes; with gray flannels, white ducks, blue jeans, or Nantucket reds; at Christmastime or on halcyon summer days. A blazer is almost always the "right" thing to wear; it is no wonder that the famous *Official Preppy Handbook* referred to the blazer simply as "the exoskeleton."

THE BIRTH OF THE BOATING JACKET

> *"The barges of the colleges, painted different colors and gilded like circus band-wagons and decorated with coats of arms and flying great flags, lined the one shore for a quarter of a mile and were covered by girls in pretty frocks and undergrads in blazers."* —Richard Harding Davis, 1892

Like victory at Waterloo, classic American and British style was born on the proverbial playing fields of England—or, in this case, its rivers. For the blazer, that staple of twenty-first-century menswear, has its origins in the rowing kit of the great British schools and universities, where the very first blazers were created in bold colors for college boat clubs.

As early as 1805, when rowing was still a leisure activity rather than a competitive sport at Oxford, informal boating clubs with their own colors and uniform codes of dress began to develop in earnest. By the 1820s, the sport had come into

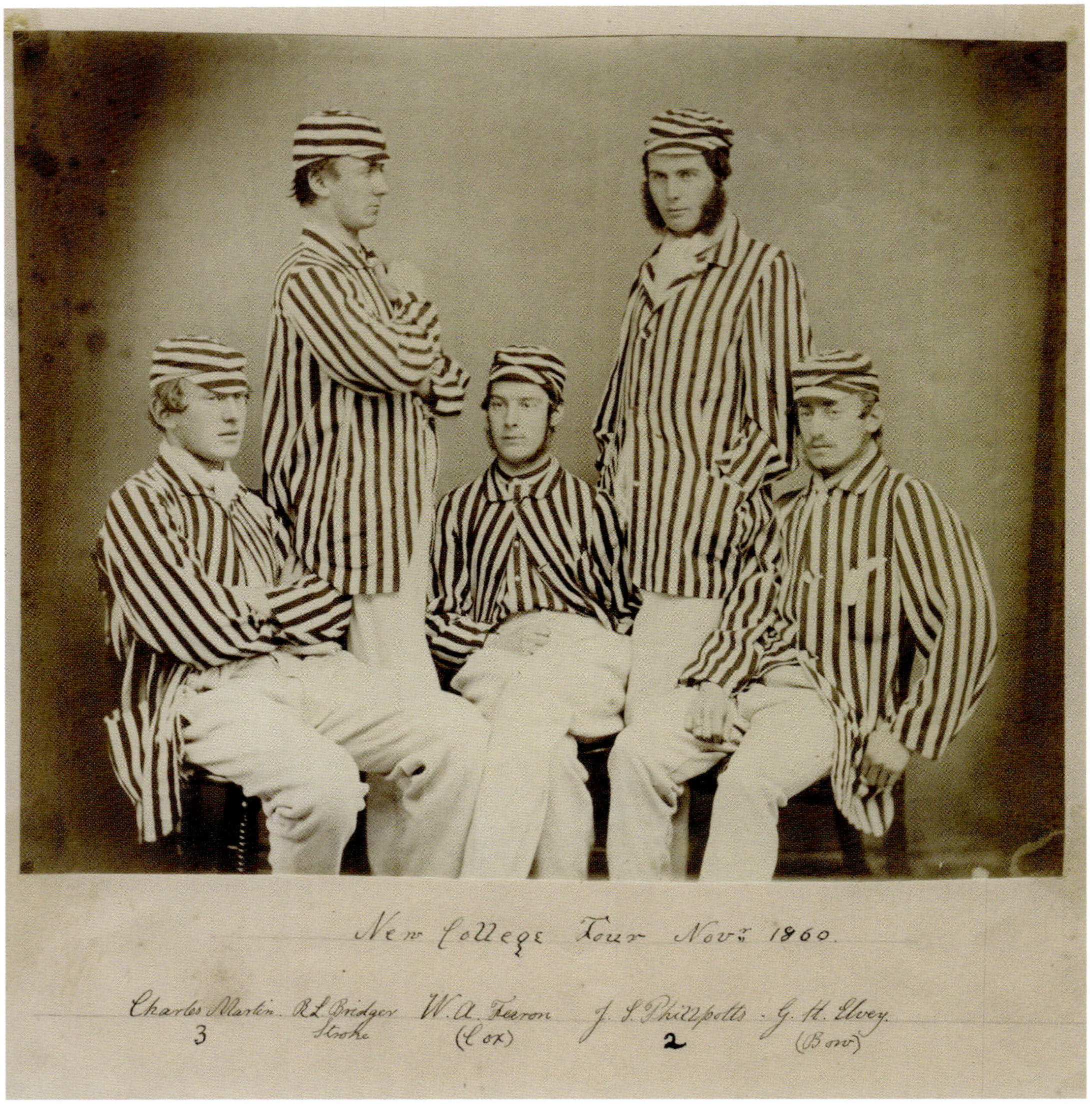

RIGHT:
Crew from New College, Oxford, 1860.

BELOW:
Amy Gentry receiving the Women's Sculling Championship Trophy from Bossie Phelps, 1932.

OPPOSITE:
The 1932 Shrewsbury School Boat Club first eight, winners of the Ladies' Challenge Plate at the Henley Royal Regatta.

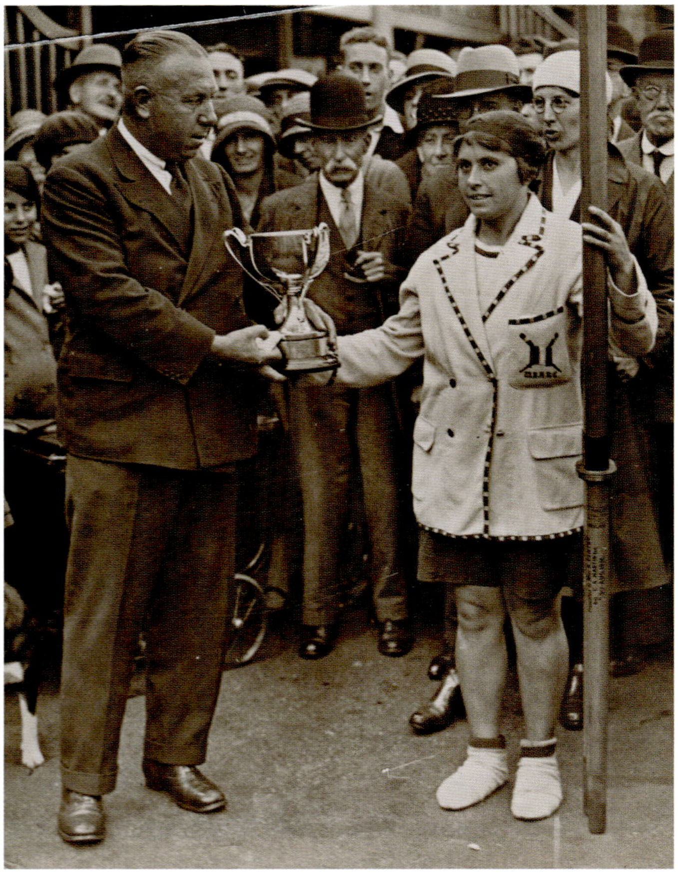

its own at both Oxford and Cambridge. Each of the many colleges within the two universities had its own boat club, and these clubs competed against each other in bumping races. (This special racing format, still used at Oxford and Cambridge, requires crews to start in single file with each crew attempting to crash, or "bump," into the crew ahead.) It was in this period, and at these clubs, that the first flannel "rowing jackets" or "boating coats" appeared.

These coats served a practical purpose, keeping oarsmen warm during chilly training sessions on the River Cam and on the Isis in Oxford. But even in this formative period, rowers seem to have developed a peculiar attachment to their jackets, not only wearing them in the boats but also incorporating them into their daily dress on terra firma.

These rowers were the world's first true student-athletes. And like their successors—the stereotypical "jocks" of twentieth-century America, who were inseparable from their hard-earned letterman sweaters or leather-sleeved varsity jackets—the earliest oarsmen probably started wearing their prototypical blazers in social settings for the sake of showing off. An 1826 publication records a fictional exchange between a landlady and a rather rude Oxford oarsman:

"Shall I take your rowing jacket, sir?"
"No, you fat piece of one-eyed womanhood! . . . I choose to go to College in this dress. Lend me my straw hat."

—*The Literary Lounger*, May 1826

By the mid-nineteenth century, rowing jackets were becoming a standard component of the Oxbridge gentleman's wardrobe. In the 1854 novel *Crewe-Rise* by John Cordy Jeaffreson, one of the characters dons his old boating coat and declares: "This is almost the only useful article of dress I took away with me from Oxford." But rowers and their distinctive jackets were also becoming targets of ire and jealousy. Oxford college authorities took measures "not to allow undergraduates to lounge about in College in their Boating dress," as the Magdalen president put it in 1859, while "Boating Snobs" were caricatured in local magazines:

If he be a Boating Snob, he will weary your ears with river "shop." . . . On Sundays, when decent people are either at Church or out walking, he lolls out of a friend's window in smoking cap and boating jacket.

—*Magdalen College School Journal*, March 1871

FROM BOATING JACKETS TO BLAZERS

"I have stood and watched it, sometimes, when you could not see any water at all, but only a brilliant tangle of bright blazers . . . when looking down into the lock from the quay, you might fancy it was a huge box into which flowers of every hue and shade had been thrown pell-mell, and lay piled up in a rainbow heap, that covered every corner."

—Jerome K. Jerome, *Three Men in a Boat*, 1890

Many of the early boating jackets were brightly colored and bound with ribbon in contrasting colors. Some were embroidered with insignia derived from collegiate heraldry and studded with brilliant, bespoke club buttons. The chosen colors and details comprised a code that revealed the college, club, and particular crew with which a rower was affiliated. The British, after all, have always had a hyper-awareness of subtle social distinctions and a flair for uniforms and pageantry. But the loud colors also served the practical purpose of helping distant spectators tell which boat was which during races.

It was one of these brightly colored designs that introduced the word *blazer* into the English vocabulary: the vivid scarlet

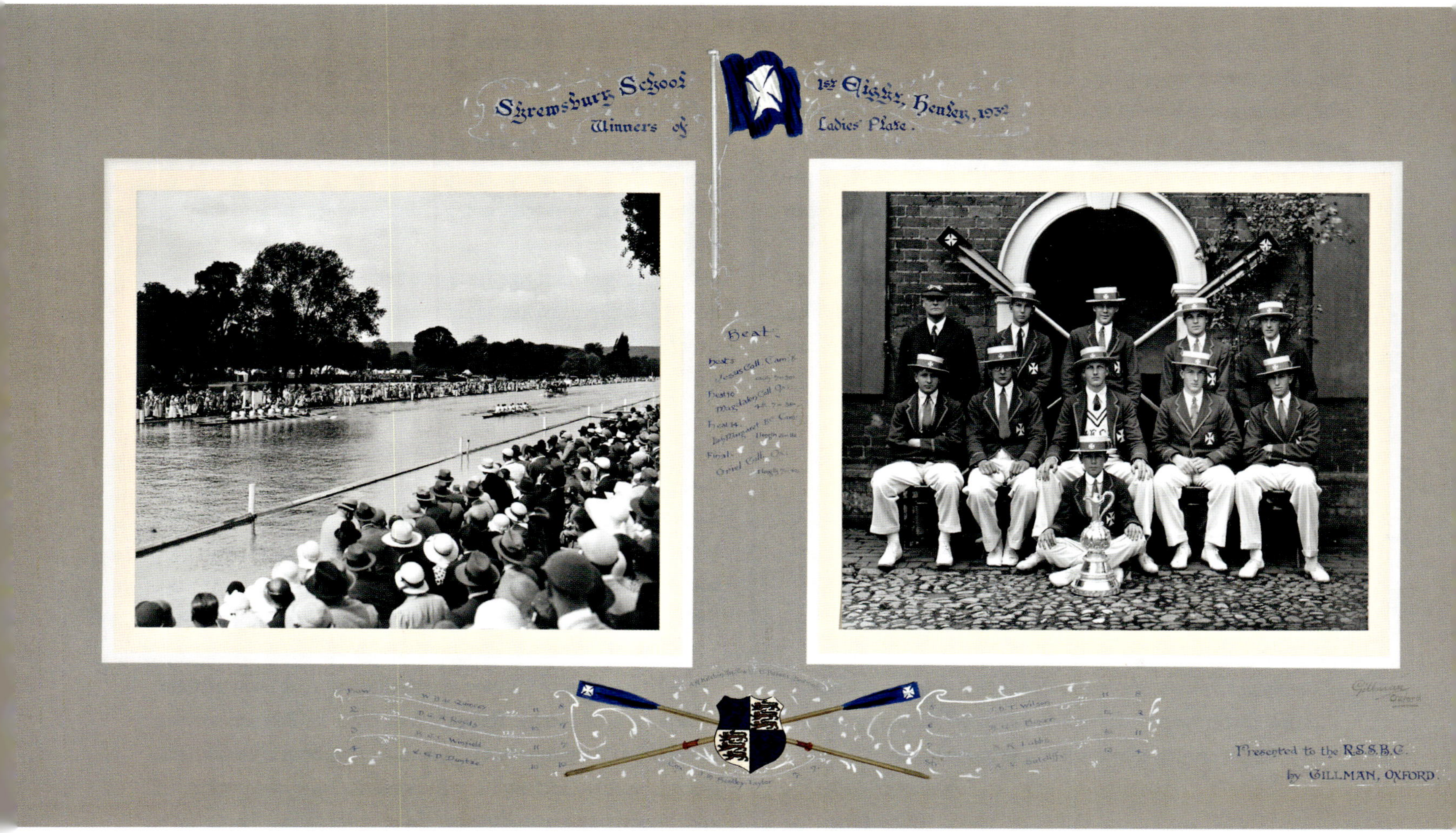

boating coats of Lady Margaret Boat Club at St. John's College, Cambridge, were nicknamed "blazers" on account of their "blazing red" hue. The first-known use of the word to refer to an article of clothing appears in the *Cambridge University General Almanack and Register* for 1852, which offers descriptions of each club's rowing uniform. These descriptions generally refer to boating jackets as flannel "coats" or "over-jerseys," except for Lady Margaret's, which is described as a red "blazer," with the word in quotation marks:

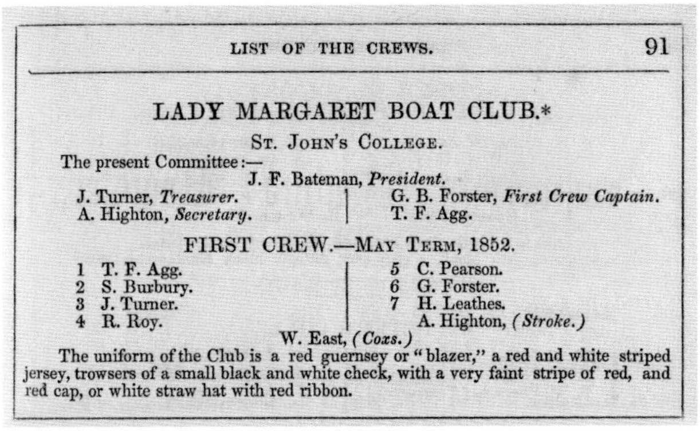
LIST OF THE CREWS. 91

LADY MARGARET BOAT CLUB.*

ST. JOHN'S COLLEGE.

The present Committee:—

J. F. Bateman, *President.*

J. Turner, *Treasurer.*	G. B. Forster, *First Crew Captain.*
A. Highton, *Secretary.*	T. F. Agg.

FIRST CREW.—MAY TERM, 1852.

1 T. F. Agg.	5 C. Pearson.
2 S. Burbury.	6 G. Forster.
3 J. Turner.	7 H. Leathes.
4 R. Roy.	A. Highton, *(Stroke.)*

W. East, *(Coxs.)*

The uniform of the Club is a red guernsey or "blazer," a red and white striped jersey, trowsers of a small black and white check, with a very faint stripe of red, and red cap, or white straw hat with red ribbon.

By the following decade, the word had become more than a slang term and could be used without quotation marks, although it still applied exclusively to the Lady Margaret jackets. It was not until the 1870 edition that the *Almanack and Register* began to refer to other colleges' boating coats as blazers.

By the 1880s, the word had traveled beyond Cambridge to the other major rowing universities, Oxford and Durham, where increasingly loud and colorful jackets were already popular among student rowers. From there, the term entered the mainstream lexicon but gradually lost its specific association with the sport of rowing; it even became possible to speak of "cricket blazers" and "rugby blazers."

In short, the word *blazer* has been appropriated and reappropriated, growing increasingly general in meaning. The popularization of this obscure jargon-word inspired one bemused Cambridge graduate to write a letter to the *Daily News* in 1889:

Aug. 22, 1889

Sir –

In your article of to-day . . . you speak of a "striped red and black blazer" . . . also of "the pale toned" ones. This is worth noting as a case of the specific becoming the generic. A blazer is the red flannel boating jacket worn by the Lady Margaret, St. John's College, Cambridge, Boat Club. When I was at Cambridge it meant that and nothing else. It seems from your article that a blazer now means a coloured flannel jacket, whether for cricket, tennis, boating, or seaside wear.

Yours faithfully,

Walter Wren.

There is an oft-repeated myth that the blazer has its origins in the jackets worn by the crew of the H.M.S. *Blazer* in the mid-nineteenth century. But this is a classic case of false etymology. Though seductively convenient, this alternate history is not borne out by the evidence.

BLAZER GLORY

"Blazers were striped, piped, and ribboned, rivalling the foppery of the Court of King Charles II. . . . I am describing the arcane to you. Only a very select few will ever have the privilege to access exclusive yacht or rowing clubs with their own secret symbols. But who can resist the blazer with its glittering buttons?" —J. J. Lee, *The Measure of a Man*, 2011

Authentic striped, trimmed, and badged rowing blazers are still worn with the greatest pride by oarsmen and -women around the world today. There are school rowing blazers, college and university rowing blazers, and rowing blazers for private and civic rowing clubs. Some blazers are affiliated with no club at all, but rather serve as prizes for the winners of particular races. This tradition has its origins in the oldest annual sporting event in the world, the sculling race for Doggett's Coat and Badge, held in London every year since 1715.

Some clubs have a single blazer design for all members. Others have many different blazers, with special distinctions for rowers in the top crew, second crew, and novice crew, or for club officers, record holders, and championship winners. Many have vast and elaborate systems that determine the blazer's color; the size or shade of the jacket's edging, or binding; the number of stripes on a sleeve; the composition of the badge; and which caps, ties, and waistcoats may be worn with the blazer.

Rowing jackets range from the understated to the absurd, and it is difficult to say which end of the spectrum is more prestigious. Those worn by the top Oxford crew are plain dark blue with matching dark blue grosgrain trim; they do not feature any pocket badge at all, out of respect for the fact that Oxford University Boat Club's blazer is the original "blue blazer." The blazers of the elite and enigmatic Cambridge Archetypals, meanwhile, are striped light blue, magenta, black, red, yellow, and indigo. The club's ties, socks, caps, scarves, and even watchbands feature the same stripes. As Jerome K. Jerome wrote of an equally gaudy blazer in 1890: "The blazer is loud. . . . There is really no other word for it."

Each nation has its own particular set of blazer rituals, which vary, of course, from club to club. In Britain, rowing blazers are de rigueur battle gear at riotous boat club dinners, garden parties, and traditional regattas. American oarsmen and oarswomen usually earn their coveted jackets only by

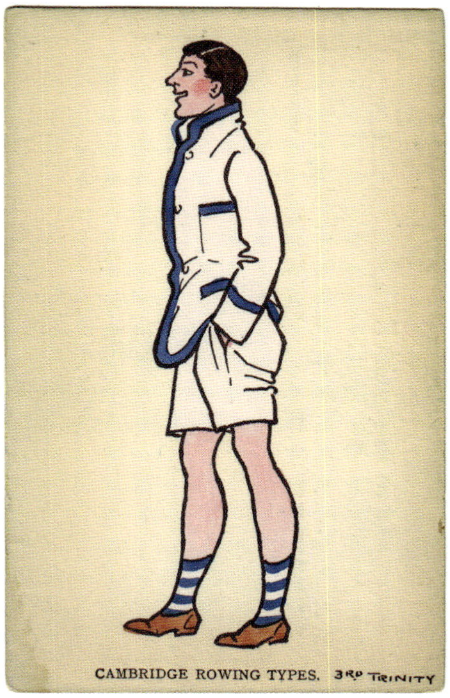

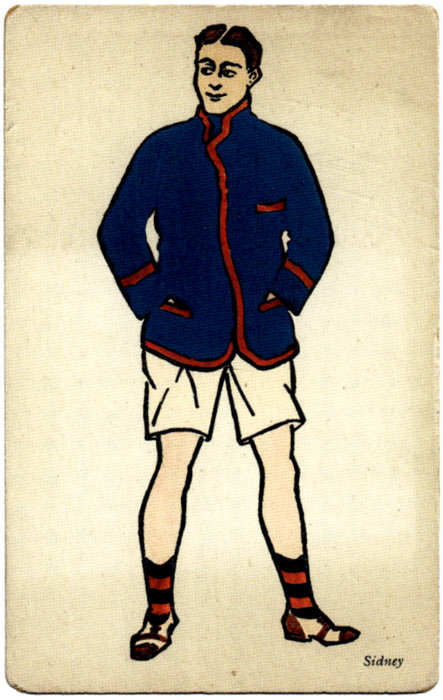

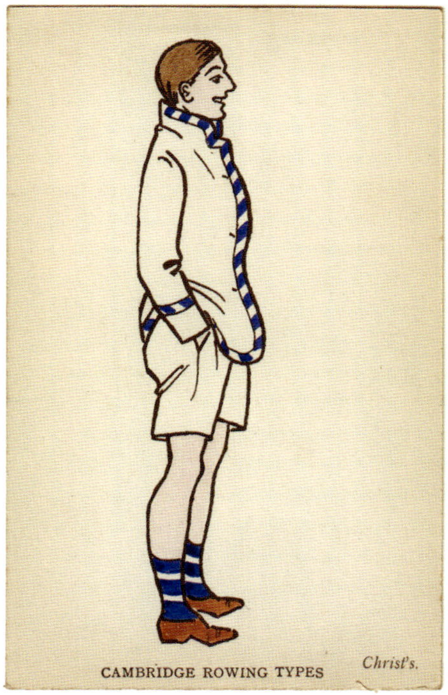

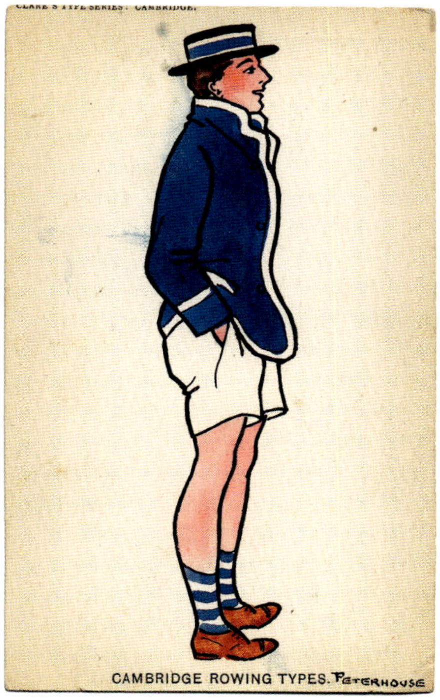

“ROWING BLAZERS

ARE TRIBAL TOTEMS,

WORN TO EMPHASIZE

BOTH COMMUNITY

and

DIFFERENCE”

Collectible cards depicting the college rowing blazers of Cambridge, ca. 1908.

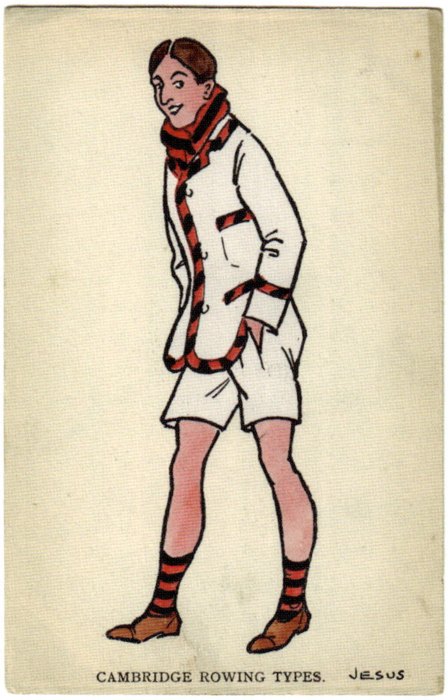

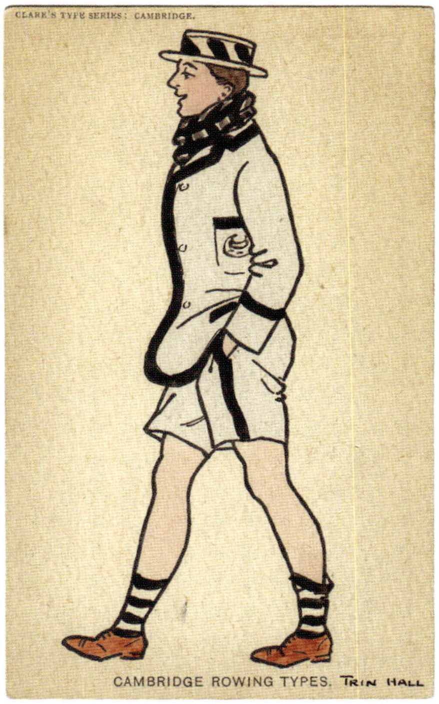

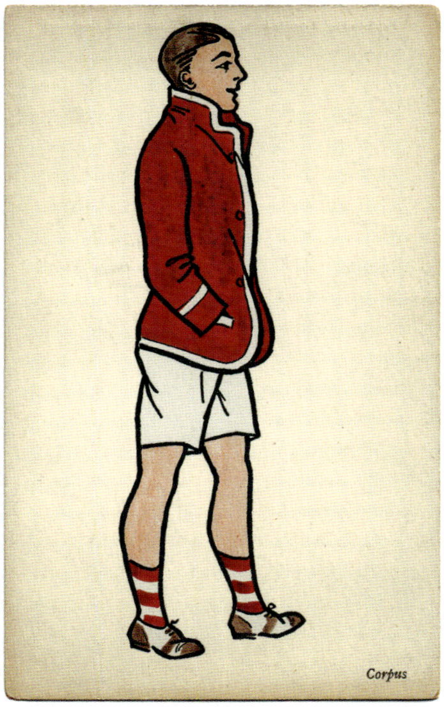

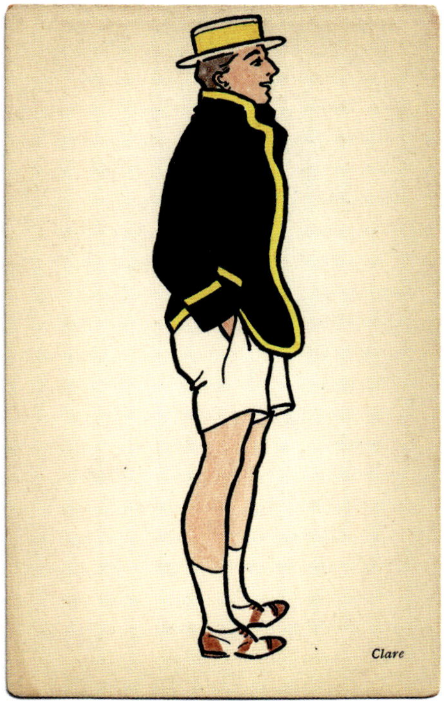

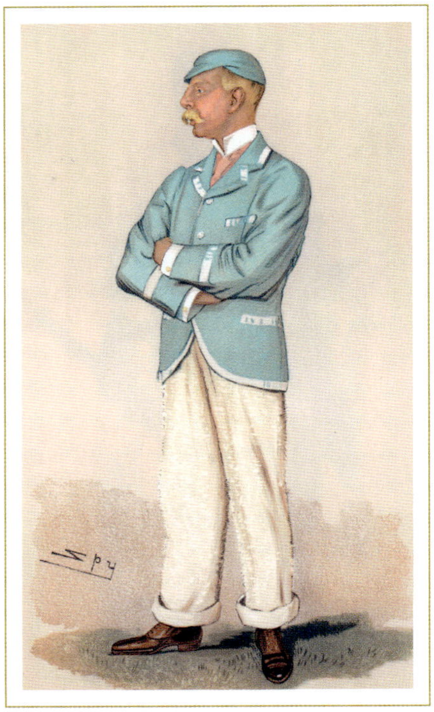

ABOVE:
Charles Thurston Fogg-Elliot, caricatured in his Cambridge University Boat Club blazer by "Spy" in *Vanity Fair*, March 22, 1894.

OPPOSITE:
Hardy Cubasch, a Cambridge Blue and world champion in the coxed pair for Australia, wears his Hawks' Club blazer and committee ascot.

winning a domestic championship or at the end of an undefeated regular season, when the crew will have blazers made up before heading across the Atlantic to compete at the Henley Royal Regatta. And in the Netherlands, rowing blazers are usually passed down from one generation of rowers to the next; they are almost universally ill fitting, threadbare, and filthy, for Dutch tradition also dictates that a blazer may not be washed until its wearer has won the nation's most prestigious regatta: the Varsity.

> *A white boating blazer (to which I was only dubiously entitled) . . . added a touch of grotesqueness to the occasion.*
>
> —Malcom Muggeridge, *Chronicles of Wasted Time*, 1972

THE MAGIC OF ROWING BLAZERS

> *"It was the rowing blazers that did it. . . . I would wear my glory with becoming modesty."*
>
> —Sir Anthony Glyn, Bt., *I Can Take It All*, 1959

Rowing blazers are treasured objects, imbued with a magical, almost sacred, aura. Almost sacred, but not quite. Thomas Merton, the Trappist monk and renowned mystic, satirized the characteristic British sentimentality for rowing blazers among other earthly artifacts:

> *Bound volumes of the Tatler . . . have gone up in smoke, and my old Punches with the Du Maurier drawings are ashes. So is the Ovid I had in school and my rowing blazer from Baliol* [sic]*!*
>
> —Thomas Merton, O.C.S.O., *My Argument with the Gestapo*, 1969

But if Merton was immune to the charms of the colorful rowing blazer, experience has shown that young ladies are not. In *Blood Over Water*, Cambridge Blue Boat oarsman James Livingston recalled: "It is astonishing what the sight of a Blues blazer can do to many a sensible, well-adjusted girl."

His report echoed Grant Allan's account in *The Scallywag*, written over a century earlier in 1895: "Faith thought she had never seen him look so handsome as he looked just then in his bright Christ Church boating-jacket. . . . A manly man seldom looks manlier than in boating costume."

Generally, however, the unwritten sartorial code of the blazer exists not to attract potential mates (although at Henley, in the words of Godfrey Smith, "men can and do work the most shameless peacock effects in their pink caps and rainbow-striped blazers"), but rather to let other rowers and cognoscenti know what one has achieved in the sport and where one's loyalties lie. Like the court liveries and heraldic devices of medieval Europe, the street gang colors of Compton, and the patches and badges of Boy Scouts and Hell's Angels, rowing blazers are tribal totems. They are ceremonial vestments, worn to emphasize both community and difference: to impress, intimidate, and influence in a game of sartorial one-upmanship. And they easily become visual measures of rank and social cachet within a given club, college, or school. Even the word *blazer* itself is a sort of reverse shibboleth for the most class-conscious sticklers of British society; as it has made its way from Cambridge argot into conventional parlance, Jilly Cooper types now insist that the only proper term is "boating jacket."

HENLEY AND THE BLAZER TRADITION

> *"When hay-scented meadows with oarsmen are crowded—*
> *Whose bright tinted blazers gay toilettes outvie—*
> *When sunshine is hot and the sky is unclouded,*
> *Oh, Henley is splendid in lovely July!"*
>
> —Joseph Ashby-Sterry, "Henley in July," 1884

The annual Henley Royal Regatta is the most prestigious rowing regatta in the world and represents the apex of the sport outside of the Olympic Games and the world championships. Like the Head of the Charles and the Oxford-Cambridge Boat Race, it is a rowing event that captures the public imagination and attracts vast international audiences. It is also, along with

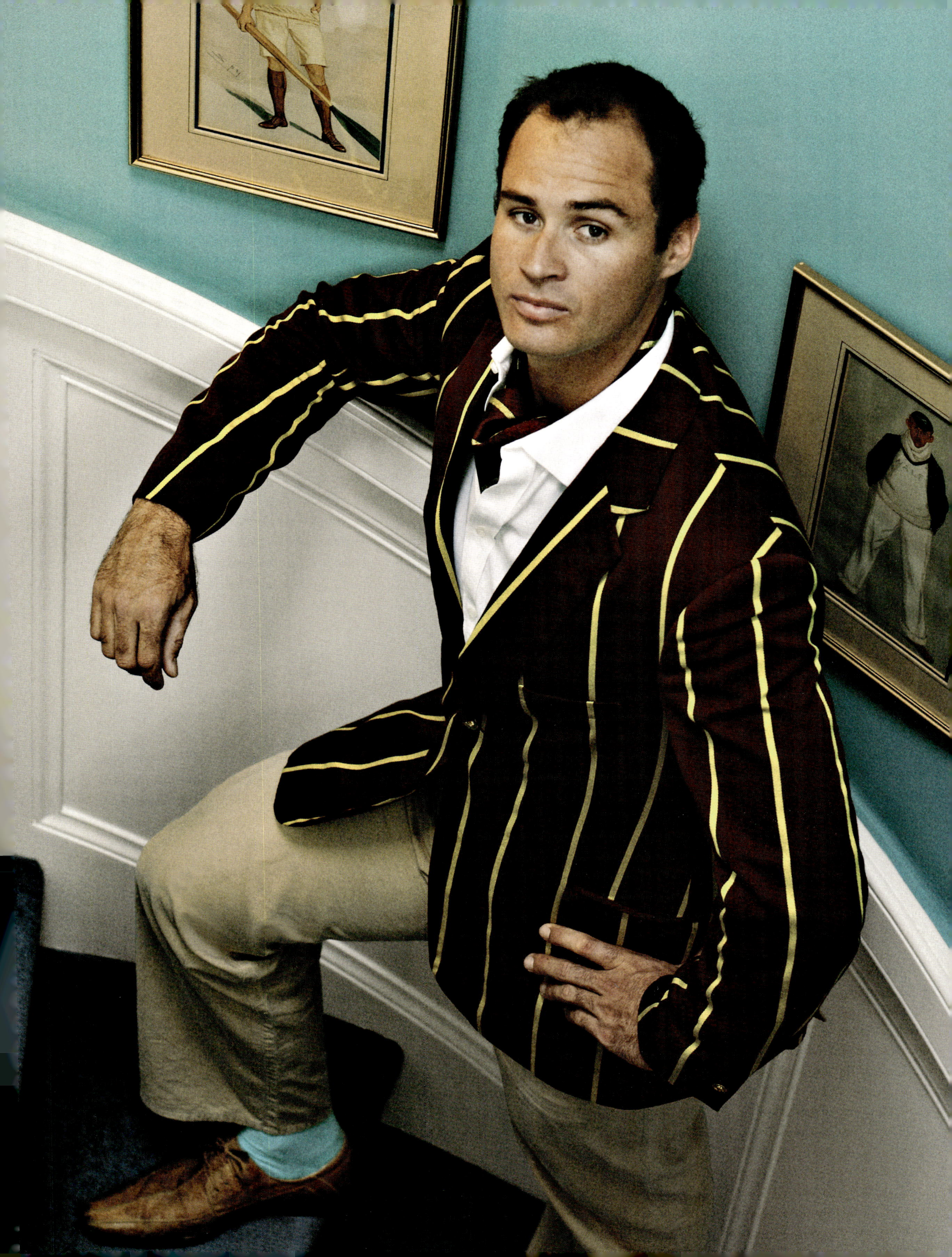

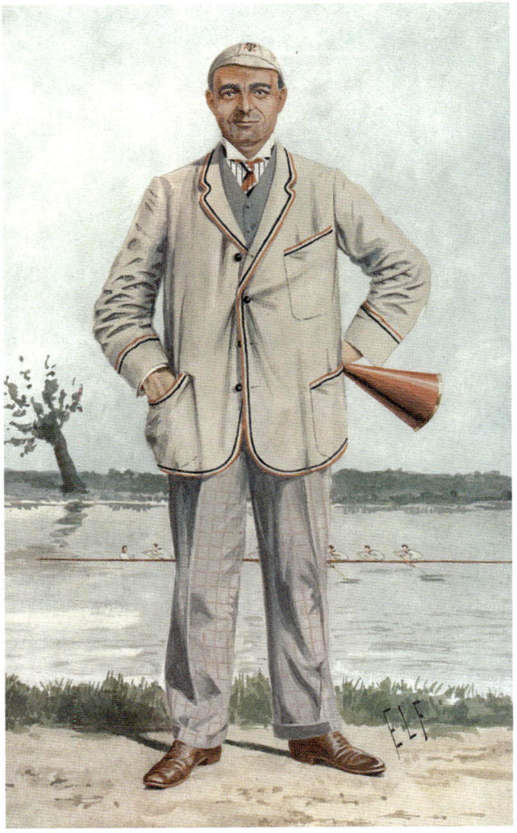

ABOVE:
Robert Henry "Bill" Forster, caricatured in his Thames Rowing Club regatta coat by "Elf" in *Vanity Fair*, July 6, 1910.

OPPOSITE:
Oriel College Boat Club, 1913.

Royal Ascot and Wimbledon, a major fixture on the British summer social calendar.

The Regatta has played a crucial role in ensuring that rowing's glorious, if quirky, blazer culture is both surviving and thriving nearly two centuries on. For the "blazerati" charged with running the Royal Regatta—the glamorous group known as the Henley Stewards—have maintained a picturesque Edwardian dress code that "encourages" ladies to wear hats; keeps hemlines several inches below the knee; and, most importantly, prevents gentlemen from removing their jackets. Henley, therefore, provides an annual five-day forum for rowers young and old to see and be seen, decked out in all of their coveted, flamboyant finery: the blazers, and also the boaters, bowties, and badges that go with them.

> *If you want to truly appreciate the Byzantine mysteries of the British class system—where the mere color of a sock, the style of a lapel braid, the direction of a tie's stripe, the initials on a brass button or the combination of hues in the band around a straw boater can instantly raise or dash one's social standing—come to the Henley Royal Regatta."*
>
> —Maureen Dowd, *New York Times*, July 4, 1993

A NOTE ON TAILORING

> *"Great care should be exercised in getting the boating-jacket properly made."* —*The Arts of Rowing and Training*, 1866

Seeing the older gentlemen at Henley sporting blazers they earned several decades and many pounds ago, one might be led to believe that rowing jackets must be ill fitting as a general rule. But a properly fitting blazer is always the most attractive. Aside from the usual Savile Row dynasties, the trade is dominated today by a small number of venerable tailoring houses, whose blazers are both beautiful and well tailored:

- A. E. Clothier, Cambridge
- The Andover Shop, Harvard Square
- Collier & Robinson, Henley-on-Thames
- New & Lingwood, Eton
- Walters, Oxford

Rowing jackets should be relatively unstructured, with patch pockets and a soft shoulder. The blazer was, after all, originally made to be worn while racing. The most traditional British versions are thick flannel (ironically making them wholly inappropriate for summer regattas—the principal occasions on which they are worn nowadays; purists will sweat and bear it). They have no vent in back and are single-breasted, three-button jackets—with cloth-covered or metal buttons, of course. The original rowing jackets had four or five buttons and closed all the way up to the collar. The more staid British alternative—just as nautical, but somewhat less inspired—is the fitted, dark blue double-breasted blazer with gilt club buttons.

The American version differs from its British counterpart in three principal ways: it is usually made of a more practical, lighter-weight material; it is usually a two-button jacket; and it often features a single vent and different types of pocket. These differences sometimes make it a little awkward to apply contrast binding to the jacket's edges and to embroider a badge on the pocket. Several years ago, a Princeton crew turned up at Henley in black blazers with thick orange trim that not only ran along the bottom edge of the blazer, but, comically, up and down the rear vent as well.

FASCINATION AND IMITATION

> *"Our blazers aroused rapturous enthusiasm."*
>
> —Lord Frederic Hamilton, *Vanished Pomps of Yesterday*, 1921

Even if the minutiae of blazerology remain mysterious to the uninitiated, outsiders have long been fascinated by the eye-catching garments. And who can blame them? Rowing jackets inevitably induce awe, joy, and wonder: unaware travelers in London's Paddington Station during Henley week imagine they must have stepped back in time, or into the dreamworld of P. G. Wodehouse.

Caricatures of distinguished oarsmen in their gaudy jackets frequently graced the pages of *Vanity Fair* in the late nineteenth and early twentieth centuries, playing on rowing blazers' colorful charm and allure, as well as on the public's captivation with the privileged world they represent. *Boy's Own Magazine* featured charts of Oxford and Cambridge Blues blazers, and cigarette companies issued series of collectible cards dedicated to rowing ties and boat club blazers. Rowing blazers are still fetishized by the press today, from tabloid spreads to articles in *GQ* and the *Financial Times*. And they continue to capture our imaginations, appearing to great effect in such films as *Chariots of Fire* and *The Social Network*.

Rowing blazers have left a deep impression on American fashion, of course, inspiring a cult of striped and piped jackets in ostentatious colors on college campuses from Cornell to Princeton in the early twentieth century. These crested "class blazers," often paired with straw boaters and worn not only by rowers but by students generally, were characteristic of the burgeoning "Ivy" look that would irreversibly transform men's style in the mid-century.

In the 1960s, striped regatta-style blazers were co-opted by the Mod movement in Britain; the more understated dark blue version, meanwhile, had become the mainstay of modern menswear on both sides of the Atlantic. The likes of The Andover Shop, J. Press, Gant, Brooks Brothers, Ralph Lauren, Tommy Hilfiger, and Hackett have practically built their brands on the blue blazer and ensured its central position in the shrine of Anglo-American fashion.

The twenty-first century has seen the blazer become as important a staple for women as it is for men, and an evergreen obsession with timeless "preppy" style has kept bullion pocket badges, outlandish stripes, and grosgrain binding in contrasting colors in vogue for both sexes.

> *Every single one of us—no matter the age or the gender or the sexual preference—owns a blue blazer.*
>
> —Lisa Birnbach, *True Prep*, 2010

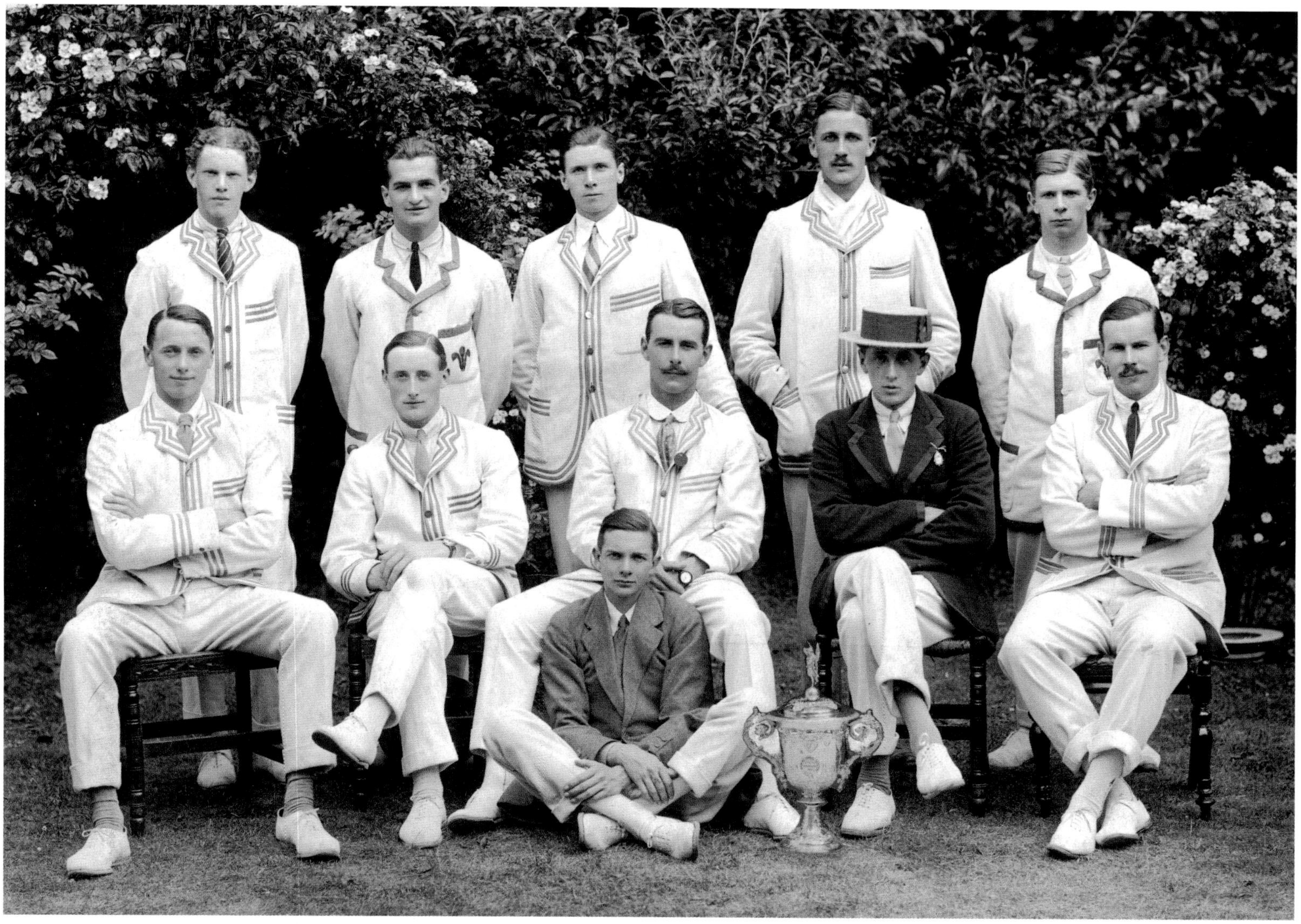

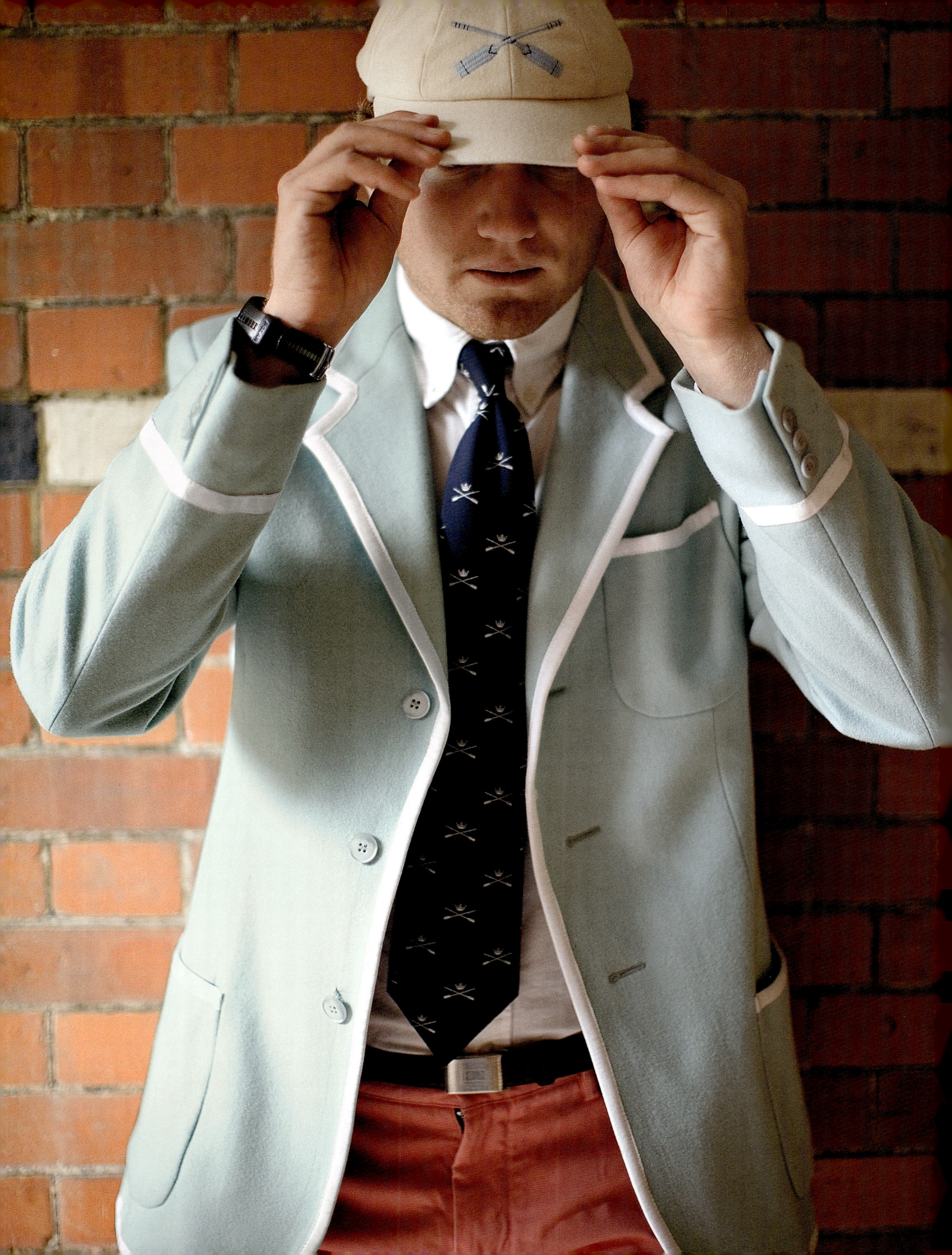

Windsor, England

Eton College Boat Club First Eight, Second Eight, *and the* Eton Vikings

CONSTANTINE LOULOUDIS, JAKE BATE, MARCUS DE WILDE

"Others will fill our places, / Dressed in the old light blue, / We'll recollect our races, / We'll to the flag be true, / And youth will be still in our faces, / When we cheer for an Eton crew, / And youth will be still in our faces, / When we cheer for an Eton crew . . ."

—William Johnson Cory, "The Eton Boating Song"

Eton College—undisputedly the poshest of posh British boarding schools—may also have been the first school to take to the water. Eton's Monarch Boat Club was established sometime in the late 1700s; the official school boat club, in 1816. And since the beginning, rowing at Eton has involved flamboyant articles of clothing.

The earliest recorded Procession of Boats—the annual rowing festival at Eton to mark King George III's birthday—was in 1793, although the practice probably began years earlier. The Procession remains, to this day, a grand and iconic occasion and is the keystone event at Eton's annual Fourth of June celebration day (which, of course, rarely falls on the actual fourth of June) for parents and friends.

Ten crews with traditional nineteenth-century names—Monarch (a unique ten-oar boat), Victory, Prince of Wales, Britannia, Dreadnought, Thetis, Hibernia, St. George, Alexandra, and Defiance—row in the Procession in clinker-built wooden racing boats. As each crew passes the crowd of spectators, its coxswain gives a command to salute, whereupon the rowers remove their oars from the oarlocks, hold them vertically, and stand upright in the boat. To the delight of the audience, these salutes sometimes result in capsizes.

The oarsmen all dress in nineteenth-century naval ratings' uniforms and straw boater hats, which school matrons (or "Dames," as they are known) decorate with weighty bouquets of fresh flowers. The coxswains of the top three boats, meanwhile, wear the full dress uniforms of Nelson-era admirals; lower boats' coxswains wear captains' and lieutenants' uniforms. Each crew also has its own color, which is used for neckties, blades, and boater hatbands; these traditionally corresponded to the somewhat less extravagant blazers and jerseys of the school's conventional racing crews (first eight, second eight, and so on).

Rowing boys at Eton are known as "wet bobs" (their cricket-playing colleagues are "dry bobs"), and the best wet bobs—those in the top boat—may wear Eton Blue blazers with white trim. Eton Blue—which is, in fact, as close to green as it is to blue—has been used by crews at the school since the early nineteenth century and has since been adopted by countless rowing and educational institutions around the world, perhaps most notably Cambridge University. Second eight rowers wear bright blue-and-white-striped blazers, while various other striped blazers are ordained for the school's many other crews. The alumni club, known as the Vikings, has a black blazer with Eton Blue trim, maroon cuffs, and a maroon collar.

OPPOSITE: Constantine Louloudis held the glamorous position of Captain of Boats at Eton. In both 2009 and 2010, he stroked the school's first eight to victory in the Triple Crown of junior rowing: the Schools' Head of the River, the National Schools' Regatta, and the Princess Elizabeth Cup at Henley. Just two years after leaving the school, he stroked Great Britain's Olympic eight to a bronze medal.

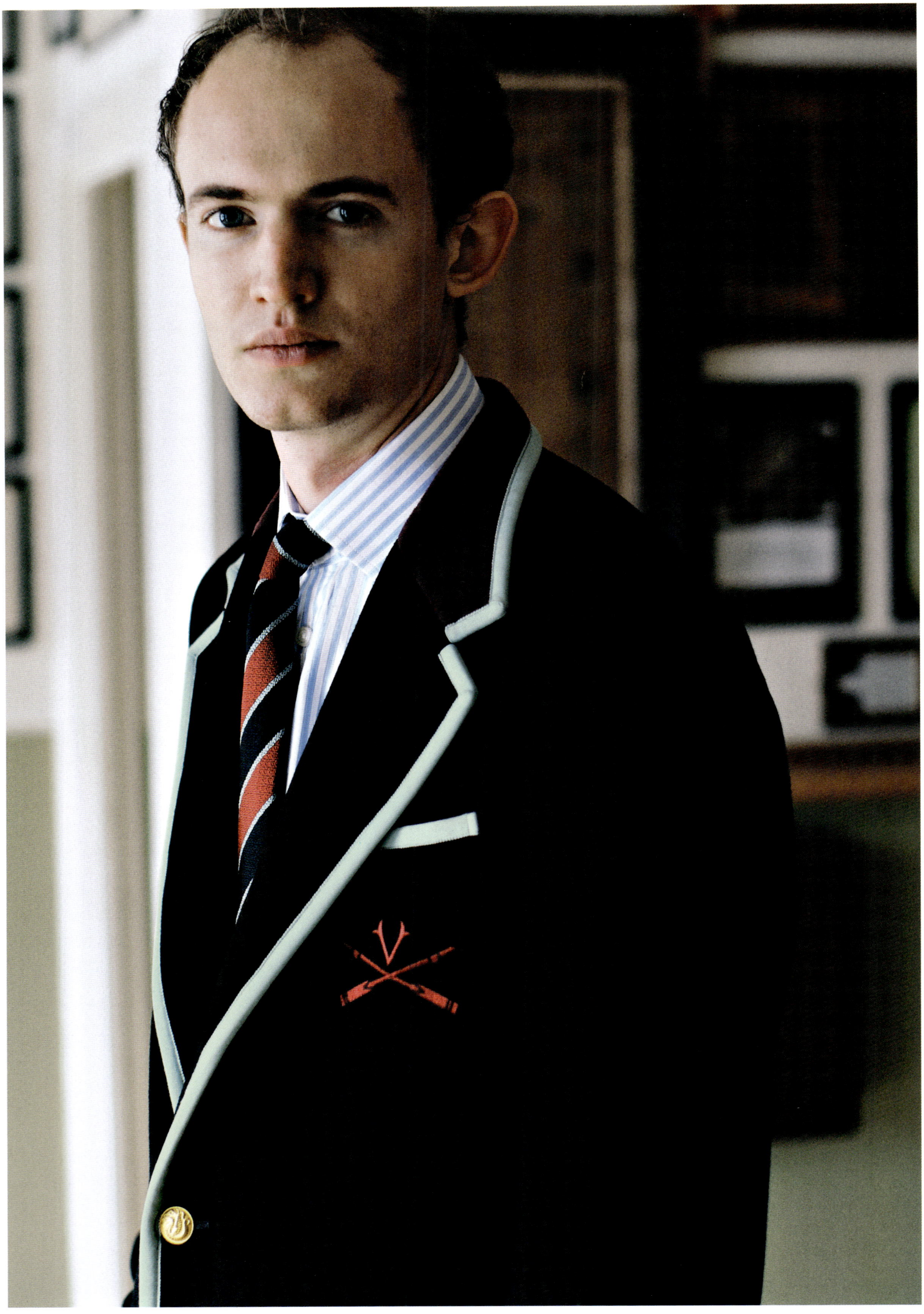

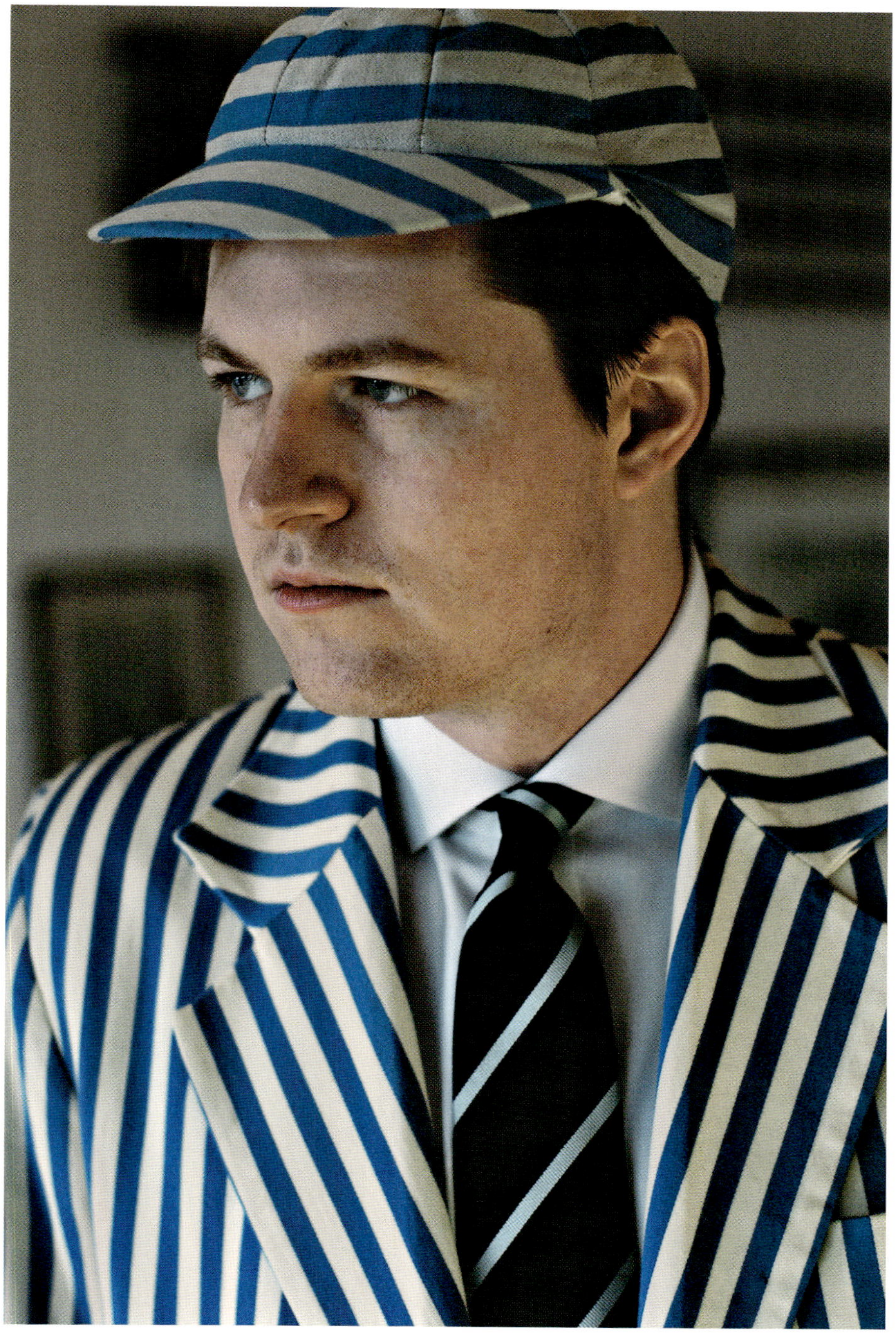

OPPOSITE:
Jake Bate, wearing the
Eton Vikings blazer.

ABOVE:
Marcus de Wilde in an Eton
second eight blazer.

OVERLEAF:
Eton boys in Nelson-era
naval uniforms and straw boaters
adorned with lavish bouquets
on the Fourth of June.

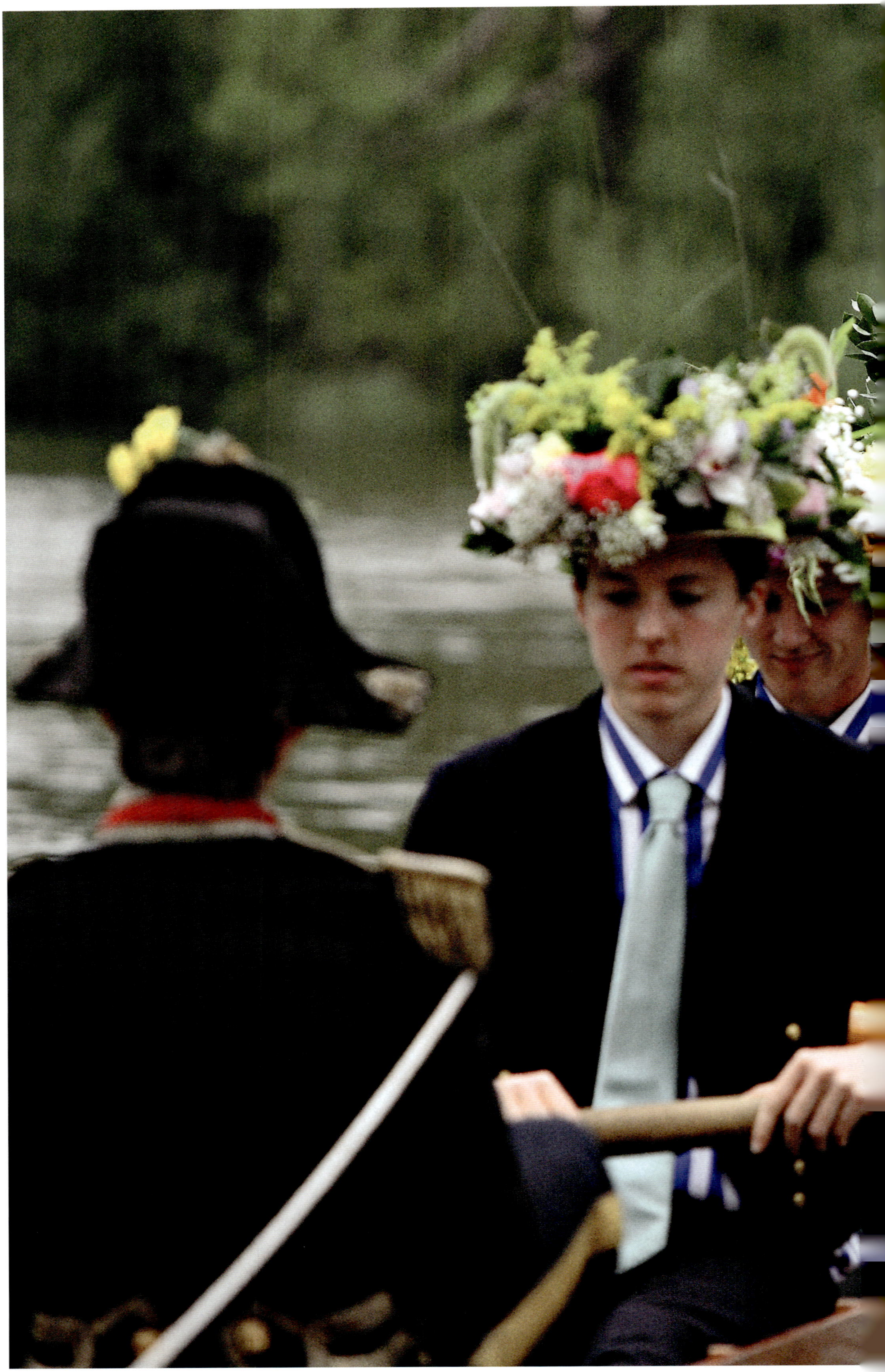

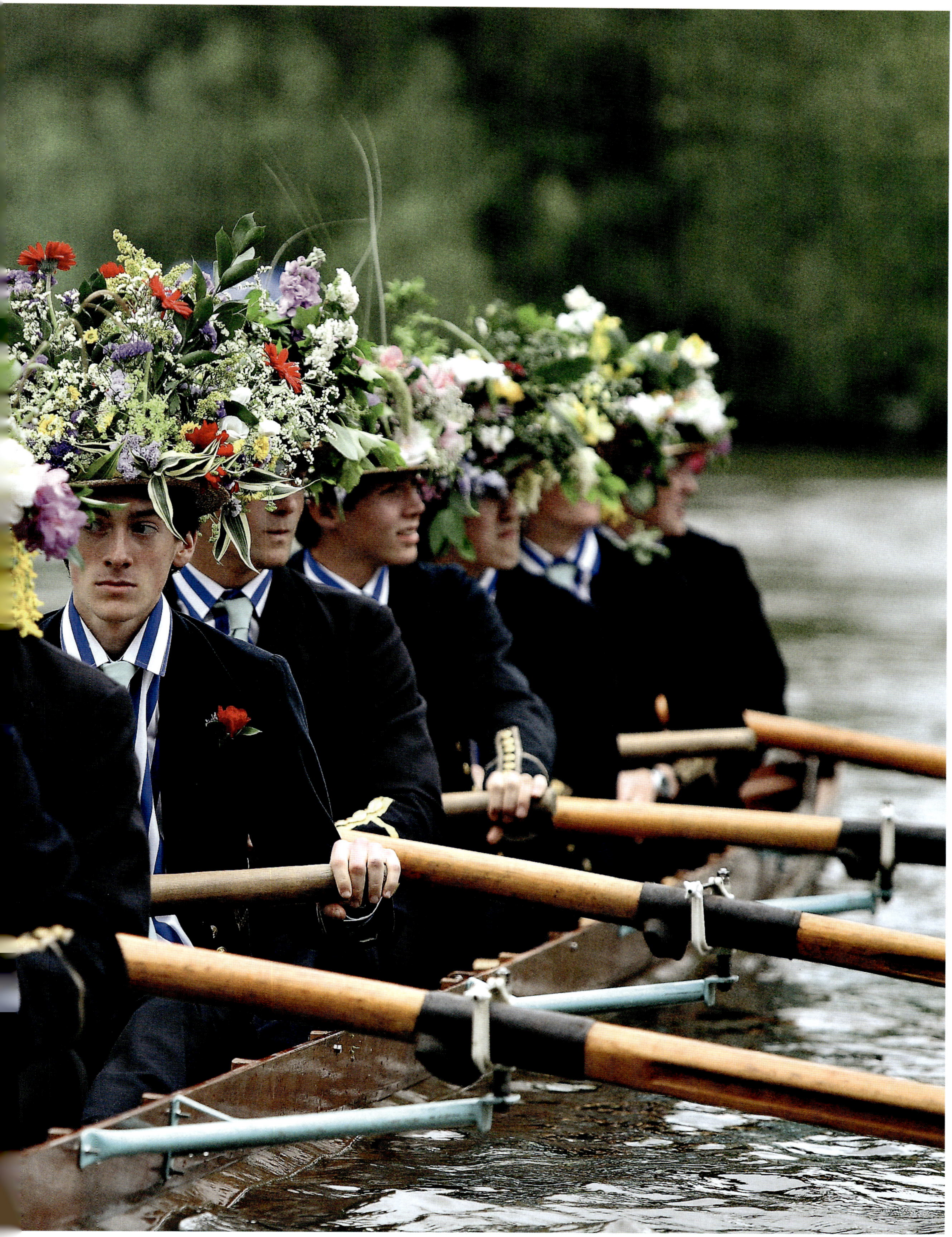

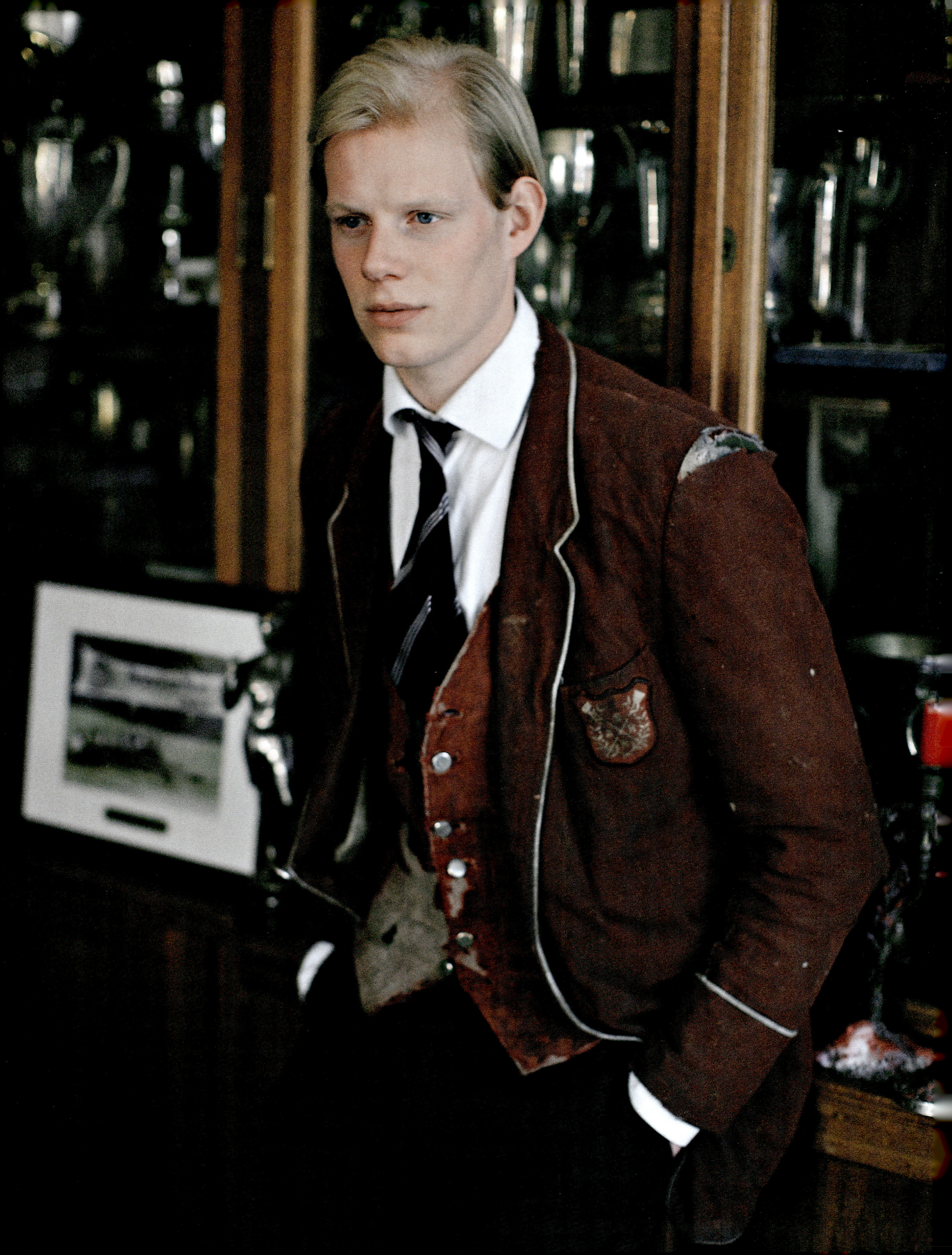

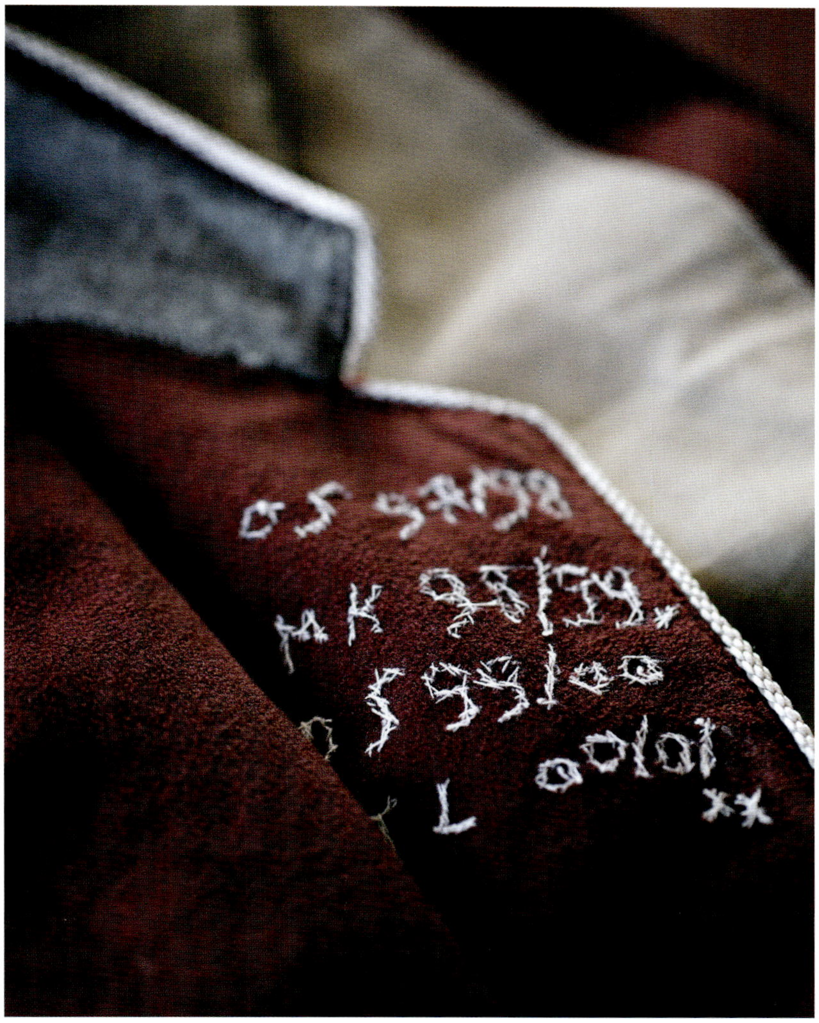

Amsterdam, Netherlands

A.S.R. "Nereus"

PHILIP VAN DE LINDE, JELMER OOR, IAN DE WOLF,
JISK VELLENGA, PHILIP D'AILLY,
KOEN MAARLEVELD, QUIRIJN KNAB, JESPER FEENSTRA

Amsterdamsche Studenten Roeivereeniging "Nereus" on the River Amstel is the most successful student rowing club in the Netherlands.

As in most Dutch rowing clubs, old blazers are passed down from one generation of rowers to the next. Each wearer stitches his initials and year inside the jacket's lapel; the older and more threadbare the blazer (and the more famous its previous wearers), the better. Invariably stained and often torn, these blazers are nevertheless worn with the greatest pride. The blazers are not only old but usually the worse for wear: they play an important role in the traditional "fights" that follow Dutch regattas, in which oarsmen attempt to wrestle each other to the ground by the lapels, often with much tattering and tearing in the process.

Moreover, the blazers can only be washed when the club wins the premier event (the men's senior four) at the Varsity race. Nereus has won thirty-eight times—far more than any of its competitors—and is the reigning champion; few, if any, crew members, however, have actually taken the opportunity to wash their jackets.

OPPOSITE: Club president Philip van de Linde wears an ancient Nereus blazer and waistcoat. **ABOVE:** At Nereus, each wearer stitches his or her initials and year on the back of the jacket's lapel. **OVERLEAF:** Jelmer Oor, Ian de Wolf, Jisk Vellenga, Philip d'Ailly, Koen Maarleveld, Quirijn Knab, and Jesper Feenstra at the Head of the Charles Regatta.

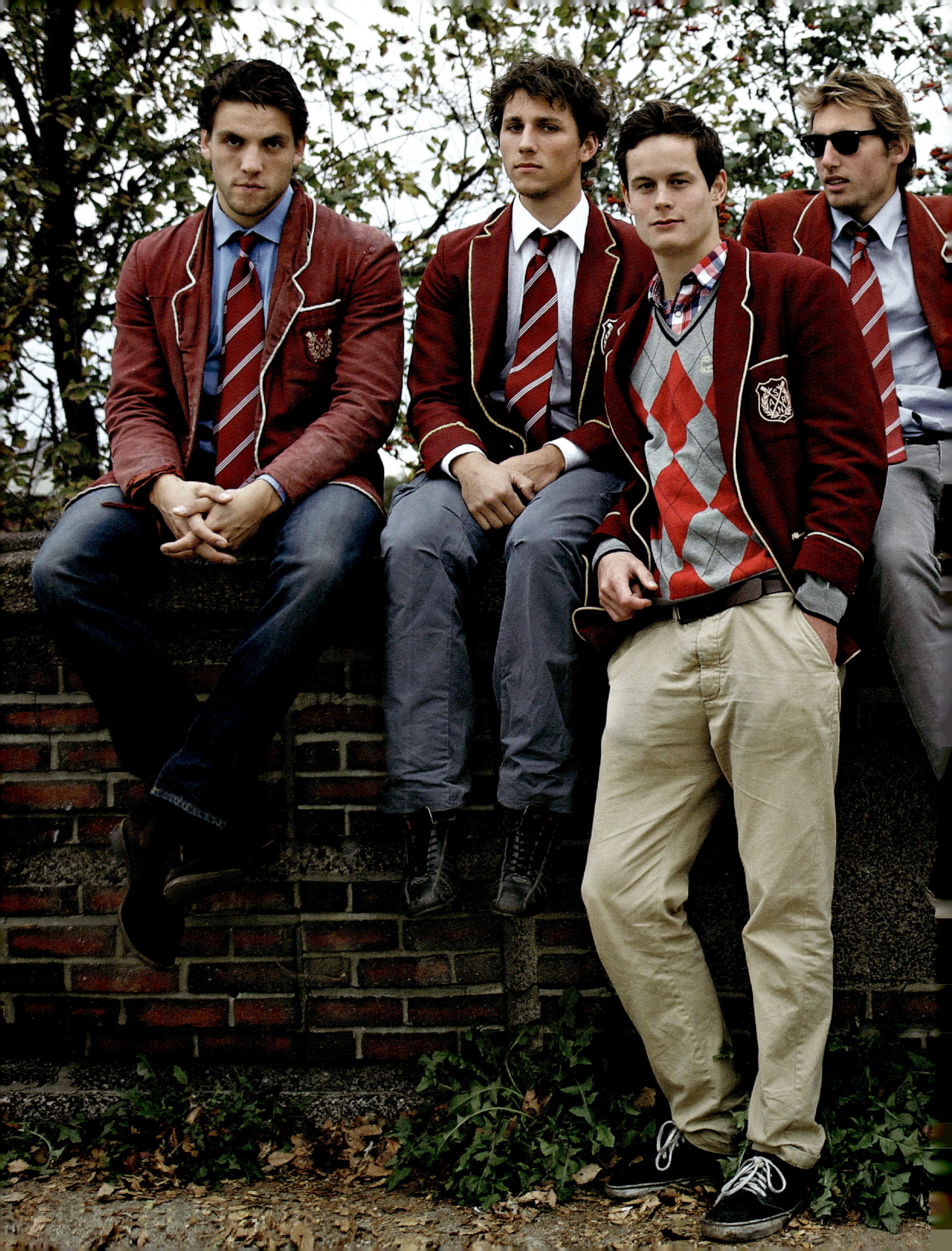

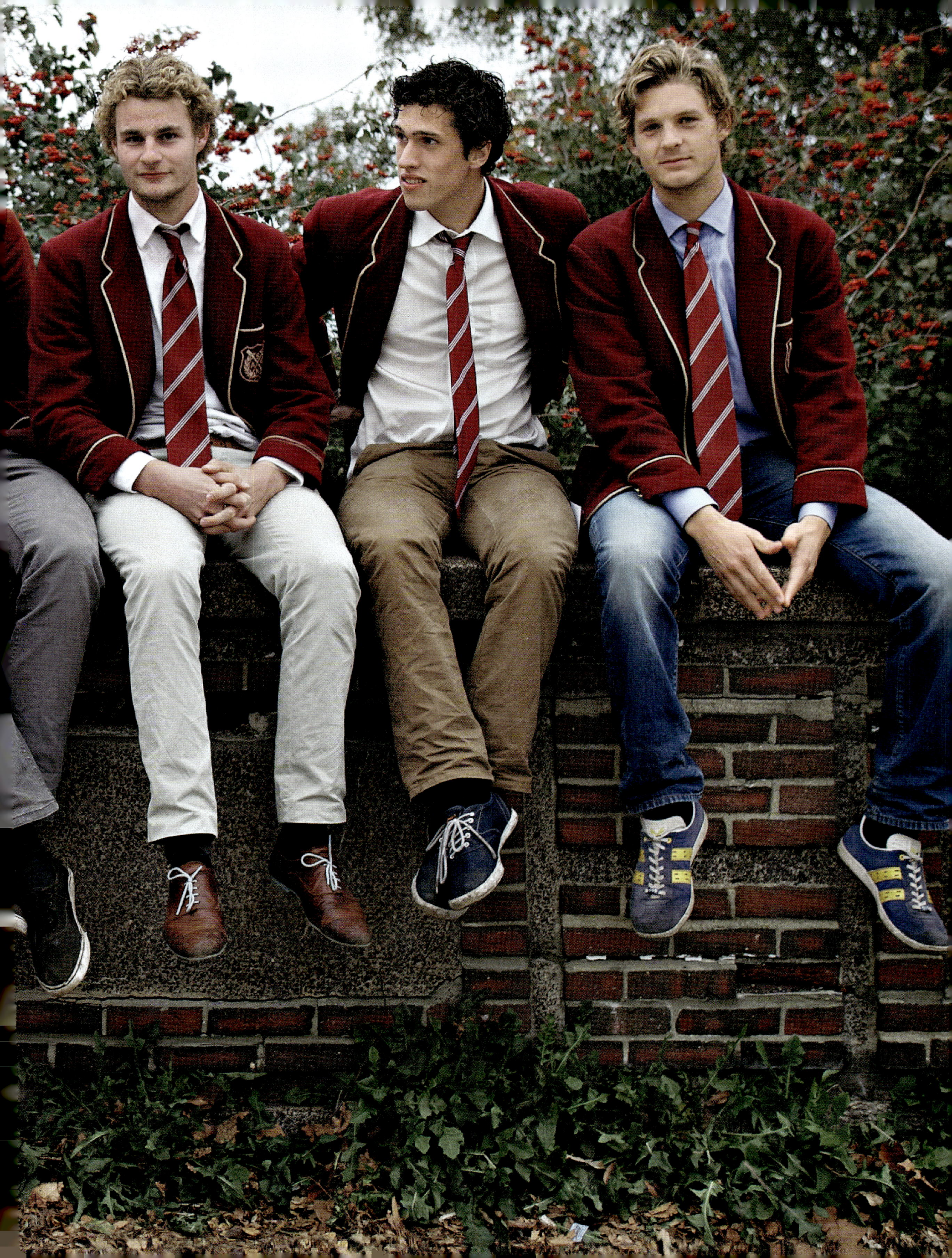

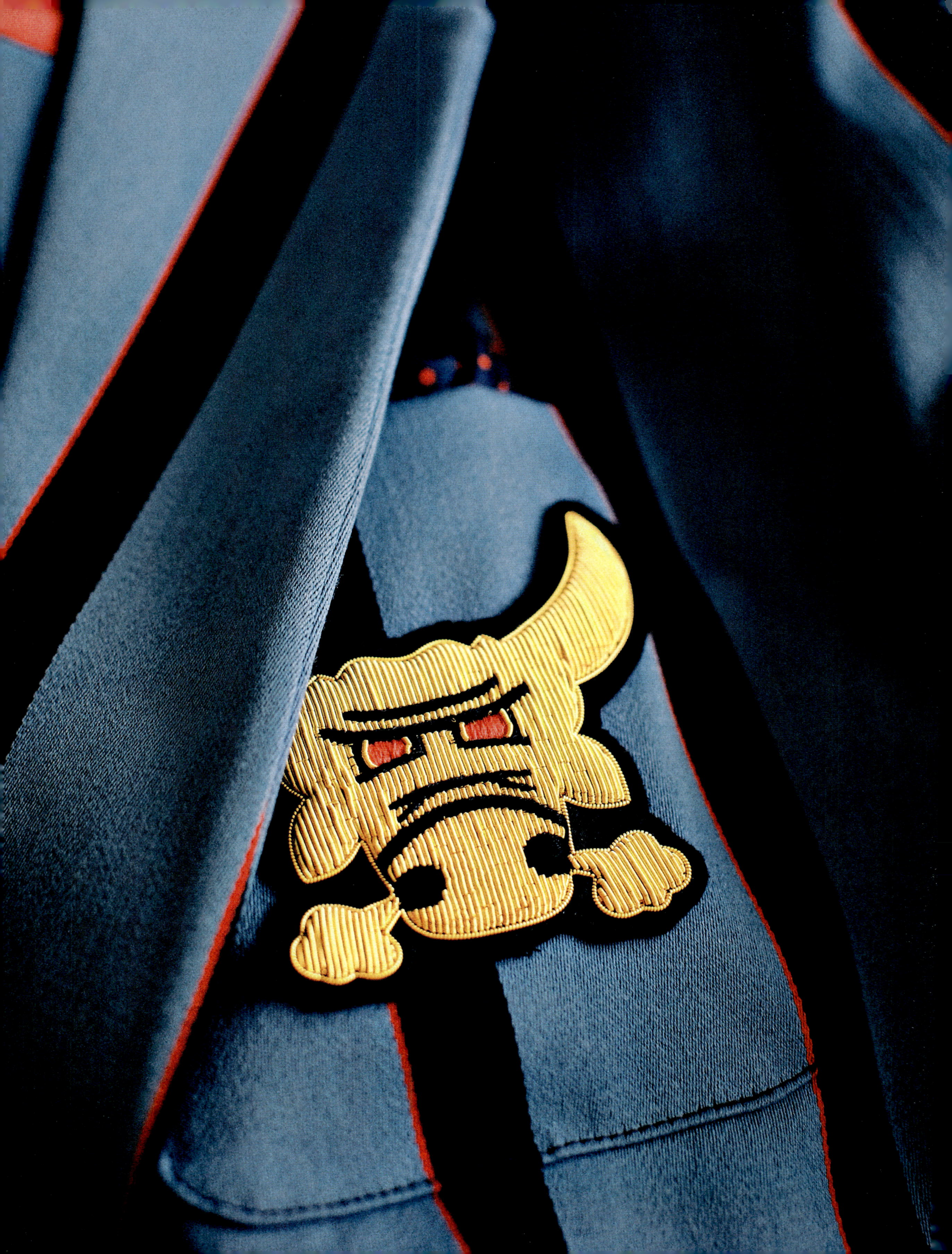

Oxford, England

Taurus Boat Club

GRAHAM BENTON, OLIVER WILLIAMS

Taurus began as the racing club for alumni and friends of Oxford Brookes University; today it is an open club linked to the university boat club.

Oxford Polytechnic became Oxford Brookes University in 1992; the following year, the student rowing club changed its blazer design from Baltic Blue (Polytechnic's color) with narrow navy-and-red stripes to burgundy, navy, and cream (the new Brookes colors). But Taurus has kept the old Poly blazer, with a Taurus bull badge in place of the Poly coat of arms on the pocket.

Graham Benton (below) has raced for Taurus at Henley twice and broken multiple indoor rowing (ergometer) world records, as well as the British Indoor Rowing Championships record for 2000 meters.

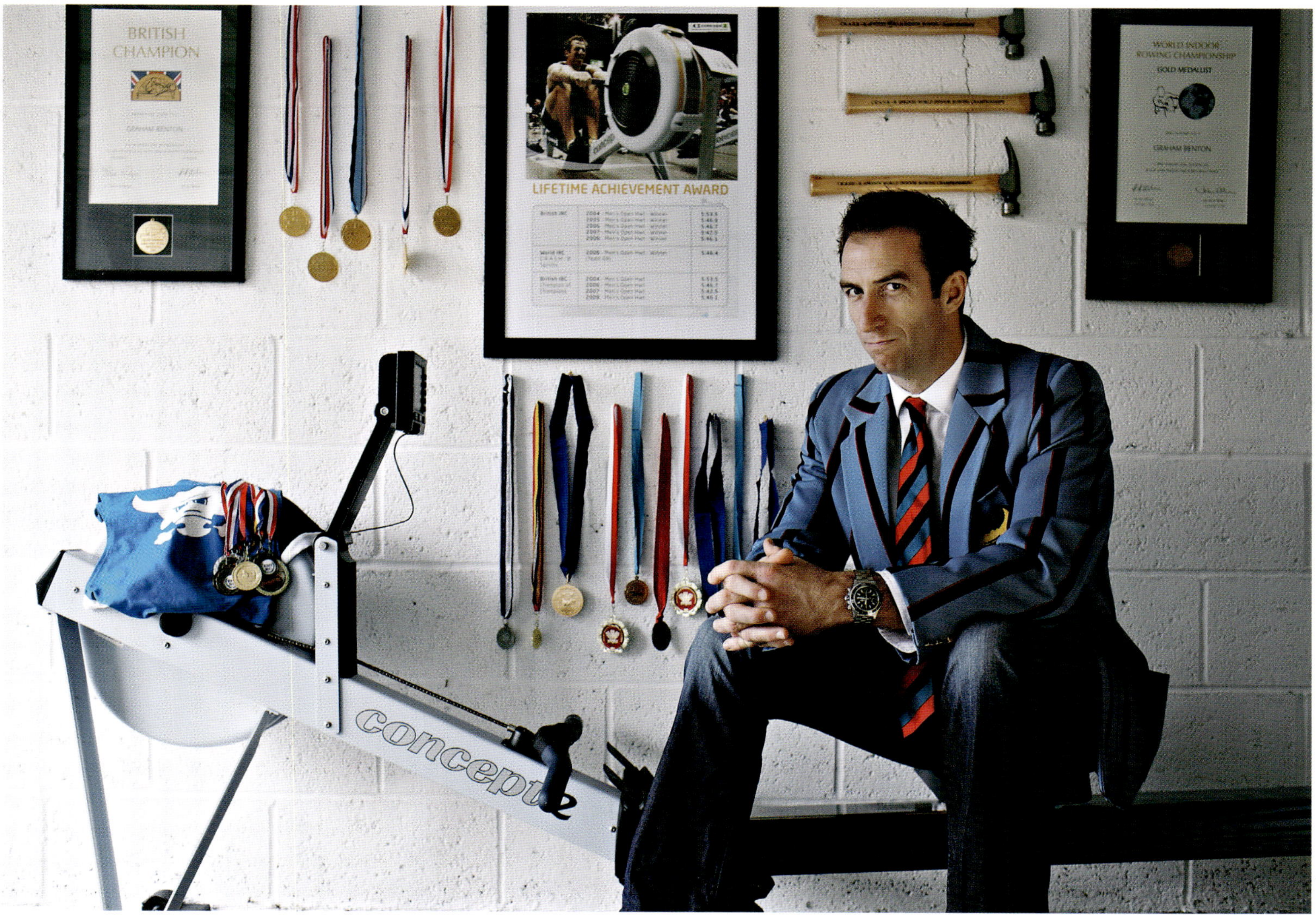

OVERLEAF: Oliver Williams wears the three-piece-suit version of the Taurus blazer.

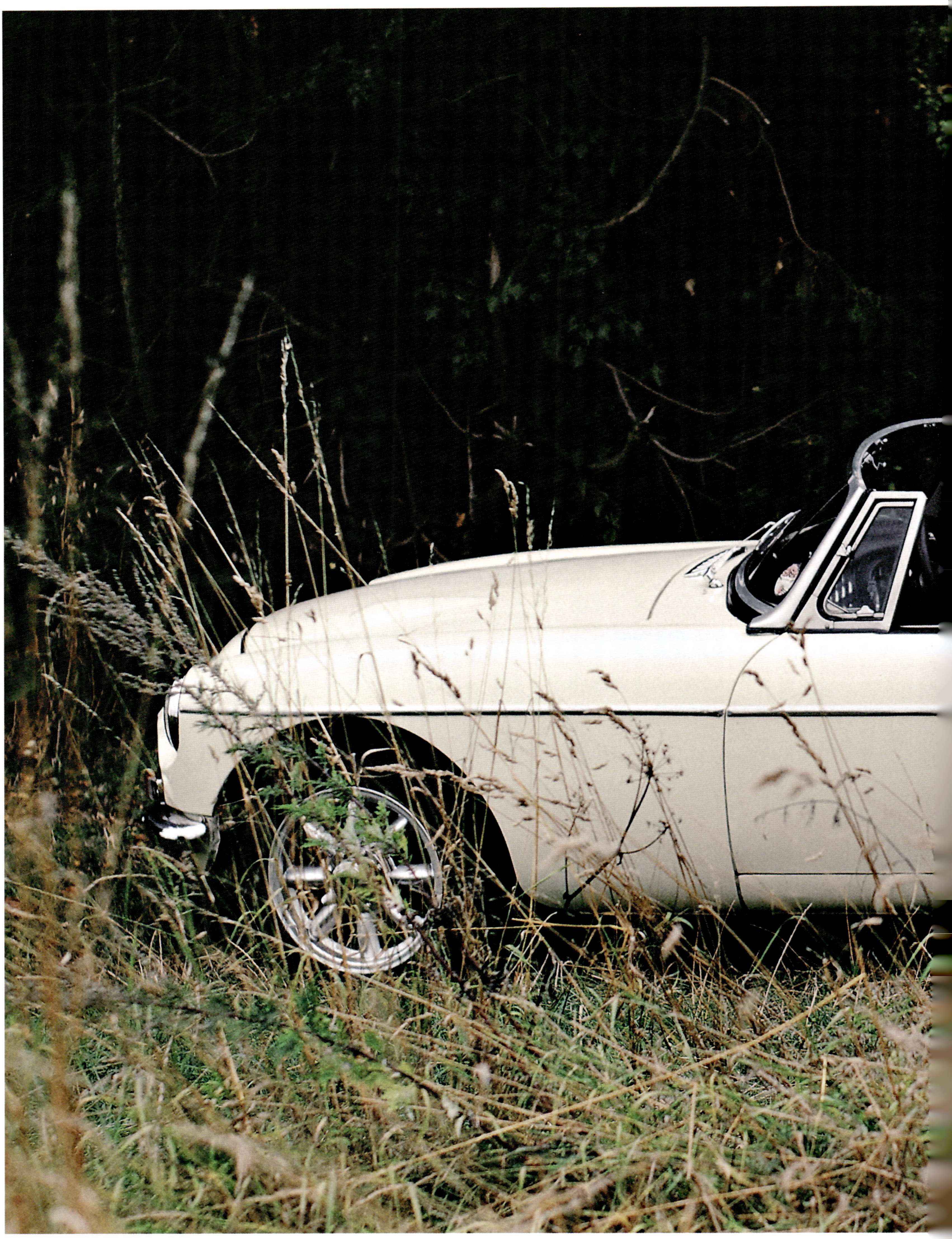

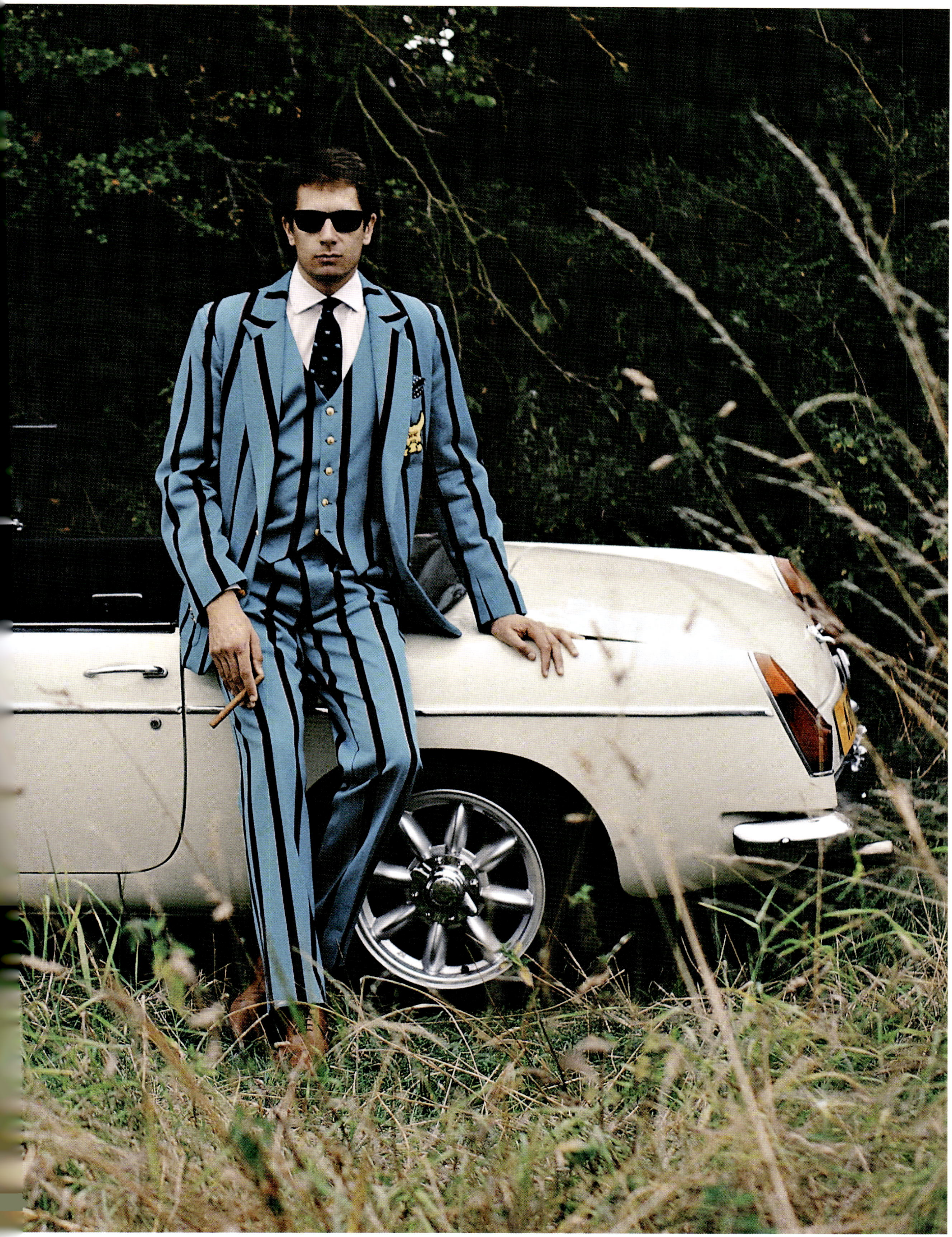

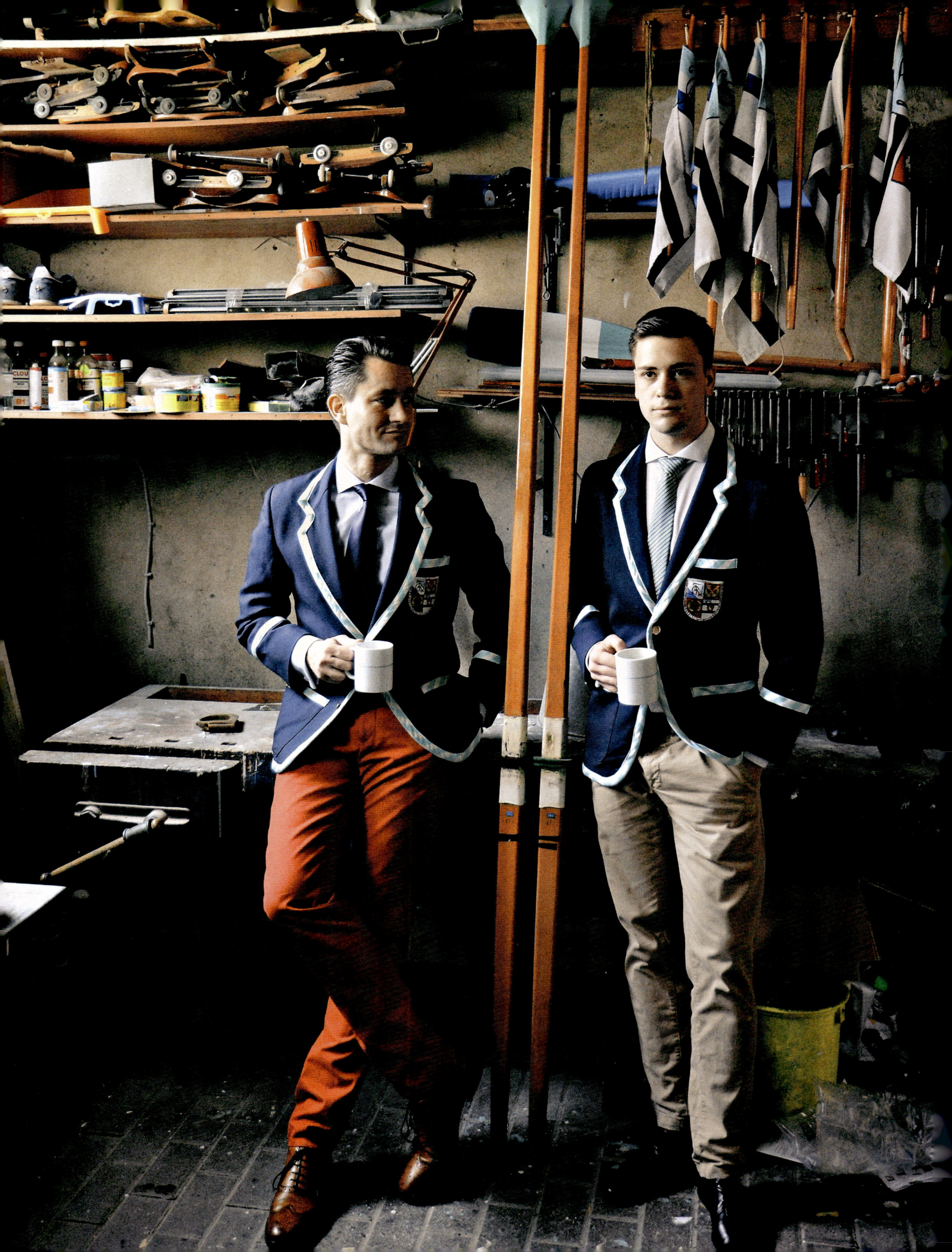

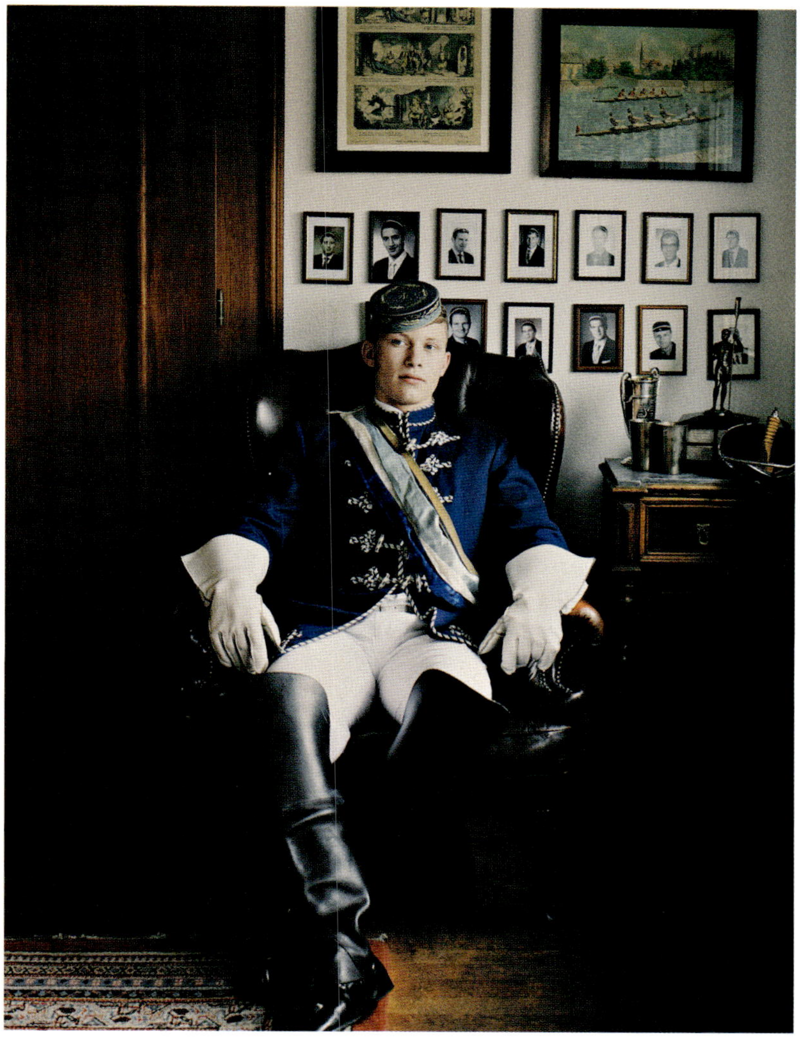

Münster, Germany

A.R.V. Westfalen

TIMO VÖLKER, CARLO BRUNOLD, ALEXANDER KRÖGER

"Our future lies upon the water. The more Germans go out upon the waters, whether it be in races or regattas, or in the service of the flag, so much the better it will be for us."

—Kaiser Wilhelm II, Speech to the North German Regatta Association, 1901

The Academic Rowing Fraternity of Westphalia *(Akademische Ruderverbindung Westfalen)* was founded by the curator of Münster University as a swimming and rowing club in 1891. Inspired by Kaiser Wilhelm's affection for the navy, there was growing enthusiasm for all things nautical among German students, and the club quickly attracted a great number of members. Many of these students were also members of various local fraternities and split their time between those and the new club.

It was therefore decided in 1904 that the club itself should become a fraternity. That same year, the club adopted the colors light blue, dark blue, and white, in homage to the colors of the Cambridge and Oxford Boat Race crews.

As is tradition in German fraternities, the club officers wear an elaborate ceremonial uniform. At A.R.V. Westfalen, this consists of a dark blue military-style jacket with appliqués in the fraternity's colors; a cap embroidered with the fraternity's *Zirkel*, or cipher; white breeches; black jackboots; and a ceremonial sword.

Out of fifteen German rowing fraternities that once existed, only A.R.V. Westfalen survives. It is also the only German fraternity with rowing blazers. Like the ceremonial uniform, the blazer is dark blue and trimmed with light blue and white. The pocket is emblazoned with the fraternity's coat of arms surrounded by the motto *Dem Vaterland ergeben, den Kräften vertrauend* (Devoted to country, confident in our strength).

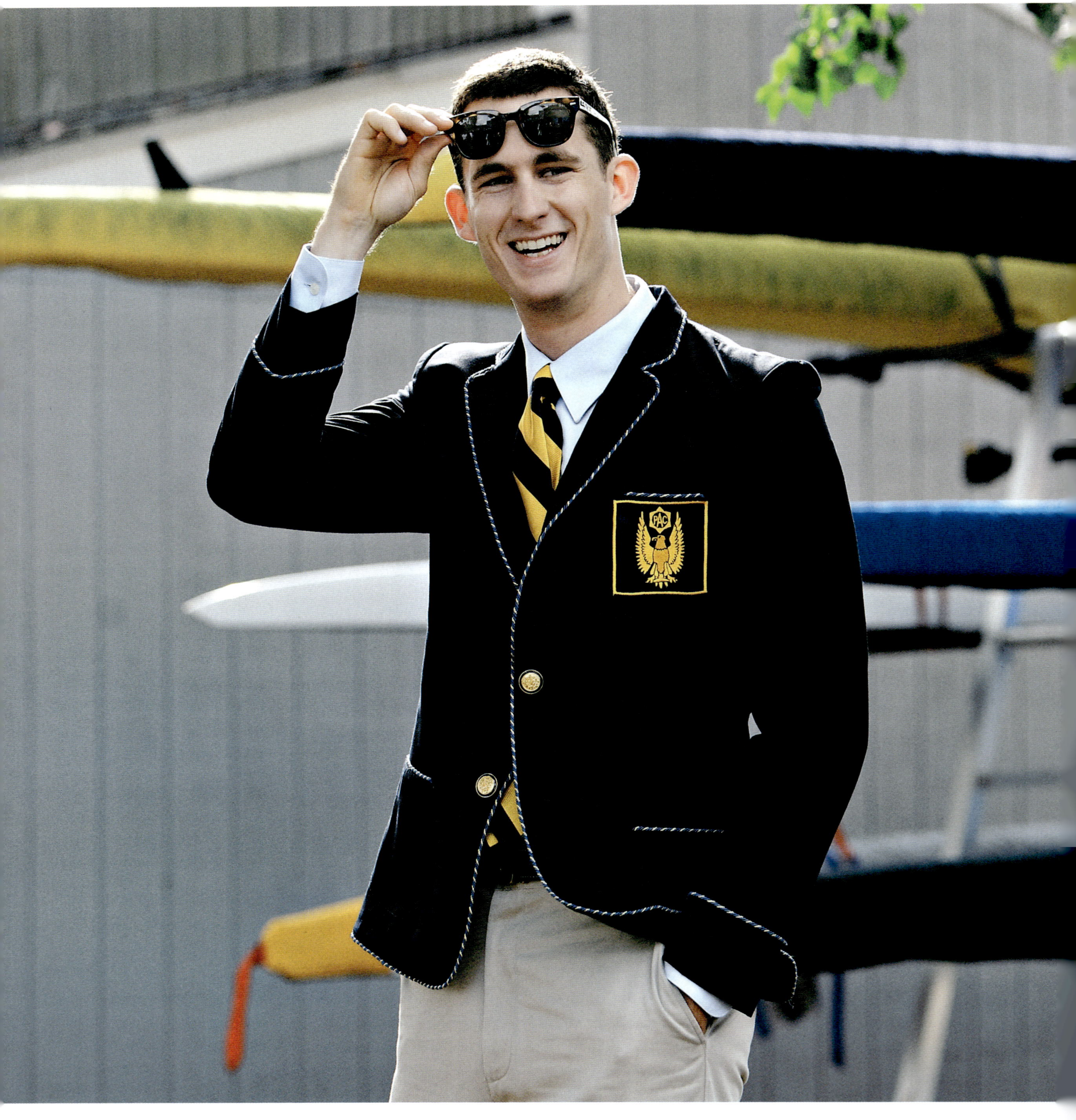
PAC

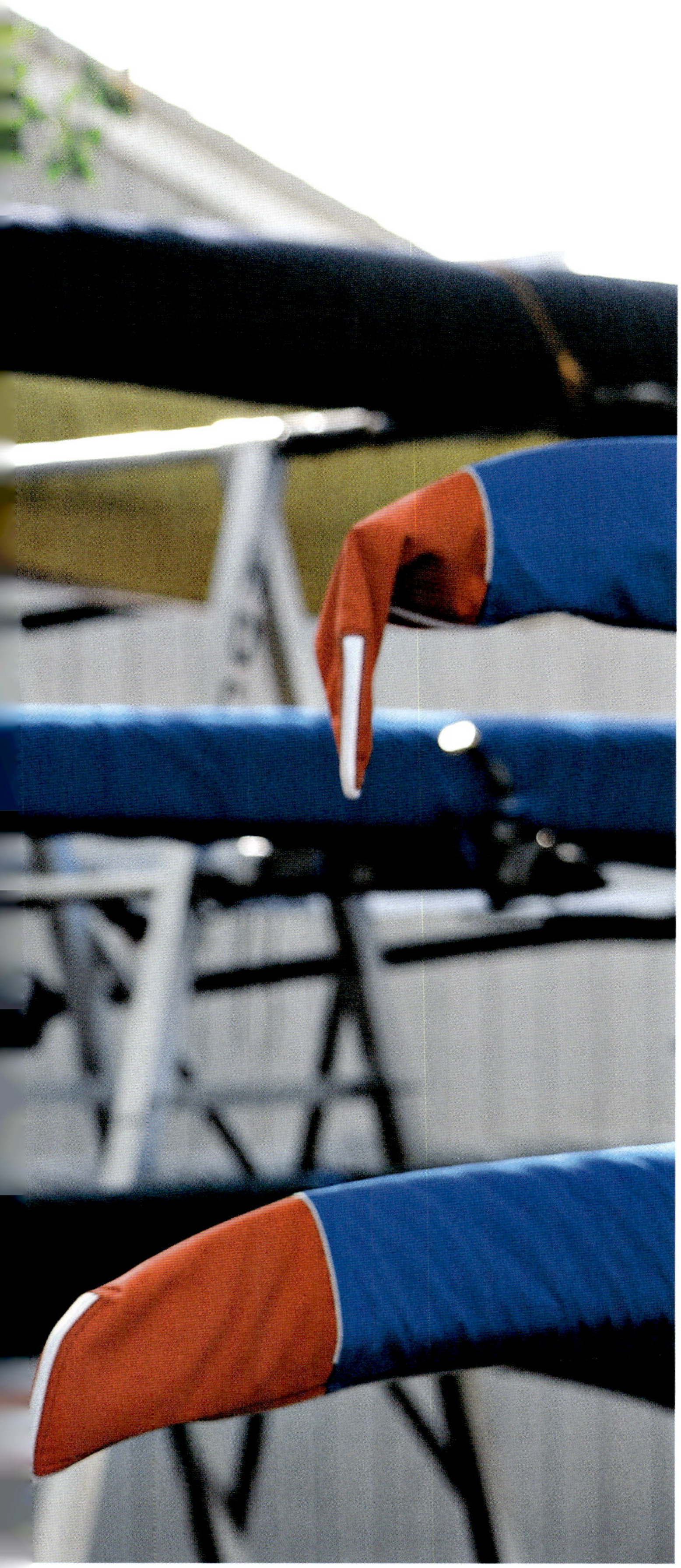

Philadelphia, Pennsylvania

Pennsylvania Athletic Club Rowing Association

TAYLOR BROWN

The Penn A.C. Rowing Association, with its navy and gold colors and stylized eagle badge, began life as West Philadelphia Boat Club in 1871. Among the many legendary figures to row for the Penn A.C., the greatest, perhaps, are scullers John "Jack" Kelly and Joe Burk.

Known as the "robot rower" and "the world's greatest oarsman," Burk was a two-time winner of the Diamond Challenge Sculls for Penn A.C. at Henley and went undefeated for forty-six straight races in 1937–40. As coach, he led Penn to victory in the Grand Challenge Cup at Henley in 1955.

He was preceded by Jack Kelly, a Philadelphia bricklayer and local sporting hero who initially sculled for Vesper Boat Club. By 1920, at the age of thirty-one, Kelly had won six national sculling titles and was unbeaten in 126 consecutive races. He set his sights on the Henley Royal Regatta that year, with every intention of continuing his winning streak. But the Henley Stewards denied his entry, citing an ongoing ban on entries from Vesper (which had run afoul of the Stewards years earlier) and an old rule that prevented manual laborers—bricklayers included—from racing. The news caused an uproar in Philadelphia, where "Kelly for Brickwork" T-shirts are still a frequent sight within the rowing community. Weeks after Henley, Kelly had his revenge: he won gold at the Olympics, beating the Henley singles champion, Jack Beresford of Great Britain, by one second. Half an hour later, he made history by winning gold in the double as well. According to legend, he mailed his racing cap to King George V with a note reading, "Greetings from a bricklayer." After leaving Vesper for Penn A.C., Kelly won Olympic gold again in 1924.

The Kelly family eventually made its peace with Henley. His son, John Jr., won the Diamond Sculls at the regatta in 1947 and 1949. And his daughter Grace presented the prizes at Henley in 1981—in her capacity as Princess of Monaco.

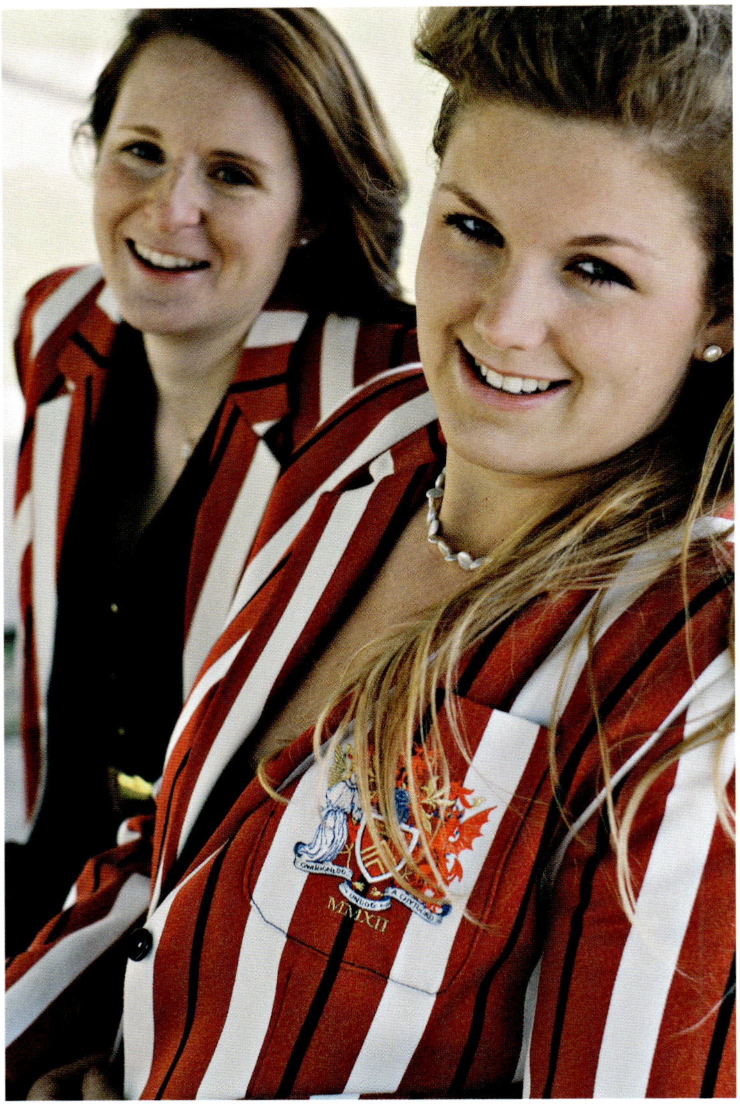

Cardiff, Wales

Cardiff University Rowing Club

PENNY CHALLANS,

AMY HILL

Oslo, Norway

Norske Studenters Roklub

DAVE STURE

The first *Norske Studenters Roklub* (Norwegian Students Rowing Club) blazers were created in 1908 to be worn by rowers at formal dinners and summer parties.

Every spring, the club inaugurates its racing season with a dual race against its rival across the Frognerkilen (a bay in the inner Oslofjord), *Christiania Roklub*. That same evening is the club's spring ball, where all male rowers are required to wear their blazers.

Dave Sture is an eleven-time Norwegian champion.

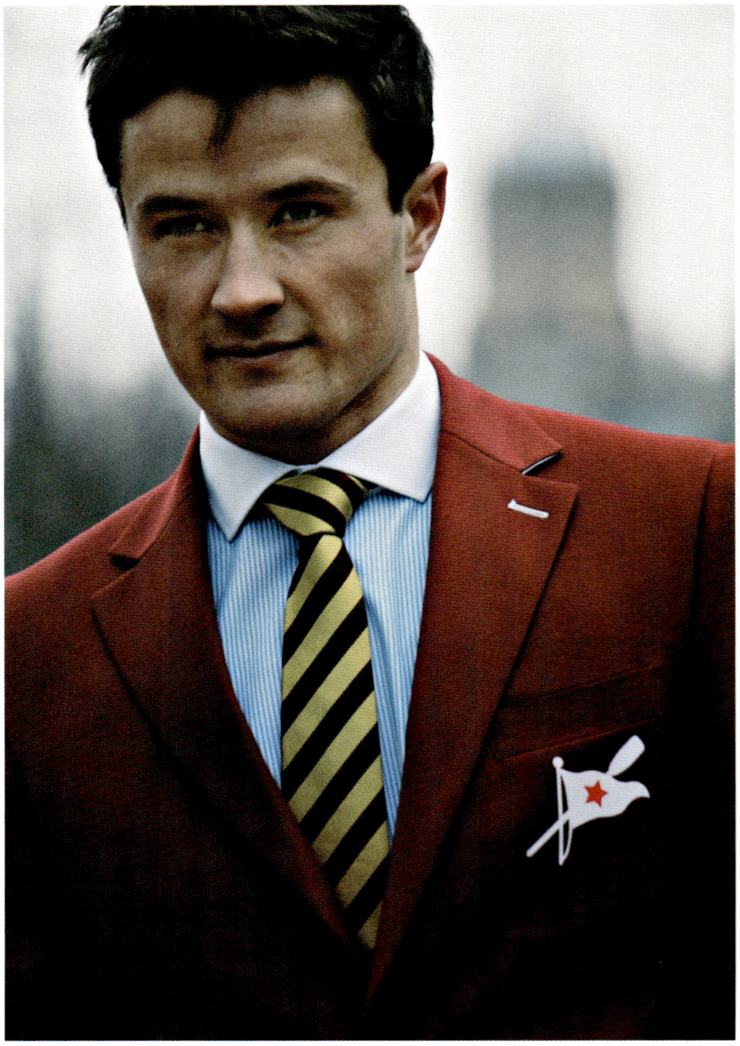

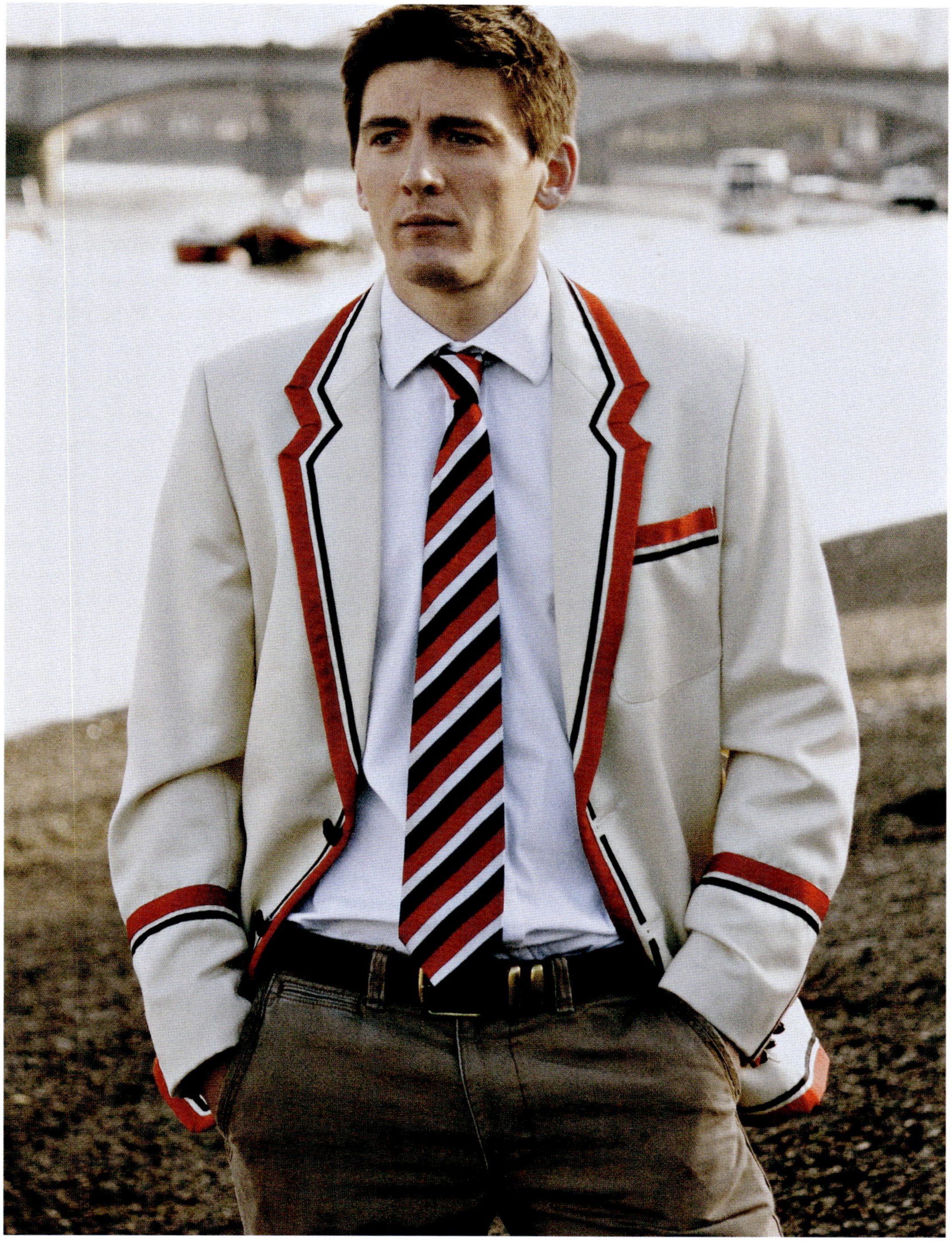

London, England

Thames Rowing Club

NICK CHALLINOR-HALFORD

Established in 1860 as City of London Rowing Club, and renamed Thames in 1862, T.R.C. began as a modest recreational club on the Putney Embankment. In its early years, it was not only a rowing club but it also organized and participated in cross-country running races and amateur boxing matches.

Today, Thames has won seventy-five Henley championships and is one of only five clubs (along with Leander Club, Oxford University Boat Club, Cambridge University Boat Club, and London Rowing Club) with the power to appoint a representative to the Council of British Rowing.

According to club rules, "Members who represent the Club at Henley Royal Regatta or Henley Women's Regatta, or who are present or past Club Chairmen, shall be entitled to wear the regatta coat, which shall be of white flannel trimmed with red and black braid and having Club buttons."

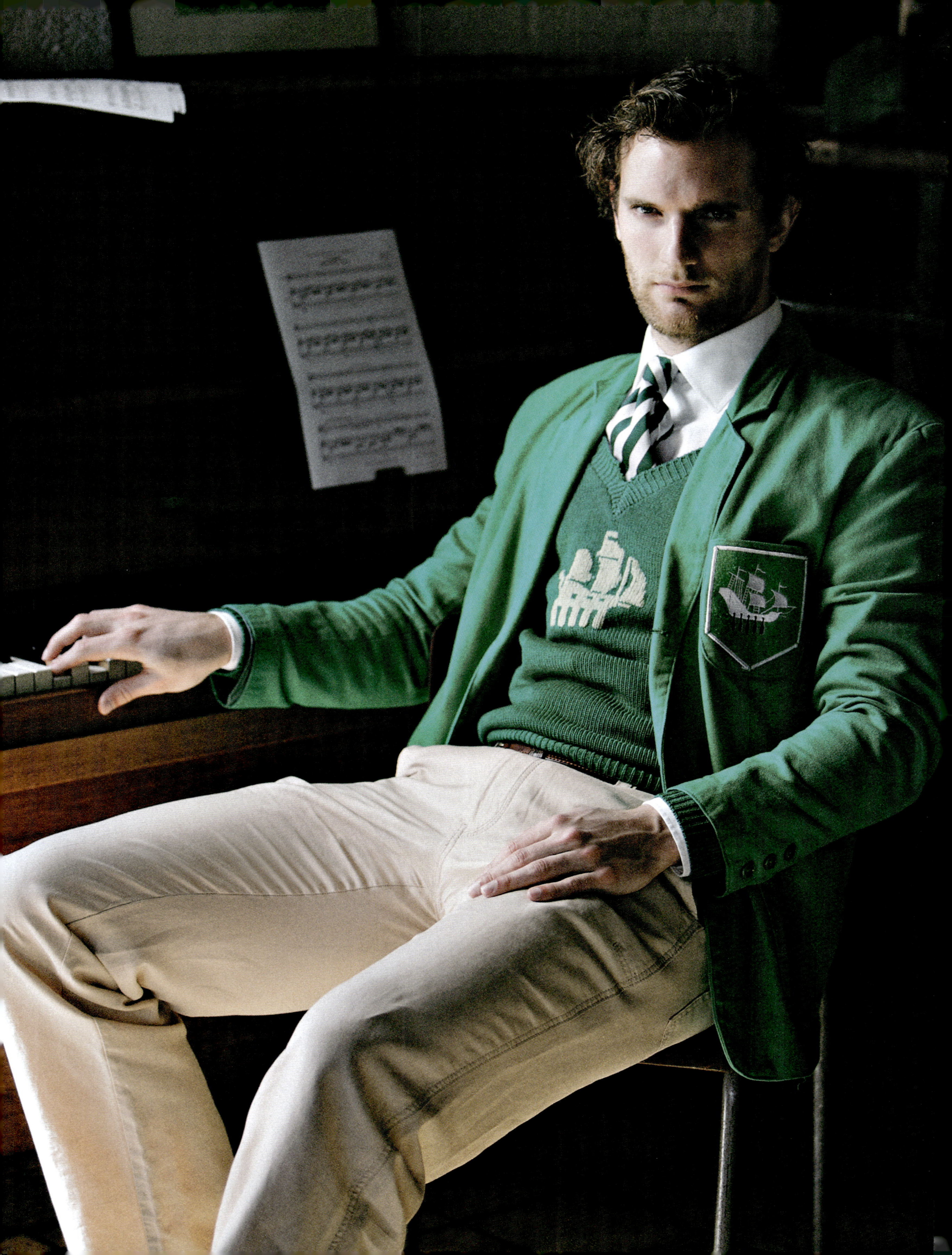

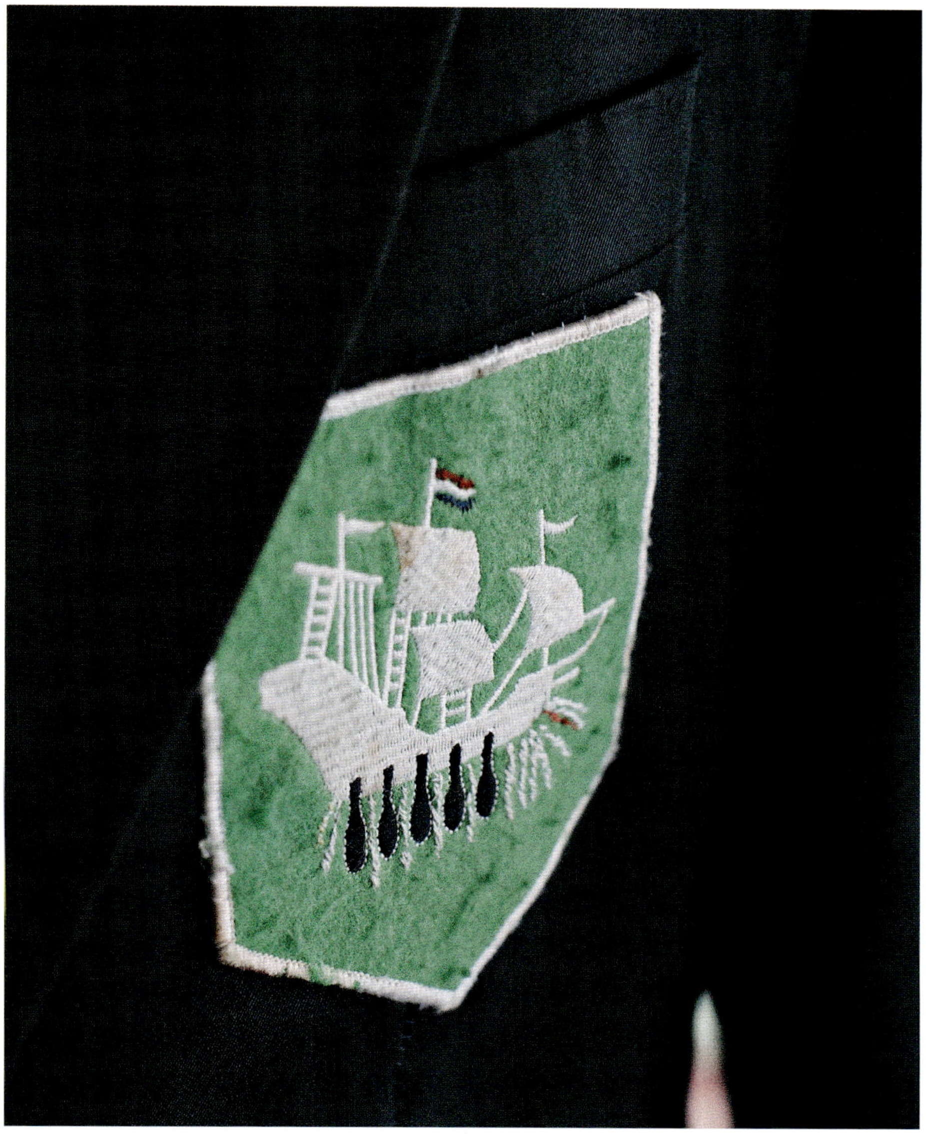

Wageningen, Netherlands

W.S.R. "Argo"

JOCHEM VAN DER HOUT

"The oars of the Argo bent like curved bows; such was the might of the hero-rowers."

—Apollonius of Rhodes, *Argonautica*, 3rd century BC

Wageningse Studenten Roeivereniging "Argo" is the student rowing club at the Dutch agricultural university at Wageningen. All members—including social members—may wear the green blazer, but only the club's serious competitors may wear the badge. The badge depicts the *Argo*, the mythical ship on which Jason and the Argonauts sailed in search of the Golden Fleece. For every race a rower wins, he may stitch a white "wave" beneath the ship on his blazer badge. And for winning a Dutch national championship, he may embroider a tiny Dutch flag on the ship's mast.

As a rower in the club's top four, Jochem van der Hout has an additional blazer and a sweater, also embellished with the *Argo*.

East Molesey, England

Molesey Boat Club

ANDY TRIGGS-HODGE MBE

"Henley has more zebras than a zoo."

—Ann Barr and Peter York, *The Sloane Ranger Handbook*, 1982

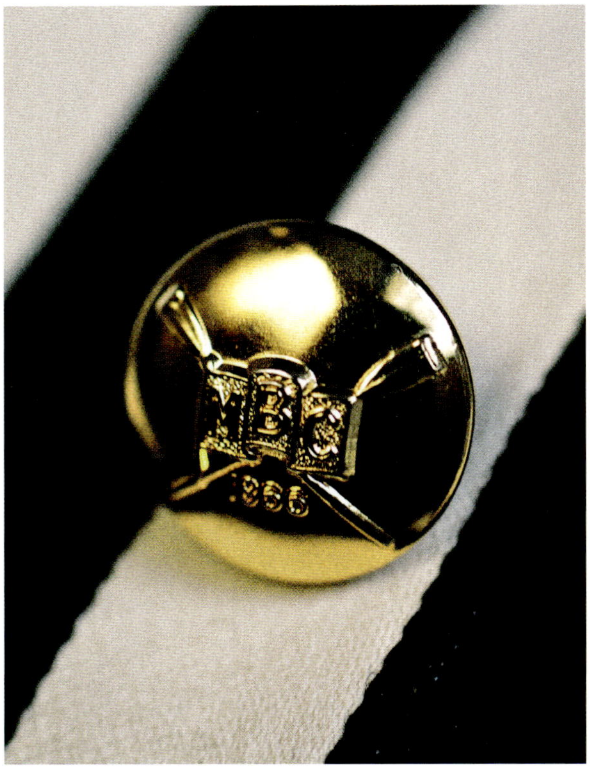

Molesey Boat Club, known colloquially as "The Black Death," rows with solid black blades and in black-and-white uniforms. The club tie features diagonal black-and-white stripes, while the "summer tie," for regatta wear, is composed of narrower horizontal stripes. The club rules state that the Molesey blazer should be either white with black binding or solid black or navy blue with M.B.C. buttons in white gold. Nowadays, however, the (apparently unofficial) striped Molesey blazer is the version most often seen on the Henley winners' podium, where Black Death oarsmen frequently appear.

One of those oarsmen is two-time Olympic gold medalist Andy Triggs-Hodge.

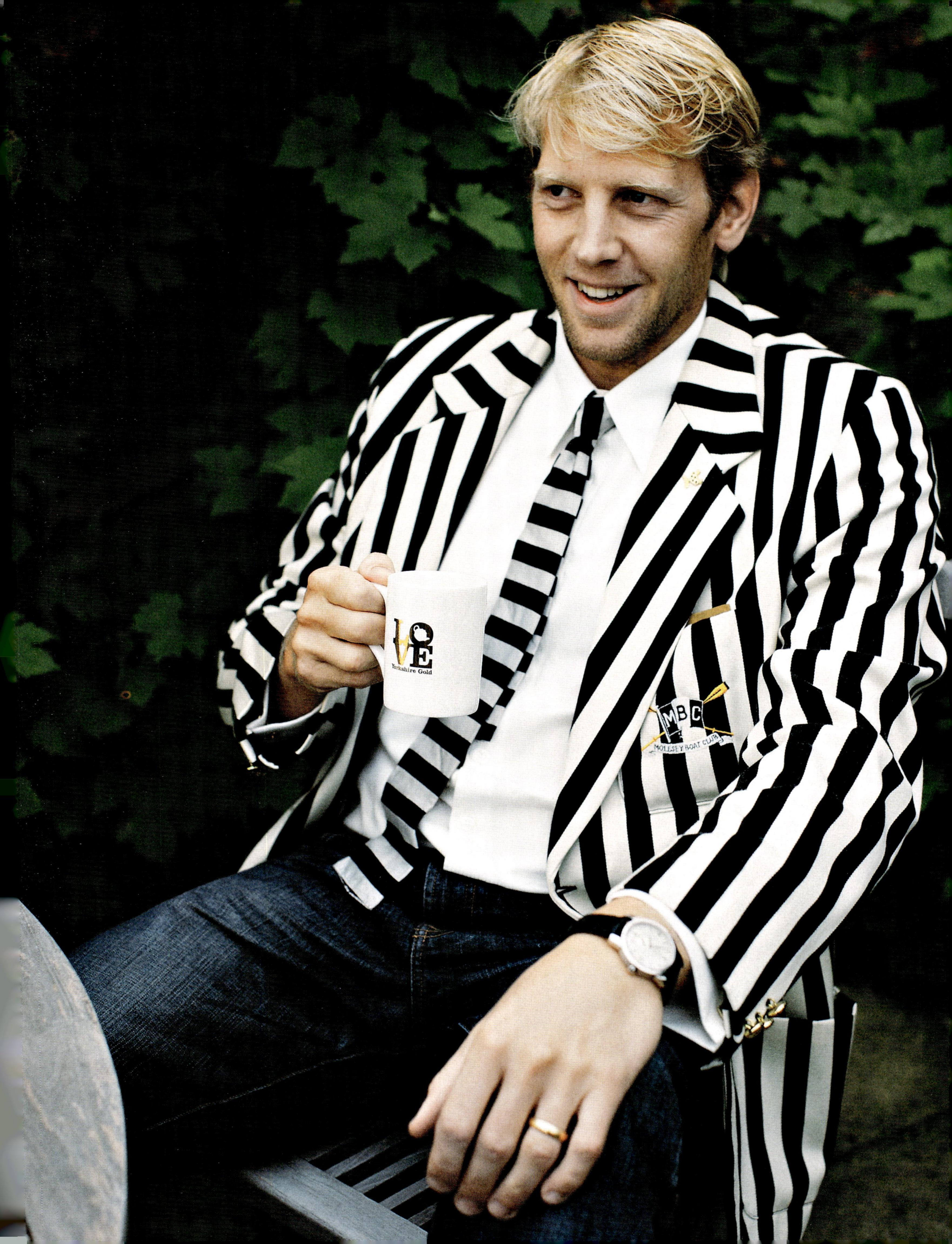
LOVE
Yorkshire Gold
MBC
MOLESEY BOAT CLUB

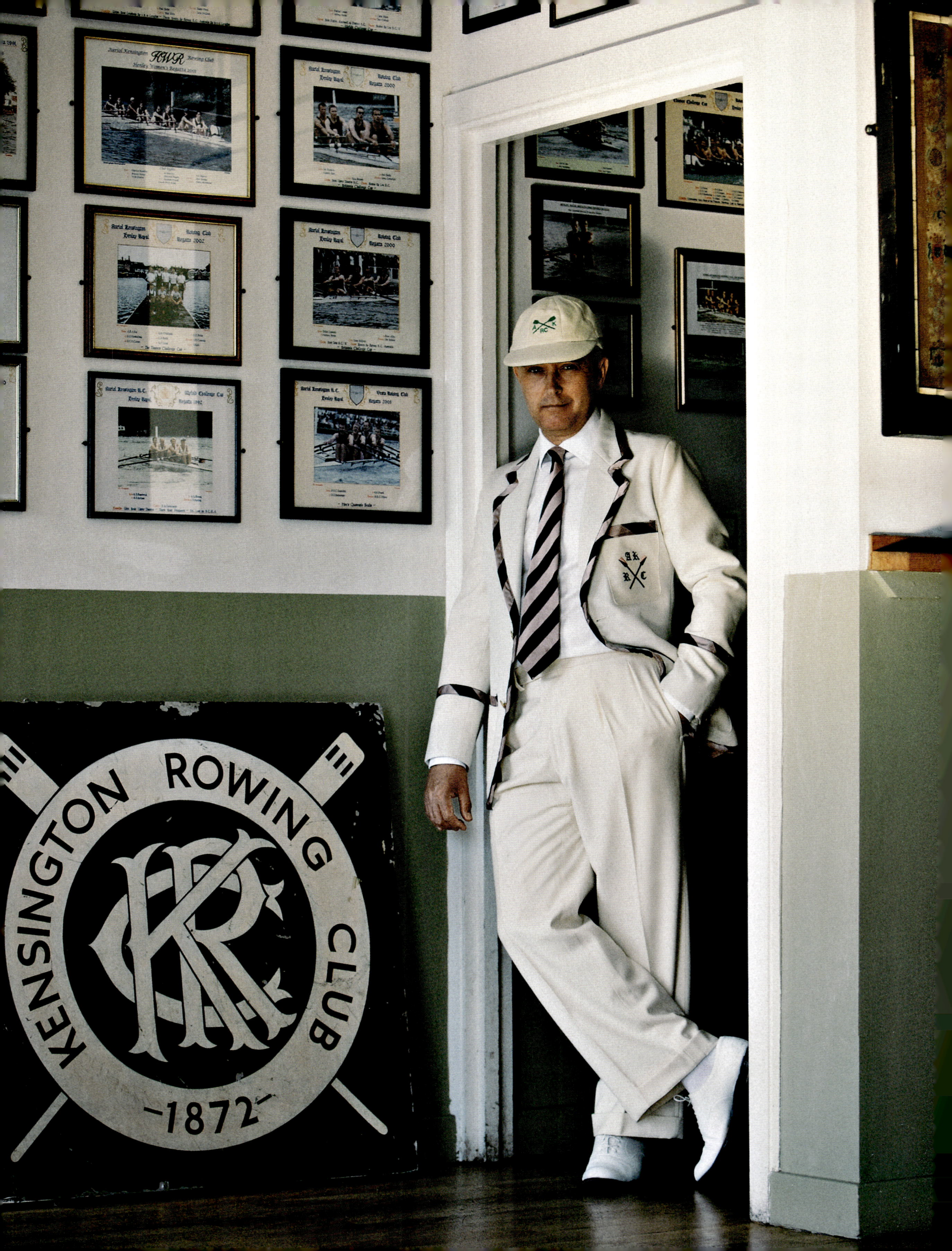
KENSINGTON ROWING CLUB
1872

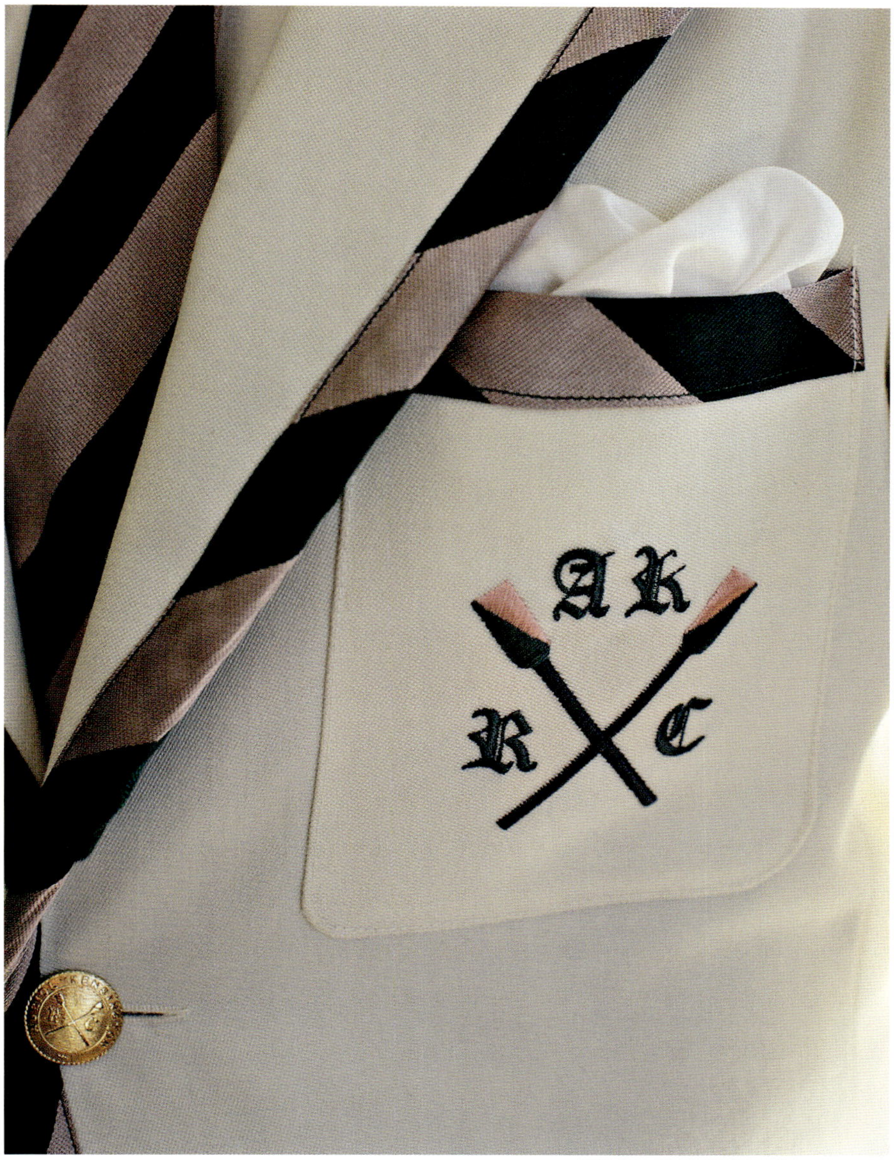

London, England

Auriol Kensington Rowing Club

TIM KOCH

Auriol Rowing Club was established by a clergyman in 1896 to promote "muscular Christianity" among working men, and never seems to have taken the subject of its blazers too seriously. The early Auriol blazers were, for the sake of frugality, perhaps, plain cream. Later versions were blue with green trim.

Kensington Rowing Club, on the other hand, was founded in 1872 and considered itself the socially superior club in Hammersmith. Like the grand clubs downstream at Putney, Kensington created strict rules to govern the wearing of blazers:

> *The official blazer for regatta crews to be White with Black and Pink facings; members who have won their "Juniors" to wear the club initials on the pocket. For other than Regatta crews the blazer to be Black, with Pink facings. The official cap to be White. Juniors to have the club initials in Pink and the Seniors the club initials with crossed oars. The club colours must not be worn on Sundays under any circumstances.*

When the clubs combined in 1981, Kensington's pink and Auriol's green were chosen as the colors of the new Auriol Kensington Rowing Club. Coincidentally (or not), it was only one year earlier that *The Official Preppy Handbook* first espoused "The Virtues of Pink and Green."

Tim Koch is an Auriol Kensington stalwart and a fount of rowing history knowledge.

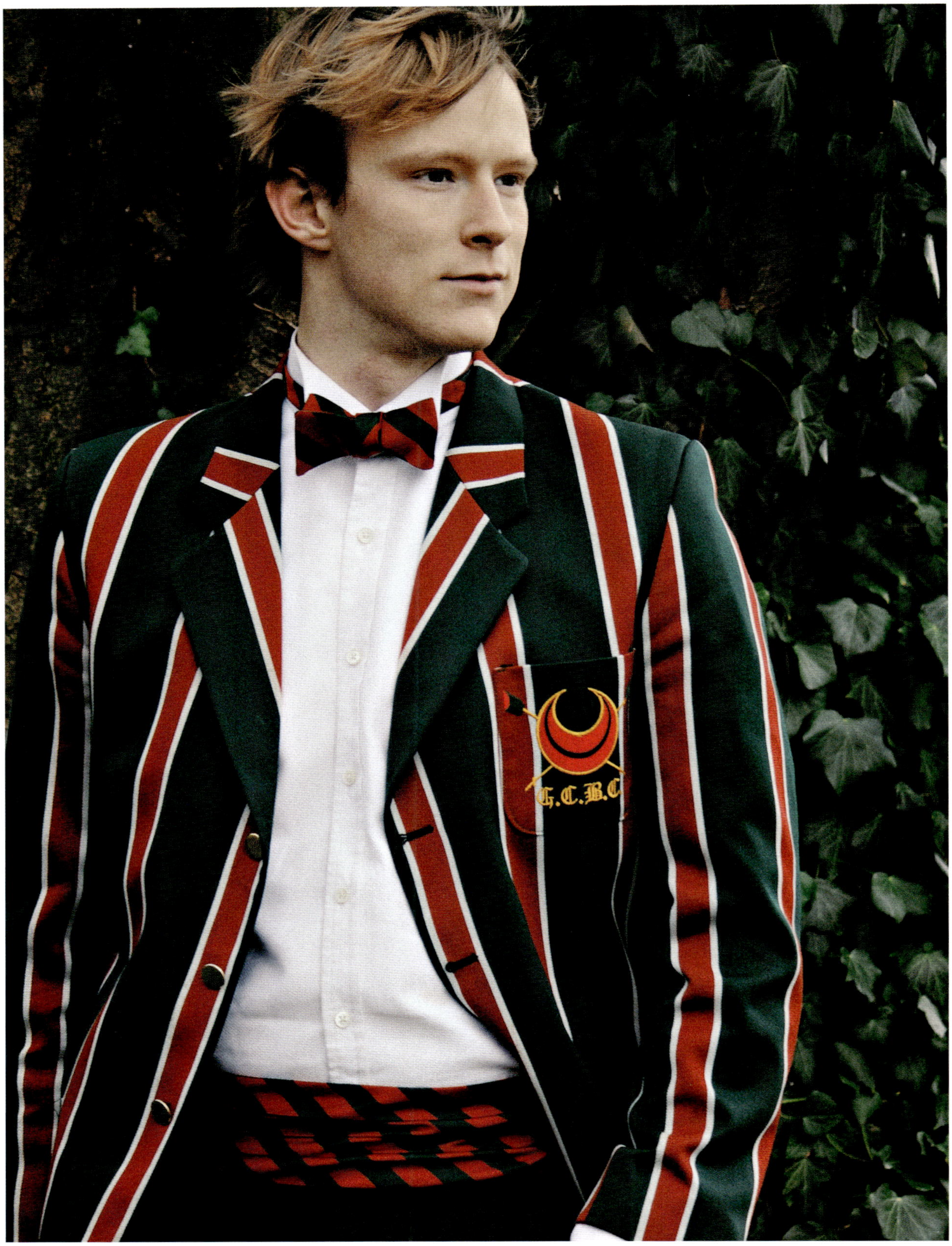

Cambridge, England

Girton College Boat Club, Cambridge

TOM HELLIER

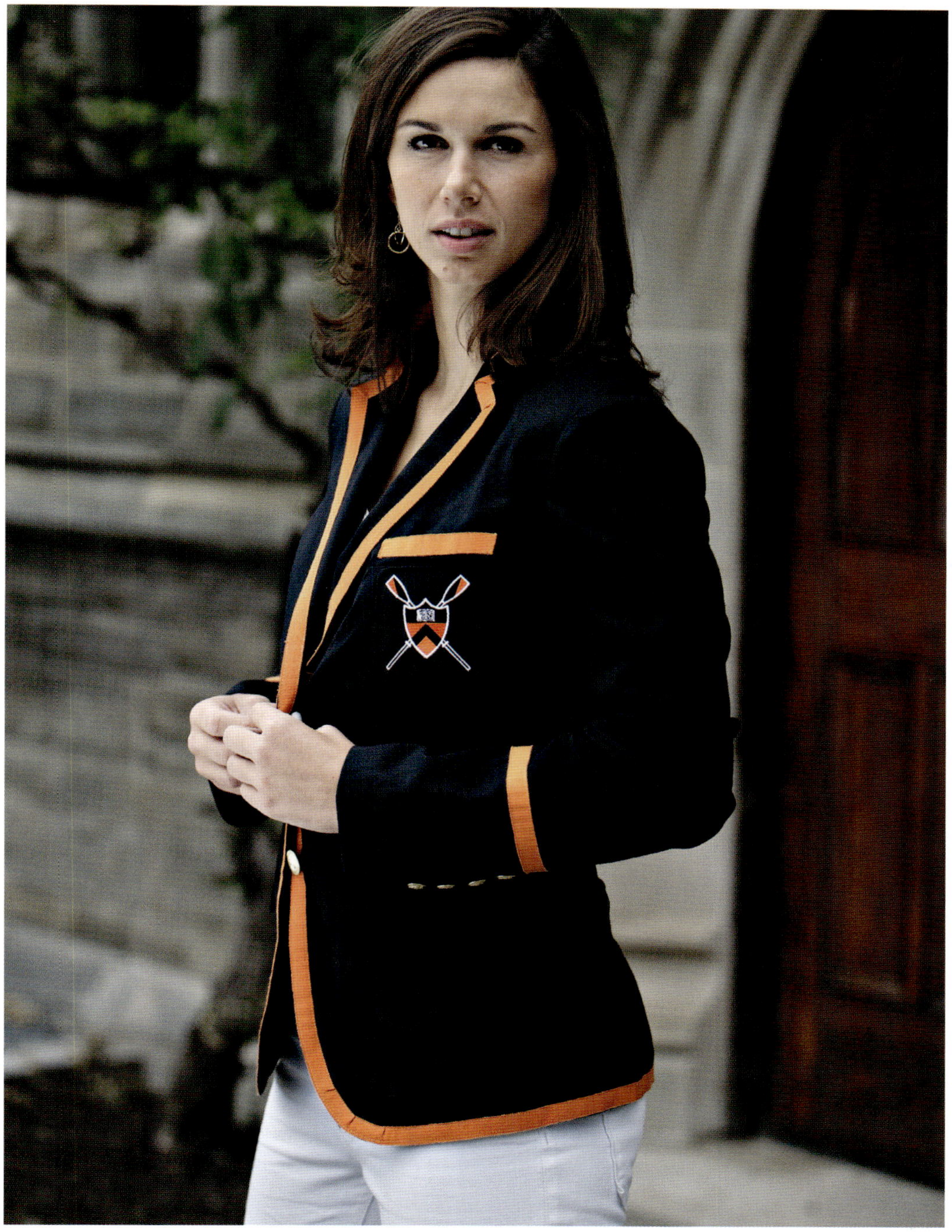

Princeton, New Jersey

Princeton University

SARA HENDERSHOT

Princeton's colors pay homage to William III, Prince of Orange and Count of Nassau, for whom the university's principal building (Nassau Hall) is named. The rowing team first donned orange and black in 1874, when the freshman crew wore hatbands in the colors.

The design of the blazer has changed over the years, and past Princeton crews often wore white or cream-colored blazers. Recent blazers, however, have been black with orange trim, each button bearing the image of a snarling tiger's face.

Sara was the captain of the Princeton women's team; she is an Olympian and a world champion in the women's four.

OVERLEAF: Princeton, in orange tops, races in lane 2 at the 2010 NCAA national championship final.

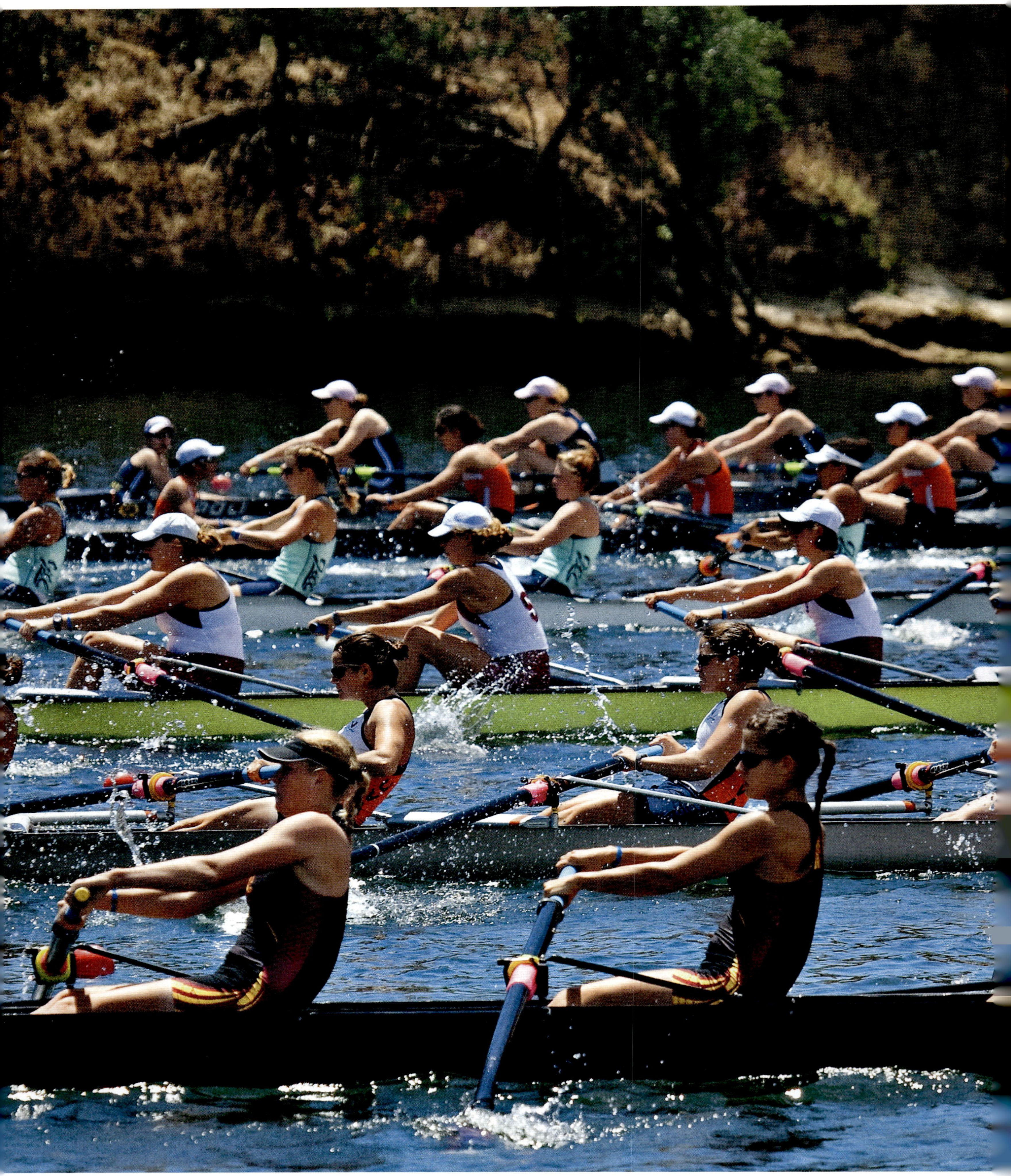

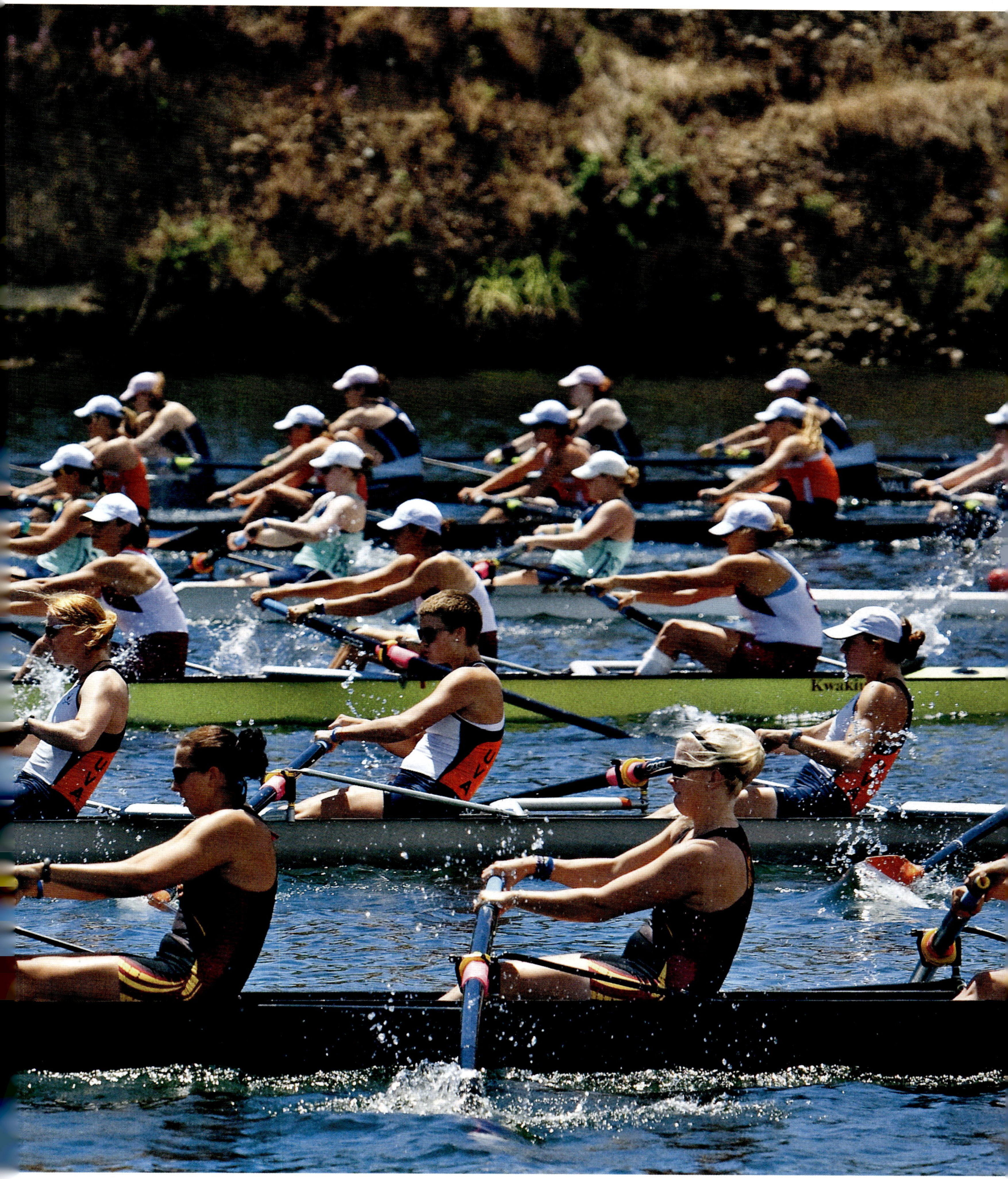

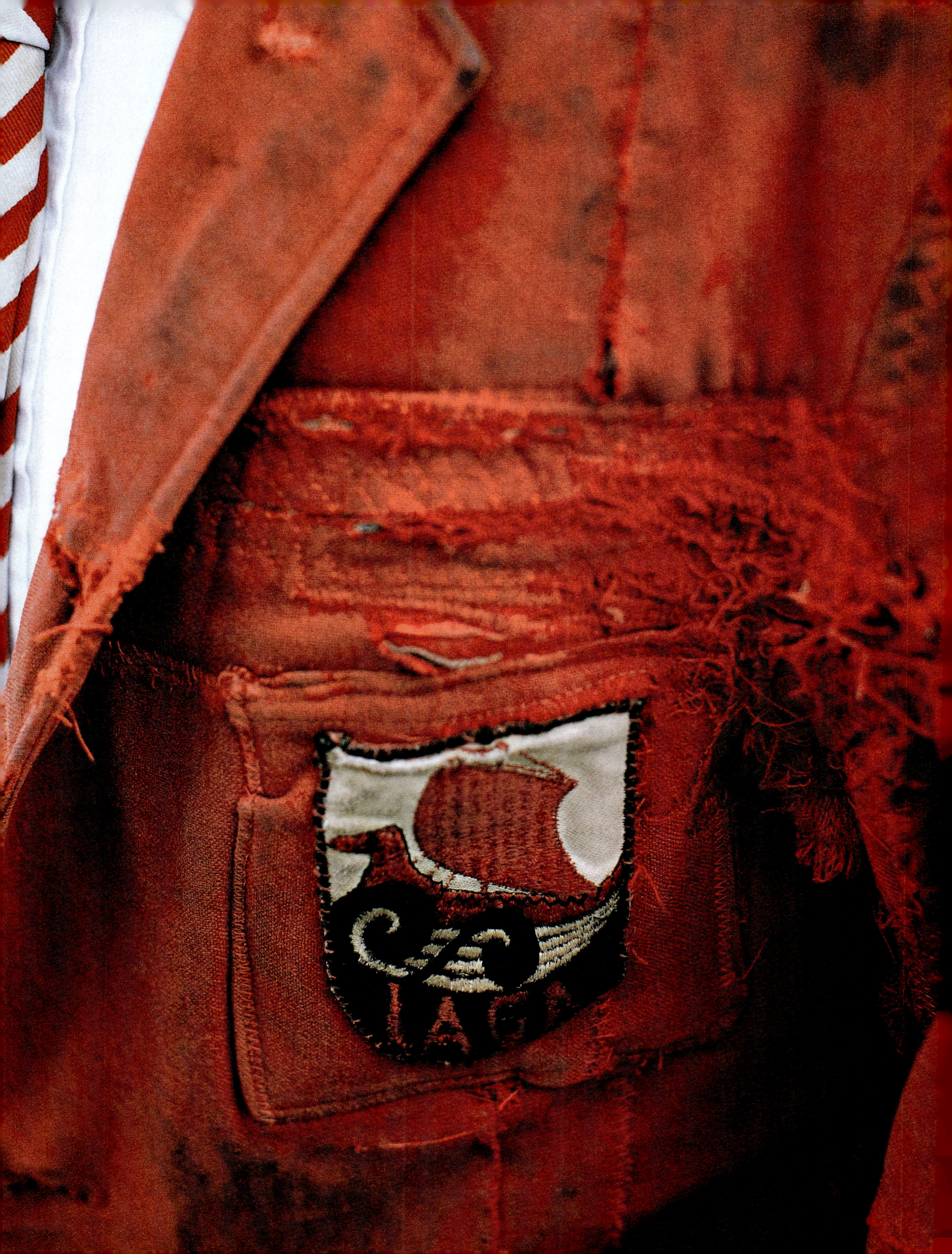

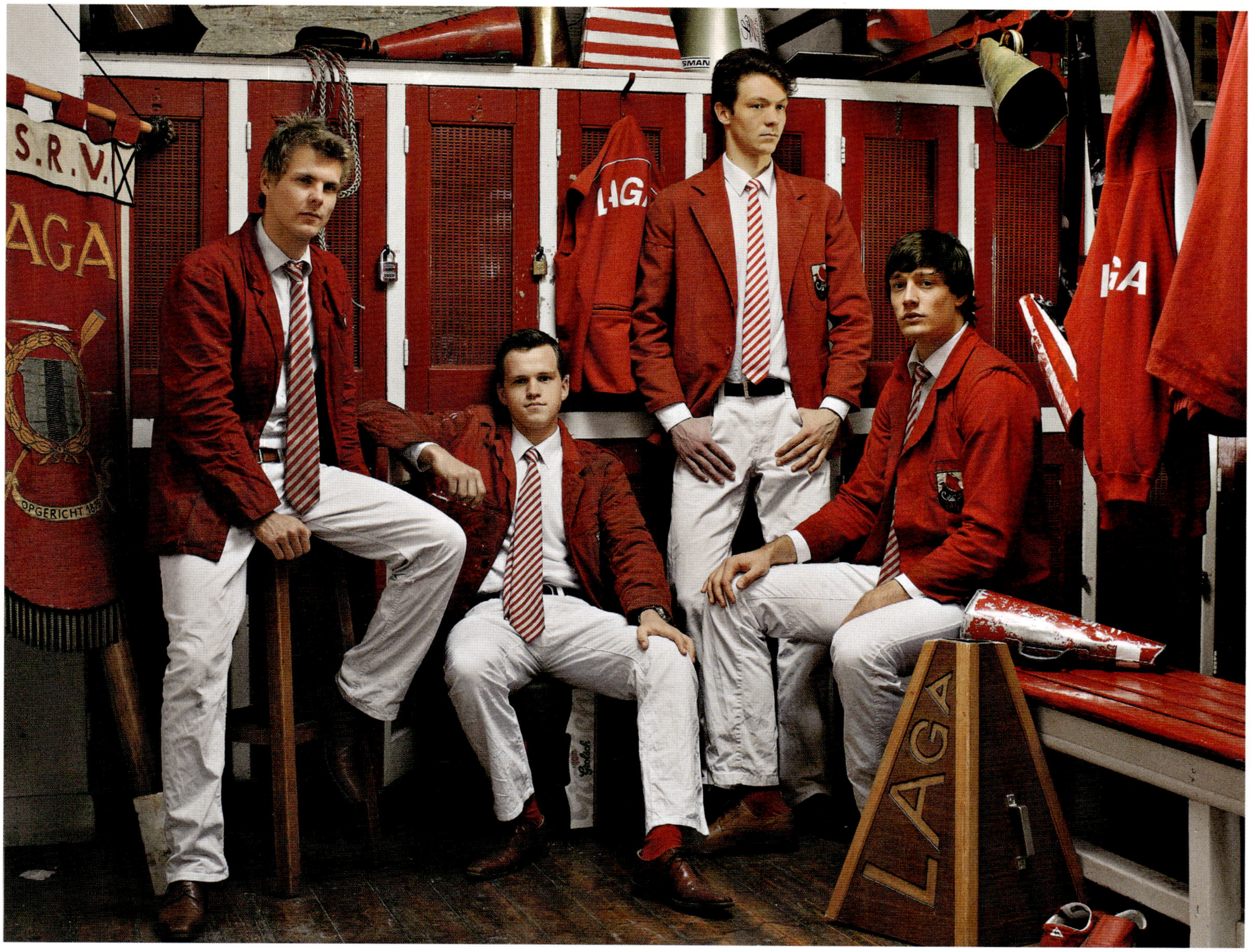

Delft, Netherlands

D.S.R.V. "Laga"

THIJS KAMPHUIS, ARNOUT DRAAIJER, JELLE VAN DER ZWAAG,
PETER EVERS, EVELIJN VINK, JURJAN DE GRAAF

Delftsche Studenten Roeivereeniging "Laga" rowers have been wearing blazers since the turn of the twentieth century, when Dutch clubs began to pick up the English blazer tradition. The club "uniform" was codified as a red jacket, white trousers, white shirt, and the red-and-white Laga tie. Each rower was responsible for stitching his own blazer badge—an image of a ship—onto his jacket.

When a rower retires, he must hand his blazer on to a new oarsman. The Laga blazers worn nowadays are decades old and famously ill-fitting. What's more, tradition dictates that a jacket cannot be cleaned until its wearer has won the most prestigious Dutch regatta: the Varsity.

ABOVE: Thijs, Arnout, Jelle, and Peter in the Laga locker room.

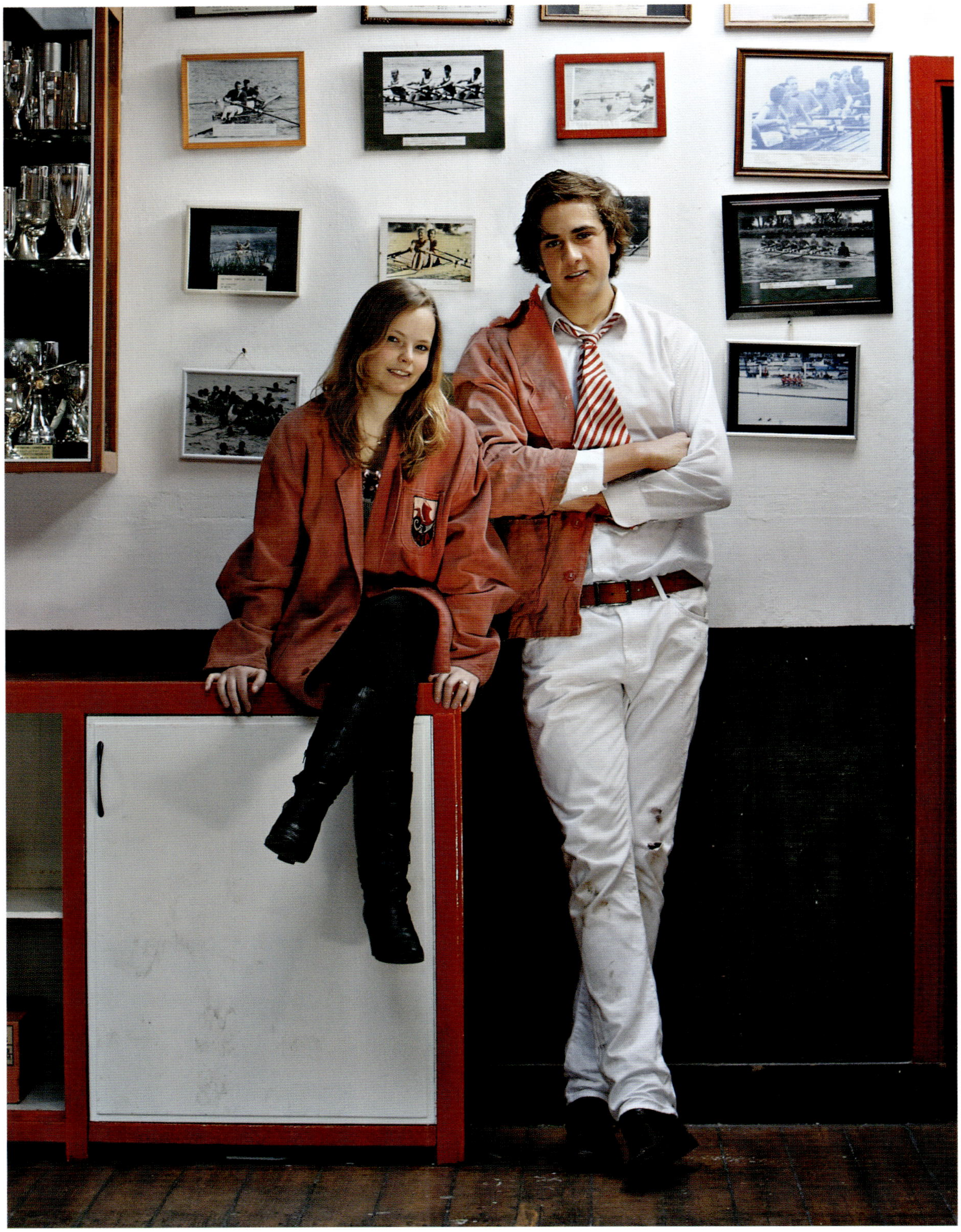

Besides being old, the blazers are often victims of the traditional inter-club fights that follow major student races in the Netherlands. The unwritten rules of these battles require participants to wrestle by grasping one another's lapels, so it is no surprise that blazers are routinely ripped in the process.

Frayed and filthy, their fibers saturated with generations of river water, sweat, and alcohol, many of the jackets have been torn apart and sewn back together countless times. Others have been less lucky: Jurjan de Graaf is not the first Laga oarsman to wake up the morning after a post-race fight with only half of a blazer.

Laga won the Temple Challenge Cup at Henley in 2013.

ABOVE: Evelijn, a coxswain, is wearing a particularly ill-fitting blazer, while traditional post-race fighting has left Jurjan with a half blazer.

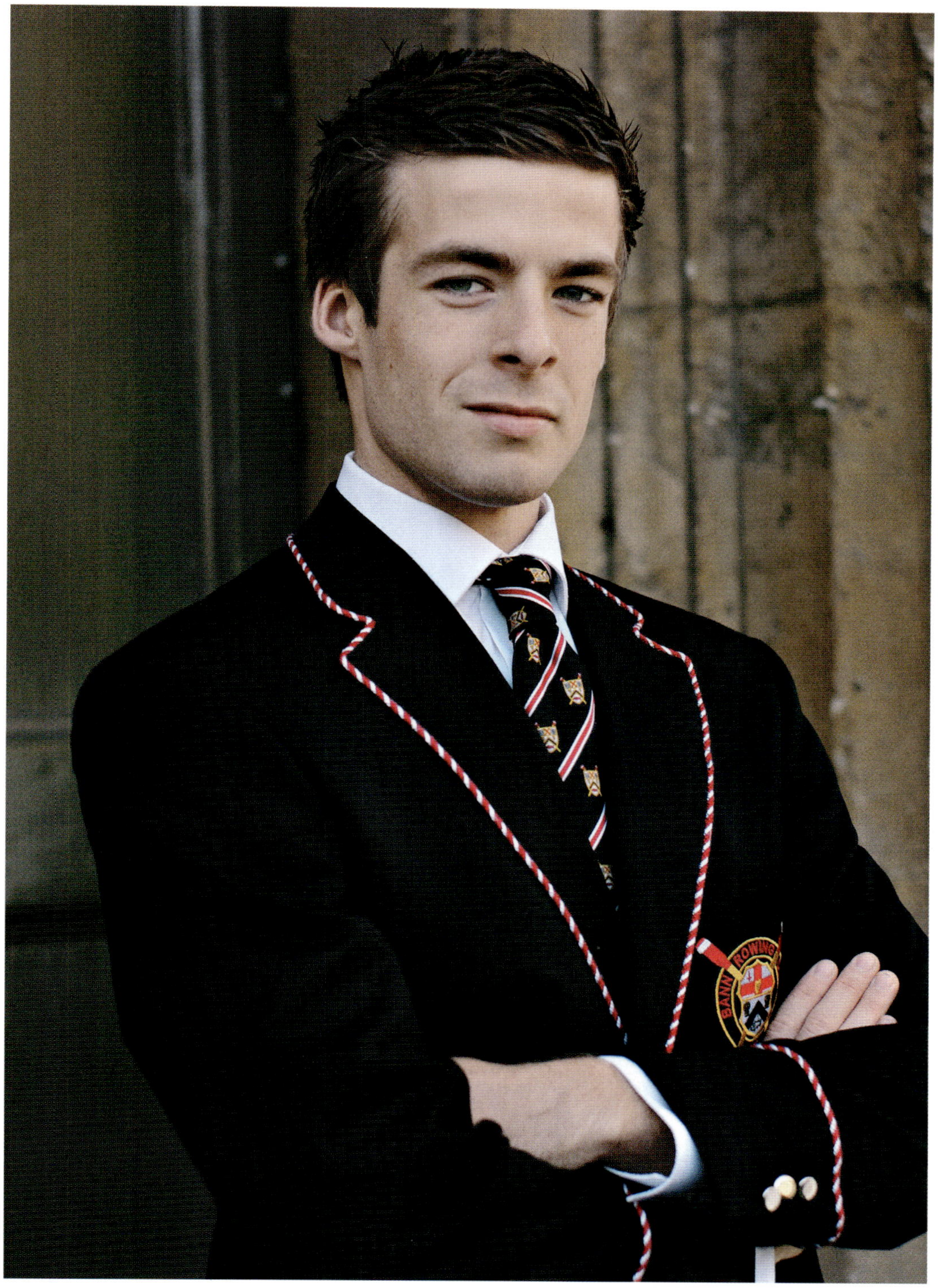

Coleraine, Northern Ireland

Bann Rowing Club

JOEL CASSELLS

Bann is a Northern Irish incubator for world-class oarsmen. Joel Cassells, who stroked the Great Britain lightweight four to a silver medal at the 2013 under-23 world championships, is the most recent rising star in international rowing to have honed his skills at Bann. He was preceded by recent Olympians Peter Chambers, Richard Chambers, Alan Campbell, and Richard Archibald.

In the past, the Bann blazer has been red with white trim, but the modern club blazers are black with narrow red-and-white piping. The badge bears the Bann Rowing Club coat of arms, a combination of the arms of Londonderry and those of Coleraine.

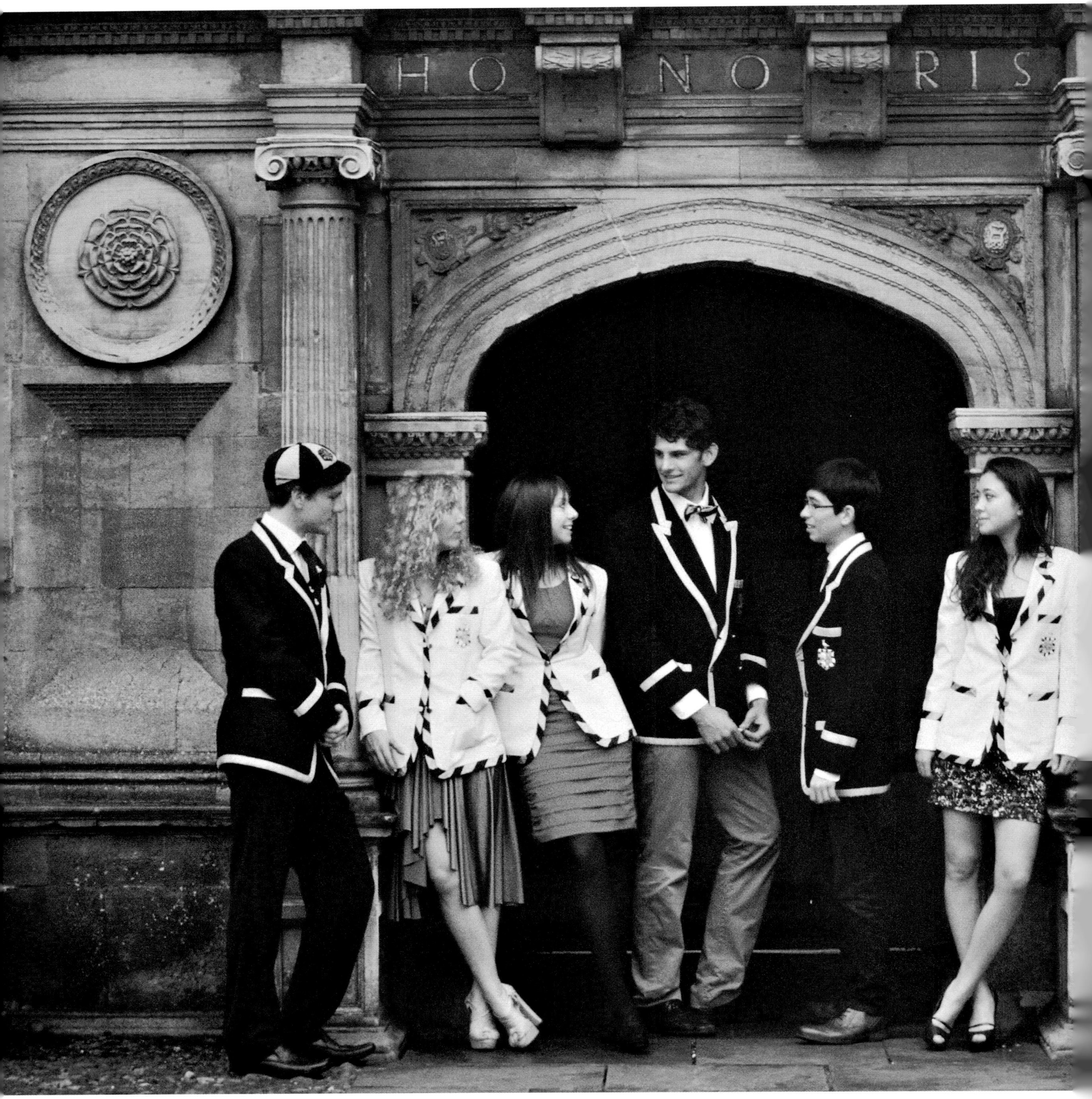
HONORIS

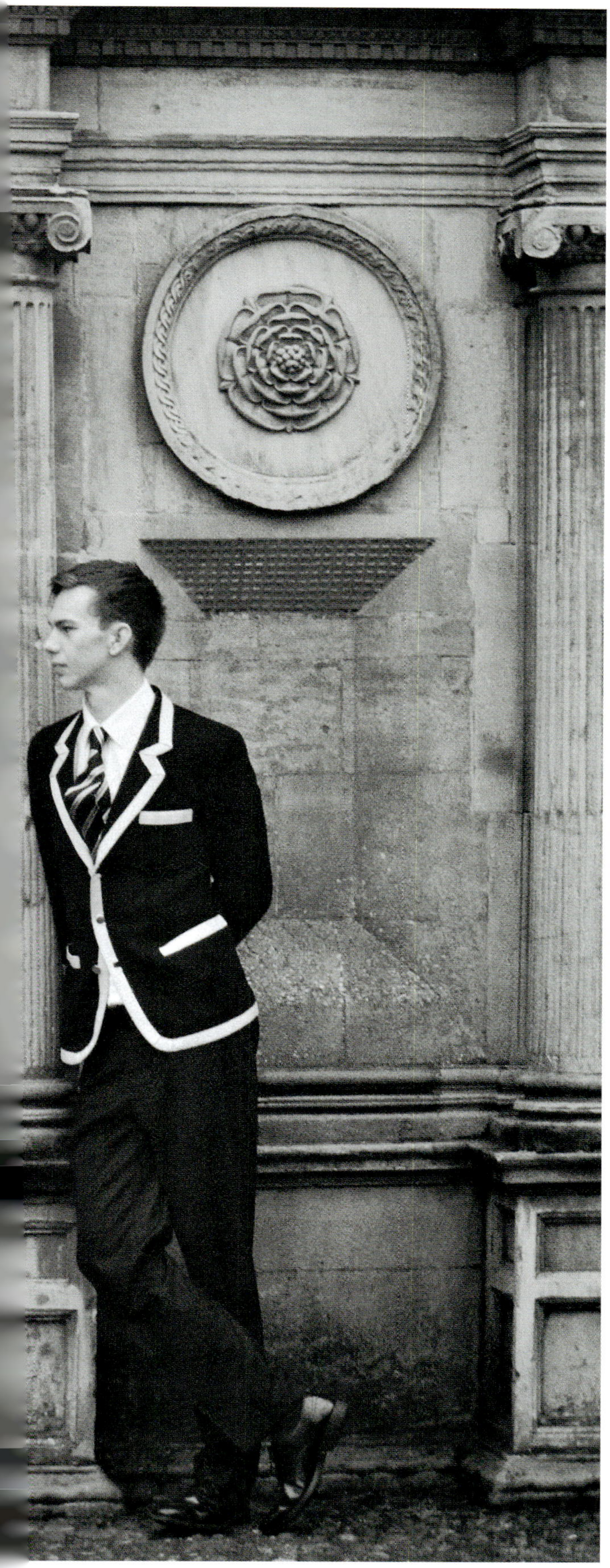

Cambridge, England

Caius Boat Club, Cambridge

GORDON BECK, JILLY TOREY,
CLAIRE OAKLEY, SAM LLOYD, JON DEAN,
EMMA WALKER, STEVE KEMP

According to myth, Caius Boat Club—the rowing club of Gonville & Caius College, Cambridge—was granted the privilege of using Cambridge University Boat Club's distinctive light green-blue color ("light blue" or "Cambridge Blue") after Caius represented the university in a fixture against Cambridge Town Rowing Club in 1844. In reality, however, Caius was using light blue as its color years before the University Boat Club adopted the same shade in 1836.

"Caius Wherry Club," as the club was initially known, was established in 1827. The founders adopted a crest—a dove bearing an olive branch—and a motto, *Labor ipse voluptas* (Work is a pleasure in itself), both of which are used today not only by the boat club but also by the college generally. Records show that in 1829, the club ordered a flag emblazoned with these symbols on a light blue silk background.

The club's jacket design changed several times over the years, but in 1870 the club settled on double-breasted black jackets with light blue (Cambridge Blue) trim. In practice, crew photographs from the late nineteenth century show a mixture of double-breasted and single-breasted blazers. This design has remained virtually unchanged since, and both double-breasted and single-breasted versions continue to be made for Caius oarsmen. The recently conceived women's blazer recalls an earlier, 1863, version of the Caius Boat Club "over-jersey": "white flannel, trimmed with the Club colours of black and light blue."

In recent years, Caius has been the most successful of the Cambridge college boat clubs, with its men's first eight holding over ten consecutive Headships (first-place finishes) in the Cambridge bumping races. Per Cambridge tradition, this entitles Caius to erect a clock tower on top of its boathouse; construction is in the planning stages.

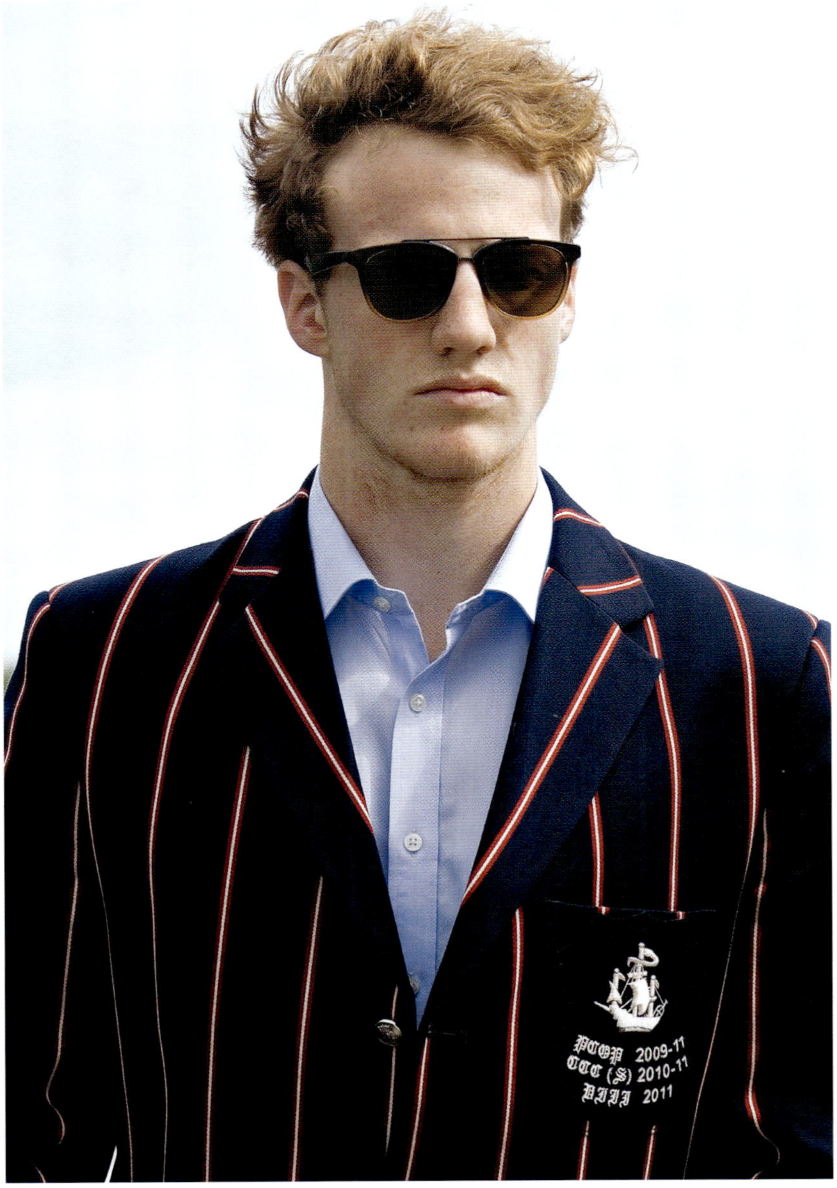

Pangbourne, England

Pangbourne College Boat Club and the Paravicini Blazer

HAMISH MILLER

"In terms of glamour and status Paravicini far outweighed being in the 6th Form. . . . It offered a private club room within which were mountains of McVities chocolate biscuits (verging on black market status) and the facility to make coffee. The icing on top of these fabulously rare privileges was the opportunity to buy the smartest striped blazer in the world."

—Lt. Col. Mike Nicholson, 2012

Rowers and other sportsmen at the Nautical College Pangbourne, now known as Pangbourne College, have traditionally been members of "Paravicini"—a club of sorts, named after the illustrious cricketer, footballer, and sometime bursar of the school, Percy de Paravicini. With membership comes the right to wear the coveted striped blazer.

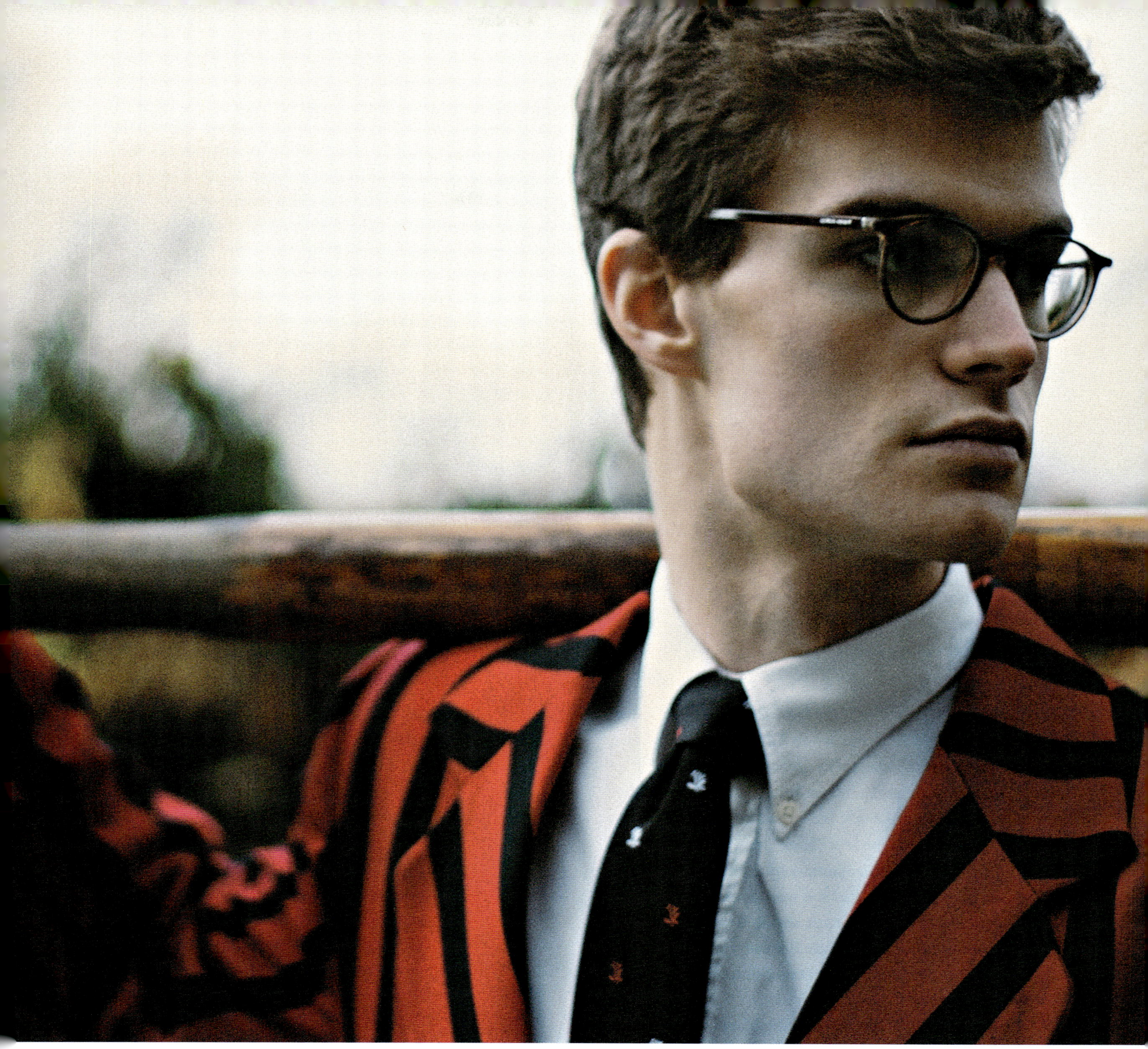

Oxford, England

Magdalen College School Boat Club

TOM GUNTER

Cambridge, England

Cambridge University Boat Club

GEOFF ROTH

In a letter dated March 12, 1829, W. Snow of St. John's College, Cambridge, wrote to his old classmate from Eton, T. Staniforth of Christ Church, Oxford:

> *The University of Cambridge hereby challenge the University of Oxford to row a match at or near London each in an eight-oar boat during the Easter vacation.*
>
> *—W Snow*
> *St. John's College*

The challenge was accepted and the first Oxford-Cambridge Boat Race was eventually held at Henley-on-Thames on June 10, 1829, when an Oxford crew in dark blue uniforms beat a Cambridge crew in mixed jerseys and pink neckerchiefs. It was not until the second boat race, held in London in 1836, that Cambridge adopted its now famous shade of "blue": shortly before racing, one of the Cambridge rowers purchased a length of light blue ribbon and tied it to the bow of the boat. Several of the Cambridge oarsmen had rowed at Eton, and it is possible that the choice of color was inspired by Eton Blue, to which Cambridge Blue is now identical. Cambridge won easily and has kept light blue as its color ever since.

Today the race is an annual event, taking place during the Easter vacation on a 4¼-mile course between Putney and Mortlake in London with more than a quarter of a million spectators lining the bank. Cambridge leads the series, with eighty-one wins to Oxford's seventy-seven (the 1877 race was declared a "dead heat to Oxford by five feet" by finish-line judge "Honest John" Phelps).

The C.U.B.C. blazer is Cambridge Blue with Cambridge Blue trim: the same color as the C.U.B.C. scarf, cap, blades, and the interior of the club's boathouse in Cambridge, where every Blue Boat crew since 1829 is listed below the word "won" or "lost." Per tradition, a C.U.B.C. blazer is never washed.

Geoff Roth rowed in the winning Cambridge Blue Boat in 2010.

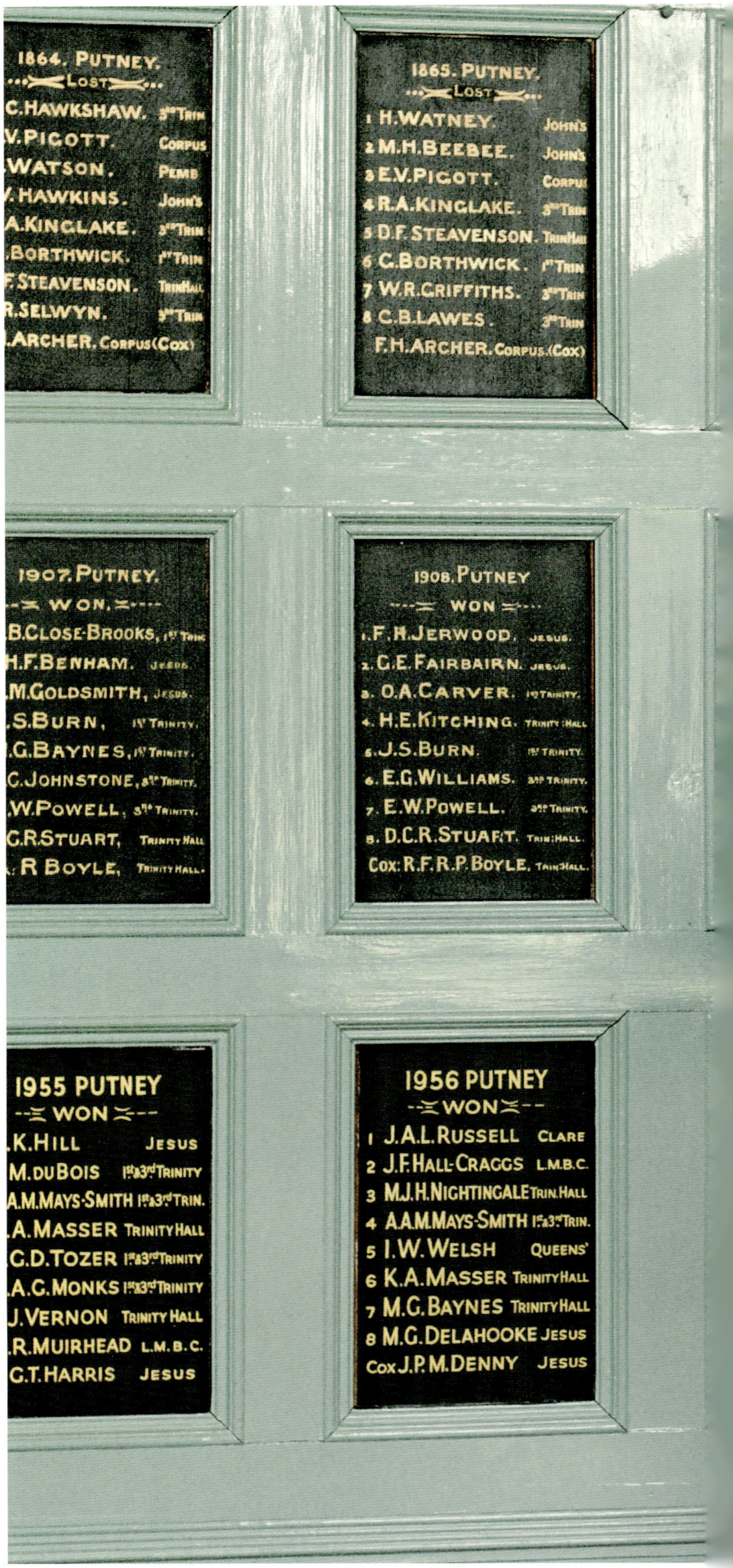

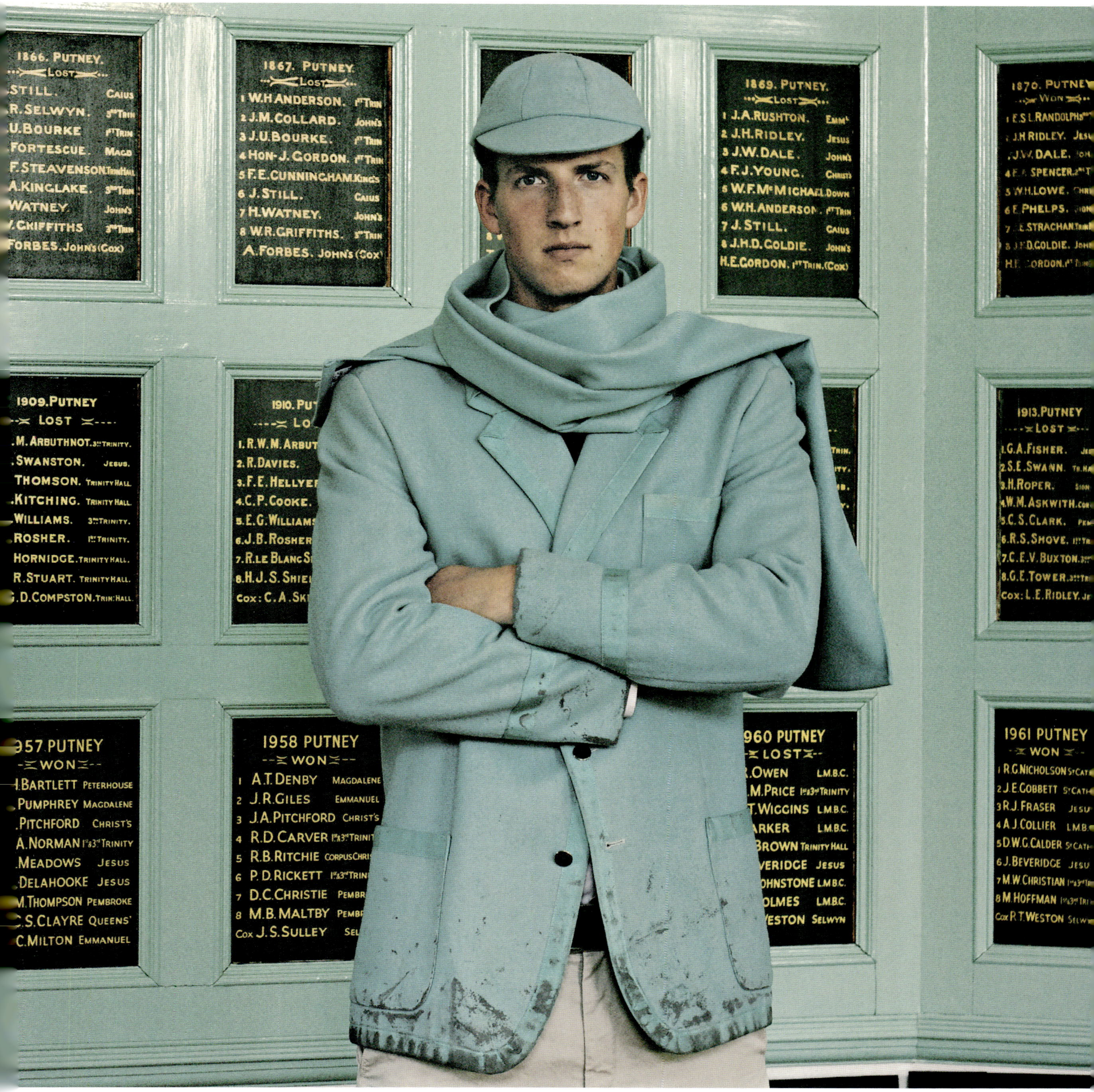

1866. PUTNEY.
LOST
1867. PUTNEY.
LOST
1 W.H.ANDERSON. 1st TRIN
2 J.M.COLLARD. JOHN'S
3 J.U.BOURKE. 1st TRIN
4 HON-J.GORDON. 1st TRIN
5 F.E.CUNNINGHAM. KING'S
6 J.STILL. CAIUS
7 H.WATNEY. JOHN'S
8 W.R.GRIFFITHS. 3rd TRIN
A.FORBES. JOHN'S (COX)
1869. PUTNEY.
LOST
1 J.A.RUSHTON. EMM
2 J.H.RIDLEY. JESUS
3 J.W.DALE. JOHN'S
4 F.J.YOUNG. CHRIST'S
5 W.F.McMICHAEL. DOWN
6 W.H.ANDERSON. 1st TRIN
7 J.STILL. CAIUS
8 J.H.D.GOLDIE. JOHN'S
H.E.GORDON. 1st TRIN. (COX)
1909.PUTNEY
LOST
1913.PUTNEY
LOST
1958 PUTNEY
WON
1 A.T.DENBY MAGDALENE
2 J.R.GILES EMMANUEL
3 J.A.PITCHFORD CHRIST'S
4 R.D.CARVER
5 R.B.RITCHIE
6 P.D.RICKETT
7 D.C.CHRISTIE
8 M.B.MALTBY
COX J.S.SULLEY
1961 PUTNEY
WON

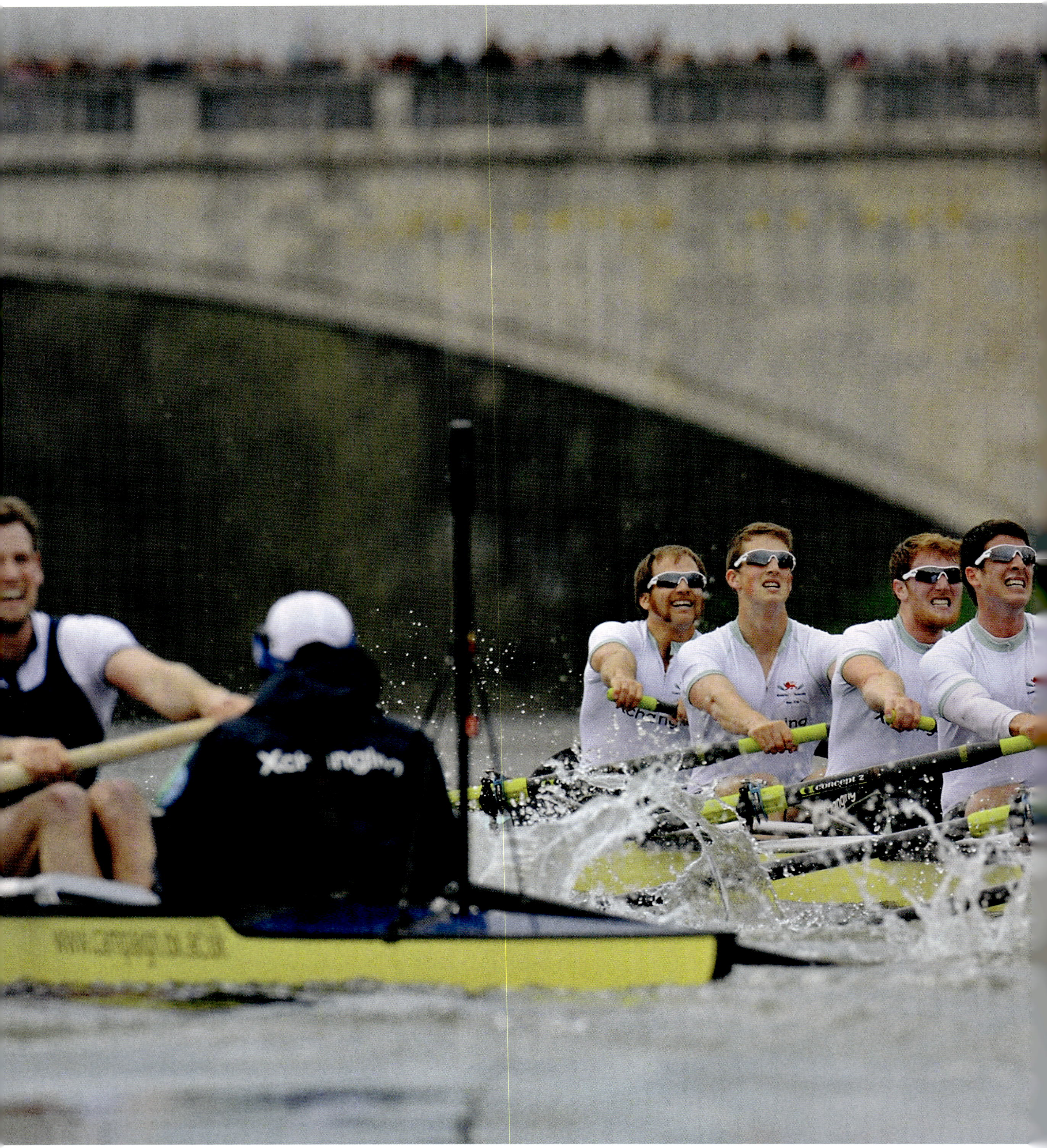

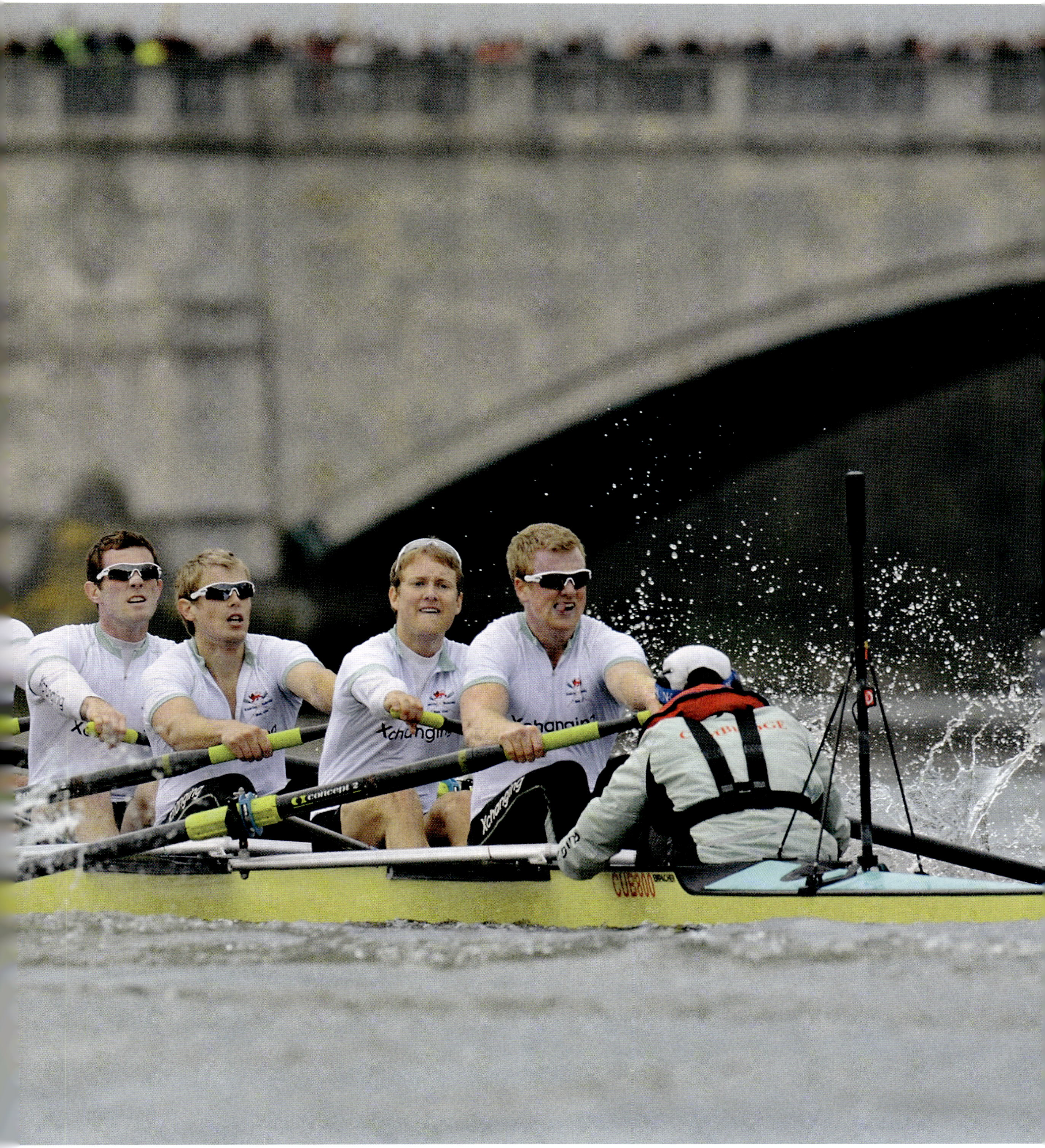

Cambridge pulls ahead of Oxford in the final mile of the 2010 Boat Race.

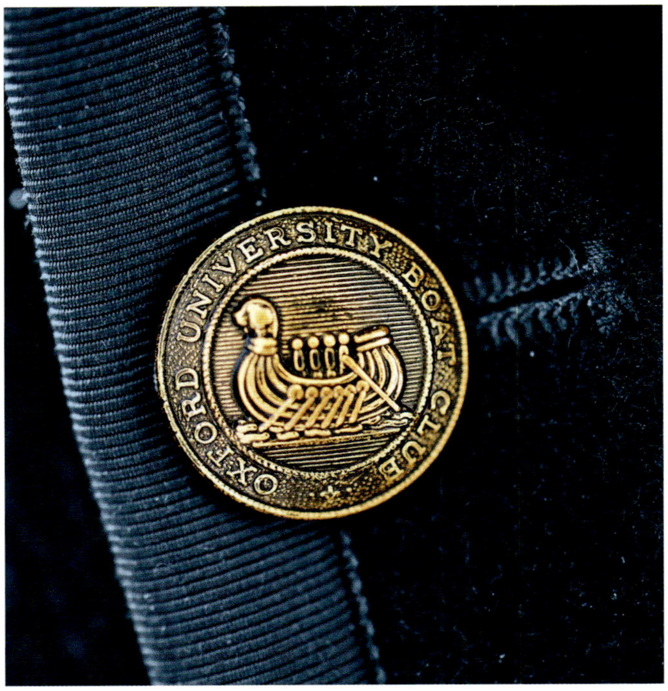

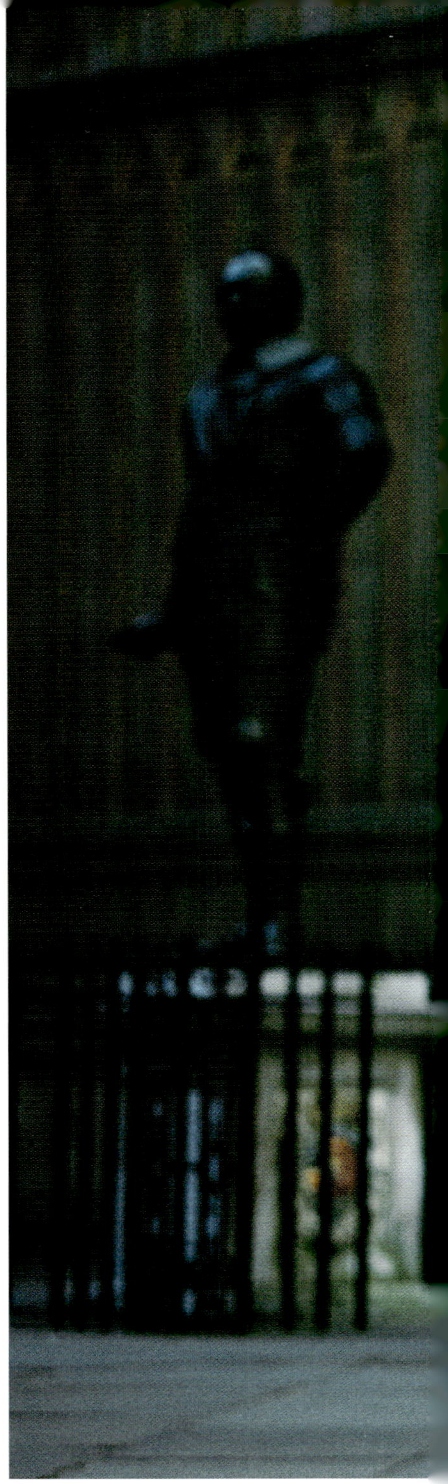

Oxford, England

Oxford University Boat Club

COLIN SMITH

> *"It is astonishing what the sight of a Blues blazer can do to many a sensible, well-adjusted girl."*
> —James and David Livingston, *Blood Over Water*, 2009

At the first Oxford-Cambridge Boat Race in 1829, the Oxford crew wore the dark blue of Christ Church, the Oxford college from which most of the crew's oarsmen (including its stroke) came. But there was not yet an Oxford University Boat Club as such. In those early years, the race was not an annual event, and for the first three Boat Races—in 1829, 1836, and 1839—the Oxford crew was cobbled together from the various college rowing clubs within the university. A few days after Oxford's embarrassing defeat in the third Boat Race, an urgent meeting of the strokes of Oxford's college crews was called. The minutes record:

> *At a meeting of the strokes and representatives of the colleges, held in the committee room, King's Yard, on Tuesday, April 23, 1839, it was resolved unanimously that a boat club should be formed for the purpose of encouraging rowing in Oxford, to be called "The Oxford University Boat Club." It was also resolved that a barge should be hired for the use of the club, and that members should be entitled to wear a club button, which was then chosen.*

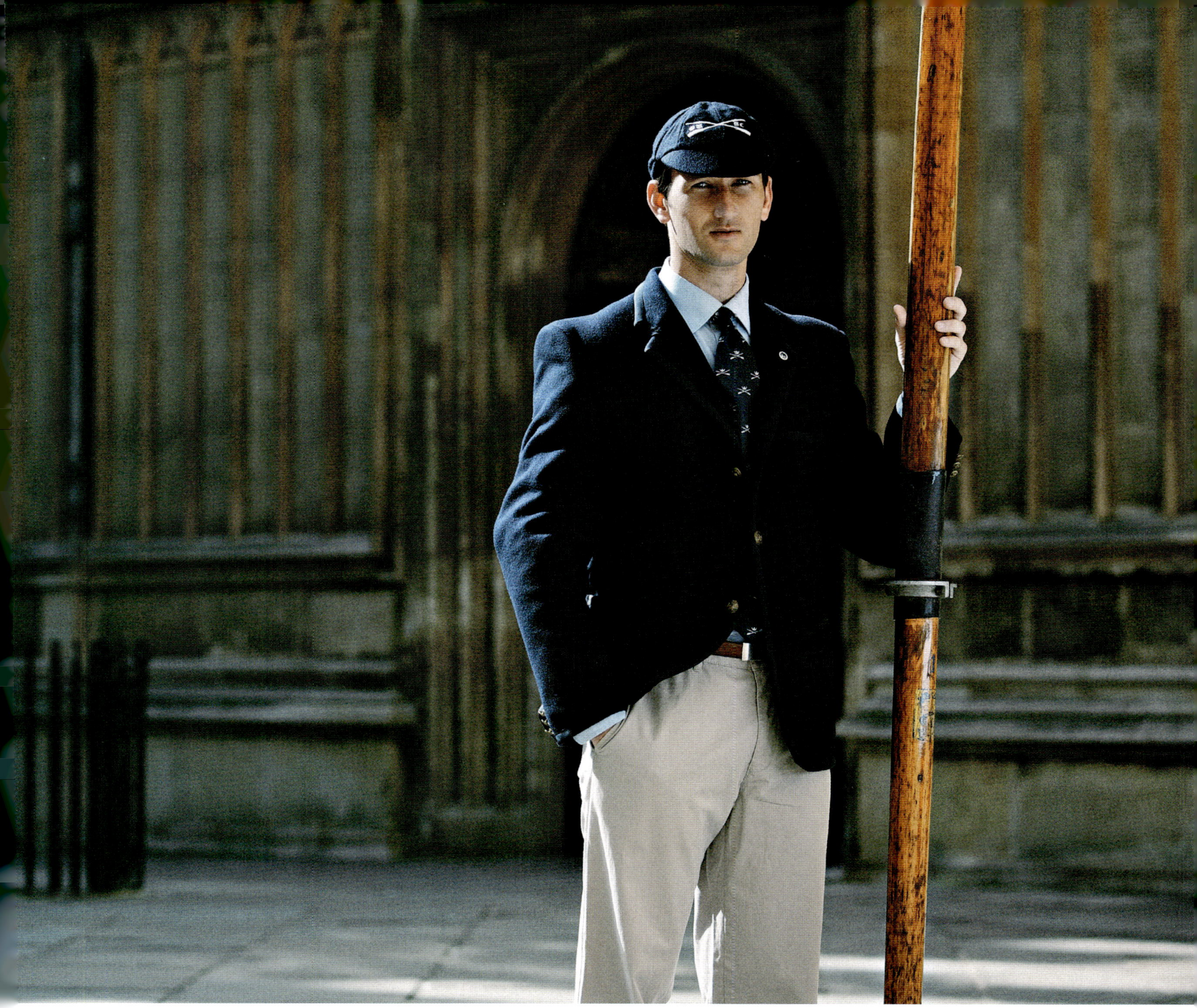

The button, which bears the name of the club and an image of a Roman galley, was to be the only distinguishing feature of the O.U.B.C. uniform.

Today, all sportsmen and -women at Oxford who have competed in a Varsity match against Cambridge are known as "Blues" and are entitled to wear a dark blue club blazer. The blazer pocket of each sport club is embroidered with its respective badge (a laurel wreath and "O.U.A.C" for the Athletics Club; racquets and "O.U.L.T.C." for the Lawn Tennis Club; etc.)—except for the Boat Club's. The Boat Club blazer pocket is plain because it is the original Blue blazer. Only the discreet buttons—in the original 1839 pattern—identify the club of the understated dark blue blazer with dark blue grosgrain trim.

According to tradition, Oxford and Cambridge oarsmen earn their blazers only when they pass the Fulham Wall, just under a mile into the 4¼-mile course, during the Boat Race; if a crew sinks before clearing the wall, or does not start the race, they will not be awarded the right to their Blue blazers.

Former O.U.B.C. president Colin Smith is a three-time Blue and two-time Boat Race winner. He also stroked the Great Britain eight to a silver medal at the 2008 Olympic Games.

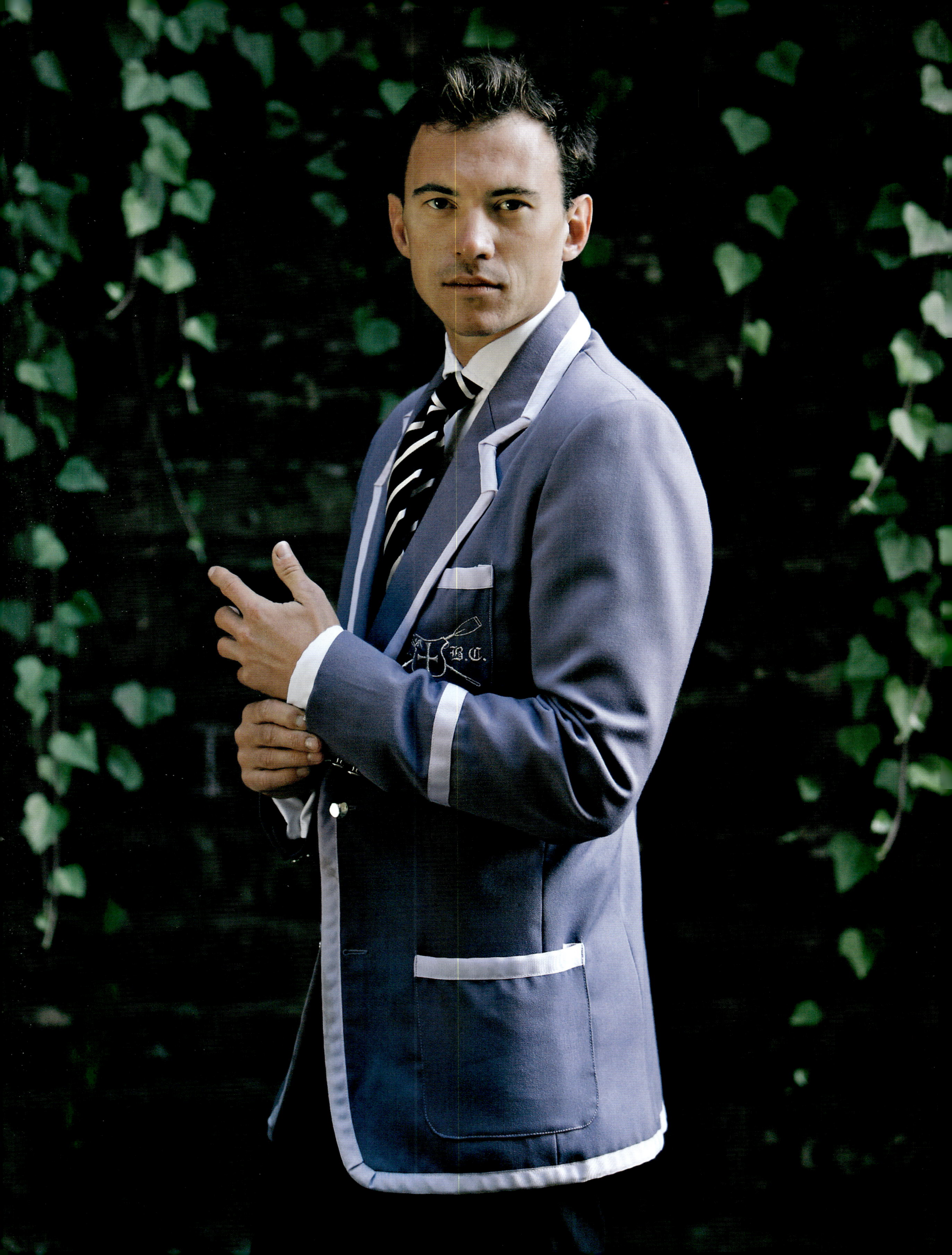
B.C.

Durham, England

Durham University Boat Club

JAMES CLARKE

"The latest novelty for the river is flannels, a blazer, and spats."

—Durham University Journal, February 21, 1885

From the eleventh to nineteenth centuries, Durham was a County Palatine—an autonomous territory ruled by prince-bishops with the authority to raise their own armies and mint their own coins.

The purple of Durham University's sporting blazers—known as Palatinate—derives from this history: purple is the color worn by Anglican bishops and was, according to some, the shade worn by the prince-bishop's armies.

Durham University Boat Club was established in 1877; the residential colleges within the university already had their own rowing clubs, but this was the first effort to pool talent and resources to create faster crews.

Rowers in Durham's top crews wear Palatinate blazers with Palatinate trim, whereas lower boats and freshmen wear Palatinate-trimmed cream or black blazers.

D.U.B.C. has won the Victor Ludorum trophy at the British University Championships for ten consecutive years. James Clarke, who rowed in several of these crews, has gone on to represent Great Britain at the 2008 Olympic Games and, most impressively, to win world championship medals in both the lightweight four and the heavyweight eight events.

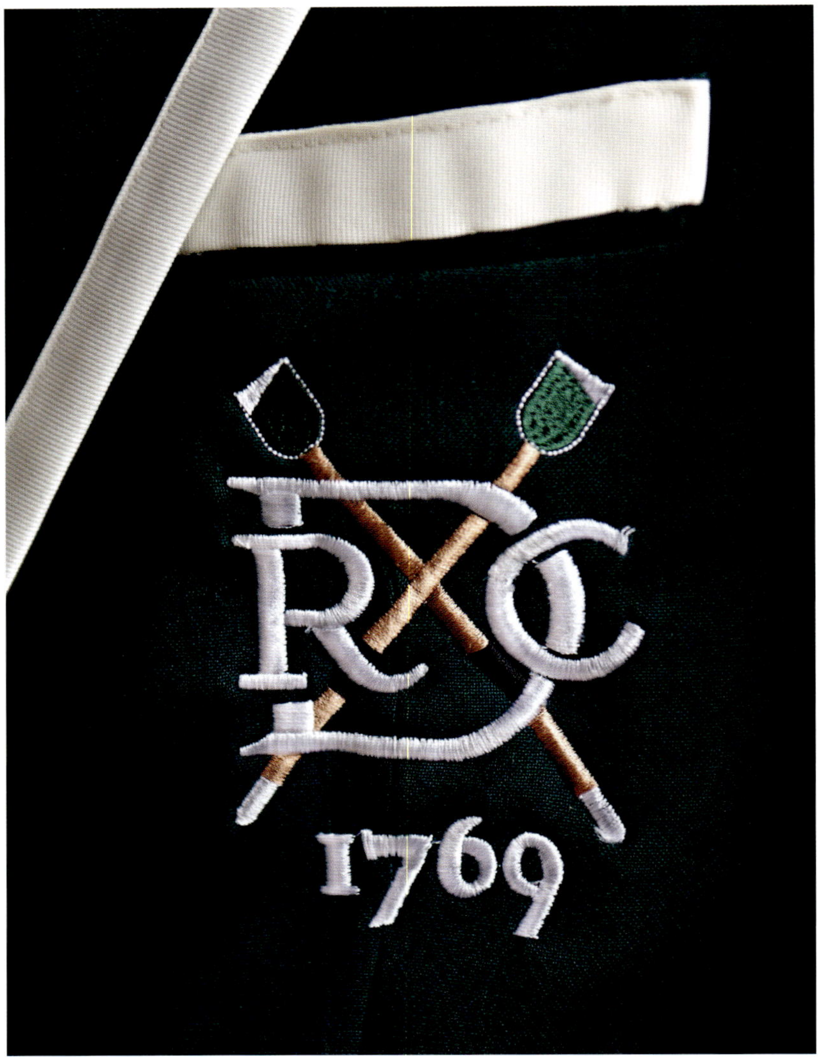

Hanover, New Hampshire

Dartmouth Rowing Club

EMERSON CURRY

"Well then here comes Dartmouth with a couple of secondhand shells with their bottoms patched, an abandoned ice house on the edge of a wilderness pond, and a tatterdemalion squad of candidates in corduroy breeches. And they go barefaced rowing, aheaving and ayanking on their hoehandles like ragamuffins on a raft." —Austen Lake, *The Boston American*, 1934

Recreational rowing at Dartmouth began in the mid-nineteenth century when students formed private rowing and canoe clubs with names like Naiad Queen Club, Phi Beta, and Camilla Club. A single rowing team for the college was finally formed in 1933, thanks to equipment donations from Exeter and Harvard.

The club remained poorly funded for much of its history, lacking "varsity" recognition from the college and relying on donated old boats from Columbia and Yale and volunteer coaches from Princeton and Boston. The cipher "D.R.C." on today's Dartmouth rowing blazers stands for Dartmouth Rowing Club, a name that pays homage to this earlier era, when rowing at Dartmouth was a "club" sport and a scrappy, student-run affair.

Emerson Curry rowed in the Dartmouth varsity lightweight crew that won the Eastern Sprints in 2007, defeating Harvard, Yale, Columbia, Princeton, and the rest of the college's East Coast rivals.

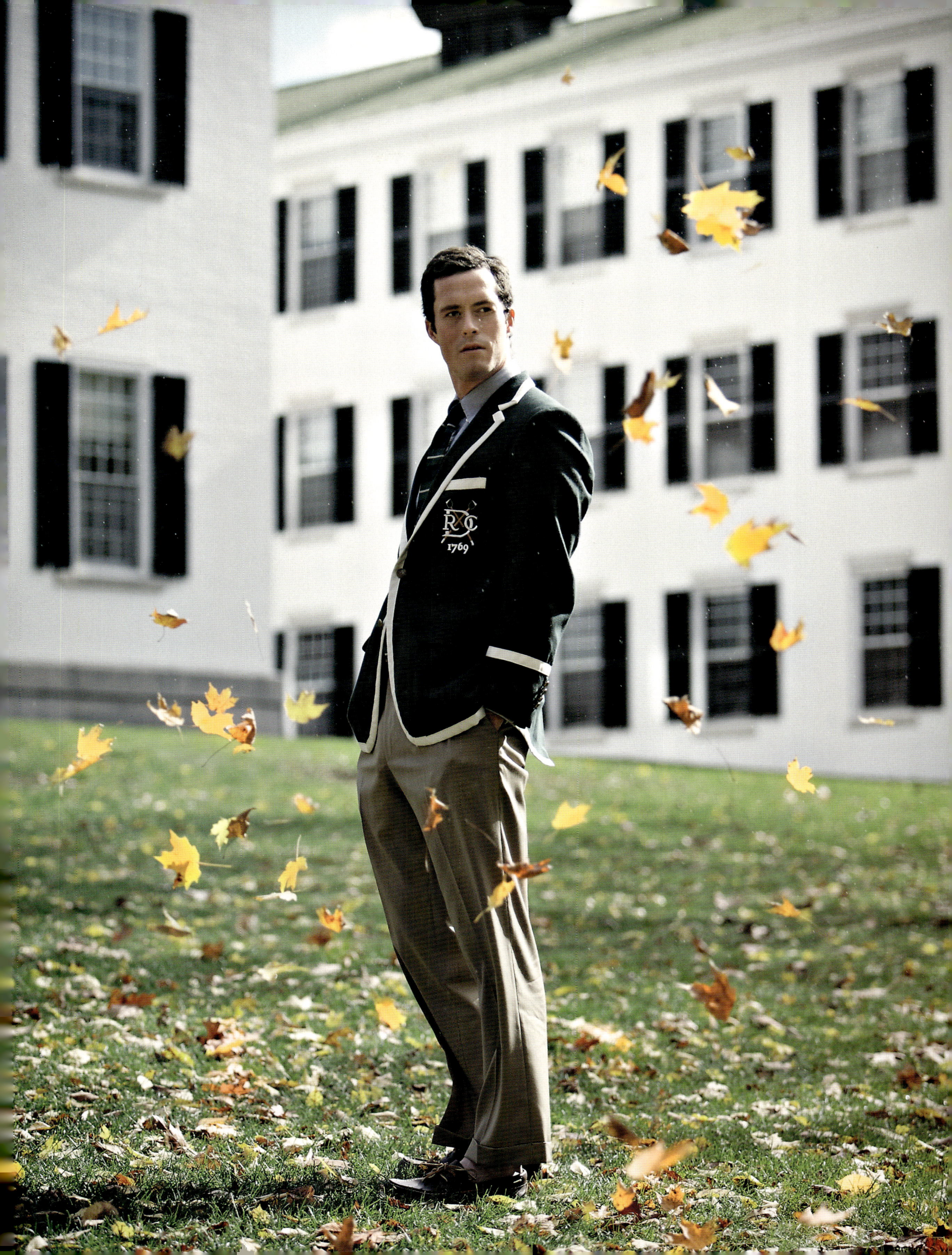
RDC
1769

Oxford, England

Wadham College Boat Club, Oxford

LUCY VENTRESS

According to an oft-repeated tale, Wadham adopted its light blue color—identical to Cambridge Blue—after defeating a Cambridge crew at the Henley Regatta. Wadham took the color as its "victory spoils," and the Wadham boating blazer and tie are, to this day, Cambridge light blue. The story is apocryphal, but there is some truth in it.

In 1849—the year usually cited for this legend—Wadham did indeed beat a crew from Trinity College, Cambridge, to take home the Henley Grand Challenge Cup (Wadham also won the Ladies' Plate and the Wyfold Cup at Henley that year). With this win, Wadham avenged their loss to a Trinity Cambridge crew ten years earlier, at the very first Henley Regatta in 1839.

But Wadham was using light blue long before their 1849 Henley victory. In fact, when they lost to Trinity in 1839, it was recorded that the Wadham rowers each wore a "light blue scarf" and a "light blue velvet" hatband. Ironically, the Trinity crew that outraced them on this occasion competed in dark blue uniforms (though light blue is the Cambridge University Boat Club color, oarsmen competing for Trinity College Cambridge wore—and still wear—dark blue).

Contrary to popular belief, then, the color of Wadham's rowing jacket does not have its origins in the 1849 Henley victory. But few have realized that another feature of the Wadham blazer is intimately connected to the 1849 crew. Wary that their tutors and college authorities would try to prevent them from competing at the regatta, the student rowers entered under false names and raced not as Wadham, but as the made-up St. John of Malta Boat Club.

The Maltese cross remains the Wadham Boat Club badge and is emblazoned on the blazer pocket; unfortunately, however, it is now often rendered as a similar heraldic emblem—the cross pattée—rather than as a true Maltese cross.

Lucy Ventress is former president of Wadham College Boat Club.

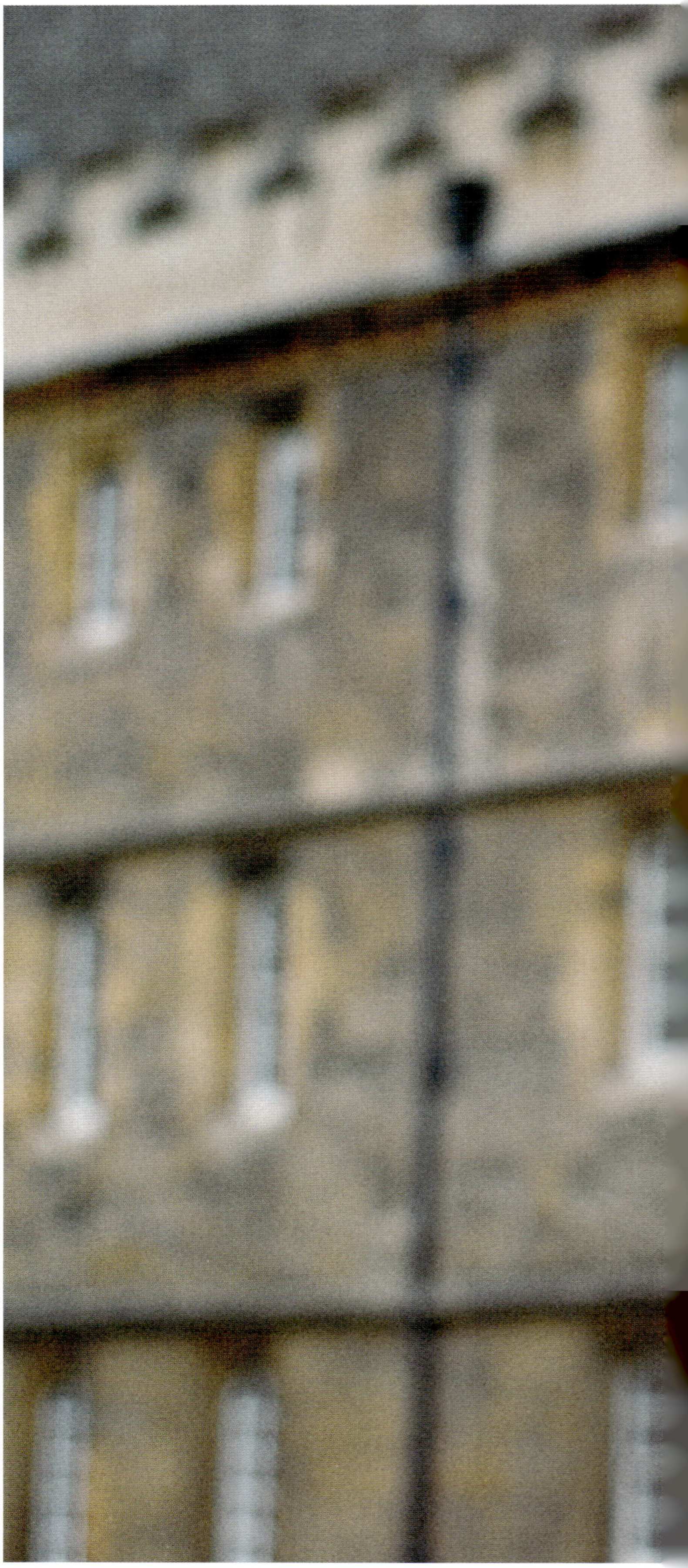

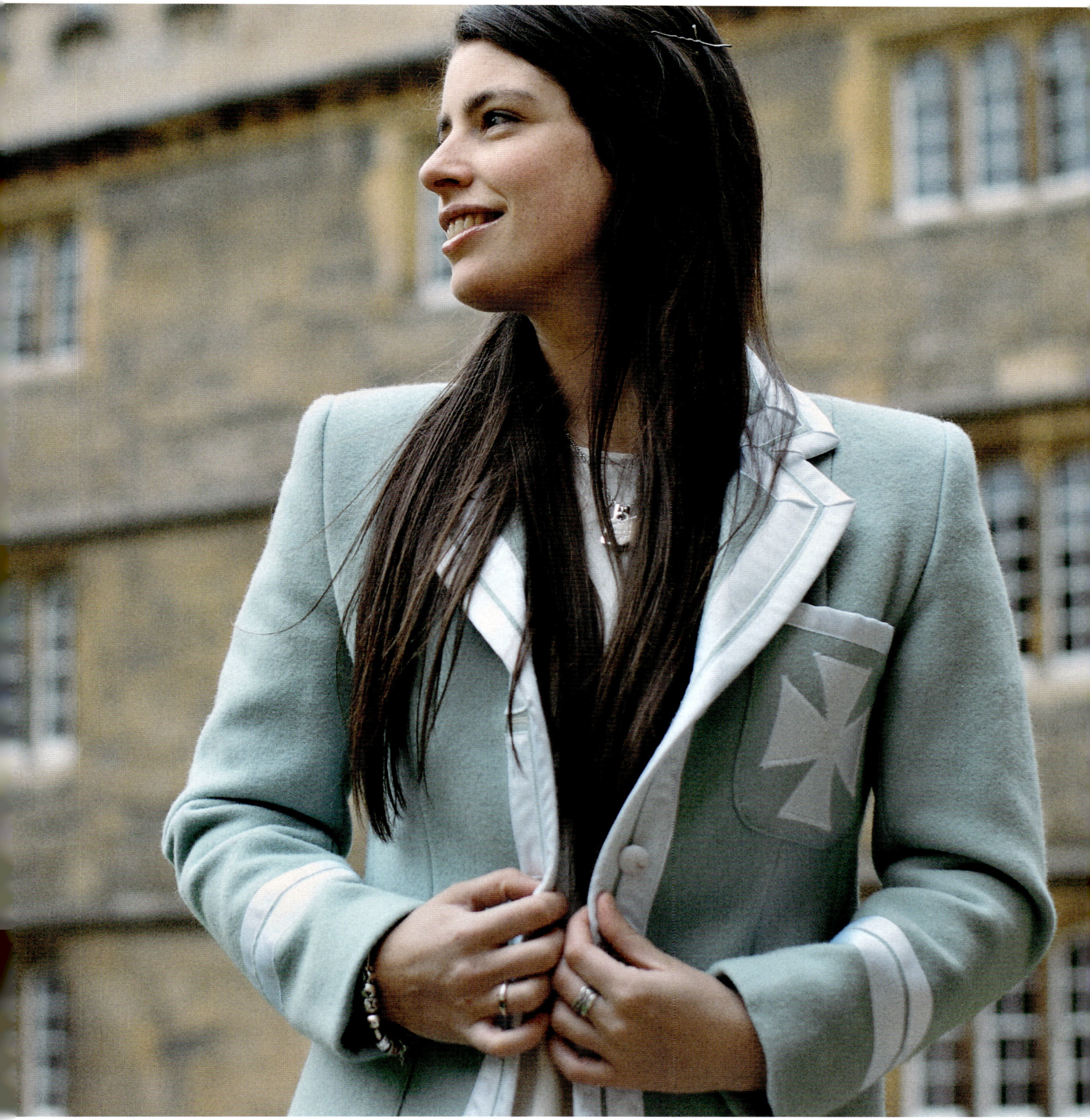

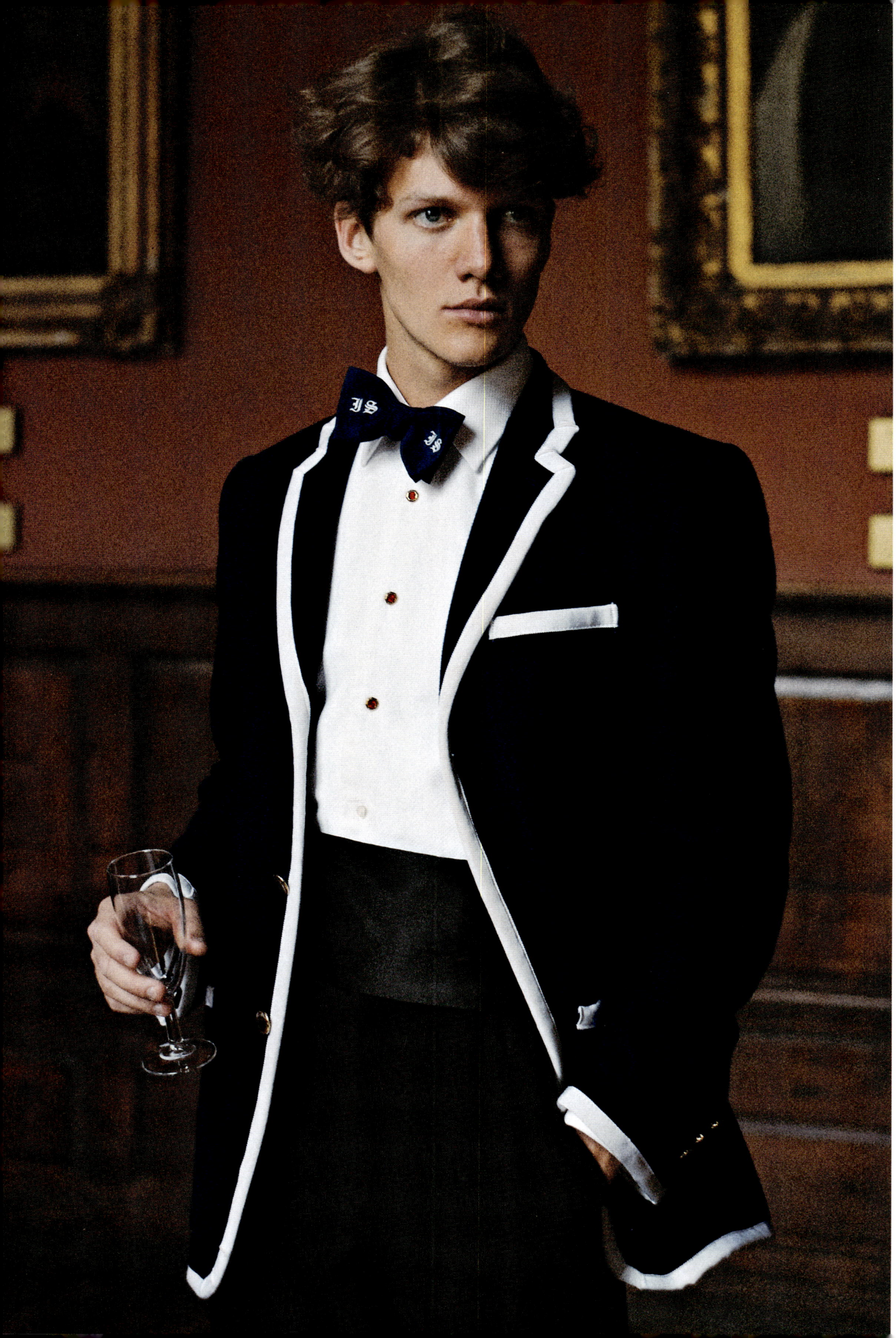
IS

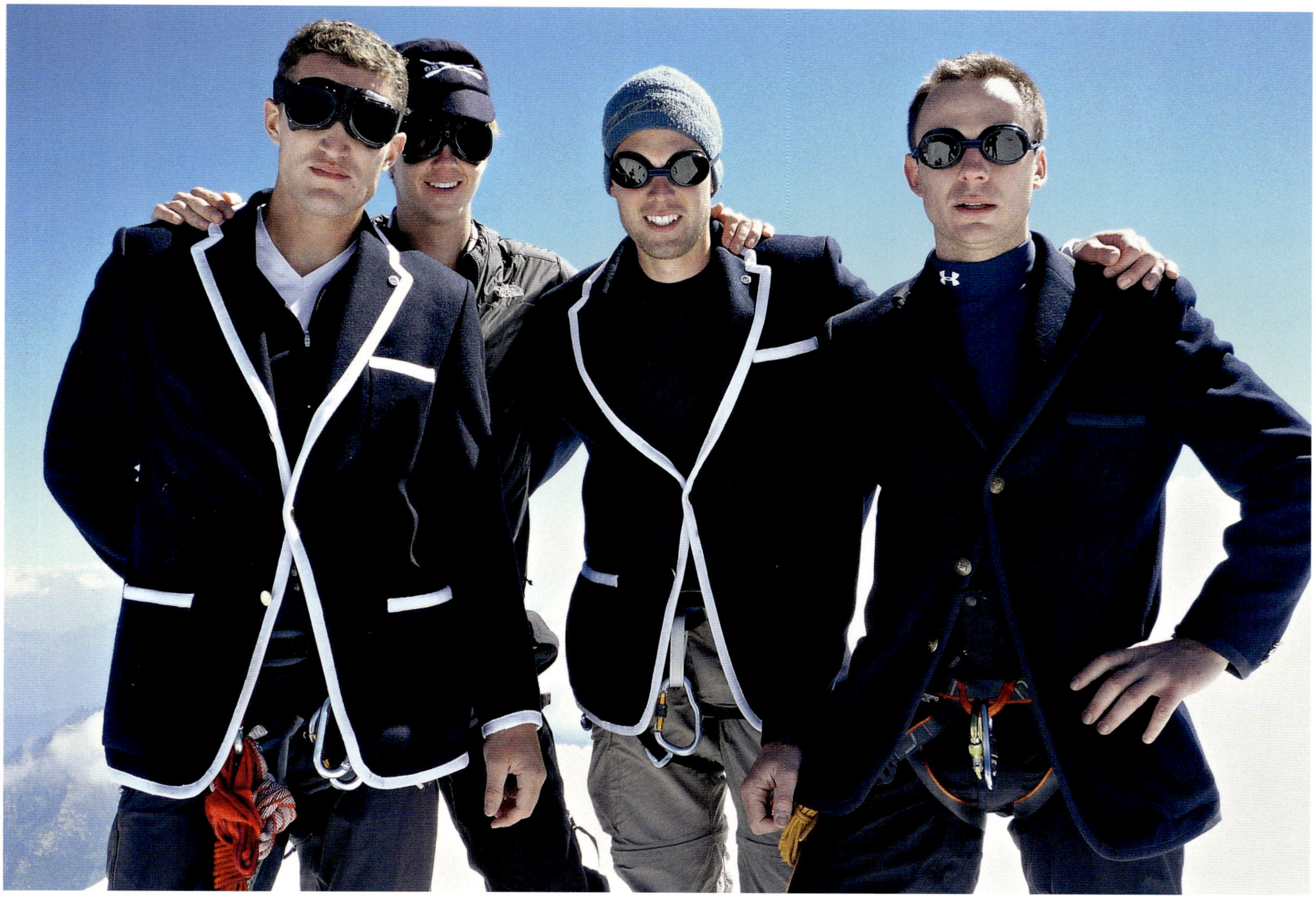

Oxford, England

Isis Boat Club, Oxford

TOMMY HILTON, ANTOINE DE WECK, BORIS LE FEBER,
BASIL GRÜTER, MICHAL PLOTKOWIAK

Isis is the second boat, or reserve crew, of the Oxford University Boat Club and is named for the stretch of the Thames that runs through Oxford. Every year, Isis races the Cambridge reserve crew, named Goldie, thirty minutes before the Oxford and Cambridge first boats take to the course. Although the first Isis-Goldie Race was not until 1965, the Isis Club dates to 1927 as a name under which Oxford rowers entered external regattas and overseas races (the racing name Oxford, or O.U.B.C., being reserved for a crew composed entirely of Full Blues).

The Isis blazer is identical to the Oxford Blue Boat blazer, except that it has plain buttons and is trimmed in white instead of blue. It is of the same thick wool flannel as the Blue Boat blazer, which makes it uncomfortable at summer regattas but apparently ideal for mountaineering outside of the rowing season.

Isis oarsmen are also entitled to wear a dark blue bowtie embroidered with the word *ISIS*, and orange socks, which commemorate a much-loved former Isis coach from Holland, René Mijnders.

OPPOSITE: Tommy Hilton sports the dark blue bowtie worn by Isis oarsmen on formal occasions.

ABOVE: Isis oarsmen Antoine de Weck, Boris Le Feber, Basil Grüter, and O.U.B.C. rower Michal Plotkowiak wore their heavy blazers to the summit of Weissmies in Switzerland.

Oxford, England

Exeter College Boat Club, Oxford

JOE JONES

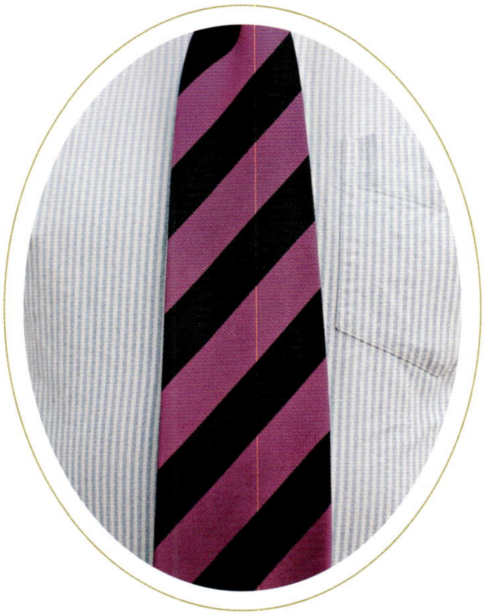

Members of Exeter College Boat Club, like members of every college rowing club within the University of Oxford, wear colorful rowing blazers: the scallop shells on the Exeter pocket replicate the scallops that appear on the coats of arms of William Palmer, college rector in the fifteenth century, and of Sir William Petre, who re-endowed the college in the sixteenth.

But the club's greatest sartorial contribution to the world—according to legend, at least—relates not to blazers but to neckties. The modern necktie, unlike the scarves and neckerchiefs that preceded it, serves no practical purpose in terms of keeping the neck warm. What it does offer is another means of demonstrating affiliation to a club or institution.

And that is what Exeter oarsmen had in mind in 1880, when, the story goes, they removed the long, narrow magenta-and-black hatbands from their straw boaters and tied them around their necks, displaying their allegiance to the boat club (without needing to wear a hat or a boating blazer) and, unwittingly, inventing the "club tie" as we know it.

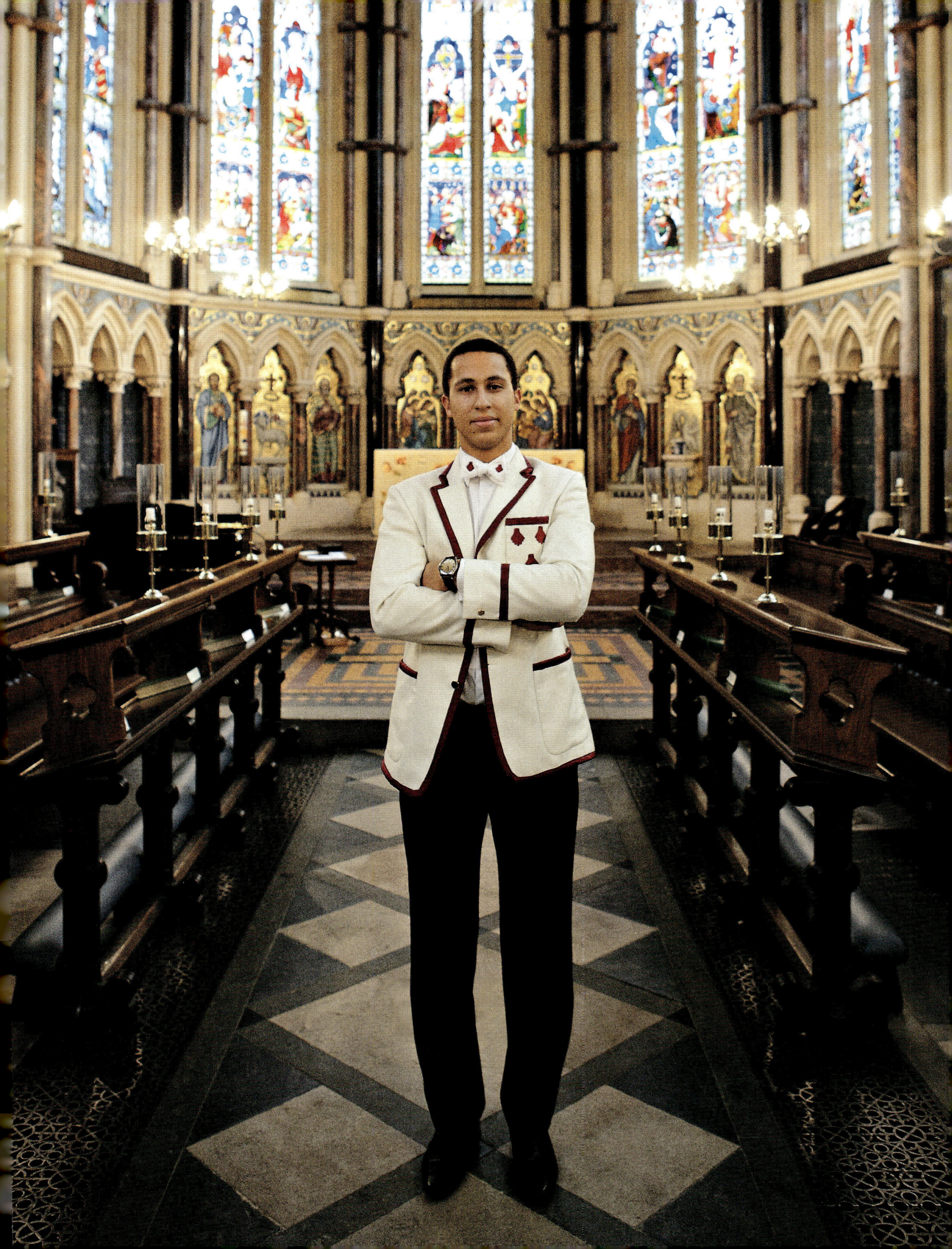

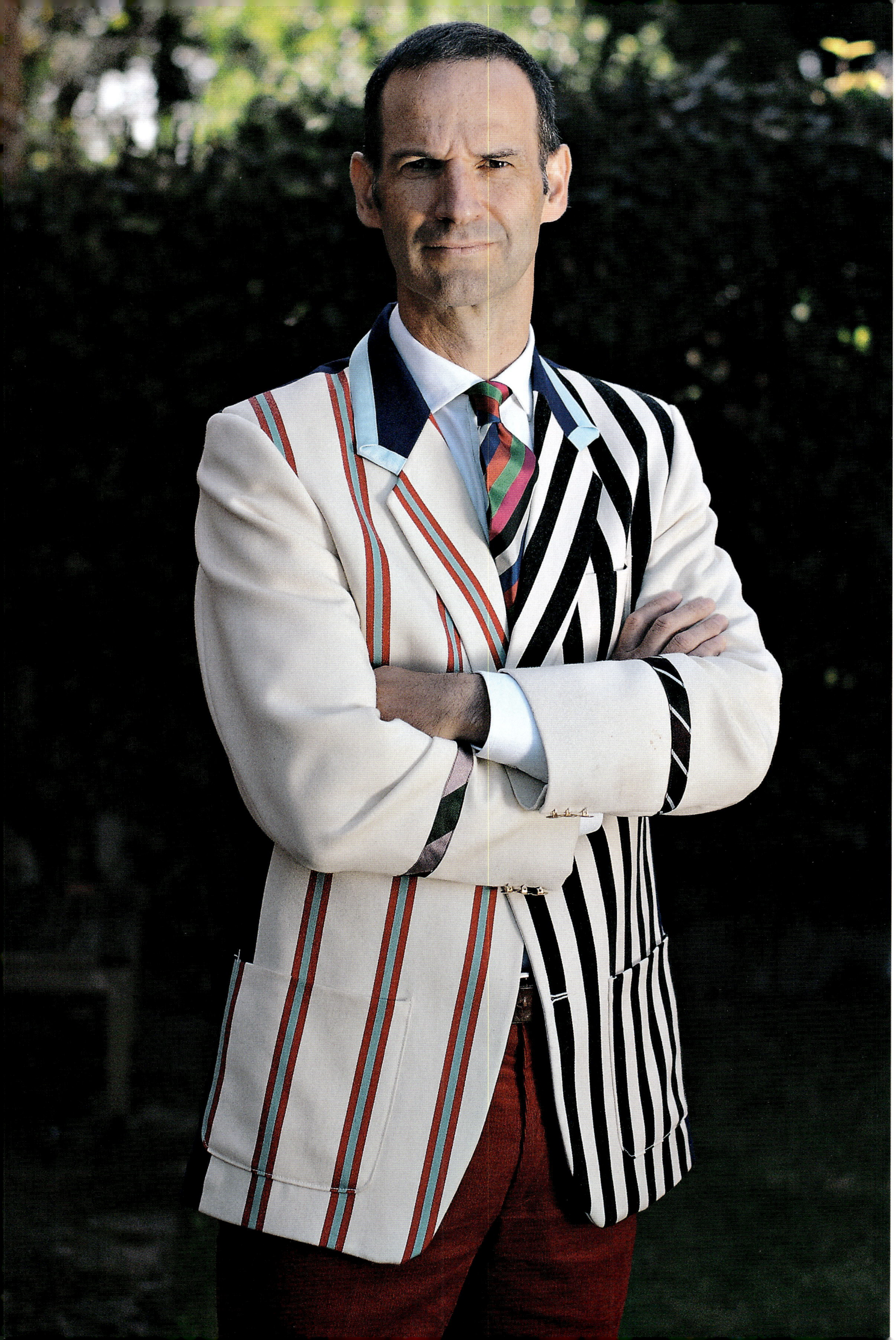

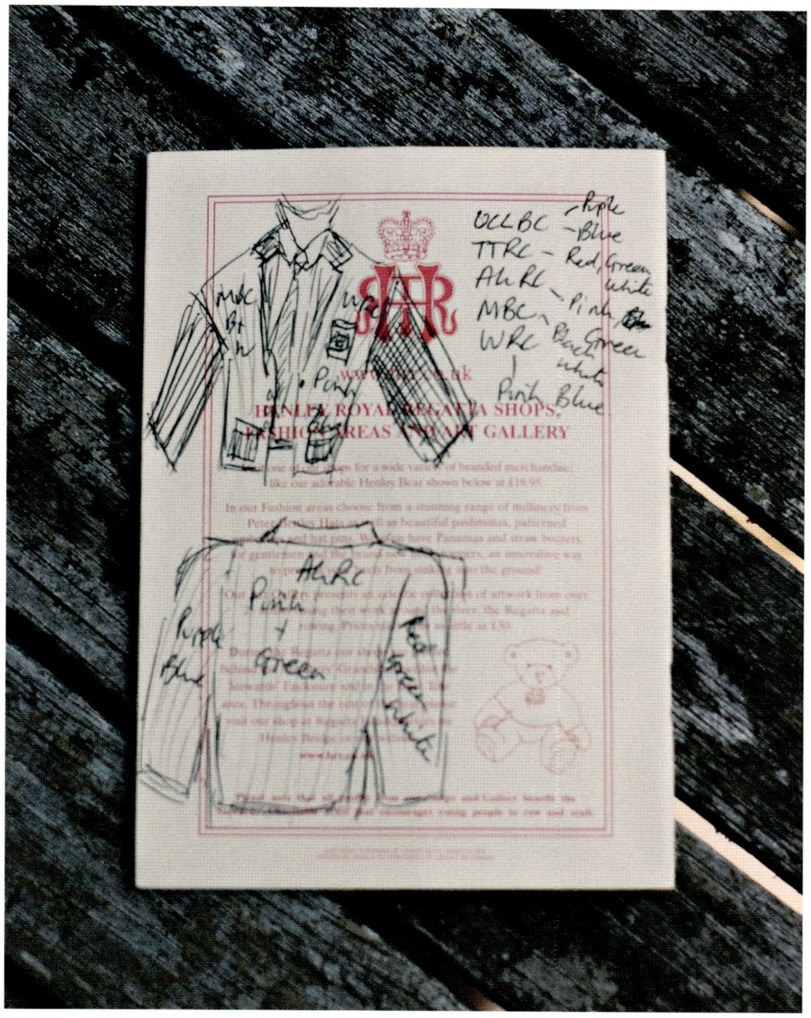

Composite Blazer and Remenham Club

PETER KING

Rowing club blazers are fundamentally tribal objects. Like the heraldic badges and liveries of medieval Europe or the gang colors of modern-day South Central Los Angeles, the blazer is a loud visual declaration of where one's loyalties lie.

But what if one has rowed for several different clubs during one's career? Many oarsmen and -women, of course, find themselves in this position and simply wear a different blazer on each of the five days of Henley.

Peter King came up with a different solution: he had a unique jacket made for himself that combines the various rowing blazers to which he is entitled. His "composite blazer" features the stripes of Molesey Boat Club and the stripes of Wallingford Rowing Club; the purple and light blue of University College London Boat Club; and a sleeve each for Auriol Kensington Rowing Club and Thames Tradesmen Rowing Club.

Peter usually wears the composite blazer with his equally colorful Remenham Club tie. Remenham is the social club for oarsmen and -women who have raced at Henley for one of seven major London rowing clubs (Kingston, London, Molesey, Staines, Thames, Twickenham, and Vesta), and the tie, of course, features the colors of each of these.

ABOVE: Peter King had the idea for his composite blazer while sitting in the sun at Henley one day. He sketched the original design on the back of his Henley program.

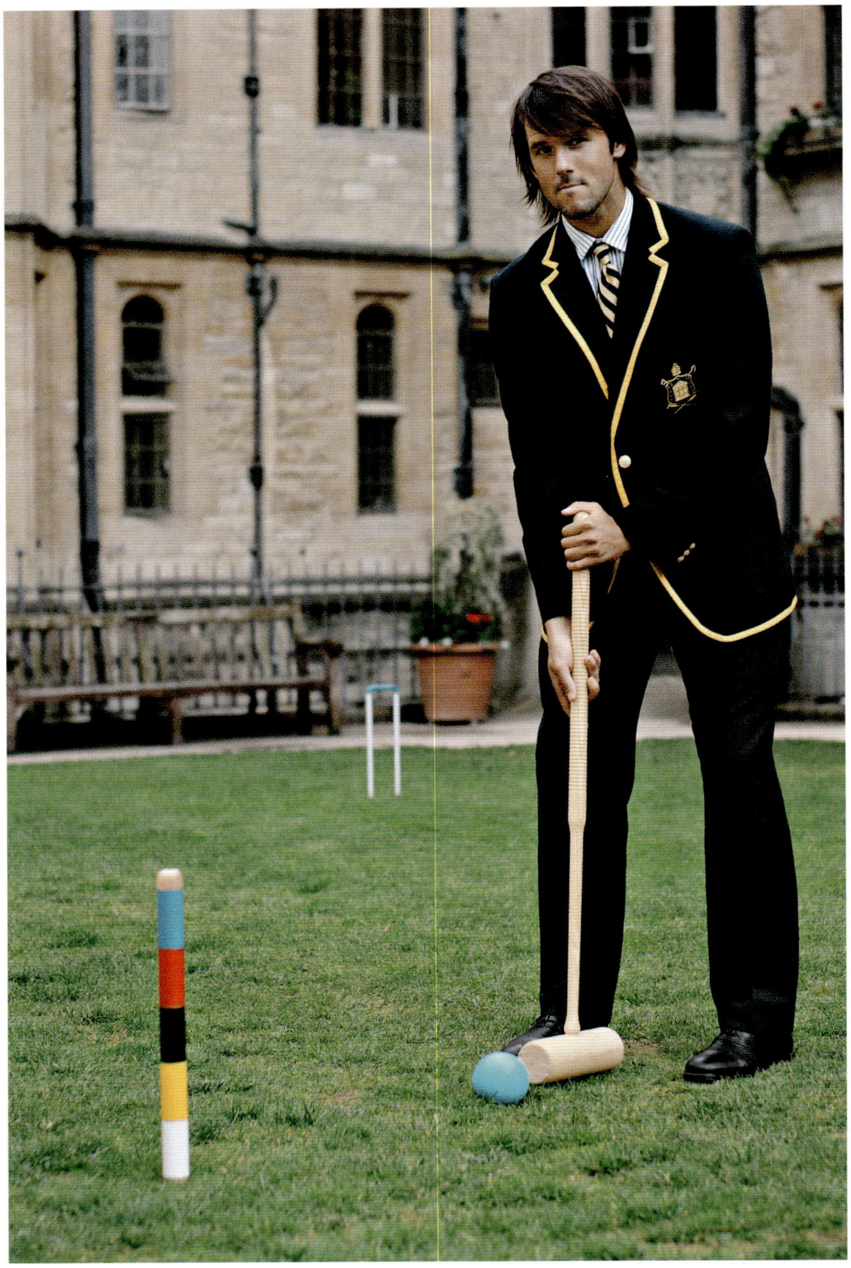

Hartford, Connecticut

Trinity College, Hartford, and Bantam Boat Club

JOHN GRAVES

Trinity has always punched above its weight in rowing. Although the New England Small Colleges Athletics Conference prevents Trinity from participating in the annual national championship race, its crews are regular contenders at the Henley Royal Regatta in England. As at many other American colleges, Trinity rowers earn their blazers when they are selected for a Henley crew.

"Trin-Trin" won its first Henley championship in 1976. Sitting in the four seat of the crew was Harry Graves, whose three sons—Tom, Peter, and John—have all gone on to row for Trinity at Henley themselves, with Tom and Peter winning in 2005.

The Graves family also has its own rowing club, Bantam Boat Club, named after the Trinity mascot. Like Trinity, Bantam is a familiar name at Henley, routinely making entries in the sculling events, including, in 2004, a quad made up of all three Graves brothers and their father.

John Graves is a member of the U.S. sculling team and raced at the 2013 world championships.

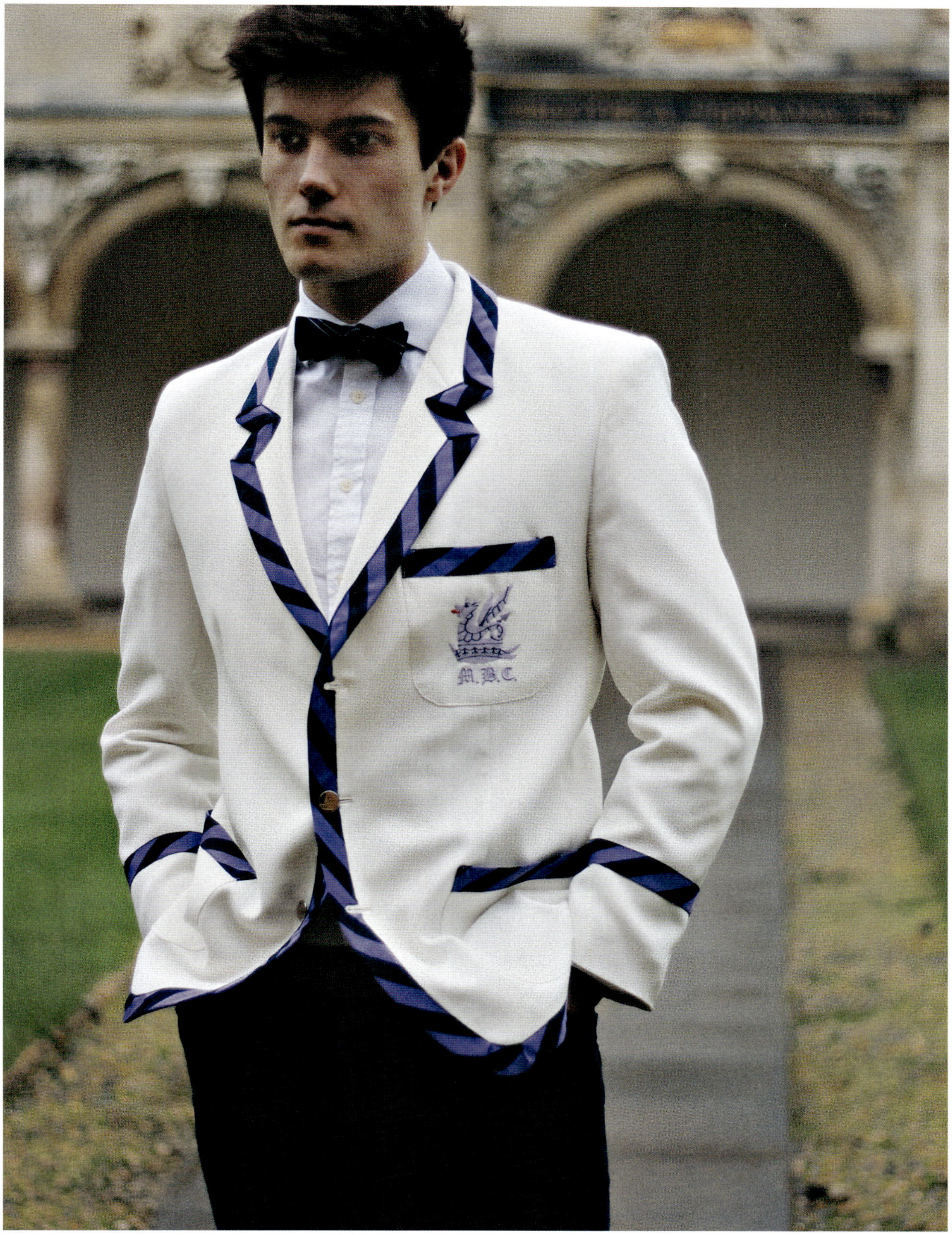

Cambridge, England

Magdalene College Boat Club, Cambridge

TOM HARGREAVES

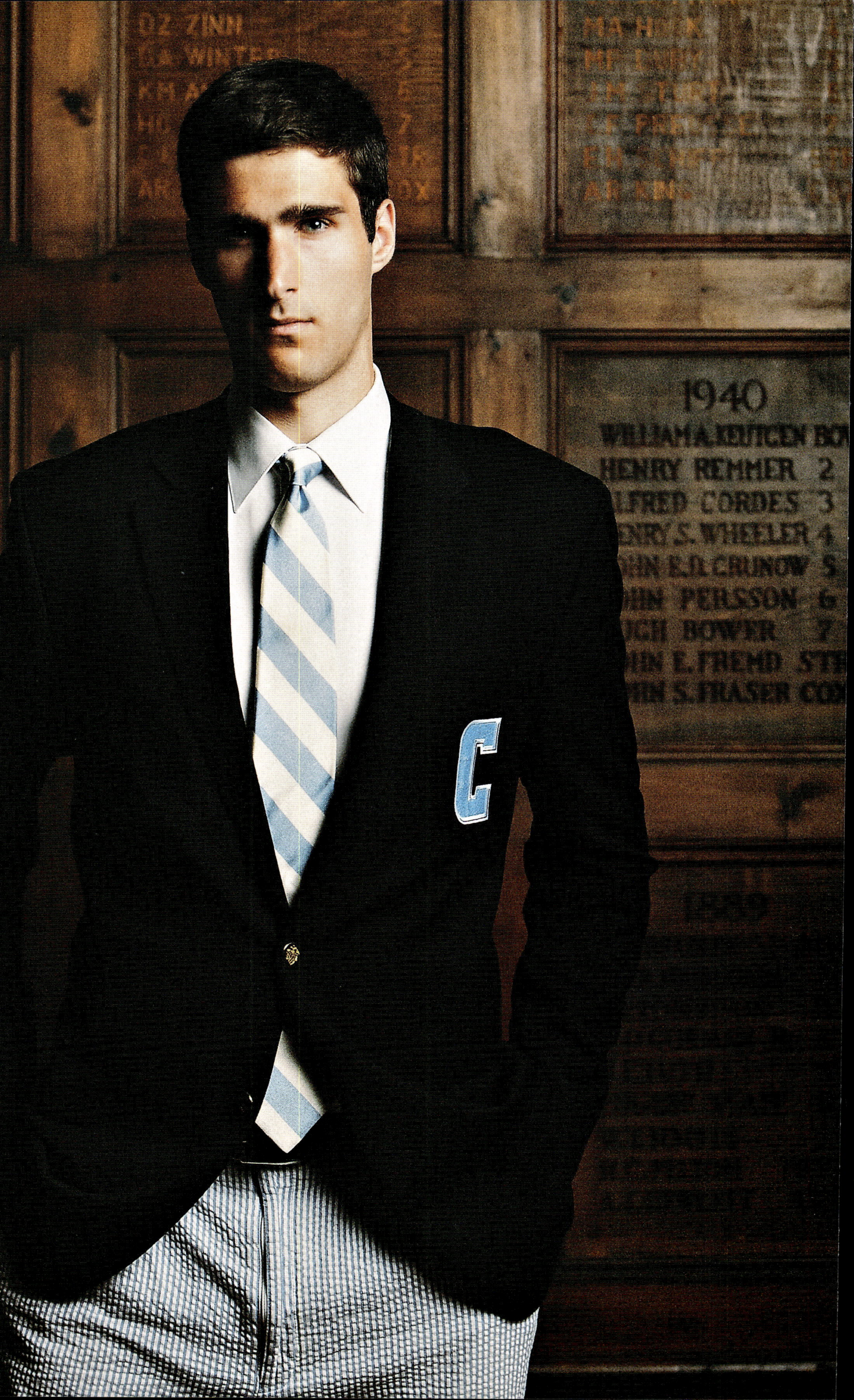
1940
HENRY REMMER 2
CORDES 3
BOWER 7

Manhattan, New York

Columbia University

STEVE LaPERLA

Six oarsmen (a four and two spares) from Columbia College in New York made history in 1878: they not only formed the first American team to compete at Henley in England but also became the first American crew to win an event at the storied Royal Regatta.

Since this initial victory, however, Columbia's appearances at Henley have been sporadic. Because of this infrequency (and because the team has blazers made only when it competes at Henley), there has been little consistency in the appearance of Columbia's rowing jackets over the years. The "King's Crown" and crossed-blades badge (a reference to Columbia's colonial-era name, King's College) has been replaced by a very American varsity letter, and though the Columbia lightweights have appeared at Henley in full light blue suits in recent years, the 2008 heavyweight crew opted for simple navy blazers.

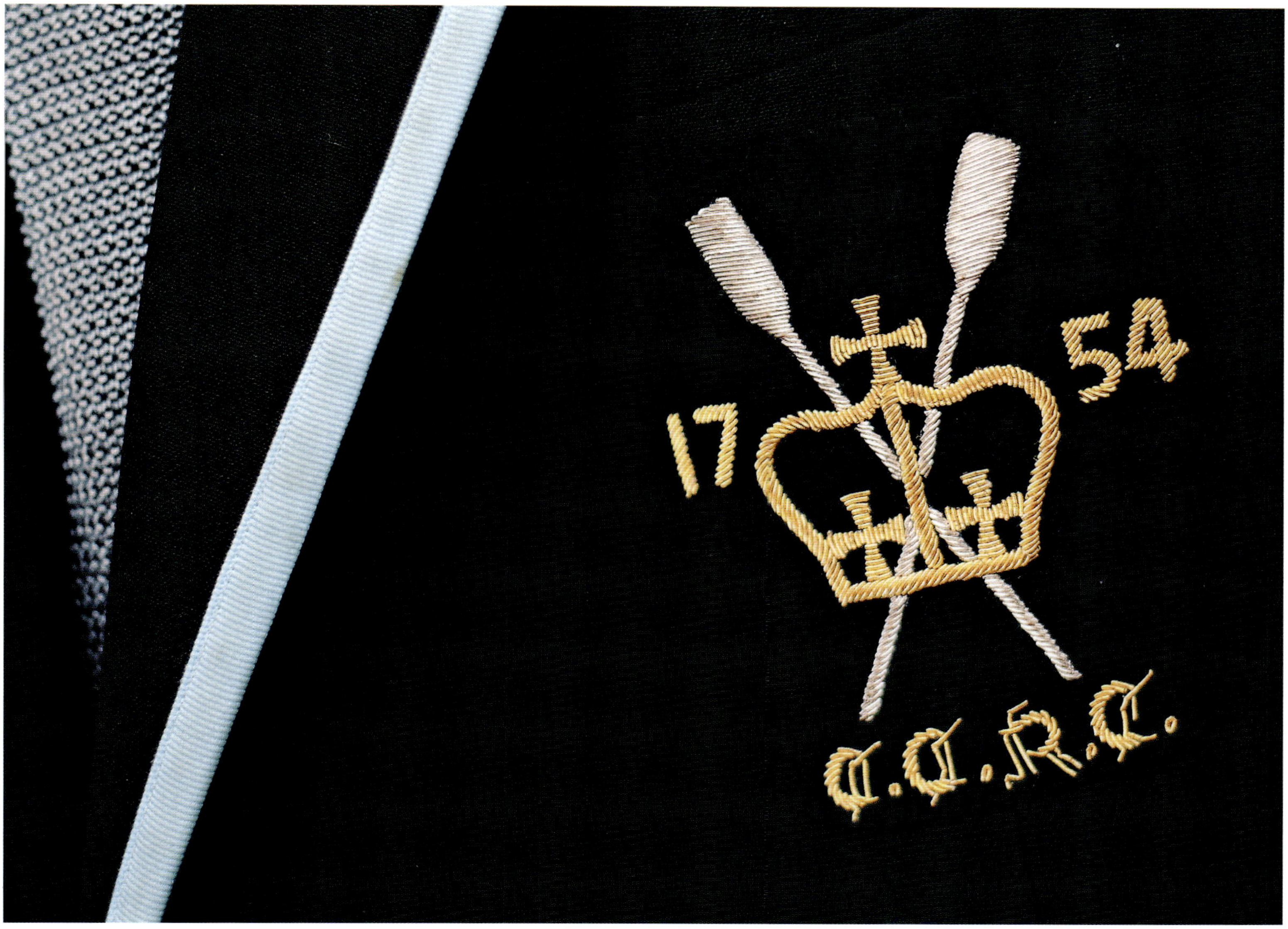

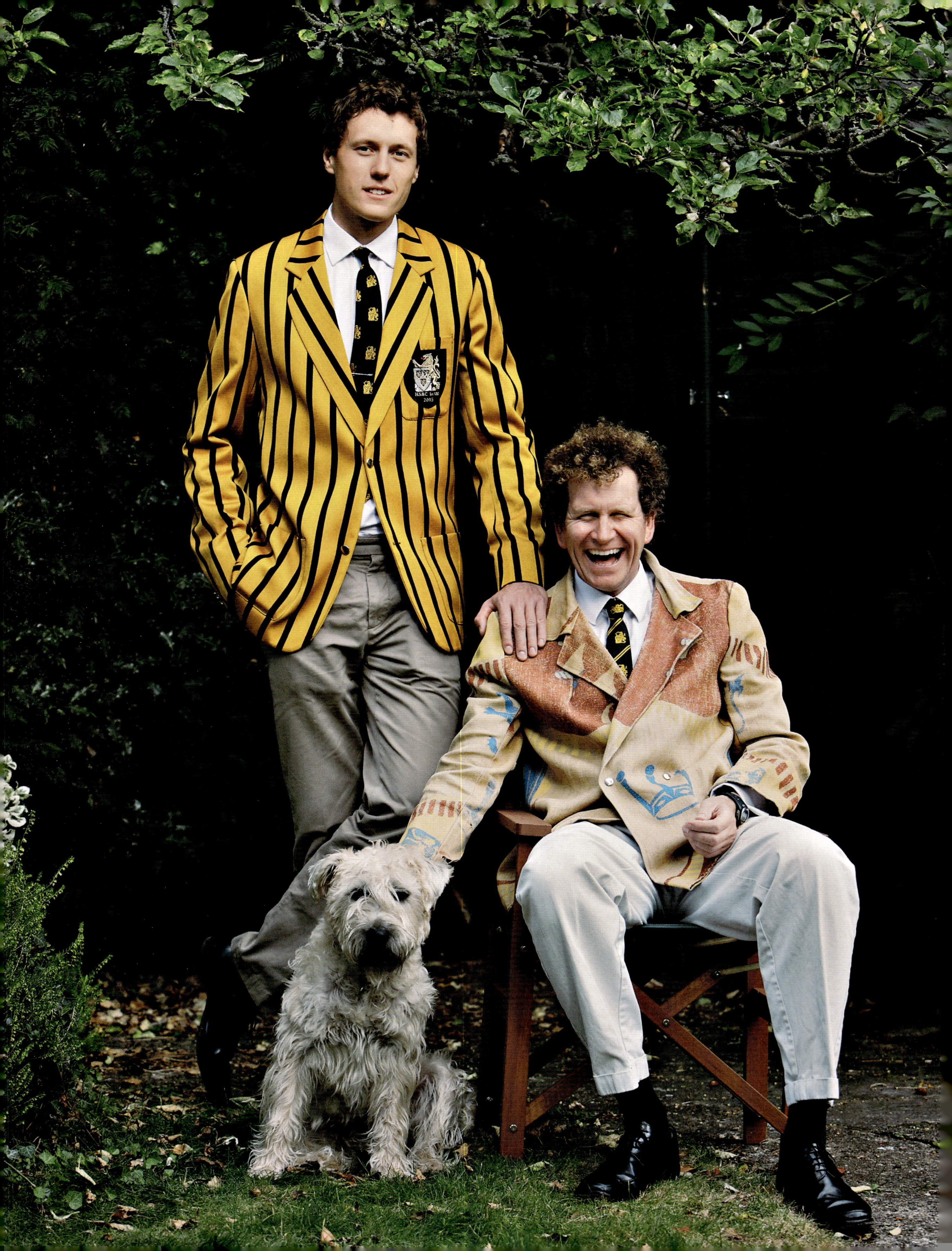
H.S.B.C
2005

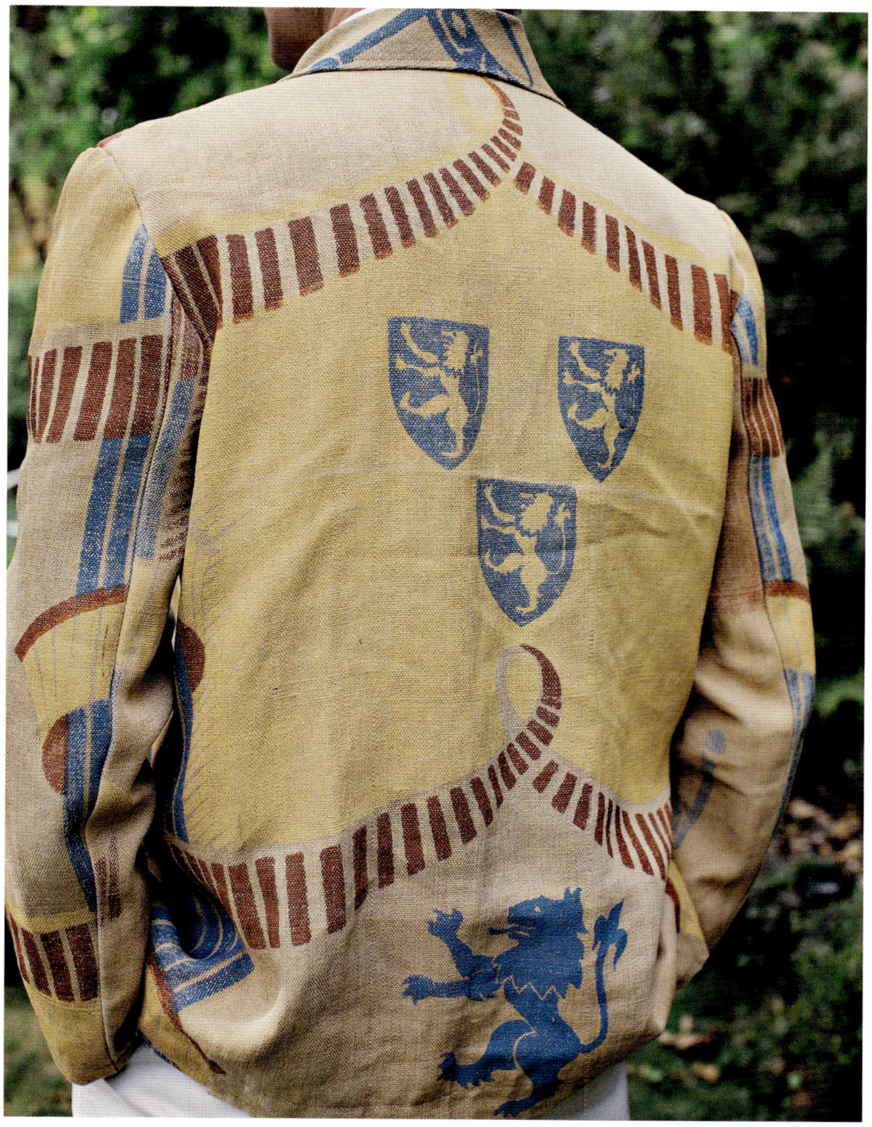

Hampton, England

Hampton School Boat Club and the Hampton Curtains Blazer

KARL HUDSPITH, JONNY SEARLE MBE

The Hampton School Boat Club blazer, with its bright yellow-and-black stripes, is a frequent sight at Henley. The Hampton Curtains Blazer, however, is seen far more rarely, for only ten have ever been made. Each Curtains Blazer is literally cut from the heavy old curtains of the school's Great Hall, which are emblazoned with crowns and lions rampant from the school's coat of arms. At Hampton, a crew is awarded Curtains Blazers for winning the "Triple" in a single year: the Schools' Head of the River Race, the National Schools' Regatta, and the Princess Elizabeth Cup at Henley. Hampton has won the Triple only twice in its history, and on these two occasions—which were in consecutive years—the entire crew was the same, with the exception of the cox. Seven of the rowers (one declined the Curtains Blazer), the two coxes, and the coach own the only ten Curtains Blazers in existence.

Karl Hudspith and Jonny Searle are Hampton graduates, former presidents of Oxford University Boat Club, and three-time Boat Race competitors. Jonny Searle (seated) won the Triple with Hampton in 1988 and 1989 and an Olympic gold medal in 1992.

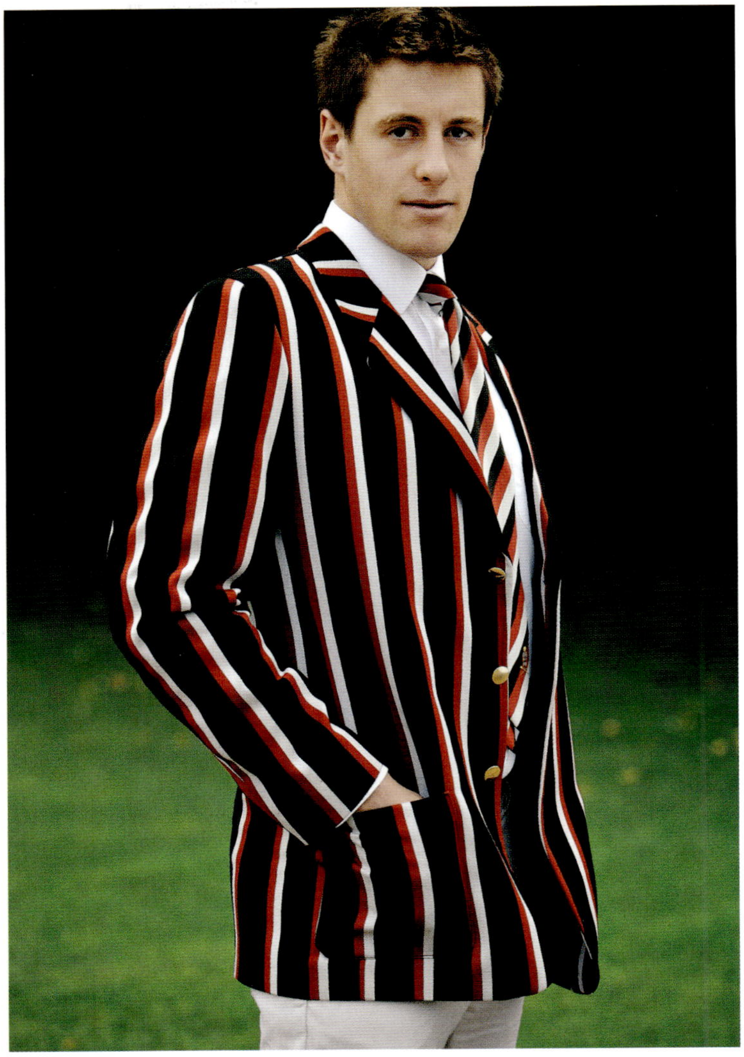

Coventry, England

University of Warwick Boat Club

DAN GARSIDE

United States Pan-American Games Team

JASON READ

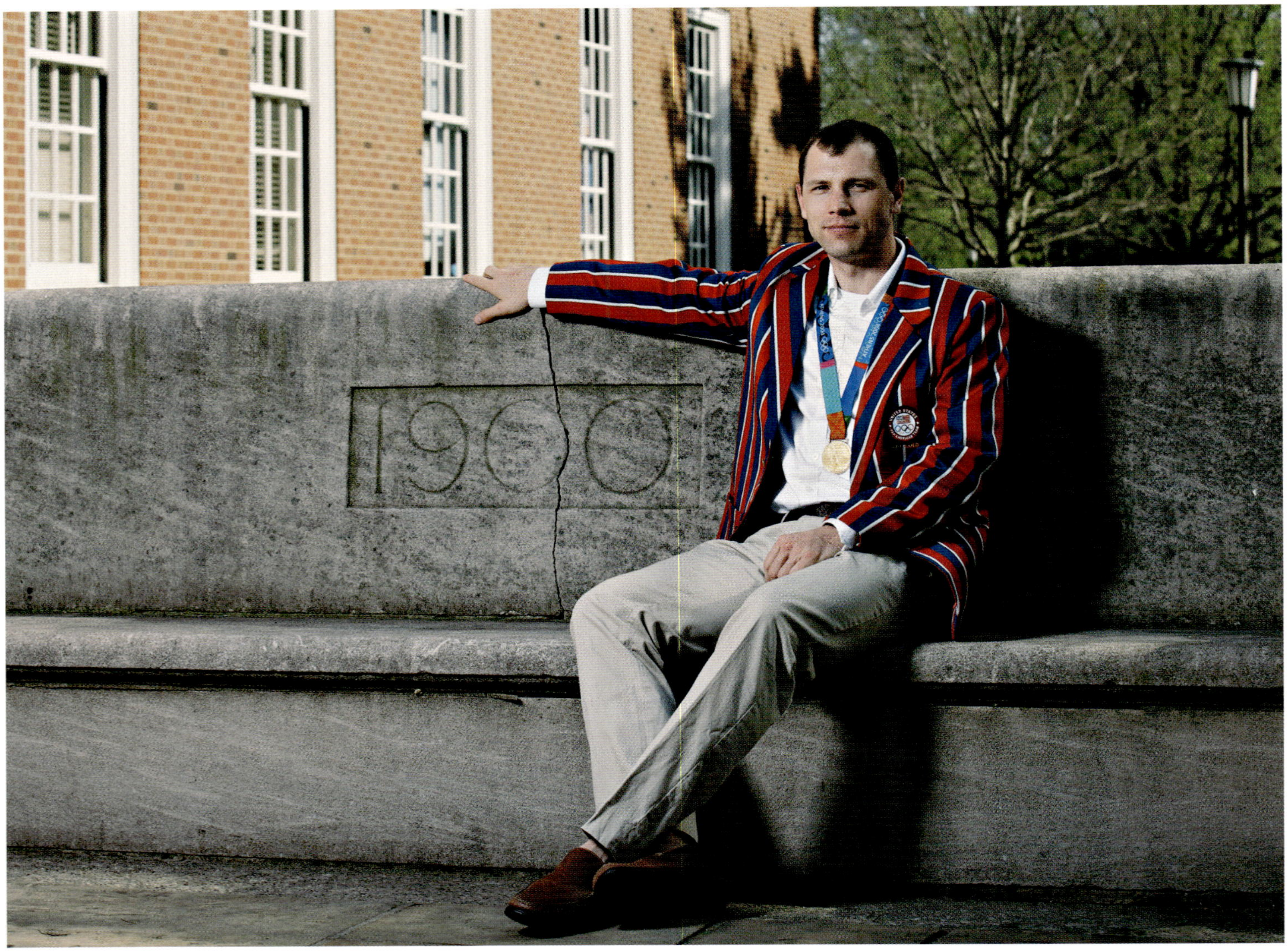

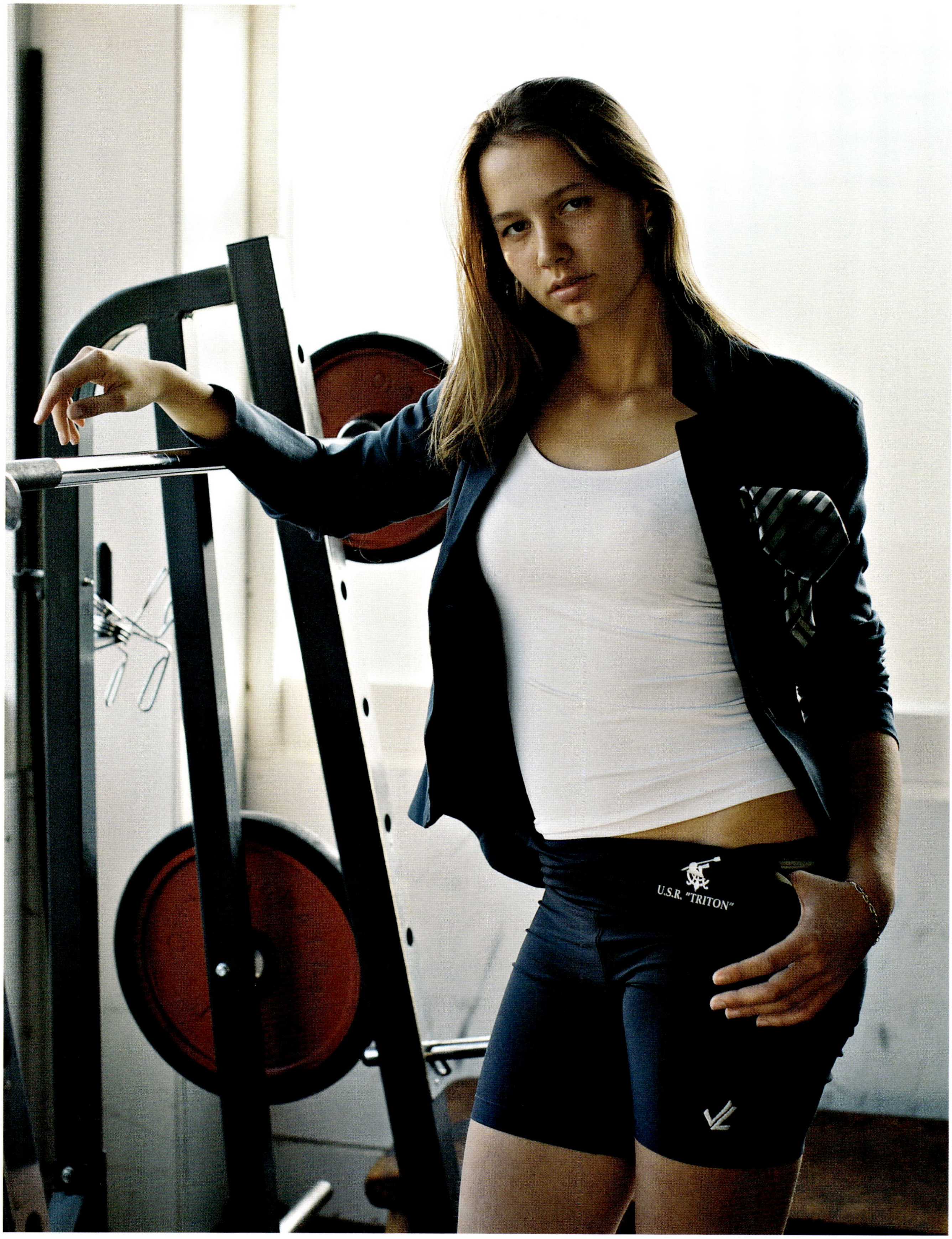

Utrecht, Netherlands

U.S.R. "Triton"

MONICA LANZ

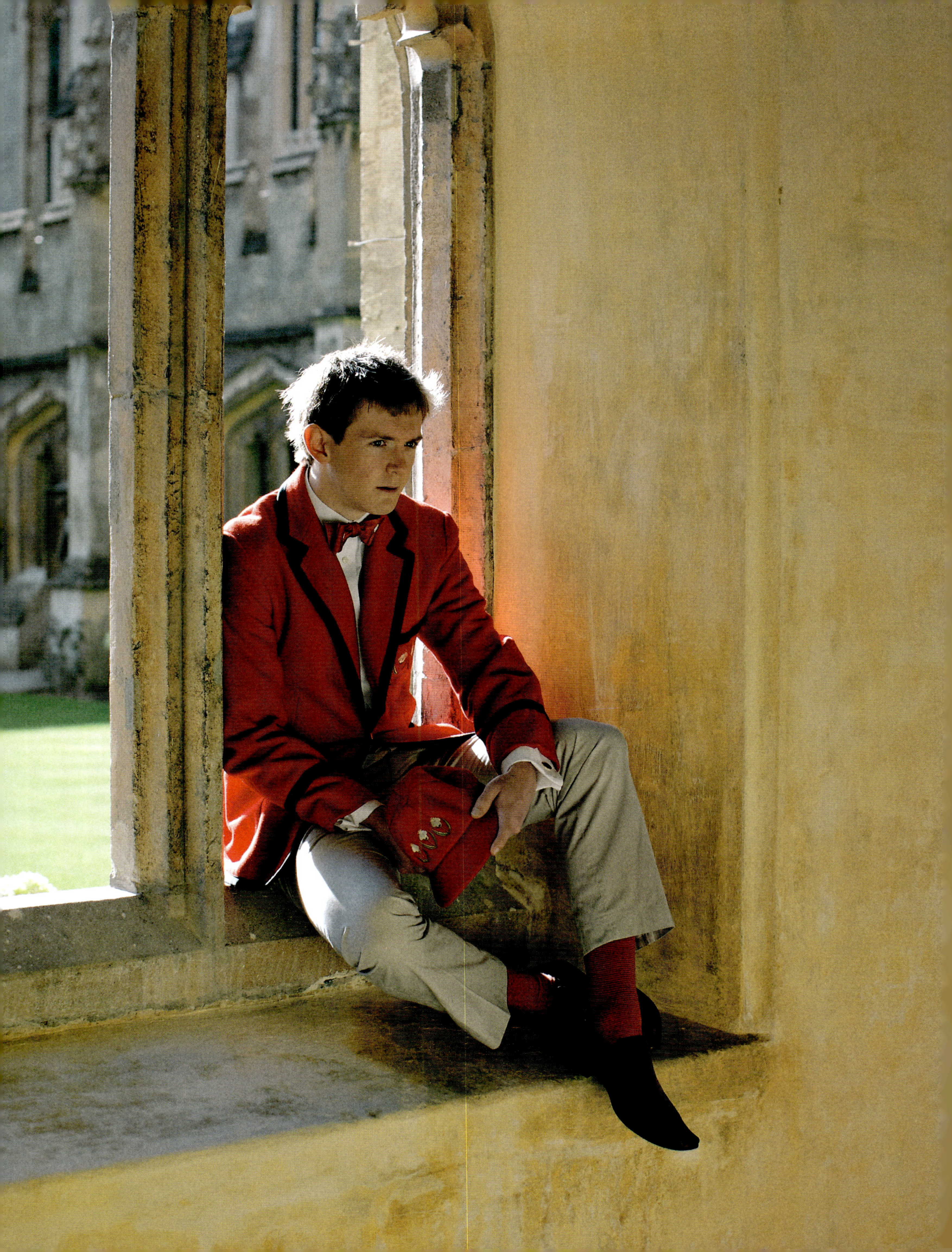

Oxford, England

Magdalen College Boat Club, Oxford

JAMES THOM

"I have given instructions to the Senior Dean not to allow the undergraduates to lounge about in College in their Boating dress."

—Frederick Bulley,
President of Magdalen College, notebook, 1859

Magdalen has generally been among the most successful Oxford college rowing clubs, the highlights of its success probably being a gold medal at the 1908 Olympics (for an all-Magdalen crew) and a gold medal in 1912 for the Olympic eight (in which all but one were Magdalen men).

The college's coat of arms is black and white and features three white lilies. But, for reasons unknown, red has been the color principally associated with Magdalen College Boat Club since its founding in 1859. The earliest Magdalen rowers wore scarlet blazers with dark blue trim and red hatbands adorned with three white lilies. Today, oarsmen in the first eight are entitled to wear blazers and hatbands with the same designs; they may also wear red bowties and red cricket-style caps with embroidered lilies.

Over time, a whole system of blazers and other accessories developed: the Magdalen second eight began wearing untrimmed red jackets and black bowties with embroidered lilies, while the first Torpid adopted caps with black-and-white concentric hoops and black-and-white-striped blazers. The stripey blazers were soon superseded by simpler white jackets with black trim and "lilied" pockets, which could be worn by any member of the boat club.

Blazers seem to have been especially popular articles of clothing among Magdalen students over the years. Even in the first year of the boat club's existence, the college president's notebook records his displeasure at the surfeit of boating gear among students. And around the turn of the twentieth century, "boating jackets" were so prevalent at the college that they were recorded separately on Magdalen laundry tariffs (and cost a penny more to clean than regular jackets). Moreover, they had a tendency to turn up in the most unexpected places: when T. E. Lawrence ("Lawrence of Arabia") was excavating at Carchemish in 1913, he was visited by his brother, who recorded, in a letter to their parents:

> *When I saw him last as the train left the station he was wearing white flannels, socks and red slippers, with a white Magdalen blazer, and was talking to the governor of Biridjik in a lordly fashion.*

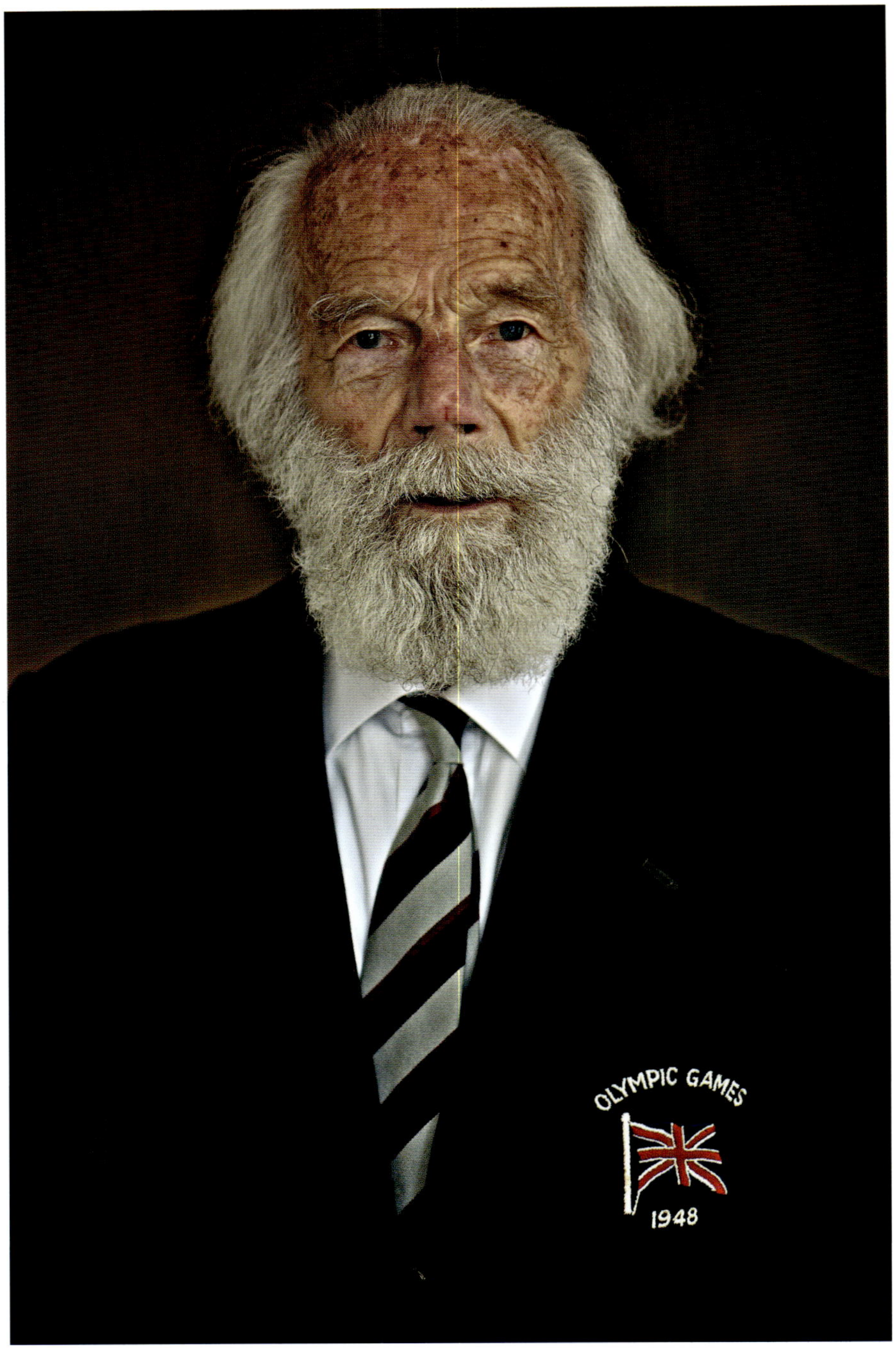

Great Britain Olympic Team

1948 and 2012

MICHAEL LAPAGE, ALEX GREGORY MBE

Alex Gregory (opposite) rowed in the Great Britain four that won gold at the 2012 London Olympics. Michael Lapage (above) also won an Olympic medal at London, but his Olympics were the 1948 "Austerity Games." A former missionary and fighter pilot, Lapage is the last surviving oarsman from the '48 Games.

Traditionally, Great Britain national and Olympic blazers featured the Union Flag on the pocket. In 2012, however, the Olympic team was outfitted in full suits, with Team GB's stylized lion emblem on the pocket.

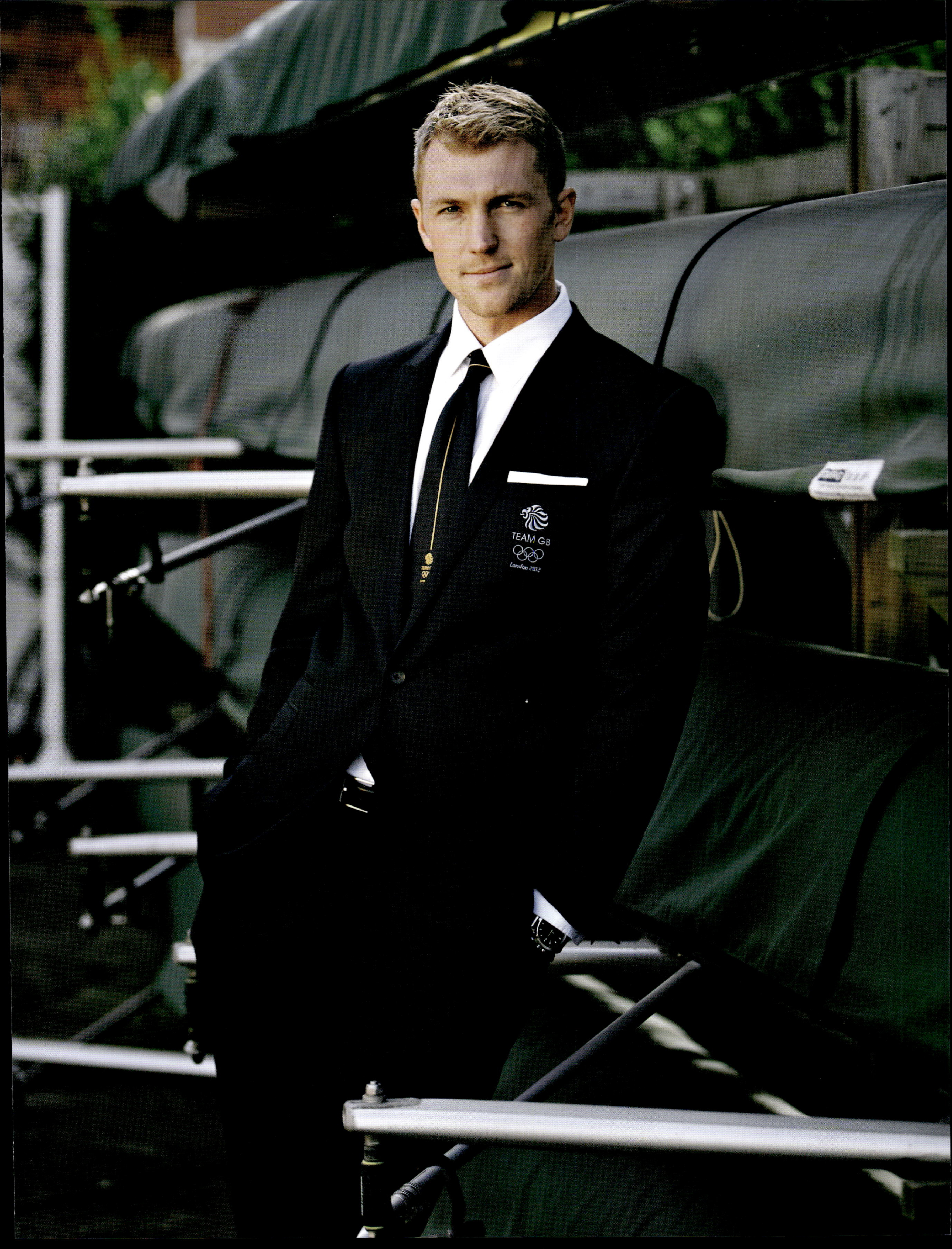
TEAM GB
London 2012

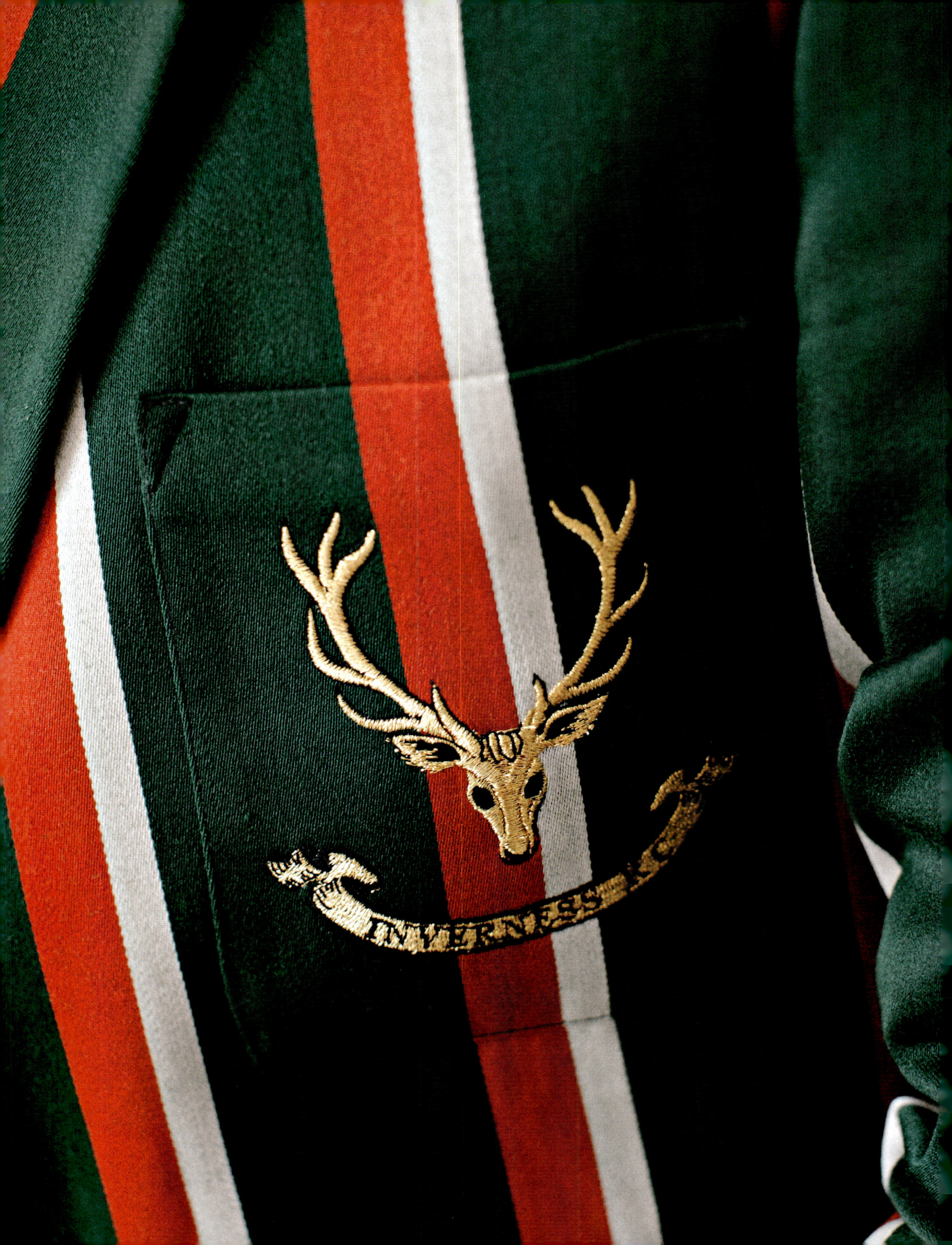
INVERNESS

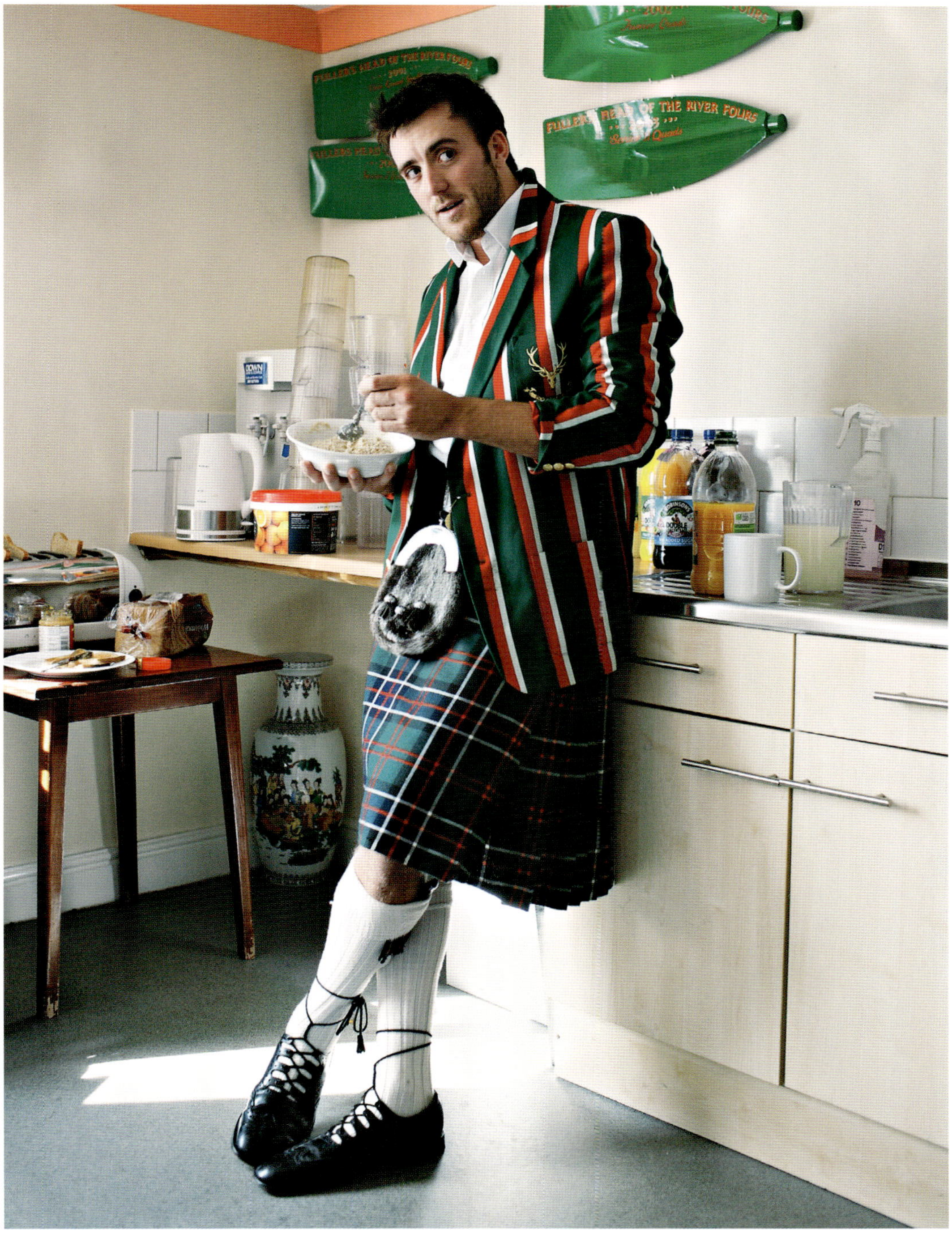

Inverness, Scotland

Inverness Boat Club

AL SINCLAIR

When he was fourteen, Al Sinclair began rowing at Inverness Rowing Club on the Caledonian Canal near Loch Ness in northern Scotland. Although he has moved south to pursue his dream of rowing on the British team, he still wears the Inverness jacket with pride. He won the Prince of Wales Cup at Henley Royal Regatta in 2011, breaking all of the course records in the process, and the Double Sculls Challenge Cup in 2012. On both occasions he donned his Inverness blazer for the prize ceremony. Al is currently in the Great Britain national squad and training for the 2016 Olympic Games.

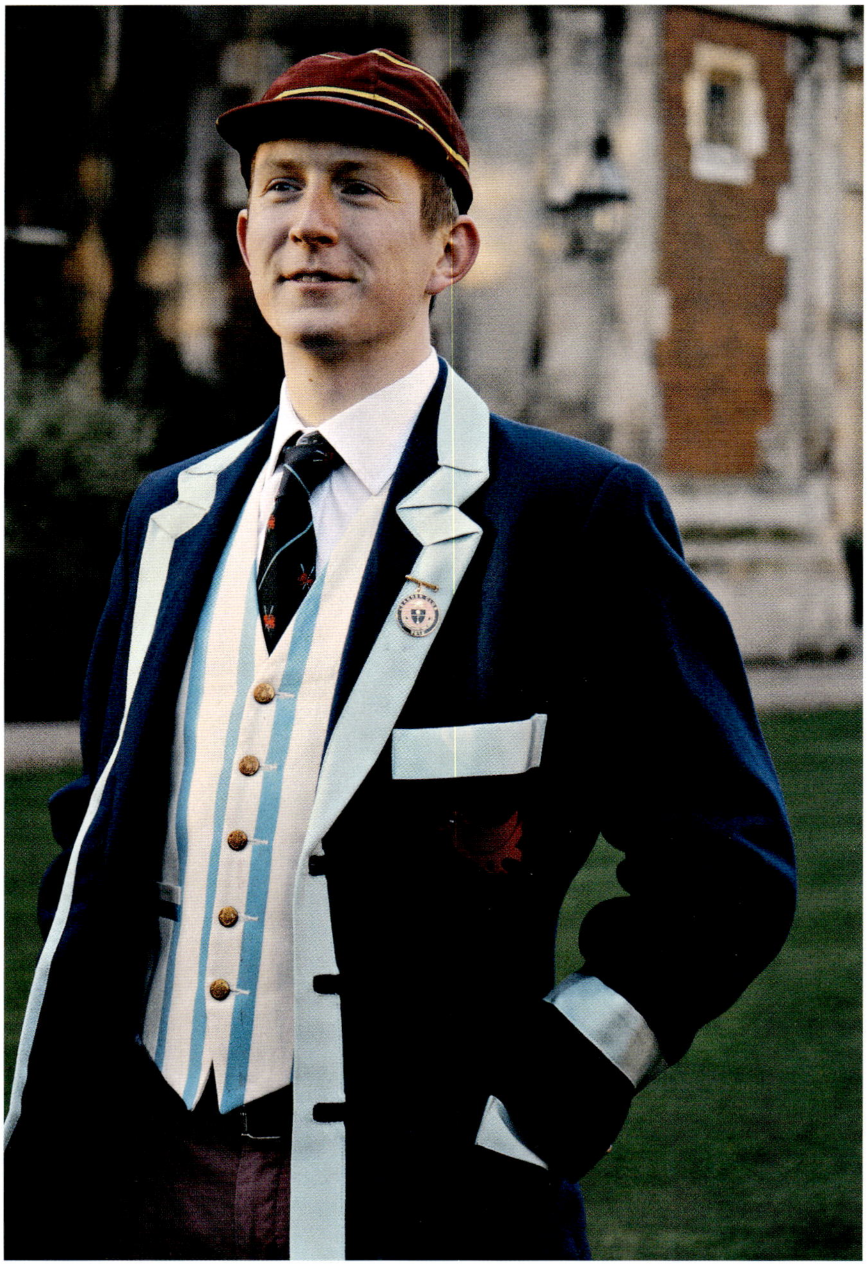

Cambridge, England

Pembroke College Boat Club, Cambridge

ALISTAIR CHAPPELLE

Pembroke is an ancient college but wasn't a regular fixture on the Cambridge rowing scene until 1856, when its crew raced in bright yellow costumes, for which Pembroke became the target of much mockery on the river. The ridicule they suffered was apparently sufficient to warrant the adoption of a more staid design: a "dark blue blazer with light blue trimmings." The blazer badge is a martlet, a footless heraldic bird from the coat of arms of the de Valence Earls of Pembroke.

ABOVE: Alistair Chappelle wears his Pembroke blazer, Cambridge lightweights waistcoat and tie, Hawks' Club cap, and Leander Club badge.

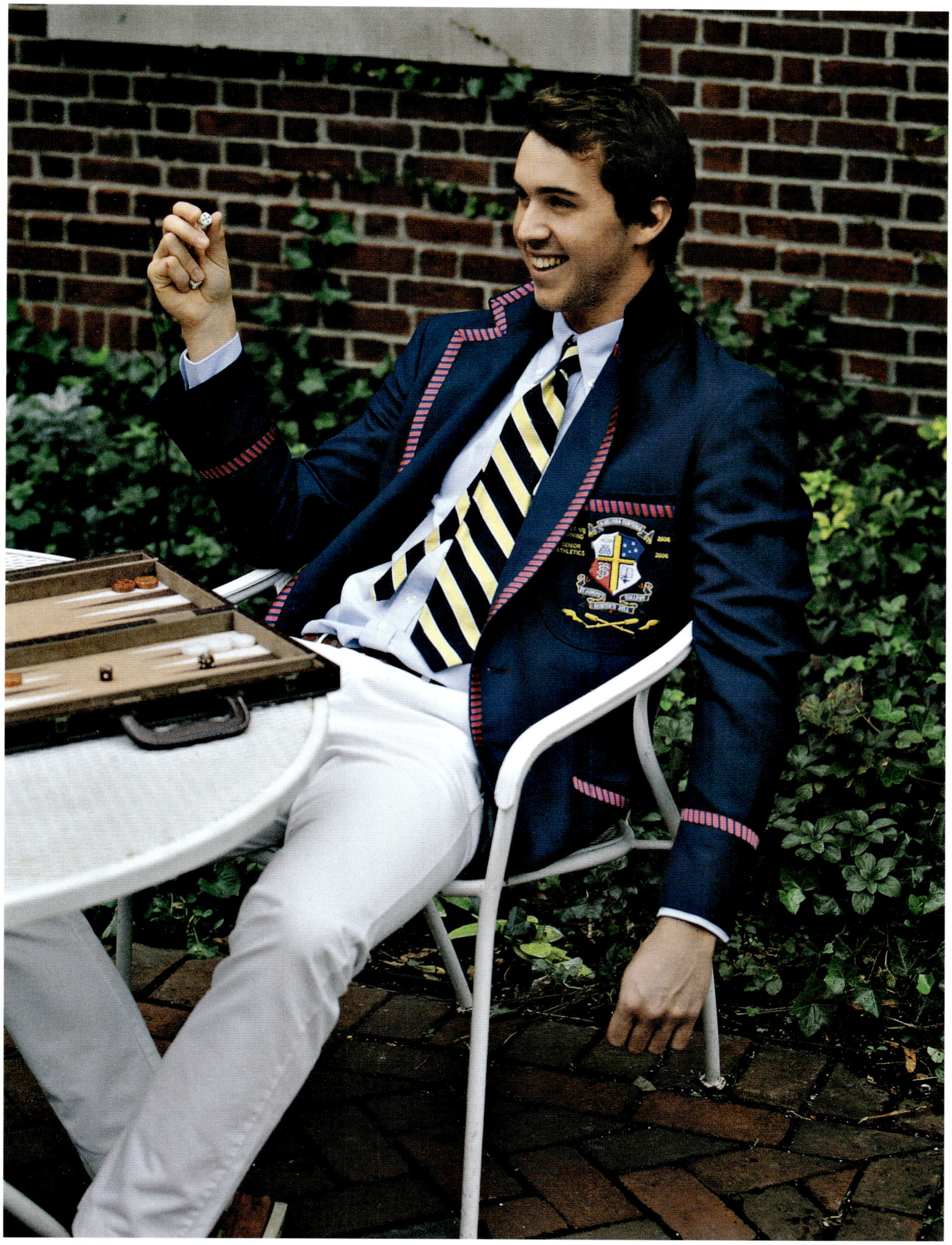

Hunters Hill, Australia

St. Joseph's College

MATT EDSTEIN

Like many Australian schools, "Joey's" awards particularly garish honors blazers to its top sportsmen; those awarded to oarsmen feature crossed blades on the pocket, beneath the school's arms.

London, England

University of London Boat Club

PAUL BENNETT, MAX GANDER,
OLLIE COOK, JAMIE COOK,
RORY BUFFACHI

Just as Oxford and Cambridge honor their top sportsmen and -women with Blues awards (manifest in the form of blazers), the University of London awards Purples. The U.L.B.C. Purple blazer is traditionally wool flannel with matching purple binding and "U.L.B.C." with crossed blades on the pocket. Newer versions feature the university coat of arms on the pocket and sometimes omit the binding: there is little rhyme or reason to these variations.

Paul, Max, Ollie, Jamie, and Rory won the Prince Albert Challenge Cup for student coxed fours at the 2012 Henley Royal Regatta.

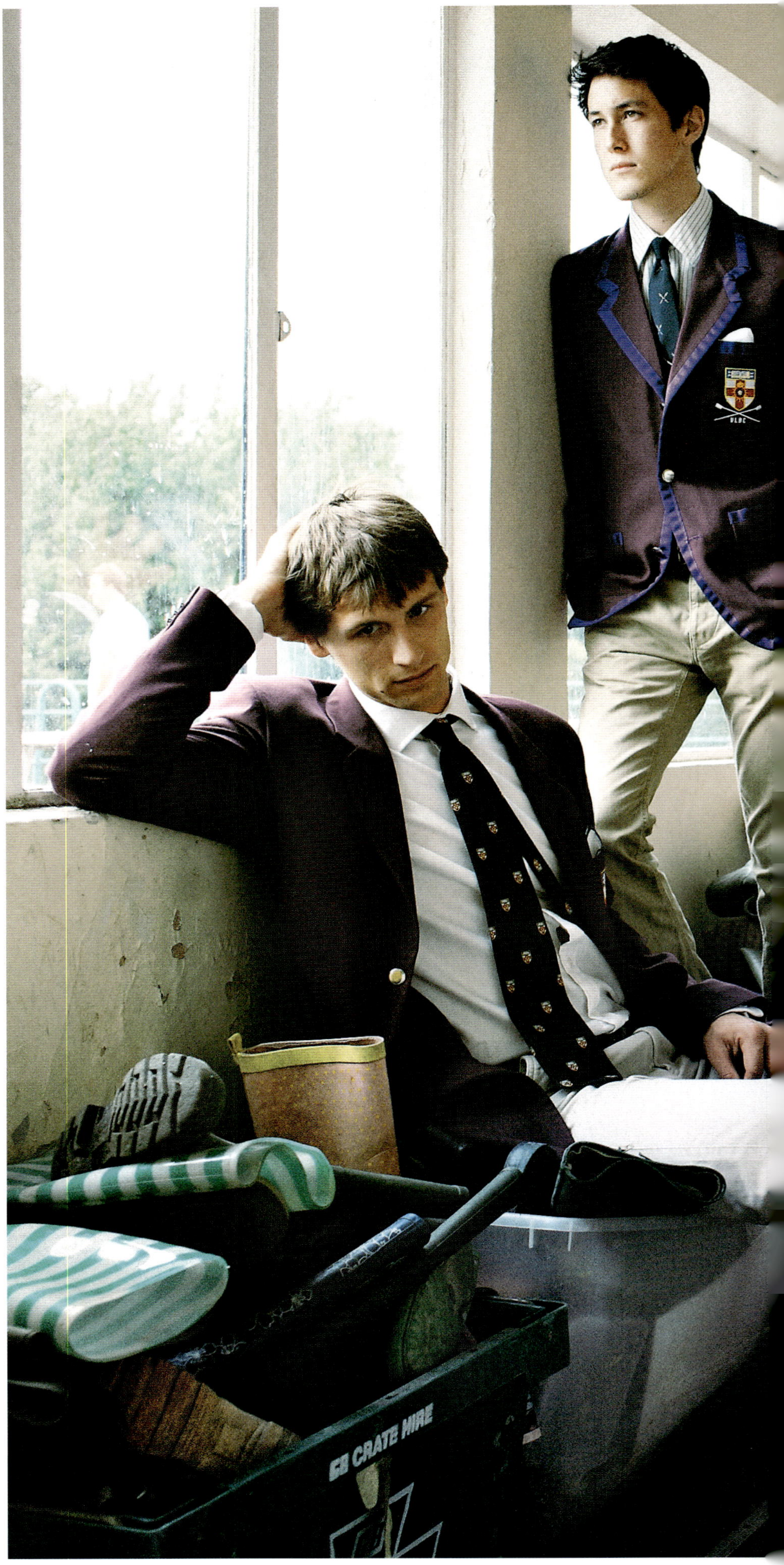

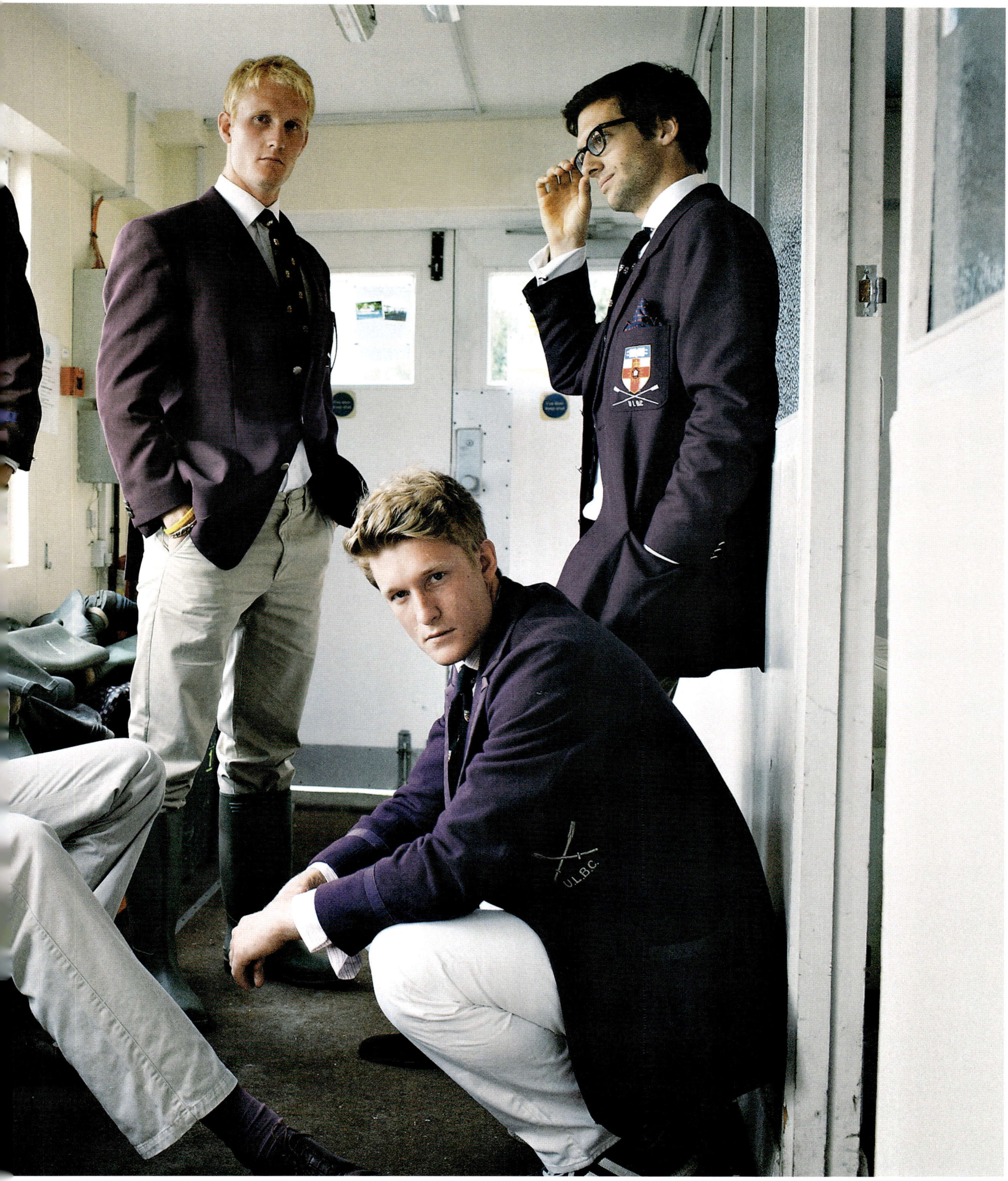
U.L.B.C.

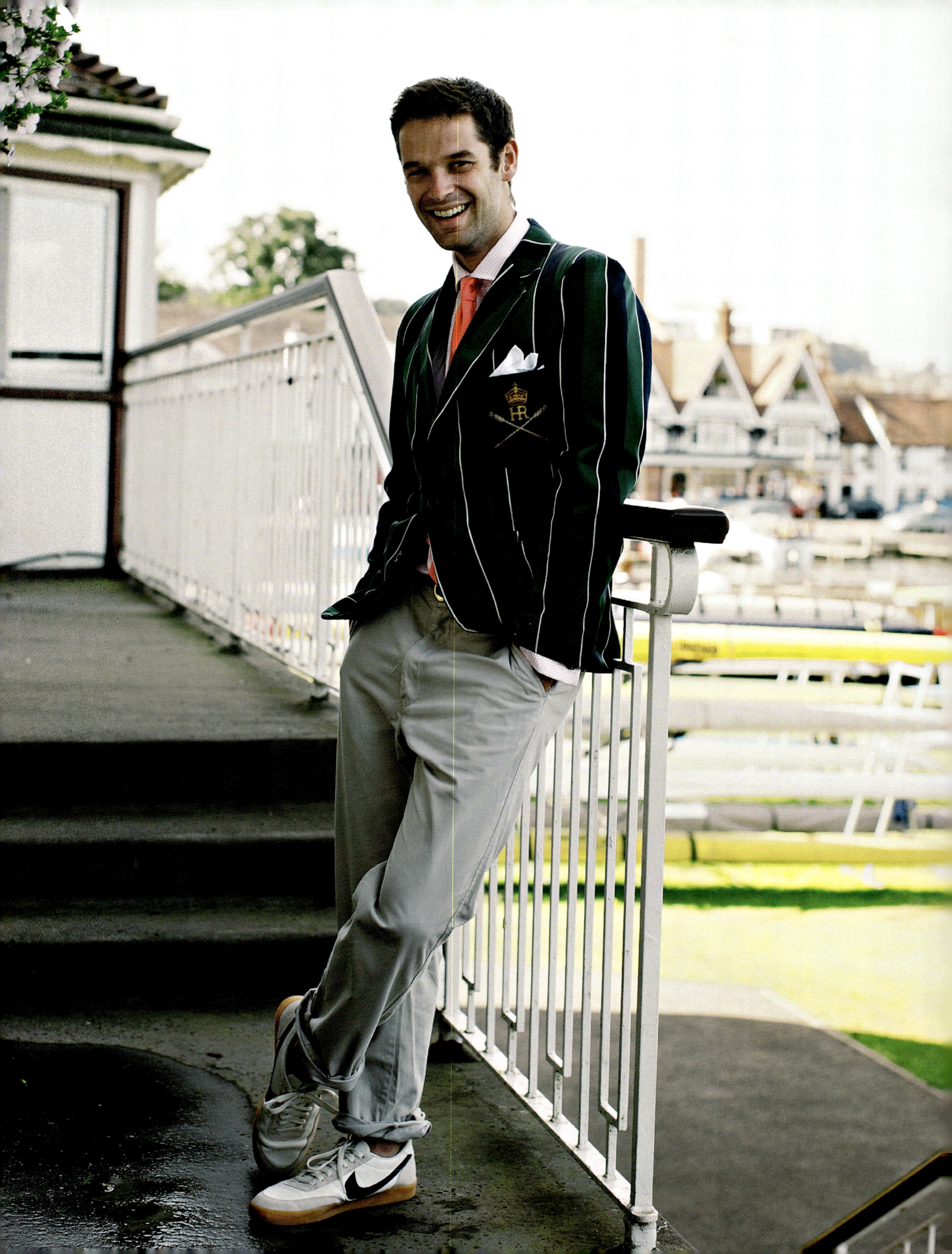
HR

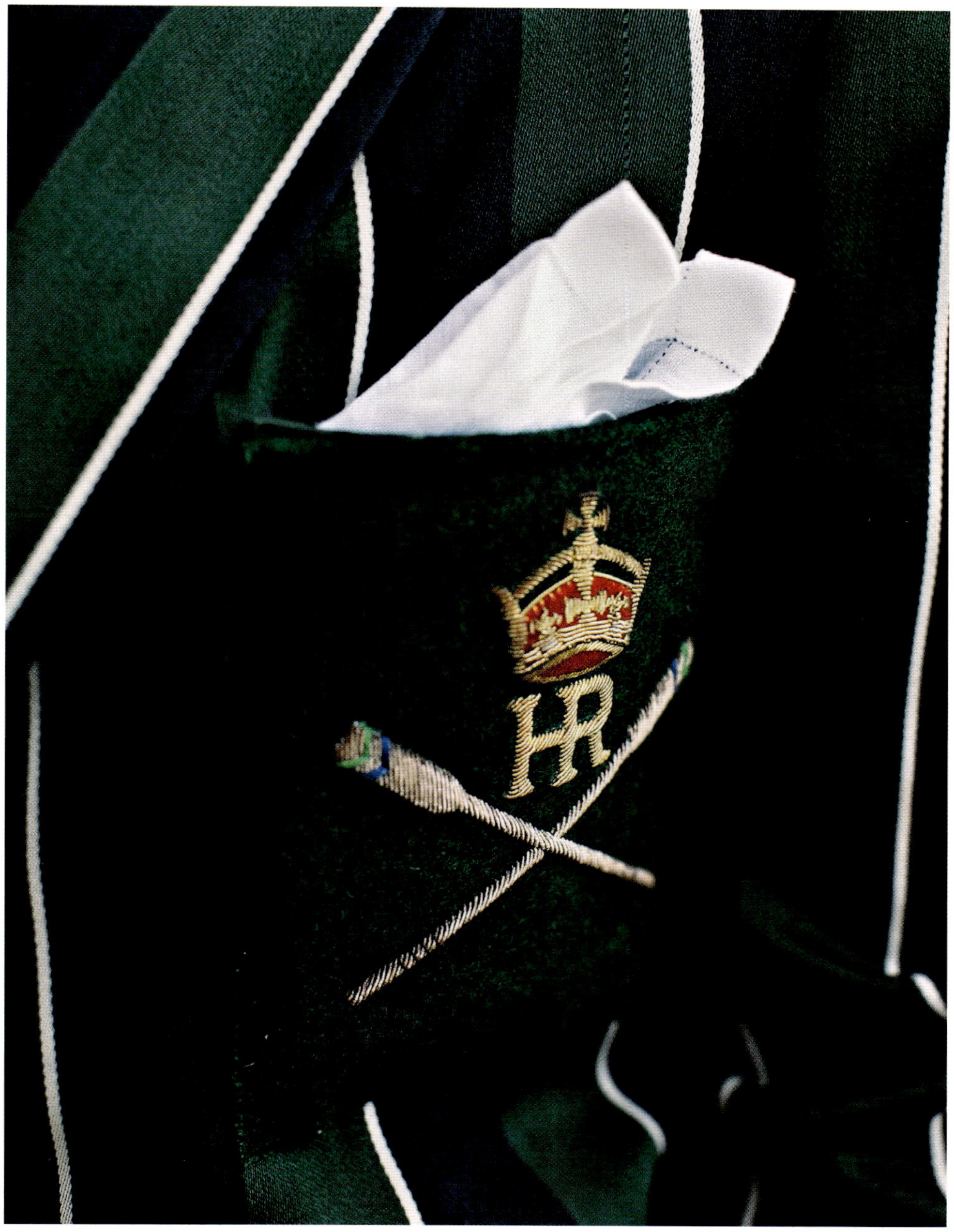

Chester, England

King's School Chester Boat Club

CHRIS BARTLEY

The green, blue, and white–striped blazer was once the sole preserve of oarsmen at King's Chester. But the sartorial privilege of the school's rowers must have been the envy of other students: like so many other British schools, the King's School Chester has appropriated its stripey rowing blazer as the general school blazer. The "HR" cipher on the blazer badge stands for *Henricus Rex:* King Henry (VIII), who founded the school in 1541.

Chris Bartley began his rowing career at King's Chester; as a member of Great Britain's lightweight four, he is a world champion and an Olympic silver medalist.

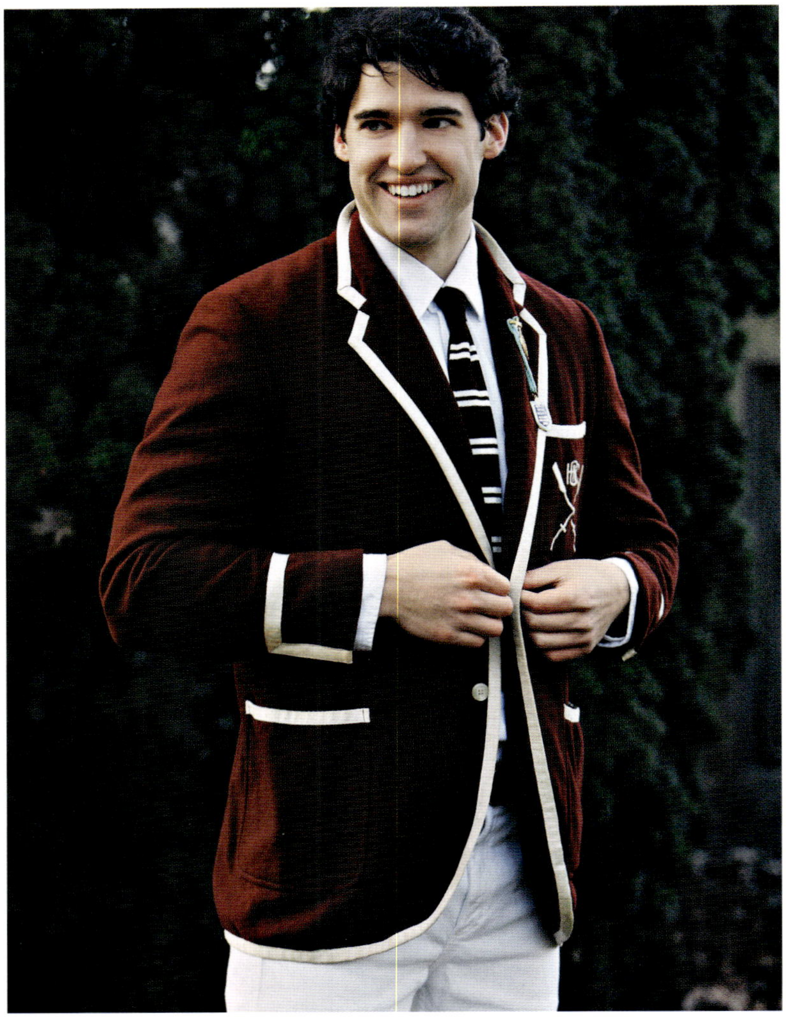

Concord, New Hampshire

Halcyon Boat Club and Shattuck Boat Club, St. Paul's School

ERIK WOELBER, SAM COOLEY

"The Halcyon jacket is maroon, the Shattuck cerulean blue, and the lapels of both are fringed with white. Straw boaters, white ducks, white oxfords, and white shirts with the Halcyon or Shattuck tie complete the after-the-race outfit. Hogwarts has Quidditch; St. Paul's has crew." —Alex Shoumatoff, *Vanity Fair*, 2006

Every student at St. Paul's School, regardless of whether he or she plans to row, is assigned to one of two boat clubs upon arrival as a freshman: Halcyon or Shattuck.

From their first race in 1871, the two clubs have enjoyed a fierce and celebrated rivalry. For decades, in fact, St. Paul's did not compete at all in interscholastic regattas, focusing instead on the all-important intramural boat races between Halcyon and Shattuck. So great was this rivalry that even when the school's oarsmen did start participating in the New England championships, they raced as two separate clubs (Shattuck took both gold and silver in 1955, and Halcyon won in 1966). When the school finally began racing as a unified team, putting all of its best rowers into a single crew for the championship races, St. Paul's dominated, winning fifteen New England championships in thirty-one years.

The Halcyon and Shattuck boat races are still held annually, and alumni and current students, sporting the ties, boater hats, and blazers of their respective clubs, turn out in droves.

To this day, the school has no rowing jacket of its own, and when St. Paul's won the Princess Elizabeth Cup at Henley in 2004, the victorious crew accepted their trophy as a motley mixture of blue Shattuck and red Halcyon club blazers.

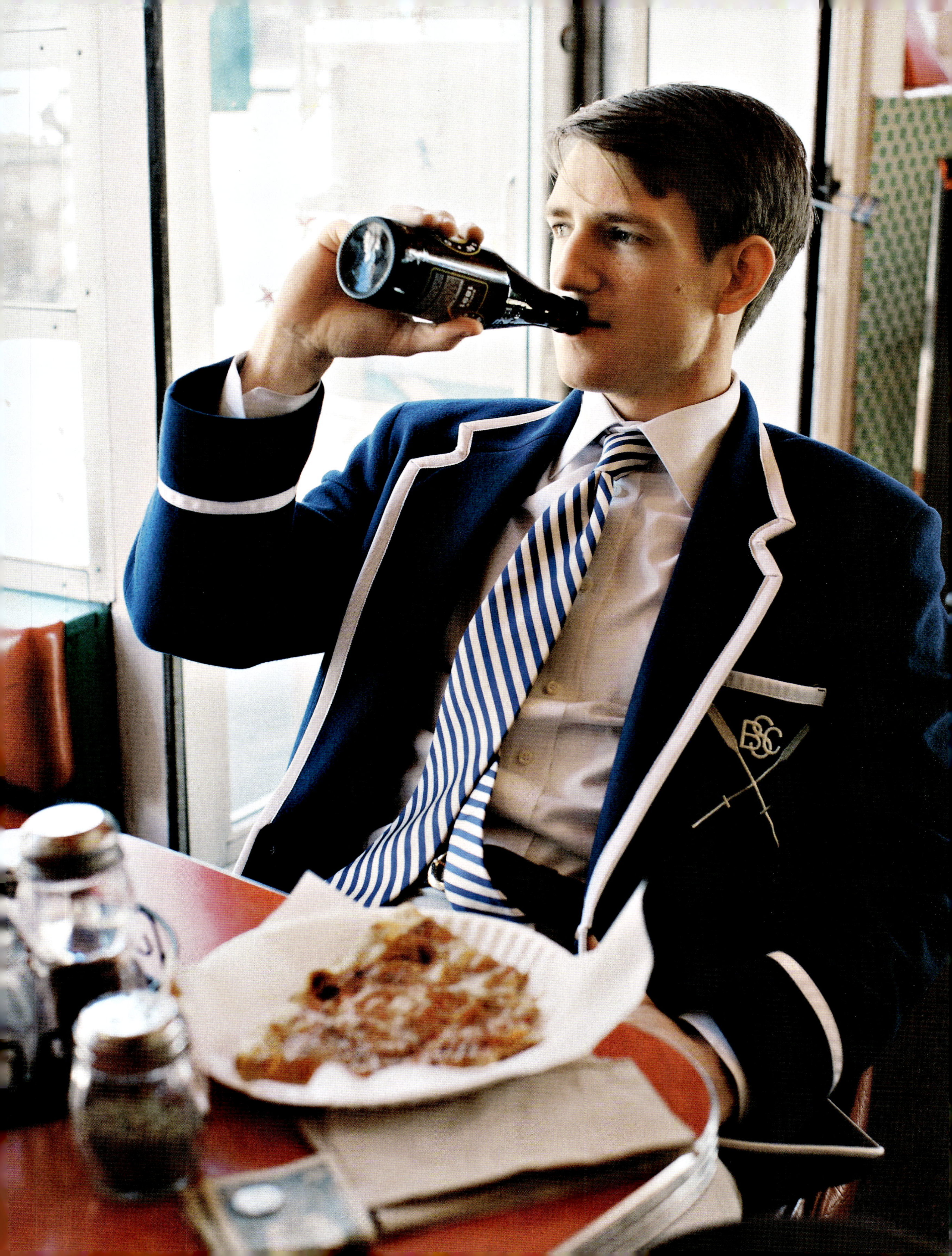
BSC

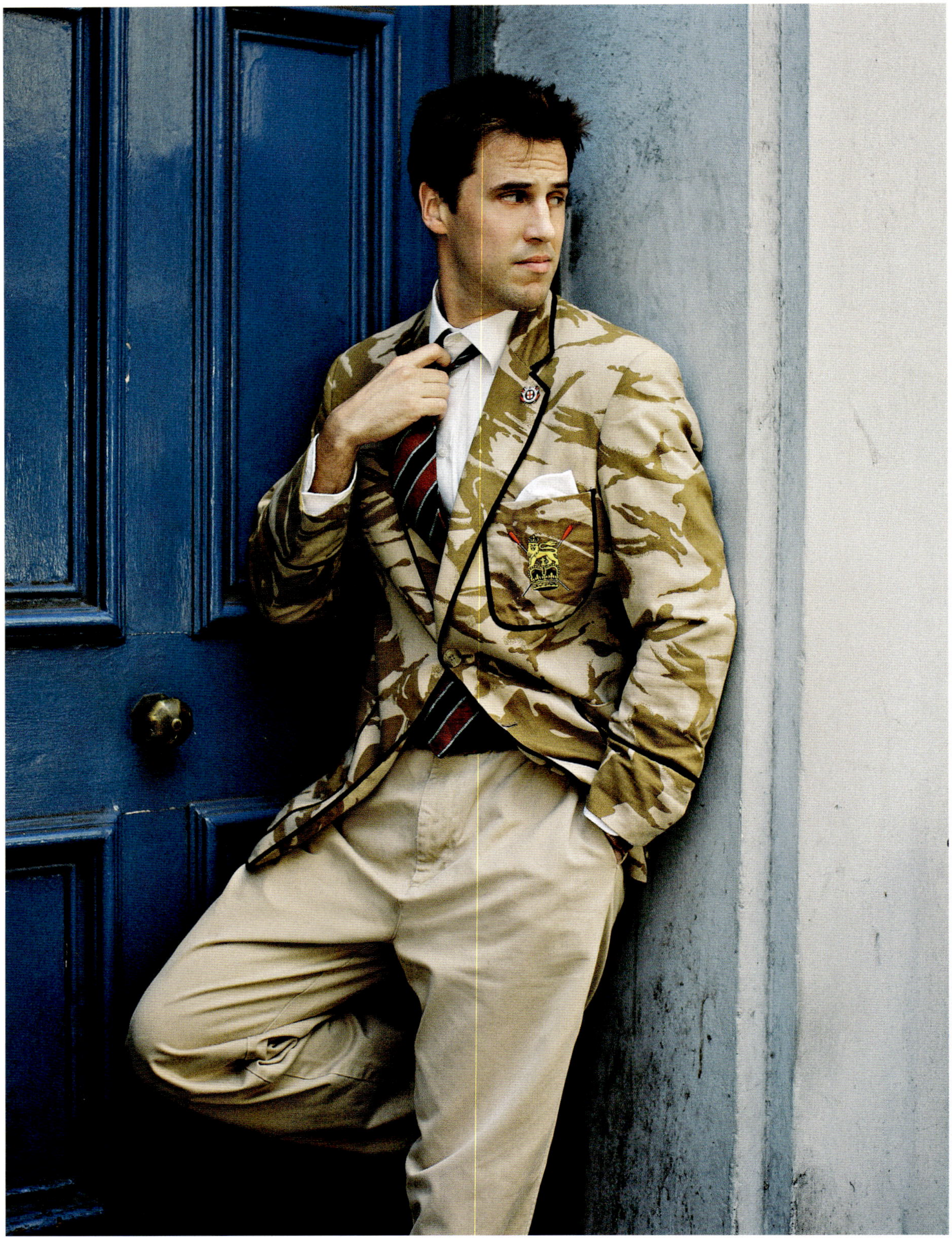

Great Britain

Army Rowing Club

NICK HEATHCOTE

Traditional rowing blazers probably owe much of their appearance to military dress uniforms, but the British Army's rowing club blazer playfully turns tradition on its head and uses the material of modern combat and utility uniforms—in this case British Army two-color desert camouflage.

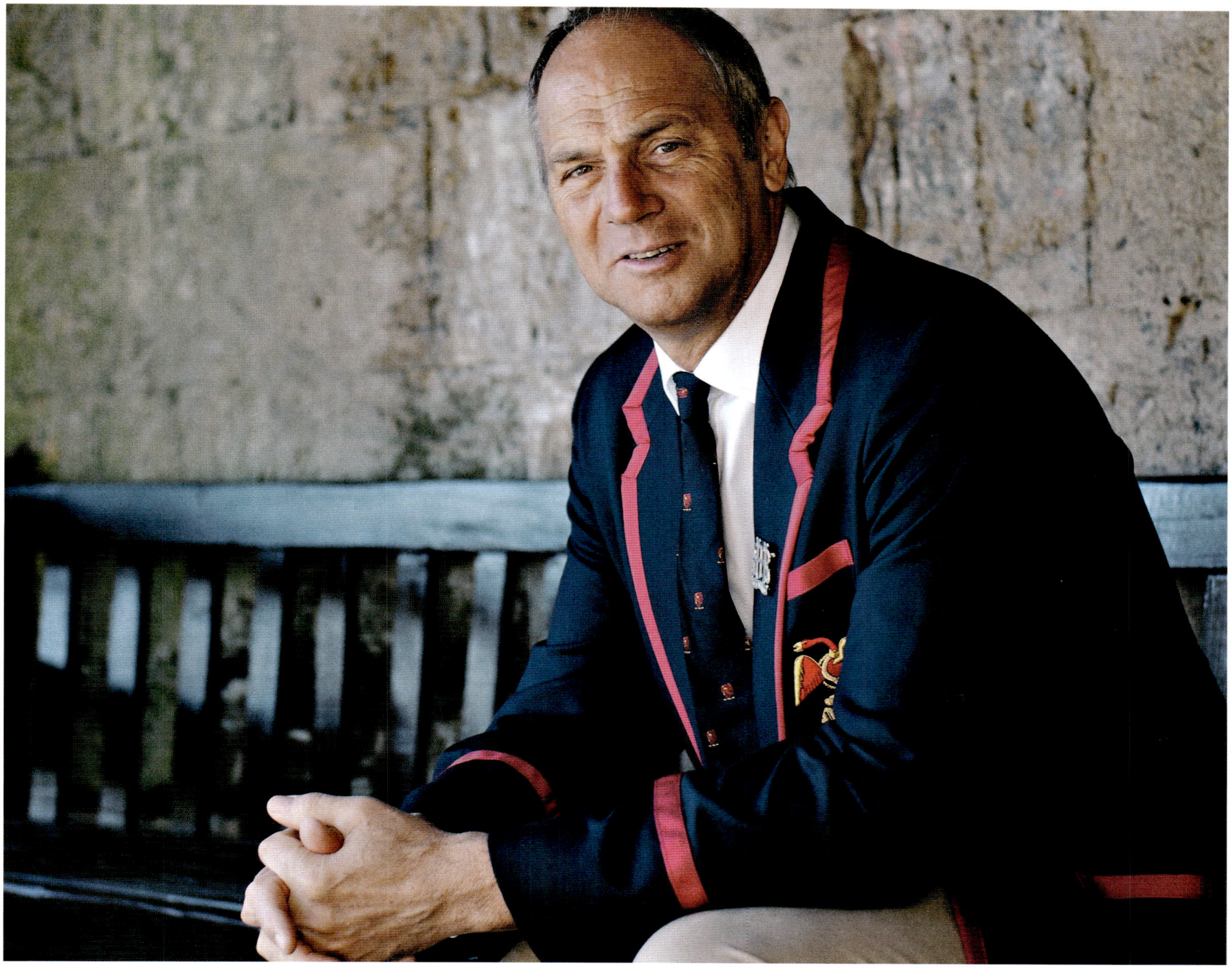

Marlow, England

Marlow Rowing Club

SIR STEVE REDGRAVE CBE DL

The current Marlow blazer pattern is the same as the one adopted in 1882: "dark blue bound with cardinal," with a chained swan on the pocket. The chained swan has a rich heraldic history, first seen as a badge of the de Bohun family (descendants of the so-called "Swan Knight") and, by marriage, of the Royal House of Lancaster in the fourteenth century; then deployed by leading families allied to the Lancastrian House, most notably the Dukes of Buckingham; and finally used in the civic heraldry of Buckinghamshire, including the coats of arms of the county and town of Marlow.

The winner of gold medals at five consecutive Olympic Games (and six Olympic medals in total), Sir Steve Redgrave is Britain's "Greatest Olympian." The gold medal he won with Matthew Pinsent in 1996—his fourth—was Great Britain's only Olympic gold in any sport that year; after the race, he famously told reporters, "Anyone who sees me in a boat again has permission to shoot me." He won his fifth and final gold at Sydney in 2000. He was knighted for services to rowing in 2001, and since 2013 has served as president of his home club, Marlow Rowing Club.

Kent, Connecticut

Kent School Boat Club

KYLE TRAUB

"No school reflects the personality and characteristics of its founder better than Kent School reflects Father Sill's. In its devotion to religion, to self-dependence, to the highest ideals of scholarship, it bears his mark indelibly. Even its prowess in crew racing stems directly from Father Sill."

—*New York Herald Tribune*, 1952

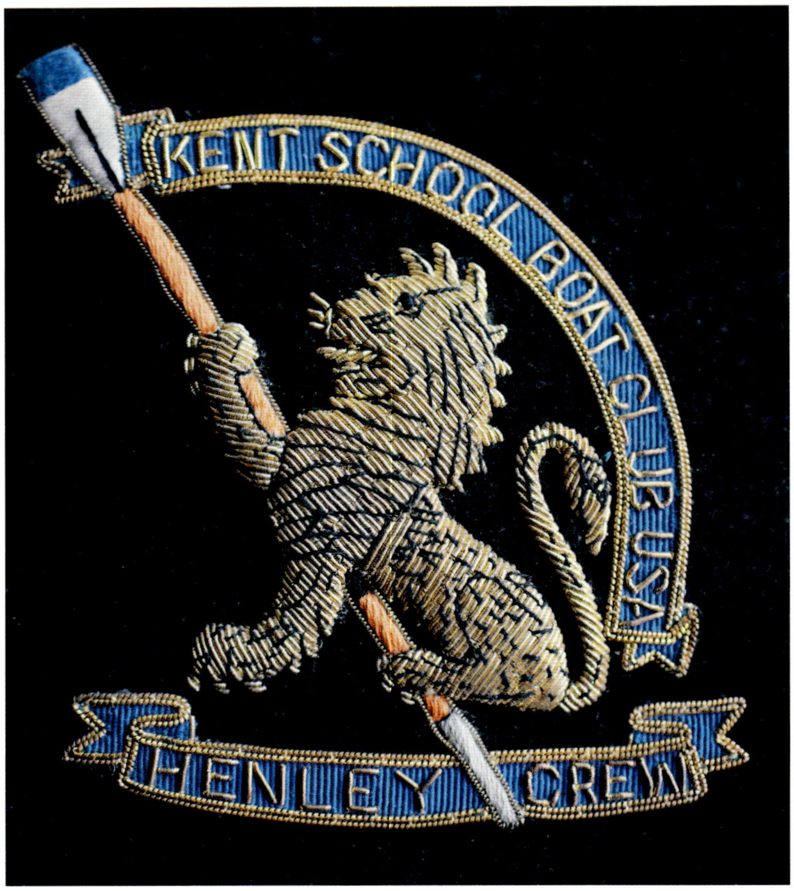

Kent School was quite literally built for rowing. The school's founder, the Reverend Frederick H. Sill, was a monk in the Order of the Holy Cross and coxed the Columbia crew to a national championship when he was an undergraduate. When he set out to found a school for "young men with slender means," he looked for a location on the banks of the Housatonic River ideally suited for rowing. And when the Boat Club was created in 1922, the monk himself served as coach; five years later, Kent became the first American schoolboy crew to compete at the Henley Royal Regatta in England. The chance to race at Henley remains the reward for Kent crews who perform exceptionally well during the regular season. The oarsmen in these crews earn one of the school's most revered honors: a coveted K.S.B.C. blazer.

Kyle served as team captain in his final year, leading Kent to a New England championship.

ABOVE: A previous version of the K.S.B.C. blazer badge.

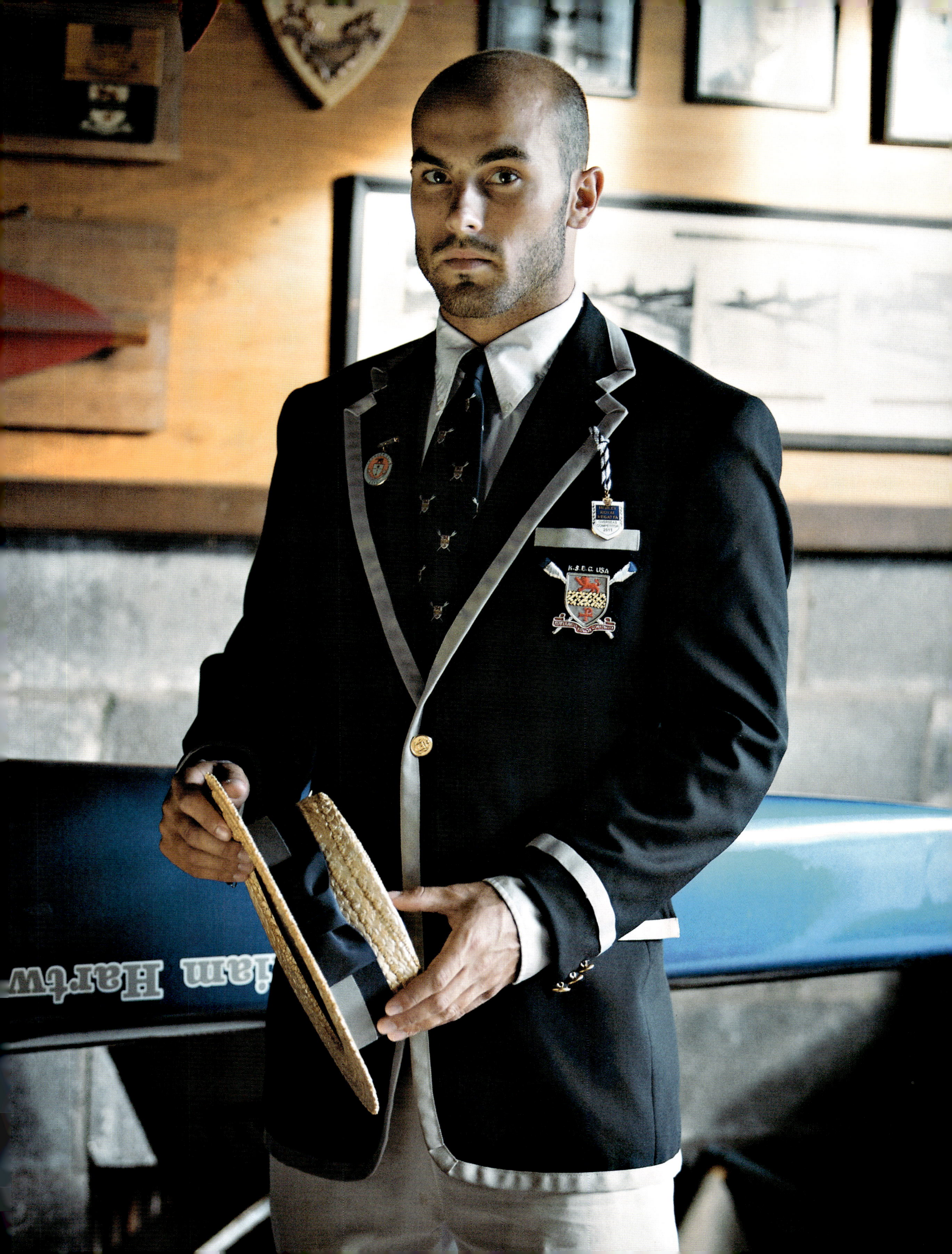
K.S.B.C. USA

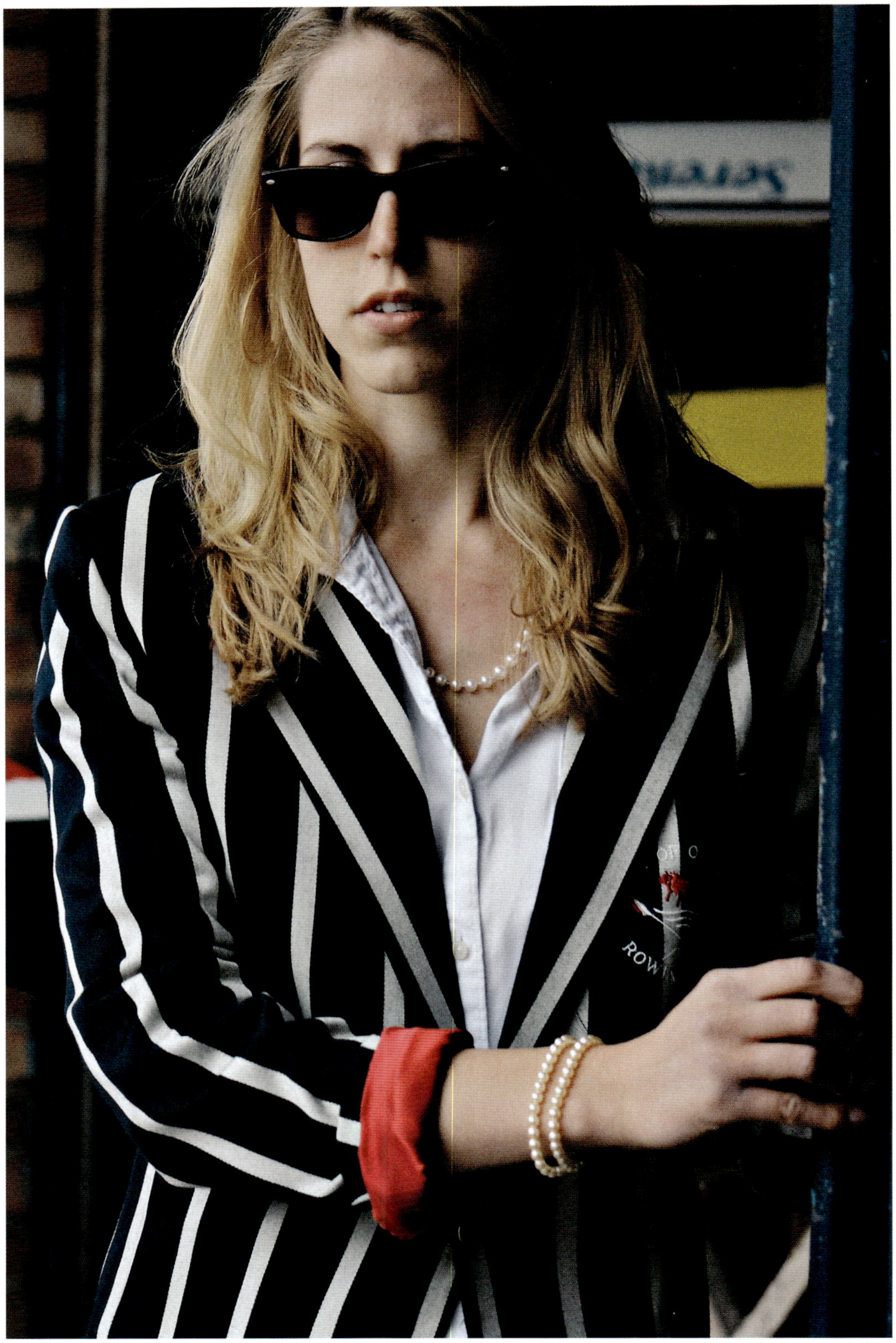

Oxford, England

City of Oxford Rowing Club

LYDIA VAN HAMEL-PARSONS

City of Oxford Rowing Club was formed from Neptune Rowing Club and Hannington Rowing Club in 1968. Its badge and colors are derived from the coat of arms of the City of Oxford, which depicts a red ox fording a blue river.

Lydia has been rowing for City of Oxford since she was eleven years old.

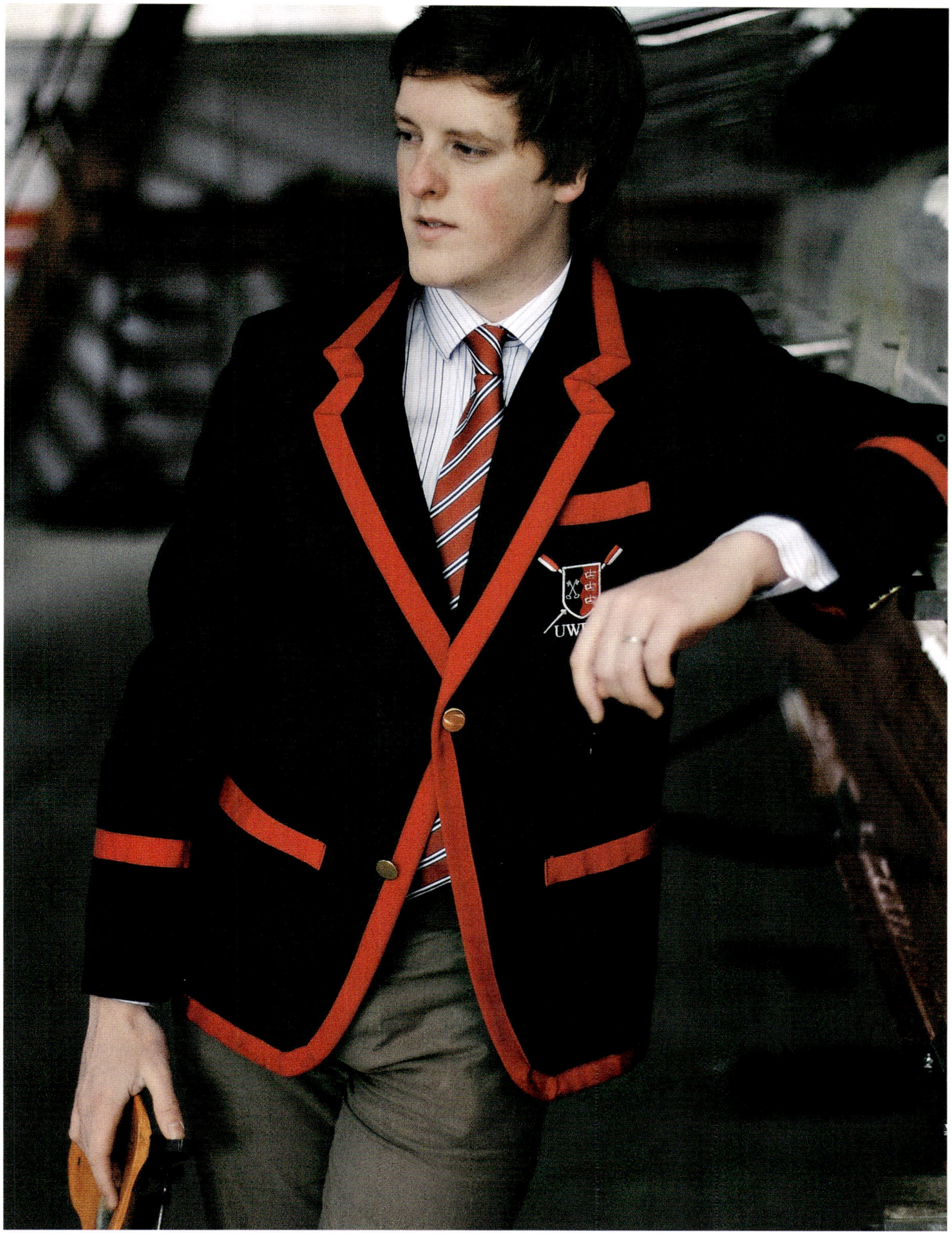

Bristol, England

University of the West of England

DAVE BORDER

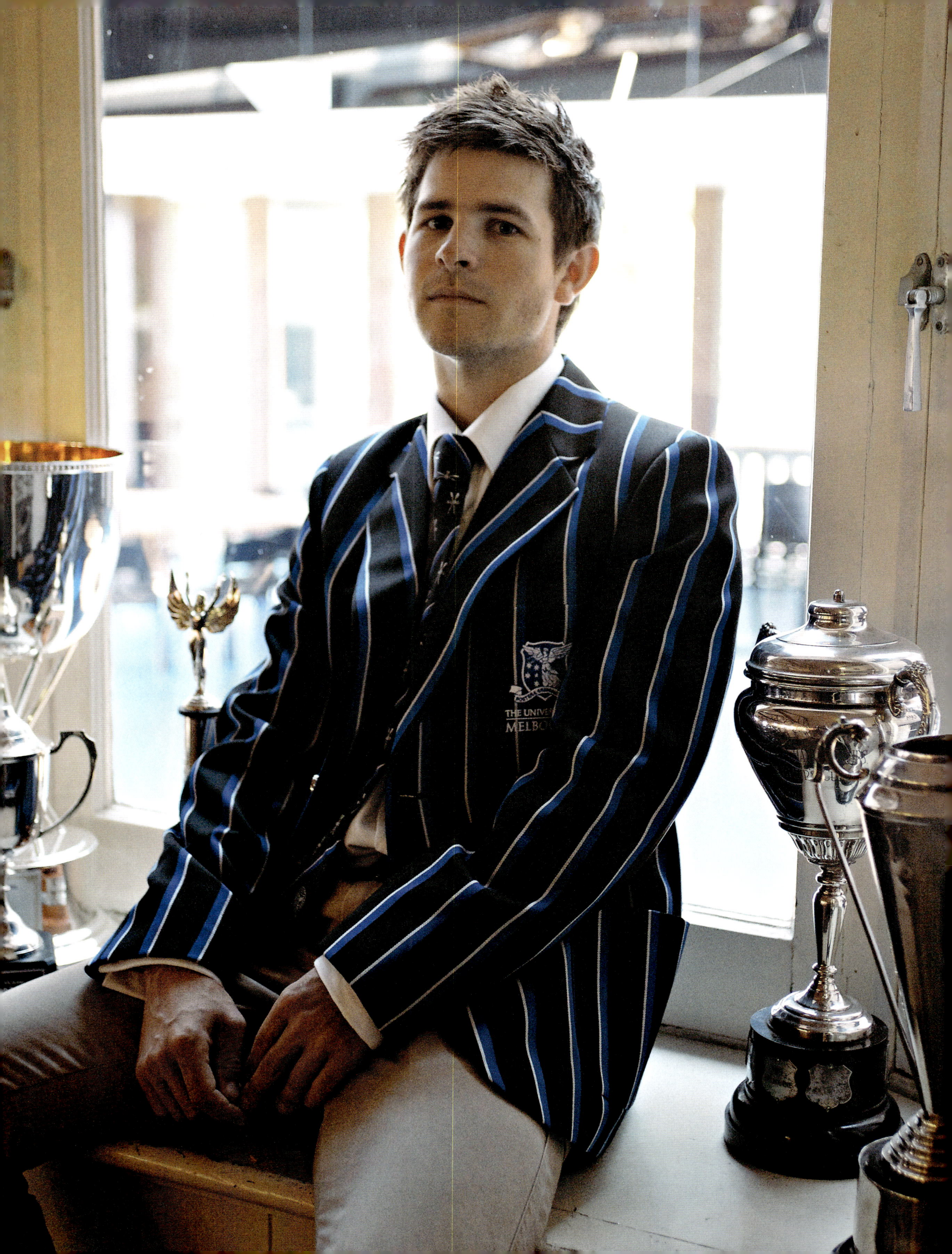

Melbourne, Australia

Melbourne University Boat Club

DAVID WEBSTER

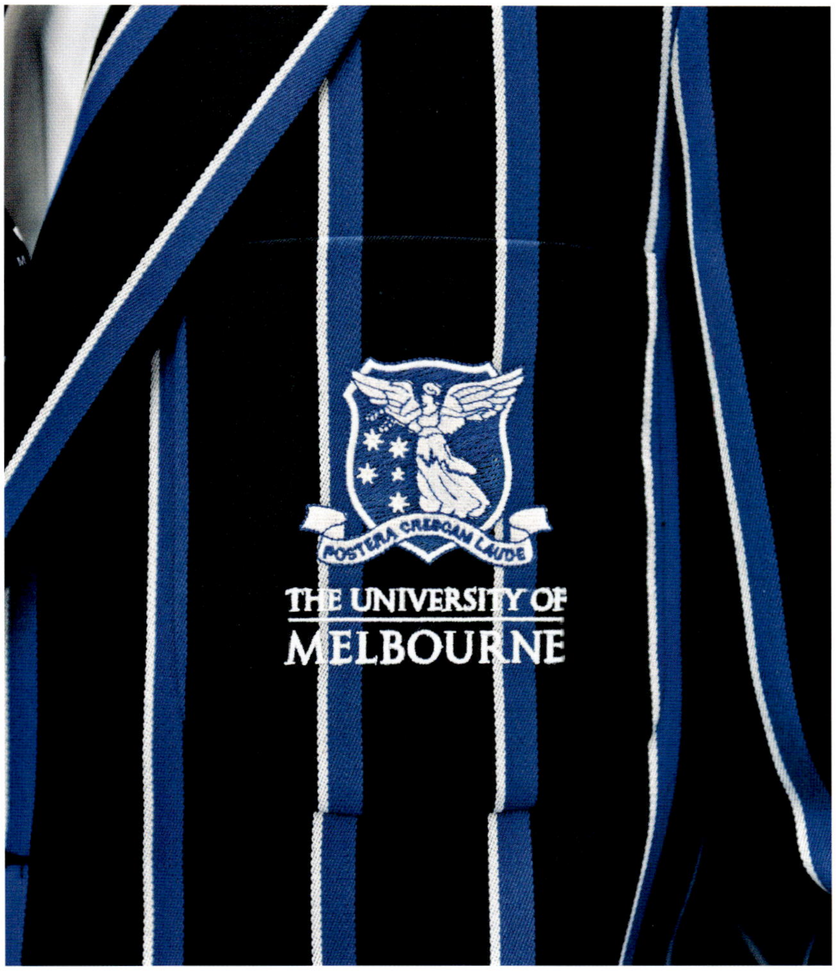

M.U.B.C., the oldest rowing club in Australia, was founded in 1859 and raced rival Sydney University for the first time in 1860.

In 1905, a meeting was held to discuss the "honour pocket" to be worn on club blazers by members of the Inter-Varsity eight. The club's blazers had been blue with black-and-white-striped trim and an image of the goddess Victory on the pocket (an allusion to the Australian state Victoria). A proposal had been made by the Sports Union to replace the depiction of Victory—which also appears on the university's coat of arms—with the club's M.U.B.C. monogram. The meeting minutes record that members were "not greatly impressed with the beauty of the [goddess] but thought that it would be a pity to abandon her." Today the winged Victory still adorns club blazer pockets, along with the full modern-day logo of the university.

David coxed for M.U.B.C. and is a world champion for Australia in both the lightweight eight and the coxed pair.

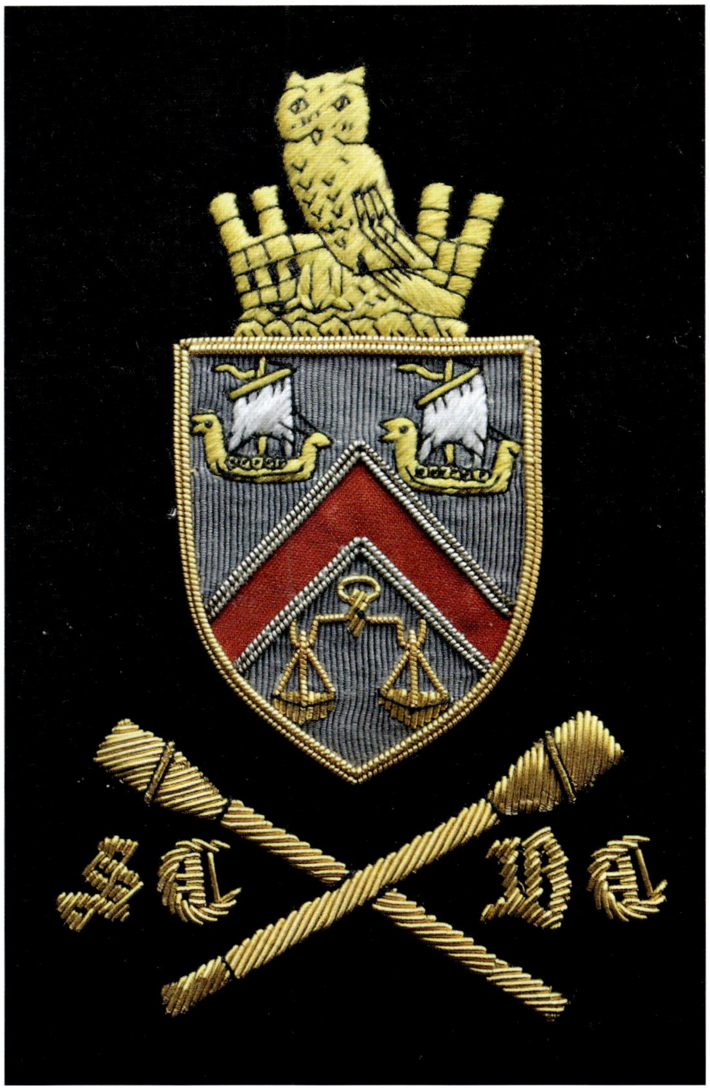

Henley-on-Thames, England

Shiplake College Boat Club

WILL SATCH

Will Satch, a world champion and Olympic bronze medalist, was born in Henley-on-Thames and learned to row at Shiplake College, where he was Captain of Boats.

Originally, only the rowers at Shiplake were allowed to wear the maroon, black, and gold–striped blazer. Each rower's blazer pocket was embroidered with an image of a ship, except for the Captain of Boats', which featured the school's coat of arms and crossed blades embroidered in gold wire.

Recently (and to the chagrin of the oarsmen, one suspects), the school decreed that all students may wear the striped blazer; current Shiplake rowers now distinguish themselves by edging their blazers with gold ribbon.

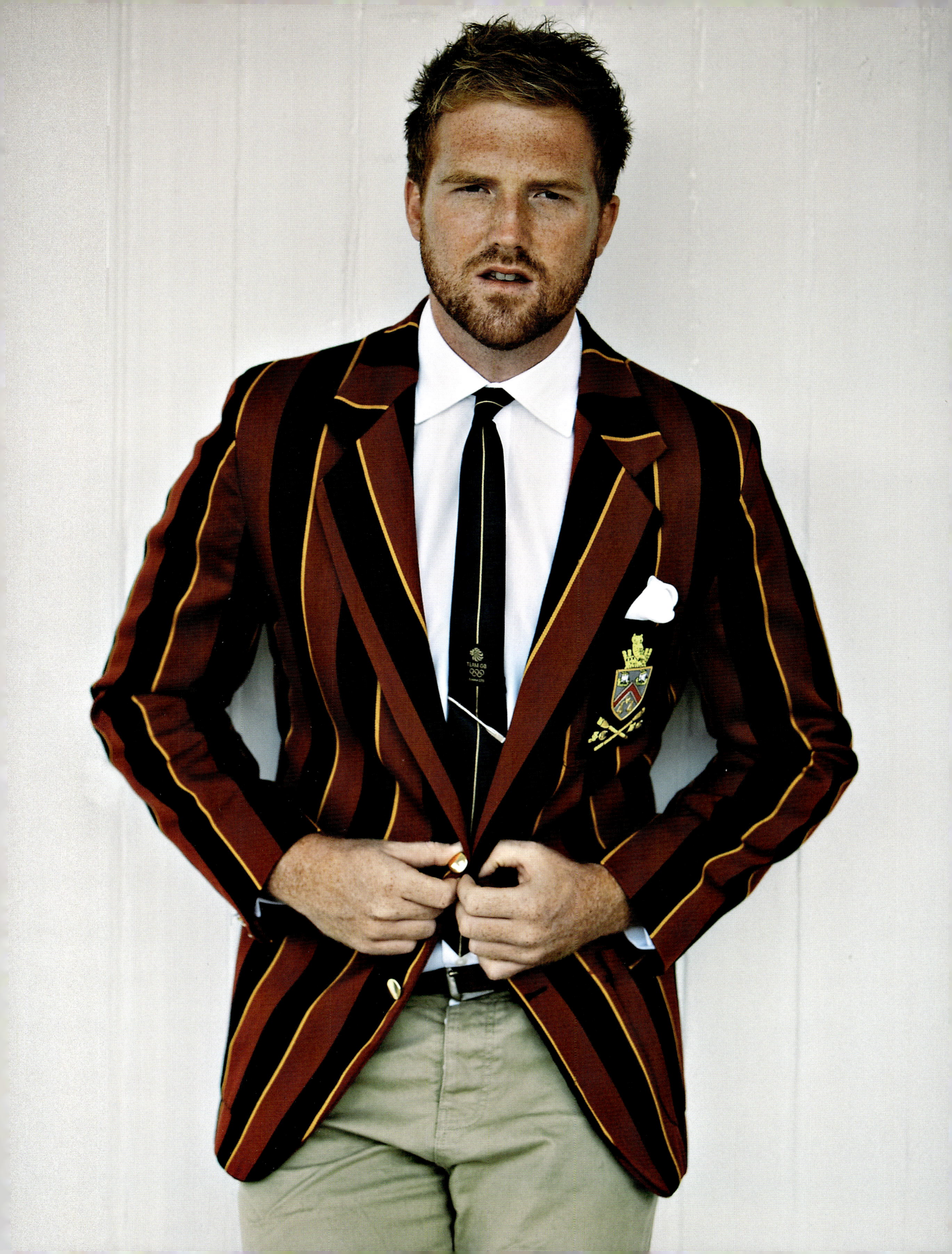

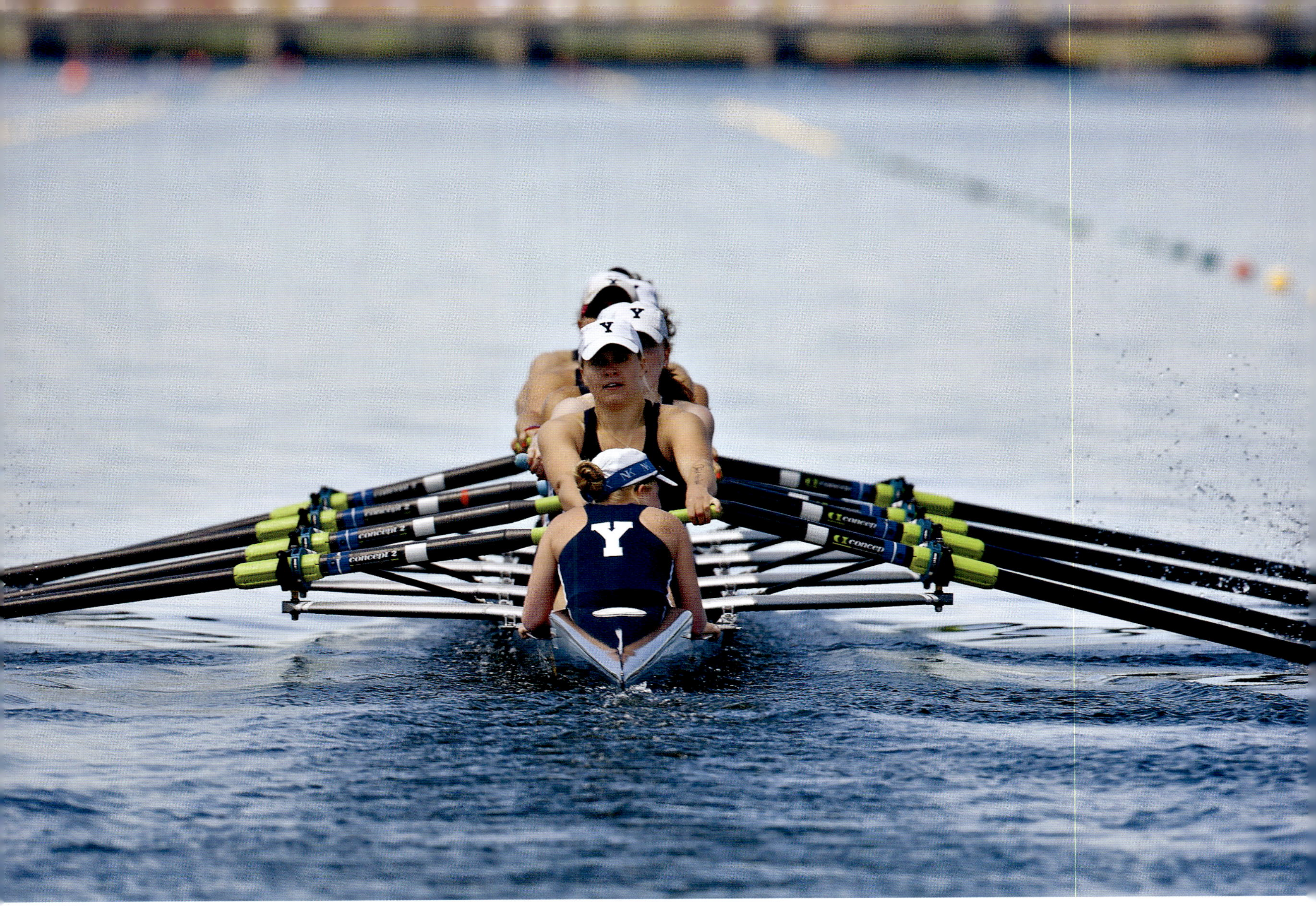

New Haven, Connecticut

Yale University Boat Club

TAYLOR RITZEL, BILL BECKLEAN

After graduating from Yale in 1839, Charles Bristed attended Cambridge University, where he was impressed by the passion for rowing and sport among British students. "If instead of the thousand and one secret societies that fritter away their time, the Yalensians would [set up] boat and cricket clubs," he wrote, "there might be some hope for them." In 1843, his vision became a reality, and the first student rowing club in the nation was formed at Yale; the first American intercollegiate sporting event, the Yale-Harvard Regatta, followed nine years later.

Yalies have rowed in blue since the 1850s, and in 1894 the university as a whole adopted the color (replacing green). Old crew photographs at Yale's Gales Ferry headquarters for the Harvard-Yale race show oarsmen wearing blue-and-white-striped blazers over their varsity sweaters, but the modern Yale rowing blazer is more understated.

The annual race between the Harvard and Yale men's heavyweight crews is the stuff of legend, and Yale has produced fabled men's crews over the years, the best of which, perhaps, was the 1956 Yale varsity eight, which won gold representing the United States at the Olympics.

But in recent decades, the women's squad has been the flagship of Yale rowing. When Title IX was passed into law in 1972, women's rowing in the United States was changed forever.

ABOVE: The 2011 Yale women's varsity crew. **OPPOSITE:** Taylor Ritzel won gold in the U.S. women's eight at the 2012 Olympics.

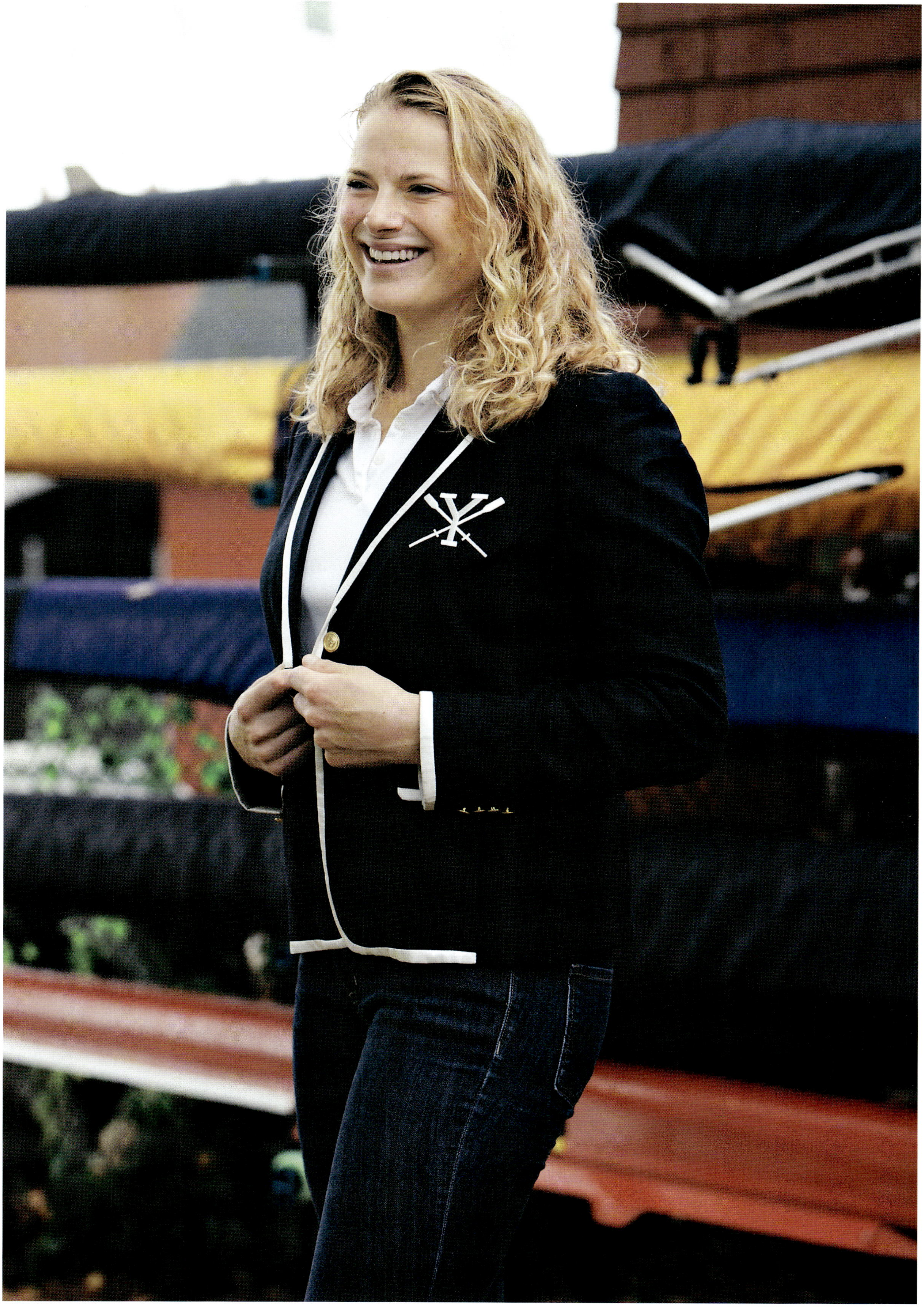

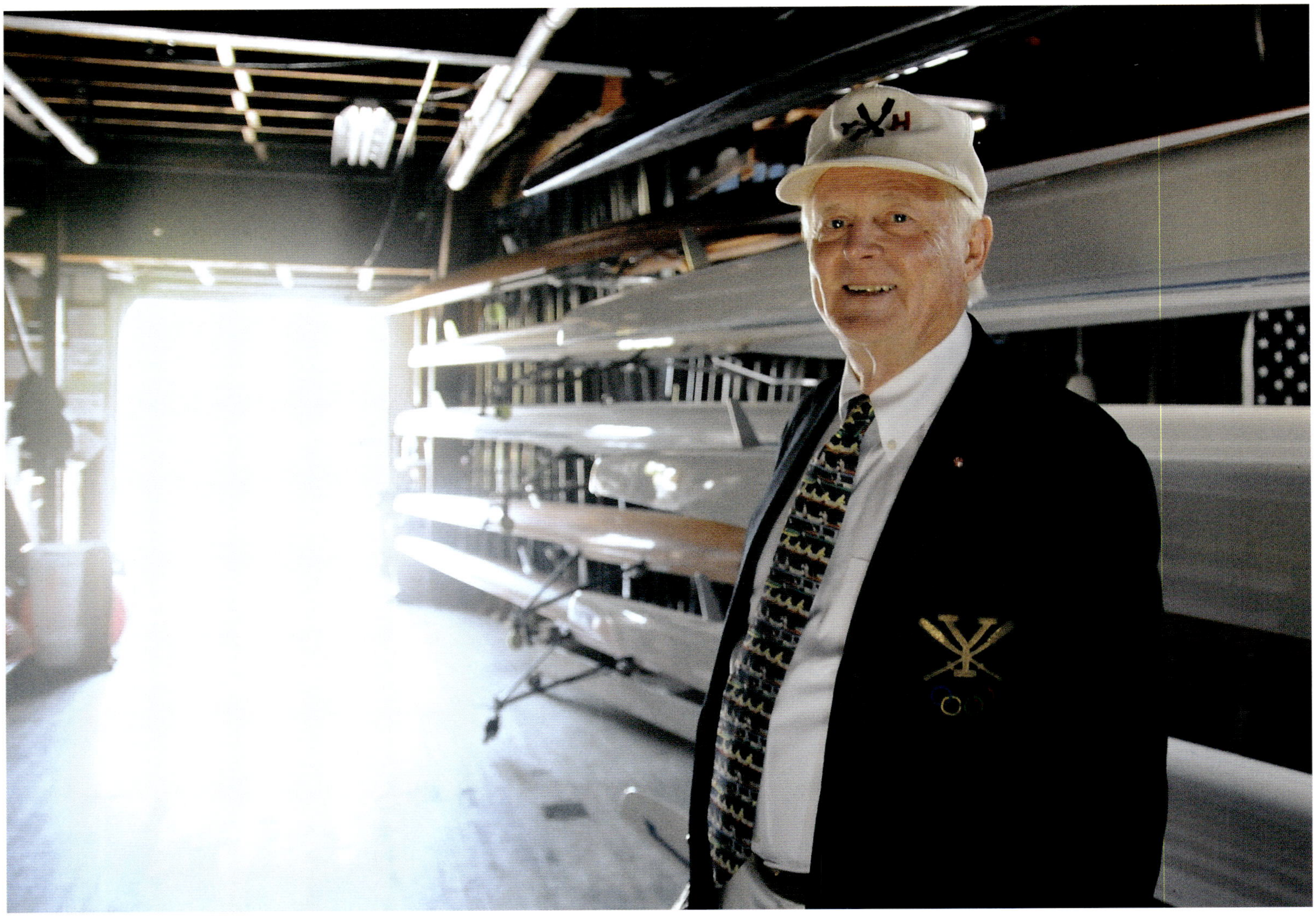

ABOVE: Bill Becklean, a member of the 1956 Olympic champion Yale varsity eight, wears the crew's special blazer badge: the varsity "Y" with crossed blades and Olympic rings. His hat is a Harvard-Yale Race umpire's cap.

Yet the new law, which guaranteed equality for women in university sports, was not always followed rigorously in the early years of its existence.

This was surely the case at Yale. In 1976, the rather unsuccessful men's squad (the Yale men had not won a Harvard-Yale Race in fourteen years) had use of cutting-edge equipment, locker rooms, and hot showers. Meanwhile, the members of the better-performing women's team—which included two of the "Red Rose Crew," the U.S. women's eight that placed silver at the 1975 world championships—were still treated as second-class citizens. Their boats were damaged and outdated; the male rowers hurled abuse at them in the weight room; and worst of all, while the men took hot showers in the boathouse every day after practice, the women had to wait, wet and freezing, on the squads' shared school bus back to campus. One of the rowers, 1976 Olympian Anne Warner, even caught pneumonia that February.

The women had had enough: on March 3, nineteen members of the Yale women's squad marched into the office of the women's athletics director, accompanied by a reporter from the *New York Times*. In unison, the oarswomen stripped off their Yale tracksuits to reveal their naked bodies, each painted with the words *TITLE IX*, while one of the rowers, Christine Ernst, read a statement:

> *These are the bodies Yale is exploiting. . . . We are not just healthy young things in blue and white uniforms who perform feats of strength for Yale in the nice spring weather; we are not just statistics on your win column. We're human and being treated as less than such.*

The story was national news by the following day. Within a week, temporary hot showers had been installed for the women, and within a year a women's locker room was built. Many of the women who participated in the protest were still at Yale in 1979 and helped the women's crew win the national championship that year.

They laid the foundations for future generations of Yale oarswomen to continue the program's winning ways. One of their successors, Taylor Ritzel (Yale '10), won three NCAA national championships and a Women's Henley title with Yale before winning gold in the U.S. women's eight at the 2012 Olympics.

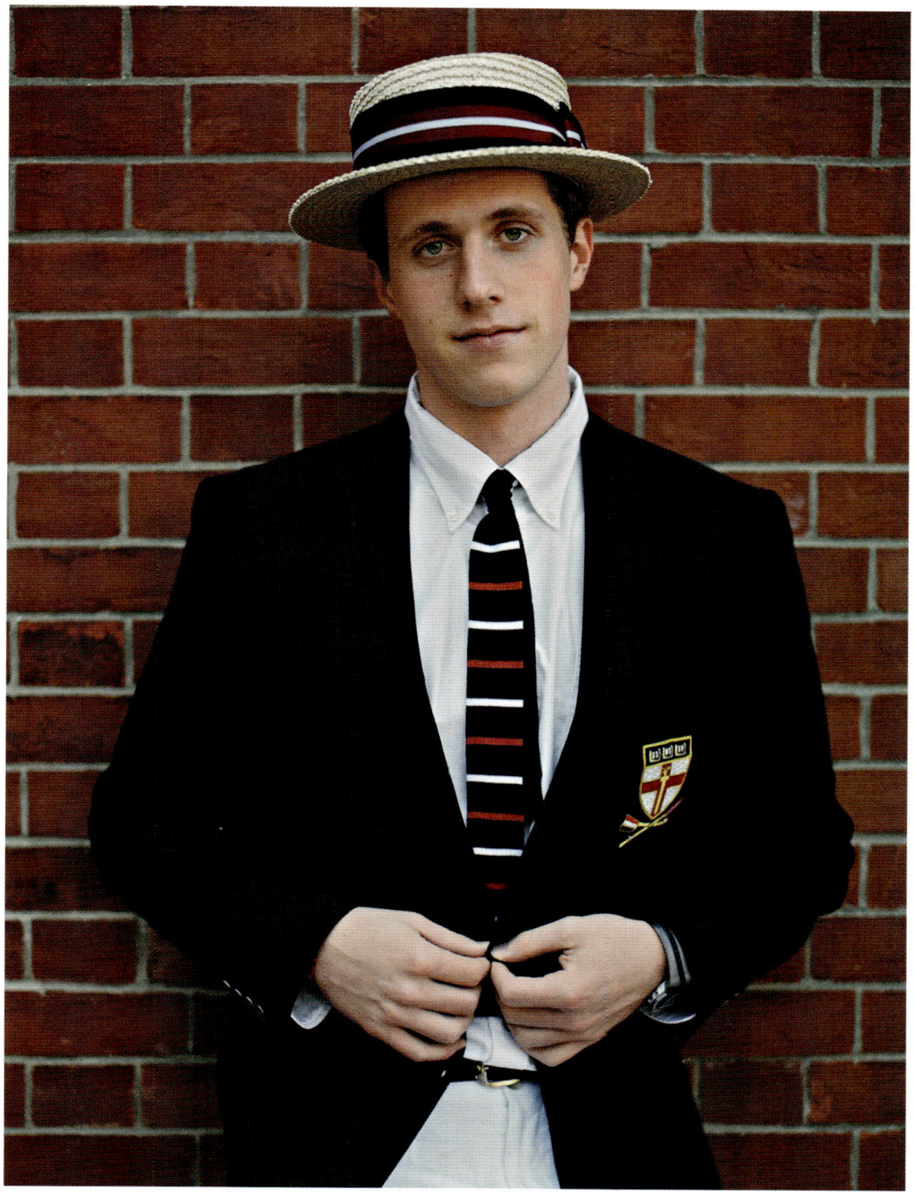

Groton, Massachusetts

Groton School

RAY DUNN

The Reverend Endicott Peabody, founder and first head of Groton School, had been a keen rower at Cheltenham College and Trinity College, Cambridge, in England; he believed that the sport was useful for instilling discipline and good moral character. So it was natural for rowing to flourish at Groton, with the support—and sometimes even the participation—of the first headmaster.

The Groton rowing jacket is straightforward and American: a navy blazer with a badge. More interesting, perhaps, is the Groton straw boater—a quintessentially English artifact worn by every Groton student at graduation—and the varsity rowing tie. In the mid-twentieth century, it was popular for students at Groton—as at many New England universities and boarding schools—to sport knit varsity ties with horizontal stripes. These ties were usually in their institution's colors, though the exact pattern of their stripes varied by sport. As the jacket-and-tie dress code disappeared at many schools and colleges, so, too, did the knit varsity tie and its subtle symbolism. In 2012, however, the Groton rowing tie was revived: Edoardo Savarelle, a Groton student from Milan, decided he liked the look of the old ties still worn by alumni and coaches, and he just happened to know a little workshop in Italy that could make them. Tabor, Choate, Brunswick, and other New England rowing schools soon followed suit, and the knit varsity tie—at least among rowers—is making its comeback in earnest.

Johannesburg, South Africa

University of Johannesburg Rowing Club

ATHENKOSI HLEKANI

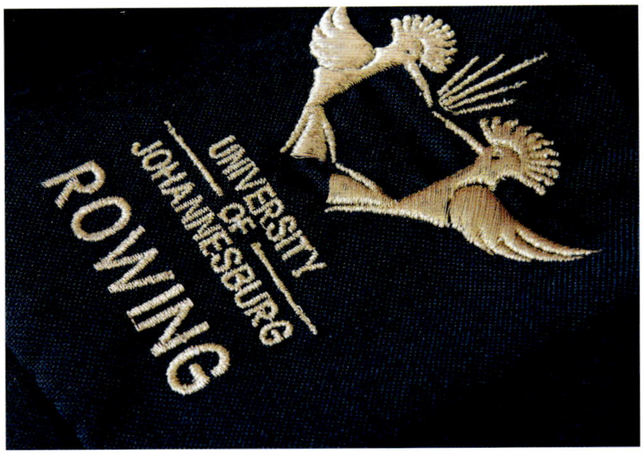

As a teenager, Athi Hlekani was offered the chance to take a swimming and rowing course through the Nemato Change a Life organization.

In his first season of competitive rowing, he did not win a single race. In his second year, however, he became one of Nemato Rowing Club's top oarsmen and accumulated an impressive record of victories. His talent earned him a sport and academic bursary at the University of Johannesburg, where he was elected captain of the rowing club. Athi has served as a youth leader in the United Nations Sport Development and Peace initiative, and is currently coaching junior rowing in South Africa.

The U.J. rowing blazer badge features African hoopoes.

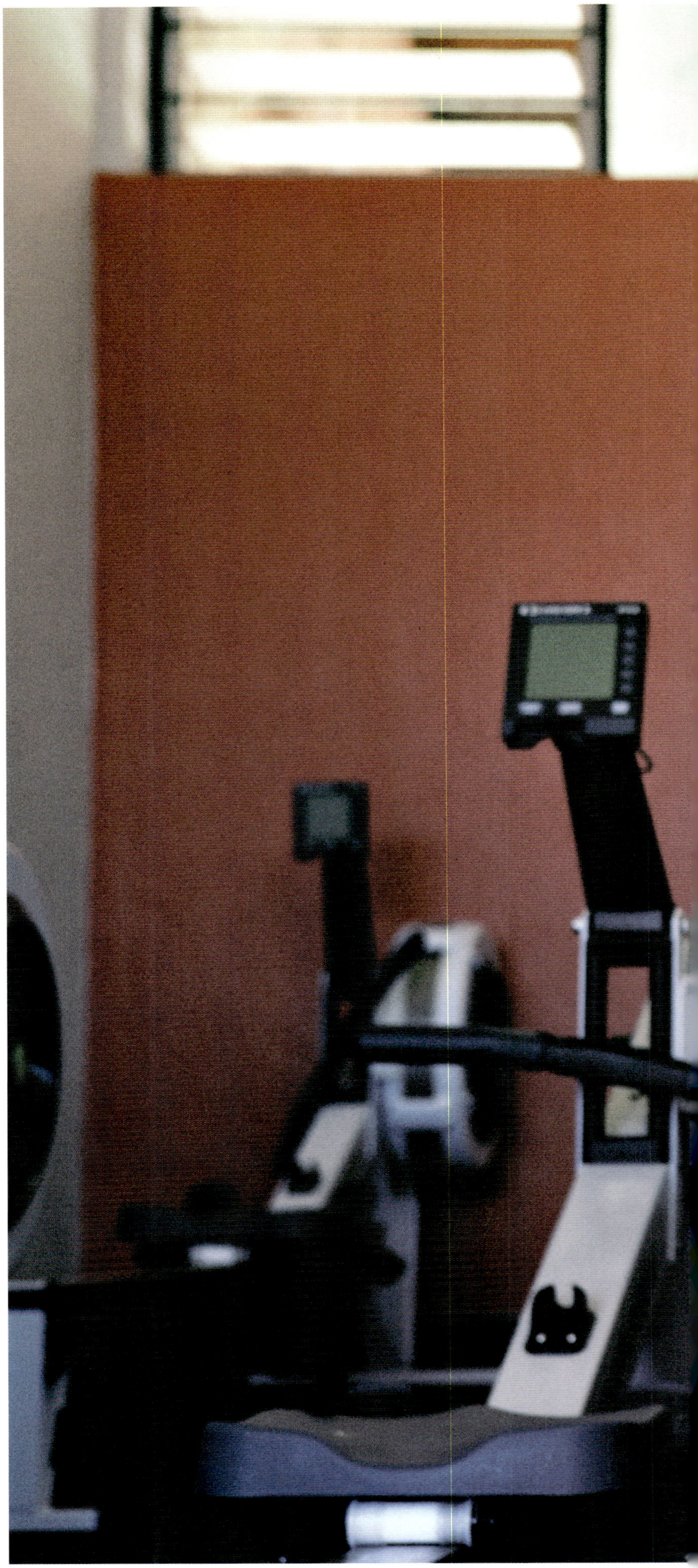

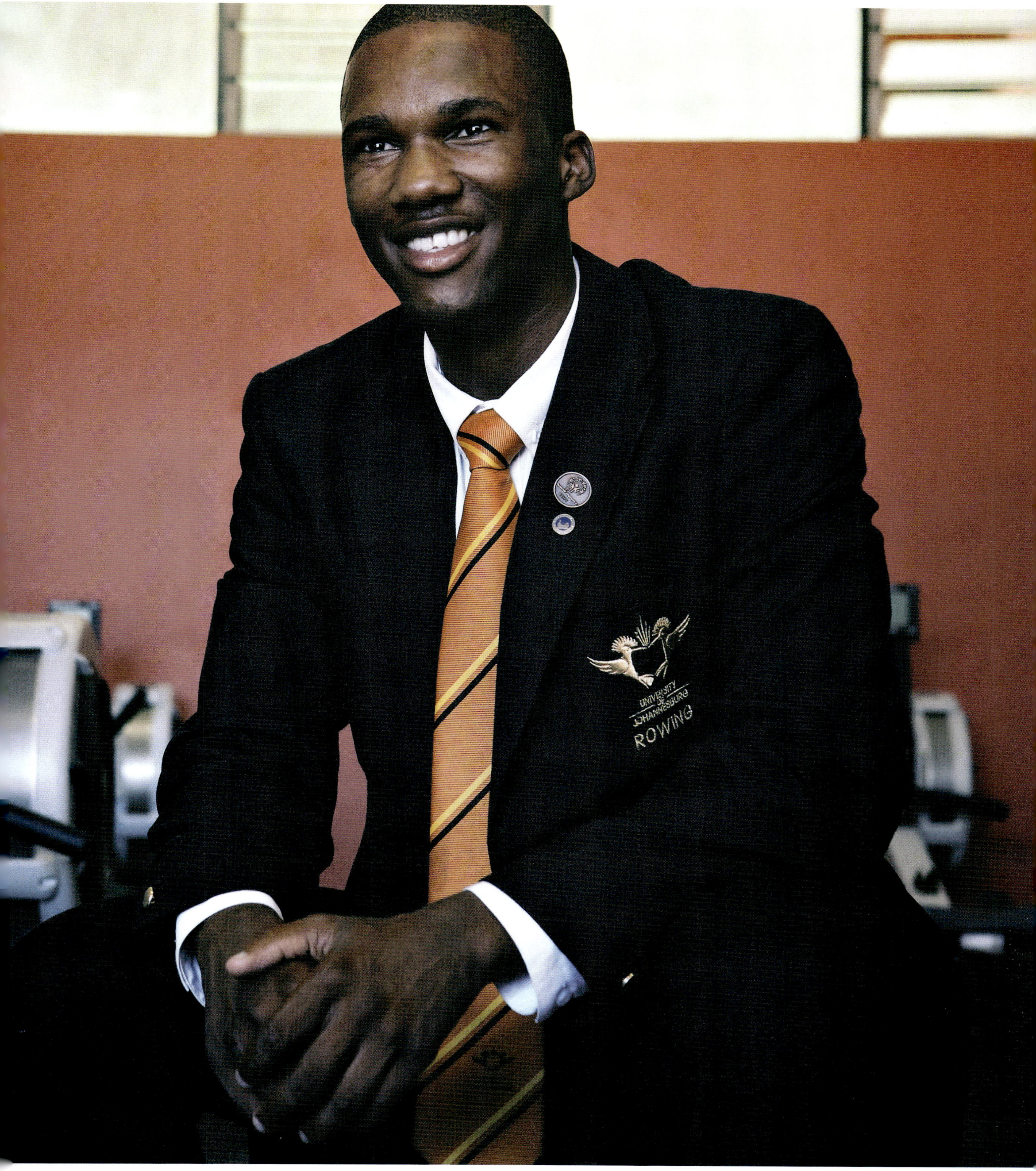
UNIVERSITY OF JOHANNESBURG
ROWING

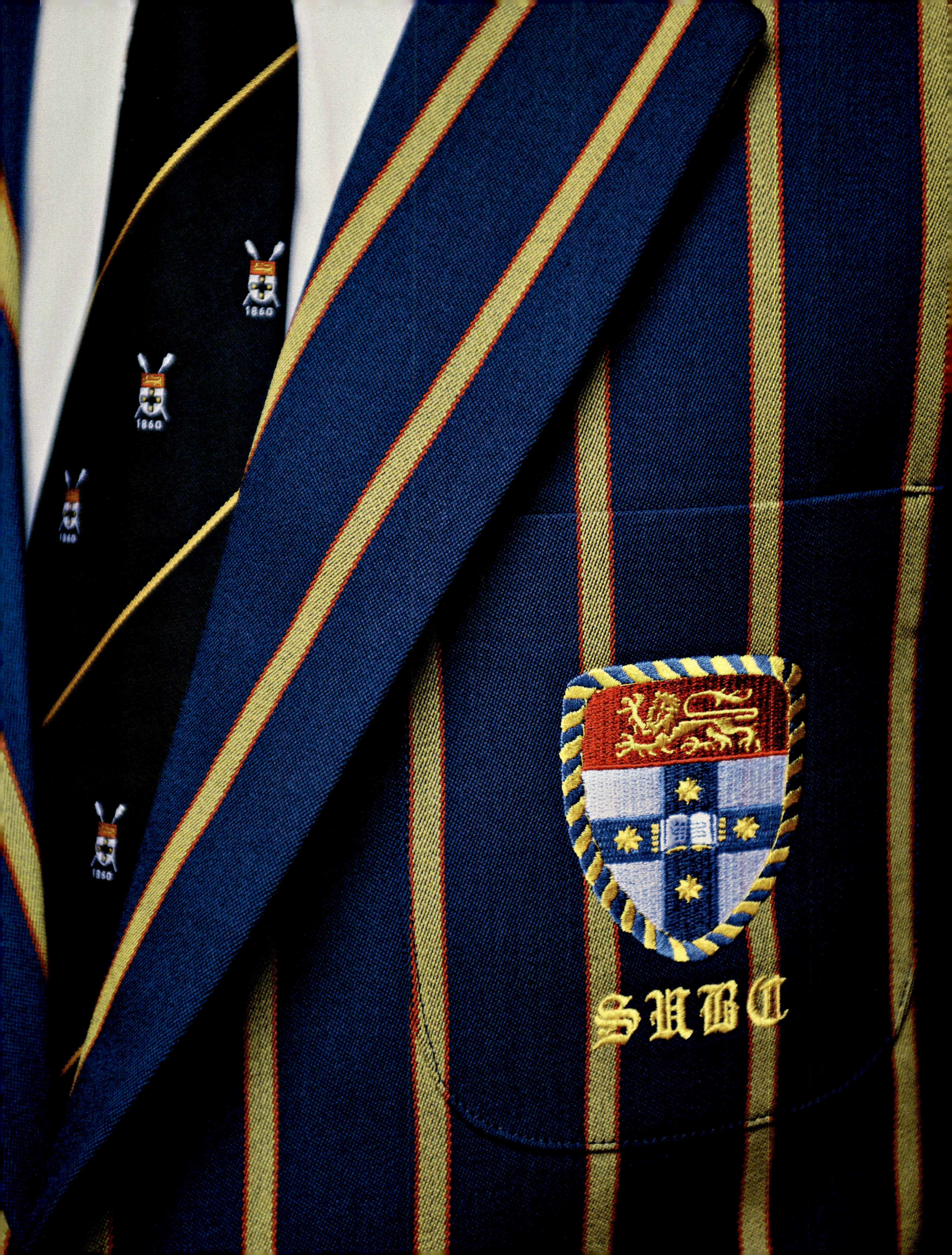
1860
SUBC

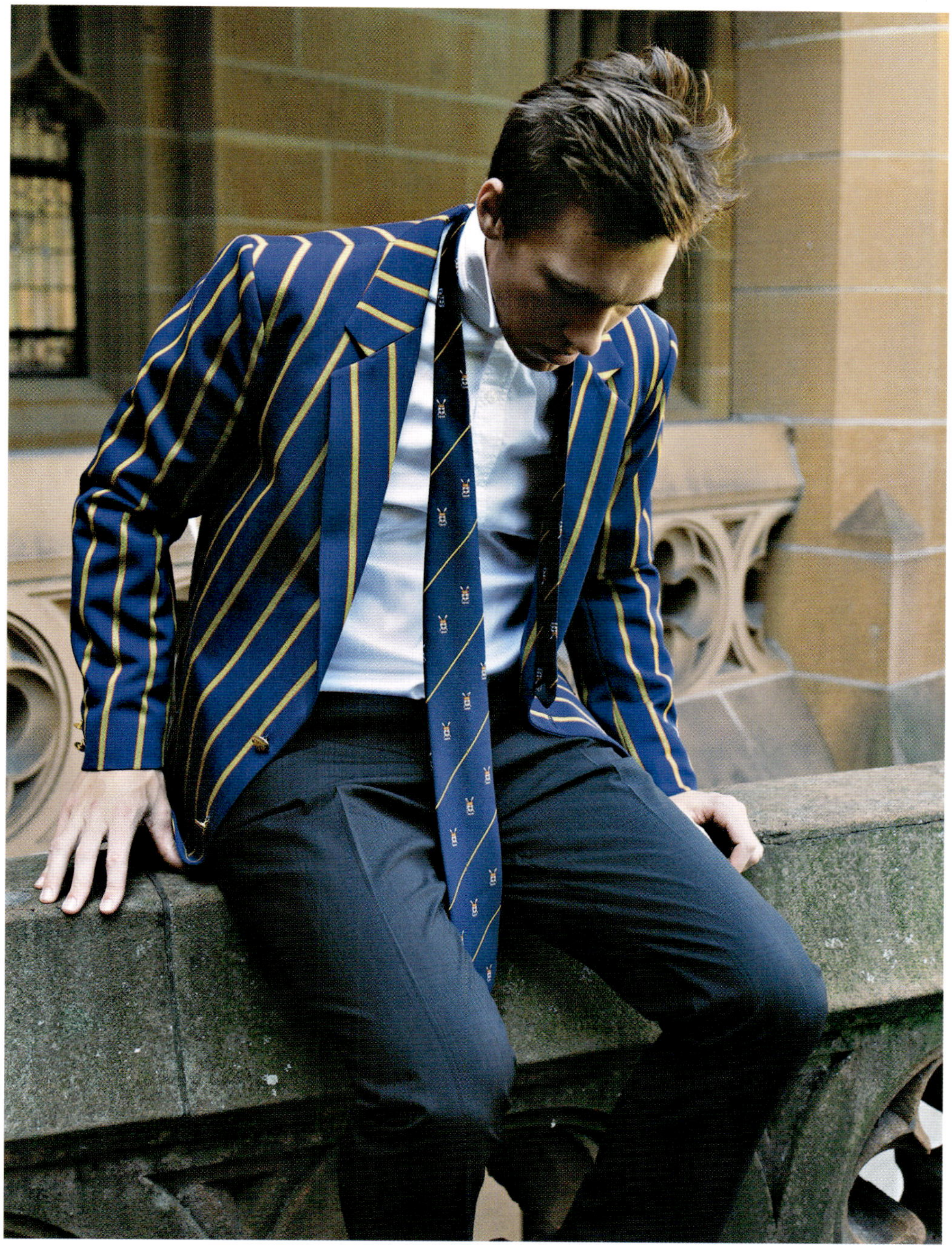

Sydney, Australia

Sydney University Boat Club

JAMES GOSWELL

The University of Sydney takes after Oxford and Cambridge, awarding "Blues" to all varsity athletes. At the annual Blues ceremony, the chancellor of the university presents each new Blue with the gold-and-blue-striped Blues blazer (known as the university "Honour Coat").

Established in 1860, S.U.B.C. first raced their rival, Melbourne University, that year. James Goswell raced in the 2011 Australian Boat Race (Sydney vs. Melbourne), earning his Blue and defeating Melbourne as well.

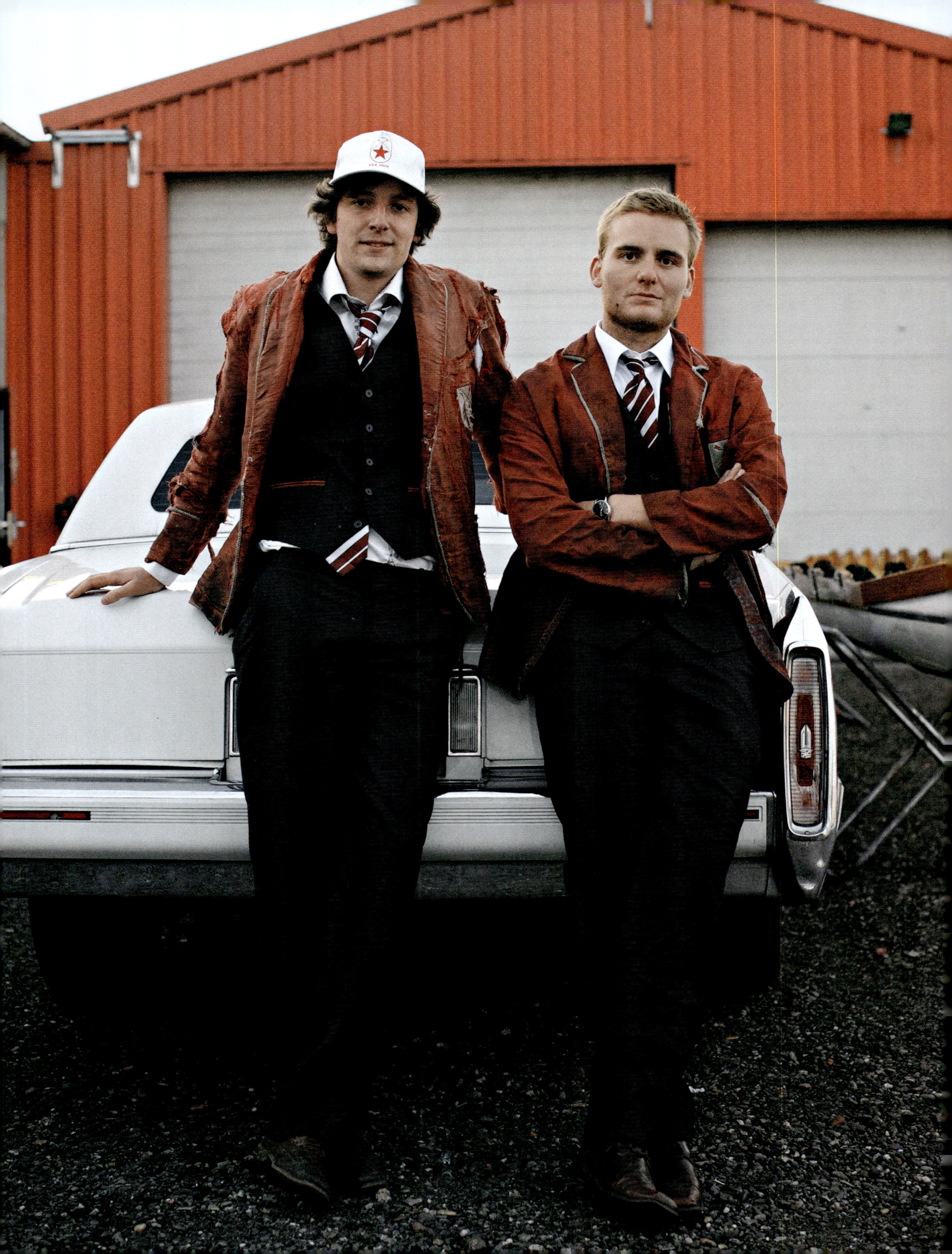

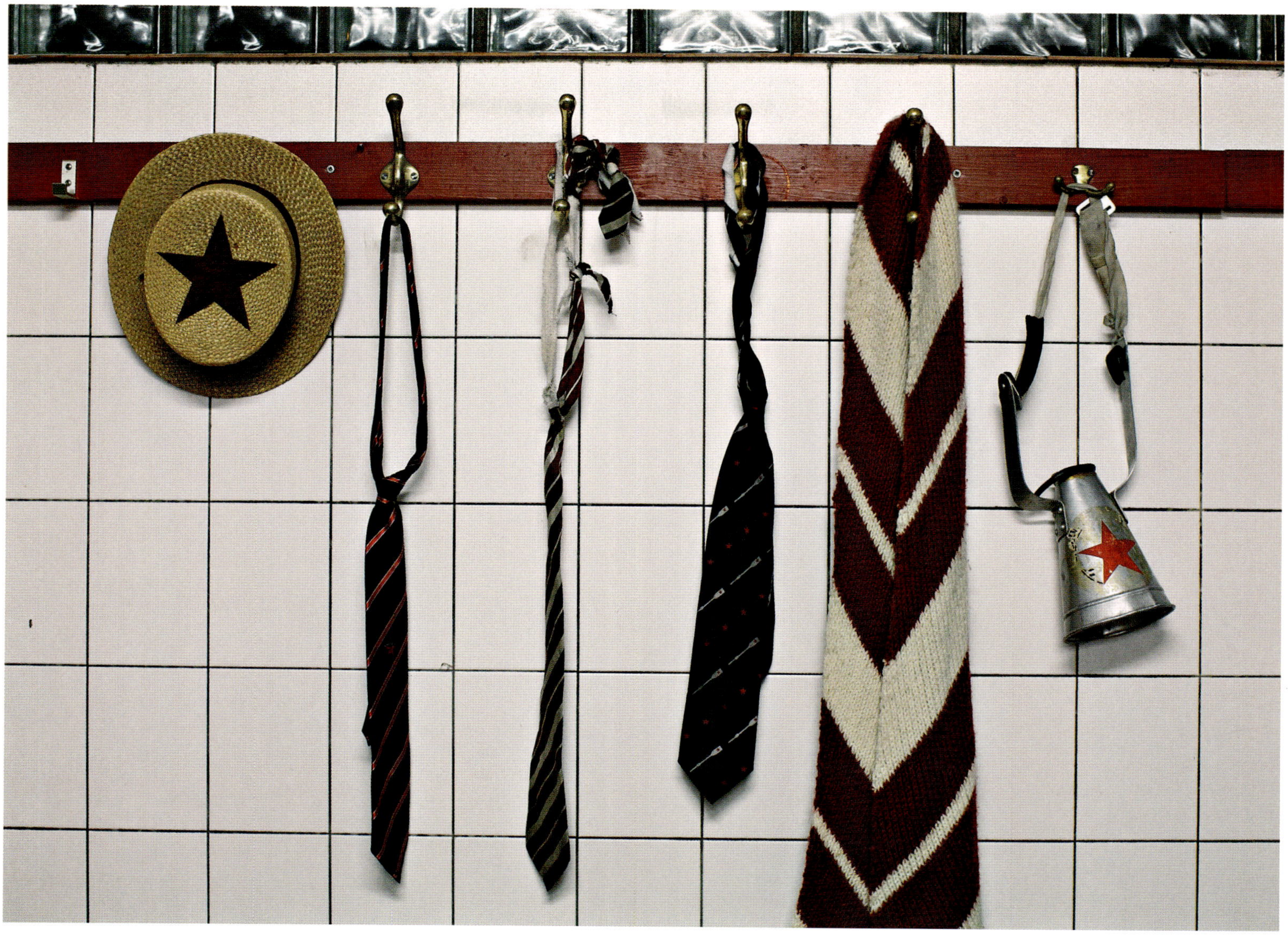

Groningen, Netherlands

G.S.R. "Aegir"

★ JOREN ZWAAN, BOB CASTELEIN ★

Groninger Studenten Roeivereniging "Aegir" is, like many rowing clubs in the Netherlands, named for a Norse deity: in this case, the rowdy, ale-brewing King of the Sea. And, as at other Dutch rowing fraternities, the racing members at Aegir wear tattered hand-me-down blazers. Unusually, however, the club's traditions largely revolve not around the blazer but around neckties and other accoutrements.

Traditionally, blazer-clad and beer-fueled "fighting" follows the major student rowing races in the Netherlands. In these vaguely organized scuffles, rowers usually grab one another by the blazer lapels and attempt to wrestle their opponents to the ground. But at Aegir, the tradition is to fight by grasping ties instead of lapels. For this reason, Aegir rowers tie their ties in tight and permanent knots. All members may wear a black tie adorned with club blades, but only racing members may wear the striped racing tie. Heavyweight oarsmen tie their tie so that a broad stripe appears on the knot, while lightweights display a narrow stripe; either way, the tie is always tied so that six broad stripes show below the knot to commemorate Aegir's six victories to date in the Varsity race.

ABOVE: In the Aegir locker room, there are five hooks reserved for the top four rowers and top coxswain in the club. Here on these hooks hang, from left to right: the *Lustrum* tie; the racing tie; the general membership tie; the club scarf (knitted by female rowers for the male rowers before the annual gala); and a coxing megaphone. Hanging to the left is a hat of the type usually worn by Aegir rowers at the Varsity.

OPPOSITE: Like most Dutch student rowing clubs, Aegir owns a rattletrap white stretch limousine for the use of club officers.

OVERLEAF: The club is known for its legendary and frequent bonfire parties.

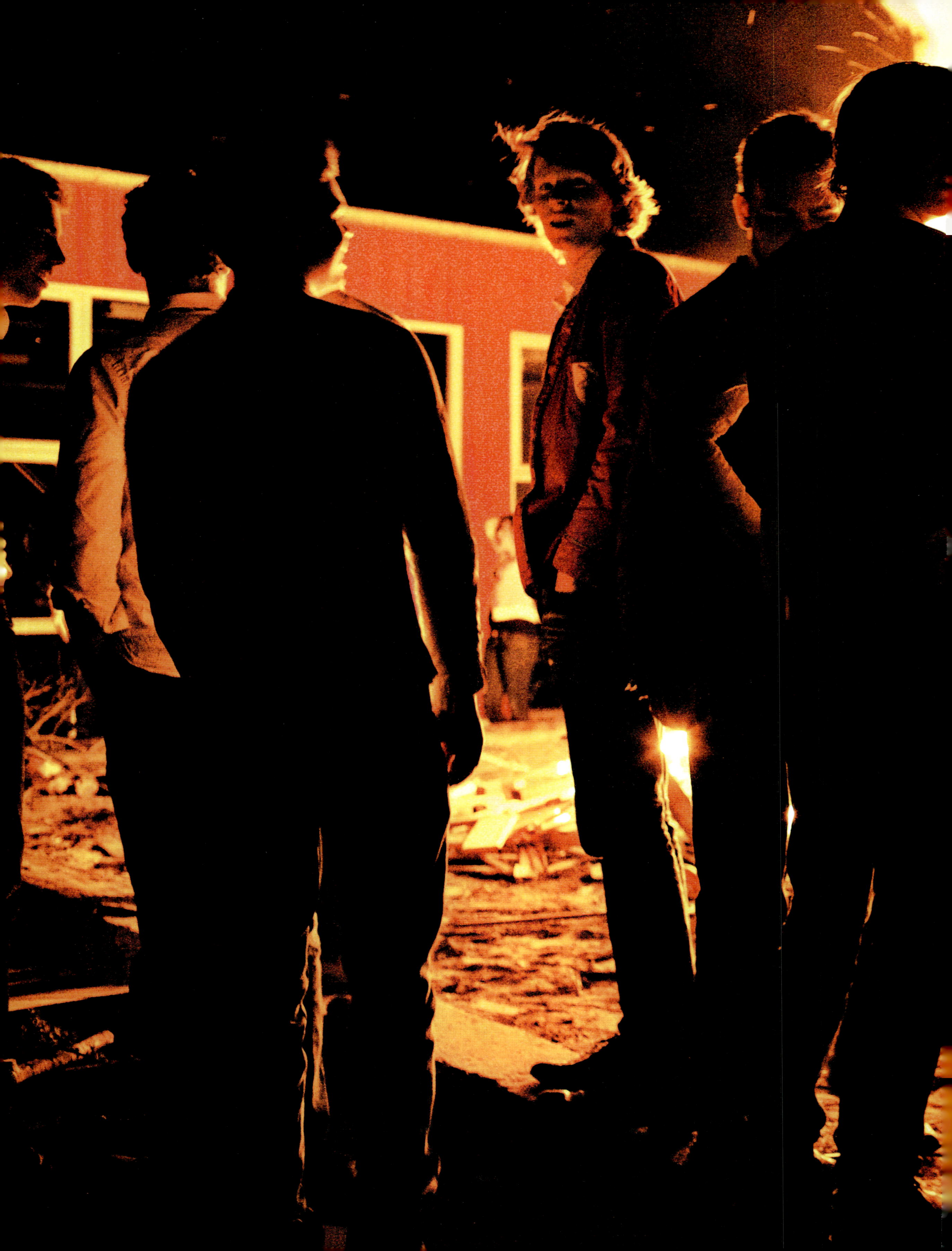

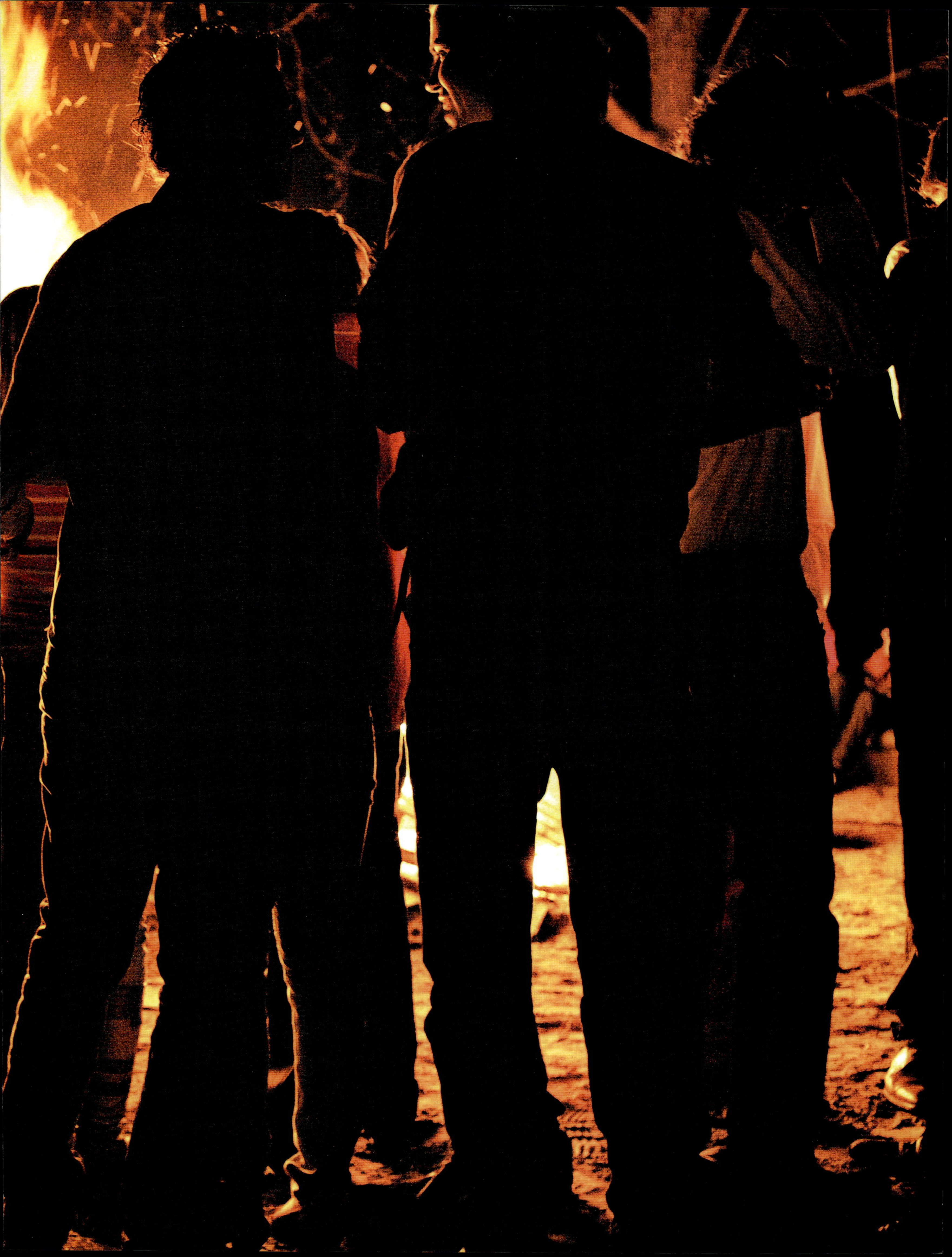

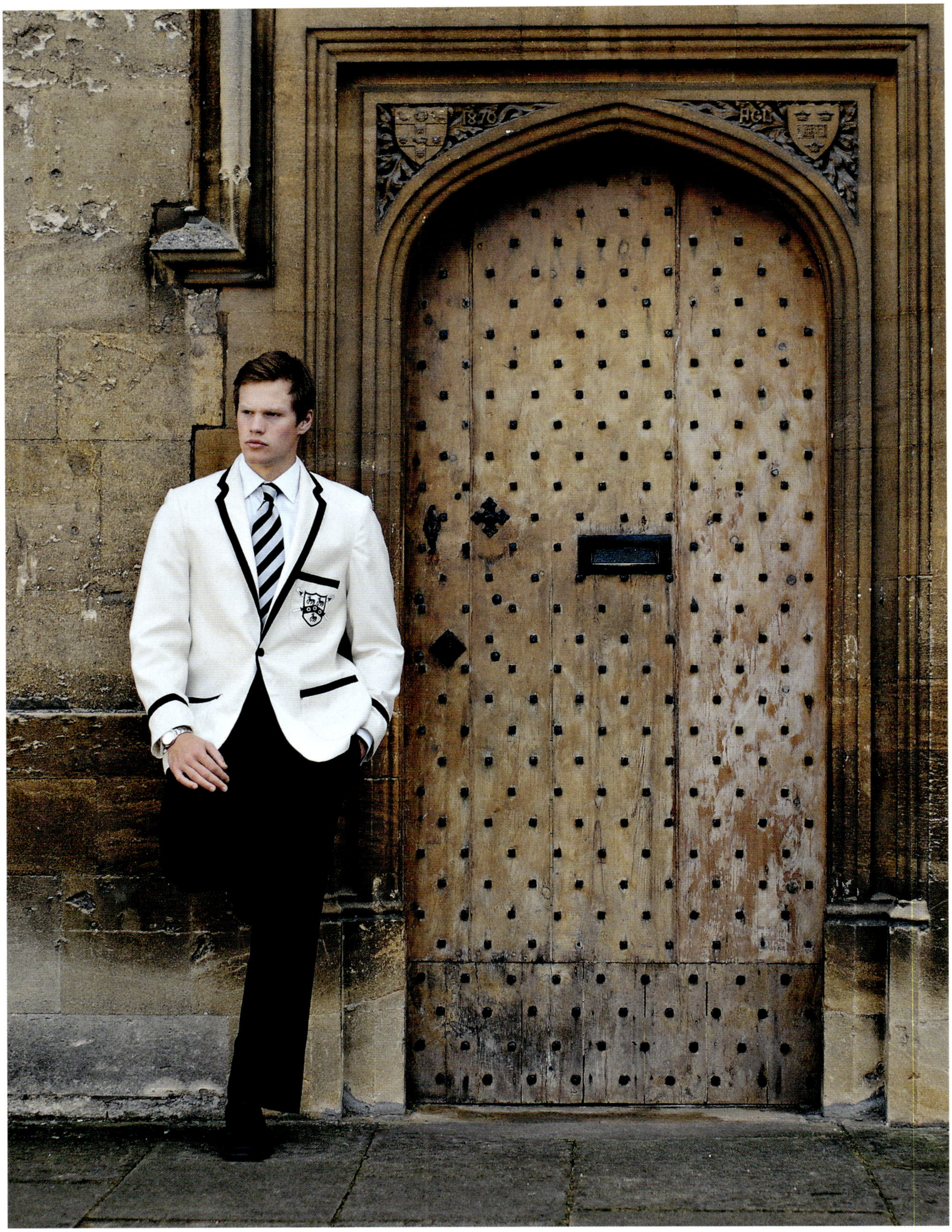

London, England

St. Paul's School, Hammersmith

GEORDIE MACLEOD

Philadelphia, Pennsylvania

Undine Barge Club

KATIE BROWN

Few American rowing clubs outside of school and university teams have rowing blazers associated with them, and fewer still have striped blazers (whereas they are commonplace in British and Australian rowing). In fact, Undine Barge Club, a quintessentially American institution, may be the only one.

The club is named for the German legend of Undine, a mythical water spirit; and Castle Ringstetten, as U.B.C.'s social clubhouse is known, takes its name from the castle in the fairy tale. Undine's boathouse is located on Philadelphia's historic Boathouse Row, the "mecca of American rowing," where the Schuylkill Navy—the association of Philadelphia's traditional rowing clubs and the oldest governing body for amateur sport in the United States—has counted Undine among its members since 1858.

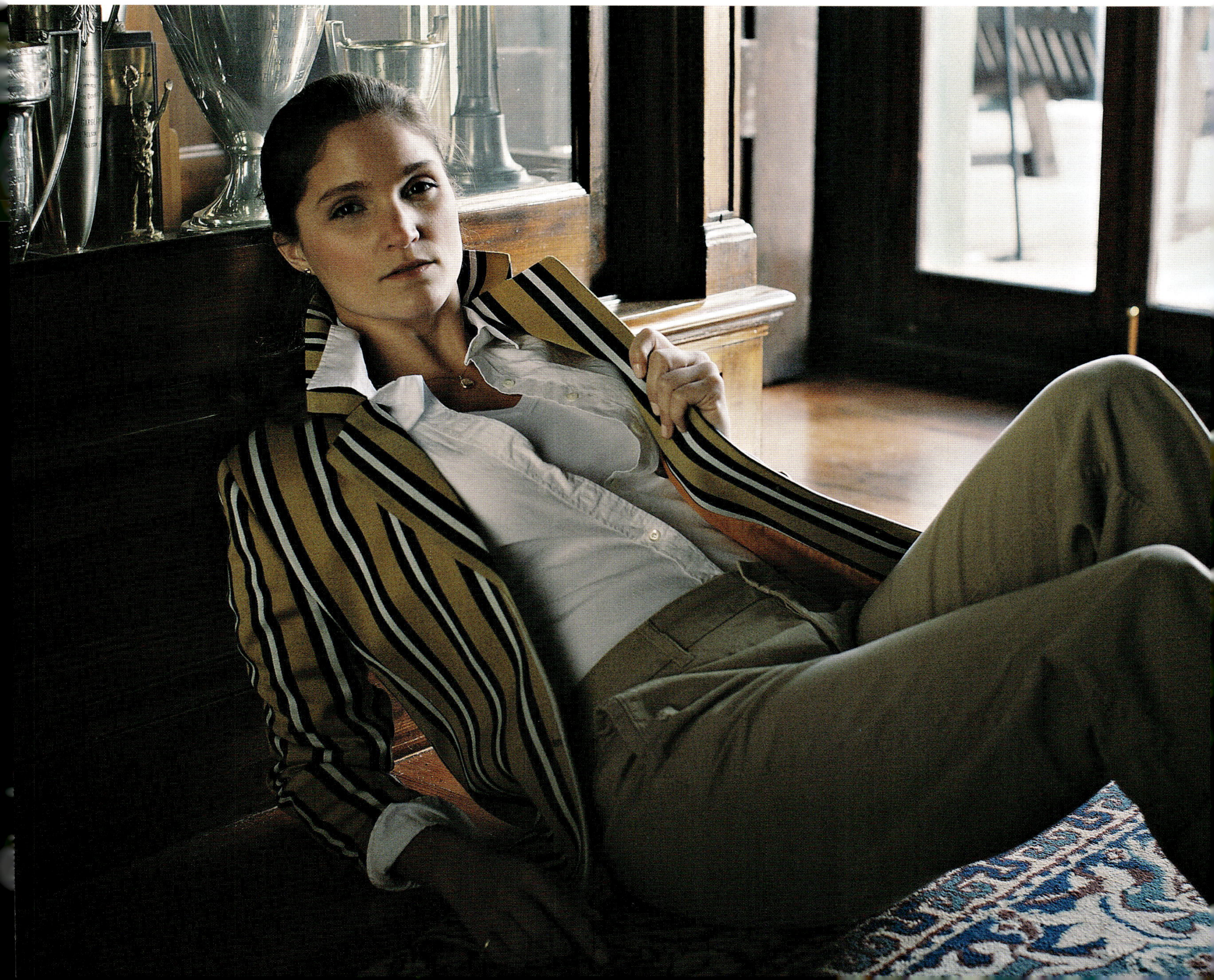

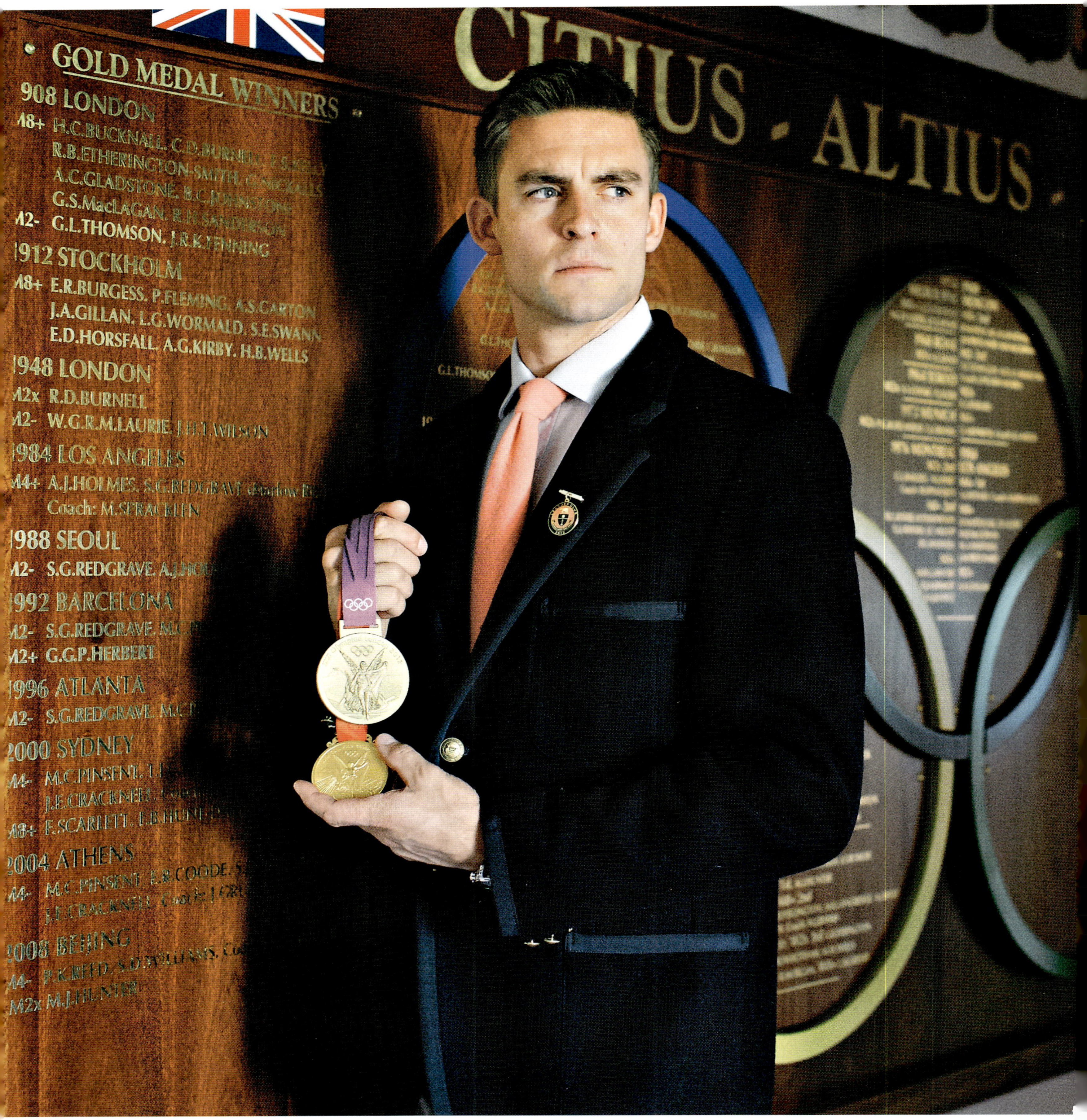

Lt. Pete Reed, shown here in his flannel Leander tie and Oxford blazer,
is a two-time Olympic gold medalist in the British men's four.

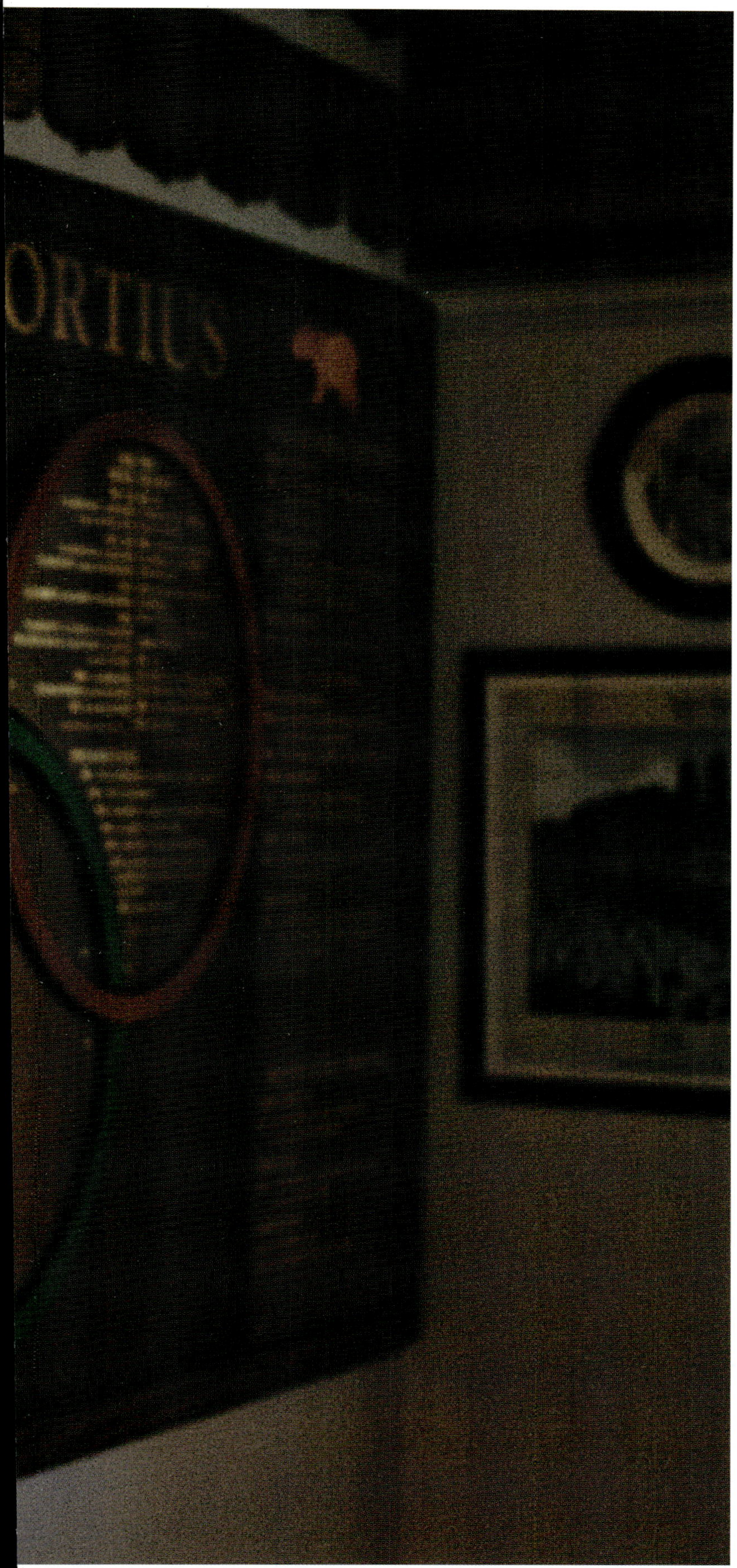

Henley-on-Thames, England

Leander Club

LT. PETE REED MBE RN

"Underneath a light straw boater, / In his pink Leander tie, / Ev'ry ripple of the water caught the Captain in the eye."

—John Betjeman, "Henley Regatta 1902"

Leander is probably the most well-known rowing club in the world. It is famous for being the home club of most of the British rowing team; for its grand clubhouse in Henley-on-Thames and close association with the Henley Royal Regatta; and for its club color—bright pink, officially called "cerise."

Leander is unusual in that it has no club blazer; members generally wear either a plain double-breasted blazer or the blazer of their original rowing club. This idiosyncrasy is the result of the club's peculiar membership qualification: to be elected a member of Leander, one must already have demonstrated a high level of rowing proficiency (usually at Oxford or Cambridge in the early years). Every Leander oarsmen would, therefore, already have a rowing blazer from his or her original club.

Members are identified instead by gilt club buttons (with two Old English letters "L.C."), pink ties (usually made of flannel), pink socks, and a range of other paraphernalia in solid pink, including scarves, pashminas, caps, sweaters, hatbands, and now even trousers. Leander is also special among British sporting clubs in that its tie is not striped but a solid color.

The first mention of Leander's distinctive color as "light crimson" was in 1840, although it is unknown when the current bright pink shade and the name "cerise" became official. But for those who are befuddled by the seemingly incongruous choice of color for one of Victorian England's top gentlemen's sporting clubs, it is worth remembering that pink was actually associated with manliness through the early twentieth century. In 1918, *Earnshaw's Infants' Department* magazine even stated: "The generally accepted rule is pink for the boys, and blue for the girls. The reason is that pink, being a more decided and stronger color, is more suitable for the boy."

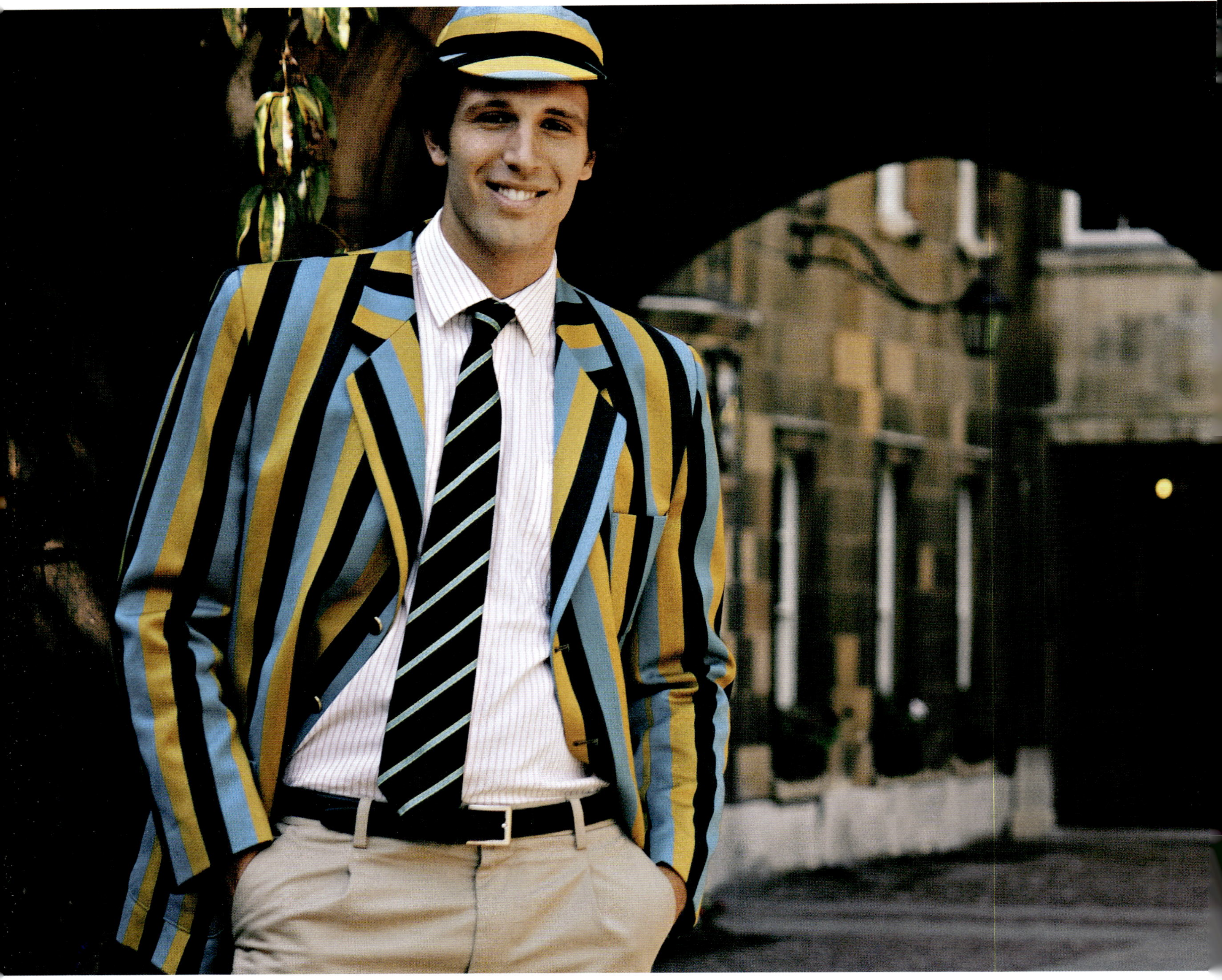

Cambridge, England

Goldie Boat Club, Cambridge

ALEX ROSS

Goldie is the reserve boat, or second crew, for Cambridge University Boat Club. Each year on Boat Race day, Goldie races Isis, the Oxford reserve crew, half an hour before the top Cambridge and Oxford boats compete. While the Cambridge Blue Boat oarsmen wear solid Cambridge Blue blazers, each member of Goldie receives a much louder blazer, striped in gold, Cambridge Blue, and British racing green.

Goldie is named for John Goldie, stroke of the Cambridge Blue Boat in 1869, 1870, 1871, and 1872 (long before the reserves race existed). The 1870 Cambridge victory ended a nine-year Oxford winning streak. Goldie Boathouse, as the Cambridge University boathouse is called, and the Goldie blazer's gold stripes also honor John Goldie.

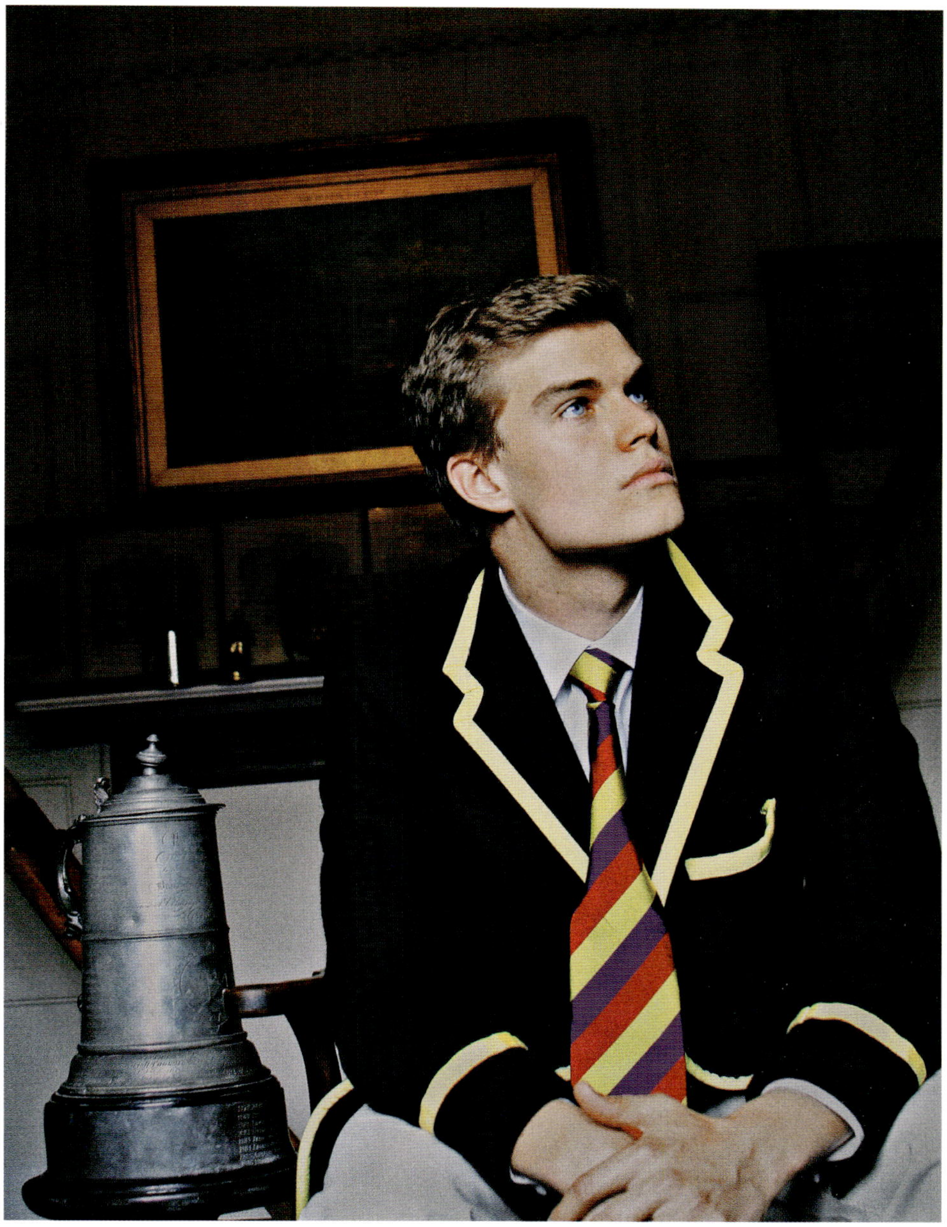

Oxford, England

Brasenose College Boat Club, Oxford

TOM GUNTER

"Yes, Childe of Ale, well named, you too can tell / The virtues of that beer you love so well;
While with nice skill, and mixture true, you float, / Beer for the crew, the water for the boat . . ."

—Brasenose College Ale Verses, 1841

In 1815, an eight-oared crew from Brasenose College, Oxford, raced against an eight-oared crew from Jesus College, Oxford, and won. This event has (rather arbitrarily, perhaps) entered the history books as the first modern race between rowing crews, and Brasenose is generally recognized as Oxford's first "Head of the River."

The club's colors are black and gold, but members of the first eight wear ties in "Childe of Hale" colors: red, yellow, and purple. It was in a costume of these colors that John Middleton, a nine-foot-tall seventeenth-century giant nicknamed "the Childe of Hale" defeated the king's champion wrestler before coming to Brasenose as the manservant of Sir Gilbert Ireland, a student at the college. A portrait of the Childe in his colorful outfit and an impression of his enormous hand hang in the college chapel and serve as inspiration to rowers in the college first boat, which is always named in his honor.

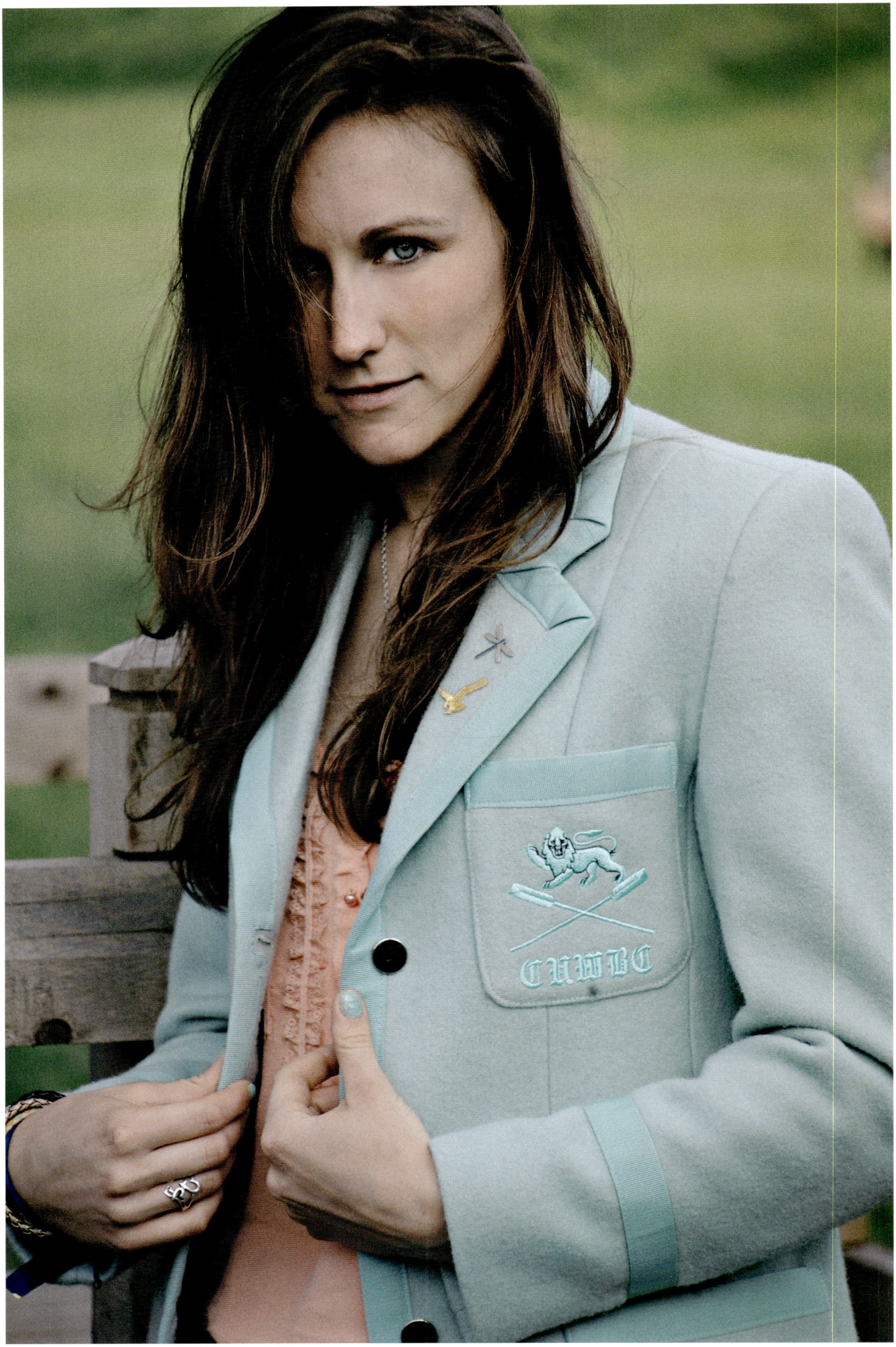
CUWBC

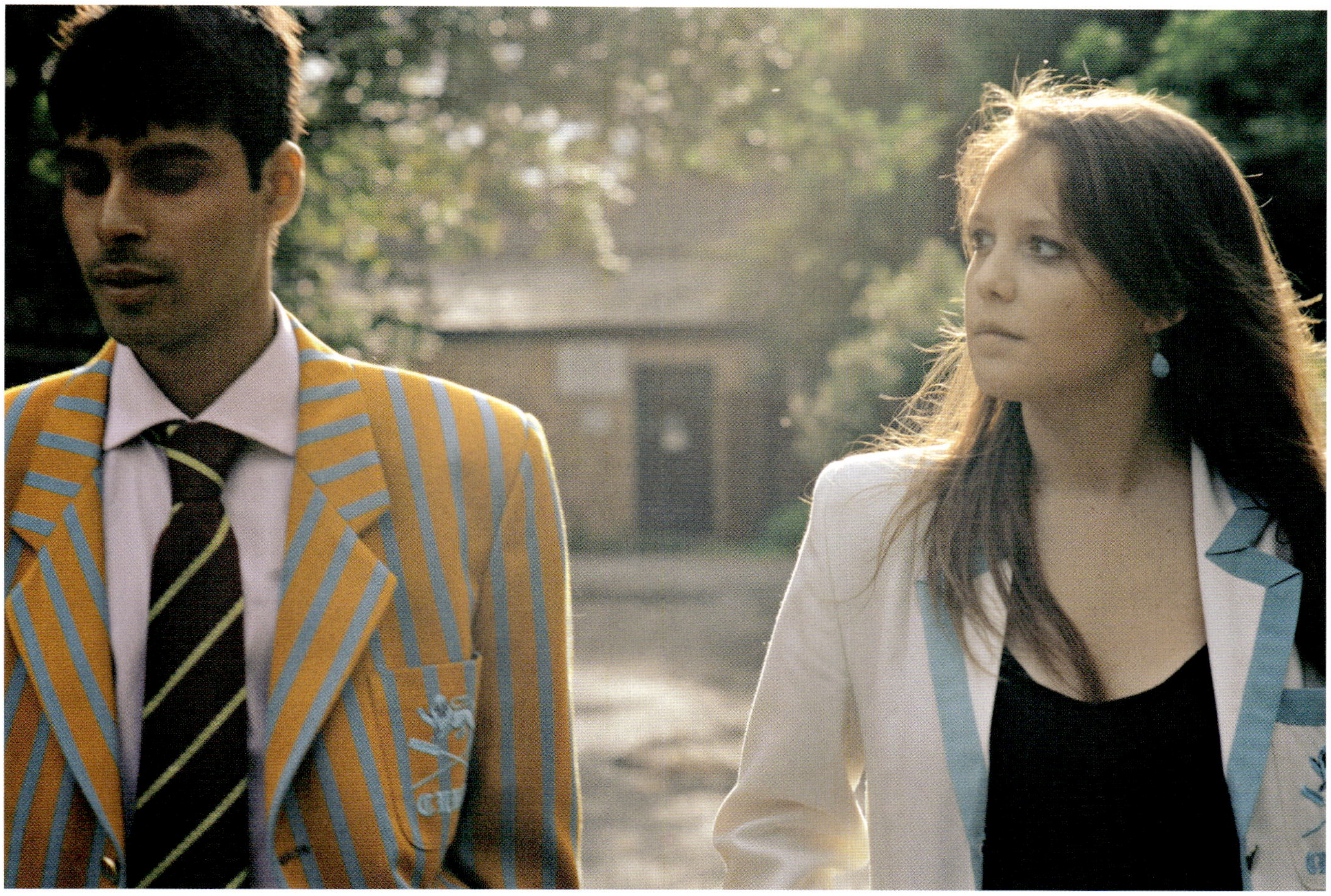

Cambridge, England

Cambridge University Women's Boat Club and Blondie

CAROLINE REID, ARAV GUPTA, BRIELLE STARK

"I personally do not approve of women rowing at all. It is a ghastly sight, an anatomical impossibility and physiologically dangerous."

—Letter from the captain of Selwyn College Boat Club to C.U.W.B.C., 1960s

The all-women's Newnham College represented Cambridge University in the Oxford-Cambridge Women's Boat Race from 1927 to 1939. In 1940, women from Girton College joined the young ladies of Newnham, and Cambridge University Women's Boat Club was born.

For most of the twentieth century, Cambridge was almost entirely male, and the female rowers—nicknamed "Sweaty Betties" or "Perspiring Persephones"—were not always made to feel entirely welcome. Nevertheless, women's rowing has been a "Blues" sport, on par with men's rowing, at Cambridge since 1941, and rowers in the top women's crew wear the same Cambridge Blue blazers as their male equivalents.

The second boat, once the club grew large enough to have one, became known as "Blondie" to correspond to the Cambridge men's second boat ("Goldie"). The club has also fielded a crew for the Lightweight Women's Boat Race since the event was instituted in 1984.

The Blondie blazer, aptly, is in a blonde-and-Cambridge Blue stripe, while the lightweight blazer is white with Cambridge Blue trim. Each of the club's blazers features a lion—from the university coat of arms—on the breast pocket.

In 2013, Caroline Reid (opposite) rowed in the Cambridge women's Blue Boat; Arav Gupta (above left) coxed Blondie (just as women may cox the men's race, men may cox the Oxford and Cambridge women's races); and Brielle Stark (above right) coxed the lightweight women's Blue Boat.

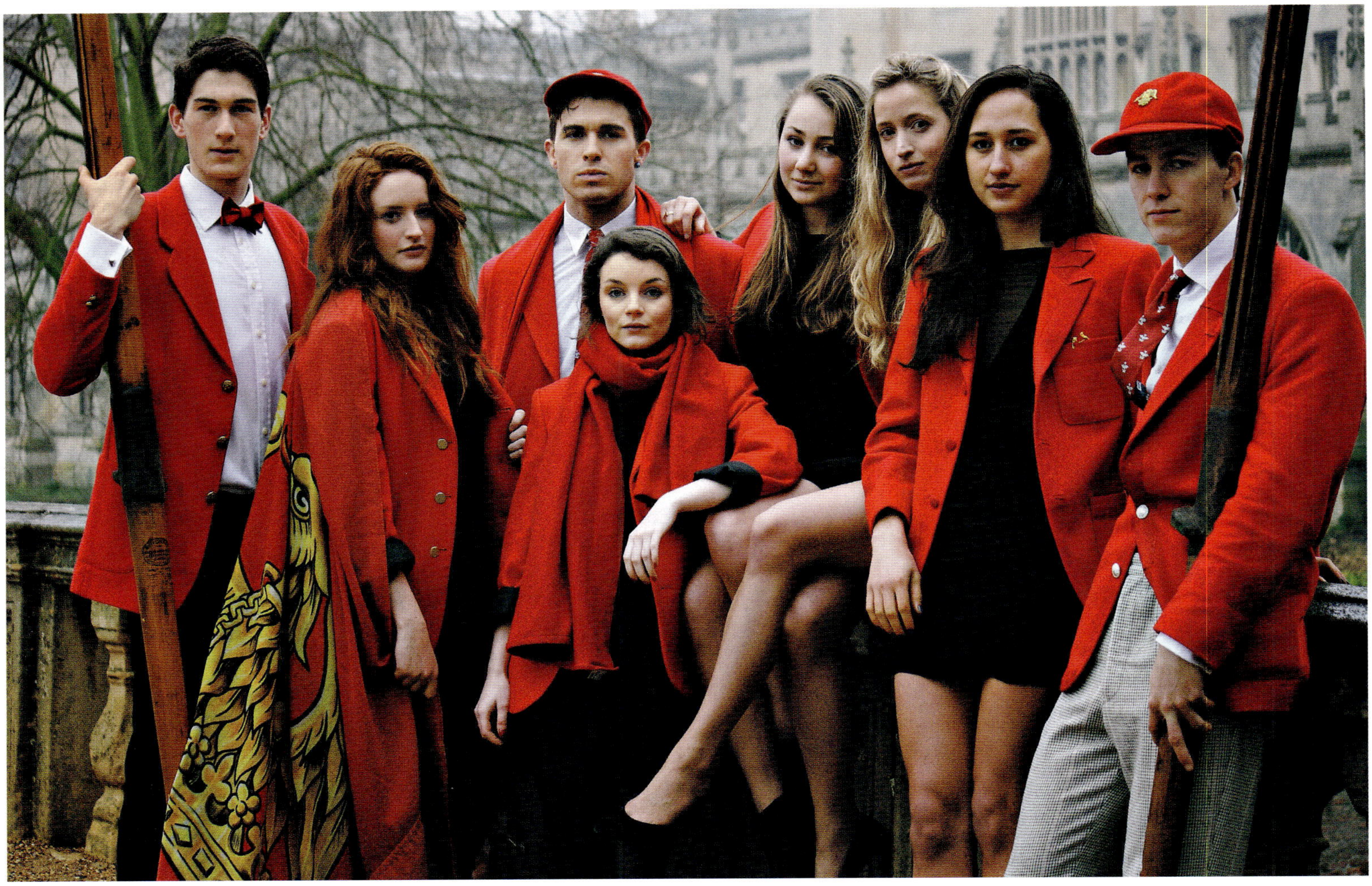

Cambridge, England

Lady Margaret Boat Club, Cambridge

TIM BORGAS, MIRANDA BOND, CARLOS SCHUSTER, VICTORIA GREEN,
ALEXANDRA BRIGHT, SOPHIE WEDLAKE, MARTINA LAGATIERRA-WELLINGTON, WILL HANDY

Just as in heraldry, which is rife with stories invented ex post facto to account for why a coat of arms features a particular tincture or charge, myths have a habit of developing around rowing blazers.

In the case of Lady Margaret Boat Club—the rowing club at St. John's College, Cambridge—the macabre, and rather absurd, story usually goes something like this: in one of the early Cambridge bumping races, the St. John's crew mounted a sword on the bow of their boat; when they bumped the crew ahead of them, the sword impaled the leading crew's coxswain. As a result, St. John's College Boat Club was banned from racing forevermore but resurfaced under the pseudonym "Lady Margaret Boat Club," whose scarlet jackets commemorate this bloody incident.

The story is pure fantasy. But what is true is that we owe the word *blazer* to Lady Margaret Boat Club. The very first "blazers" were the blazing red rowing coats of the L.M.B.C. The first known use of the word to refer to a jacket of any kind is a description of the Lady Margaret uniform in the *Cambridge University General Almanack and Register* for 1852.

By the following decade, the word had become more than a slang term and could be used without quotation marks, and by 1870, the boating jackets of other Cambridge colleges began to be called blazers as well. The expression traveled across to Oxford and up to Durham, where it was picked up by rowing clubs on the Isis and the River Wear. By the end of the twentieth century, a blazer was any colorful jacket at all—for rowing, cricket, rugby, or tennis. Today, the term may refer to a navy blue reefer, a school uniform coat, or a stripey regatta jacket, and the blazer is a staple of every gentleman's wardrobe (and many ladies' too). But the original "blazers" will always be the bright red flannel jackets still worn by Lady Margaret rowers.

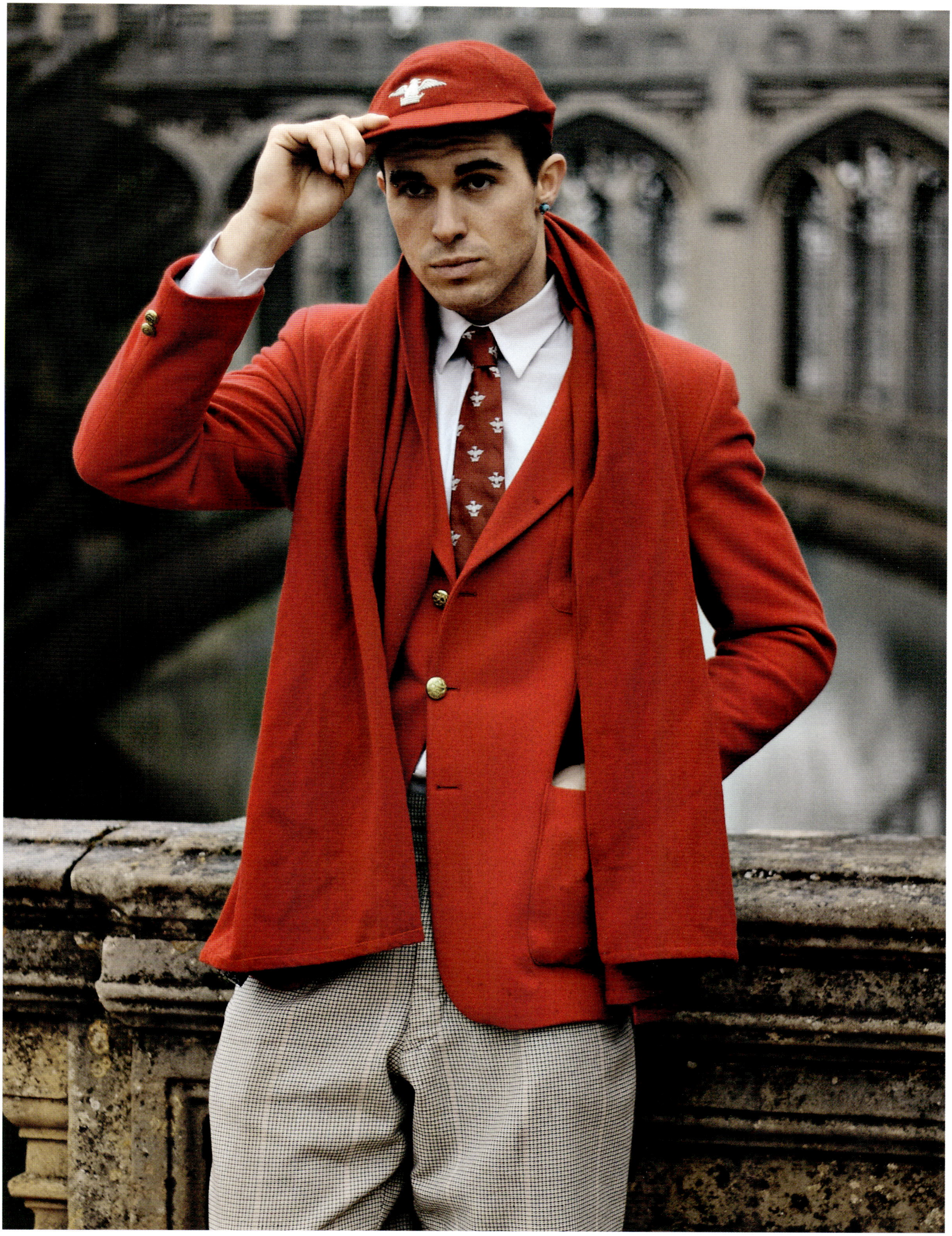

The L.M.B.C. blazer is traditionally worn with a matching cap and sponge-bag (checkered) trousers. Rowers in the top crews may wear red grosgrain trim and gilt buttons emblazoned with the crest of the college's foundress, Lady Margaret Beaufort.

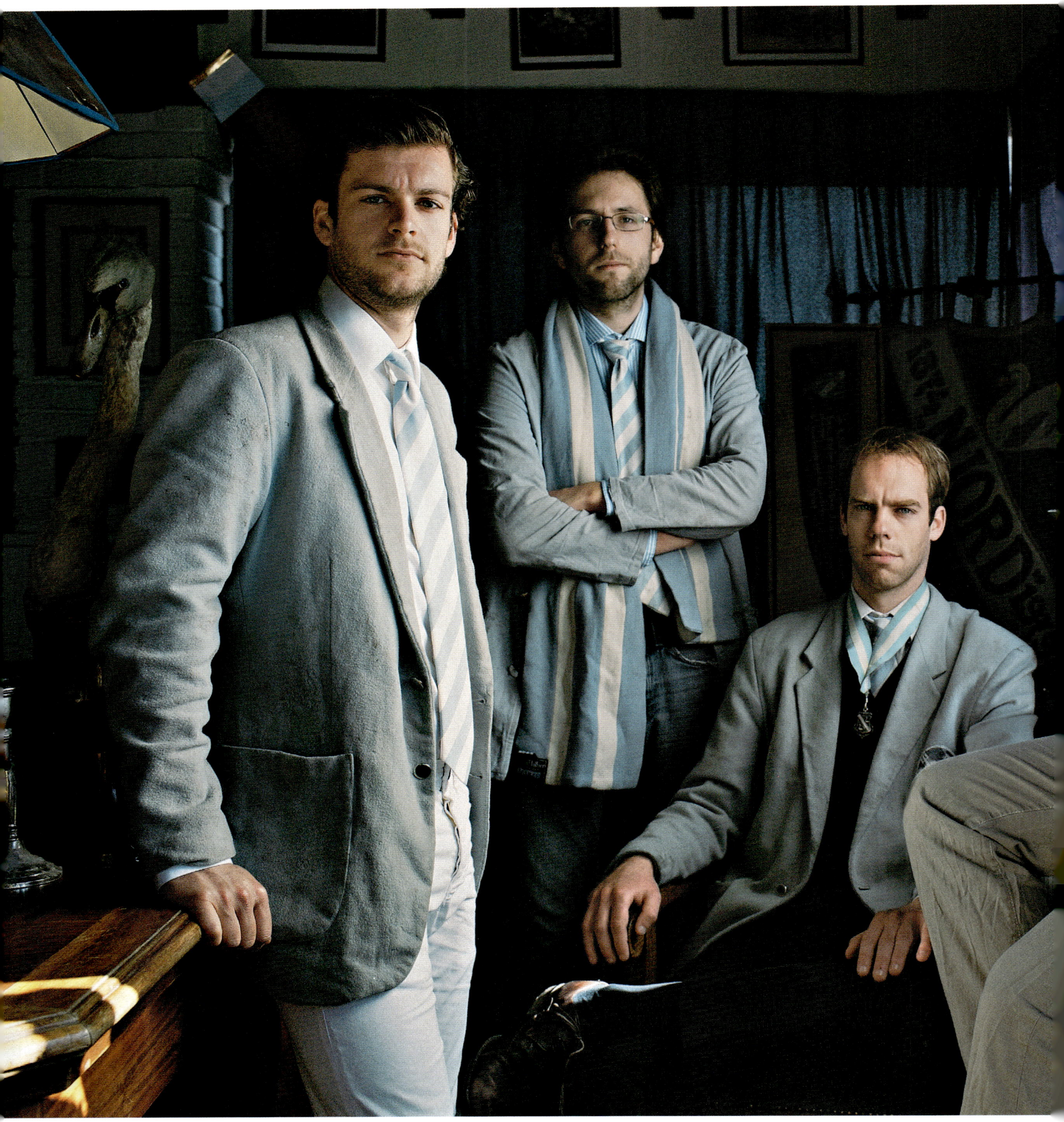

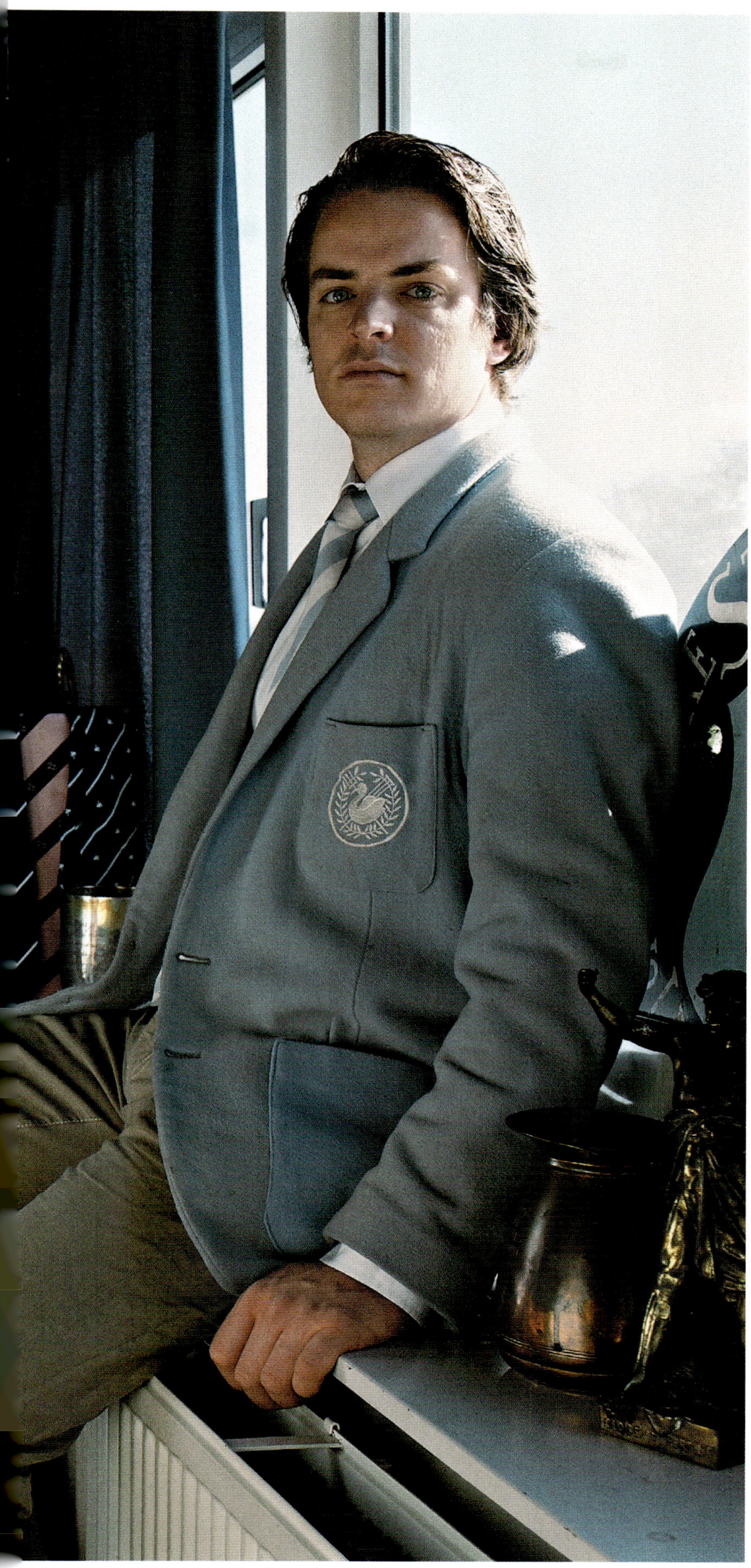

Leiden, Netherlands

K.S.R.V. "Njord"

PAUL FOKKINGA,
MICHIEL JONKMAN,
MAARTEN VAN DER HORST,
SEBASTIEN OLDENBROEK

Koninklijke Studenten Roeivereeniging "Njord" in Leiden is the oldest student rowing club in the Netherlands and the only one to be granted "Royal" *(Koninklijke)* status by the crown. Njord takes its name from the Norse god of the sea, whose attribute is the swan. An image of a swan therefore appears on the club's blazer pockets (in front of a trident, a blade, and a laurel wreath).

An elaborate set of traditions governs Njord's blazers and other accoutrements. A rower is given a club scarf for his or her first race, and the light blue-and-white-striped tie is presented to rowers for completing the Duinloop, a running race.

Components of the blazer badge may be added or colored, depending on the wearer's rowing achievements. Rowers who have raced abroad may embroider the club's name above and below the blazer badge. Those who have won a major sprint race may color the swan's eye black, and the beak may be colored orange to indicate a first-place finish in any major regatta's premier event. A red trident denotes a win against the club's rival, D.S.R.V. Laga, at Laga's quinquennial Lustrum Regatta. The highest achievement in Dutch student rowing—a victory in the men's senior coxed four at the Varsity—entitles a rower to color the badge's laurel wreath gold.

As at other Dutch clubs, the blazers are handed down from retiring rowers to new rowers. A rower may, therefore, inherit a blazer that indicates achievements he has not yet earned; in such cases, the rower must repaint these parts of the badge white or tape over them.

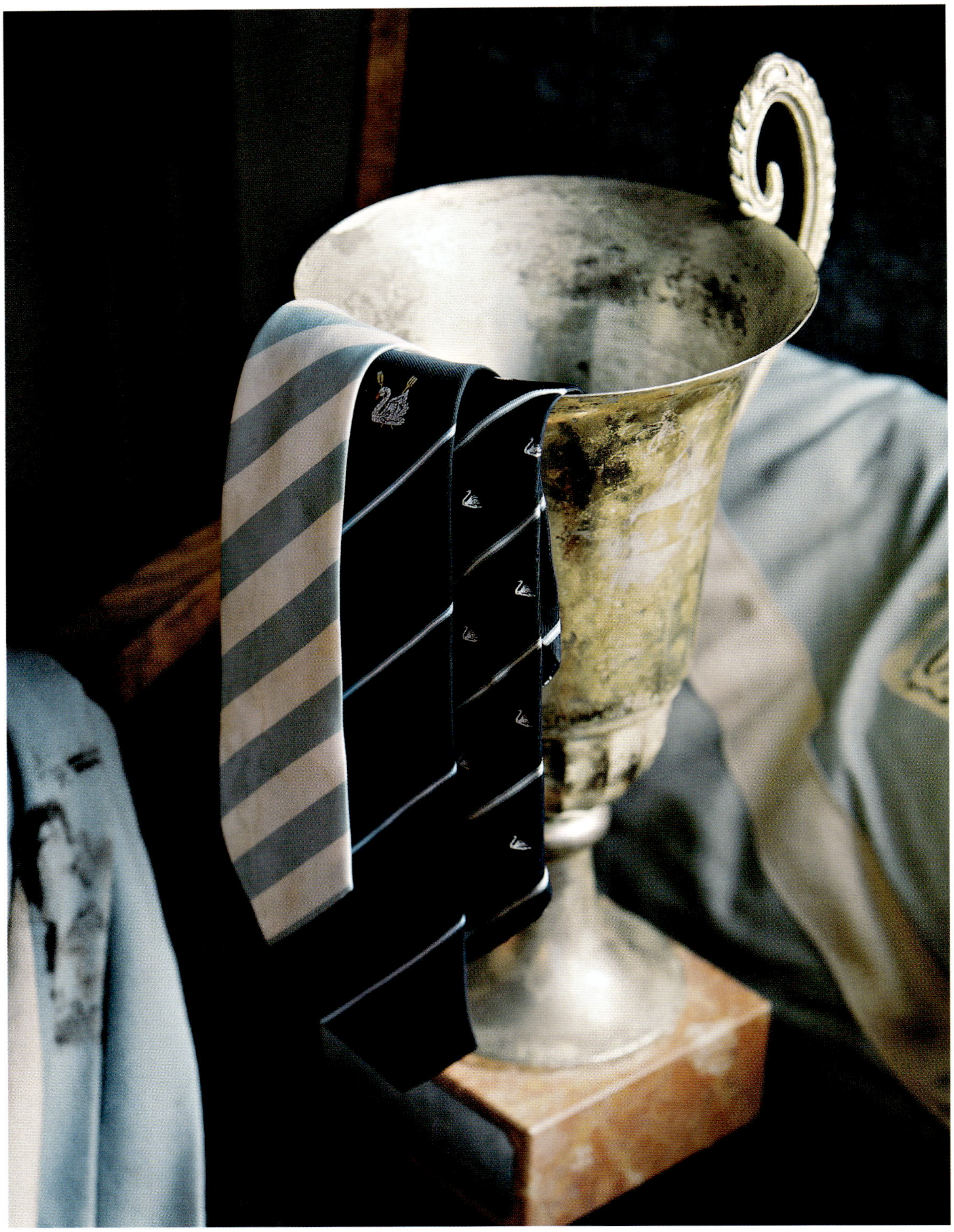

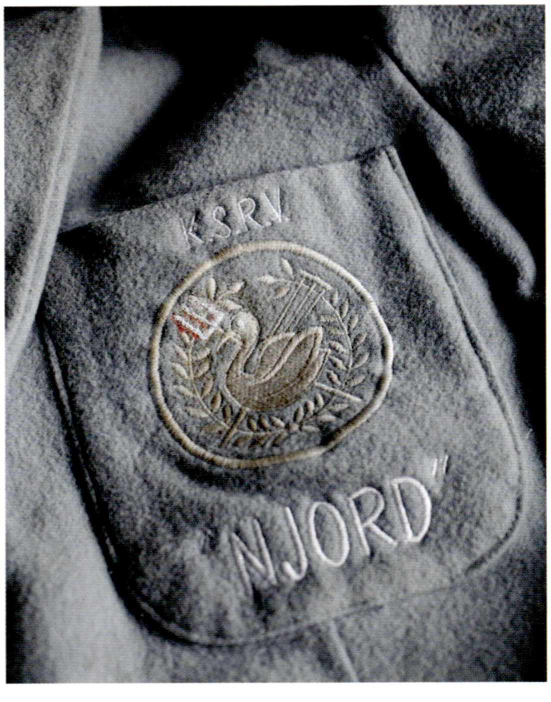

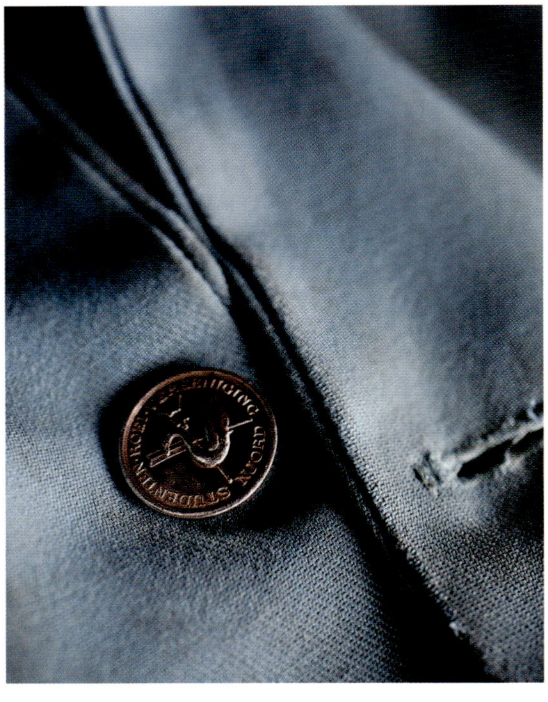

TOP:
The Duinloop tie, the general membership tie, and the old members' tie.

BOTTOM FAR LEFT:
The red trident on the badge indicates a win against rival club D.S.R.V. Laga.

BOTTOM LEFT:
A blazer button that predates Queen Juliana's grant of the title Royal (Koninklijke) to the club in 1974.

OPPOSITE:
The current wearer of this blazer has taped over the embroidered club name and the trident on the badge, indicating that he has not yet earned the achievements entitling him to these embellishments.

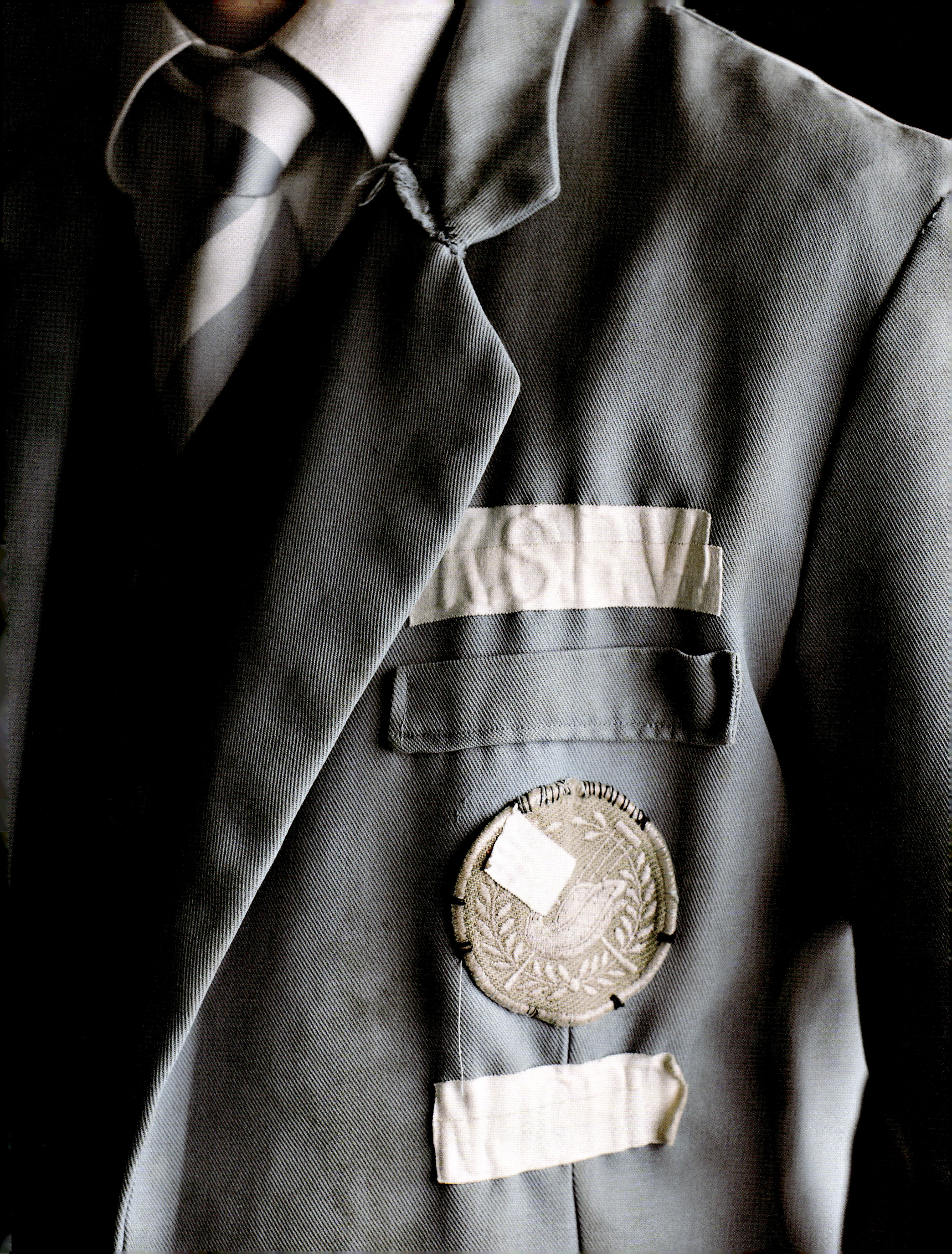

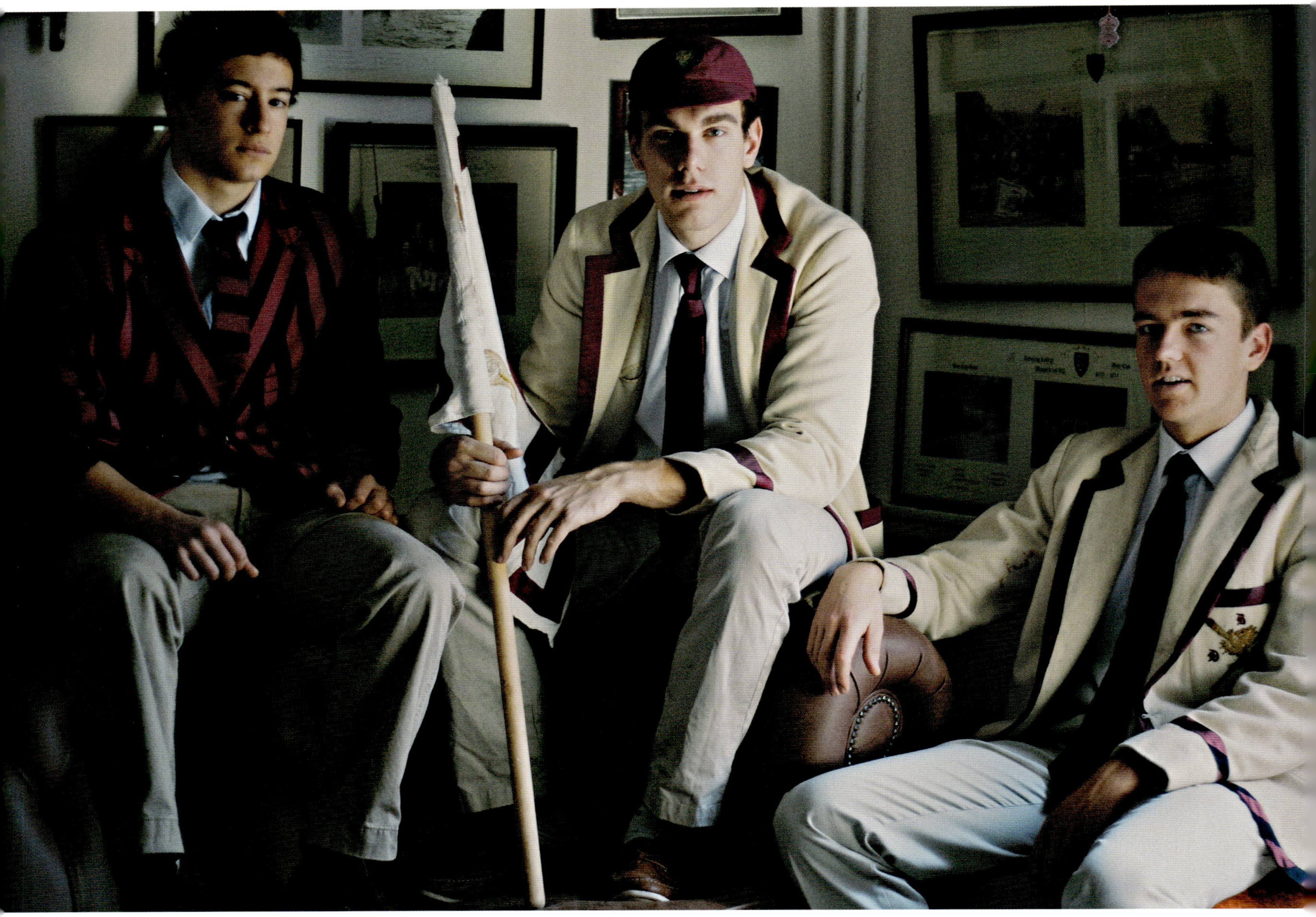

Cambridge, England

Downing College Boat Club, Cambridge, and the Downing Tribe

PEDRO VILA DE MUCHA, MIKE WHETNALL, STUART McPHAIL

Downing College Boat Club adopted the colors magenta and black in 1866, and its blazers are cream with magenta-and-black-striped trim. A golden griffin, from the college coat of arms, adorns the blazer pocket, and members of the first eight may wear blazers with solid magenta trim. The boat club tie is composed of diagonal magenta-and-black stripes, while the Downing Tribe's tie is horizontal stripes of the same colors.

The Downing Tribe is the boat club's riotous alter ego. Under the leadership of an oarsman elected as "Chieftain," the Tribe holds an infamous annual garden party on Suicide Sunday (the first Sunday after the end of Cambridge's summer term), playing host to some seven hundred blazer-clad students and alumni for a day of wanton debauchery. Only the Tribal Chieftain is entitled to wear a fully striped magenta-and-black blazer.

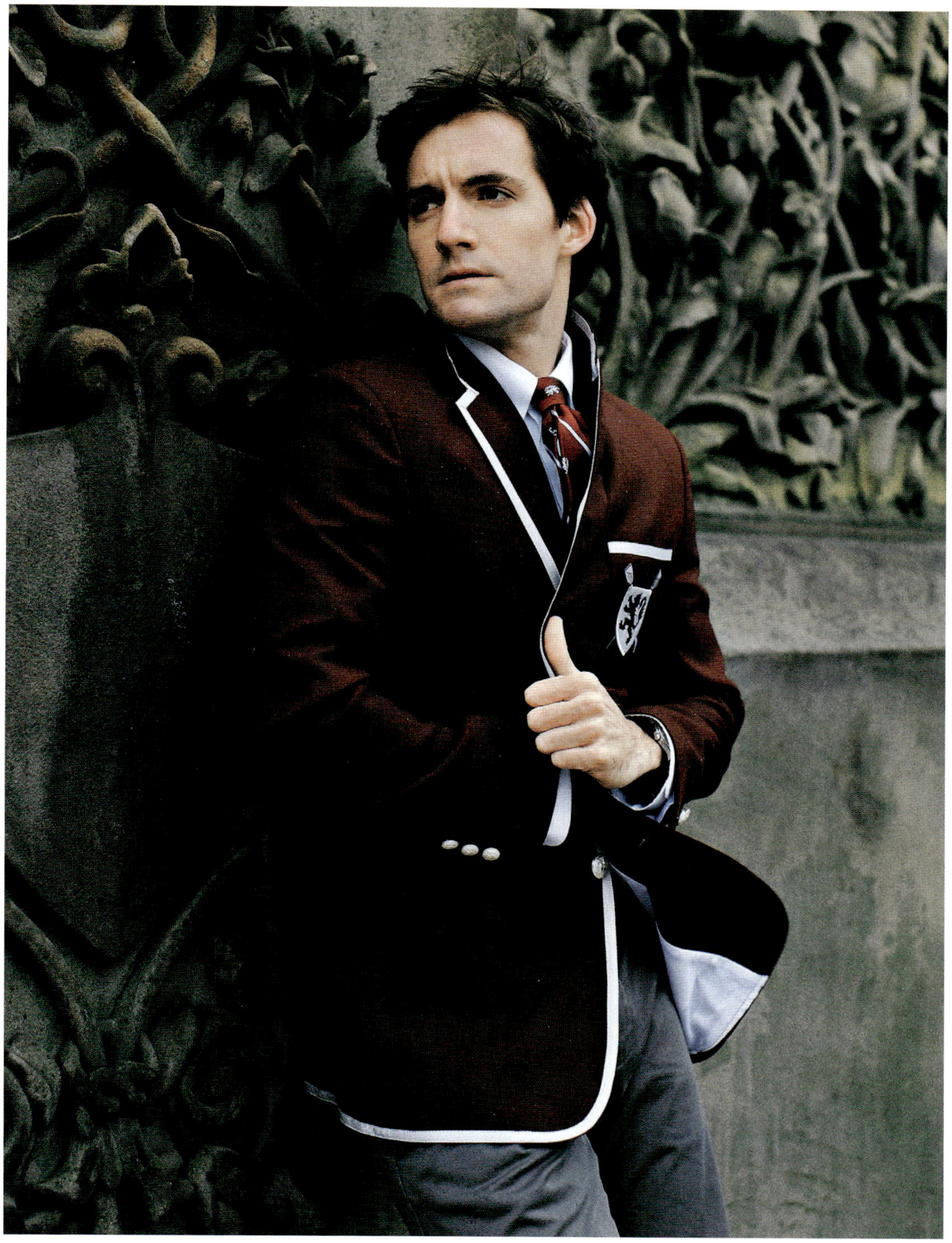

Exeter, New Hampshire

Phillips Exeter Academy

TYLER CALDWELL

Phillips Exeter has always been a grand feeder school for Harvard. When the academy's first oarsmen took to the water in the 1860s, they imitated Harvard's rowers, who had been wearing crimson since 1858. The maroon-and-gray blazer is a recent innovation, however; Exeter crews competing at Henley have traditionally worn simple navy blazers with Exeter badges.

Madison, Wisconsin

University of Wisconsin

KENNY McMAHON

"Participation in the Henley Regatta leaves its character on an oarsman like an indelible dye on a piece of cloth. To have rowed at Henley is to realize that not to have rowed at Henley is like not having rowed at all. It is the fulfillment of recognition, of applause, of win or lose in the absolute sense." —Randy Jablonic, 1986

Wisconsin has rarely raced at the Henley Royal Regatta in England, and when it has, it has found little success. Legendary coach Randy Jablonic, who led "Wisco" to four national championships between 1968 and 1997, nevertheless appreciated the regatta's magic and history.

In 2008, Wisconsin won the points trophy at the Eastern Sprints and won the national title in the varsity eight for the first time in eighteen years. When reporters asked Jablonic's successor, coach Chris Clark, if he would be taking his crews to Henley, he replied, "Nope. We've won the national championship. What more do you want?"

The squad did not race at Henley but did commission Henley-style blazers to commemorate their championship season.

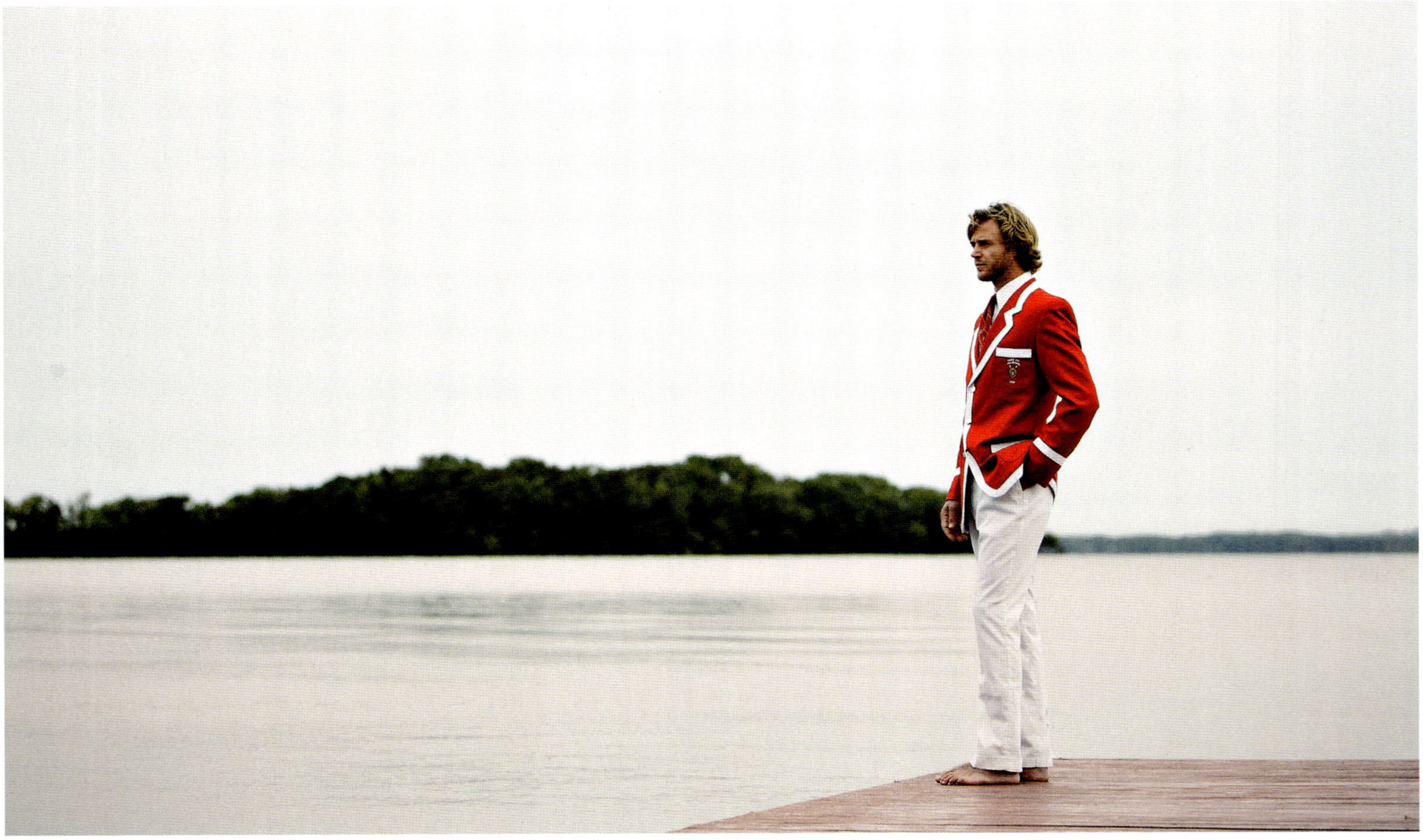

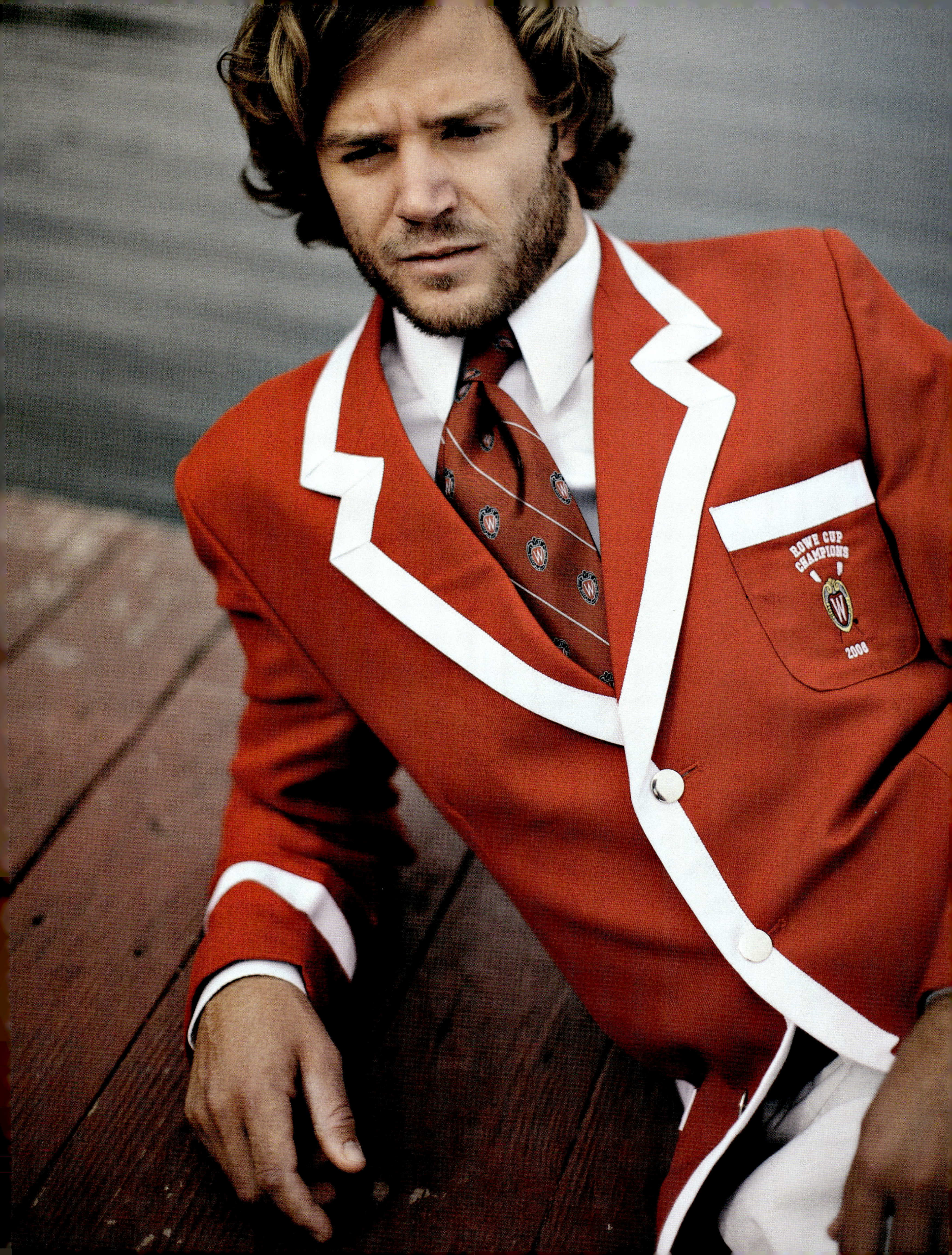
ROWE CUP
CHAMPIONS
2006

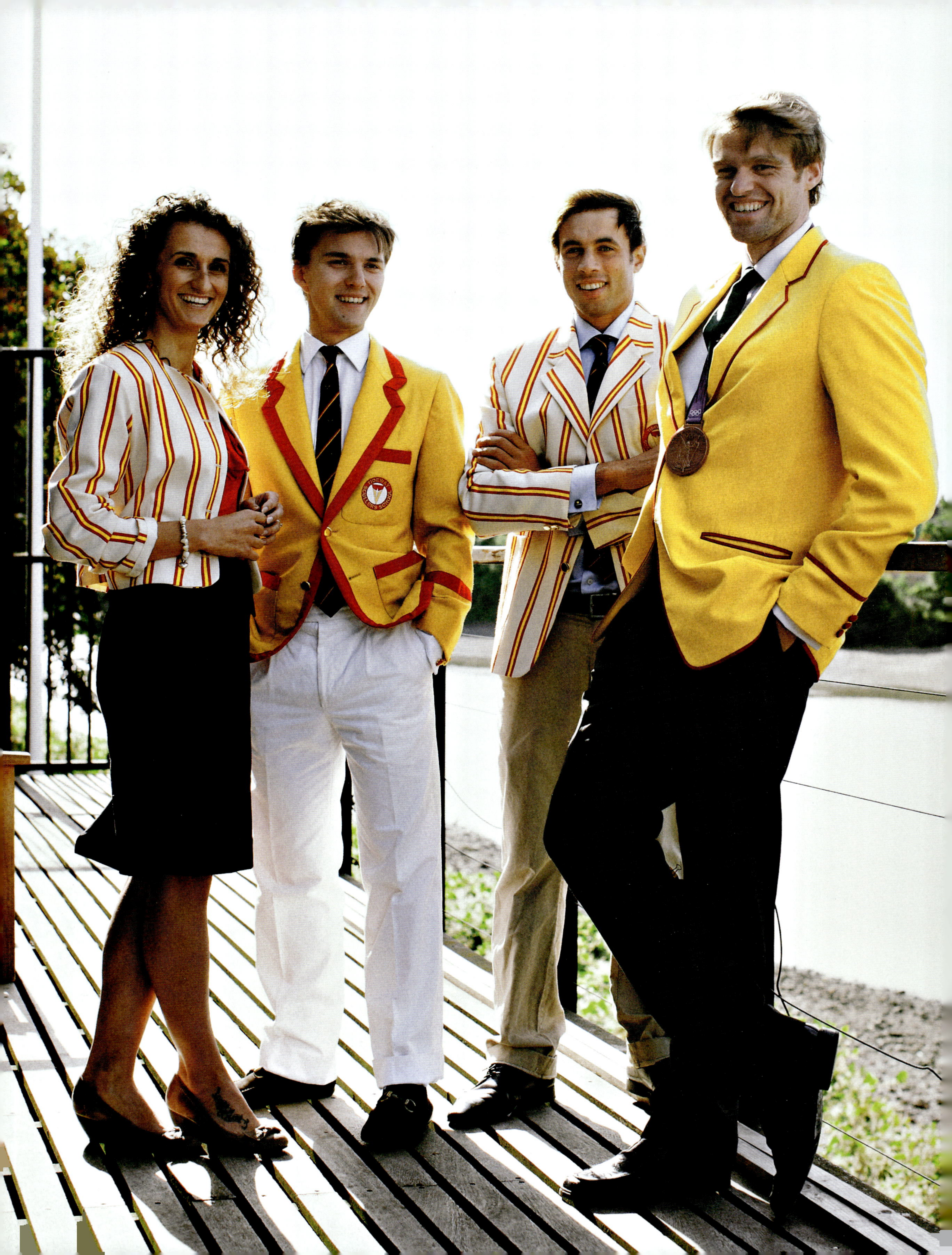
TIDEWAY
SCULLERS SCHOOL

London, England

Tideway Scullers School

ELAINE JOHNSTONE, FREDDIE FOKS, NATHAN O'REILLY, ALAN CAMPBELL

"... the hugely successful Tideway Scullers School, that loose fraternity of top British scullers which dominated the national rowing scene ..." —Daniel Topolski, *Boat Race*, 1985

The Barry family is a sculling dynasty like no other. Ernest Barry and his nephew Bert defended the professional sculling championship of the world a combined six times between 1912 and 1920; Bert's brother, Lou Barry, held the title "champion of the Thames" in 1936, and all three were winners of the Doggett's Coat and Badge sculling race. Lou's son, Bill Barry, won the British amateur sculling championship, the Wingfield Sculls, in four consecutive races, 1963–66, and won a silver medal at the 1964 Olympics.

Lou Barry firmly believed that two-oared sculling, especially in singles (one-person boats) was the best training, even for sweep oarsmen (that is, rowers who race in crew boats with one oar each), and that crew boats should be chosen based on sculling ability; with this in mind, he began the Tideway Scullers School as an informal training group in 1957.

Rowers from all over the Thames Tideway came to join the group for coaching and training in single sculls. They would be told where to meet on the river and to look out for Lou Barry's coaching launch, which would be flying the red-and-yellow "Man Overboard" flag.

Today, T.S.S. is coached by Lou Barry's son, Bill. True to its founder's vision, the club counts the world's best scullers among its members, including Alan Campbell. Like his coach, Alan is a four-time winner of the historic Wingfield Sculls race and an Olympic medalist: he took home bronze in the single sculls in 2012 (fellow T.S.S. member Mahé Drysdale won the gold for New Zealand).

Alan and Mahé were both part of a grand experiment undertaken by Bill Barry in 2009: the Tideway Scullers Great Eight. The Great Eight brought the top eight scullers in the world together in one crew to compete in the Head of the River Race in London and the Head of the Charles Regatta in Boston. The Scullers crew won both events, defeating many of the world's best sweep oarsmen: this result, no doubt, would have made Lou Barry very happy.

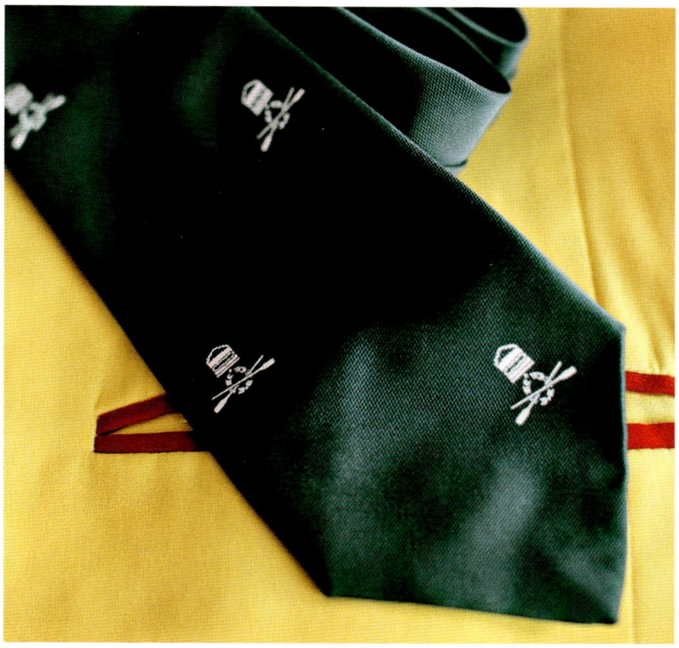

ABOVE:
Alan Campbell's Tideway Scullers School blazer and the award tie given to him for winning the Wingfield Sculls, Great Britain's amateur sculling championship.

OVERLEAF:
The Tideway Scullers Great Eight racing at the 2009 Head of the Charles Regatta.

Red and yellow are the club's colors in homage to Lou Barry's "Man Overboard" flag, and feature on all Tideway Scullers blades and blazers. But there is no standard T.S.S. blazer. Because of the club's emphasis on single sculling, each member may design his or her own particular blazer.

Alan Campbell's is yellow with narrow red piping and no badge. "I don't need a club badge on my pocket because everyone already knows I'm Tideway Scullers through and through," he says. "You could cut me in two, and you'd see, I'm all red and yellow inside."

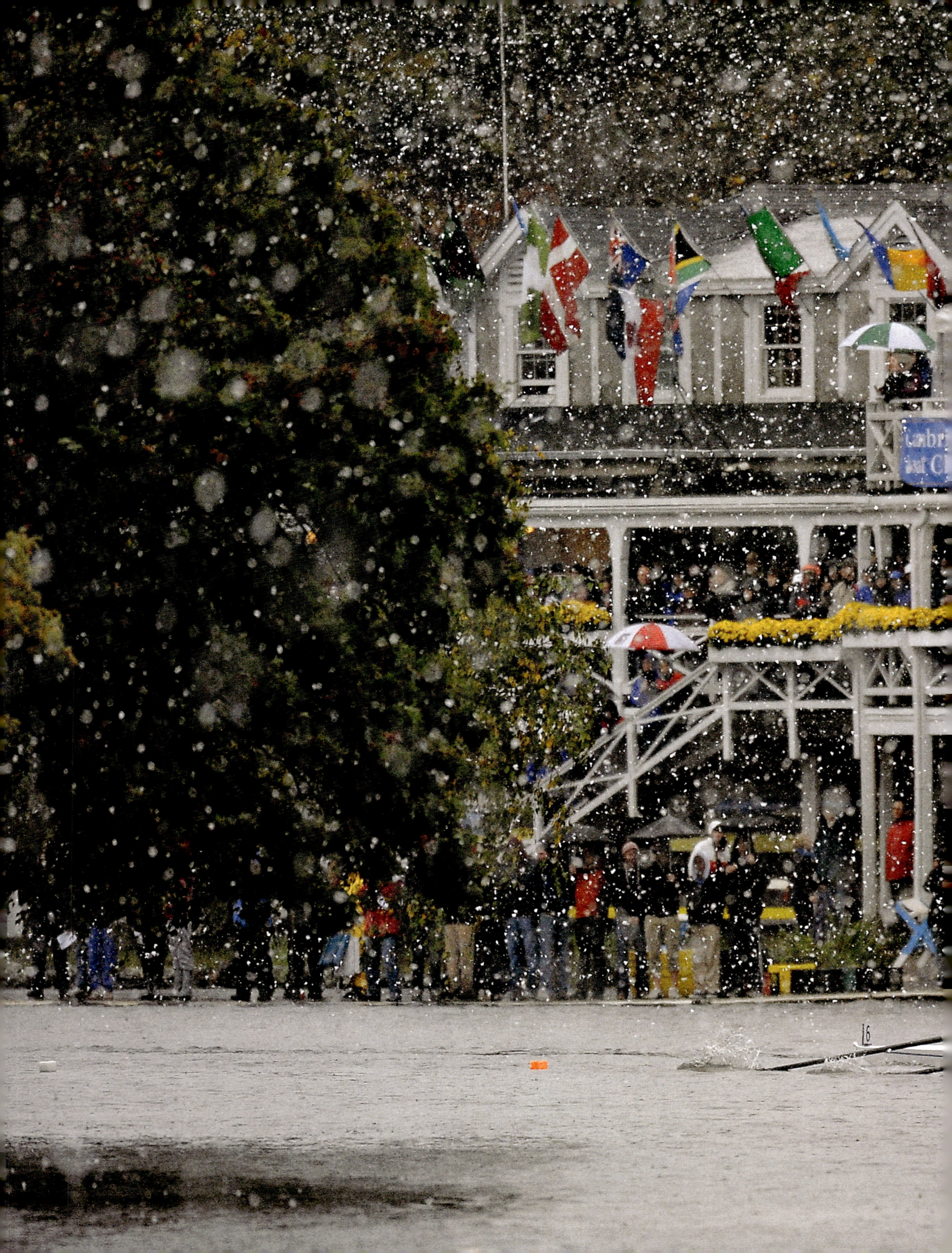

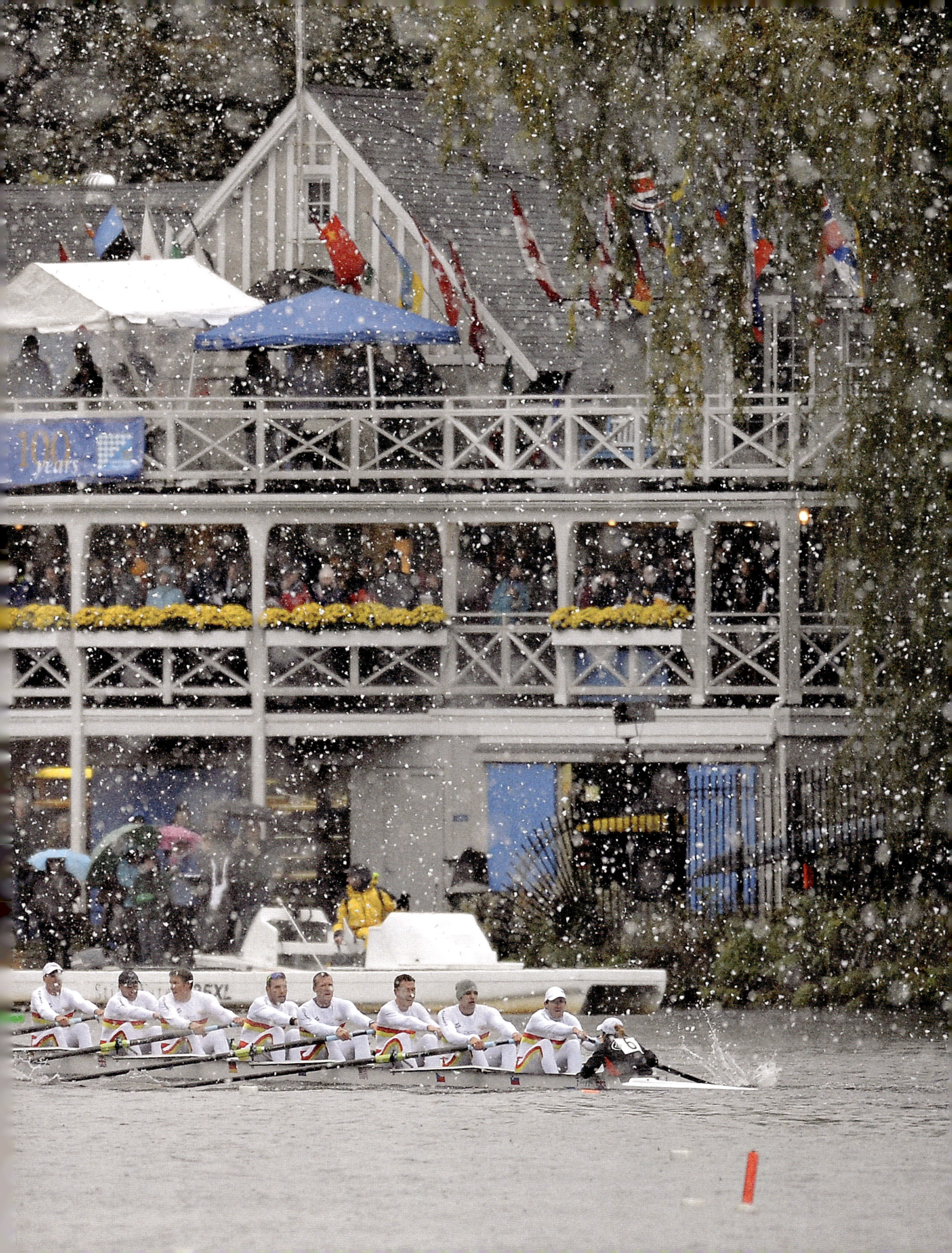
100
years

Oxford, England

New College Boat Club, Oxford

DAVE WHIFFIN

Despite its name, New College was founded in 1379. But its rowing colors, according to a much-repeated myth, date to 1912. The Olympic Games were held in Stockholm that year. In those days, each nation could enter multiple crews in the same event, and the Olympic championship was a Henley-style series of single elimination dual races. Those were also the days when Oxford college crews were Olympic caliber. So it was that there were two Great Britain entries for the eight that started on opposite sides of the draw and met in the final: one of these crews was from Leander Club and Magdalen College, Oxford; the other was from New College, Oxford.

The Olympic course at Djurgårdsbrunnsviken, Sweden, featured a slight bend, and apparently one of the lanes was favored. According to the legend, it was customary for crews to toss a coin for lanes before the race, and, in gentlemanly fashion, the winner of the toss was to offer the choice of lanes to their opponents, who were, in turn, to decline politely. New College won the coin toss before the final and, following the ritual, the story goes, offered the Leander-Magdalen crew their choice of lanes. Rather than courteously refusing, however, Leander-Magdalen accepted and promptly chose the advantageous lane for themselves.

The New College crew put up a valiant fight but fell behind at the bend and lost by 3.5 seconds. King Gustaf V of Sweden, who had witnessed the race and the preceding events, was horrified by the unsportsmanlike conduct of Leander-Magdalen during the coin toss. The king wanted to console and honor the losing crew and so, it's said, he granted New College Boat Club use of the colors of Sweden's Royal House of Bernadotte: purple and gold. The club has used purple and gold blades, purple racing uniforms, and purple-trimmed blazers ever since.

New College did indeed lose to Leander-Magdalen in the final of the 1912 Olympics, but much of the rest of this amusing story seems to be fictional. Among other small problems with the tale, there is the fact that the colors of Sweden's Royal House are not purple and gold. New College's colors, however, *were* purple and gold (sometimes recorded as violet and orange) long before the 1912 Olympics. Purple and gold trophy blades from the nineteenth century even hang in the New College boathouse, and photographs of the crew taken in Stockholm show the coxswain, J. D. Walker, wearing a New College blazer that is no different from the current design.

In his diary, the bitter New College captain, Arthur Wiggins, did complain about being in the disadvantaged lane for the final, but he says that none of the crew found out about it until they arrived at the starting platform ready to race. He mentions nothing of a coin toss but does speculate that their unfavorable lane draw might have been the result of "a bit of very dirty work somewhere. . . . Had we had the other station," he goes on to write, "I firmly believe that we should have won."

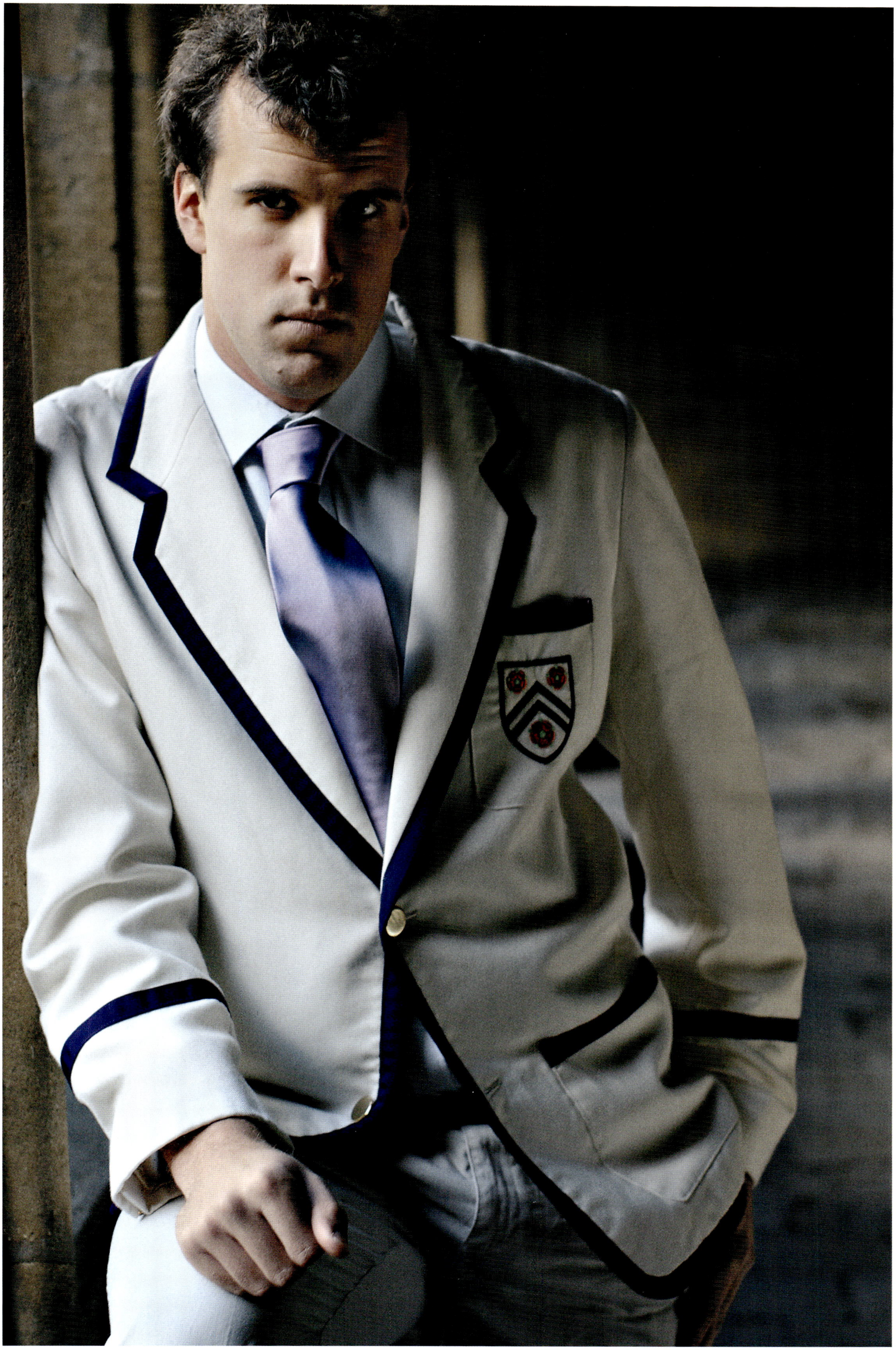

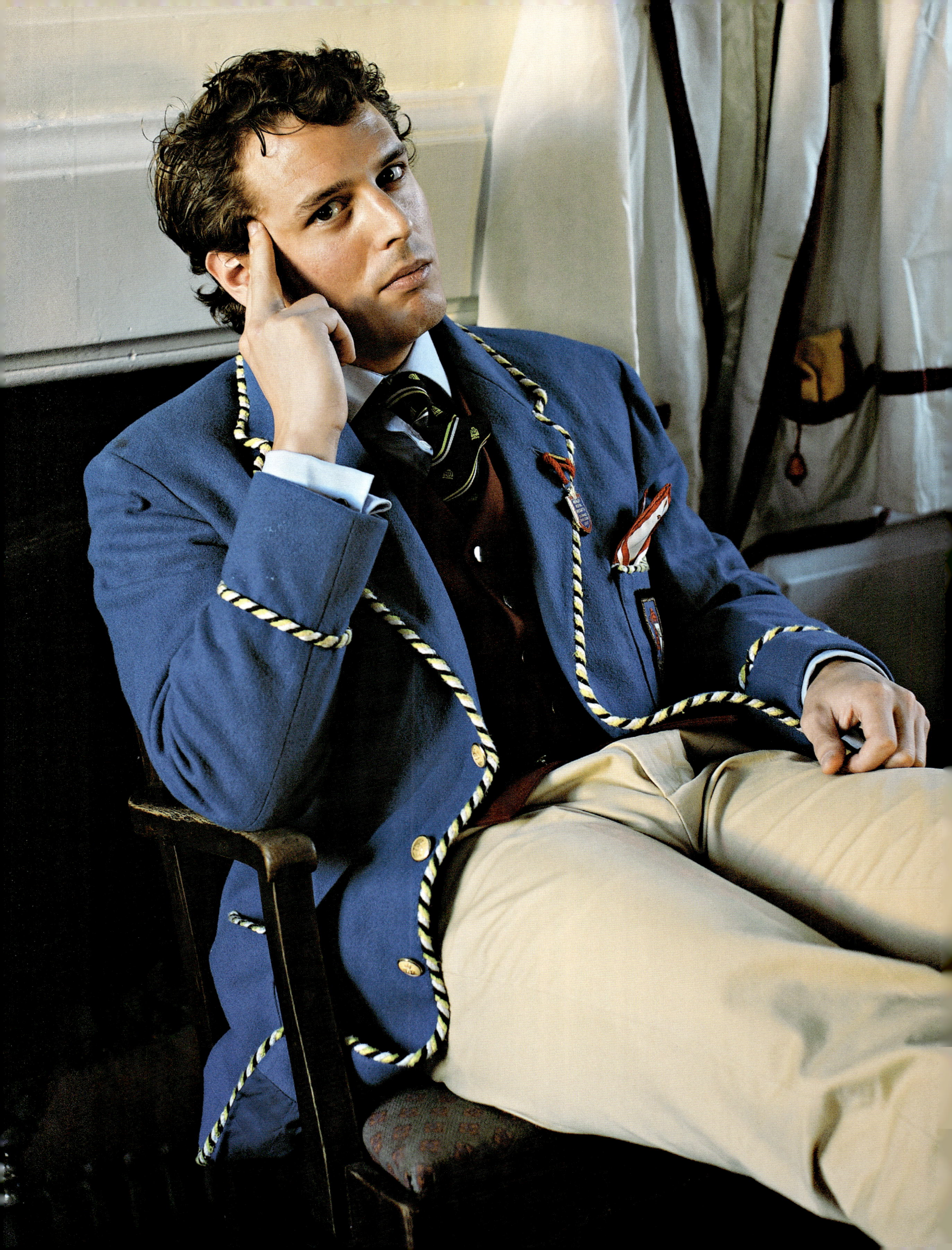

Woodcote, England

Oratory School Boat Club

and the

Oratory Cardinals

MAXIMILIAN LAU

Oratory has never been a great power in the rowing world, but the boys pursue it with joy and enthusiasm. The first eight are awarded bright blue blazers trimmed in the school colors: black, yellow, and white. The active alumni rowing club, the Oratory Cardinals, has its own blazer, which is cream with cardinal trim. The badge is the coat of arms of the school's founder, the Blessed Cardinal Newman.

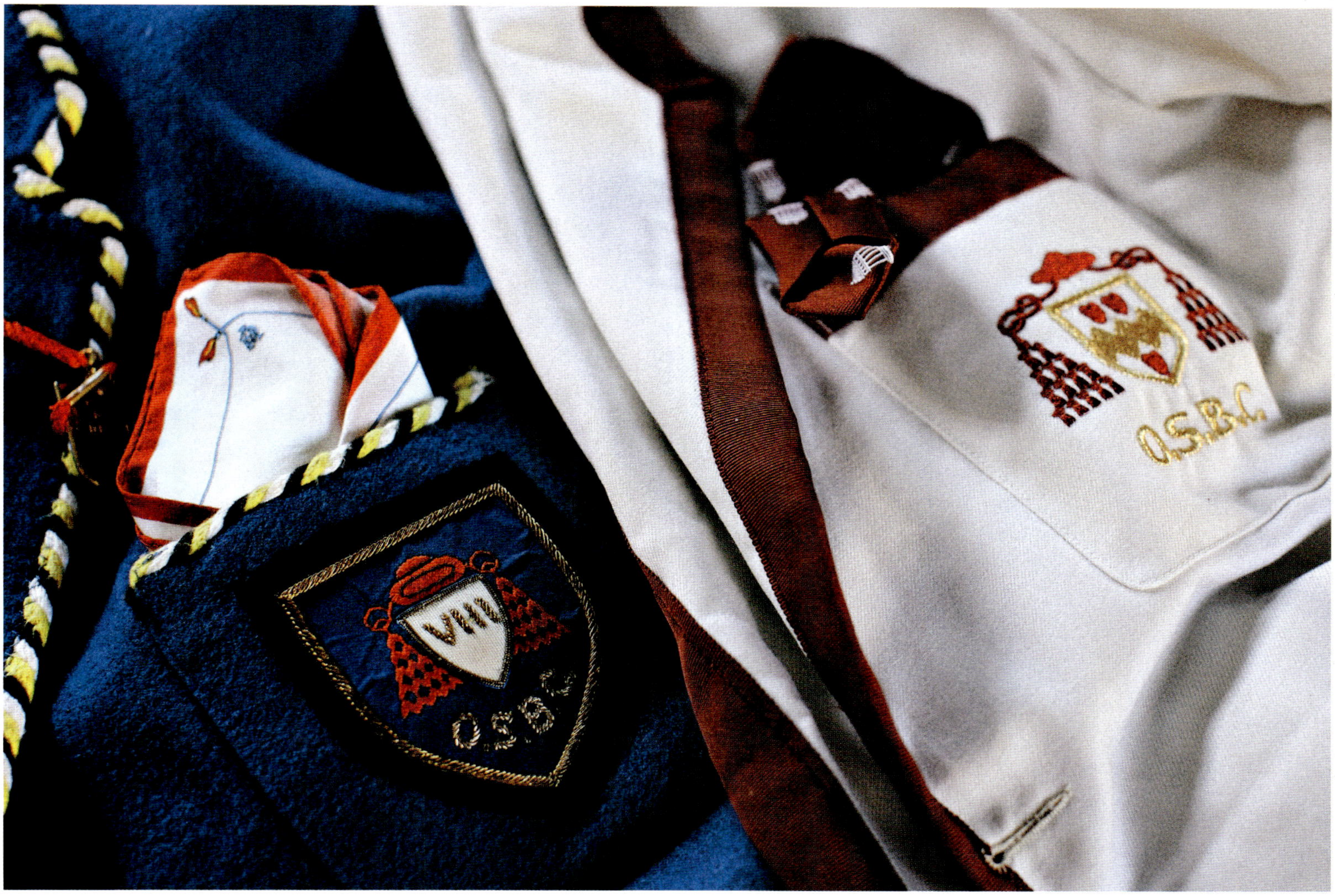

Cambridge, England

Jesus College Boat Club, Cambridge

RICARDO HERREROS-SYMONS,

EDMUND BRADBURY

"Mileage makes champions" is a phrase coined by Steve Fairbairn, the great Jesus College oarsman and coach who founded the Head of the River Race in London. Fairbairn was largely responsible for the near invincibility of Jesus College Boat Club in the early twentieth century.

Jesus remains near the top of the pile in the world of Cambridge rowing, and its oarsmen wear white flannel blazers trimmed in black and "Jesus red." Tradition holds that on race day, crew members walk from the college to the boathouse together wearing white shorts, a zephyr racing jersey, and Jesus socks.

Ricardo (left) is president of J.C.B.C., and Edmund (right) is the fourth in his family to row for Jesus in the last thirty years.

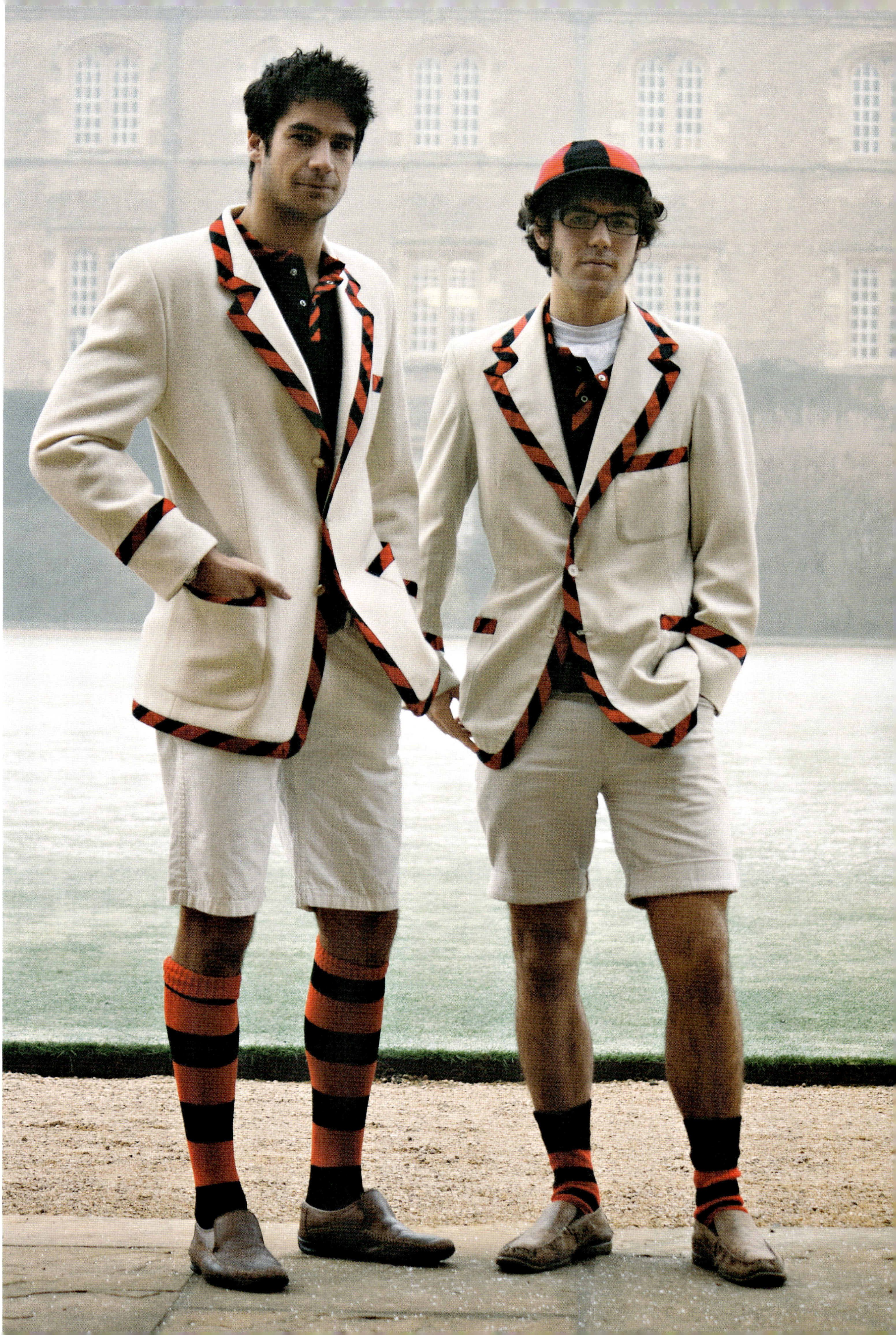

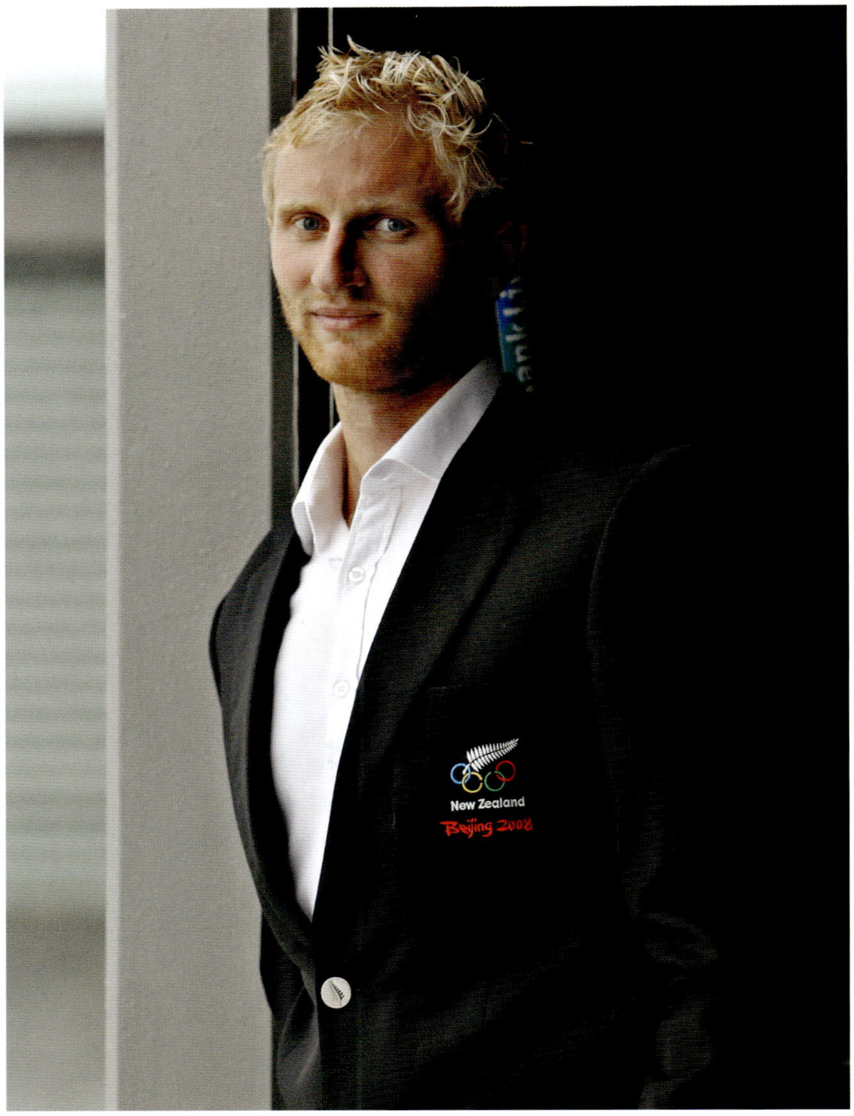

New Zealand Olympic Team *and the* New Zealand Red Coat

HAMISH BOND MNZM, ERIC MURRAY MNZM

Most rowing blazers correspond to clubs. But, like the famous green blazer given to winners of the Masters Golf Tournament, some rowing blazers are awards or prizes. The New Zealand "red coat" is one such blazer. Inspired, perhaps, by the red Doggett's Coat, the New Zealand Amateur Rowing Association presents a red jacket emblazoned with its badge to each winner of the national championships, while victorious coaches are given similar green coats. "Winning a red coat" is synonymous with winning a national title in Kiwi rowing circles.

Hamish Bond and Eric Murray won gold in the men's pair at the 2012 Olympics, where they set the world and Olympic record time (beating the ten-year-old record set by James Cracknell and Matthew Pinsent by nearly six seconds). Some consider them to be the greatest sweep oarsmen in history.

ABOVE: Hamish Bond is wearing the New Zealand Olympic blazer.
OPPOSITE: Eric Murray wears a red coat emblazoned with the New Zealand Amateur Rowing Association badge.

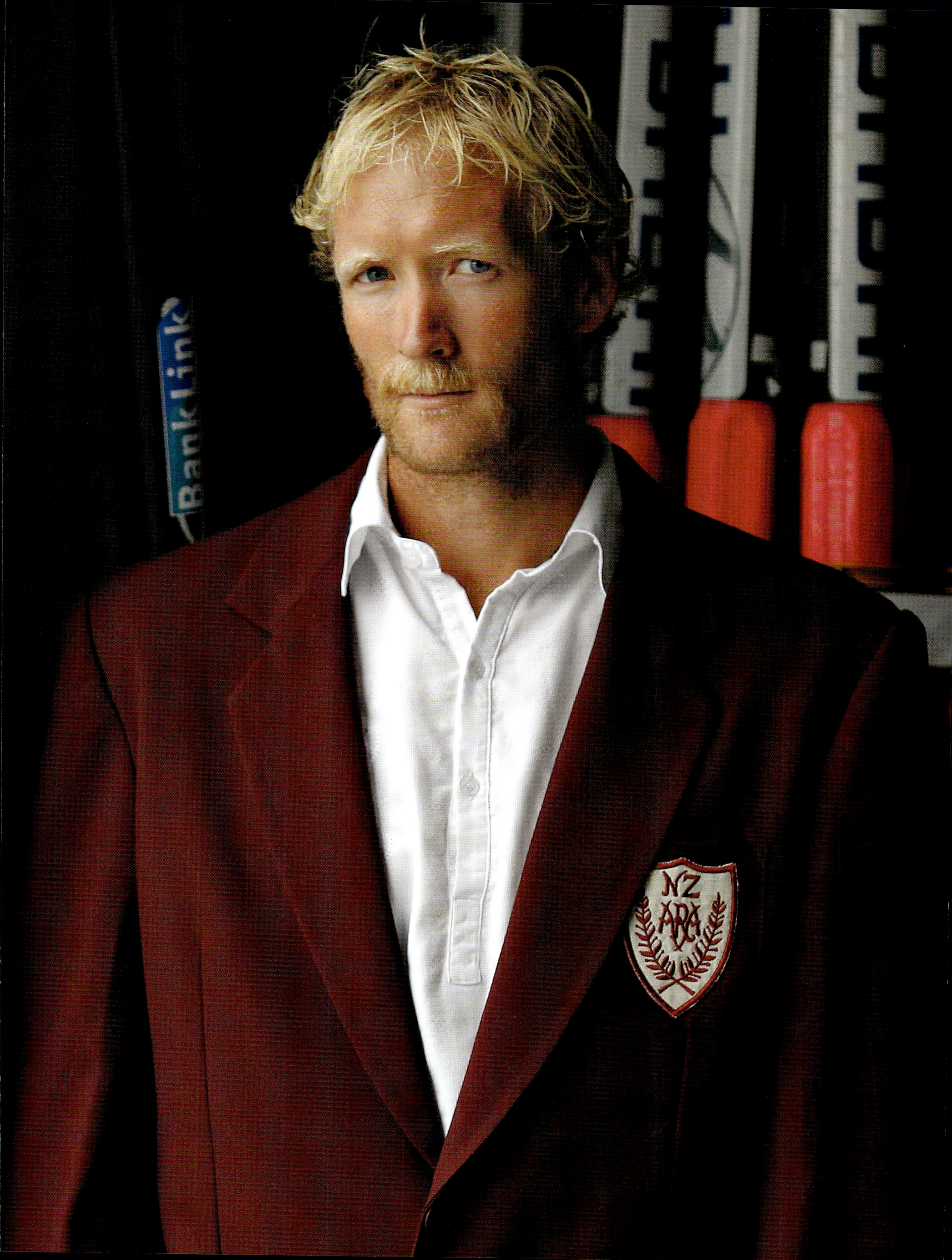
BankLink
NZ
ARA

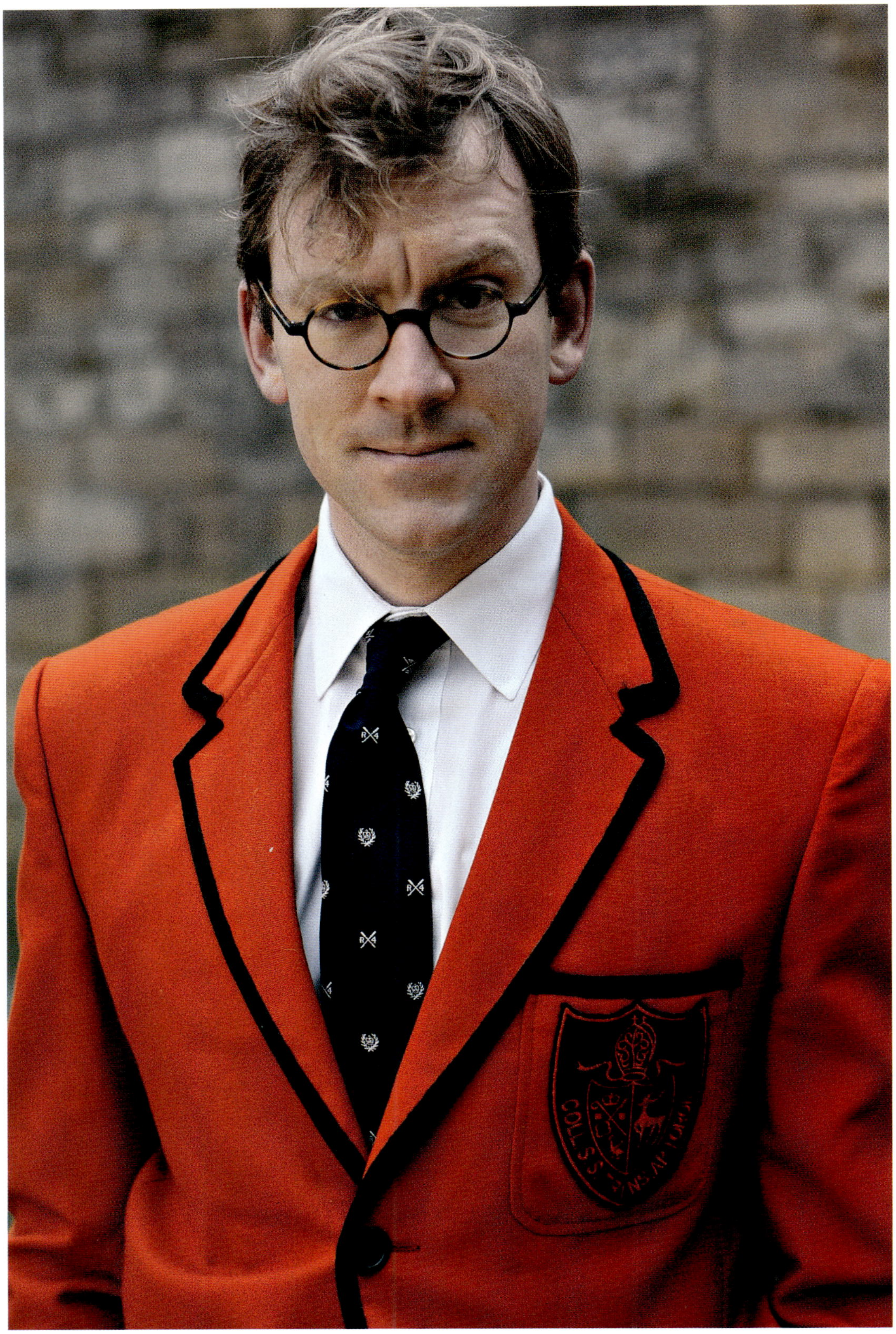

Toronto, Canada

Trinity College, Toronto

MICHAEL RICHARD JACKSON BONNER

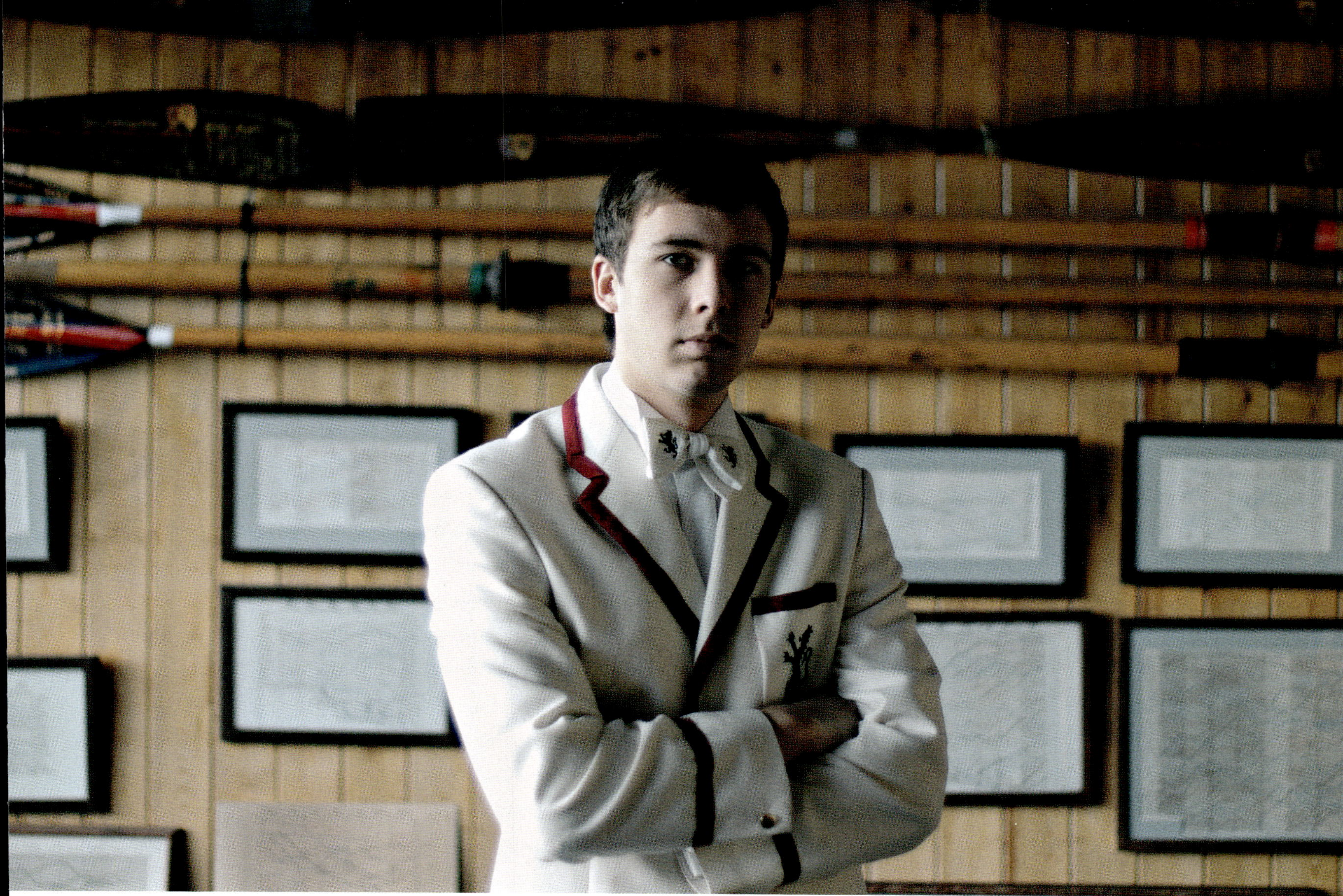

Oxford, England

Balliol College Boat Club, Oxford, and the Gordouli Blazer

ROB WADSWORTH

Balliol College, Oxford, has a long-standing rivalry with its neighbor, Trinity College. A group of Trinity men once padlocked every Balliol gate from the outside, effectively besieging the whole college; on another occasion, Balliol students managed to turf the entire Trinity Junior Common Room floor, complete with daffodils.

In earlier years, these exchanges sometimes had a nastier flavor. Many of Trinity's "pranks" took aim at the relatively high number of foreign students at Balliol; Balliol responded in the 1890s with the rather mean-spirited "Gordouli" song. Gordouli was the nickname of a half-Italian student at Trinity—Arturo Galletti di Cadhilac—who did not fit the stereotype of the Anglo-Saxon Trinity man. It became tradition for Balliol oarsmen to assemble in their blazers outside of Trinity's gates after Boat Club dinners to sing the Gordouli song:

Gordoooouli!
He's got a face like a ham!
Bobby Johnson says so
And he ought to know!

(The Trinity retort is: "Balliol, Balliol, / They can't row! / John Legge says so, / And he ought to know!")

The singing tradition continues to this day, and the Balliol boating jacket is always known as the Gordouli Blazer.

Oxford, England

Oriel College Boat Club, Oxford

WILL ZENG

Oriel's success since the 1970s is unparalleled in the world of Oxford rowing: in the final quarter of the twentieth century, Oriel was Head of the River in Summer Eights in all but six years and Head in Torpids every year but three (Summer Eights and Torpids are Oxford's two principal college races).

Rowing blazers, naturally, are prized possessions and important indicators of social cachet at Oriel. They have also occasionally been involved in the mischief made by rival colleges: when an Oriel captain's blazer goes missing, it can usually be found the following week in Christ Church's Tom Quad, where the statue of Mercury will inevitably be wearing it.

There is a wide range of symbols and accoutrements associated with Oriel rowing. The Prince of Wales's feathers badge on the blazer pocket began as a hat badge in the club's earliest years and reflects Oriel's great royalist tradition: the college was the first royal foundation in Oxford, hosted the Privy Council during the English Civil War, and has the Queen as its current official Visitor.

Members of the first eight wear three blue stripes on their blazer sleeves; second eight and first Torpid rowers, two stripes; and all others, one. The concept, like blazers themselves, developed from racing kit to slightly more formal terrestrial dress. Oriel's top crews have worn three stripes on their race jersey sleeves since the mid-nineteenth century.

A stylized tortoise is the symbol of the men's senior crews, whose members are entitled to wear dark blue tortoise ties and waistcoats. This emblem has been used since the 1930s, when the boat club's beloved pet tortoise had even its parturitions recorded in the *Times* ("On May 28, 1938, at Oriel College, Oxford, to Georgina, wife of O.C. Testudo—a son").

Will Zeng rowed for Oriel in 2012 and was part of the crew that successfully defended Oriel's Head of the River title in Summer Eights. Earlier that year, he rowed in the Oxford-Cambridge Boat Race and nearly decapitated a rogue swimmer (the protester Trenton Oldfield) with his blade. This race was also famous for the clash of oars that left Oxford wallowing in Cambridge's wake with only seven functional blades.

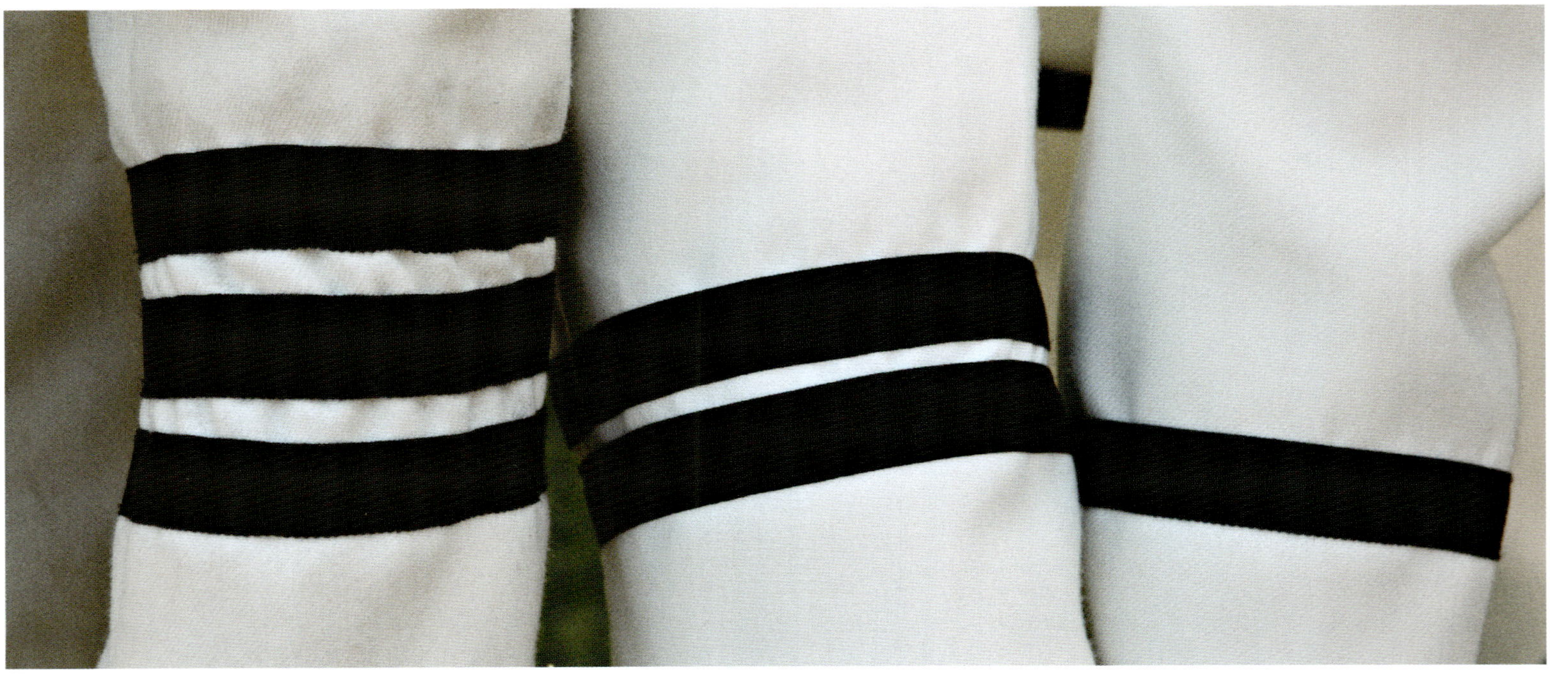

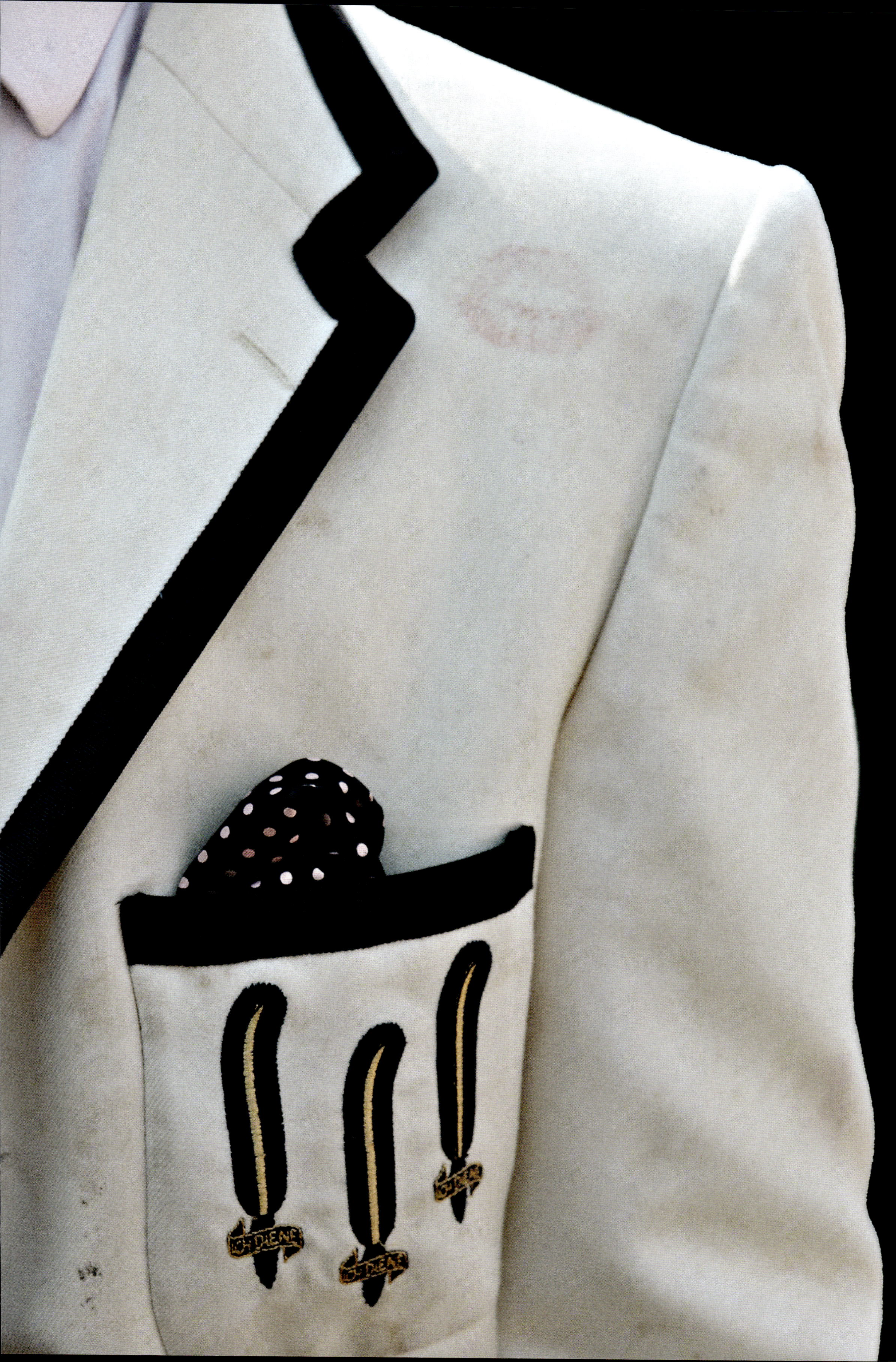
ICH DIENE

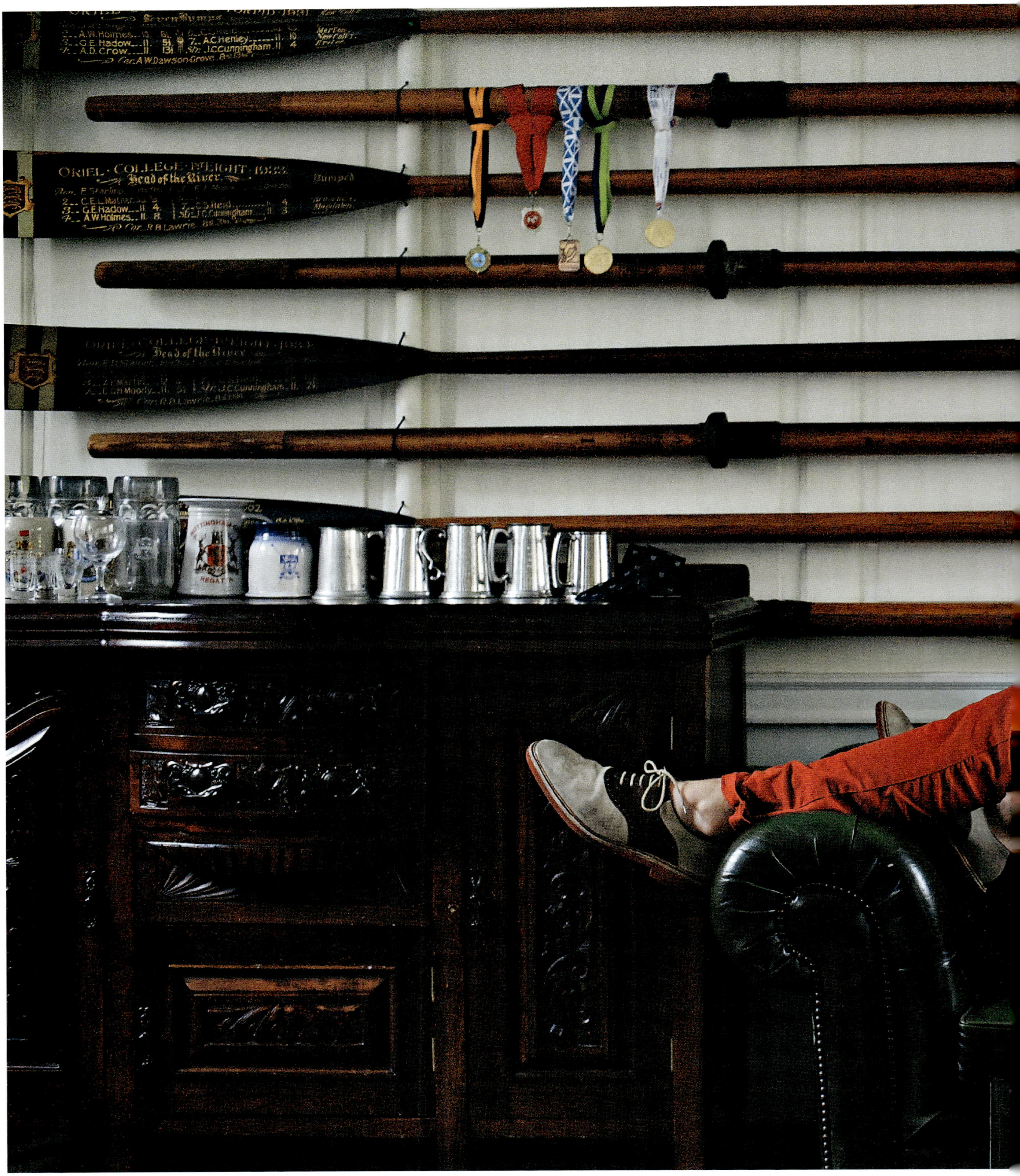
ORIEL · COLLEGE
Head of the River
G.E.Hadow
A.W.Holmes

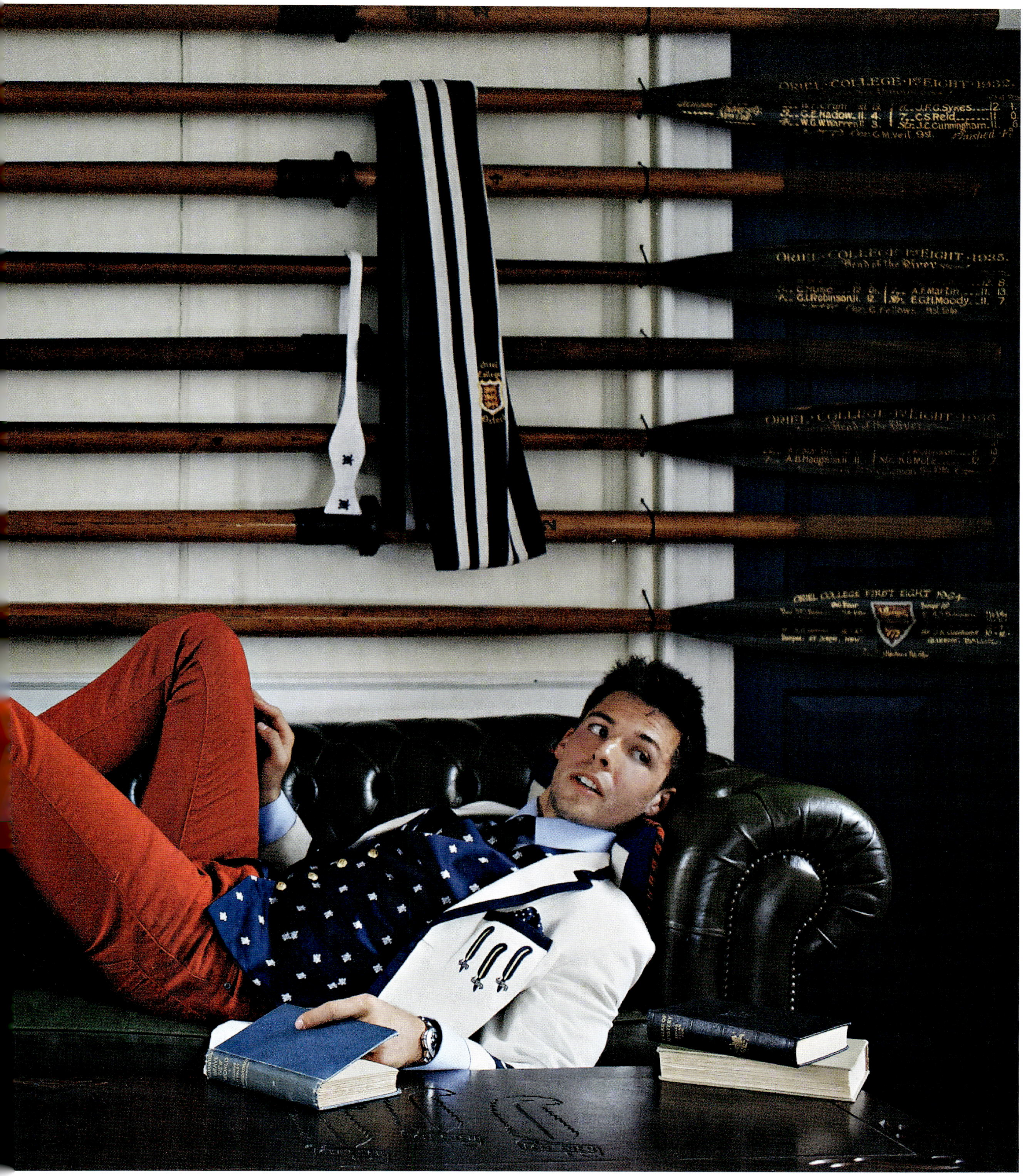

Will Zeng lounges in "One-One," as the rowing captain's room in Oriel College is known.

Washington, D.C.

Georgetown University Boat Club

CHARLES DE PENTHENY-O'KELLY, MICHAEL HENNESSY,
HENRY HOFFSTOT, TIM BROUGHTON

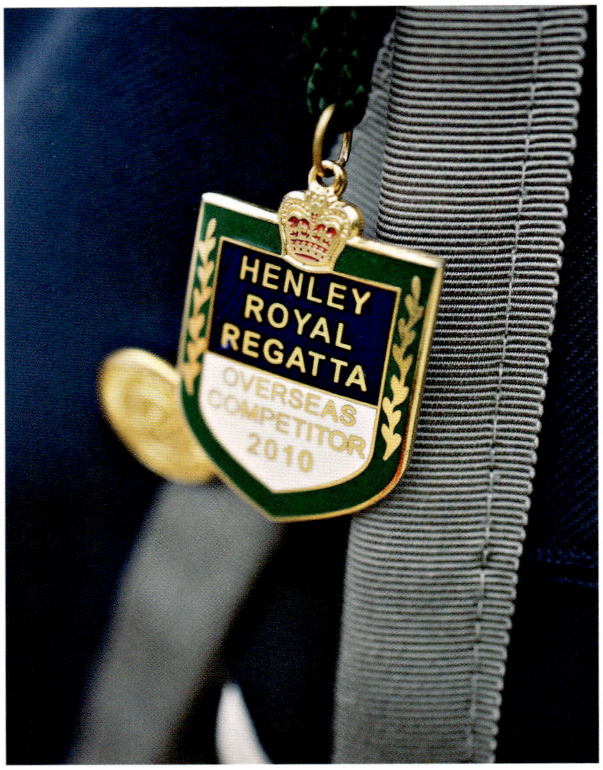

"Give way, give way, no man shall say
We're laggards at the oar;
No dame shall flush, nor maiden blush
For Georgetown's honest fame.
Hurrah! then, boys, hurrah! hurrah!
The Blue and Gray forever."
—The Georgetown College
Boat Song, 1876

When a group of students founded Georgetown University Boat Club in 1876, one of the club's first acts was the appointment of a committee to select racing colors. A report in the *Georgetown College Journal* announced:

> *These gentlemen have decided on Blue and Gray as appropriate colors for the Club and expressive of the feeling of unity that exists between the Northern and Southern boys of the College.*

The boat club received enthusiastic support from the university community and beyond. Young ladies studying at the nearby Visitation Academy presented the club with a hand-sewn flag, half blue, half gray, and embroidered with the Latin *Ocior Euro* (Swifter than the wind) above the letters "G.U.B.C." Their letter to the club read:

> *May this little flag ever wave over true and noble hearts! May success ever attend you, and while old Potomac echoes back the shout of merry voices, may it carry your bark—"swifter than the wind"—down its rippling waters.*

In the following years, the blue-and-gray boat club flag was displayed at important university events, and—as at so many universities—the rowing colors were eventually adopted by the university as a whole. Georgetown's rowing blazers are, of course, blue and gray, as are their blades.

Charles, Michael, Henry, and Tim are the most recent oarsmen to represent Georgetown at the Henley Royal Regatta; Henry and Tim won the Britannia Challenge Cup at the regatta in 2013.

OVERLEAF: Charles, Henry, Michael, Tim, and, barely visible behind them, their coxswain, Carly Heitlinger, racing at the 2010 Henley Royal Regatta.

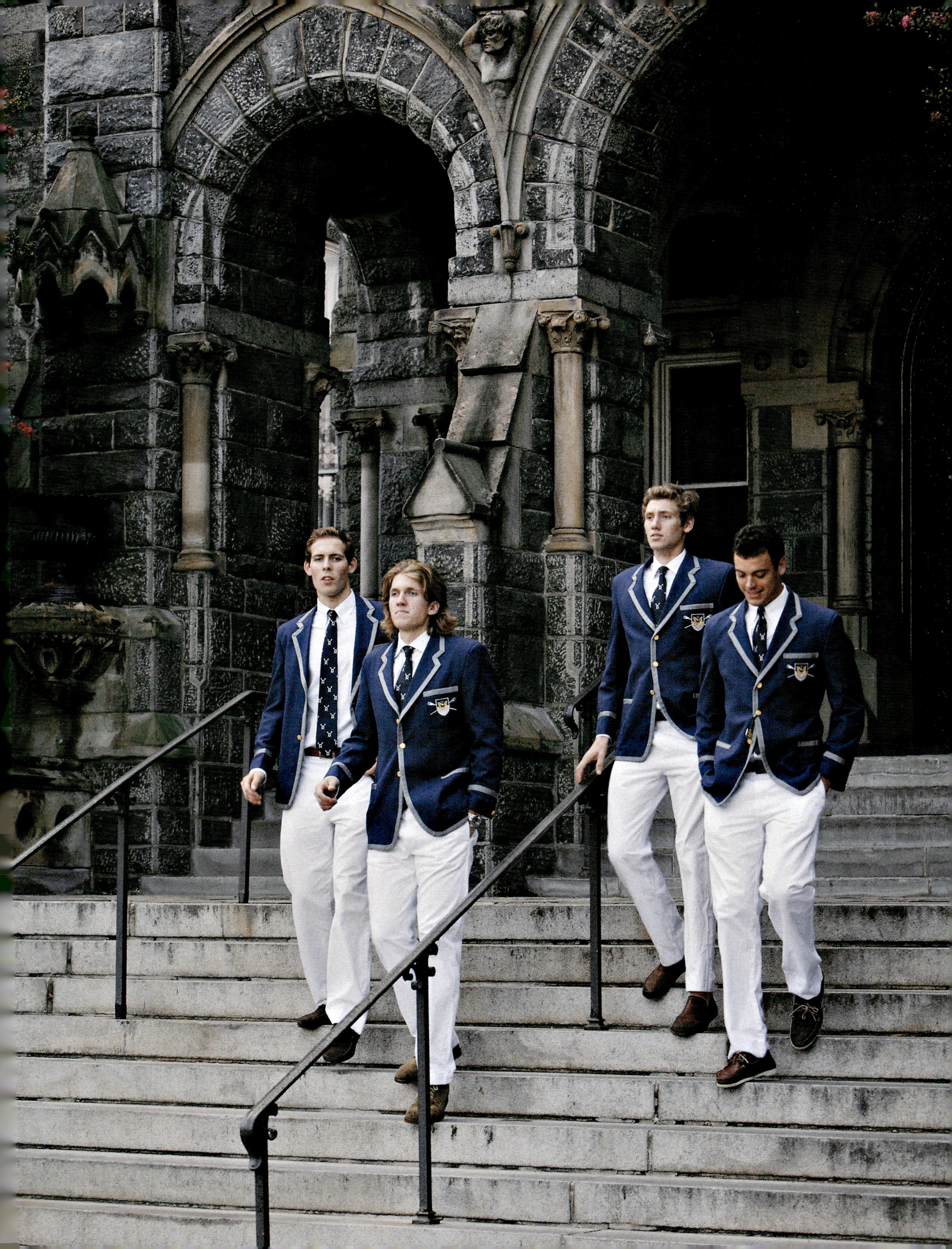

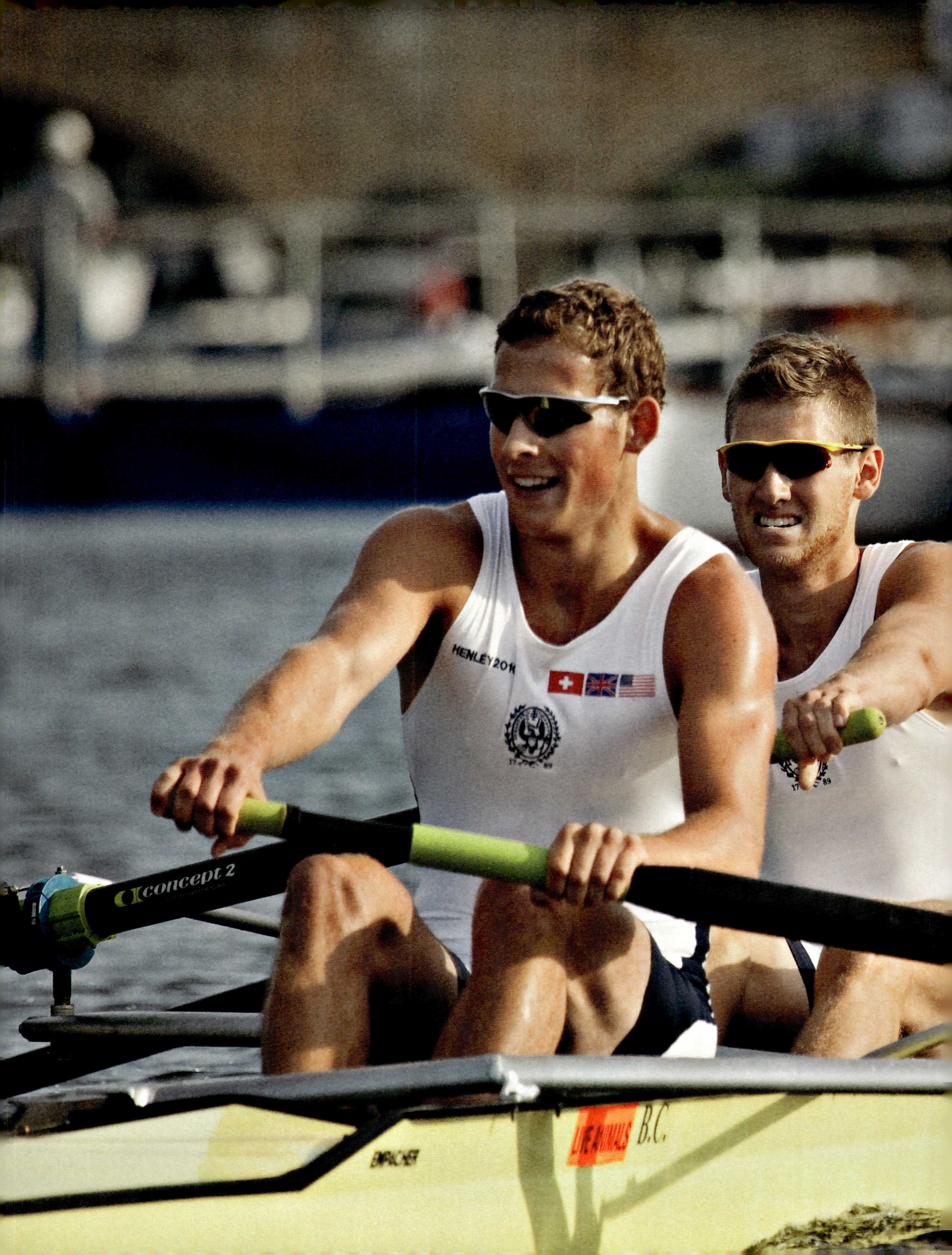
concept 2
B.C.

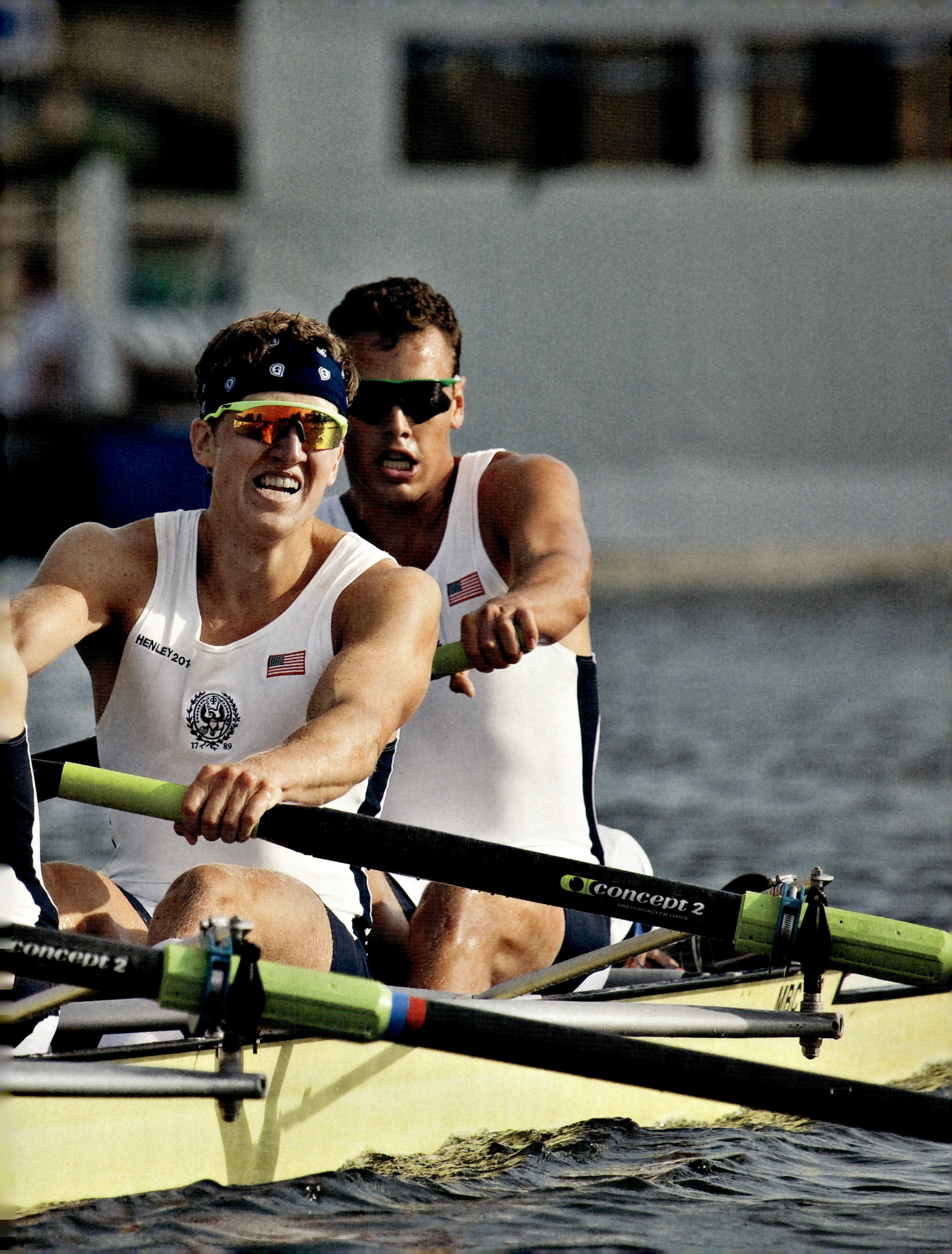
HENLEY201
concept 2
concept 2

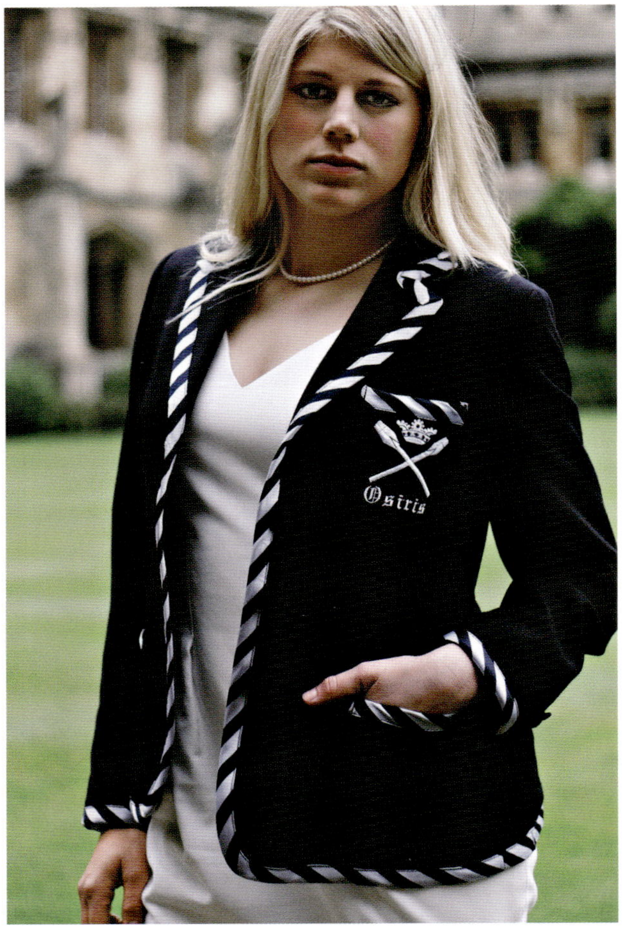

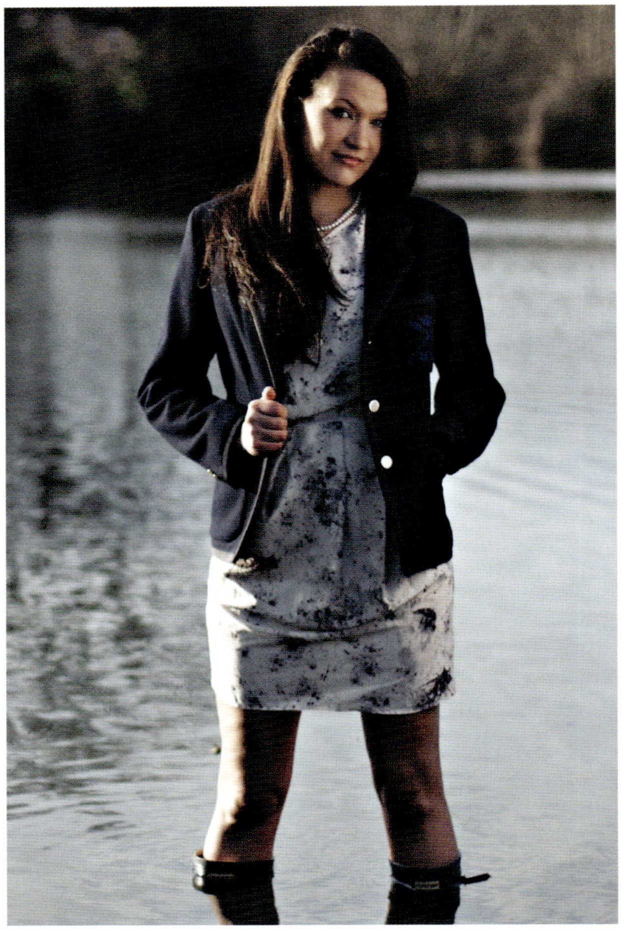

Oxford, England

Oxford University Women's Boat Club, Osiris, and Oxford University Lightweight Women's Rowing Club

AMY VARNEY, MIA VAN MANEN, SIMONE PAULSON, AMY SHARKEY

The first Oxford-Cambridge "Ladies' Boat Race" was held in 1927 on the Isis in Oxford. According to the *Times*, "large and hostile crowds gathered on the towpath" to observe the spectacle with a mixture of curiosity and snide disapproval. This "race," between Oxford University Women's Boat Club and Newnham College Boat Club, Cambridge (representing Cambridge University), was not actually a race at all; rather, it was a "time and style contest" in which the two crews were not even allowed on the water at the same time.

Today, of course, the Oxford and Cambridge women's boats compete in an annual side-by-side race like their male counterparts. To parallel the race between the men's reserve crews for Oxford and Cambridge, known as "Isis" and "Goldie," respectively, a women's reserve race is now also held between "Osiris" and "Blondie." The Lightweight Women's Boat Race, first contested in 1984, is the most recent addition to the Oxford-Cambridge varsity boat races.

The O.U.W.B.C. blazer is almost identical to the one worn by the Oxford men's Blue Boat. Whereas the men's version (the original blue blazer) has a plain pocket, the women's version sports a blazer badge: a crown and crossed blades. The Osiris blazer is dark blue with blue-and-white-striped binding.

The Oxford Lightweight Women's blazer is usually trimmed in white, but occasionally lightweight crews are given "discretionary Full Blues" (awarded for winning the lightweight boat race and finishing within 4 percent of the time of the winning openweight Blue Boat). These blazers are the same blue-on-blue as the Oxford men's and women's heavyweight crews.

ABOVE LEFT: Amy Varney in her Osiris blazer. ABOVE RIGHT: Mia van Manen in her O.U.W.B.C. blazer and Wellington boots during the 2014 Oxford floods. OPPOSITE: Simone Paulson and Amy Sharkey in their lightweight Half-Blue blazers.

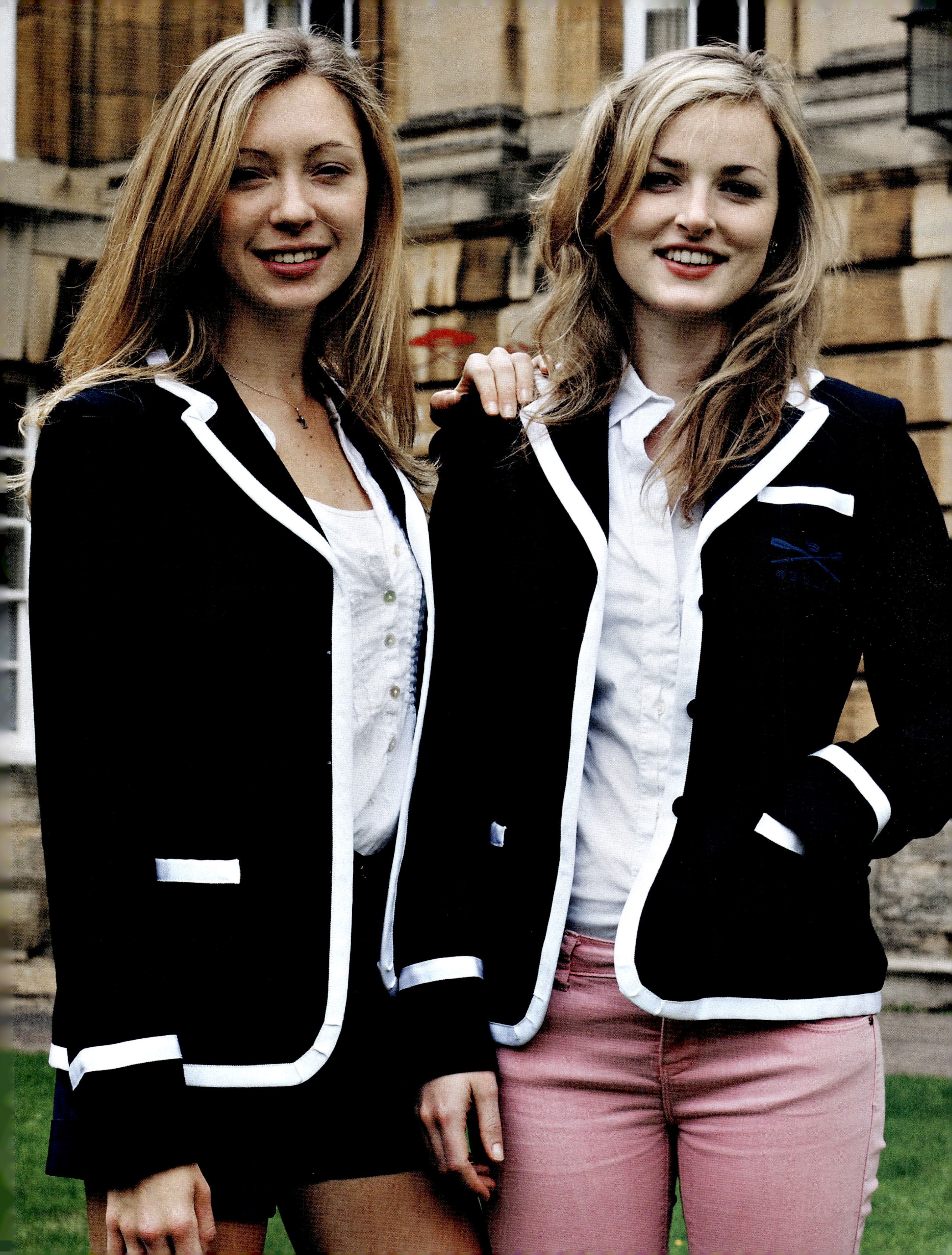

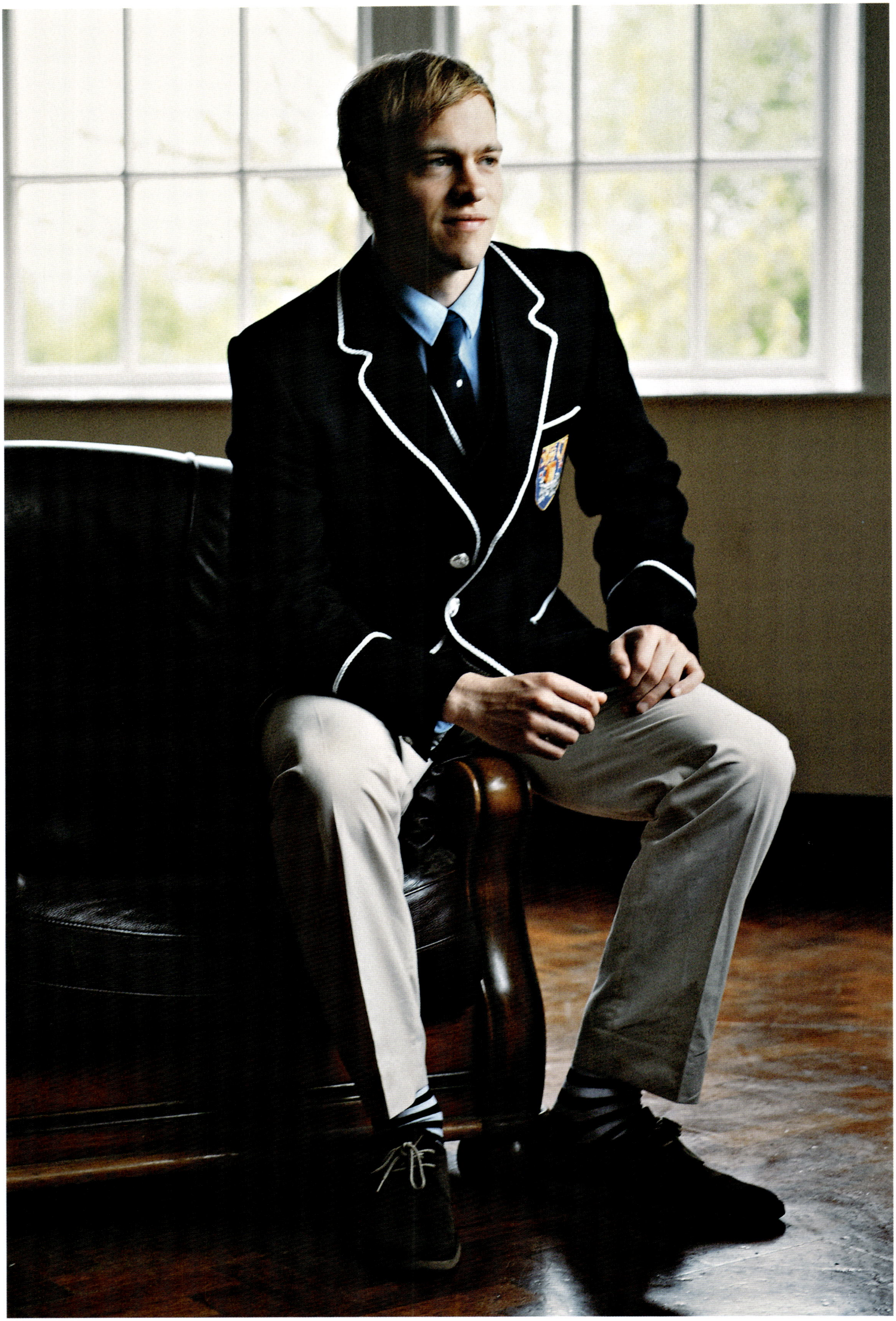

Dublin, Ireland

Dublin University Boat Club

LUKE ACHESON, CATHAL DOLAN

In the 1860s, Ireland's ancient university was home to two rival rowing clubs, confusingly named Dublin University Rowing Club and Dublin University Boat Club. The Rowing Club, which raced in blue, was the older of the two; the Boat Club, which raced in black and white, had been formed by a group that opposed the Rowing Club's alleged discrimination against Roman Catholics. The Boat Club flourished, becoming the first Irish club to win a title at the Henley Royal Regatta, among other achievements, while the Rowing Club fell into decline.

The Boat Club finally absorbed the crumbling Rowing Club in 1898, although the takeover was diplomatically billed as a merger. The matter of blazers and colors was not irrelevant in discussions about this takeover. According to club records, Boat Club Captain F. Hannyngton declared that there would be no "amalgamation in any form" if the Rowing Club tried to bring any "tomfoolery about blue blazers" into the negotiations.

The Boat Club stood on far firmer ground in the so-called "amalgamation" and was able to keep both its name and its black-and-white blazers. It did, however, add a very narrow blue stripe to its black-and-white ties in the spirit of goodwill. It is recorded that when one old Boat Club member saw the new tie years later, he brusquely remarked that the blue stripe was "no improvement."

For the club's centenary in 1936, a set of extremely elaborate regulations relating to blazers and other trappings was laid down; improbably, these rules are still rigorously followed today. They detail with ruthless precision the official patterns not only for a racing singlet, tie, black-and-white-striped socks (each sock stripe must be ⅝ inch wide), cable-knit sweater, flannel muffler, and woolen scarf for all club members, but also for distinctive blazers, caps, ties, waistcoats, dress waistcoats, trousers, singlets, and sweaters to be worn by members of the Senior Eight, Junior Eight, and Maiden (novice) Eight. In fact, the only provision for personal liberty in the lengthy set of regulations is the line: "width of trouser bottoms as desired."

The sections of this byzantine code that relate to blazers are among the most straightforward and are as follows:

> *The [Senior] blazer shall be of black flannel, with white cord piping round the edges and above the cuff. Three large silver buttons on the front, and four small silver buttons on the cuff. No dates or initials shall be worn. The badge shall be worn on the pocket, and shall be 4 ins. high by 3 ins. wide.*
>
> *The [Junior] blazer shall be of white flannel with black cord piping. Three large black buttons in front and three small ones on the cuff. The same badge as on the Senior Blazer.*
>
> *The [Maiden] blazer shall be black and white flannel in vertical stripes, each stripe shall be 2 ins. wide. Black cord piping shall be used, and three large black buttons in front and two small ones on the cuff. The same badge as on the Senior Blazer.*

OPPOSITE: Luke Acheson wears the Senior blazer and club socks.

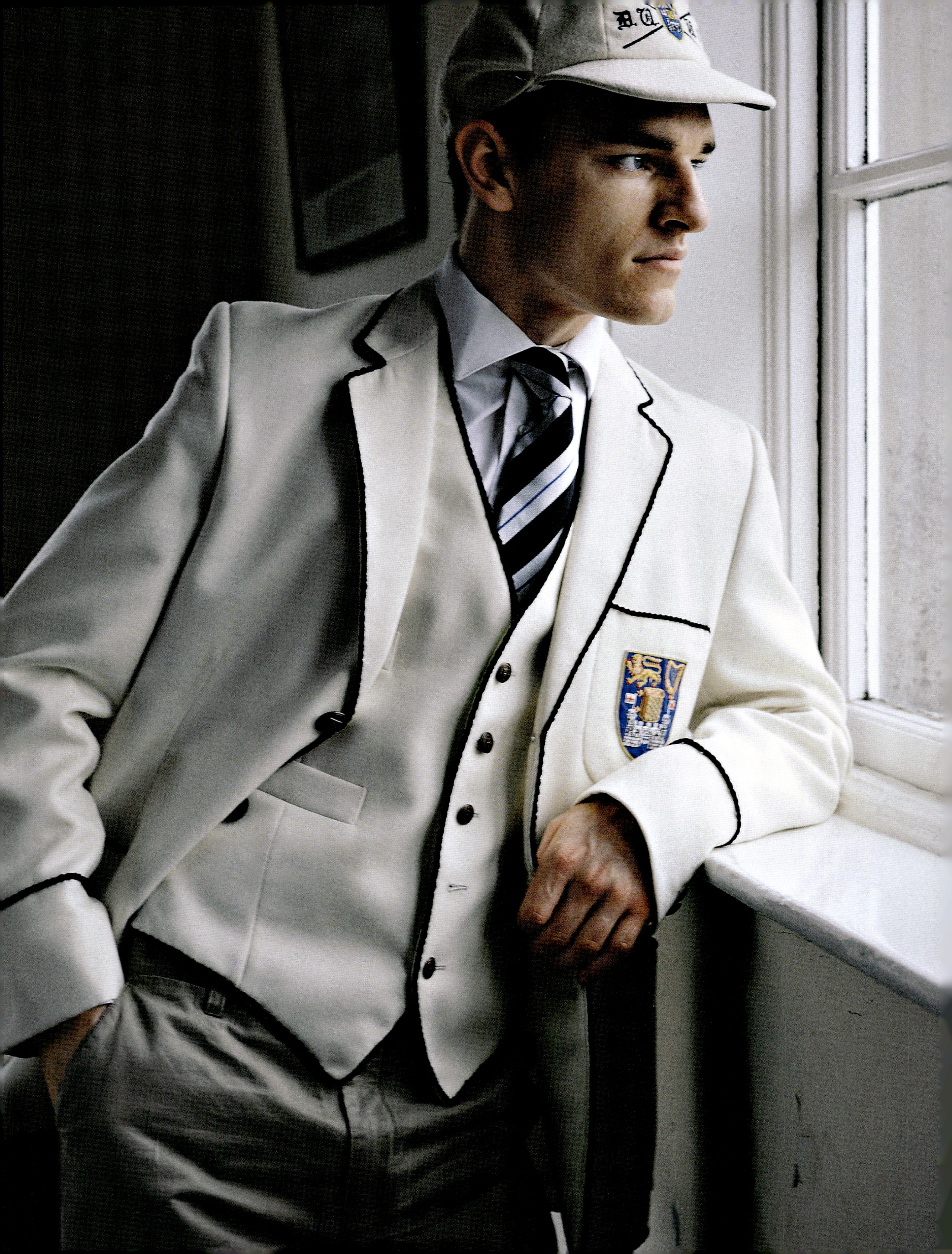

OPPOSITE:
Cathal Dolan wears the Junior blazer, waistcoat, cap, and club tie.

RIGHT:
The Maiden blazer.

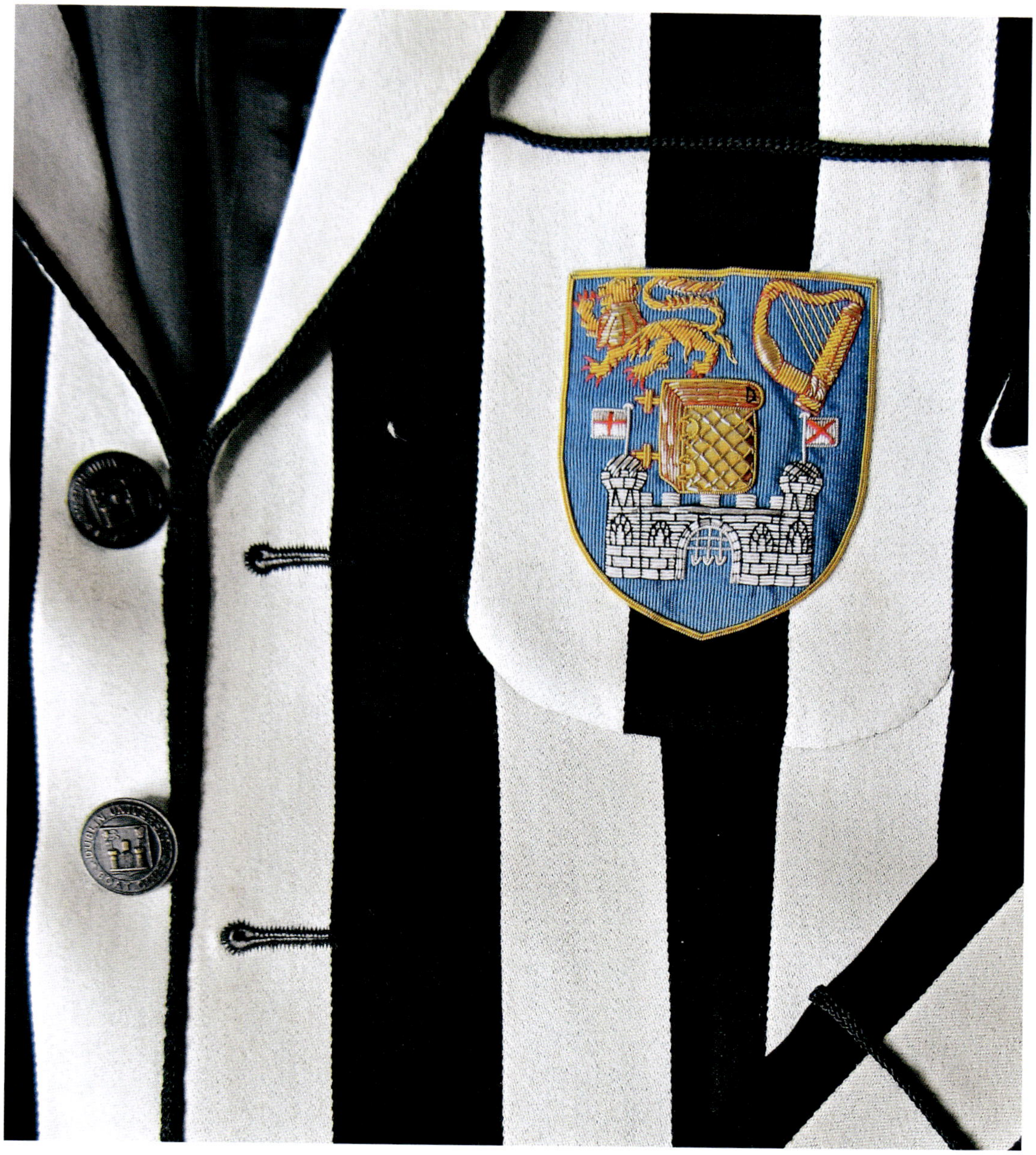

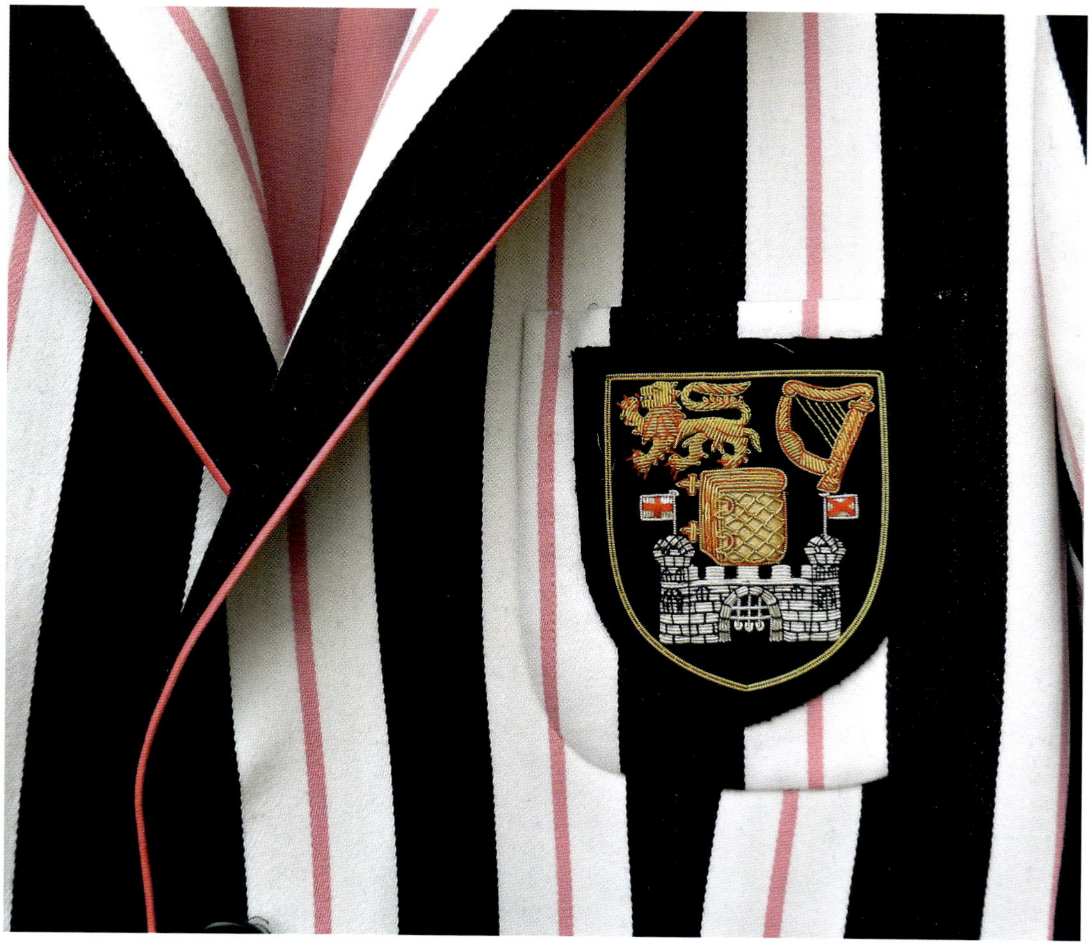

LEFT:
The Dublin University Ladies Boat Club blazer is similar to the D.U.B.C. Maiden blazer, but with pink piping and additional pink stripes.

Cambridge, Massachusetts

Buckingham Browne & Nichols School

JACK CARLSON

The first American schoolboy crew to compete at the Henley Royal Regatta in England was from Kent School (in 1927), but the first to win came from Browne & Nichols School two years later. The B&N crew had white-trimmed black blazers made especially for the historic trip.

Nicknamed "Brawn & Knuckles" by fans and rivals, the school was rarely beaten in the twenties and thirties, and their regular races against the likes of Kent, Tabor, M.I.T., Union Boat Club, Rindge Technical School, and the Harvard freshmen were covered enthusiastically by the *Boston Globe*—too enthusiastically for the tastes of Headmaster George Nicholas, who told the paper in 1929, "We deplore the over publicity given to schoolboy athletics."

When the all-boys Browne & Nichols merged with the all-girls Buckingham School in 1974, the amalgamated school adopted Buckingham's blue-and-gold colors, but the rowing team maintained B&N's black-and-white blades and uniforms.

Since the first trip in 1929, the school has made many journeys to Henley—the most recent in 2004—and also has the distinction of being the first, last, and only American school crew ever to compete in the Soviet Union.

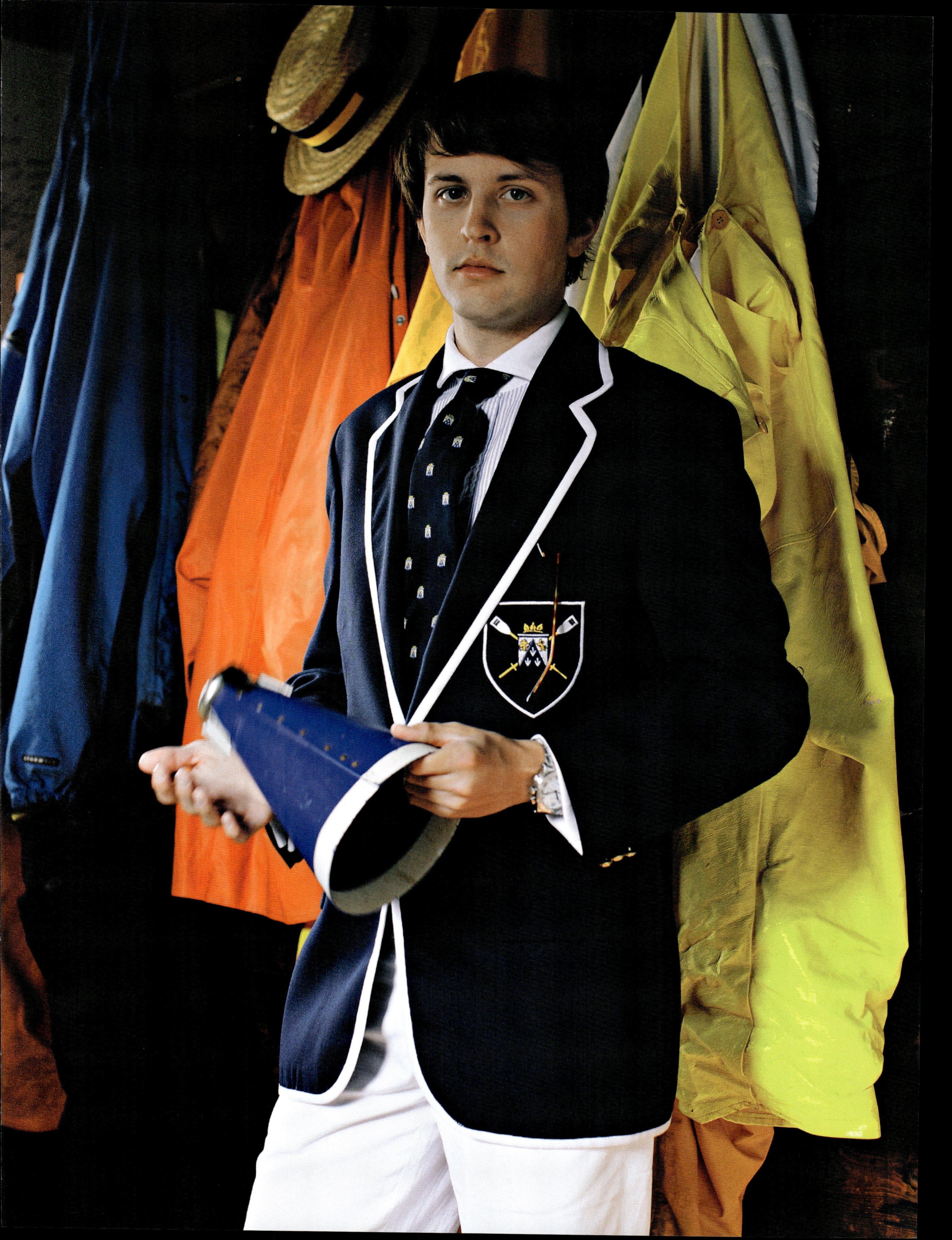

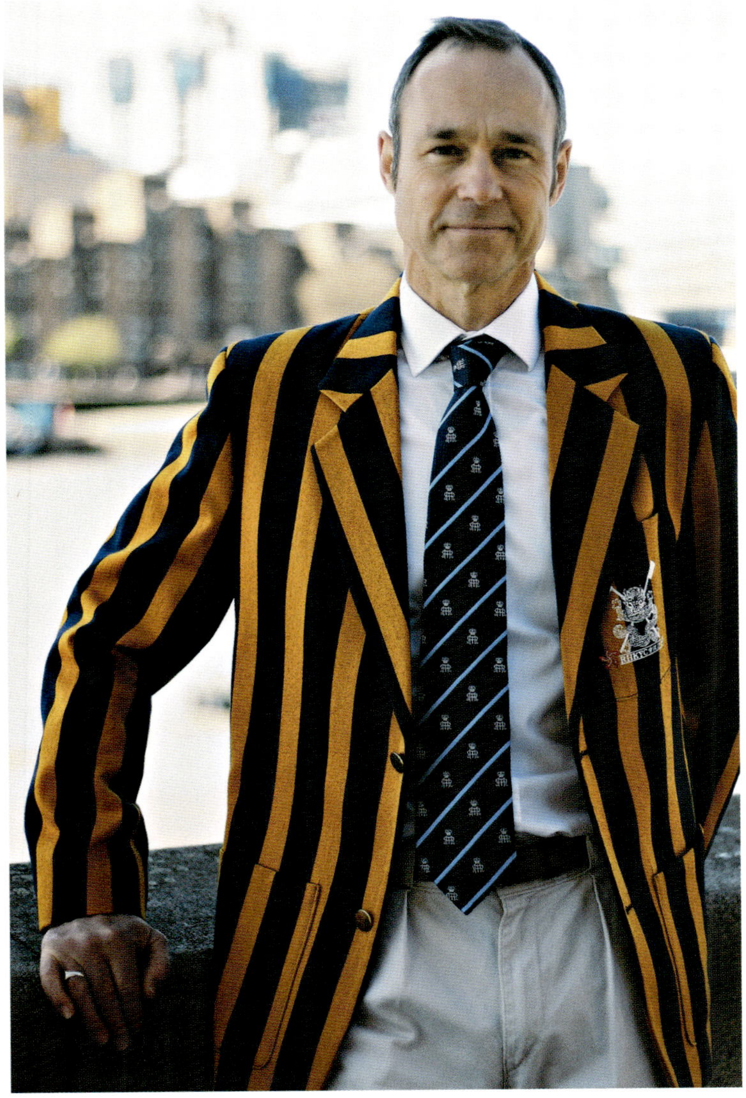

Kellett Island, Hong Kong

Royal Hong Kong Yacht Club

MARK NORTHWOOD

In 1837, a group of hearty rowers established the first modern athletic club in China, Canton Rowing Club, in what is now Guangzhou. It is reported that for fun, they would occasionally row the nearly hundred miles through pirate-plagued waters to Hong Kong. The community of Far Eastern rowing clubs was soon expanded to include Hong Kong Boat Club, which amalgamated with Royal Hong Kong Yacht Club in 1905. Mark Northwood has represented the blue and gold at major regattas in Hong Kong, the United States, and Great Britain.

Bewdley, England

Bewdley Rowing Club

ALEXANDER "TEX" HOLDEN-SMITH

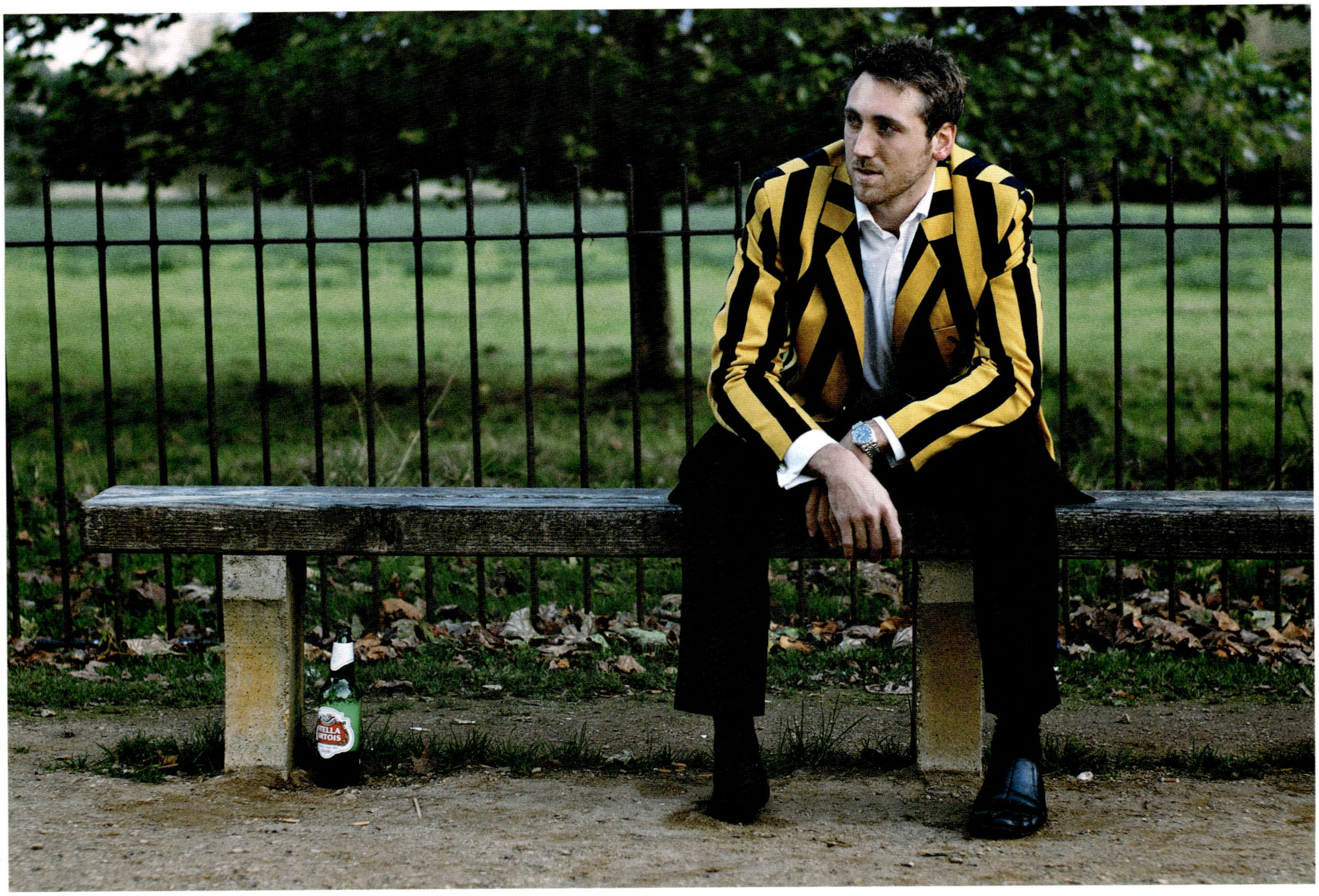

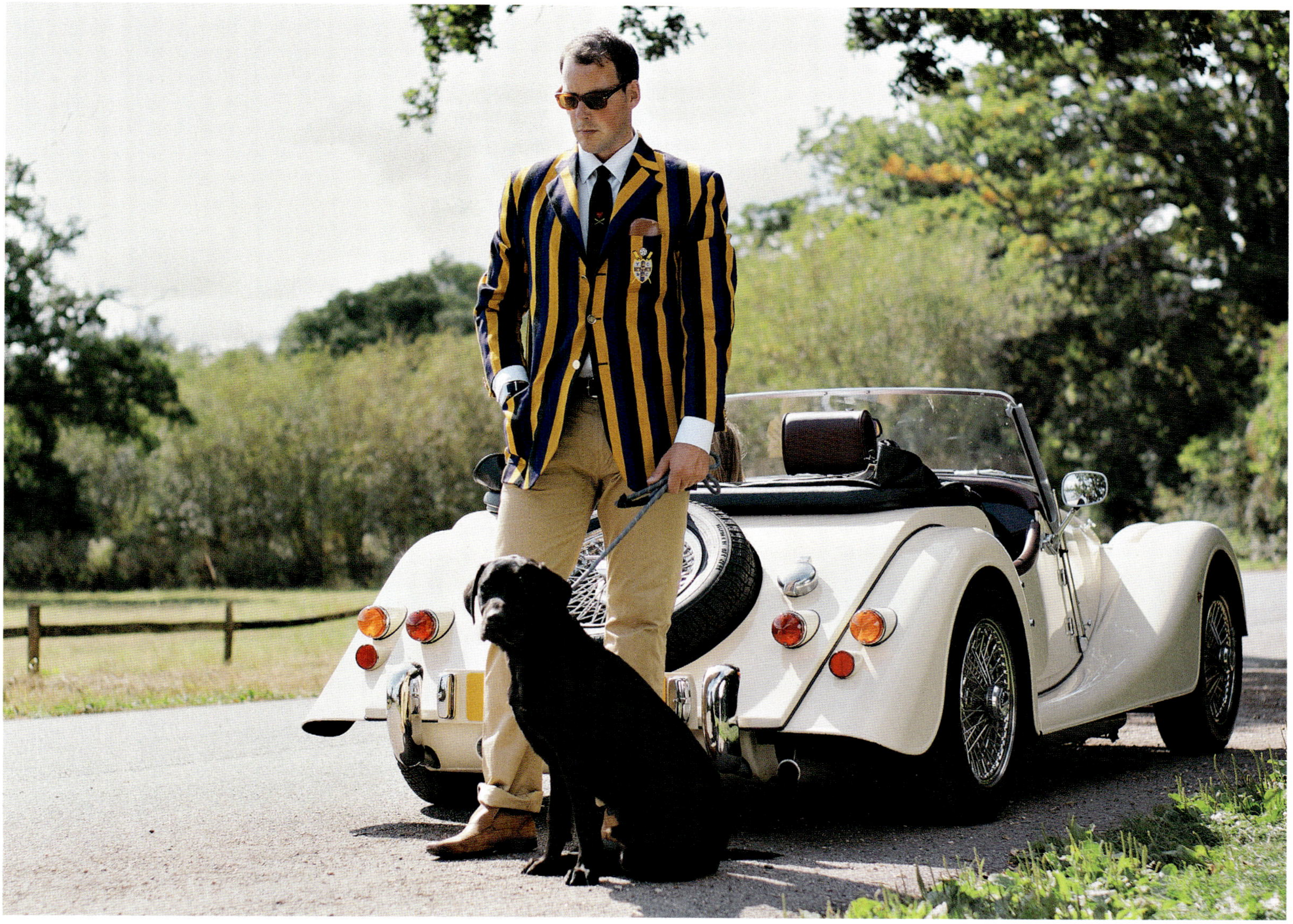

York, England

York City Rowing Club

WILL TODD

Cambridge, England

Clare Boat Club, Cambridge

JOEL JENNINGS, ANNIE ELKINGTON

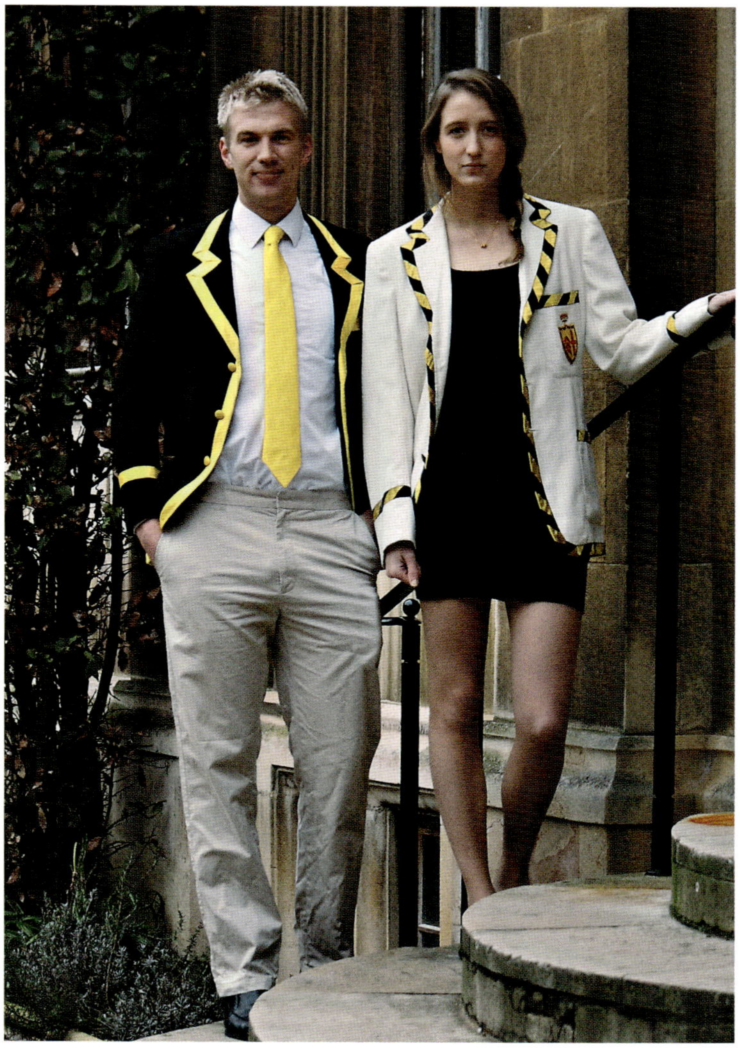

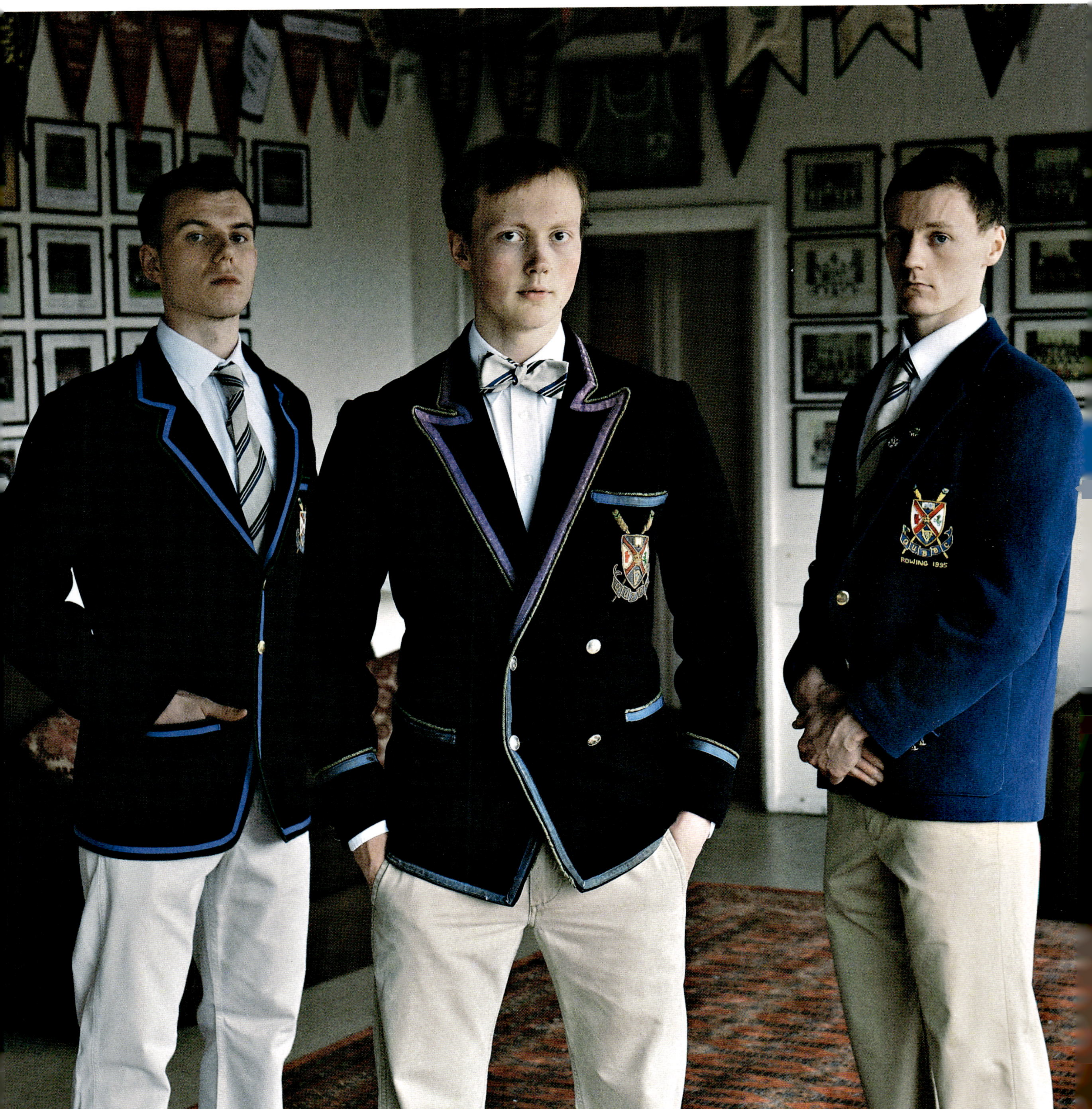
Q.U.B.B.C
ROWING 1995

Belfast, Northern Ireland

Queen's University Belfast Boat Club

PETER GILLANDERS, ANDREW LITTLE,
CHARLES CUNNINGHAM

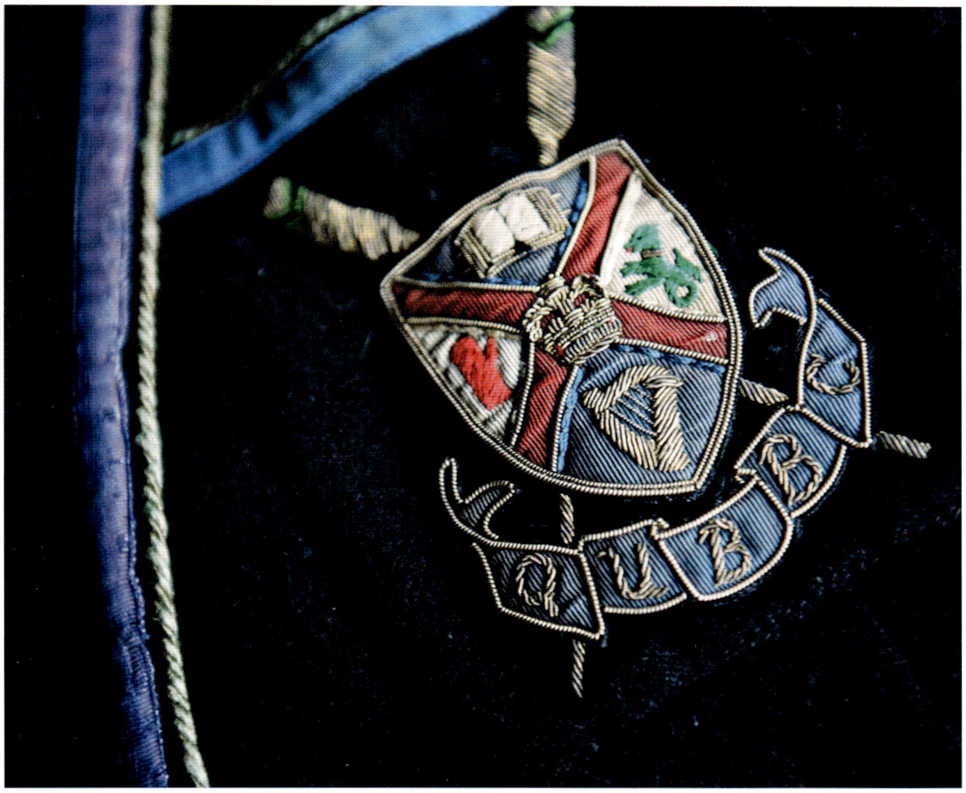

Blazers have been important to Queen's University Belfast Boat Club since rowing was established at the university in 1931–32. One of the club's first acts was the decision to use white blazers with black-and-green edging. At the time, the full university colors—royal blue, emerald, and black—were reserved for well-established sports. By 1936, the club had started its switch to black blazers and had begun using royal blue in its colors.

There are three versions of the Queen's University Belfast blazer today. The first is the standard club blazer: black with blue and emerald trim, club buttons, and badge. The second is the Captain's blazer: a double-breasted variation on the club blazer with purple trim on the lapels. And the third is the Blues blazer, solid royal blue, awarded to rowers who have received a "Blue"—the university's top sporting award.

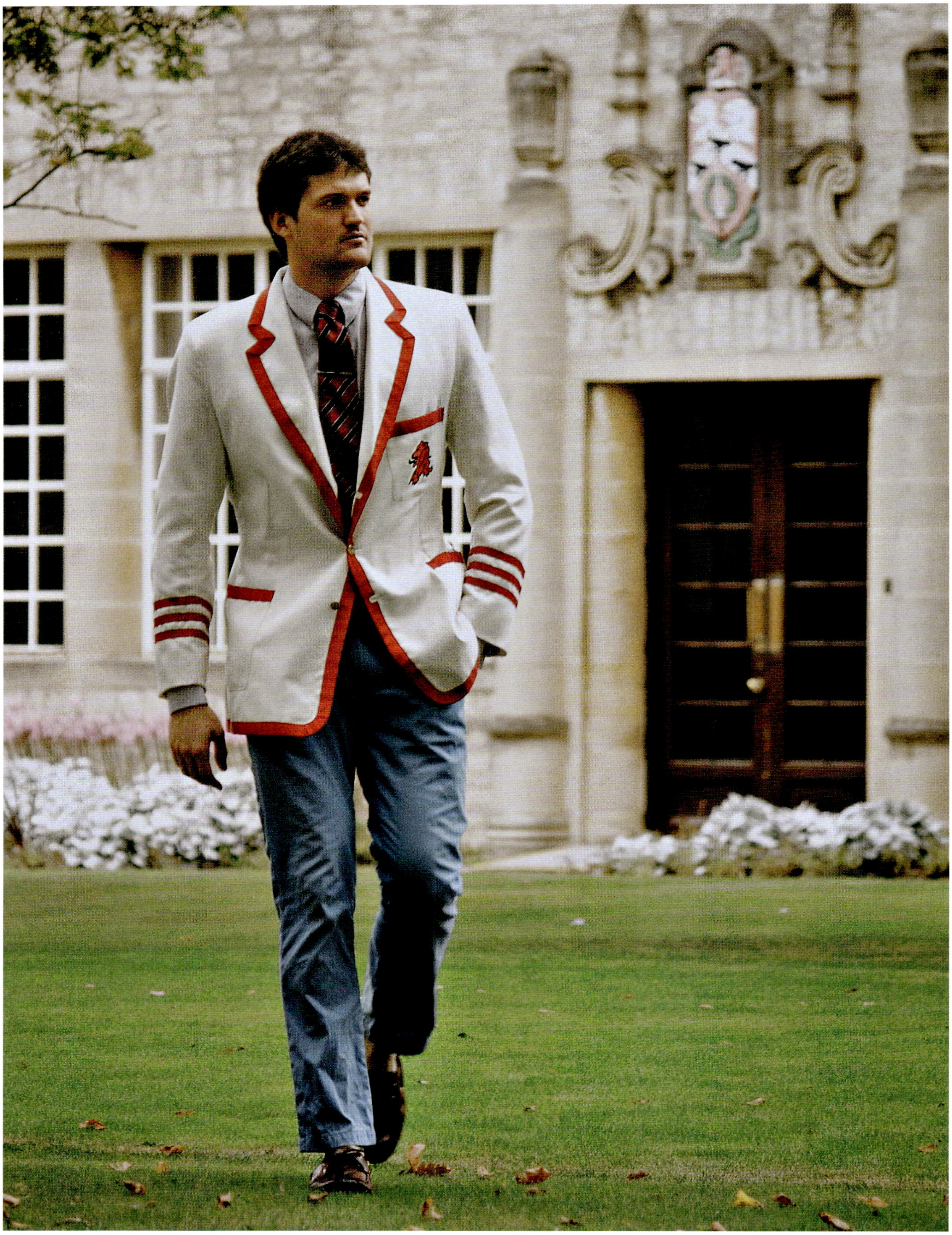

Oxford, England

St. Anne's College Boat Club, Oxford

BEN MANSFIELD

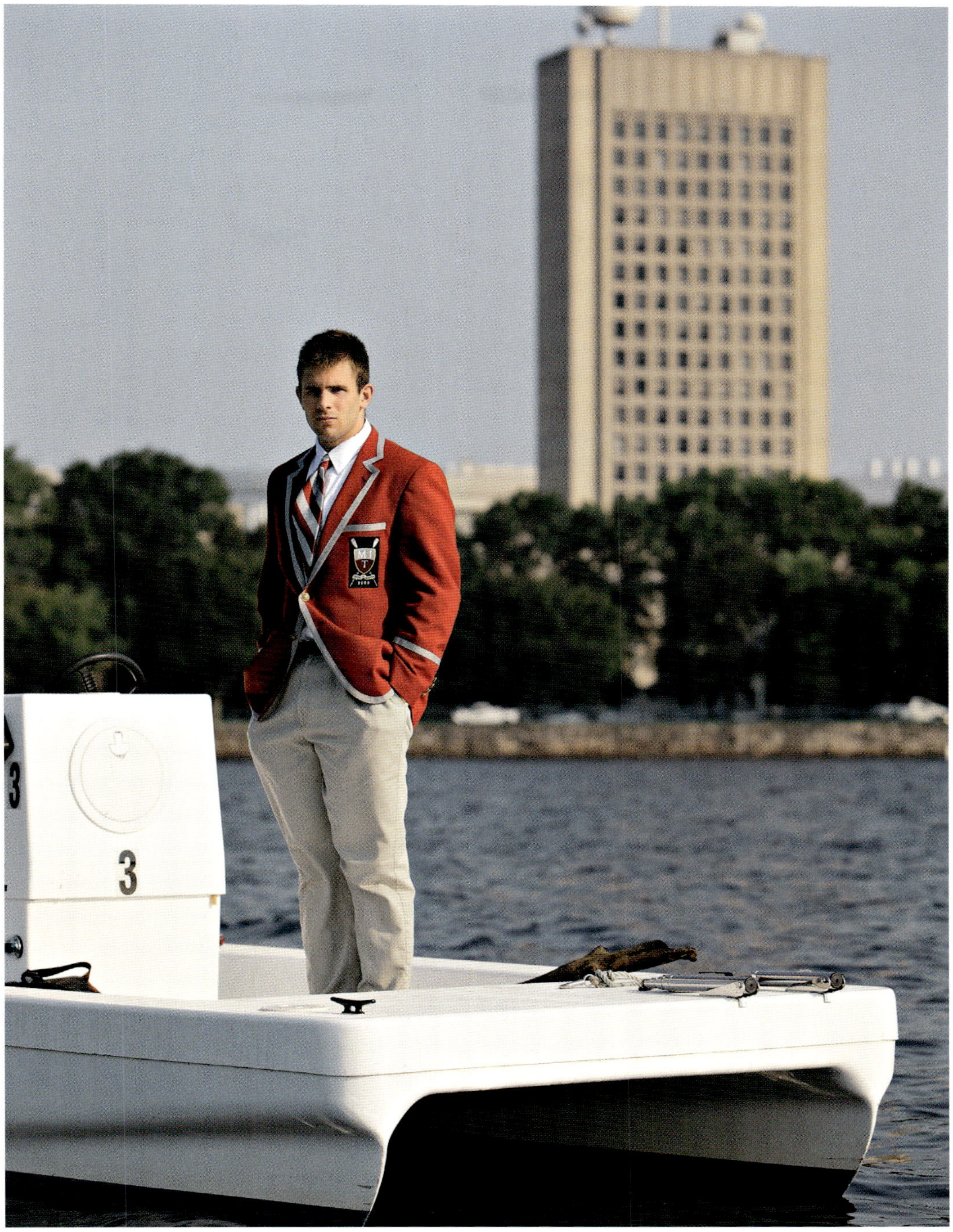

Cambridge, Massachusetts

Massachusetts Institute of Technology

LUCAS GOODMAN

Although M.I.T.'s rowing program has a storied history, in recent years the team has often struggled to compete with its opposition in the Eastern Sprints league. In 2009, however, the varsity heavyweight eight recaptured a bit of the club's past glory, defeating Princeton for the first time in thirty-four years and making it through a round at the Henley Royal Regatta.

OVERLEAF: The Engineers racing at Henley in 2009.

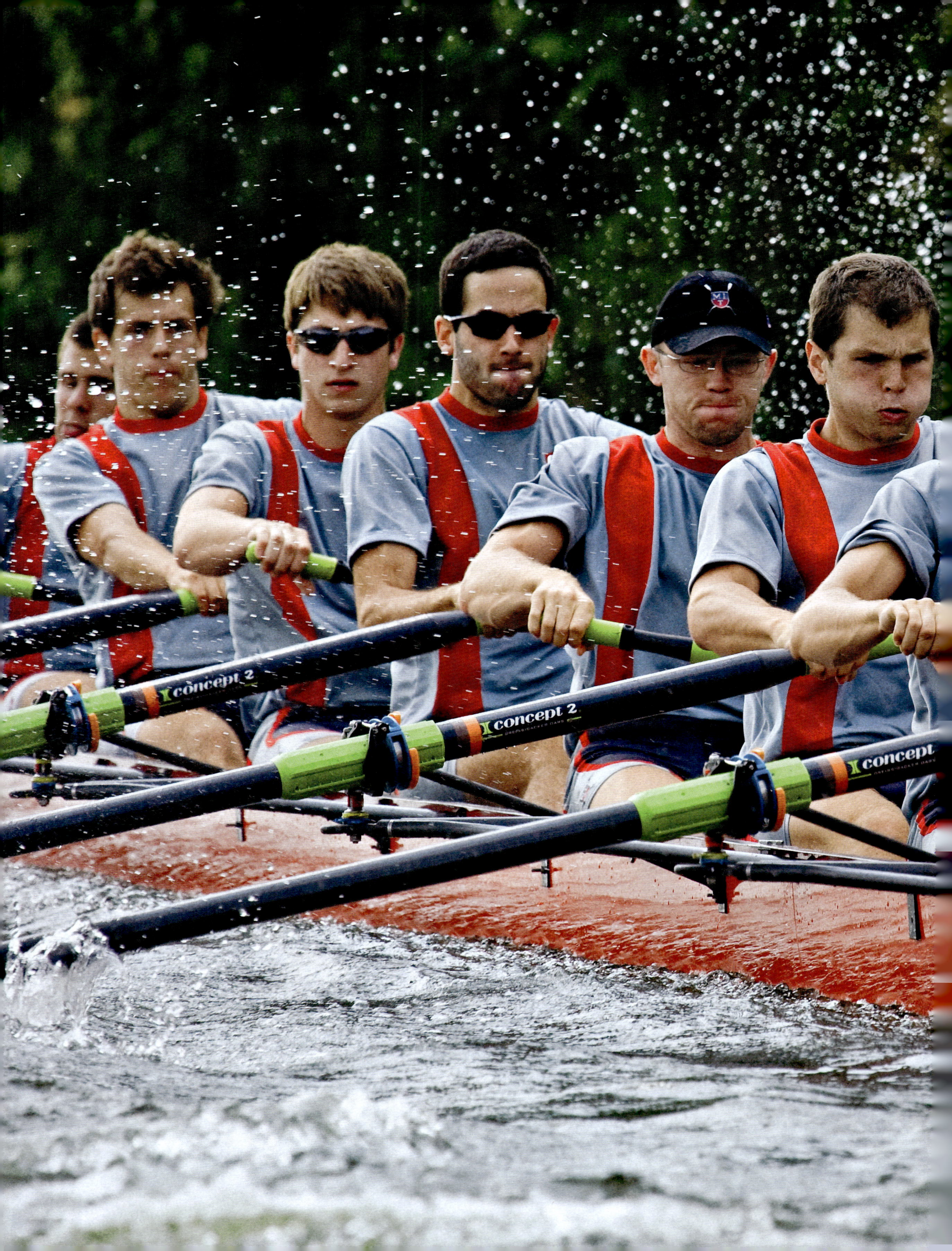
concept 2
concept 2
concept

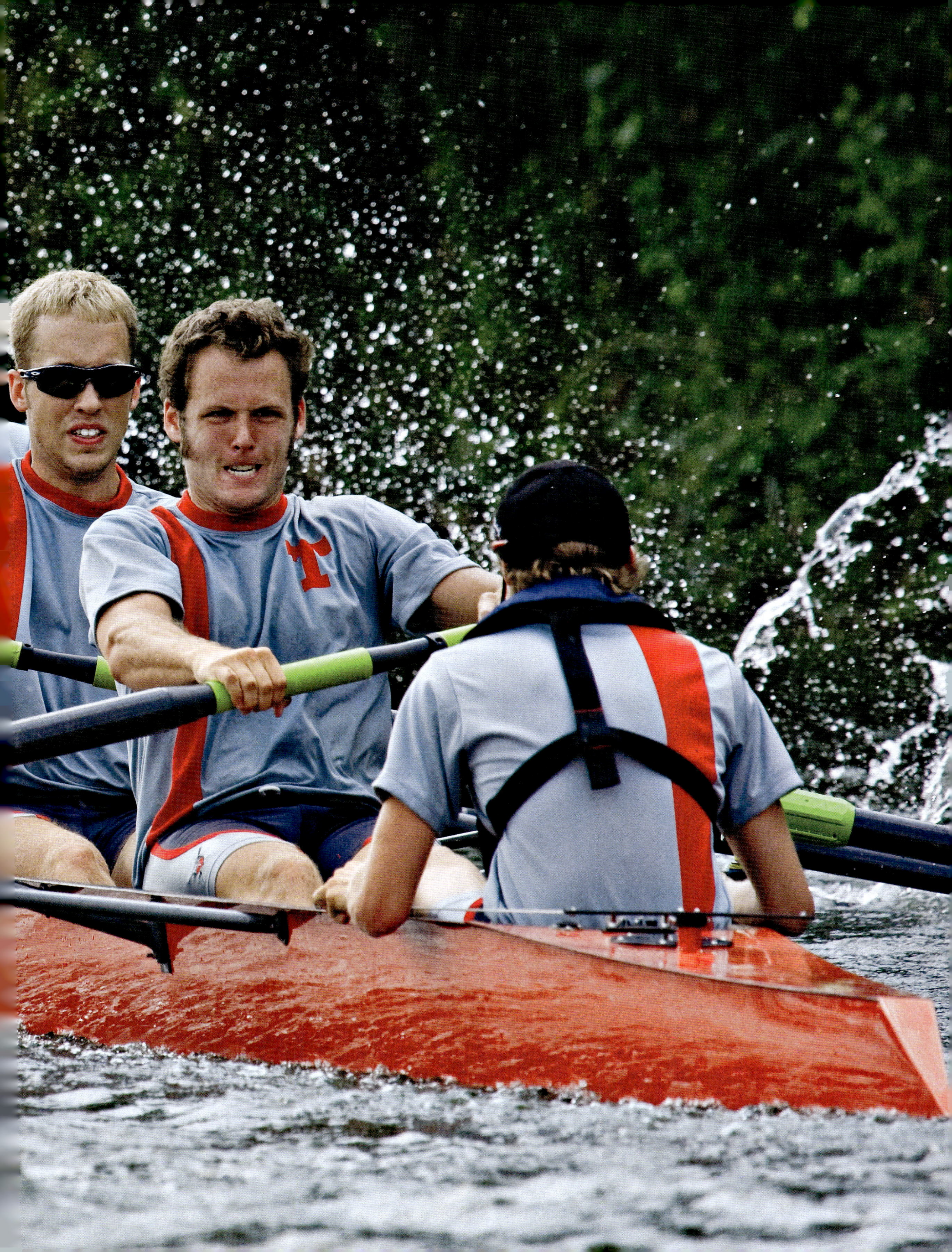

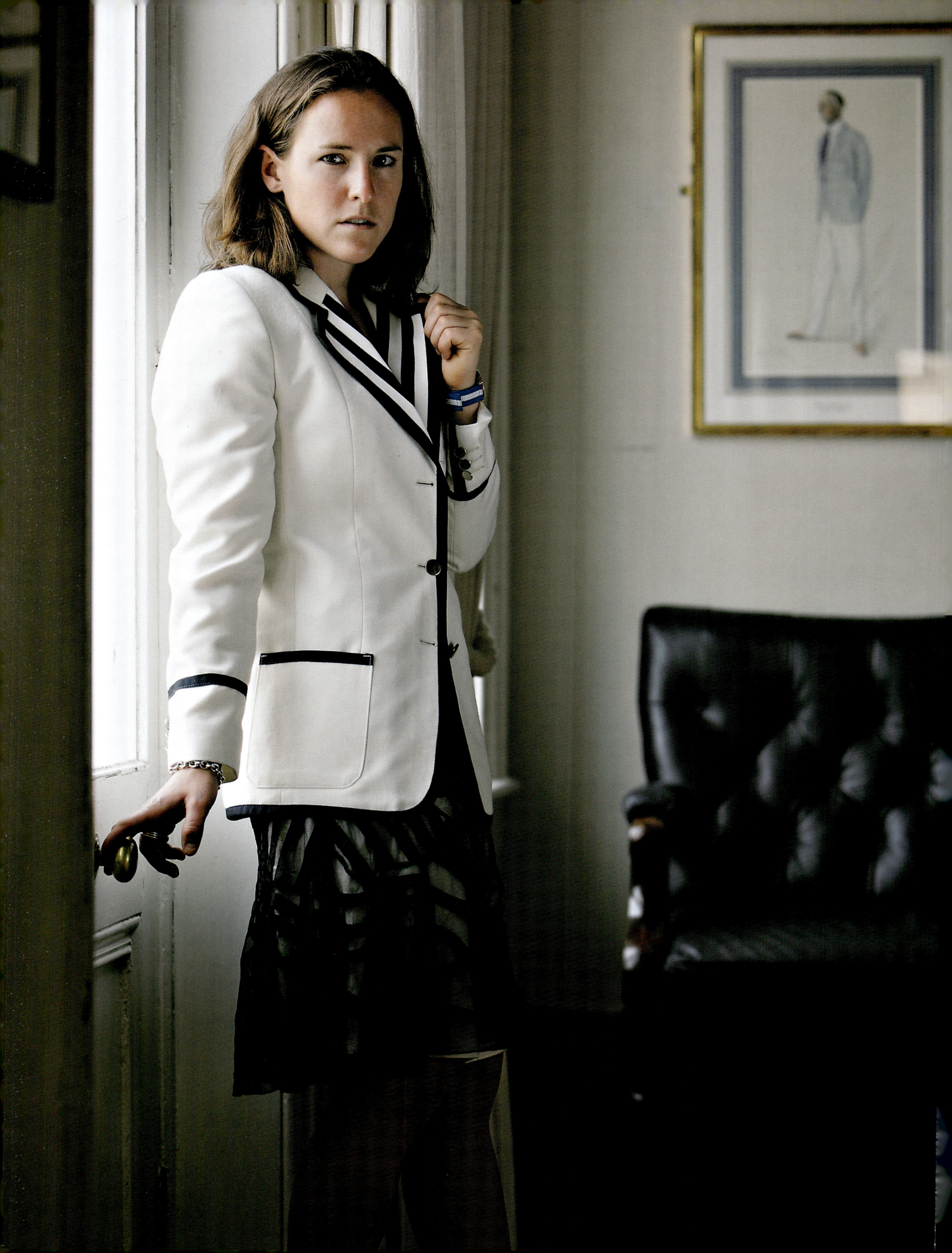

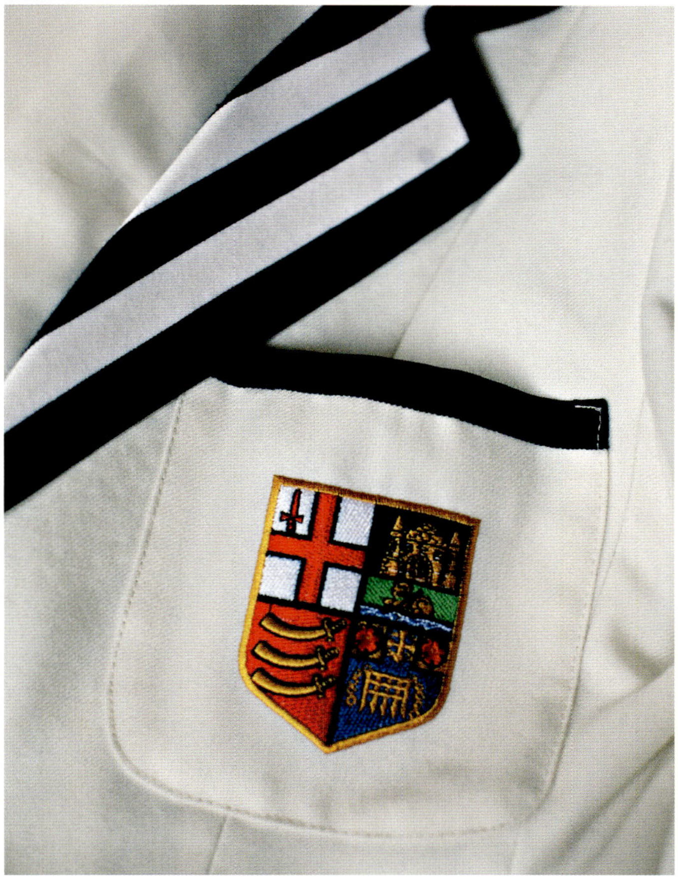

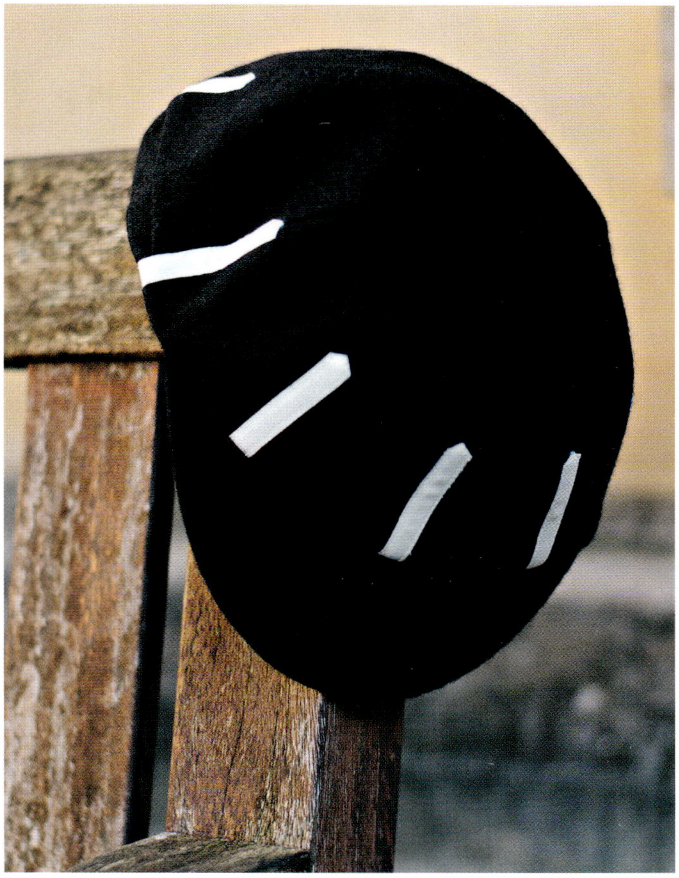

London, England

London Rowing Club

SOPHIE HOSKING MBE

Except for the pocket badge, which is a fairly recent (and unofficial) addition, the London Rowing Club blazer has remained virtually unchanged since the club's beginnings in the 1850s. The jacket is distinctive primarily for its blue-and-white-striped lapel facings. The L.R.C. cap —dark blue with white "blade" tabs—is also unmistakable and is frequently seen at Henley, worn by members on the bank and in racing crews. 1960s Formula One legend Graham Hill rowed in twenty Henley finals for London (winning eight) and famously used the London Rowing Club cap design on his racing helmet.

Sophie Hosking is a longtime member of London Rowing Club and an Olympic champion for Great Britain in the lightweight women's double sculls. With her partner Kat Copeland and under the guidance of London Rowing Club coach Paul Reedy, she won Britain's first gold medal in a lightweight women's event.

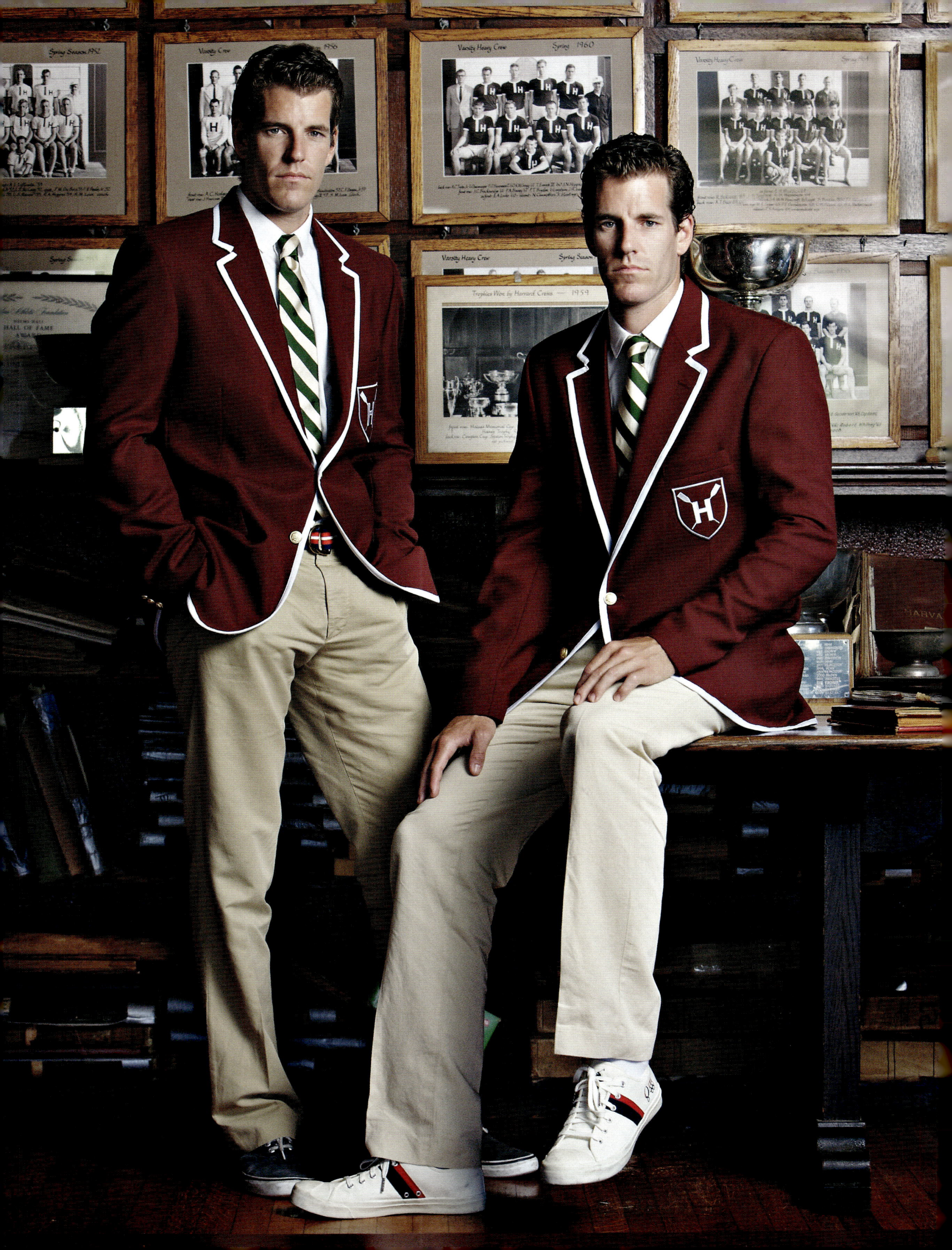
Spring Season 1952
Varsity Crew
Varsity Heavy Crew
Spring 1960
Varsity Heavy Crew
Trophies Won by Harvard Crews — 1959
HALL OF FAME

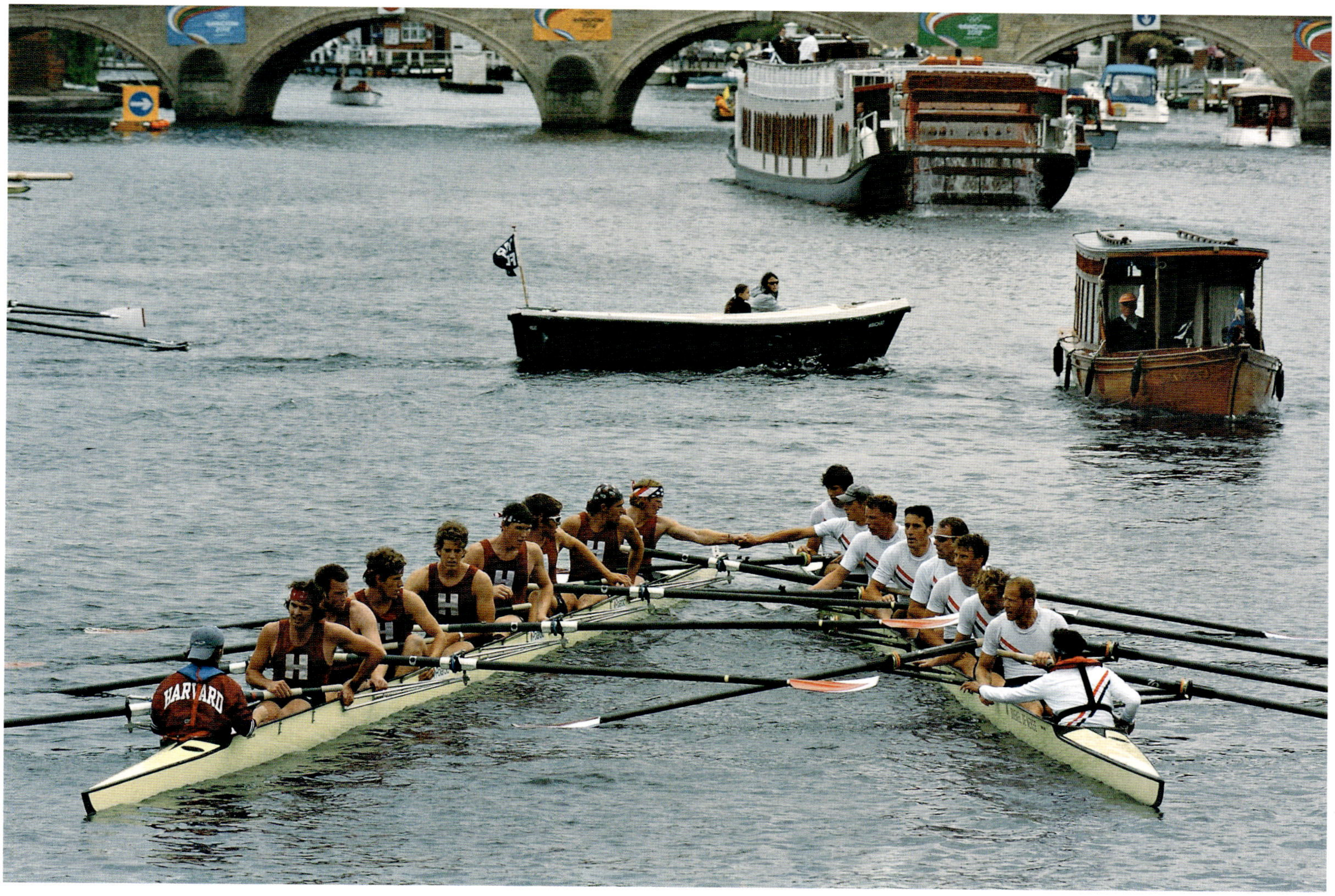

Cambridge, Massachusetts

Harvard University Boat Club

TYLER WINKLEVOSS, CAMERON WINKLEVOSS

On August 3, 1852, America's first intercollegiate sporting event was held on Lake Winnipesaukee in New Hampshire. Sponsored by the Boston, Concord & Montreal Railroad, it was also the first instance of corporate involvement in American college sports. The event, the first-ever Harvard-Yale Race, featured three crews: the *Oneida* from Harvard, and the *Shawmut* and the *Undine* from Yale. The Harvard crew, wearing blue and white, won, with the Yale *Shawmut* crew, wearing red and white, finishing second.

It was not until the 1858 Beacon Cup Regatta in Boston that Harvard adopted its famous crimson. The Harvard oarsmen realized that they would be racing no fewer than fourteen other crews and decided—for the sake of their large cheering section on the shore—that they needed to adopt a vibrant uniform "other than the underclothes in which they customarily rowed," as Harvard historian Samuel Morison put it. Two of the Harvard rowers (and scions of two of Boston's oldest Brahmin families), Charles Eliot—later president of the university—and Benjamin Crowninshield, paid a visit to E. E. Hovey and Company to request "handkerchiefs of strong, fast color." They chose a "handsome red of certain Chinese silk handkerchiefs," which they wore as bandannas.

The Harvard rowing blazer has changed its appearance slightly over the years. At various times, Harvard crews have worn black-and-crimson-striped blazers, cream-colored blazers, and plain crimson blazers. In the modern era, however, Harvard heavyweight crews have consistently worn crimson blazers with narrow white trim and the block "H" and crossed

ABOVE: The Harvard crew and the Dutch Olympic eight pull their boats together and shake hands after racing in the final of Henley's Grand Challenge Cup in 2004.

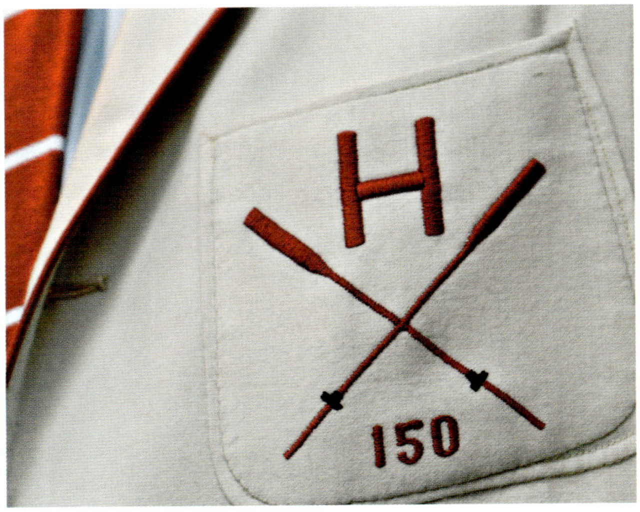

blades on the pocket. Captains wear an inverted version of this jacket (white with crimson trim), while lightweights have the number "150" (lbs.), their original weight limit, embroidered beneath the "H."

Cameron and Tyler Winklevoss earned their crimson blazers representing the university in the premier event at the Henley Royal Regatta, the Grand Challenge Cup, in 2004. After winning the Harvard-Yale Race and the American national championship, their Harvard crew raced at the Rowing World Cup in Lucerne before losing narrowly to the Dutch Olympic eight in the Henley final; this race, and Cameron and Tyler's Harvard blazers, were immortalized in the film *The Social Network*.

ABOVE:
A Harvard lightweight captain's blazer.

RIGHT:
Tyler and Cameron in Harvard's Newell Boathouse.

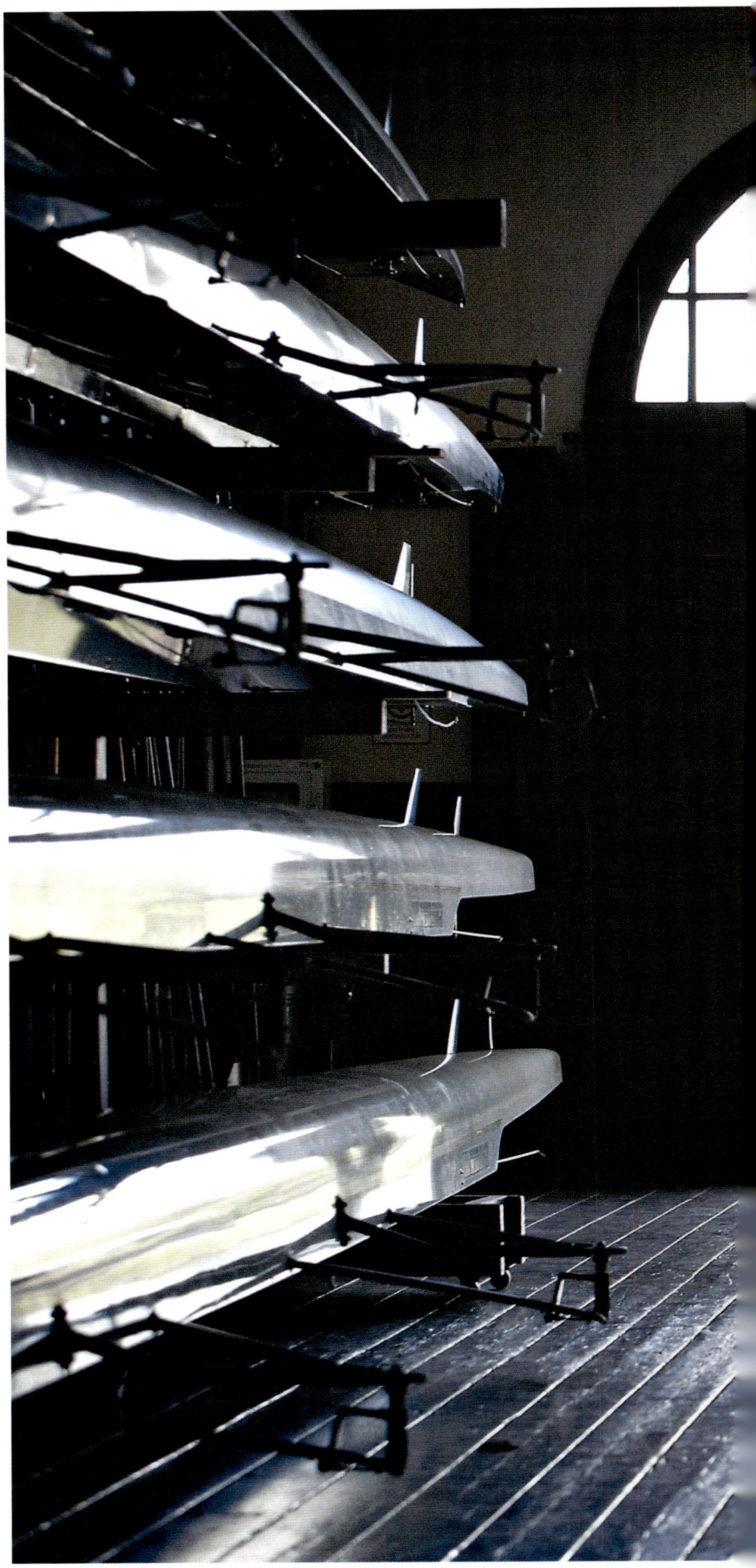

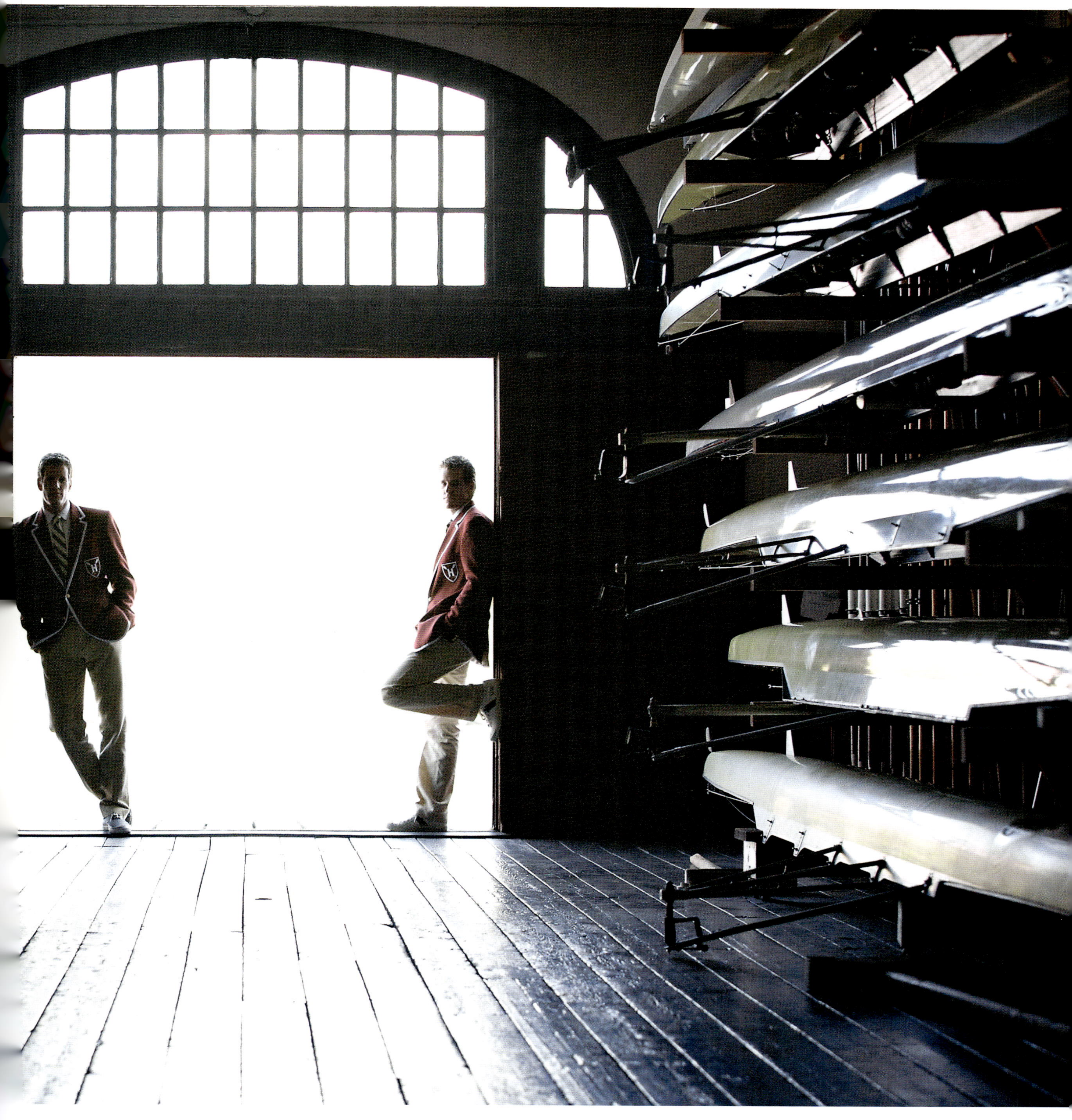

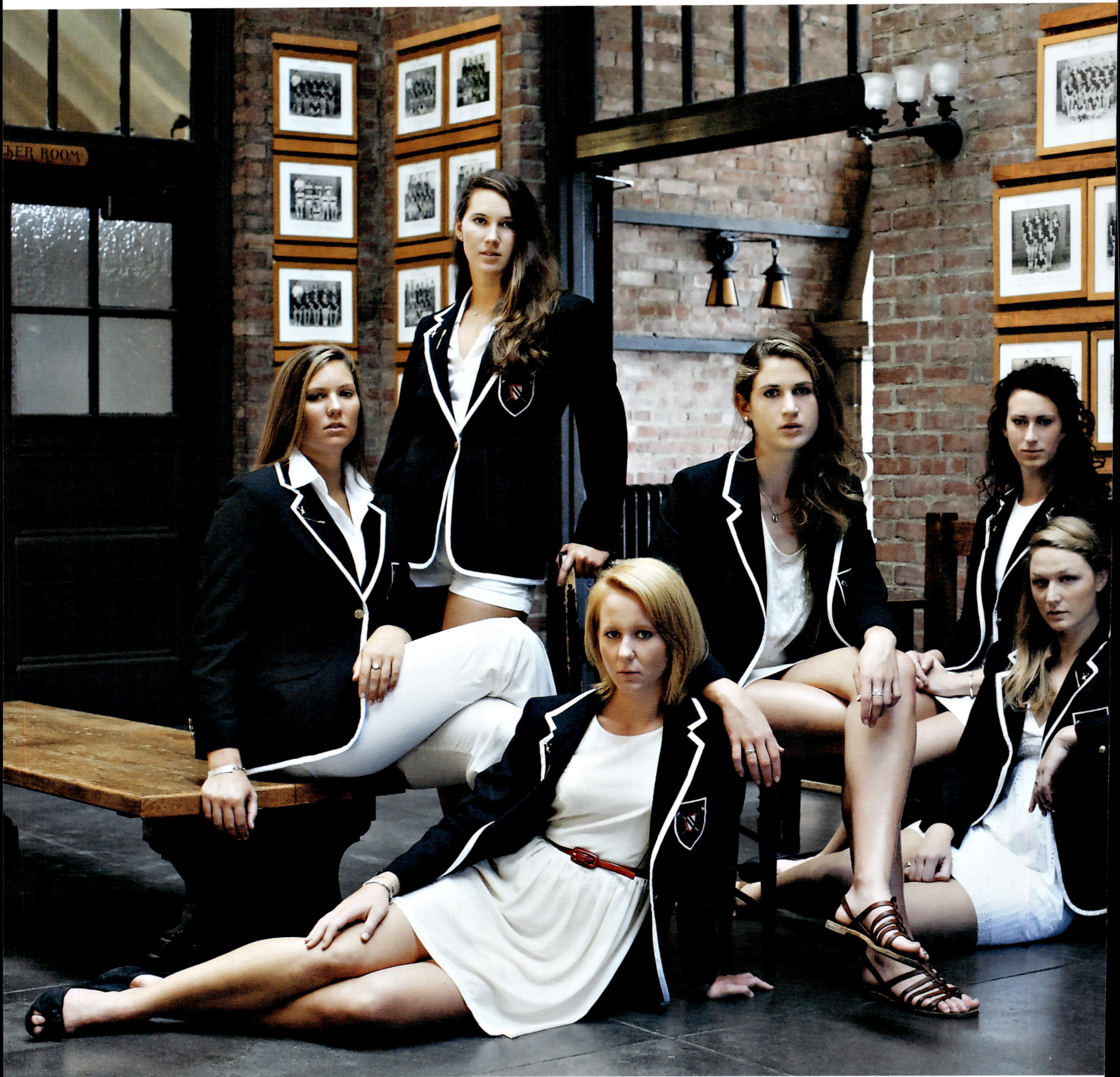

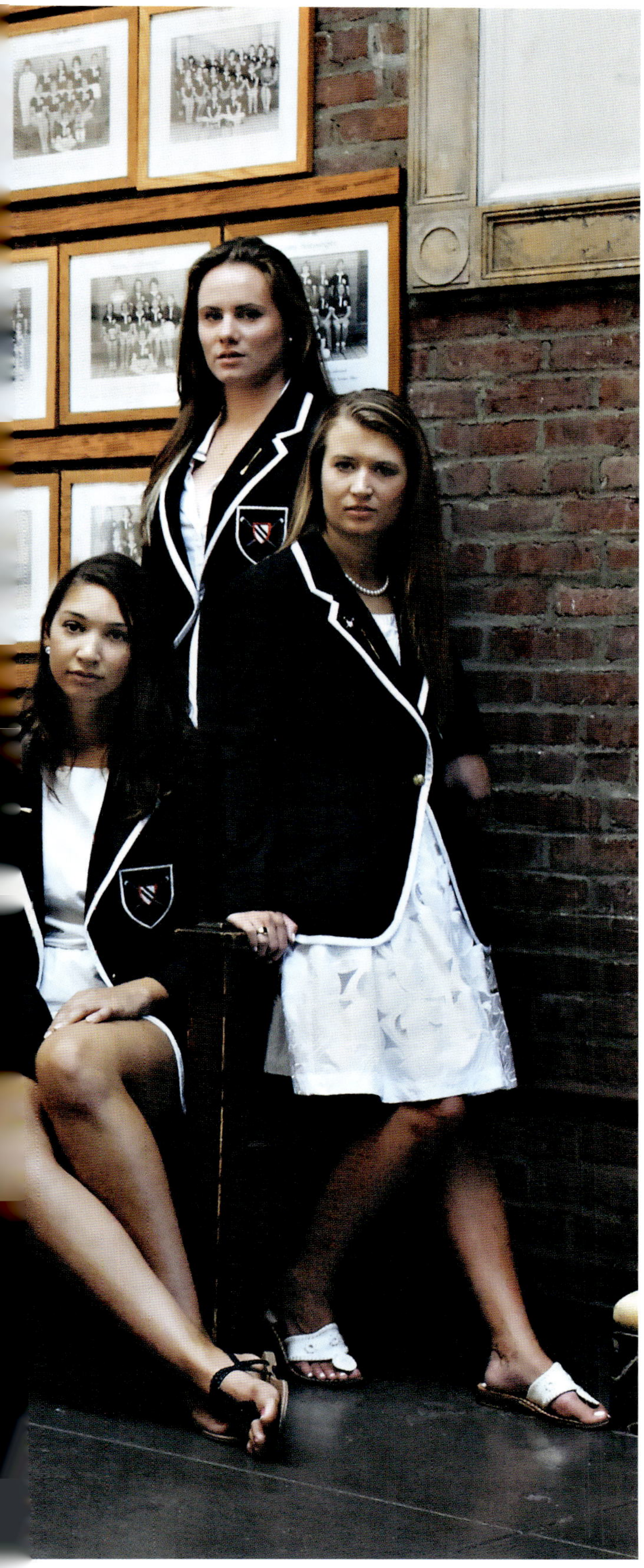

Cambridge, Massachusetts

Radcliffe

COURTNEY DIEKMA, SHELLEY PEARSON,
LUCY GRINALDS, MIMI TANSKI,
JENNA GREGOIRE, LIZ SOUTTER, SCOUT MORAN,
MARY MAGINNIS, JILL CARLSON

Before 1977, there were two undergraduate colleges within Harvard University: Harvard College for men and Radcliffe College for women. When the two combined, each women's sports team in the university was allowed to decide if it would continue to compete under the Radcliffe name and with Radcliffe's black-and-white colors, or wear crimson and compete as Harvard. Every team—with one exception—chose to adopt the name and notorious crimson of Harvard. Only the women's rowing team voted to stick with tradition: in doing so, they hoped to honor the Radcliffe women who had founded the team six years earlier.

Today, Harvard's oarswomen continue to compete under the Radcliffe banner, racing with black-and-white blades and in black-and-white uniforms proudly emblazoned with the old Radcliffe College coat of arms.

The 2012 Radcliffe varsity crew won the inaugural Ivy League Championship regatta, earning their blazers and a chance to compete for the Remenham Challenge Cup, the only event for women's eights at the Henley Royal Regatta.

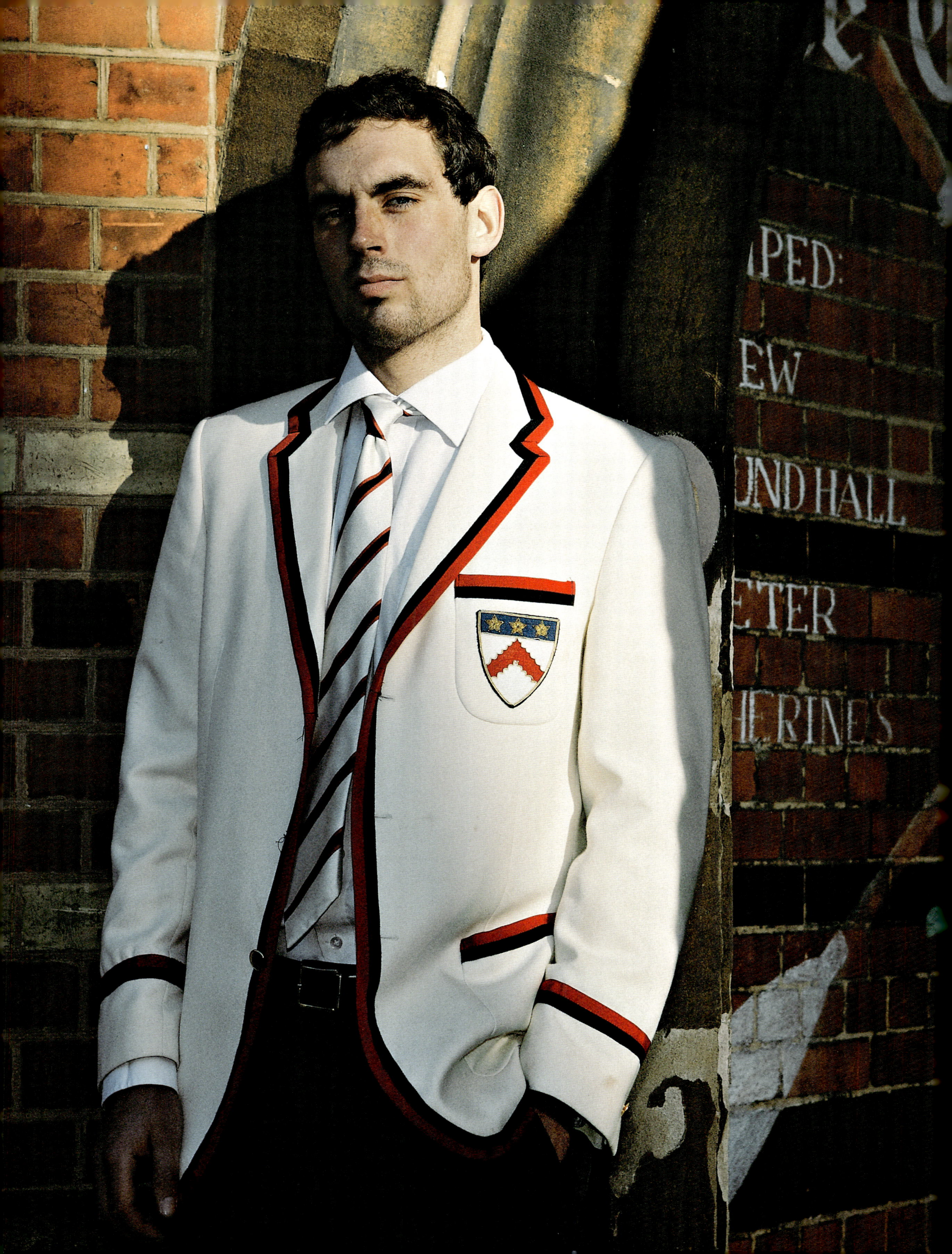
PED:
EW
UND HALL
ETER
HERINES

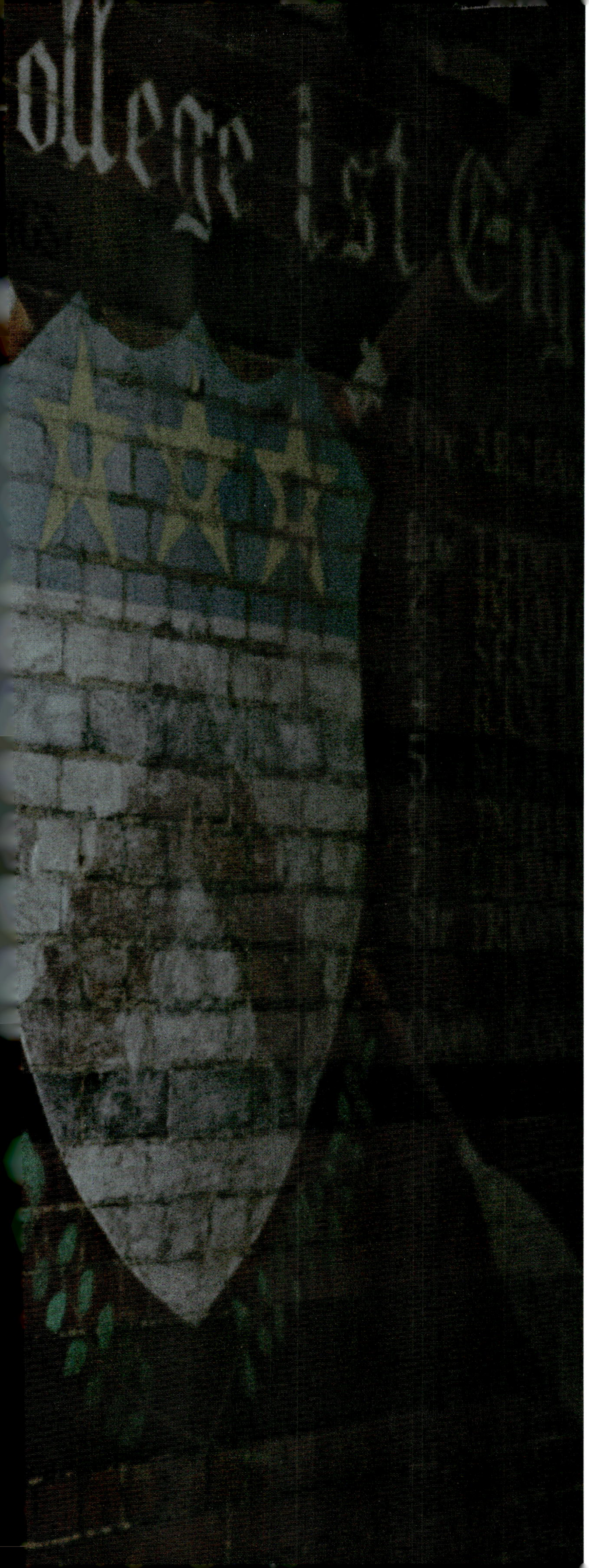

Oxford, England

Keble College Boat Club, Oxford

JULIAN BUBB-HUMFRYES

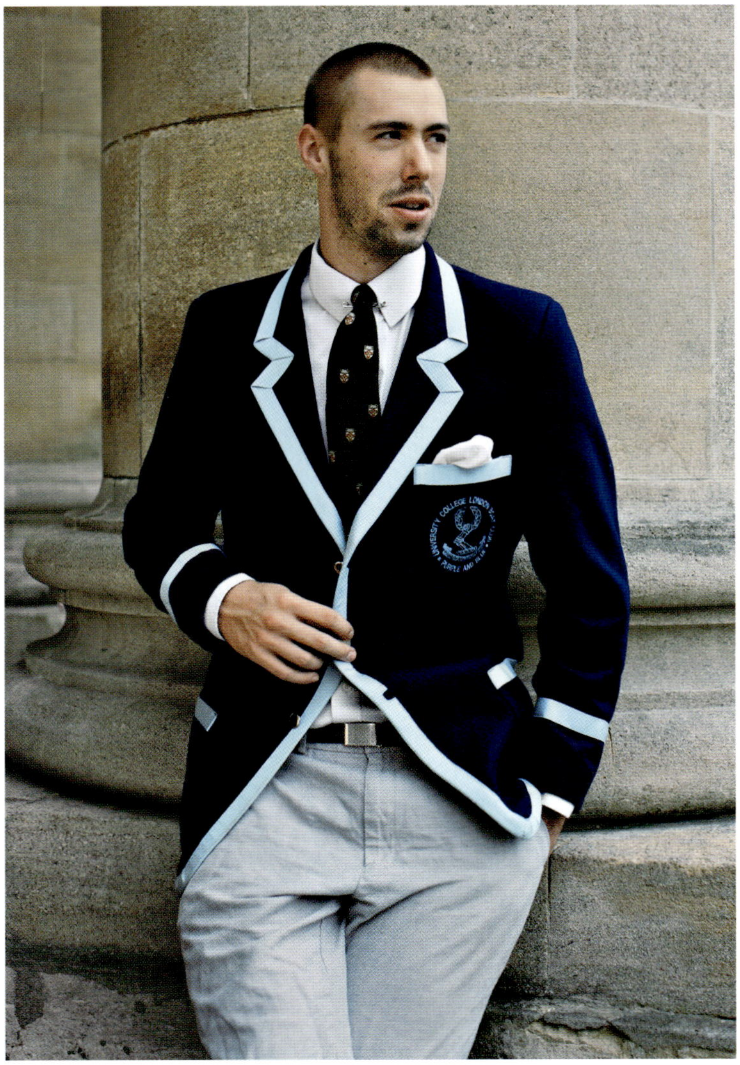

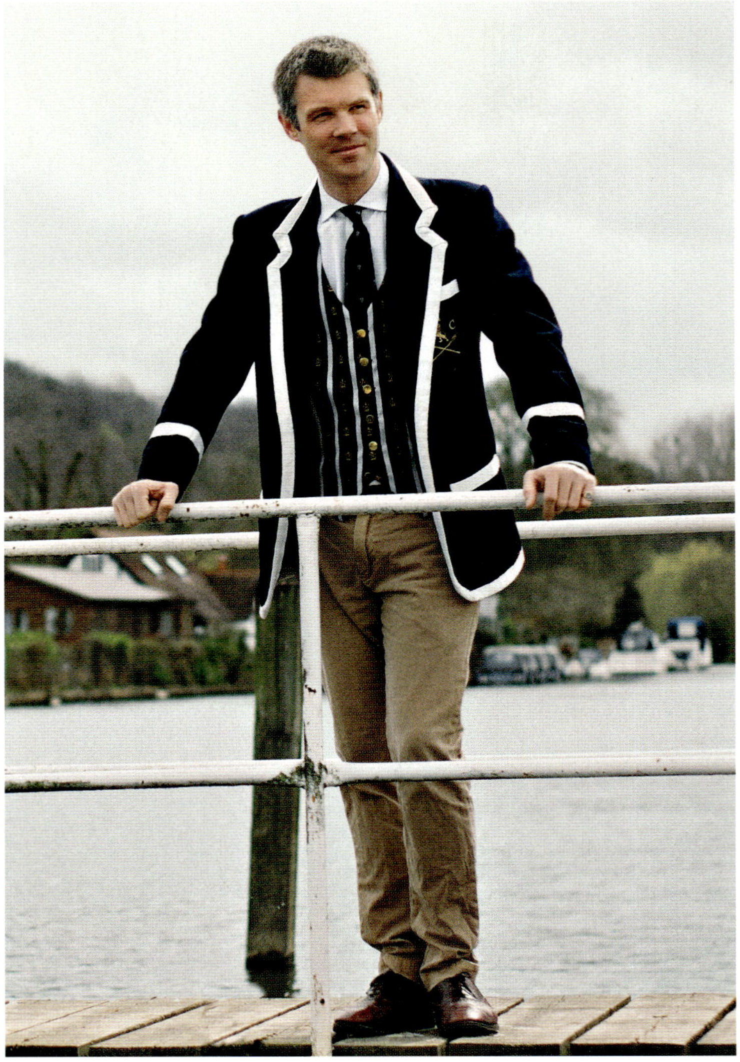

CLOCKWISE FROM TOP LEFT

London, England

University College London Boat Club

ALEX DAVIDSON

Henley-on-Thames, England

Henley Rowing Club

NICK MEAD

York, England

University of York Boat Club

JAMES PADMORE

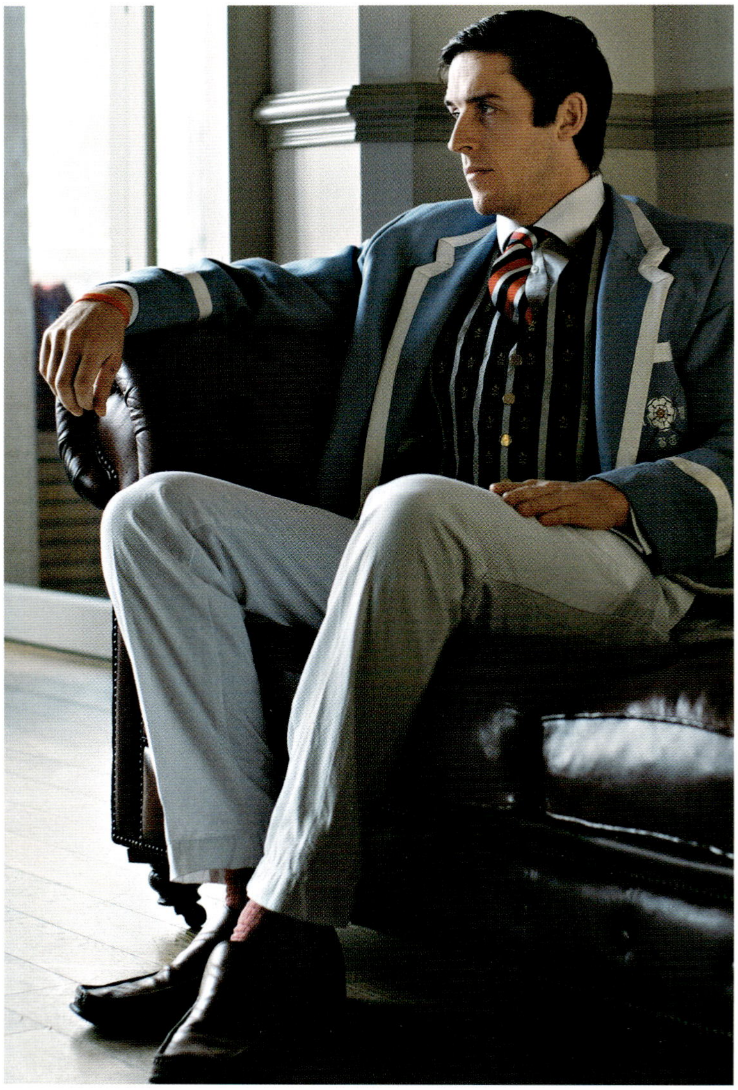

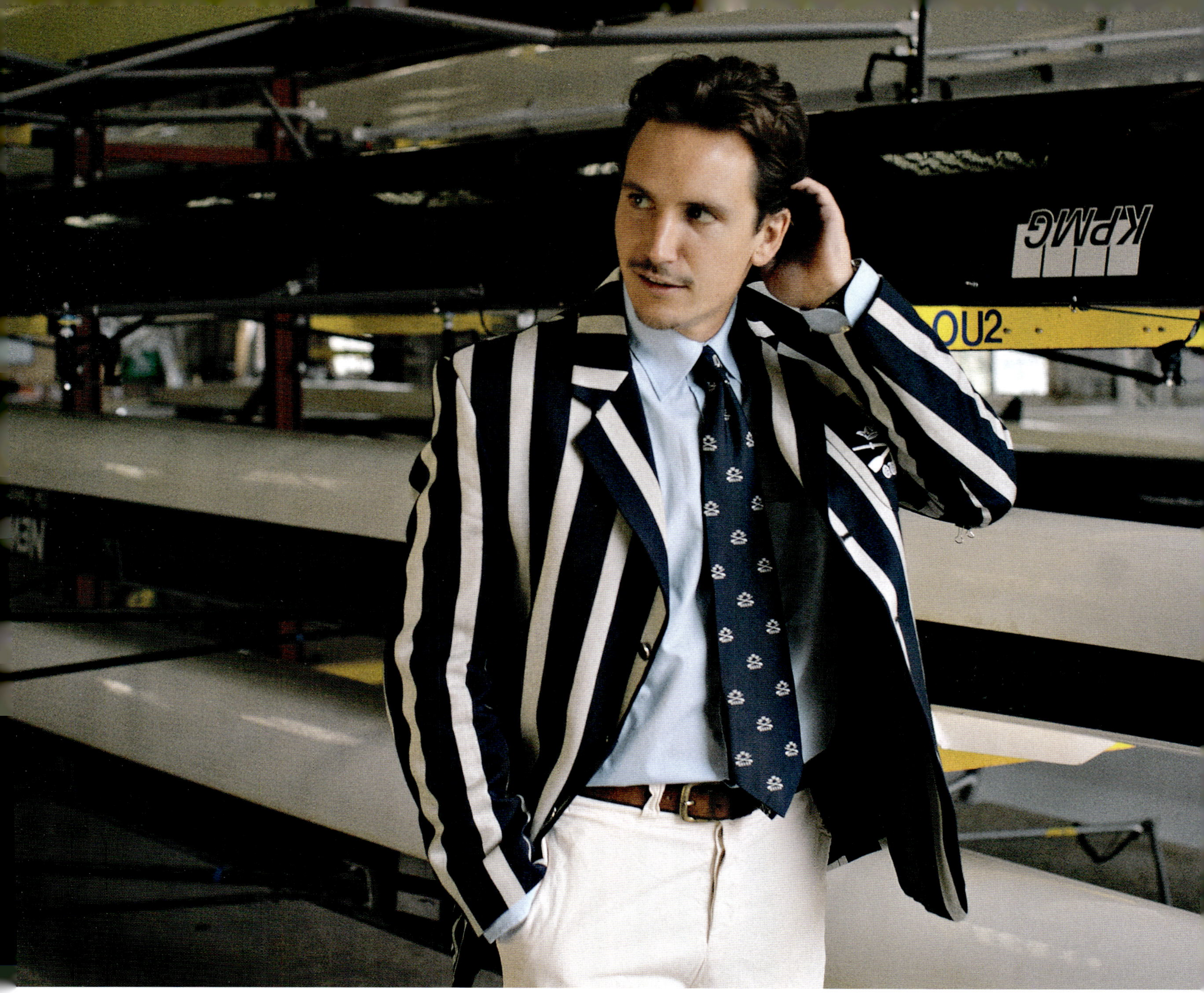

Oxford, England

Oxford University Lightweight Rowing Club

BODO SCHULENBURG

The Oxford University Lightweight Rowing Club was formed in 1975 to accept a challenge from Cambridge for the first Oxford-Cambridge Lightweight Boat Race. In the early years, the Oxford lightweights wore dark blue blazers with white trim, before switching to the broad Oxford Blue-and-white stripes they wear today. Cambridge leads the series, 23 to 16, although Bodo Schulenburg has done his part to reverse the trend; he has helped Oxford to win twice as a rower and once as a coach.

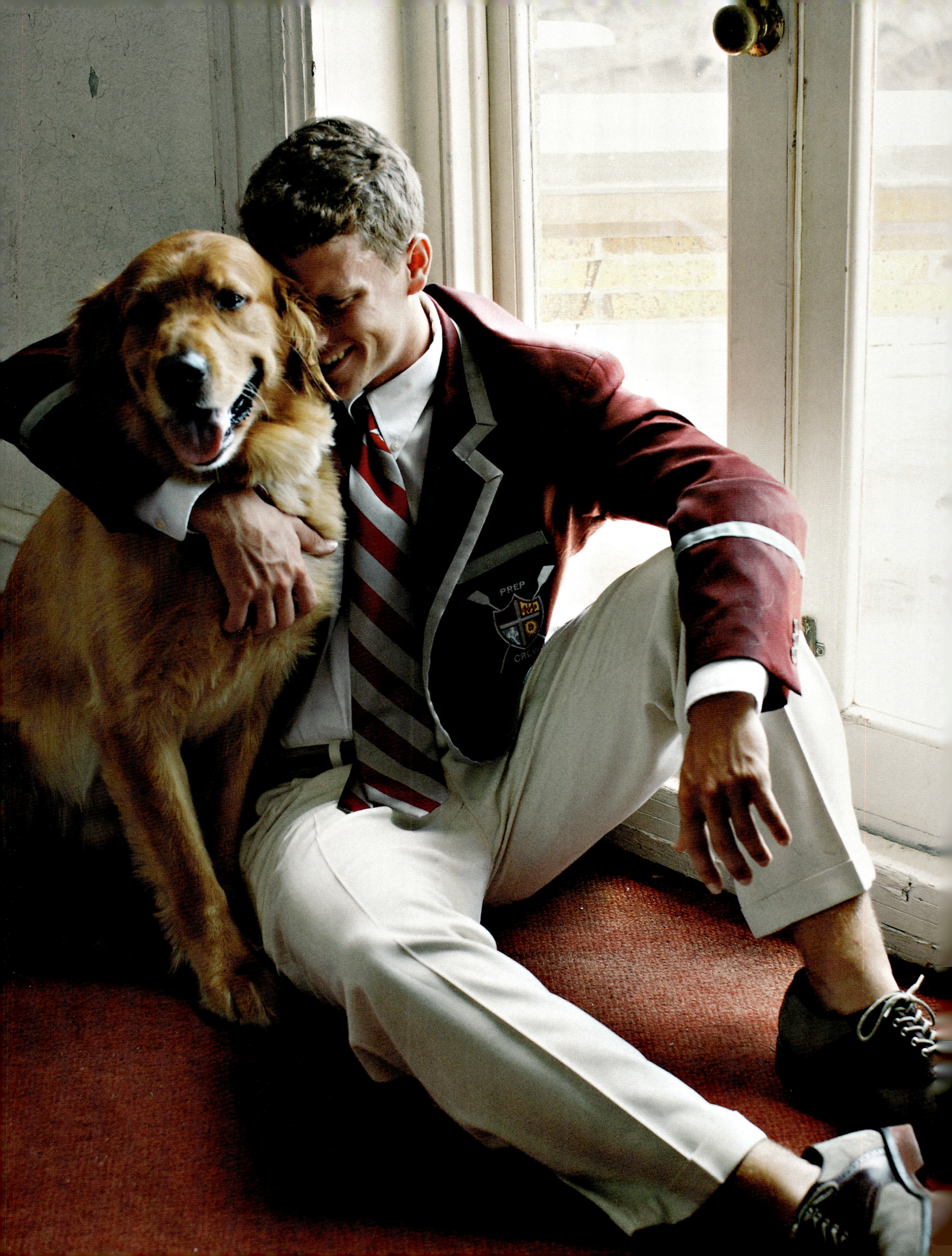
PREP

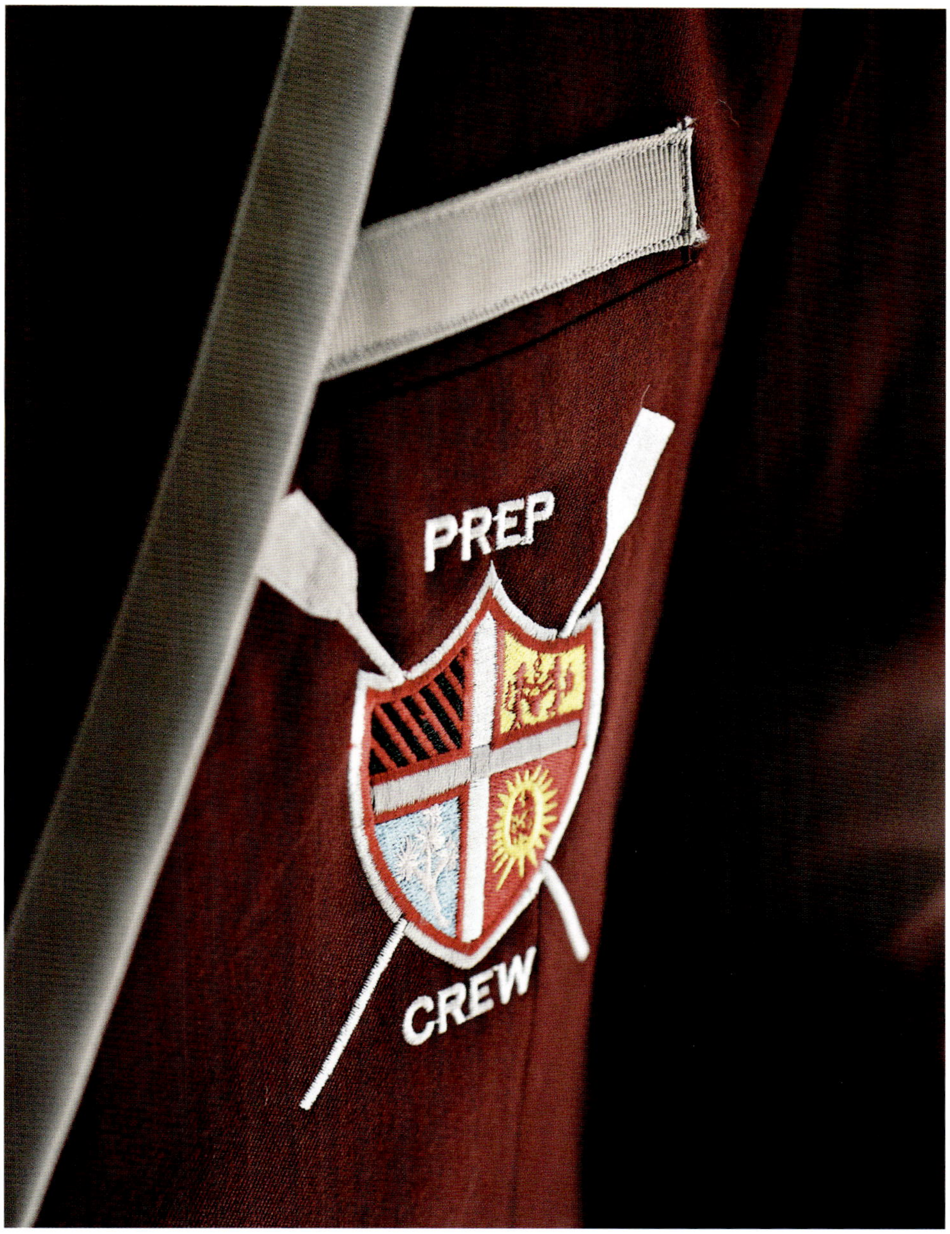

Philadelphia, Pennsylvania

St. Joseph's Preparatory School

DEAN HILL

"The Prep" is a powerhouse in U.S. high school rowing and has been one of the most regular American contenders for the Princess Elizabeth Cup at Henley in recent years. An all-boys Jesuit day school in the heart of Philadelphia, it contrasts nicely with many of its rowing rivals: co-ed, rural, Episcopalian or secular New England boarding schools.

Dean Hill was a three-time Stotesbury Cup winner and three-time Scholastic Rowing national champion at St. Joe's Prep. He stroked the Prep crew to the semifinals at Henley in 2010.

Amsterdam, Netherlands

R.S.V.U. "Okeanos"

ROMMERT BERGSHOEFF,
BORIS LE FEBER

Roeivereniging van Studenten aan de Vrije Universiteit "Okeanos" is one of the newer student rowing clubs in the Netherlands. Its members train alongside the Dutch national squad on the world's first man-made rowing lake, the Bosbaan.

Okeanos rowers wear a red, white, and green–striped blazer, while the club president wears a similar waistcoat beneath a navy tailcoat with lapels in the club colors.

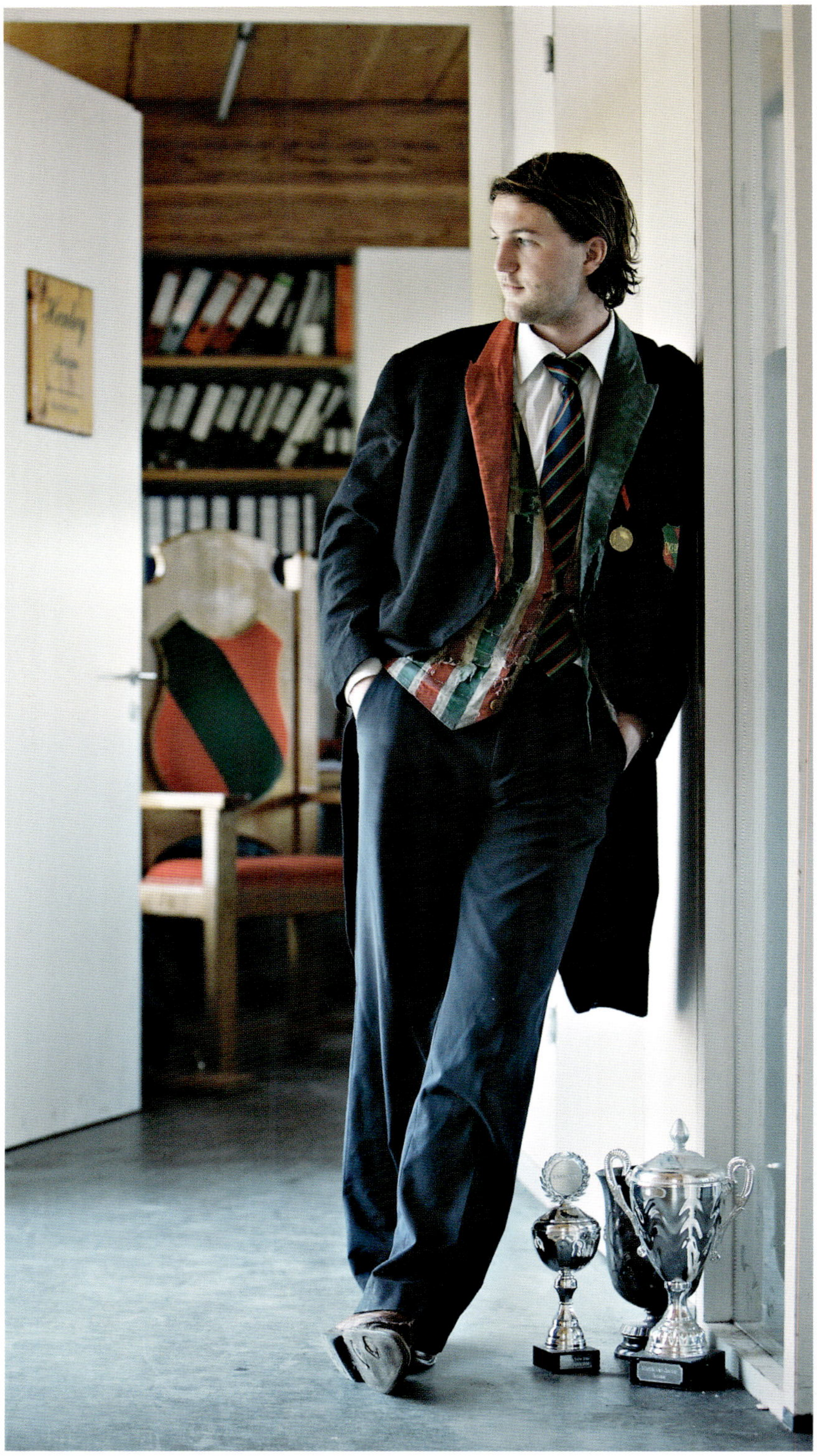

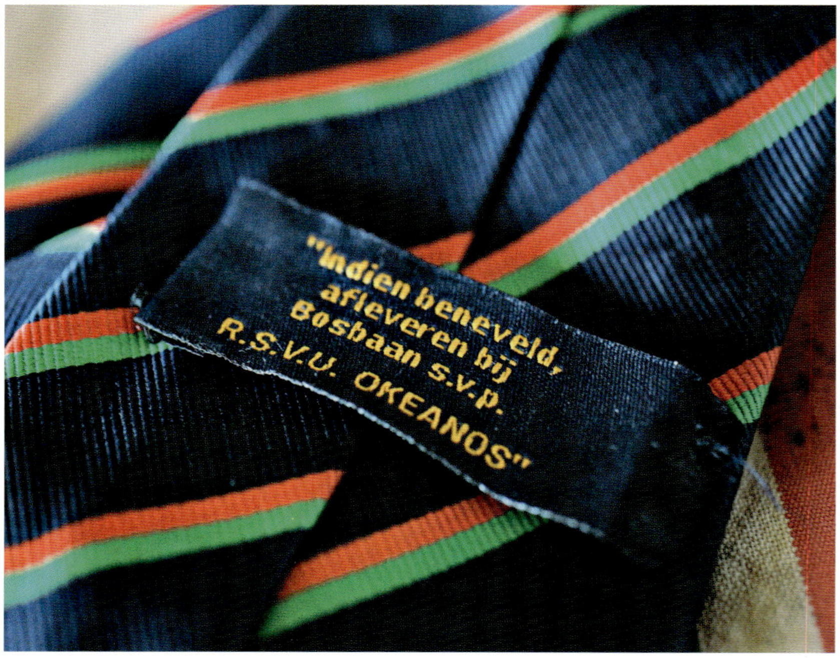

ABOVE RIGHT:
Okeanos president Rommert Bergshoeff.

RIGHT:
The tag on the back of the club tie reads: "If tipsy, please return [this rower] to R.S.V.U. Okeanos, the Bosbaan."

OPPOSITE:
Boris Le Feber wears the tie of *Dispuut Stercus Tauri*, a society within the club.

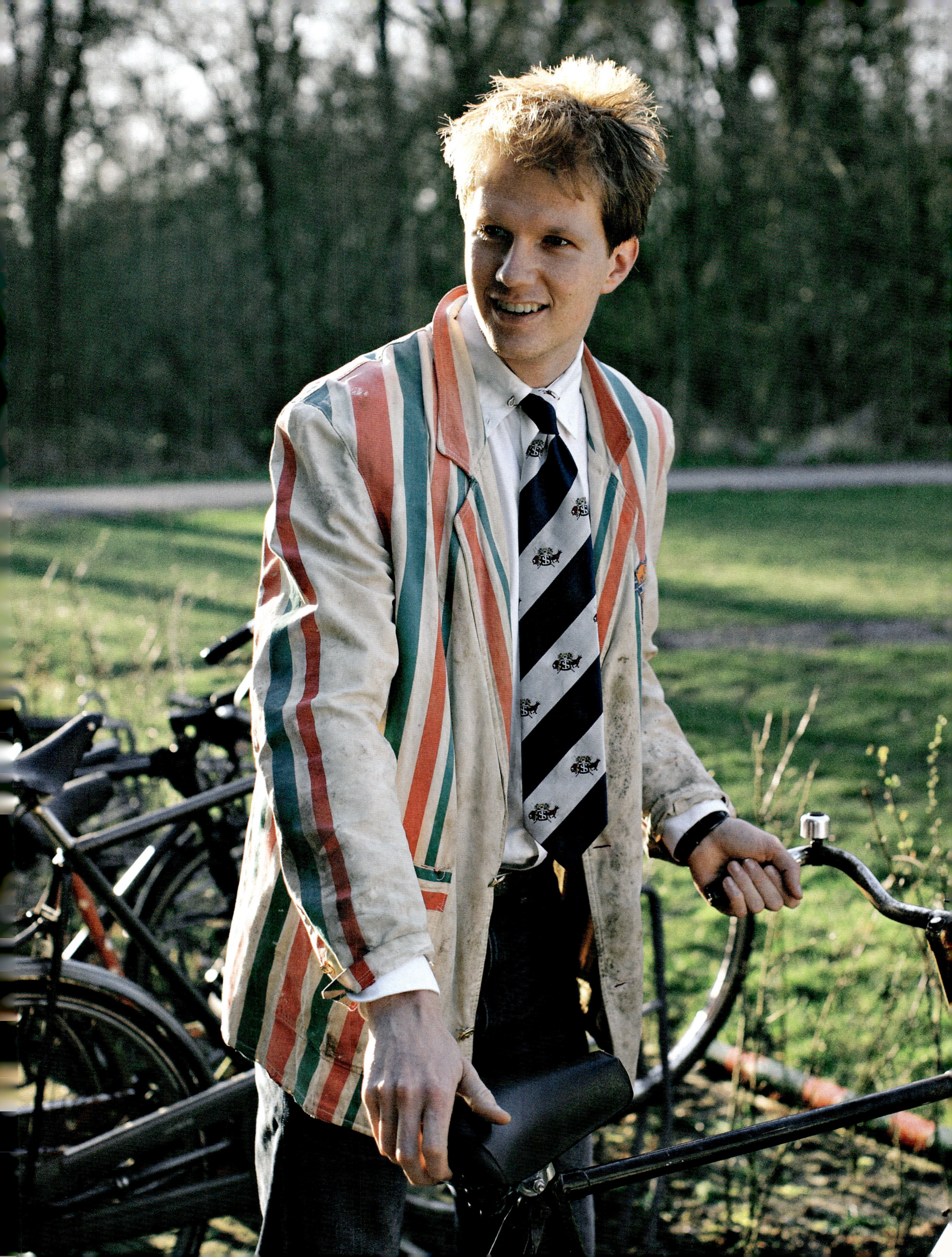

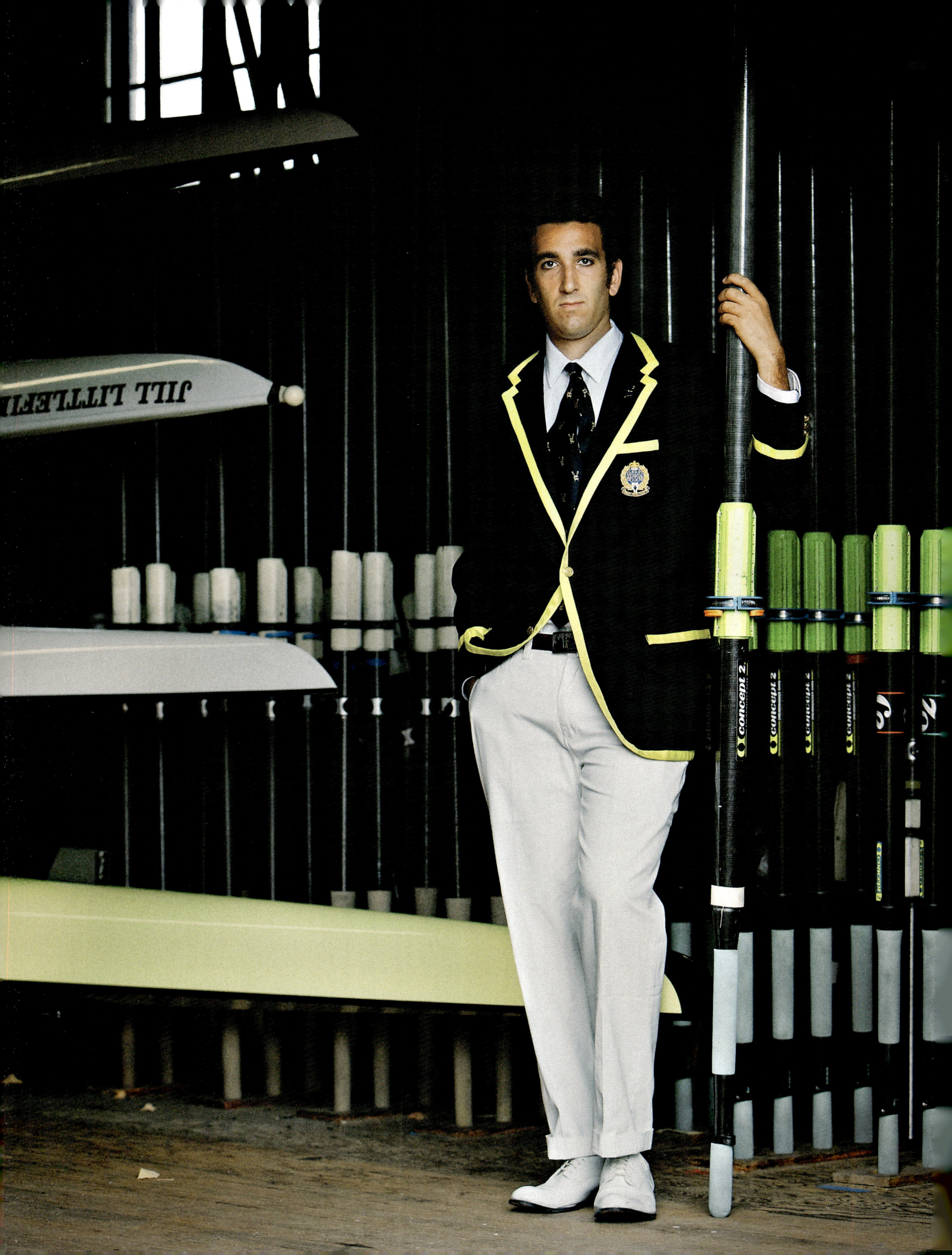
concept 2

Berkeley, California

University of California, Berkeley

NAREG GUREGIAN

Although the East Coast is the birthplace of American rowing, Cal is one of the most historic and successful university teams in the nation. Under legendary coach Ky Ebright, Cal represented the United States at the 1928, 1932, and 1948 Olympic Games, winning gold on every occasion.

Two of the most traditional fixtures on the Cal rowing calendar today are the Schoch Cup—the annual varsity race against the University of Washington—and the Class Day Race, in which senior, junior, sophomore, and freshman crews battle for the privilege of earning a coveted belt buckle prize.

Nareg Guregian won the Temple Challenge Cup at Henley with the Cal freshmen in 2007 and won a U.S. national championship with the varsity crew in 2010; he has rowed in the U.S. national squad since graduating.

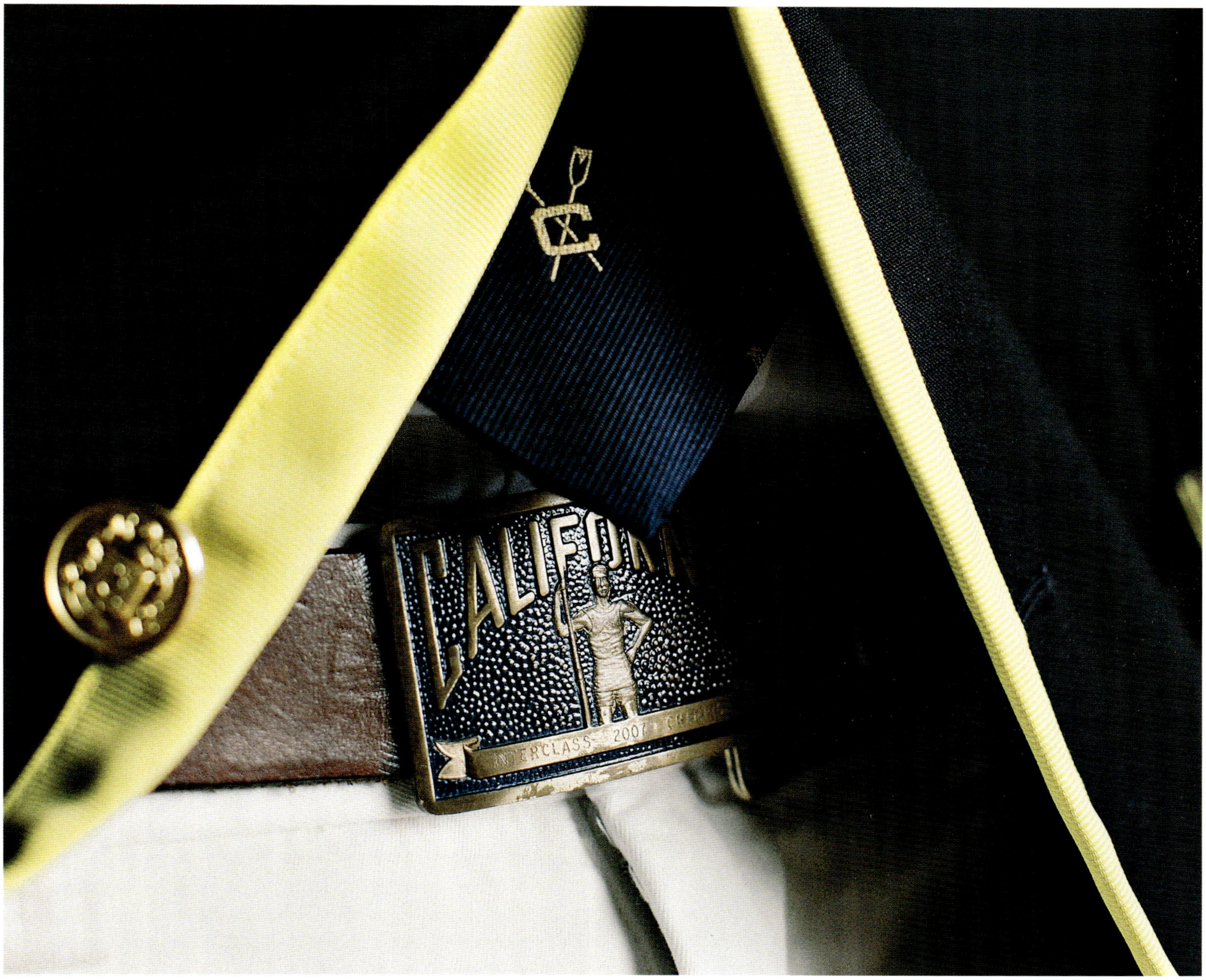

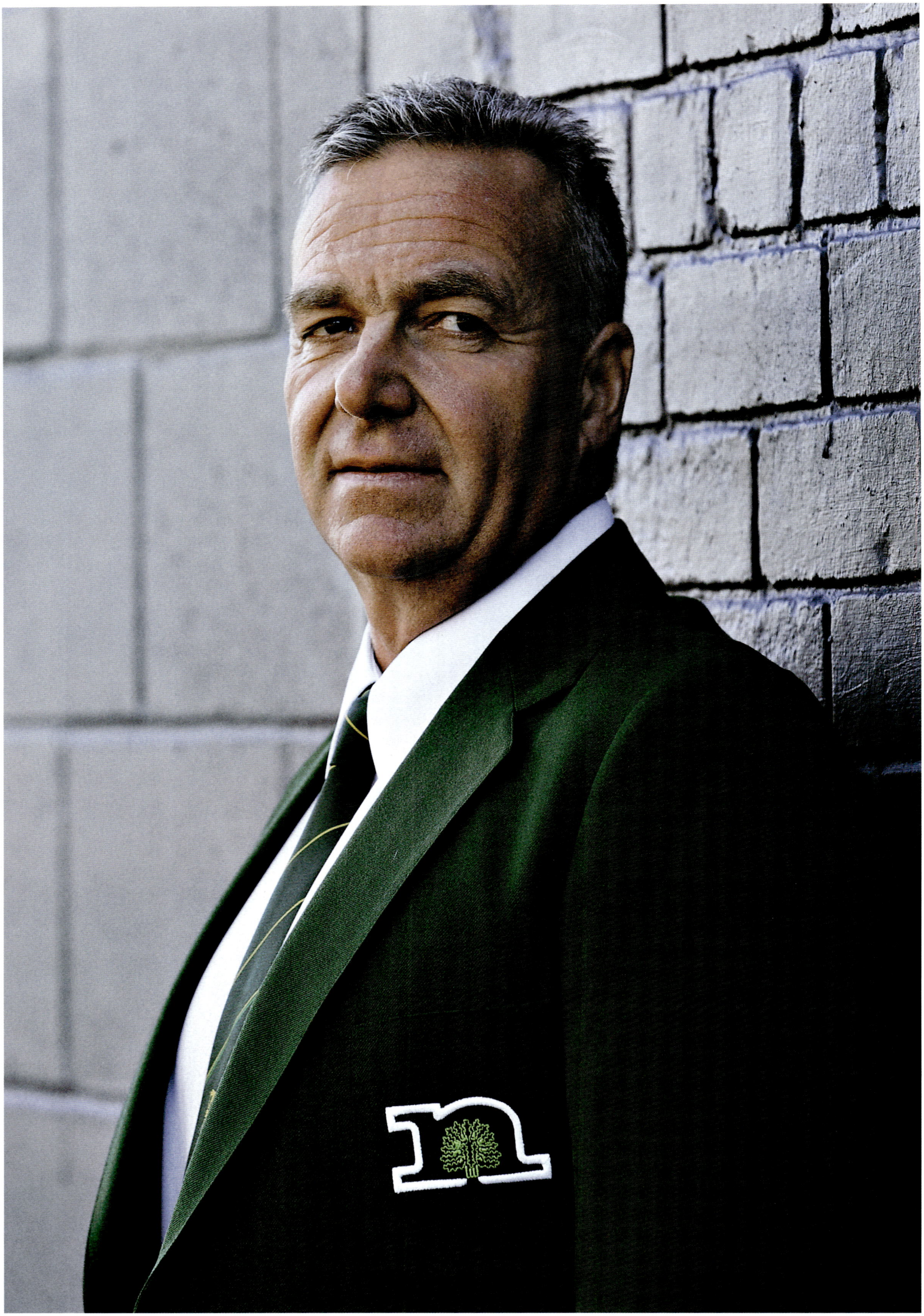

Nottingham, England

Nottinghamshire County Rowing Association

CHRIS BATES

Notts County Rowing Association is long extinct, but its most famous race is immortalized in Henley lore. The 1989 Henley Royal Regatta was a classic: ten records were broken; grudge matches and unforgettable duels were the order of the day; and, as it was the 150th anniversary of the regatta, the program was filled with festivities and special events for past winners. The regatta culminated in the final of the Ladies' Challenge Plate, in which the all-lightweight Notts County faced the undefeated Harvard heavyweights. "Notts County will need divine intervention to beat Harvard," read the headlines. And divine intervention came: the lightweight underdogs annihilated Harvard by five lengths and broke the course record they had set the previous day.

But as the County rowers broke out the Champagne, changed into blazers for the prize-giving, de-rigged their boat, and downed a few cans of ale, the Harvard crew lodged an appeal with the Stewards to have the race re-rowed: a branch, apparently, had become stuck on the Harvard boat's fin during the race. The appeal was successful, and the Notts County crew were informed that they should stop drinking immediately and would be required to re-row the race at 8 o'clock that evening, after the prize ceremony for the other events. As the sun set, an almighty roar erupted in the Stewards' Enclosure, which had, by then, been opened to the public—Notts County beat Harvard for the second time that day, this time by two-thirds of a length. Bursting with aggression and barely dipping below forty strokes per minute all the way down the course, they broke the course record they had set less than three hours earlier. One of the N.C.R.A. oarsmen, Peter Haining, rowed the last ten strokes with one hand, pumping his fist in the air with the other.

Notts County was a famously motley crew. Nicknamed "the green slime," they were also the first to wear Lycra unisuits (now standard). But their blazers were far less avant-garde. "We didn't have any blazers or anything before we entered for Henley," recalled their coach, Ray Sims. So they asked the Nottinghamshire County Council what they might be able to offer, "and they produced bus conductors' uniform[s] that had started life as rent collectors' jackets. They had the oak tree symbol of the county, and came in a great assortment of sizes, but none of them fitted us properly. They were £10 apiece, but I don't think they ever charged us."

Chris Bates is one of the oarsmen from the famous 1989 Notts County crew.

Oxford, England

Oxford Brookes University Boat Club

RORY COPUS, PETER CHAMBERS,
OLIVIA CARNEGIE-BROWN, SCOTT DURANT,
HENRY BAILHACHE-WEBB, SCOTT SMITH,
YASMIN TREDELL, OLIVER STAITE, TEX HOLDEN-SMITH,
LOUIS PATERSON, JAMES MARTYN SMITH

Oxford Brookes has often been called a rowing club with a university attached. And indeed, Brookes is not only one of the most successful university boat clubs in Britain but also one of the nation's top rowing clubs of any type.

Brookes won its first Henley Royal Regatta title in 1993, just a few months after the university was born: Oxford Polytechnic had become a full university the previous September, changing its name to Oxford Brookes and its colors from Baltic Blue to burgundy, navy, and cream. The '93 crew still wore striped Baltic Blue blazers at the prize-giving, but the rowing club adopted the new colors for its blades, racing kit, and blazers the following year. Since then, Brookes has raced in burgundy and navy, and has claimed victory in a staggering total of twenty-four Henley events in twenty years.

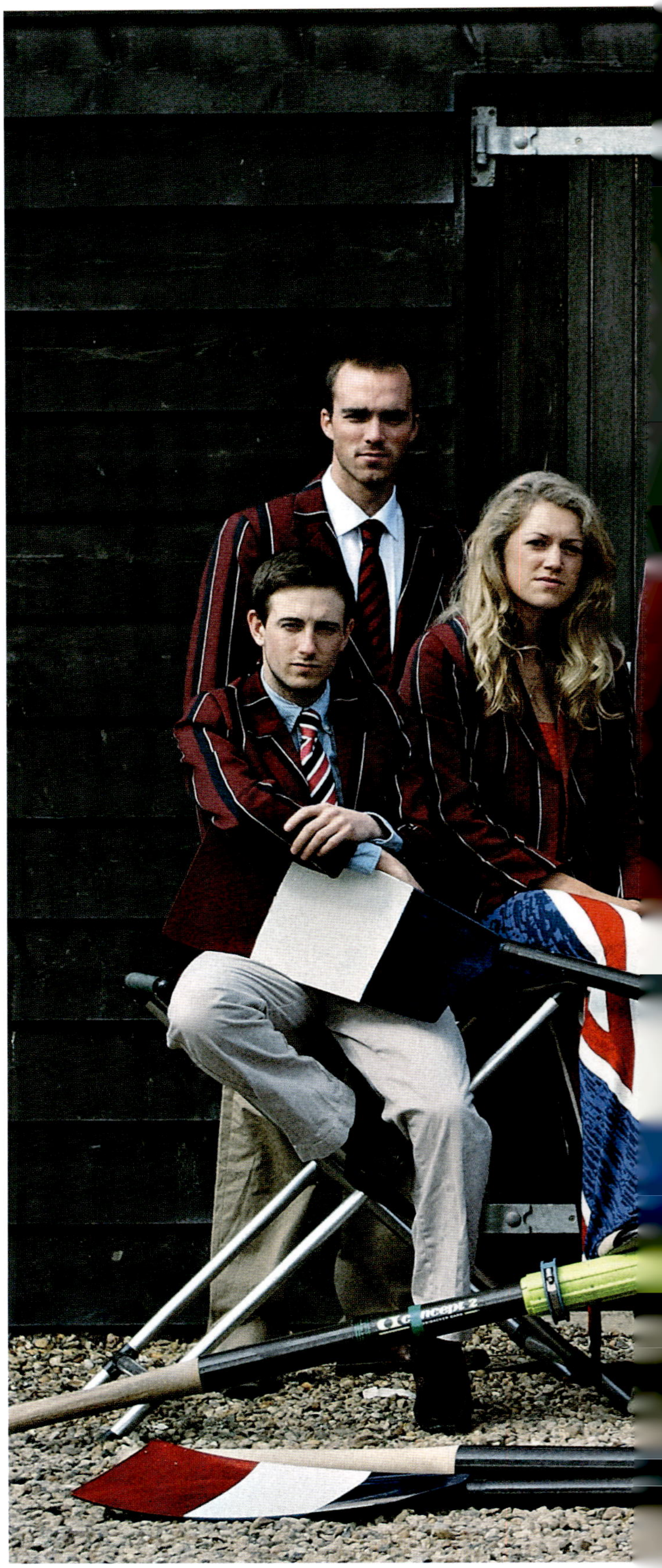

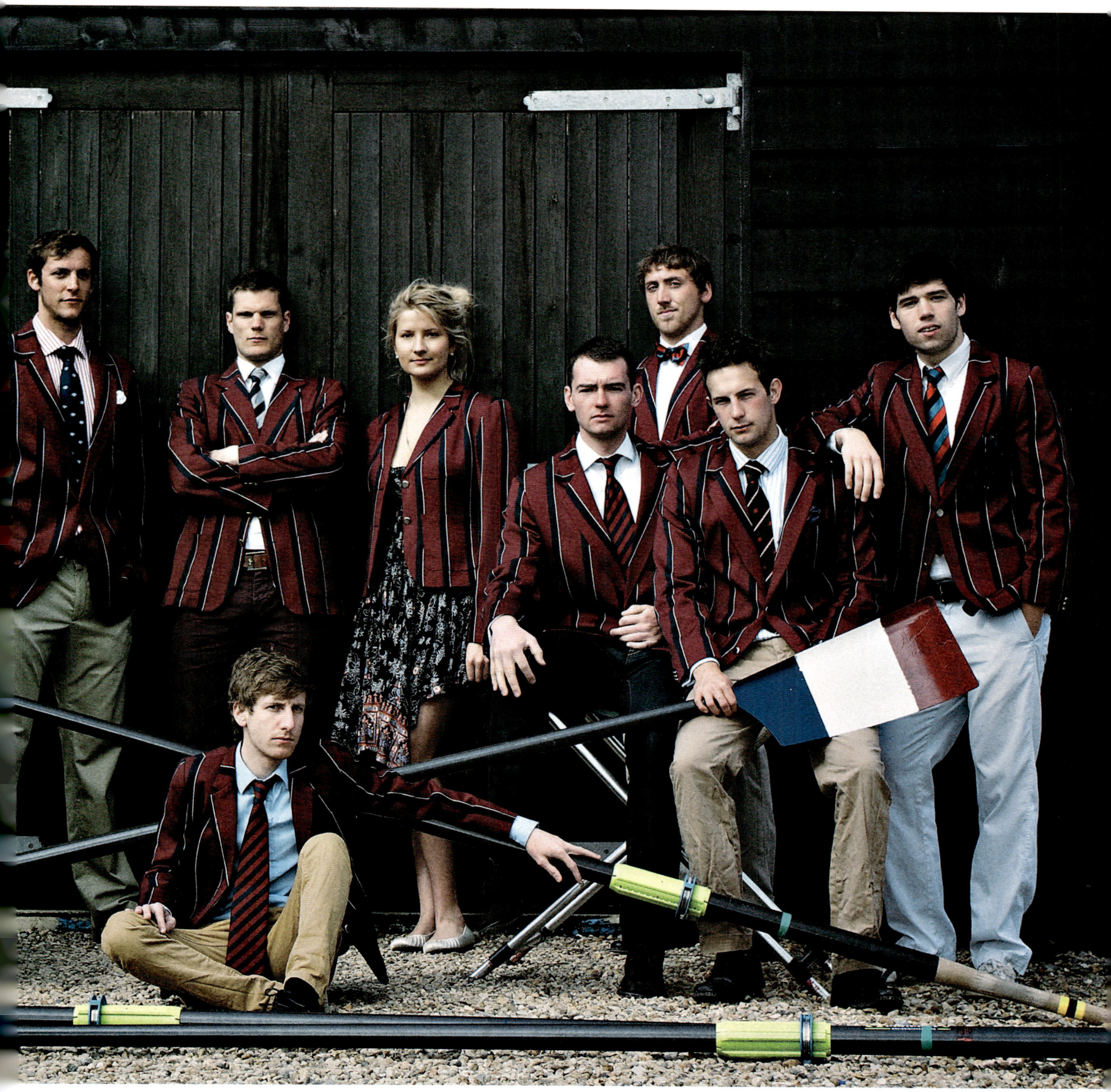

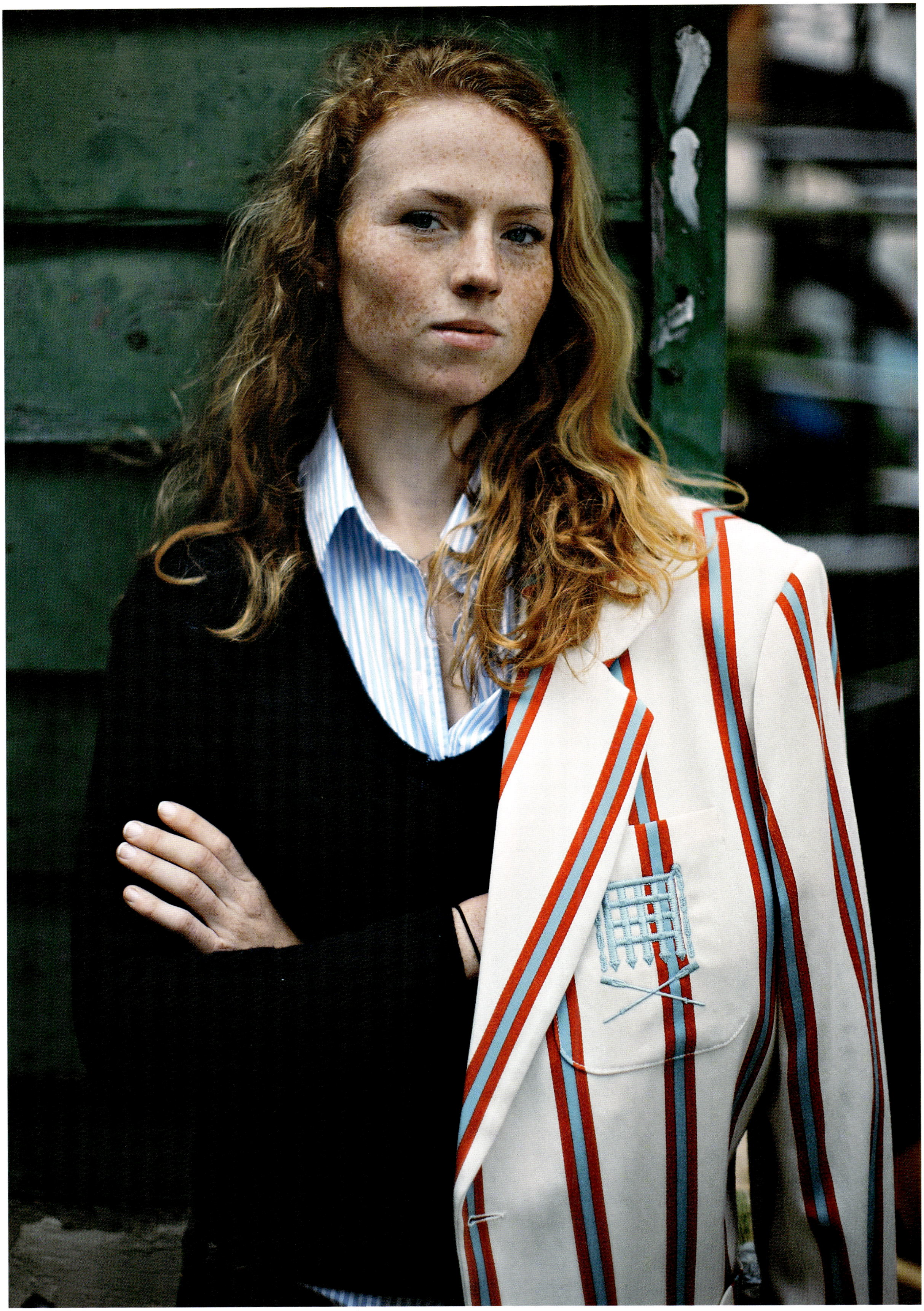

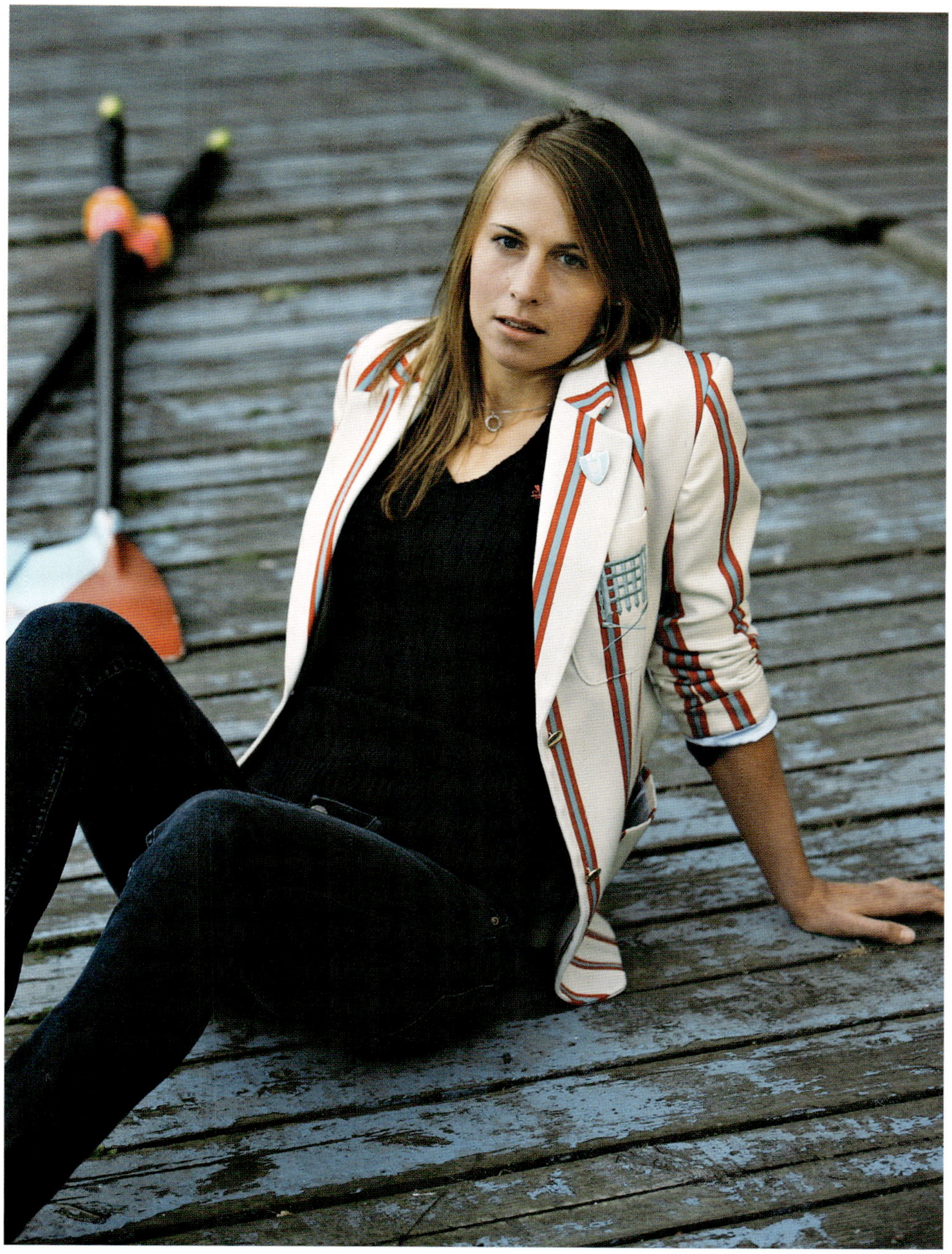

Wallingford, England

Wallingford Rowing Club

BRIANNA STUBBS, ELLIE PIGGOTT

Ellie Piggott (above) and Brianna Stubbs (opposite) won gold together in the lightweight women's double sculls at the under-23 world championships in 2013. They train at Wallingford Rowing Club on a picturesque stretch of the Thames where Oxford Brookes and Oxford University also train.

The club's badge, a portcullis, or castle gate, has been a symbol of the town of Wallingford for centuries and probably referred originally to Wallingford Castle, erected in the eleventh century and destroyed in the seventeenth.

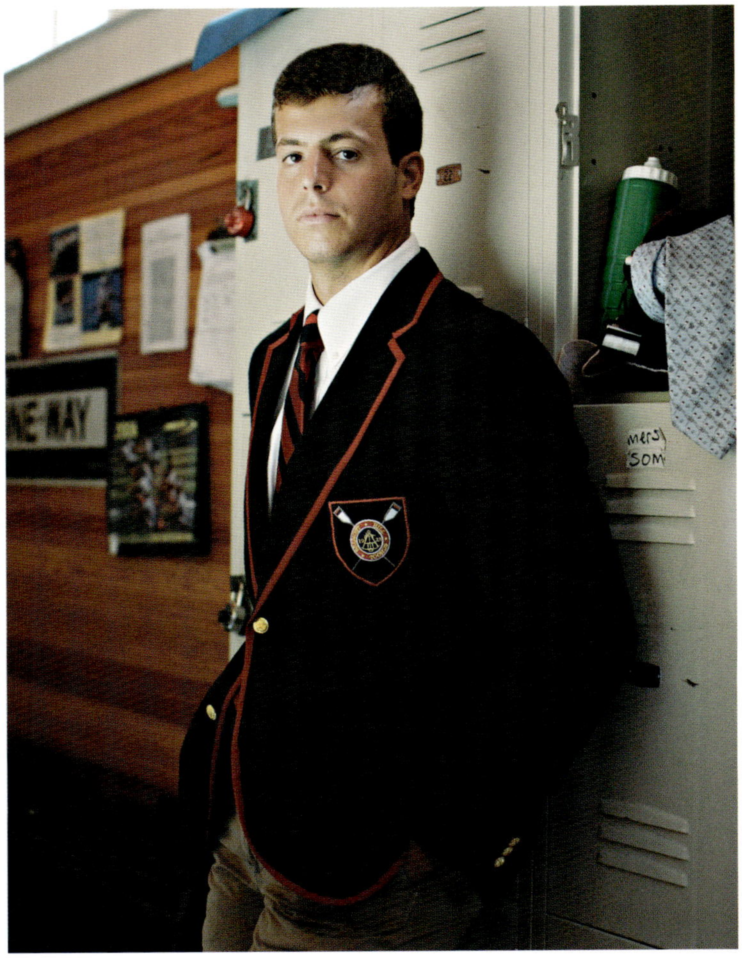

Belmont, Massachusetts

Belmont Hill School

MIKE DiSANTO

Belmont Hill School rowers earn their red-edged blazers—and the opportunity to race against top school crews from around the world at the Henley Royal Regatta—by putting in especially strong performances at the New England Interscholastic Rowing Association Championships and national championships.

In his four years at Belmont Hill, Mike DiSanto won three New England first boat championships and a national title. As team captain in his final year, he led Belmont Hill to a "sweep"—victories in the first, second, third, and fourth boat events—at the New England championships: a first for Belmont Hill since the race was founded in 1947.

Newcastle, England

Newcastle University Boat Club

GEORGE LAUGHTON

Few rowing clubs have adapted their blazer badges from beer logos. But the Newcastle University Boat Club badge, which appears on its blades and blazers, is the Blue Star, which has its origins in the logo of Newcastle Brown Ale. Since 1928, each bottle of Newcastle Brown has featured a five-pointed blue star to represent the five founding breweries of Newcastle. The star was appropriated by both the boat club and the now-defunct professional soccer team Newcastle Blue Star F.C.

Newcastle's Blue Star blades race in the highest echelon of British university rowing today, and N.U.B.C. is a feeder for the Great Britain national squads.

George Laughton is a gold medalist at both the World University Championships and the European University Championships.

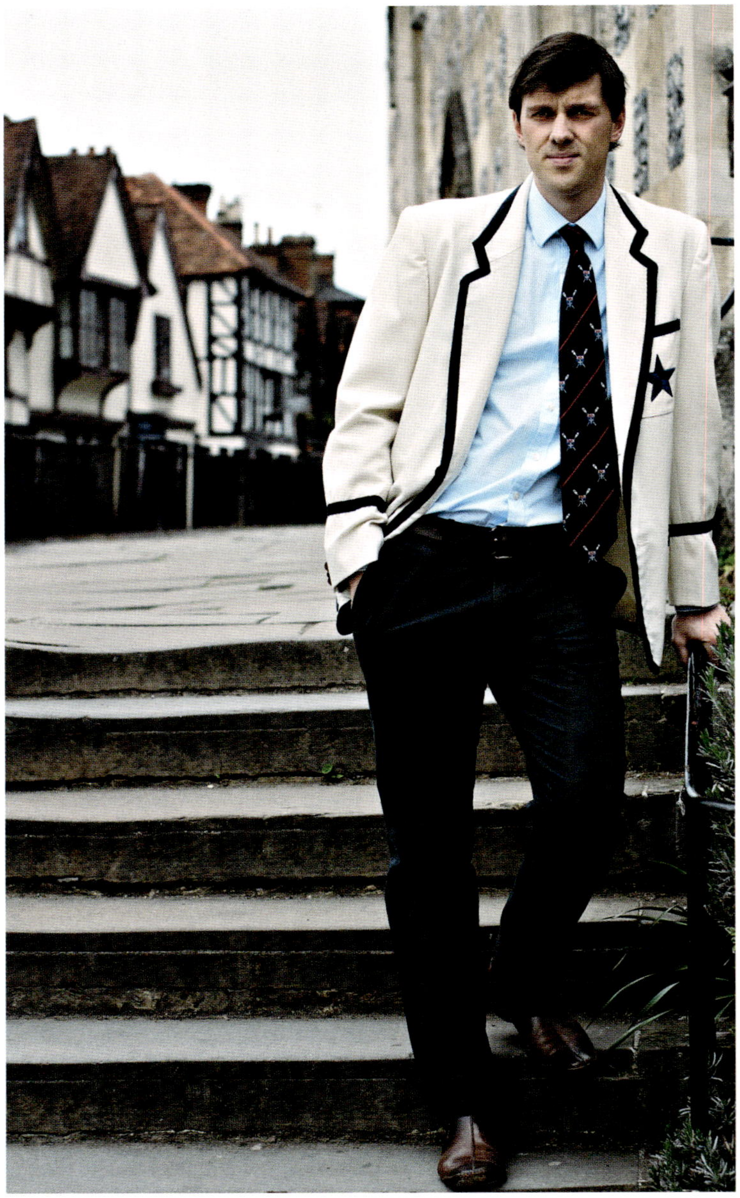

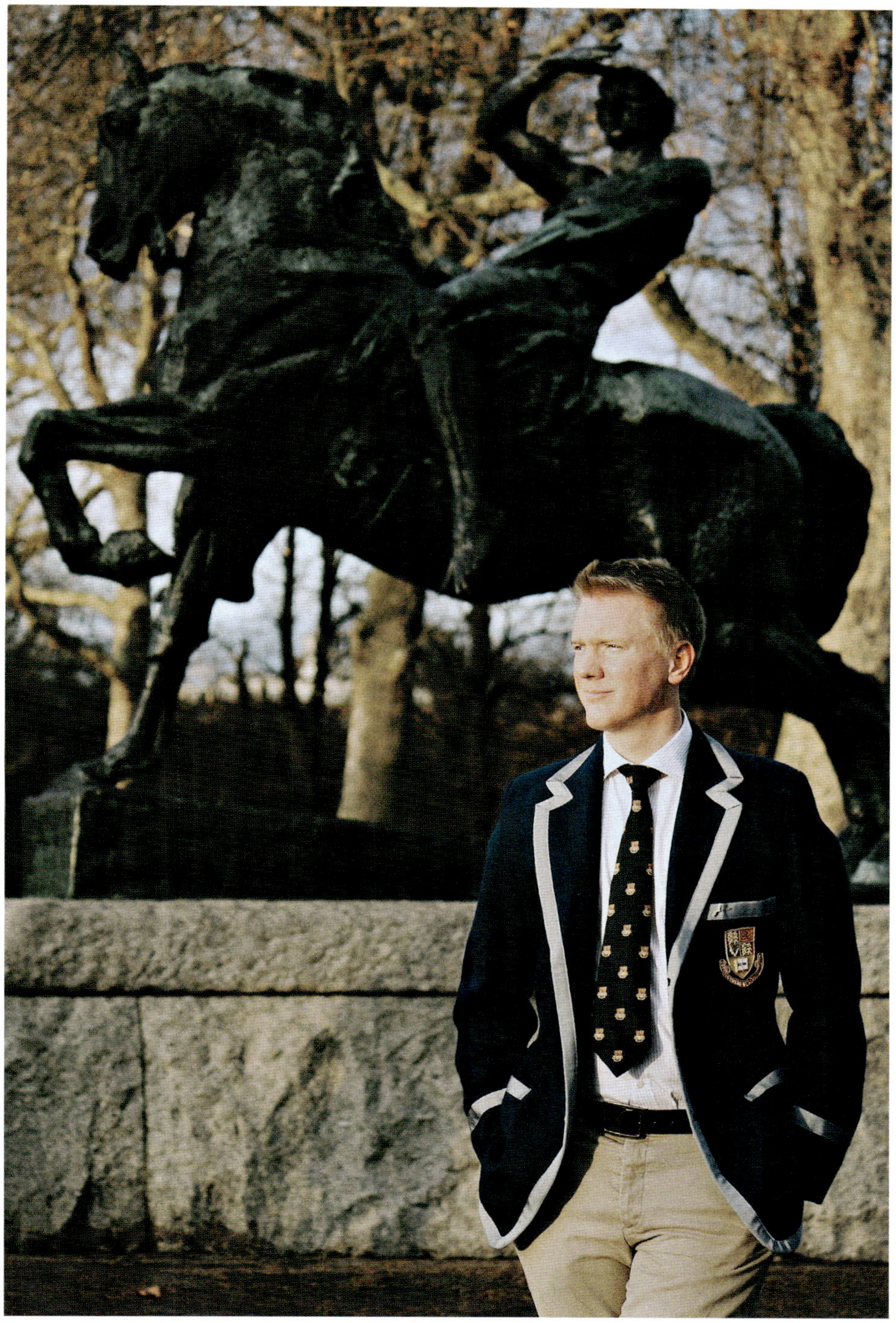

London, England

Imperial College Boat Club

SIMON HISLOP

Imperial College Boat Club has won twenty Henley Royal Regatta titles since the club was founded in 1919. Simon Hislop rowed in two of these winning boats, in 2004 and 2006.

Simon's 2004 crew won the inaugural men's student coxed fours event at Henley, and when the event became a permanent fixture at the regatta, Imperial celebrated their win by donating a trophy for the event. The crew chose an apt name for the new trophy, the Prince Albert Challenge Cup: Prince Albert was not only instrumental in the creation of the Imperial College of Science, Technology and Medicine in the area of London now known as Albertopolis, but was also the first royal patron of the Henley Royal Regatta.

Only those Imperial oarsmen who have won Henley, finished in the top ten in the Head of the River Race, or rowed at the senior or under-23 world championships are eligible to wear the blue-and-gray club blazer.

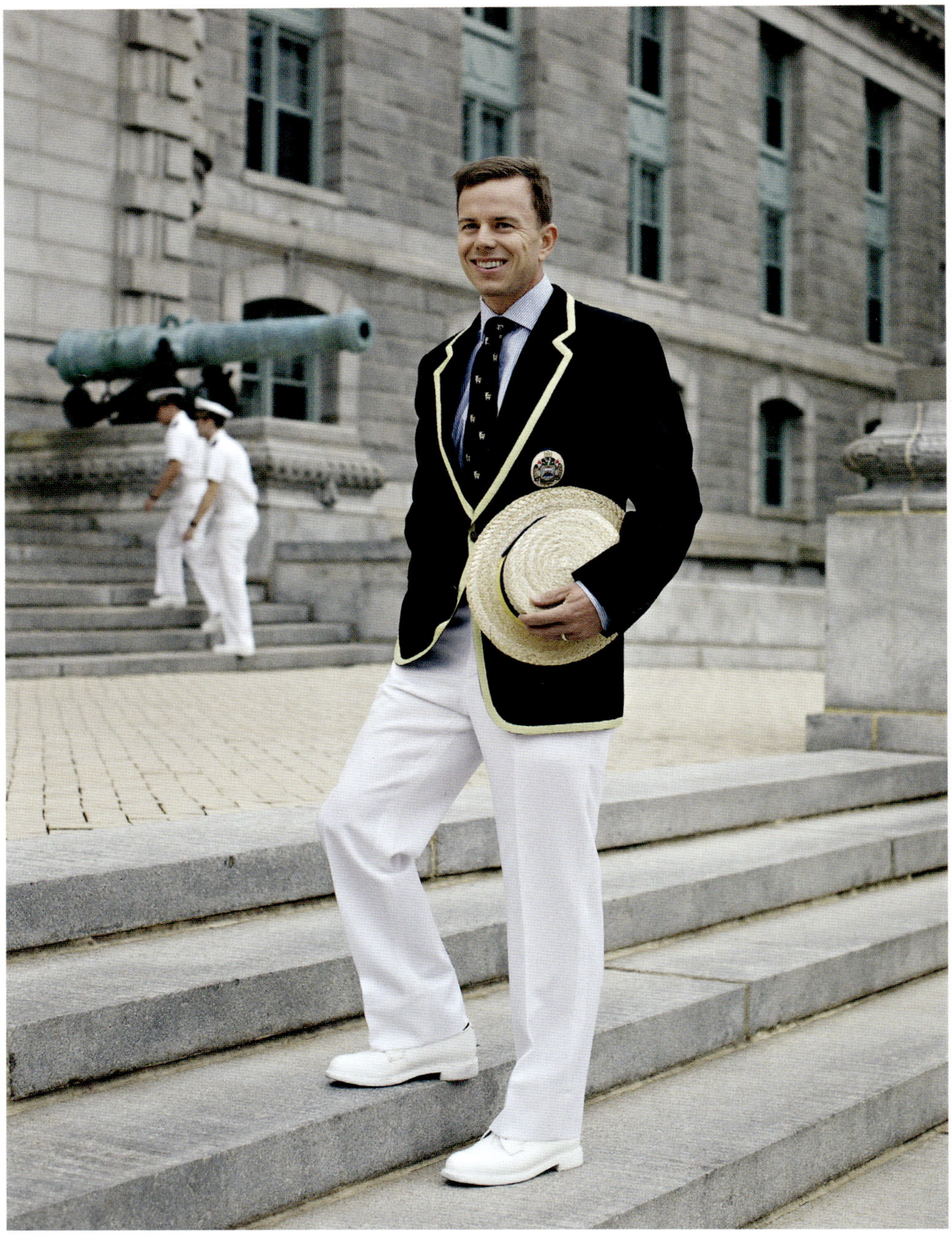

Annapolis, Maryland

The United States Naval Academy

LT. JIMMY SOPKO

"Sitting in the classrooms of Academic Hall, the crew midshipmen listened to history professors tell of how the Academy's rowing tradition sprang from its roots in warfare . . ."

—Susan Saint Sing, *The Wonder Crew*, 2008

The U.S. Naval Academy rarely makes an appearance at the Henley Royal Regatta in England. But in 2004, the Navy lightweight eight's undefeated record in the regular season carried on through the Eastern Sprints and the national championships; the Midshipmen took gold in both events. Their run took them all the way to Henley, and to the semifinal of the Temple Challenge Cup. Between races, the crew swanned around the Stewards' Enclosure, either in their Navy rowing blazers or in full dress whites.

Lt. Jimmy Sopko rowed in the '04 crew and served as a Surface Warfare Officer aboard the U.S.S. *Ford* before rowing on the U.S. national team from 2009 to 2012.

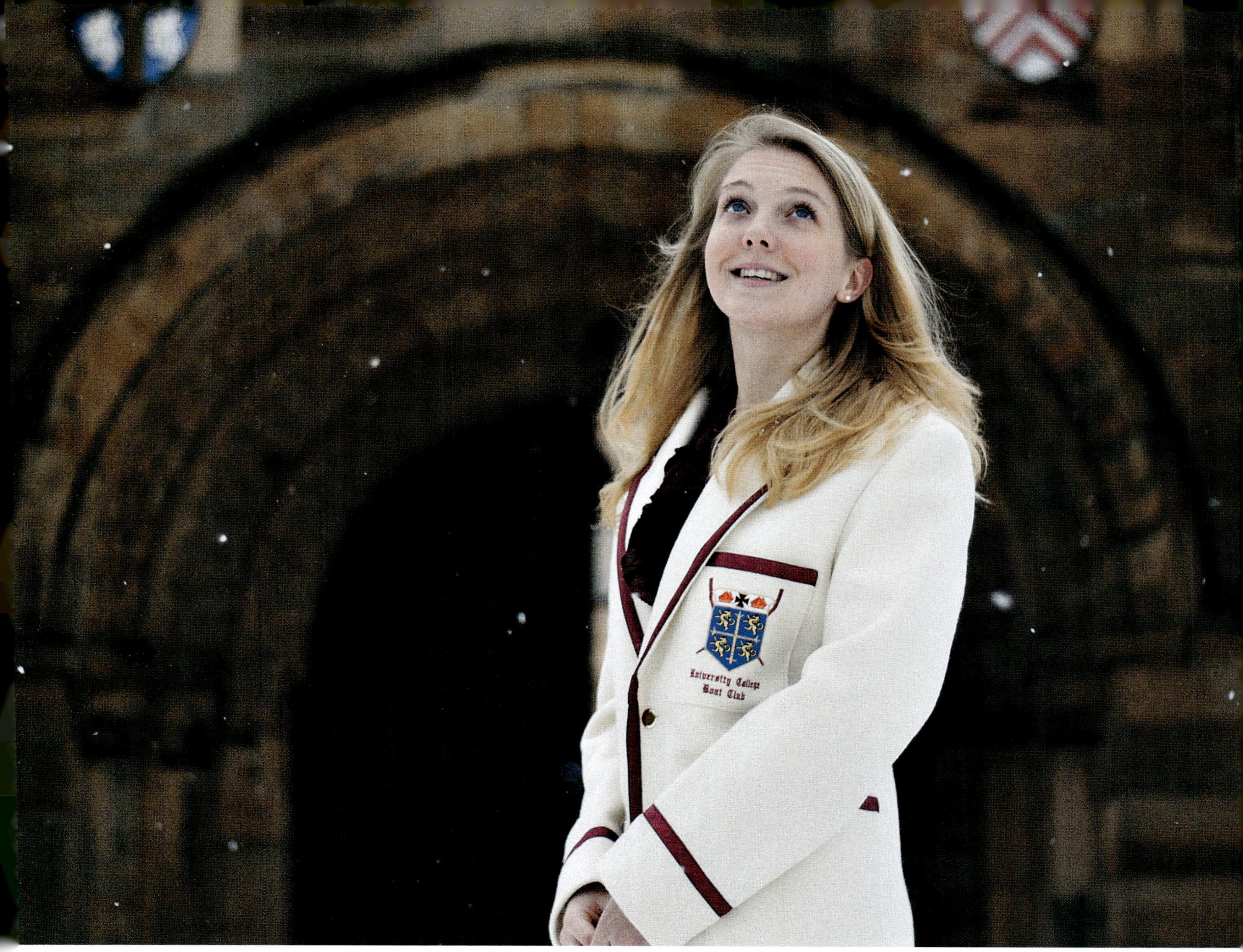

Durham, England

University College Boat Club, Durham

LOUISA SPENCER

Like Oxford and Cambridge, Durham is a collegiate university: the student body is divided into residential colleges, and each college has its own boat club. But when rowing began at Durham—just two years after the university was founded in 1832—University College (or "Castle," as it is colloquially known) was the only college. U.C.B.C. therefore predates Durham University Boat Club by over four decades; in fact, the club is the oldest student society of any type in Durham, and the oldest rowing club in the North of England. The very first Durham Regatta—one of the earliest rowing regattas in Britain—was held in 1834 to commemorate the Battle of Waterloo and consisted of a race between the county sheriff's crew and a six-oared University College crew.

Consciously fashioning itself on Oxford and Cambridge prototypes (although the club itself predates many Oxbridge college boat clubs), U.C.B.C. is highly traditional, and among these traditions is the wearing of blazers. Castle rowers have worn the cardinal-and-white jackets since the nineteenth century; current and former first boat rowers may wear two cardinal sleeve stripes, while all other members wear one.

Louisa Spencer rowed for Castle and stroked the Durham University women's eight at the Henley Women's Regatta.

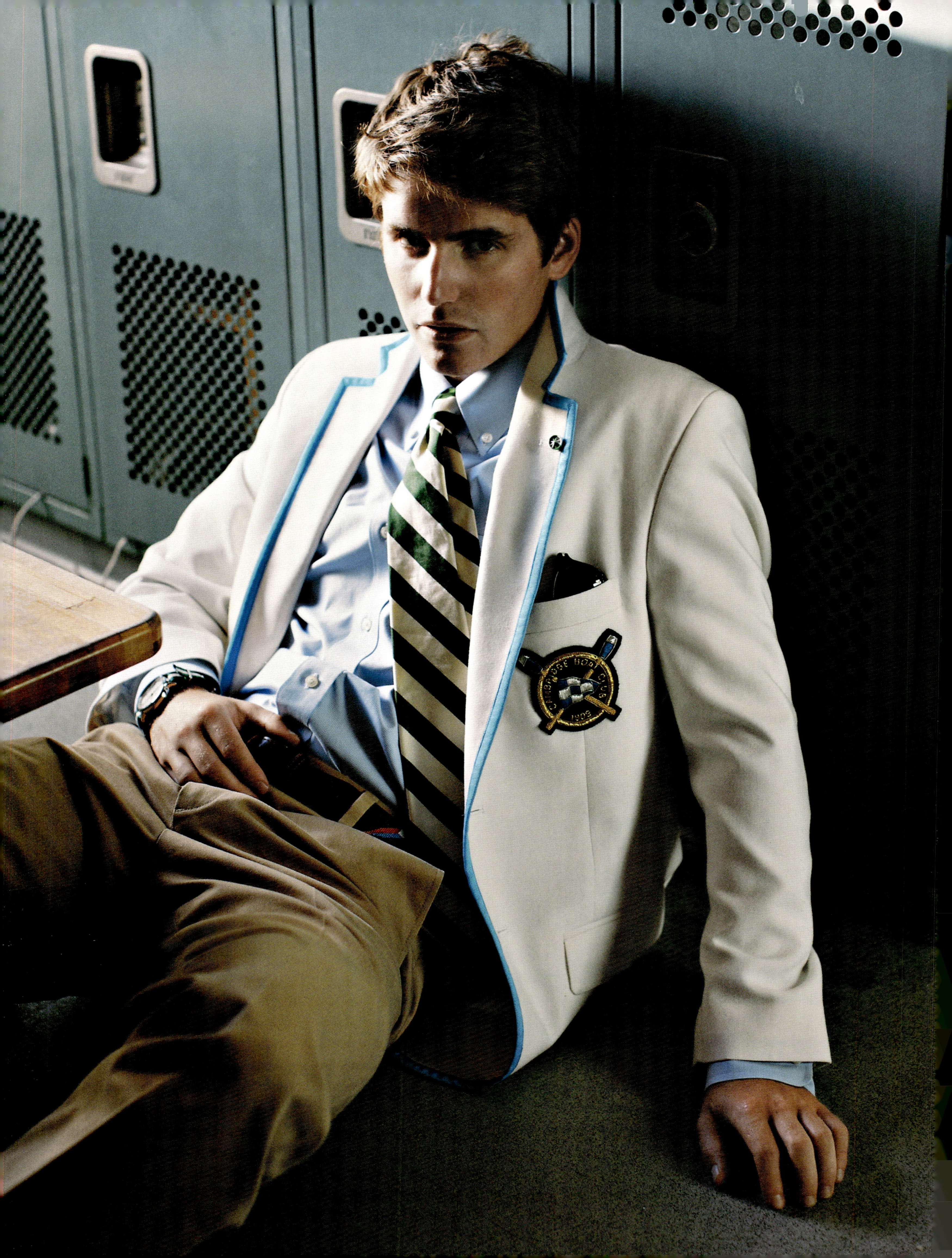

Cambridge, Massachusetts

Cambridge Boat Club

ANDREW CAMPBELL JR.

Cambridge Boat Club was established on the banks of the Charles River in 1909 to "encourage athletic exercises, boating and yachting and to establish and maintain a place for social meetings." For decades, however, the club was first and foremost a posh social club. It was not until the 1960s, when the club established the Head of the Charles Regatta and began to host national-team hopefuls, that competitive rowing became a focus.

Today, C.B.C. serves as headquarters for the Head of the Charles—now the largest two-day rowing event in the world. The club is also the current training site and home club for several elite and national-team scullers, including U.S. lightweight single sculler and under-23 world champion Andrew Campbell Jr.

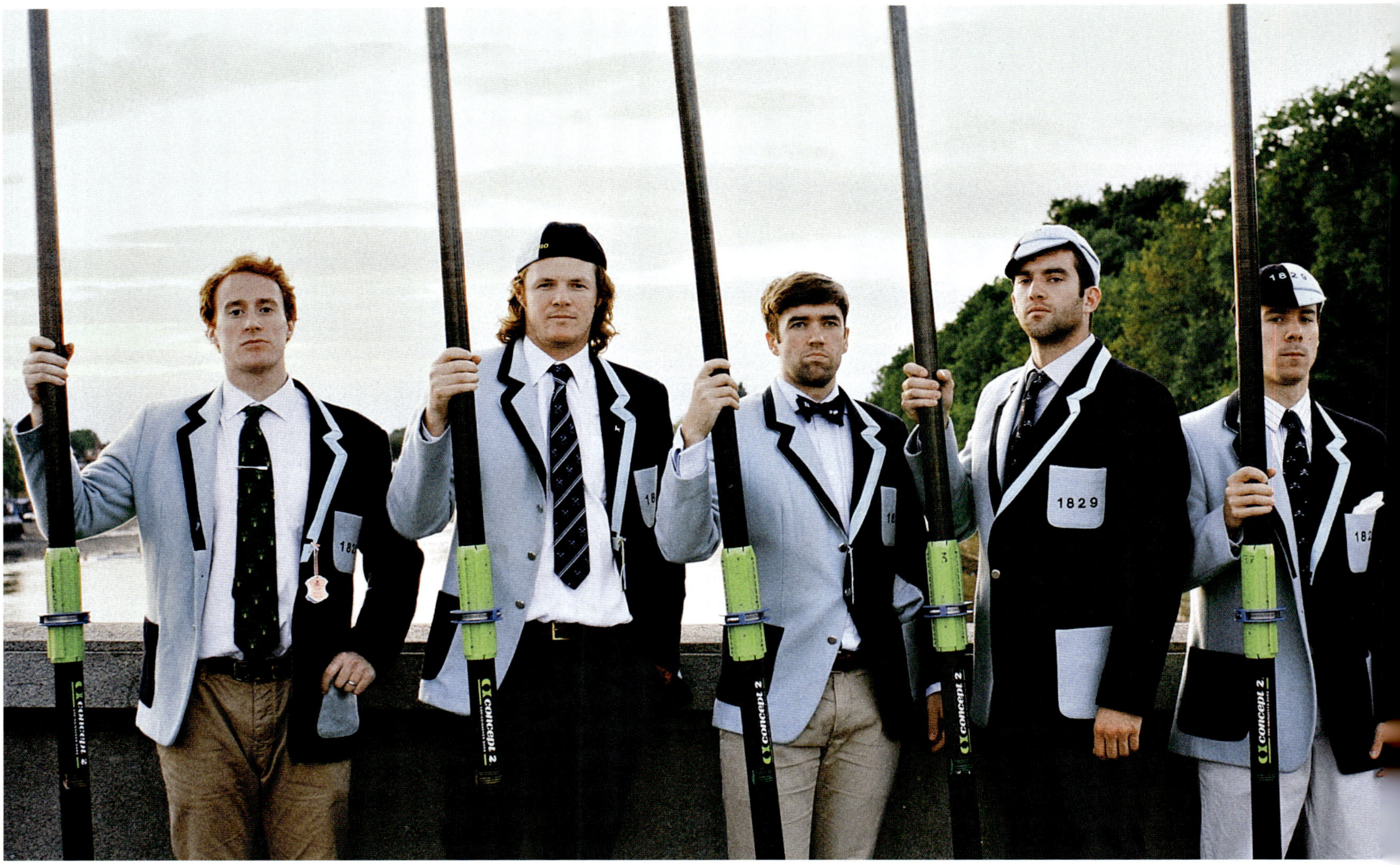

London, England

1829 Boat Club

MARK VICKERS, RODNEY STEPHENS, LUCAS DALGLISH,
ROBIN EJSMOND-FREY, JONNY MATHEWS, HENRY MORRIS

Bosporos is the name of the Oxford University Boat Club alumni (old boys') rowing club, and Crabtree is its Cambridge counterpart. To assemble more competitive crews for Henley and other events, however, the Oxford and Cambridge old boys occasionally forget their differences and join forces under the banner of "1829 Boat Club." The club is named for the year of the first Oxford-Cambridge Boat Race, and its blazer is a combination of Oxford's dark blue and Cambridge's light blue, with counterchanged trim and pockets.

1829 won the Thames Challenge Cup at the Henley Royal Regatta in 2010 and the Wyfold Challenge Cup in 2007.

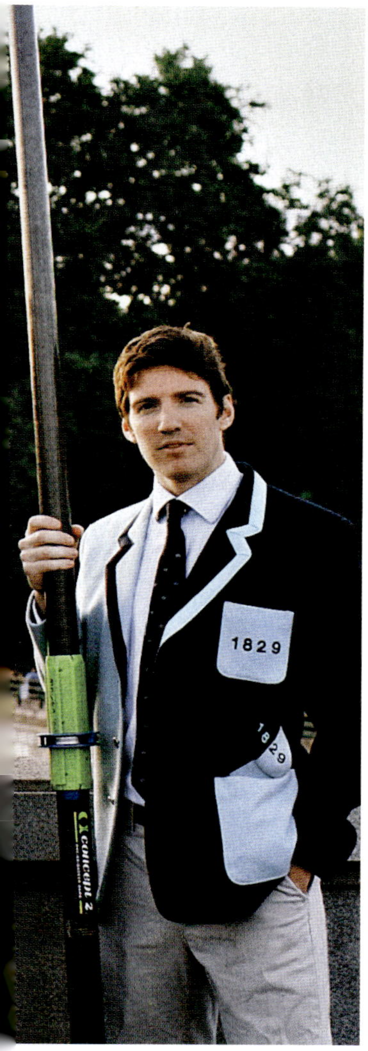

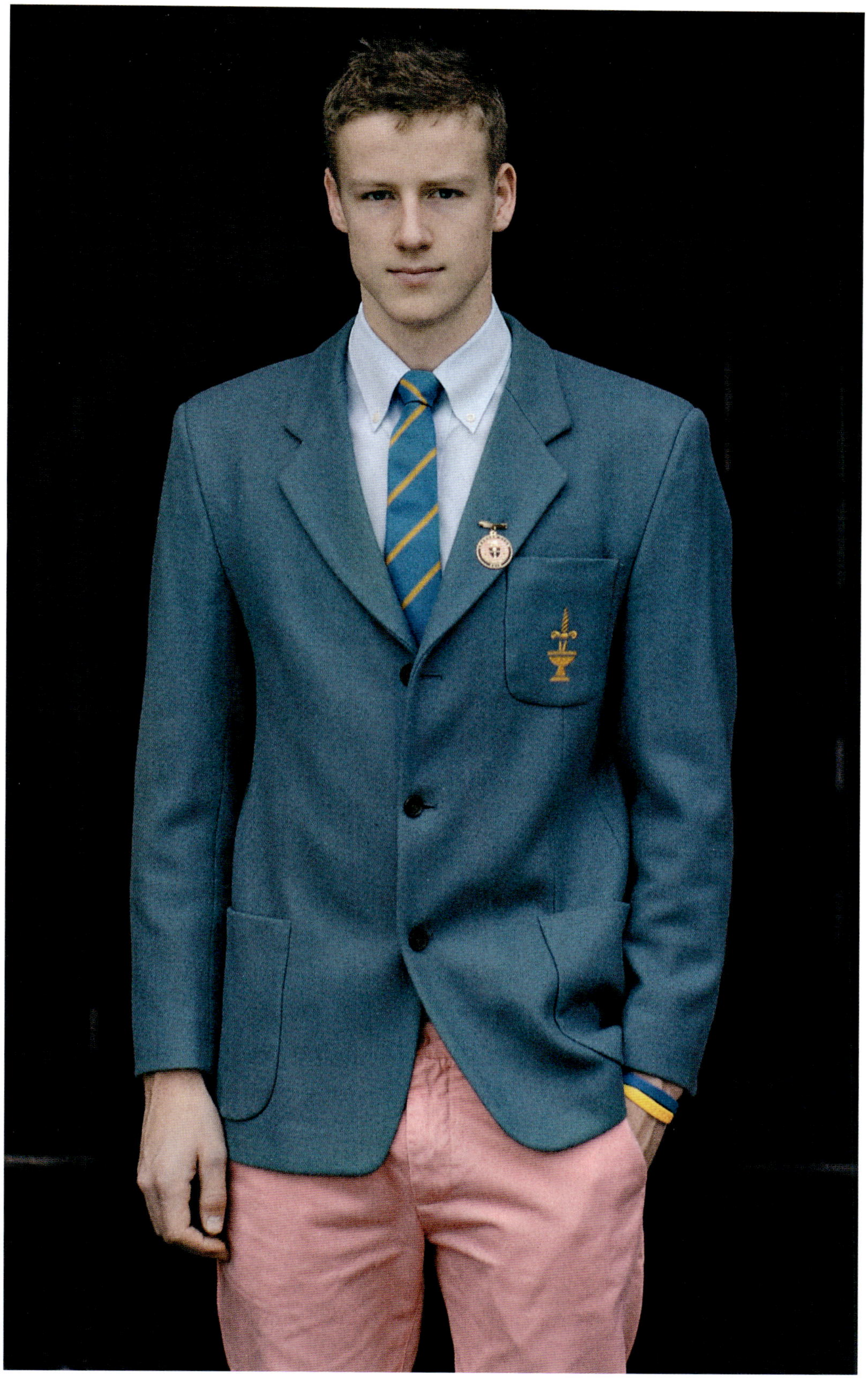

Oxford, England

St. Edward's School Boat Club

CAMERON MacRITCHIE

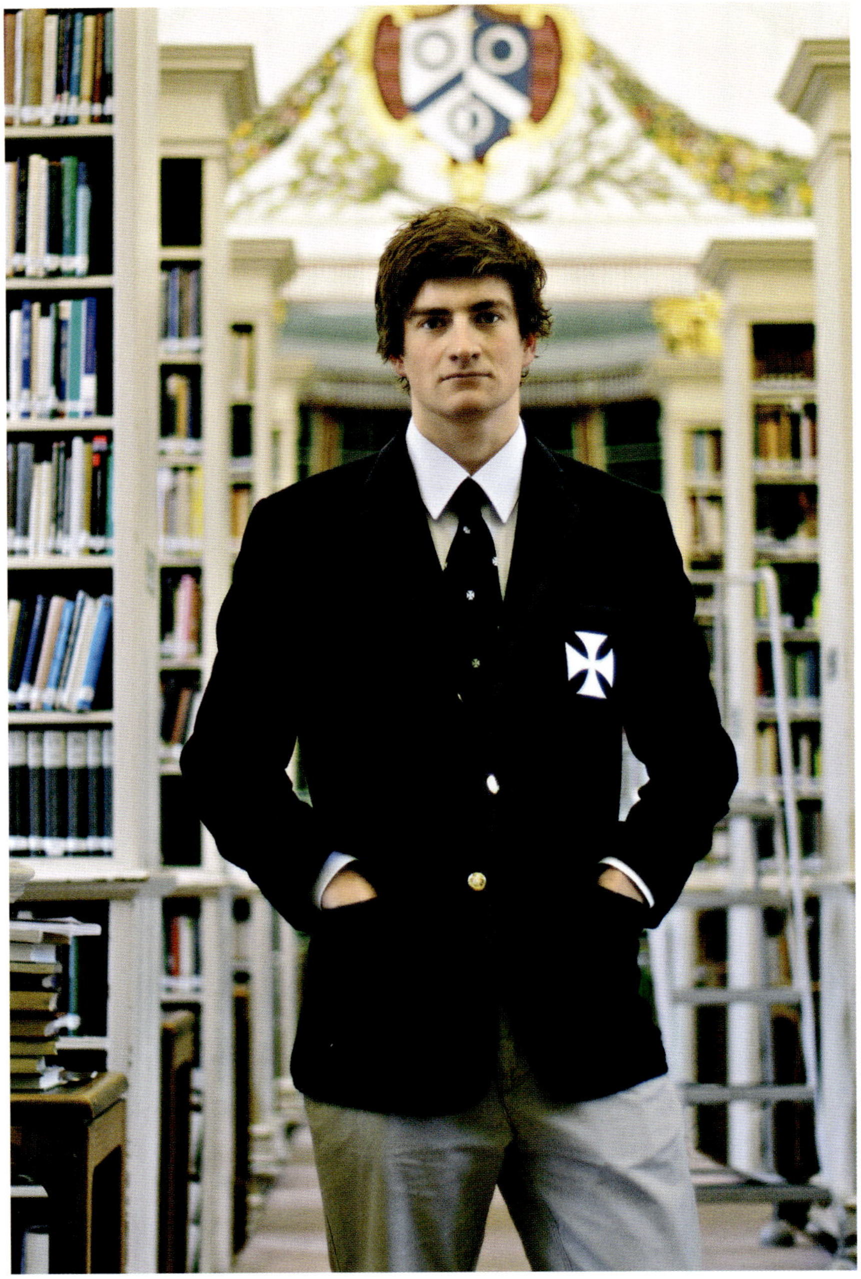

Shrewsbury, England

Royal Shrewsbury School Boat Club

KRIS BLAKE

The Royal Shrewsbury School Hunt (the world's oldest cross-country running club) and the R.S.S.B.C. are the only two sport clubs at the school that have the designation "Royal." The R.S.S.B.C. is also one of the school's most successful sporting clubs.

In 1866, the club's original constitution, written by the boys themselves, declared that their uniform would be "a straw hat with a dark blue ribbon and a white jersey trimmed with dark blue with a blue Maltese Cross on the front." Since then, blue and white have been the club's colors, and the "Maltese Cross" (actually a cross pattée) has been the club's badge. When the Blackburn Rovers Football Club was established by Shrewsbury alumni a few years later, they adopted the same colors and emblem.

Shrewsbury first boat rowers now wear dark blue flannel blazers with dark blue trim: the blazer is identical to those worn by the Oxford Blue Boat, except for the white cross on the pocket.

Old Salopians (as the school's alumni are known) may race for the alumni boat club, Sabrina Club, and wear an entirely different blazer composed of narrow chocolate, royal blue, and silver stripes.

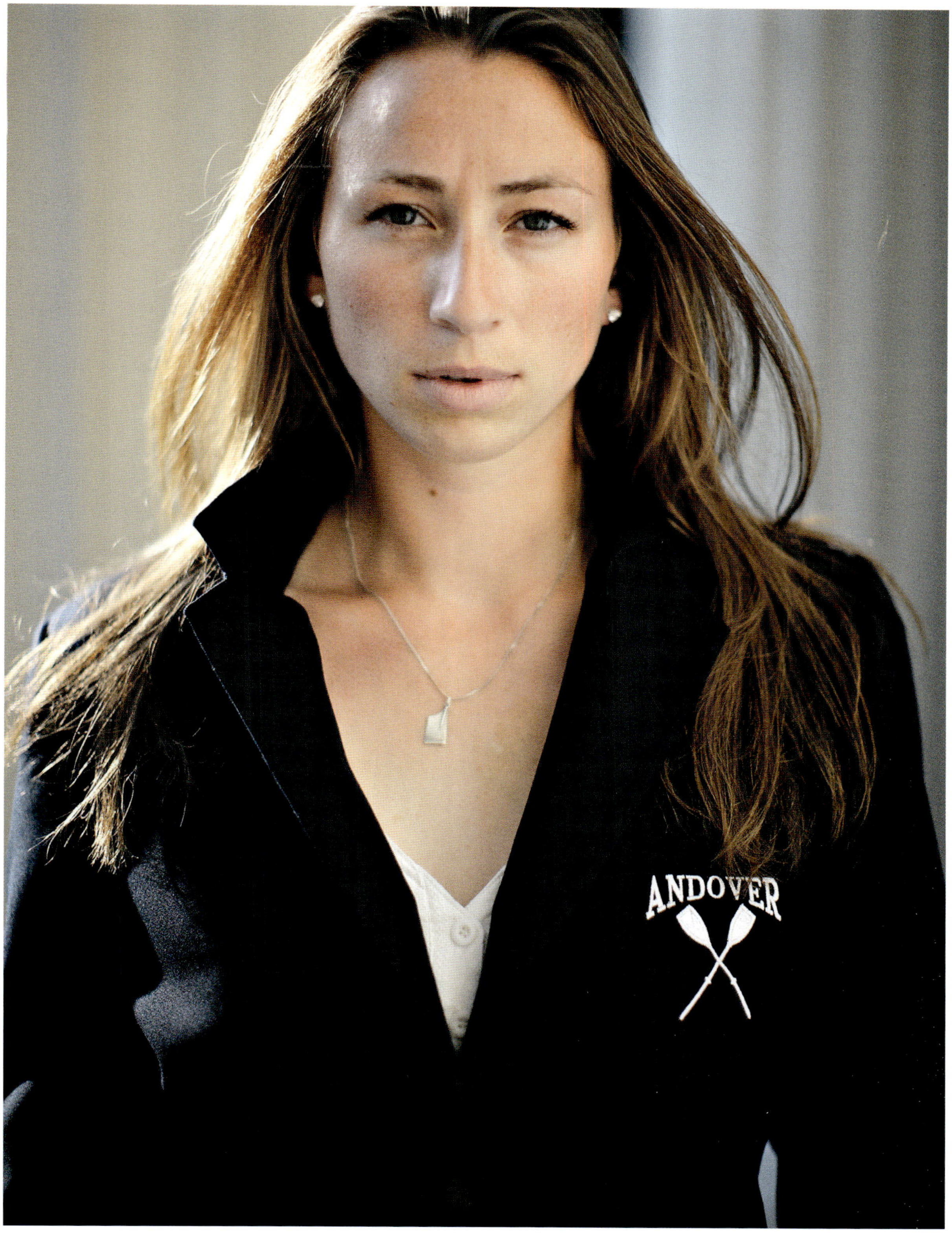

Andover, Massachusetts

Phillips Academy Andover

LIV COFFEY

The daughter of an Olympic rower, Liv led Phillips Academy to an appearance at the Women's Henley Regatta in her senior year at Andover. She has gone on to row for Radcliffe and for the U.S. team, winning a world championship in 2013.

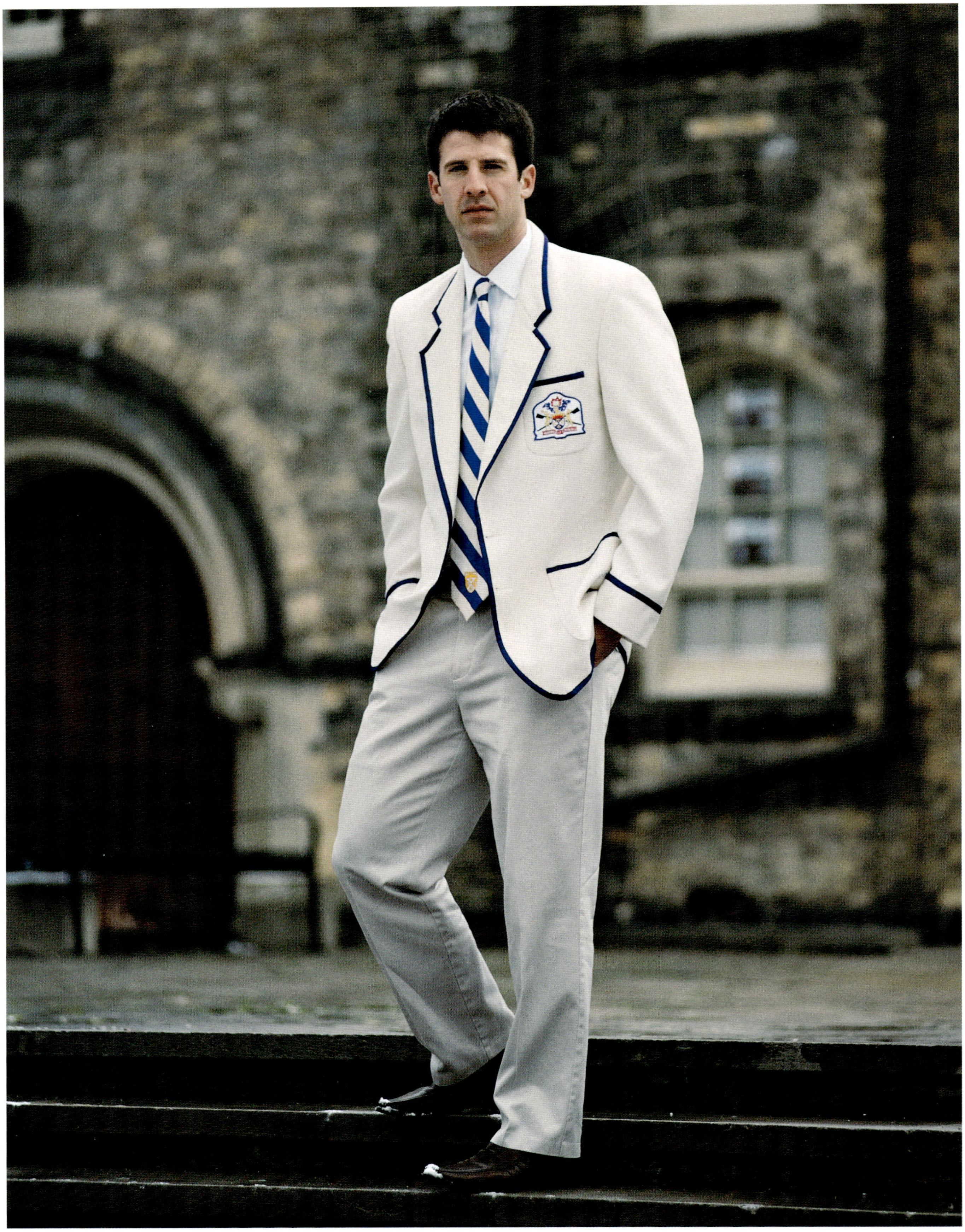

London, Canada

University of Western Ontario

PETER McCLELLAND

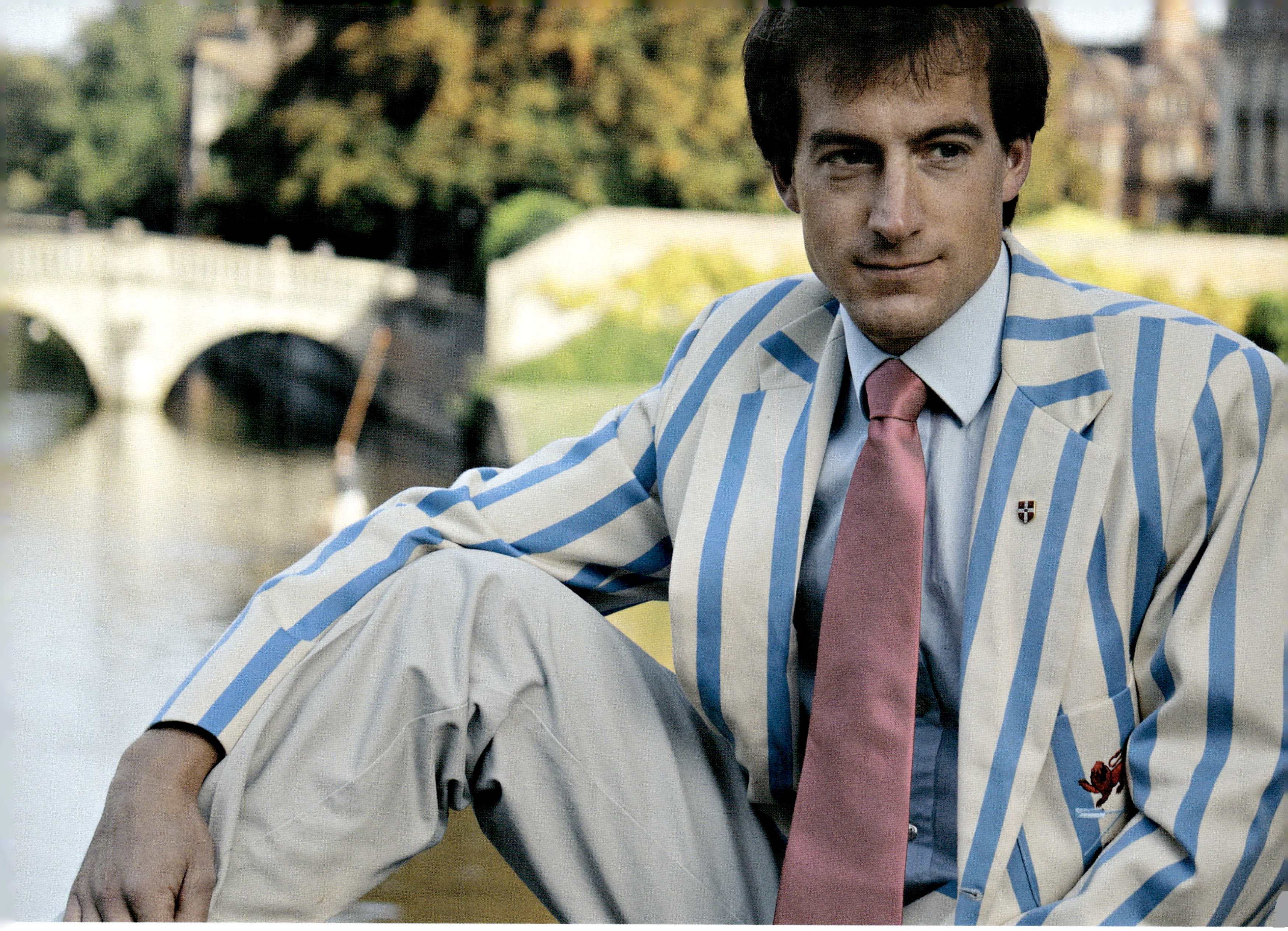

Cambridge, England

Cambridge University Lightweight Rowing Club

CHARLIE PITT-FORD

Great Britain first gave official recognition to lightweight-division rowing in 1974. A few months later, on Sunday March 23, 1975, the first Oxford-Cambridge lightweight race was held. Like its heavyweight counterpart, the first Lightweight Boat Race was organized by an undergraduate at St. John's College, Cambridge, who challenged Oxford to an eight-oar match on Henley Reach.

The race became an annual event, and over time additional Oxford vs. Cambridge races were added to the program of what is now known as the Henley Boat Races: a women's race; a lightweight women's race; and races for the women's and lightweight men's reserve crews.

As at Oxford, lightweight rowing is deemed to be a "Half-Blue" sport at Cambridge, and so C.U.L.R.C. Blue Boat oarsmen wear white-and-Cambridge-Blue-striped jackets.

Charlie Pitt-Ford raced for Cambridge in the Lightweight Boat Race three times, winning twice.

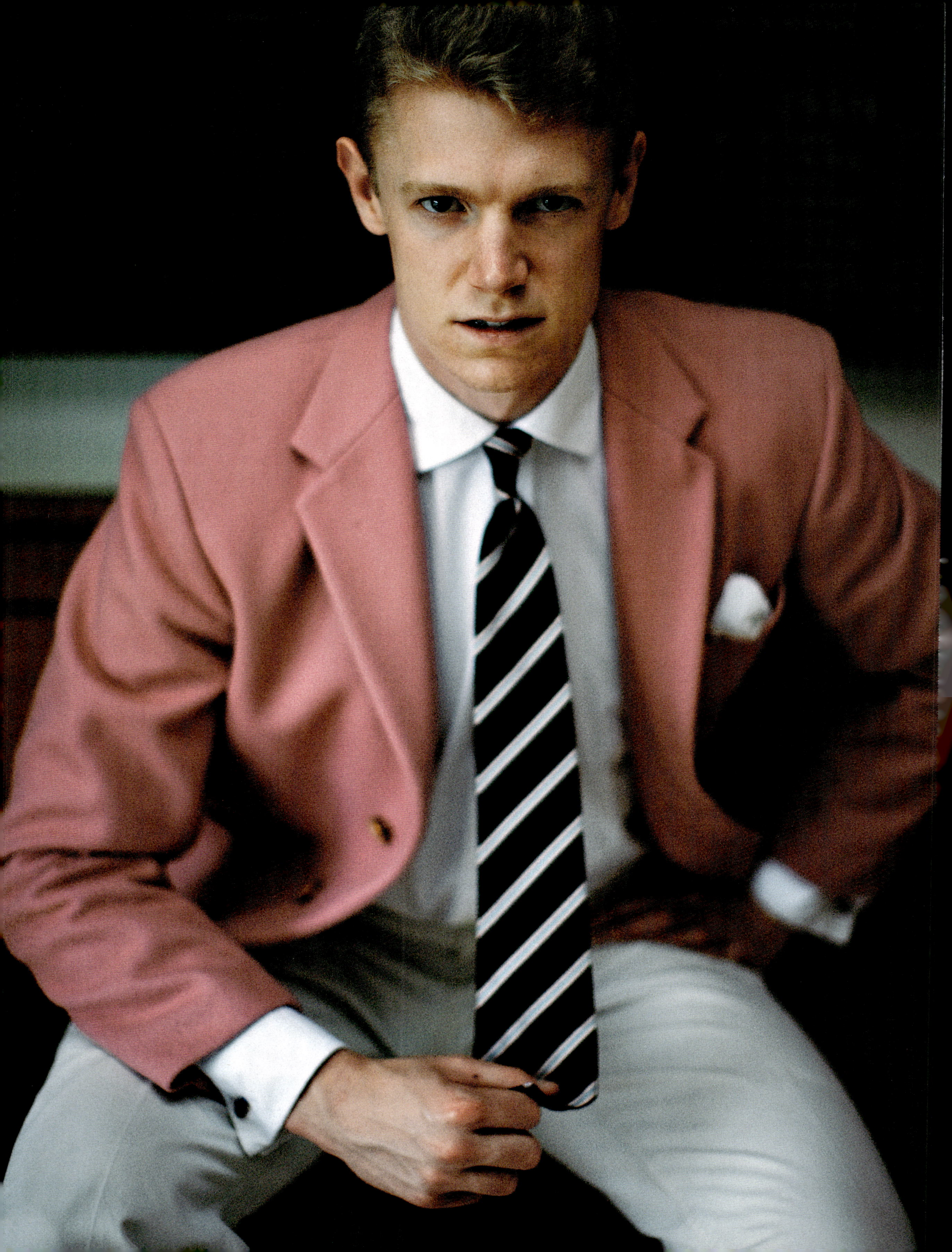

London, England

Westminster School Boat Club

DAN RIX-STANDING

Along with Eton, Westminster School was one of the first to take up rowing; records from the early eighteenth century praise the rowing talents of individual students. As an organized sport, rowing—or "water," as it is known at Westminster—began at the school in the 1790s.

Westminster and Eton boys had been attempting to arrange a match race since 1818, but the schools' headmasters were able to avert such a contest—which was, in their view, an entirely inappropriate activity for young gentlemen—for a full decade.

Eton and Westminster finally raced on the Thames in 1829 (the same year as the first Oxford-Cambridge Race), but the headmasters persisted in their efforts to prevent the race from becoming an annual event by locking students in their rooms on race day, threatening rowers with expulsion, and deploying a range of other underhanded tactics.

Both crews wore light blue in the 1835 race, but for the next race, in 1837, Westminster adopted its famous pink so that spectators would be able to tell which crew was which. One of these spectators was the ailing King William IV, who attended against the advice of his doctors. Bundled in a great white coat and hoping for an Eton victory, he watched from his carriage. As soon as he saw the Westminster crew pull ahead, he allegedly shut the blinds of his carriage in disgust and ordered the carriage back to Windsor Castle, where he stayed until his death (attended by a team of Westminster-educated physicians).

Westminster's school color is still pink, and Westminster rowers wear soft pink flannel blazers. Dan Rix-Standing won the Fawley Cup with Westminster at the 2009 Henley Royal Regatta.

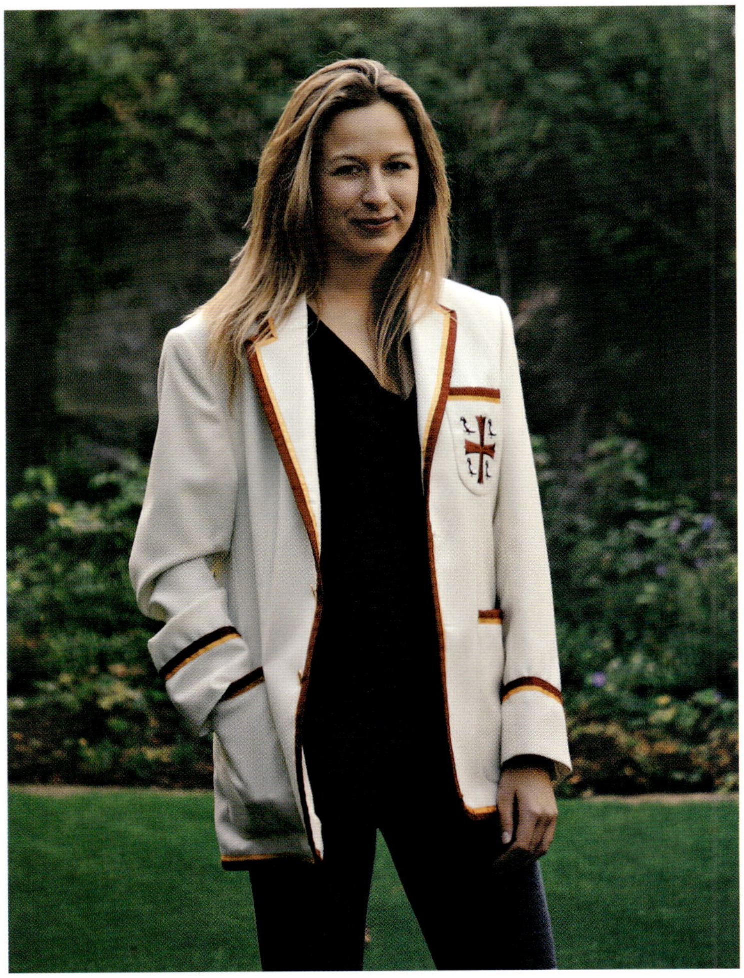

Oxford, England

St. Edmund Hall Boat Club, Oxford

ANNA HEIMBICHNER

•

"Teddy Hall" reigned women's rowing at Oxford from 2006 to 2009, holding the top position—the women's Headship—in Summer Eights.

In 2004, as a visiting student from the University of California, Anna Heimbichner stroked the women's first eight to a meteoric rise from ninth to third in the Oxford University bumps charts. In 2006, back at the Hall as a graduate student, Anna stroked the boat to the Headship before relinquishing the stroke seat in 2007 to take the coxswain's position; steering and making the calls, she and the crew successfully defended Teddy Hall's Headship.

London, England

Vesta Rowing Club

KATHRYN HEDGES

•

"Vesta Rowing Club . . . Established in 1871. Election by ballot of members, one black ball in three to exclude. . . . Colours, crimson and black stripes oblique."

—Charles Dickens Jr., *Dickens's Dictionary of the Thames*, 1881

Kathryn Hedges won the women's senior eight event at Henley Women's Regatta in 2010, earning herself a Vesta honours cap. According to club rules: "An honours cap shall be awarded at the Club's expense to all Active Members who win, whilst representing the Club, an Open Senior rowing or sculling race. This cap shall be of Club crimson embroidered with the Club flags and the year of the award."

All members may wear the club blazer: white flannel with club buttons and trimmed with the club ribbon.

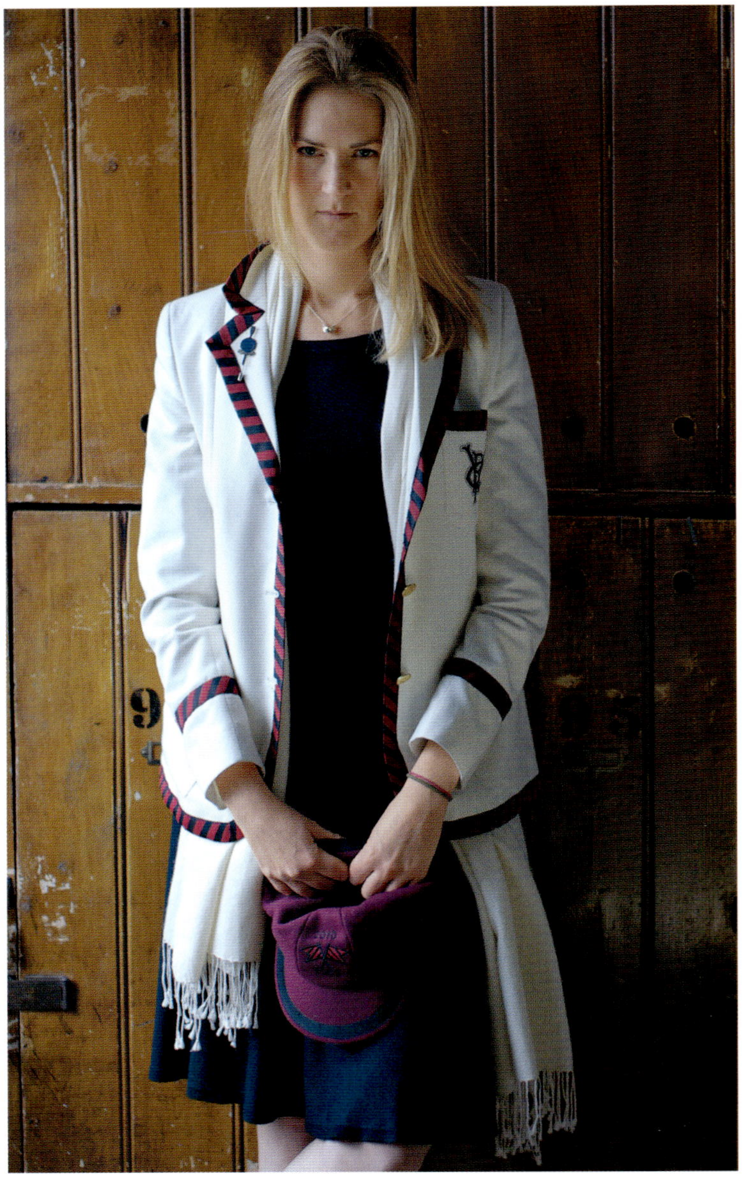

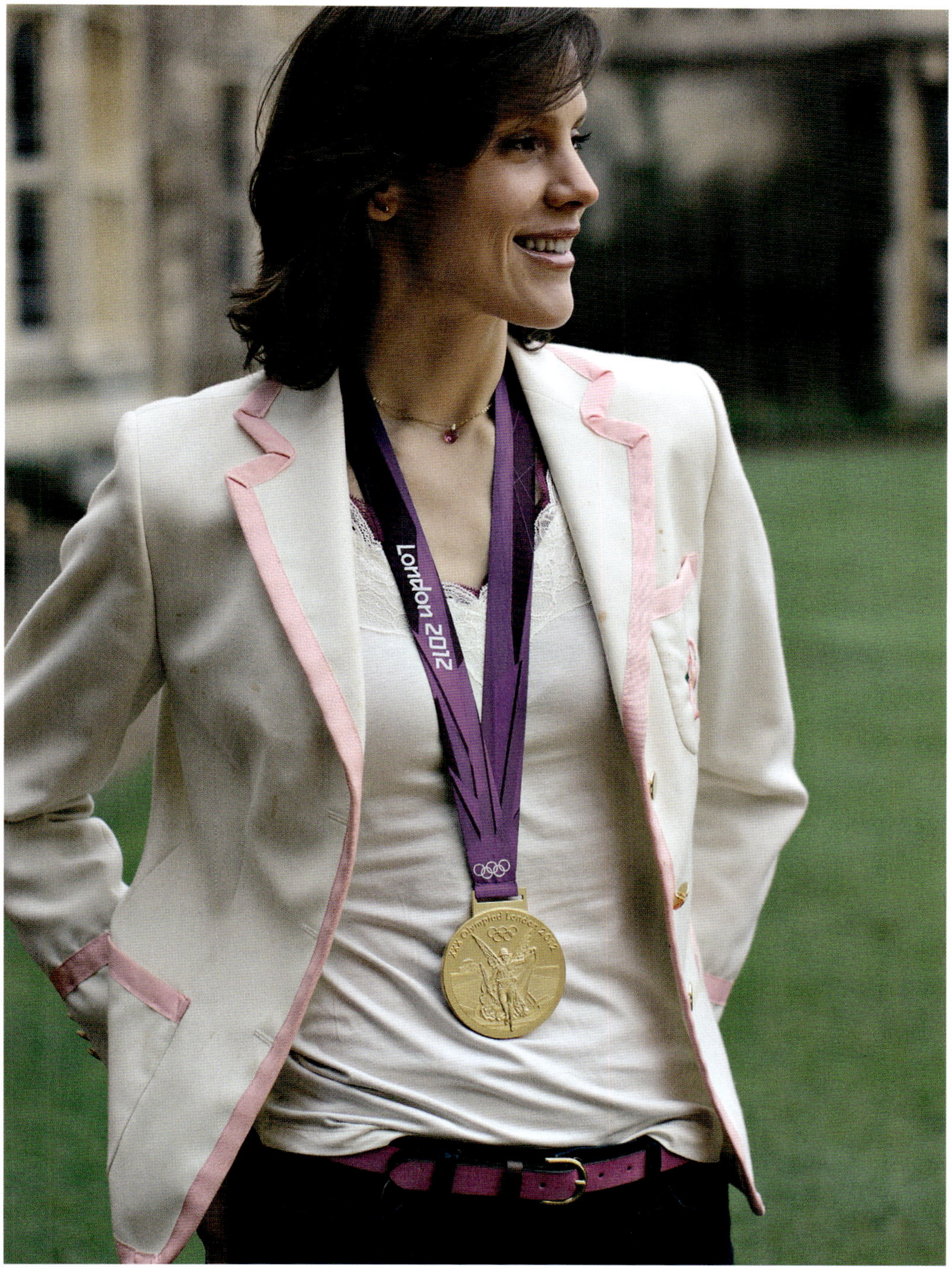

Oxford, England

Pembroke College Boat Club, Oxford

CARYN DAVIES

Since the mid-nineteenth century, Pembroke College Boat Club has used the rose—from the college coat of arms—as its emblem and various shades of pink and red as its color.

In recent years, Pembroke has been one of Oxford's most successful boat clubs in both men's and women's events. The club caused an uproar in 2013, when its men's first boat was stroked by visiting student Caryn Davies, a three-time Olympic medalist with the U.S. women's team. With seven male rowers behind her, and racing against all-men's crews (several of which contained male Olympic medalists), Caryn led Pembroke to the Headship in both of the major Oxford bumping regattas: Torpids and Summer Eights. She is America's most successful female Olympic rower ever.

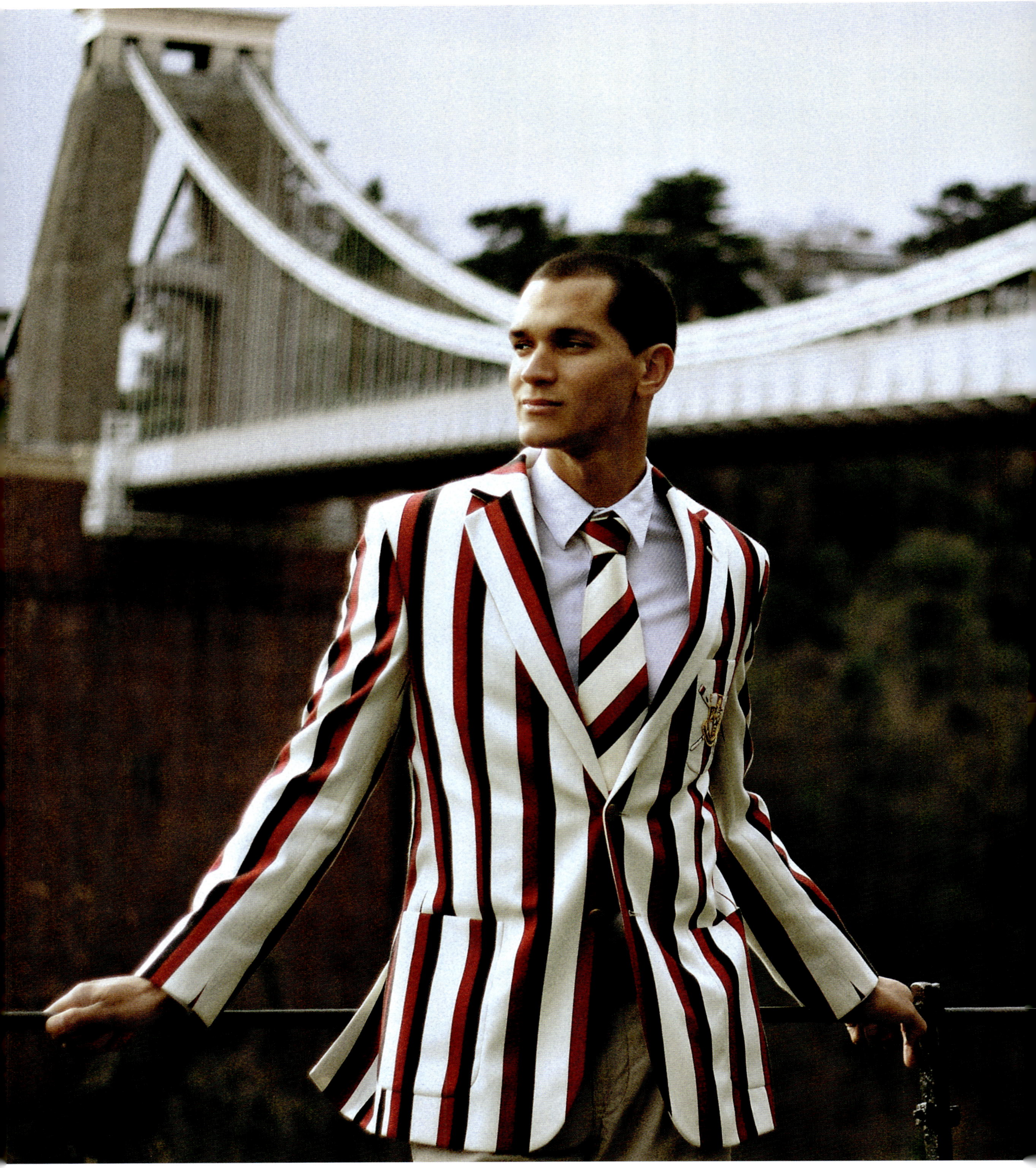

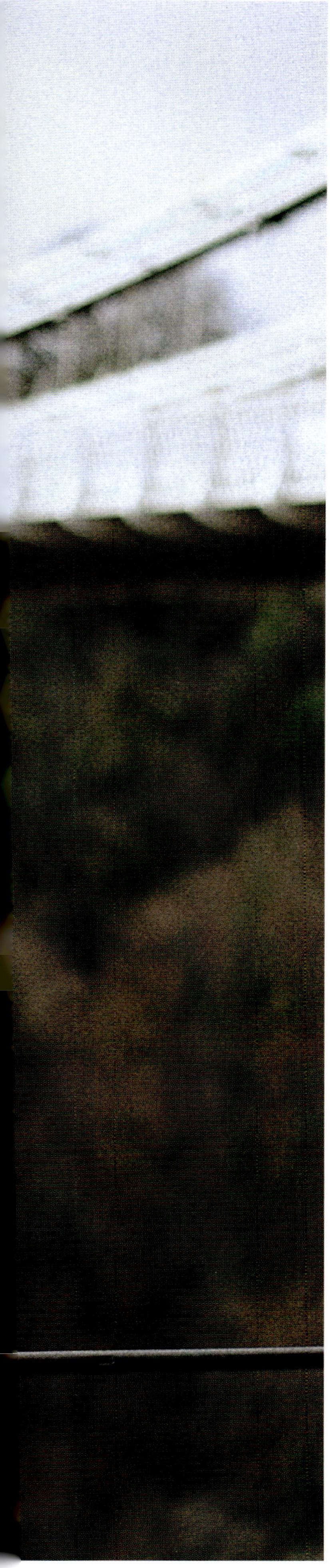

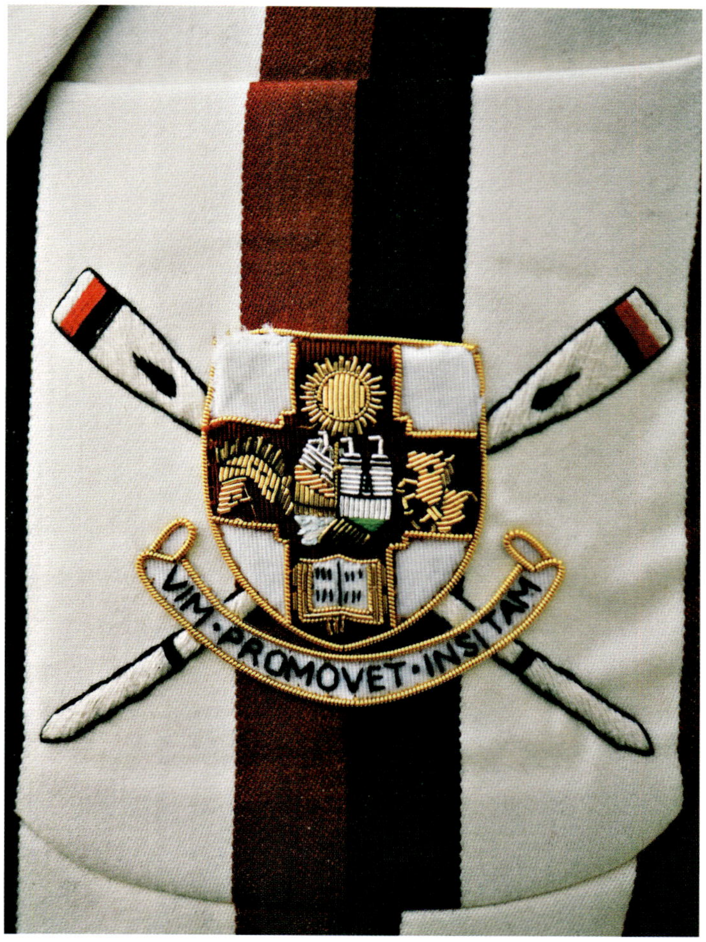

Bristol, England

University of Bristol Boat Club

JAMES DIAZ-SOKOLOFF

University of Bristol Boat Club was established in 1909, the same year that the university obtained its Royal Charter. Only those who have represented the club at Henley or performed "extraordinary service" for the club may wear the blazer.

James Diaz-Sokoloff, who has twice represented the university at Henley, stands in front of Bristol's famous Clifton Suspension Bridge.

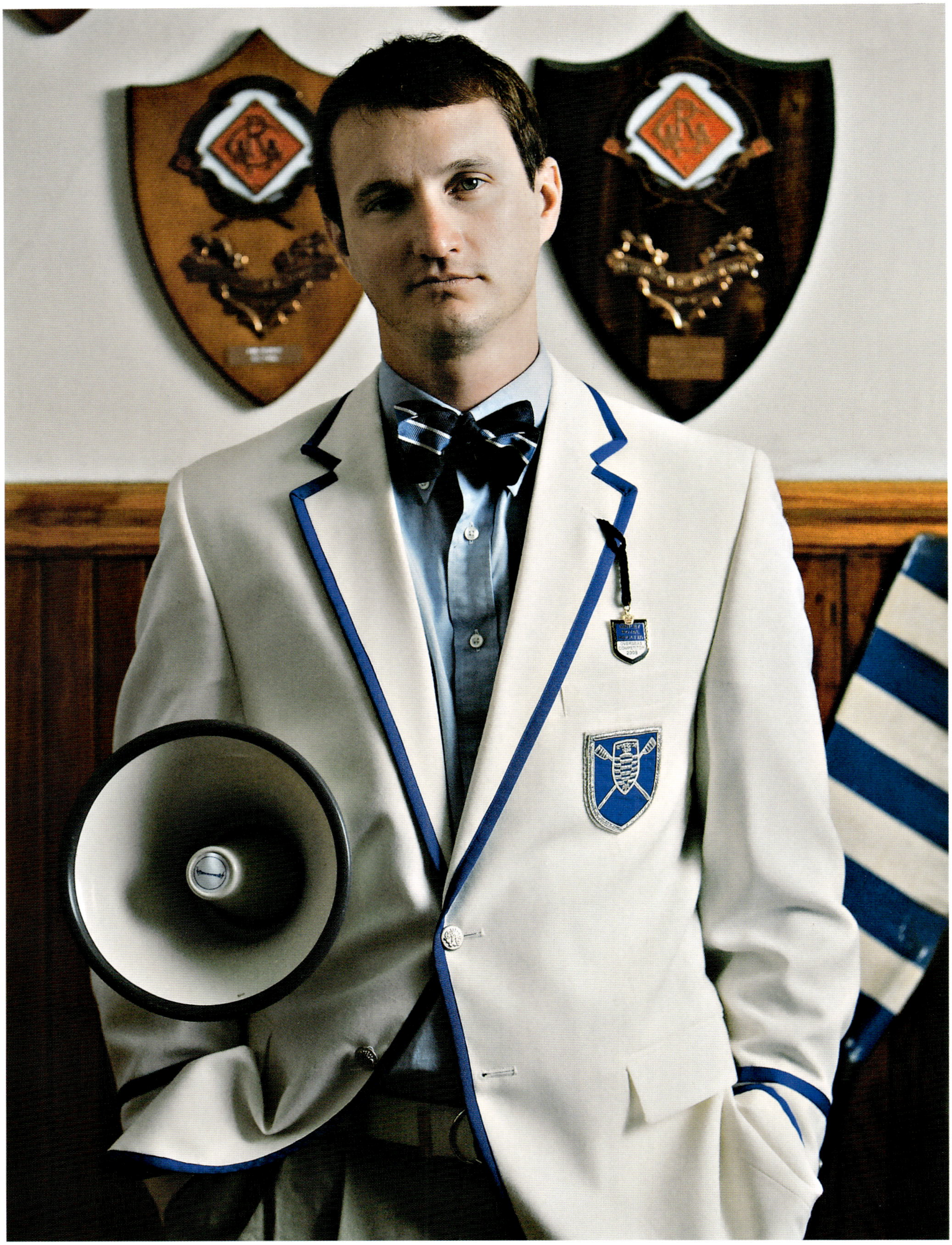

Cambridge, Massachusetts

Riverside Boat Club

JEFF FORRESTER

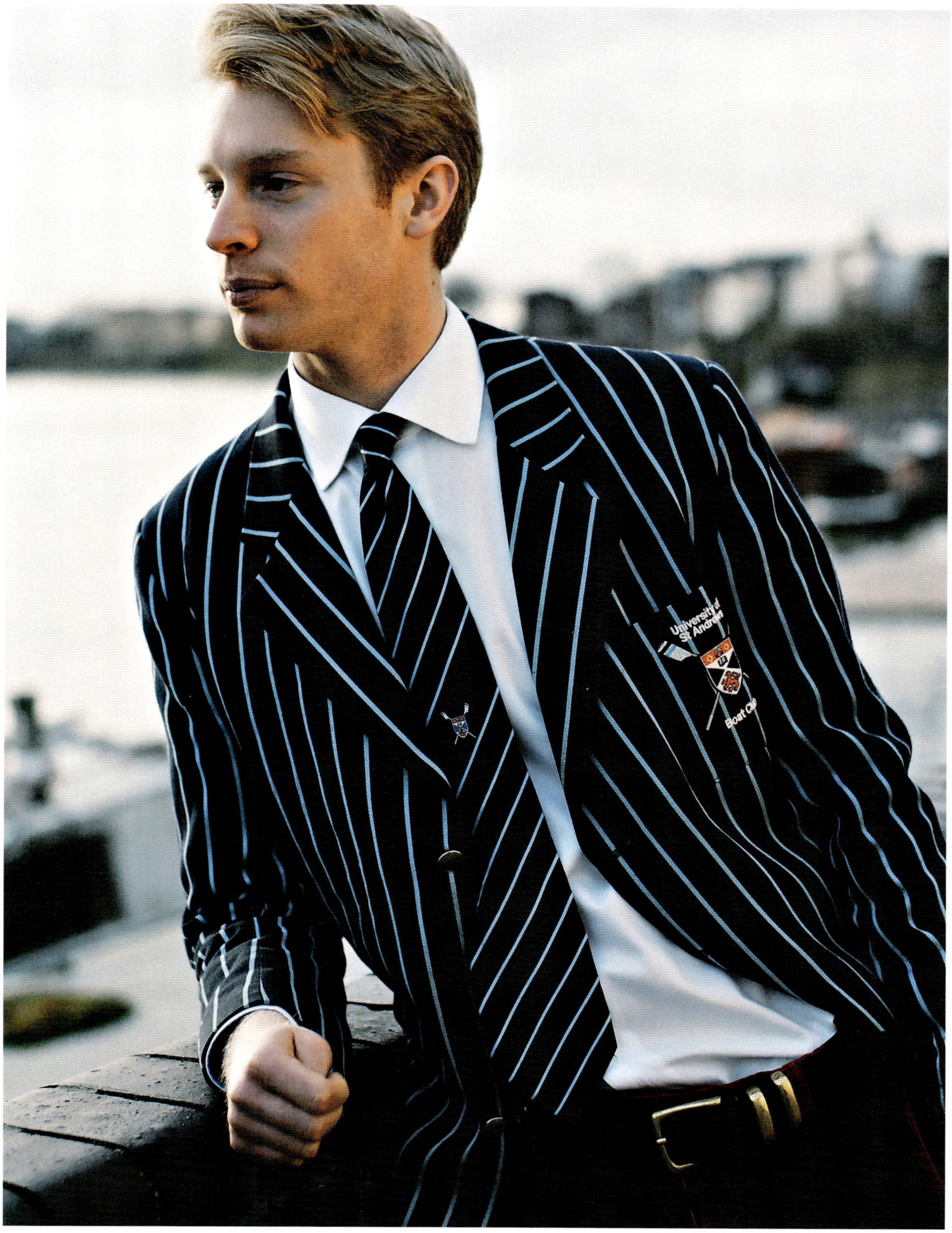

St. Andrews, Scotland

University of St. Andrews Boat Club

MICHAEL DARCY PLANT

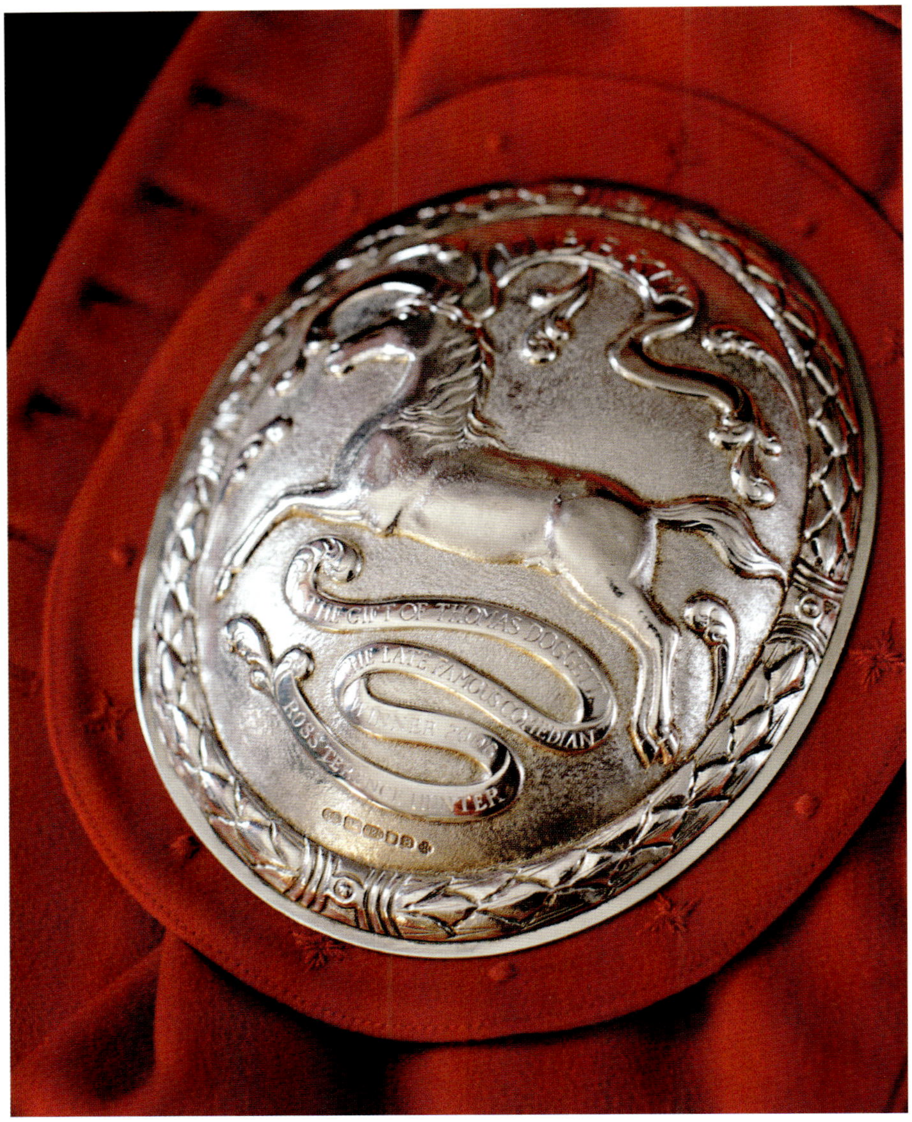

London, England

Doggett's Coat and Badge

ROSS HUNTER

"I was the pride of all the Thames, / My name was natty Jerry, / The best of smarts and flashy dames / I've carried in my wherry: / For then no mortal soul like me / So merrily did jog it, / I lov'd my wife and friend, d'ye see, / And won the prize of Doggett: / In coat and badge so neat and spruce, / I row'd, all blithe and merry, / And every waterman did use / To call me Happy Jerry."

—Charles Dibdin, "Happy Jerry" song, ca. 1774

For centuries, Londoners relied on licensed Thames watermen—the taxi drivers of their time—and their wherry boats to travel within the metropolis. Travel by road was often slow and unsafe, and until Putney Bridge opened in 1729, London Bridge was the only road crossing of the Thames downstream of Kingston. But rowing on the Tideway could also be a difficult and dangerous affair, and so as early as 1193 the Corporation of London was tasked with licensing boat operators on the Thames. Since the sixteenth century, watermen have had to complete formal apprenticeships to earn their licenses.

Comedian, writer, actor, theater manager, and ardent supporter of King George I, Irish-born Thomas Doggett was a larger-than-life character in early eighteenth-century London. He was also a frequent customer of the watermen, using their services to travel between his theater in the City and his rooms in Chelsea.

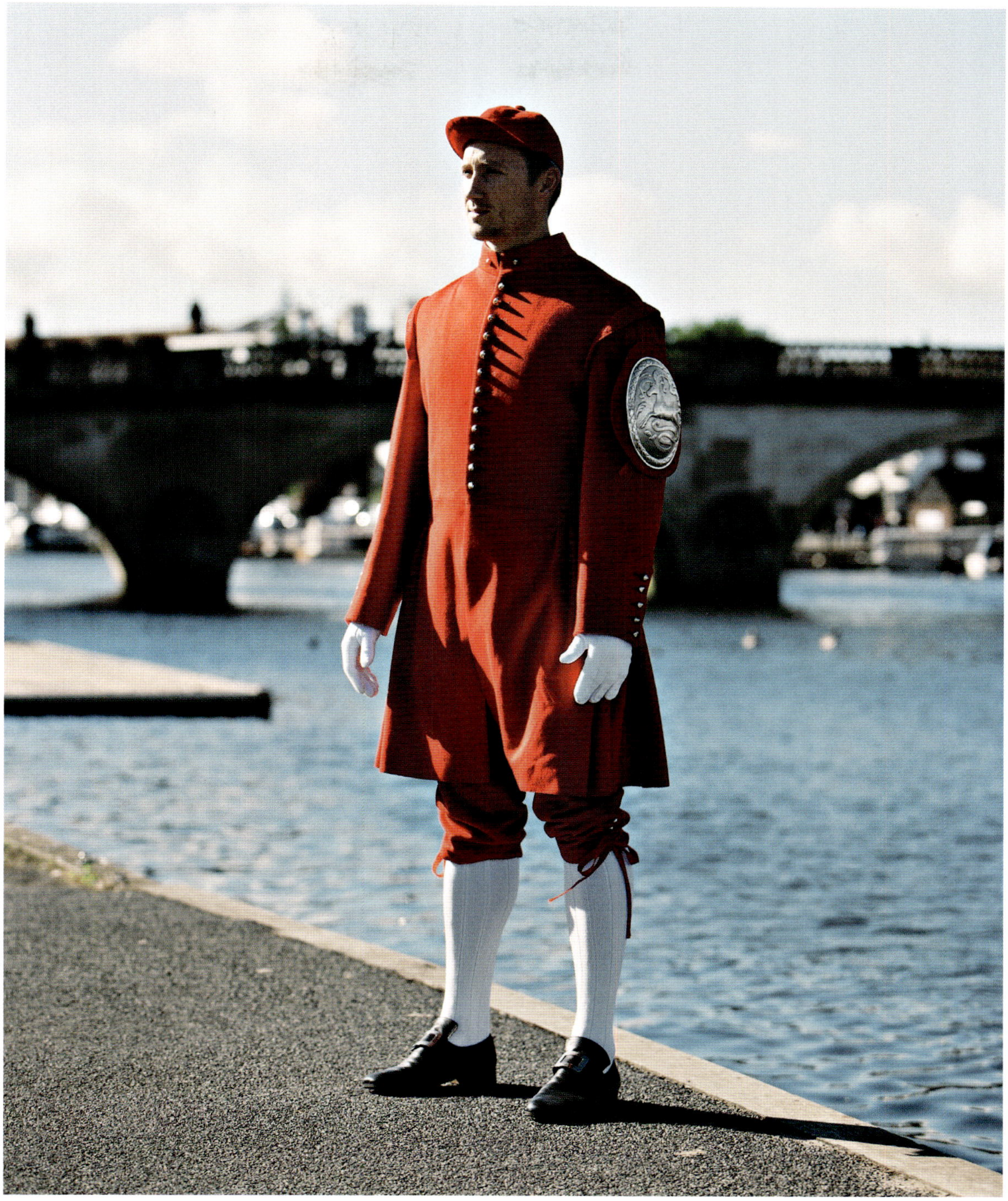

One particularly tempestuous evening, according to legend, Doggett wished to hire a waterman to row him home. In spite of the stormy weather, unfavorable tide, and turbulent water, a young waterman who had just completed his apprenticeship volunteered for the task and brought Doggett safely home. Doggett was so impressed by the fellow that he decided to fund an annual race for recently licensed watermen. According to another version of the story, the comedian decided to sponsor the race after he actually fell into the Thames and was saved from drowning by the young waterman.

Whatever his true inspiration, in 1715 Doggett established a race for newly initiated watermen from the Old Swan Inn near London Bridge to the White Swan Inn in Chelsea. The race was held on the first anniversary of King George I's coronation, and the winner's prize, donated by Doggett, was a traditional waterman's coat and an ostentatious silver badge emblazoned with the word LIBERTY and the wild horse of Hanover, in honor of George I and the new royal House of Hanover.

Doggett made the Coat and Badge wager an annual event and organized the race every year until he died in 1721, when he left instructions and funds for its continuation "for ever." The race has been managed by the Worshipful Company of Fishmongers since then and can claim to be the oldest continually staged annual sporting event in the world.

Today, the course and the prize remain the same, but watermen compete for the Coat and Badge in modern sculling boats. Ross Hunter won the Coat and Badge in 2006, completing the four-mile, five-furlong course in 25 minutes and 27 seconds. Ross learned to row at Poplar, Blackwall & District Rowing Club—the traditional rowing club for Thames watermen and lightermen.

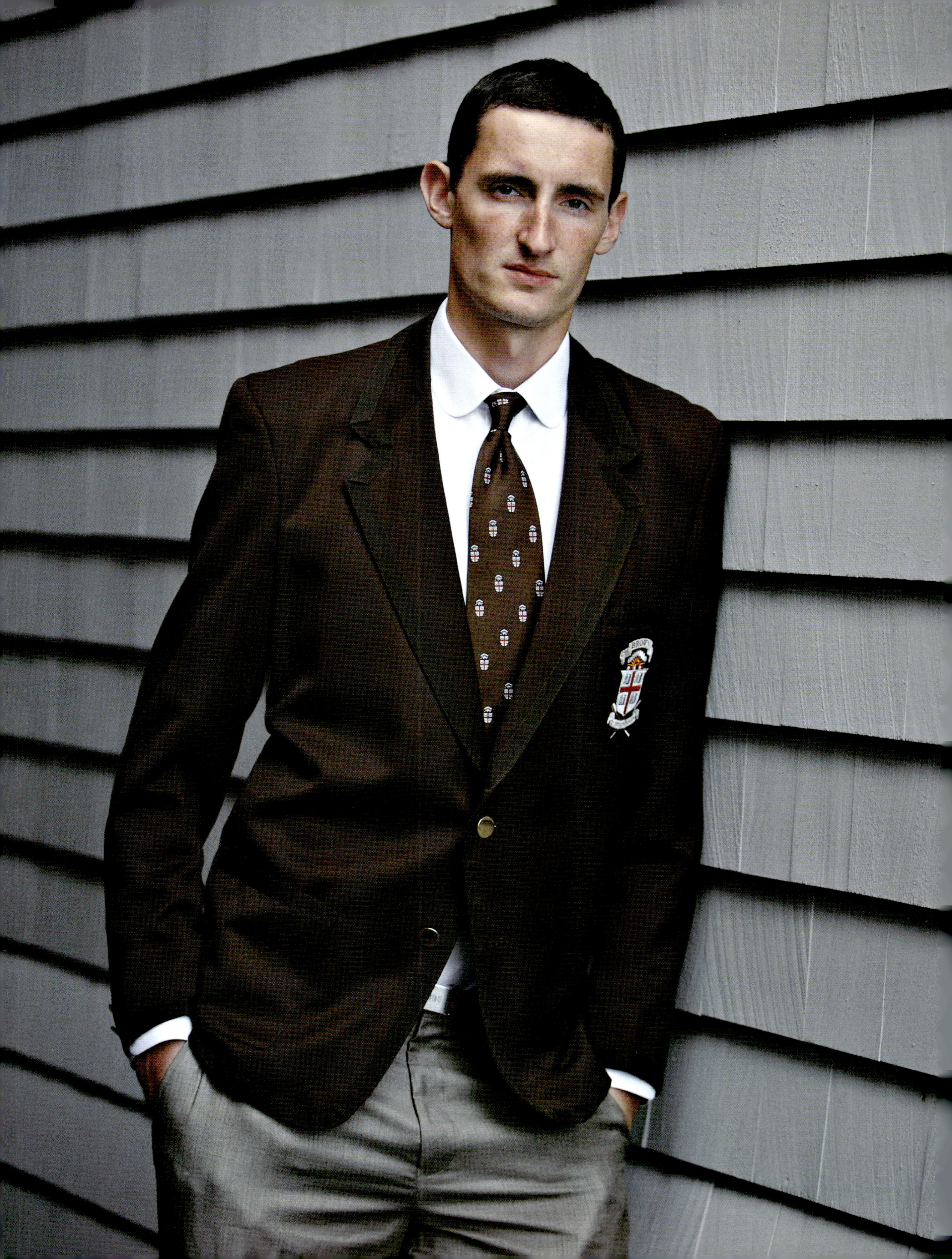

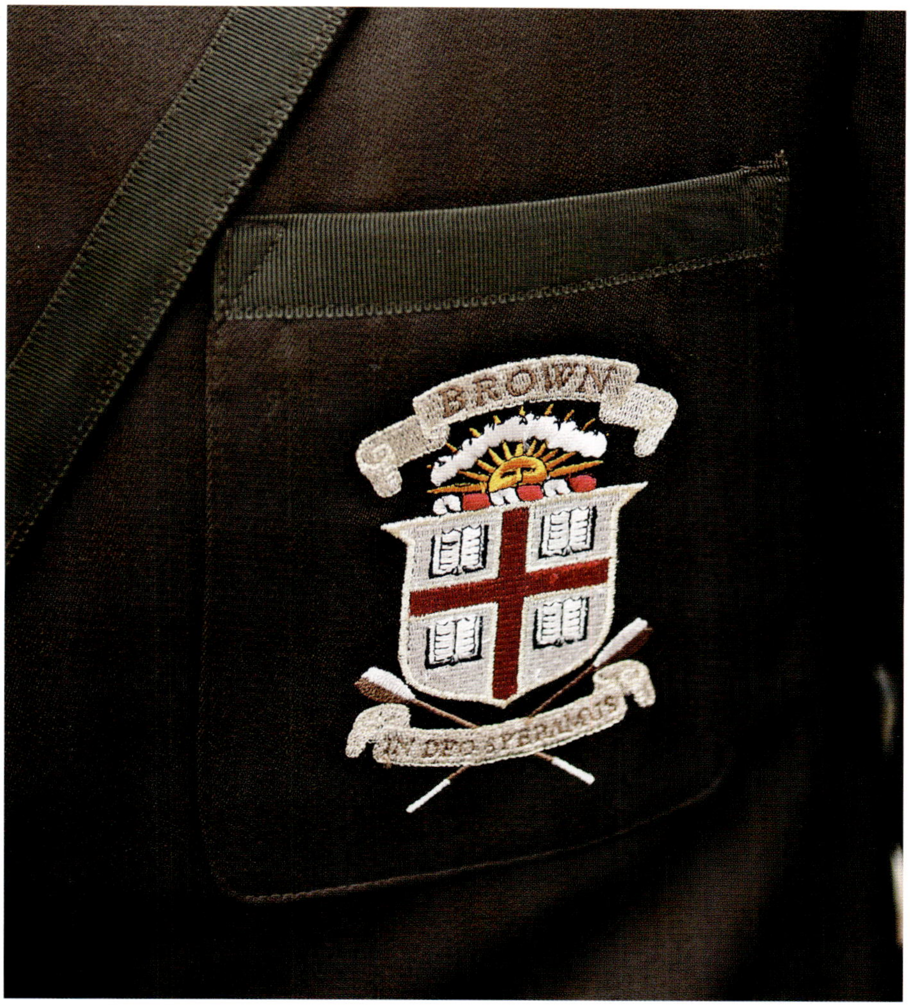

Providence, Rhode Island

Brown University Boat Club

MATT WHEELER

"The general opinion seems to be that [the color] brown should be adopted. . . . Nothing could be more appropriate for Brown-bred boys. . . . It is the very mark of hardihood, of pluck, of soberness—if you will—but of victory." —Brown Paper, 1866

Brown's Henley jackets imitate the monotone blazers of the top Oxford and Cambridge crews, which are blue with matching blue trim. The university's color may seem an obvious choice, but it was not always so. In 1859, Brown's first oarsmen (and very first intercollegiate athletes) lost a race to Harvard and Yale on Lake Quinsigamond in Worcester, Massachusetts, while wearing a lurid uniform of checkered trousers, salmon silk shirts, and blue skullcaps. Seven years later, seal brown was adopted as the official college color.

In 2009, for the first time in the history of the regatta, Brown emerged victorious in every major event at the Eastern Sprints championship (on Lake Quinsigamond), winning the second freshman eight, first freshman eight, varsity four, second varsity eight, and varsity eight events. Matt Wheeler rowed in the varsity eight, which beat Harvard by one second to cap off Brown's perfect regatta. The varsity crew went on to capture the Ladies' Challenge Plate (for men's eights) at the Henley Royal Regatta.

OVERLEAF: Brown's 2009 varsity eight powering ahead of a Leander-Molesey composite and taking their last strokes in front of the Steward's Enclosure in the Henley final.

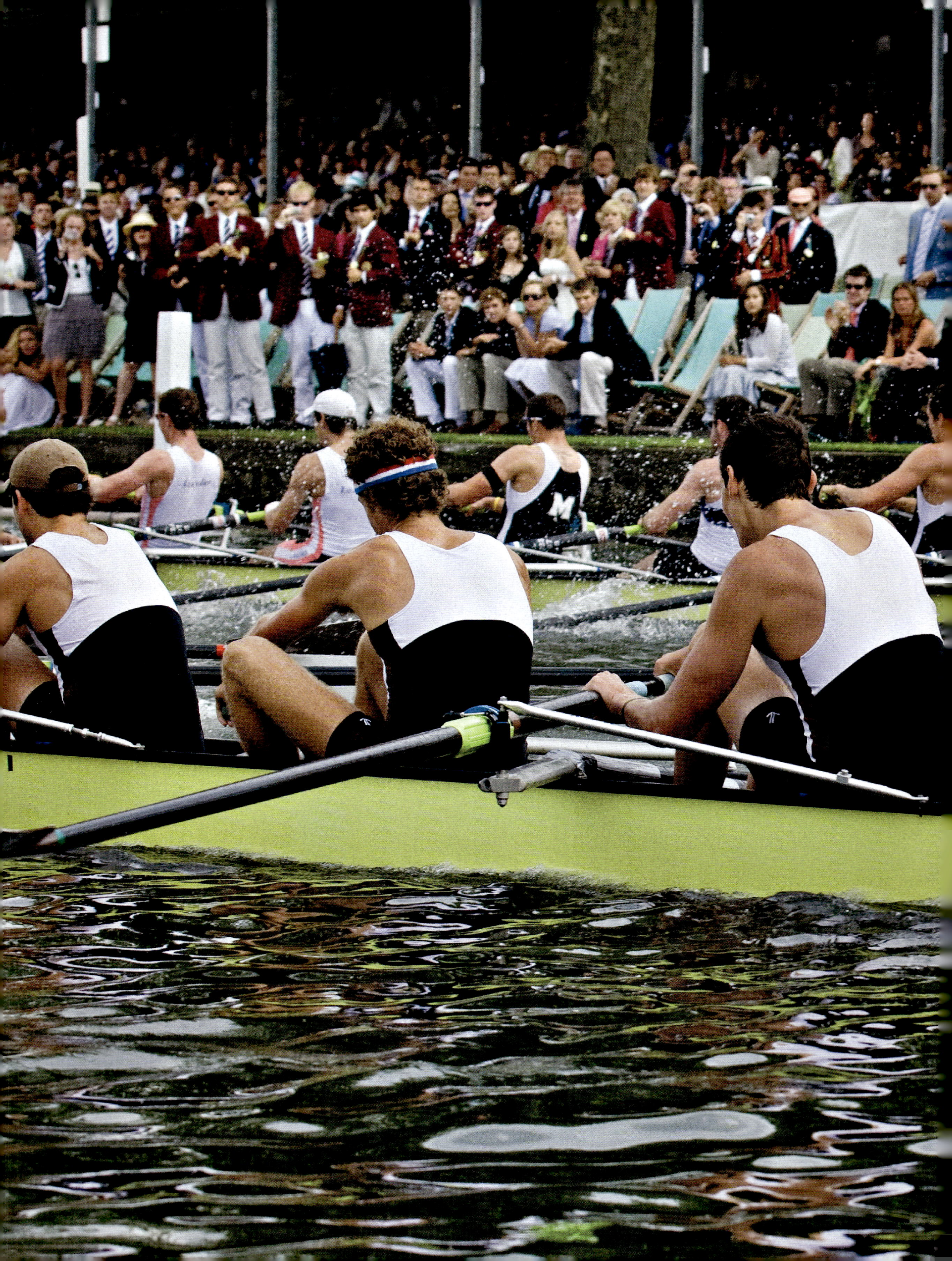

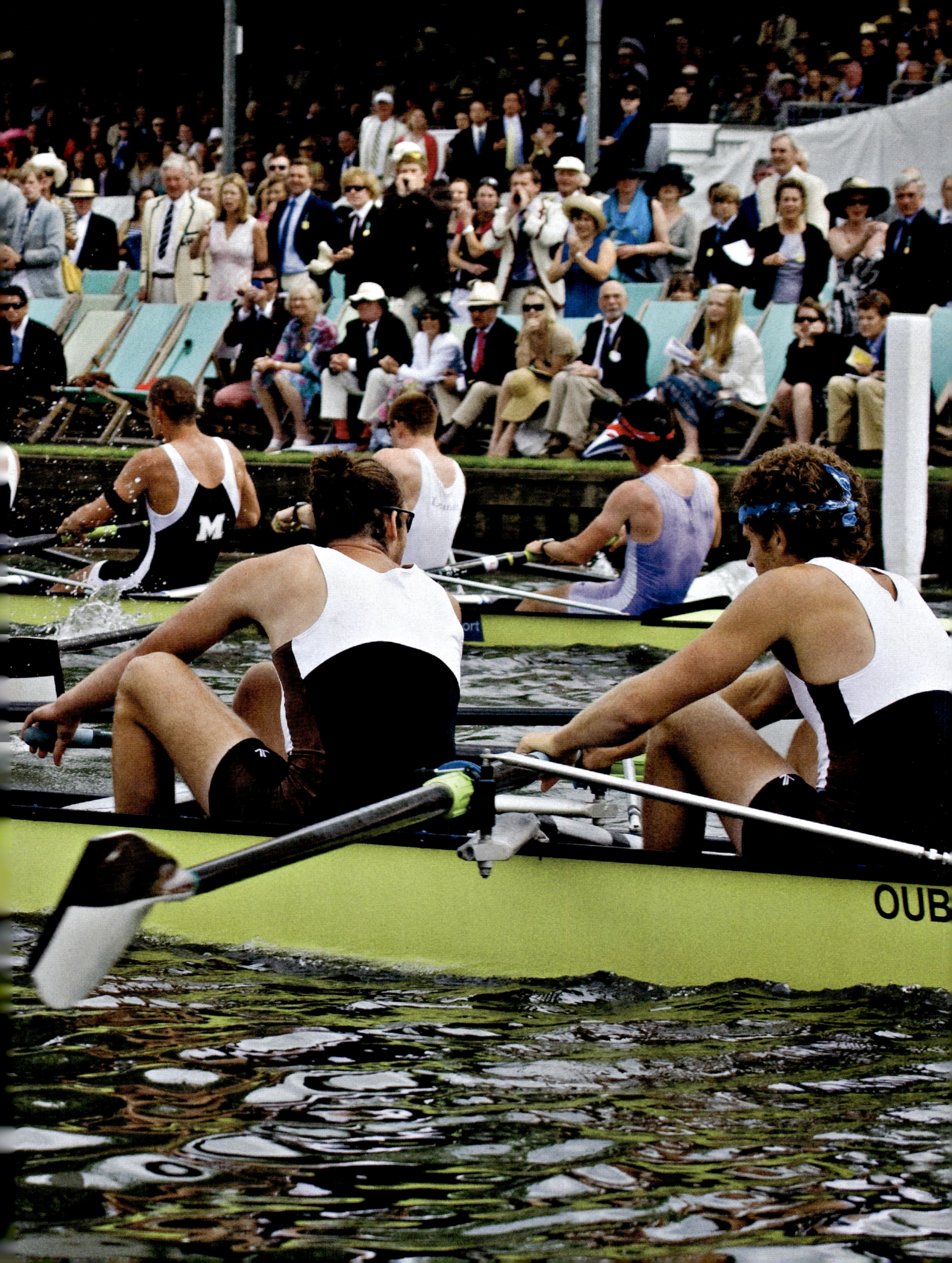
M
OUB

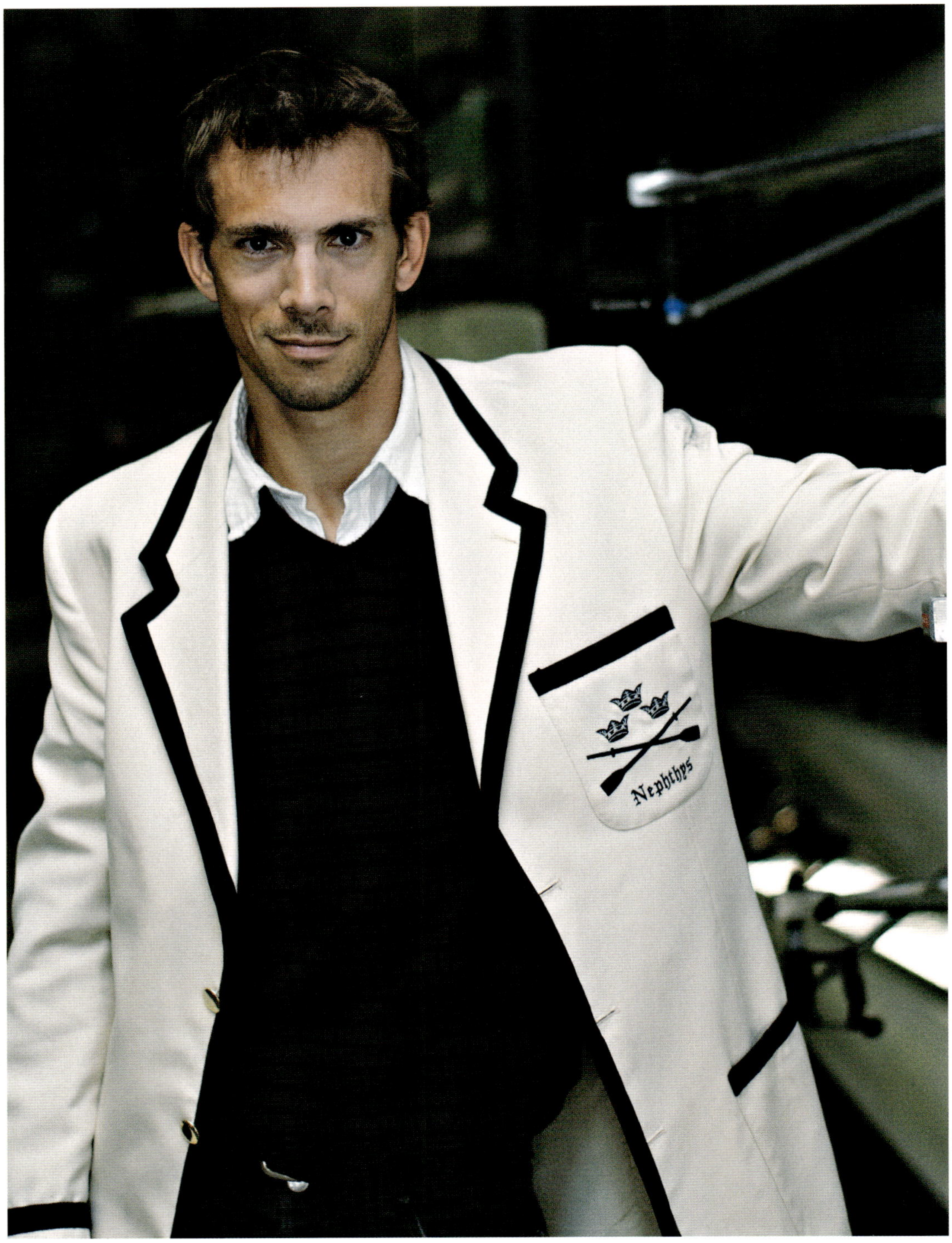

Oxford, England

Nephthys Boat Club, Oxford

PAUL MATTICK

The Oxford lightweight reserve (second) boat, like the Oxford openweight men's and women's reserve crews, Isis and Osiris, respectively, takes its name from an Egyptian deity.

Paul Mattick stroked the Nephthys boat in 2003, losing to the Cambridge lightweight reserve crew, Granta. Paul never made the lightweight first boat (the lightweight Blue Boat, as it is known) and was not rated very highly by his coach at Oxford, who once repeated the word "no" to Paul on every stroke of a twenty-kilometer training session. After that frustrating session, Paul came off the water and made a rather ambitious promise to himself that one day he would row on the British national team.

Today, Paul is an Olympian and has won two world championships with the Great Britain lightweight squad.

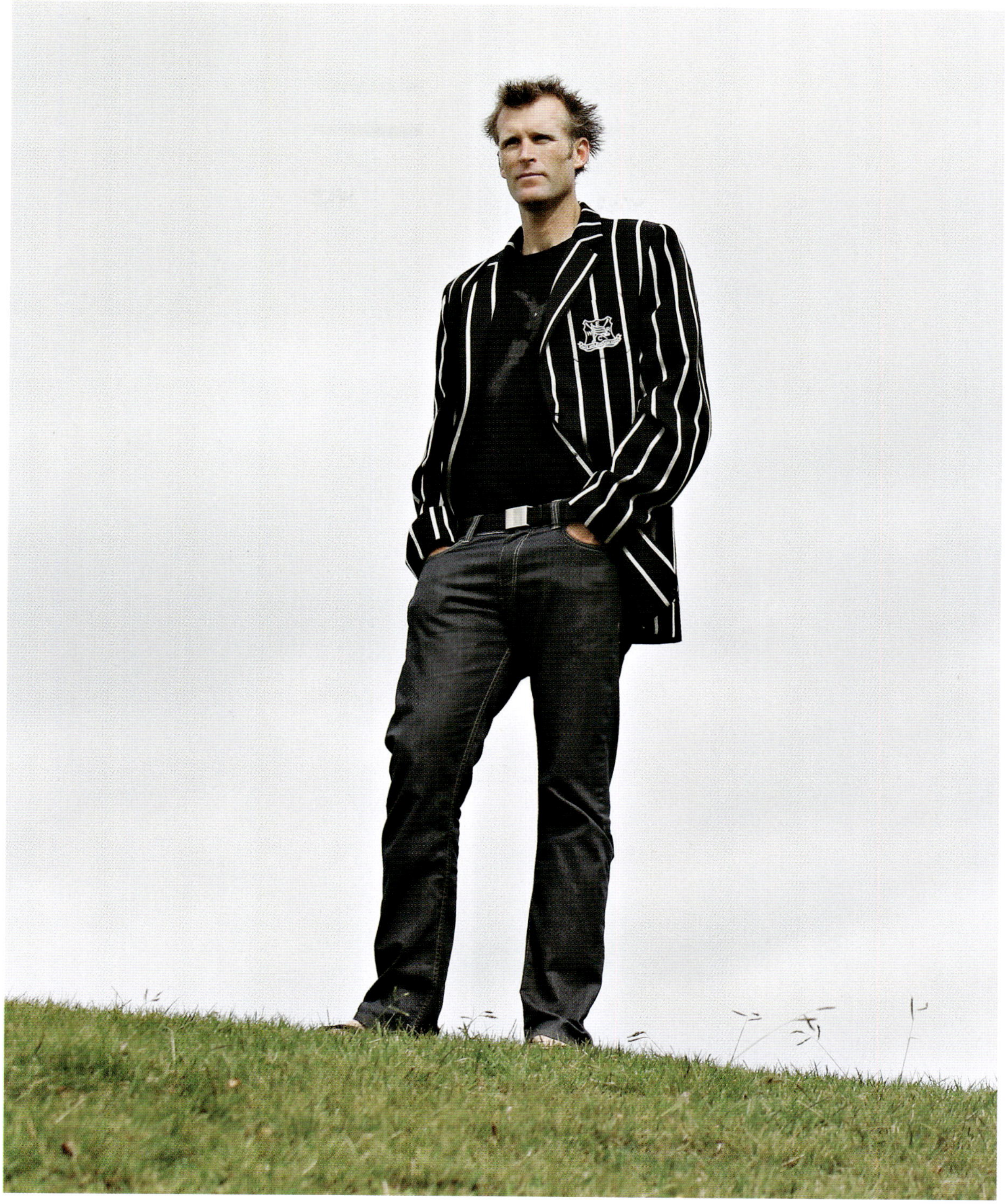

Auckland, New Zealand

West End Rowing Club

MAHÉ DRYSDALE MNZM

Mahé Drysdale won the 2012 Olympic title for men's single sculls representing New Zealand. With five previous world championships to his name, he also holds the world record time in the single scull (6:33.35).

Mahé has also won the Diamond Challenge Sculls at the Henley Royal Regatta three times, representing West End Rowing Club of Auckland, New Zealand. Like the New Zealand national team, West End's colors are black and white. The club's motto, *"Ake, ake kia kaha,"* means "Forever, forever be strong" in Māori.

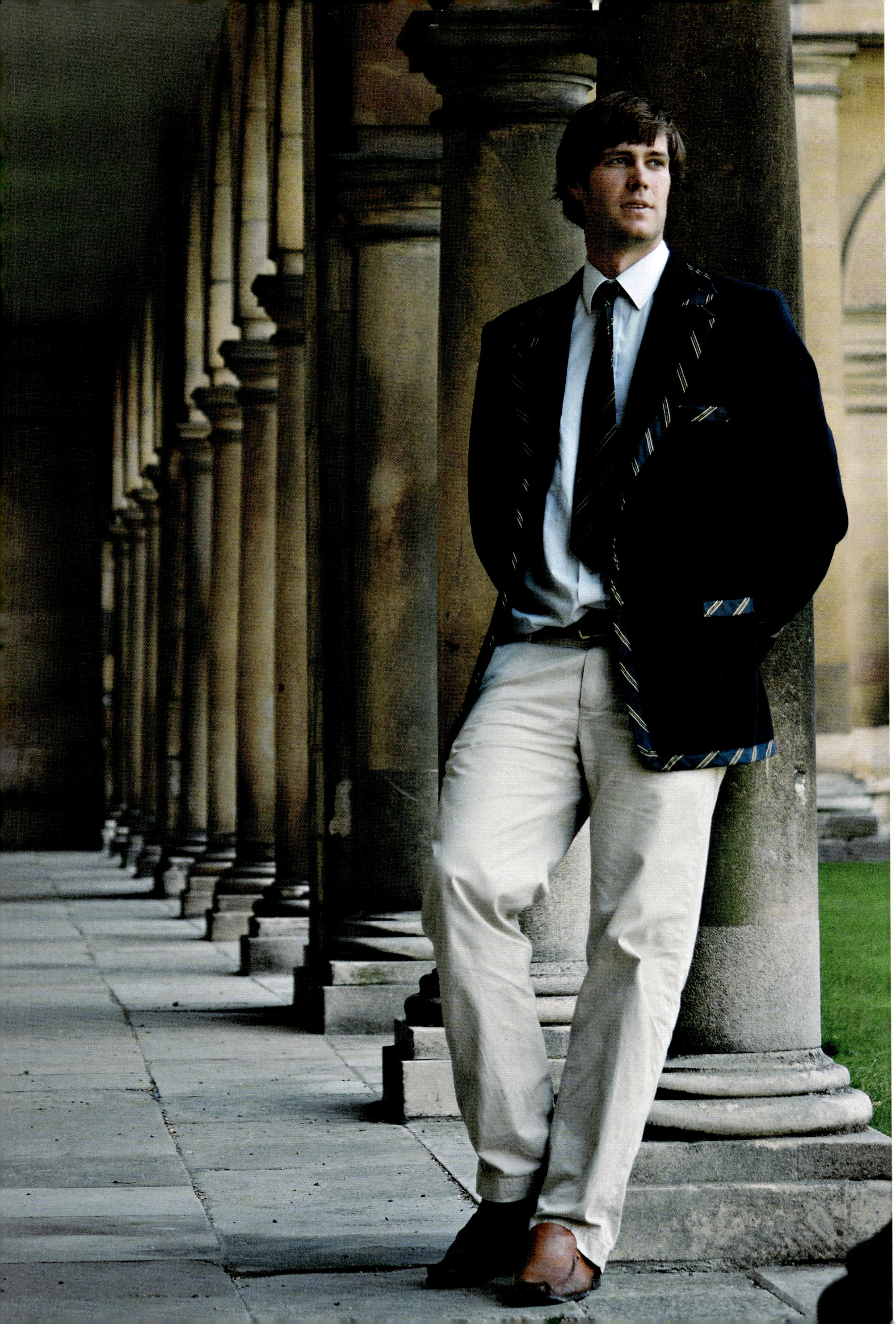

Cambridge, England

First & Third Trinity Boat Club, Cambridge

JAMES STRAWSON

Cambridge's largest college, Trinity, was once host to no fewer than three separate boat clubs: First Trinity, the college's general rowing club; Second Trinity, for Simeonite scholars (known as "Reading Trinity" or the "Hallelujahs"); and Third Trinity, for alumni of Britain's foremost rowing schools, Eton and Westminster. All three were highly successful, holding at one time or another the Headship in the Cambridge May Bumps, and First Trinity won the Grand Challenge Cup at the first-ever Henley Regatta.

Second Trinity, drawing as it did from a very small pool of students, was short-lived. The remaining two clubs amalgamated after World War II, by which time the elitist nature of Third Trinity and the impracticality of having two separate rowing clubs in a single college were considered archaic.

The combined club, First & Third Trinity, uses the original First Trinity blazer for its top crew in the May Bumps: a dark blue coat trimmed with dark blue ribbon. Aside from its buttons, it is identical to the Oxford University Blue Boat blazer, and according to a cheeky rumor at Trinity, Oxford's Boat Race crew must ask the captain of First & Third for permission to borrow their uniform each year. In truth, because of the similarity to the Oxford blazer, many First & Third oarsmen only wear the club's junior blazer, designed for the Lent Bumps crew, which is dark blue with blue-and-gold-striped binding.

James Strawson rowed for First & Third Trinity between 2006 and 2011 and went Head of the River in both the Lent and May Bumps races.

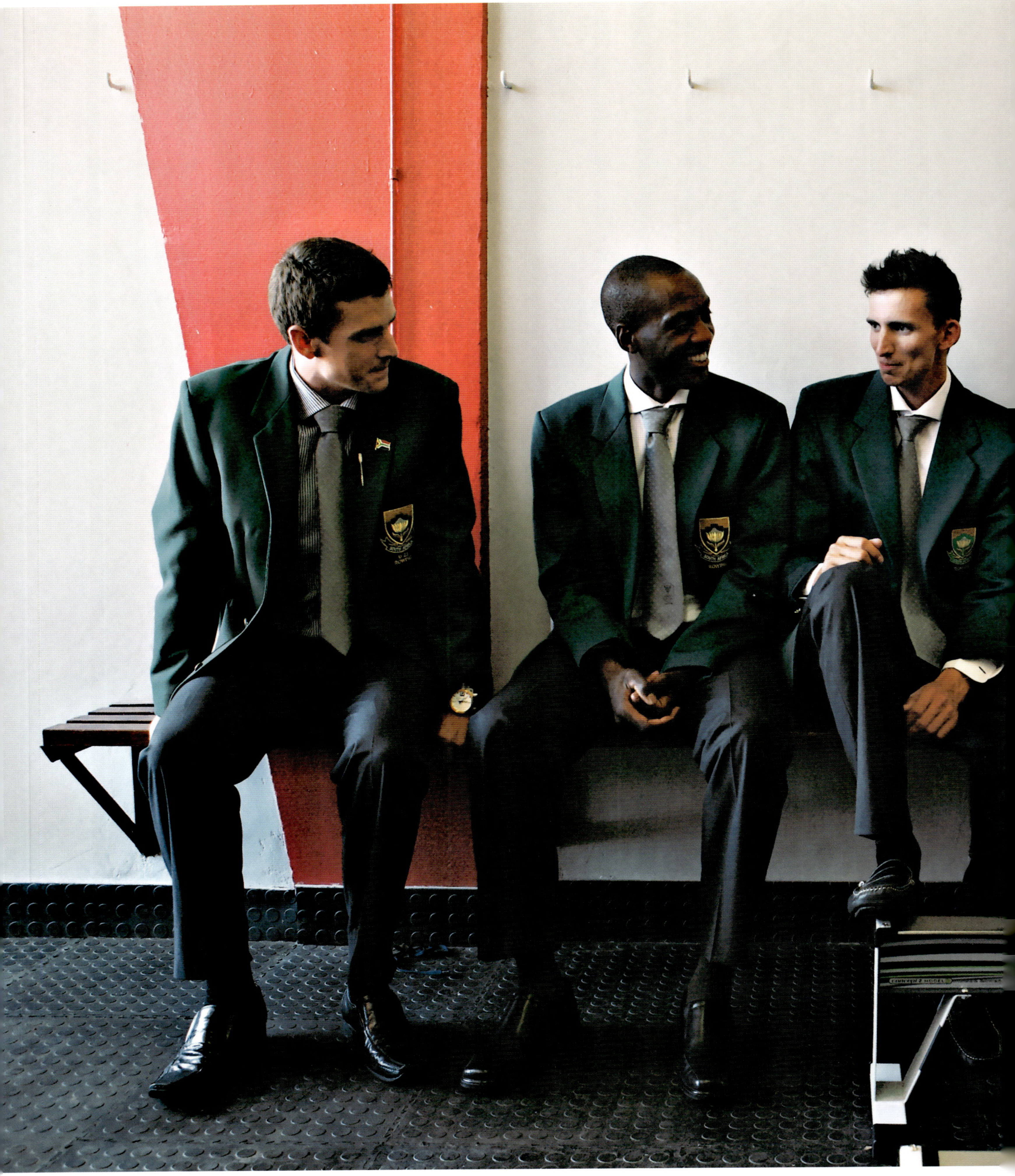

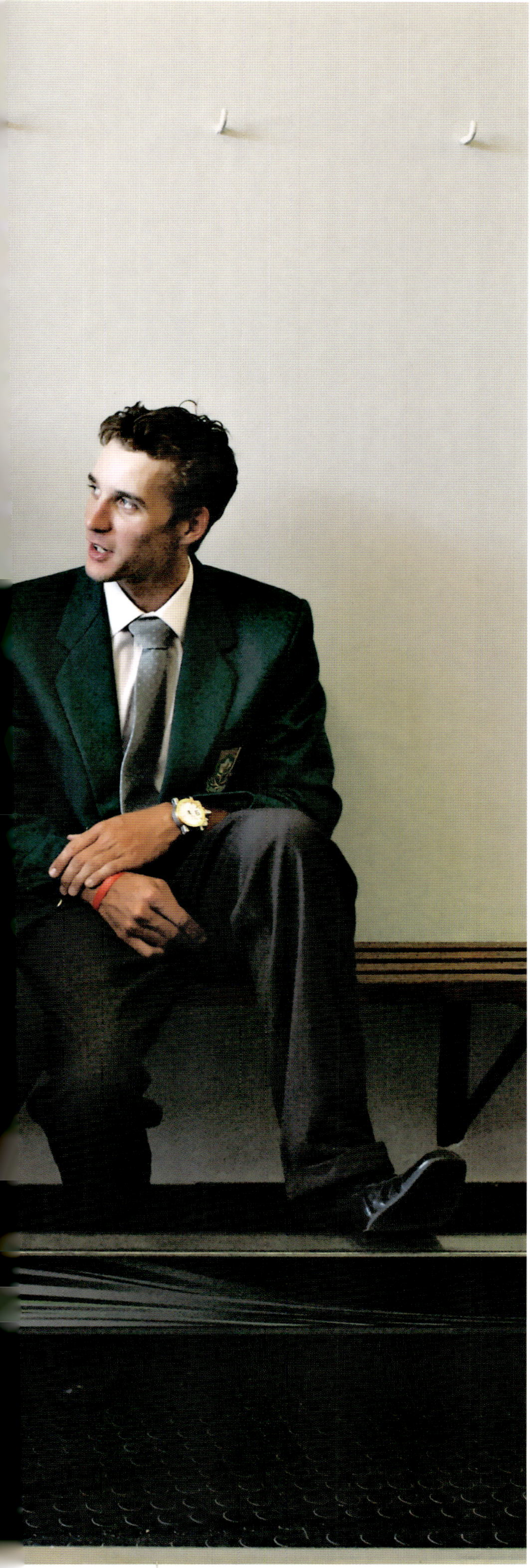

South African Olympic Team

MATT BRITTAIN,
SIZWE NDLOVU, JOHN SMITH,
JAMES THOMPSON

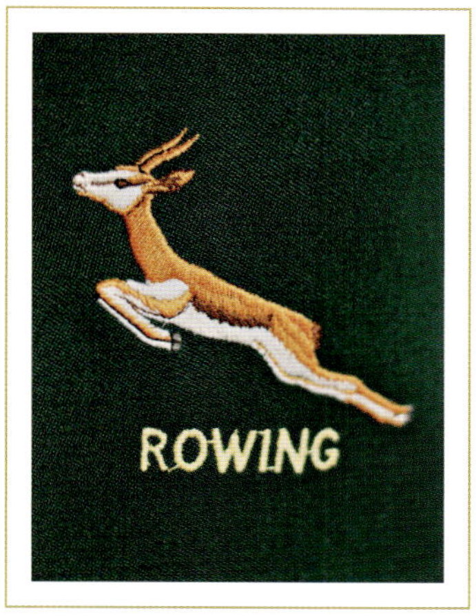

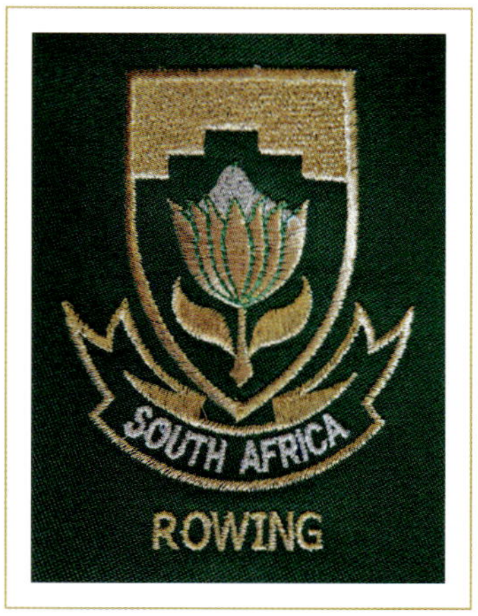

The leaping springbok, adopted as the South African rugby team's badge in 1906, soon became the symbol of all South African national sporting teams. Until 1994, sportsmen, including rowers, who represented South Africa on the international stage were traditionally awarded green blazers with the springbok motif.

With the abolition of apartheid and in the spirit of change and new beginnings, the African National Congress government voted to replace the springbok as the nation's sporting emblem with the king protea flower. President Nelson Mandela famously intervened to allow the rugby team to retain its springbok badge, but all other national teams—including rowing—adopted the protea. A shield emblazoned with a king protea is now the blazer badge on all non-rugby international and Olympic sporting blazers in South Africa.

In 2012, the South African lightweight four won gold at the London Olympics. With this victory, Sizwe Ndlovu became the first black rower to win an Olympic gold medal, and South Africa earned its first-ever Olympic championship in the sport of rowing.

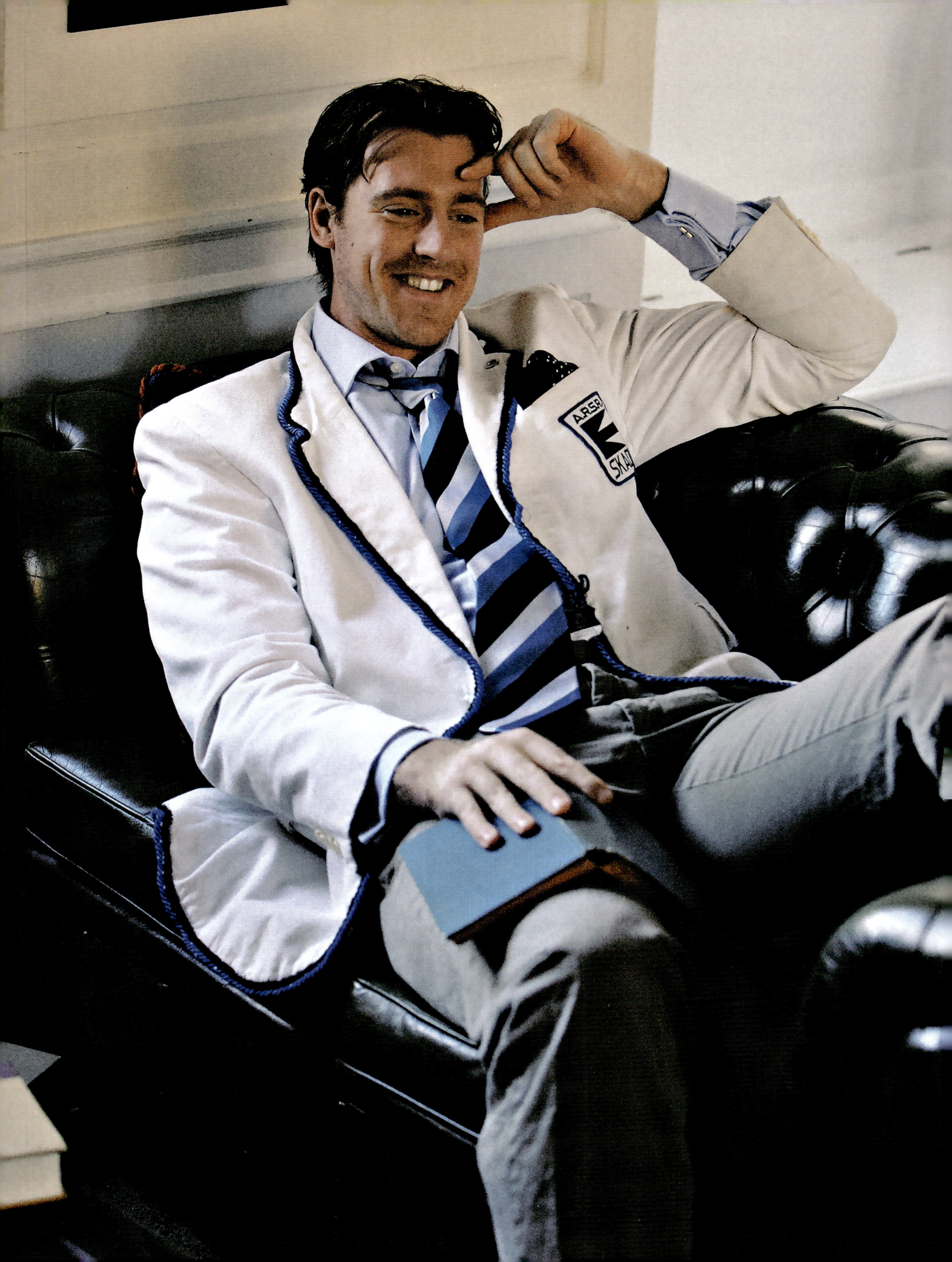
A.R.S.R.

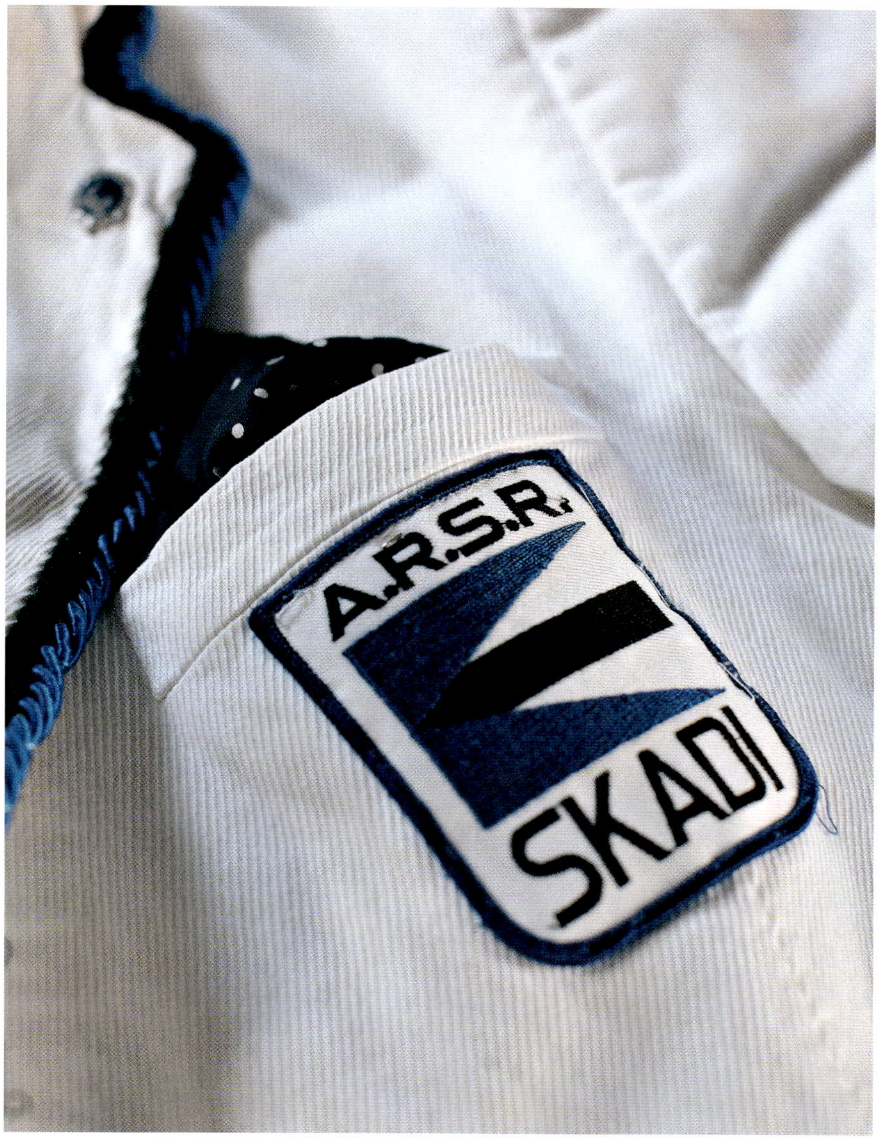

Rotterdam, Netherlands

A.R.S.R. "Skadi"

ROEL HAEN

Based in Rotterdam and named for the Norse goddess Skaði, *Algemene Rotterdamse Studenten Roeivereniging "Skadi"* is one of the traditional Dutch student rowing clubs.

After Skadi merged with a neighboring club, "Hades," the new club kept the Skadi name but adopted the blue and black colors of Hades. Today Skadi rowers earn their blue, black, and white ties after completing a 25-kilometer row and other initiation rites.

Blazers, of course, also play an important role in the club's hierarchy. According to club rules, all members—including social members—may wear a plain black blazer, but only racing members may wear the Skadi badge (an image of the club's flag and blade design) on their blazer pockets. Skadi rowers who have won an event at the Varsity races may wear black blazers with white trim, and those who have won the premier event at the Varsity (the men's coxed four) may wear distinctive white blazers with bright blue-and-black trim.

A Grand Challenge Cup winner at Henley, Roel Haen reached the pinnacle of Dutch student rowing five times in a row, winning the Varsity with Skadi in the men's coxed four in 2006, 2007, 2008, 2009, and 2010.

OVERLEAF:
According to tradition, when a club wins the Senior Four at the annual Varsity race, its members on the bank strip off their clothes (except for the club tie) and swim to the winning crew.

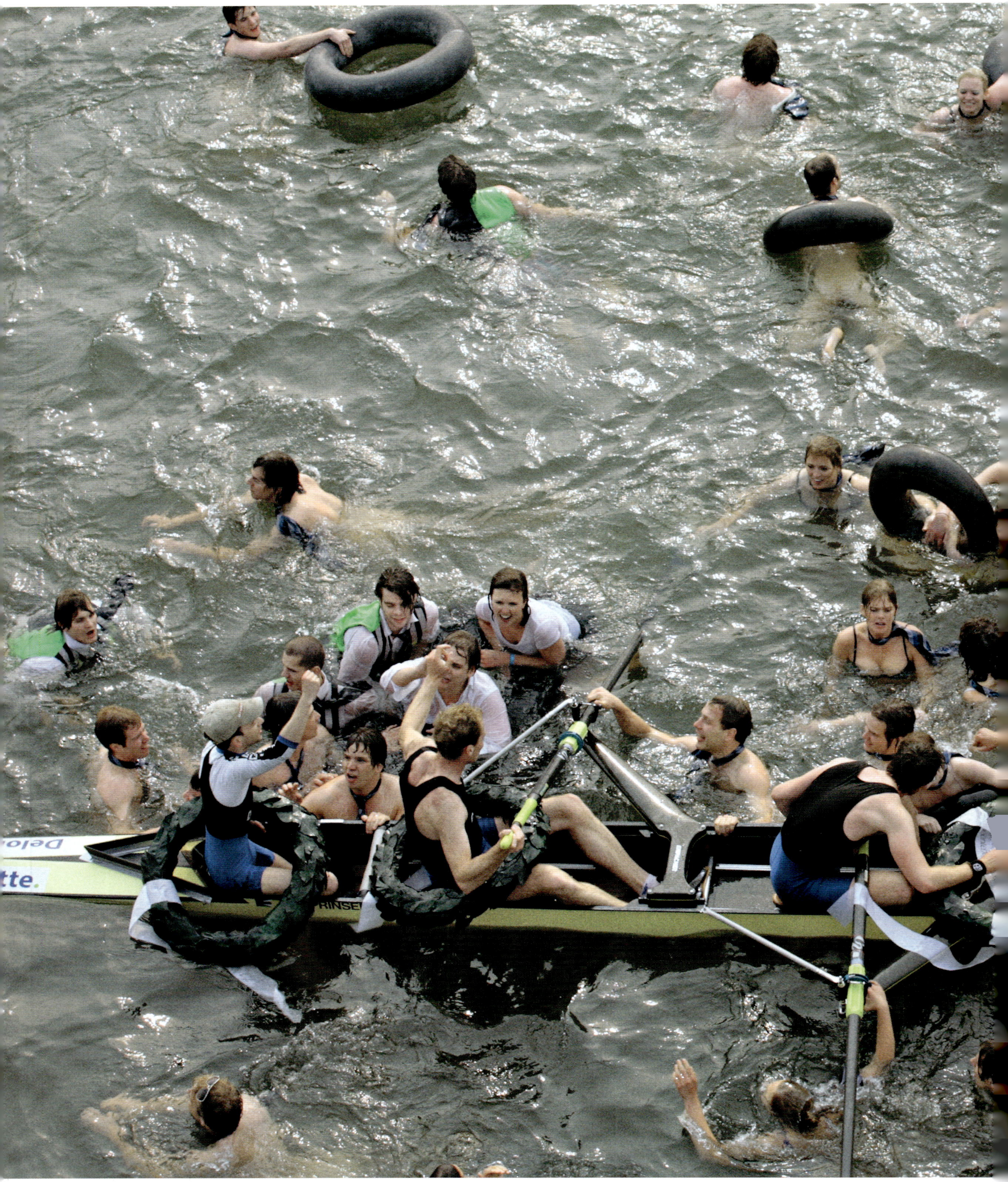

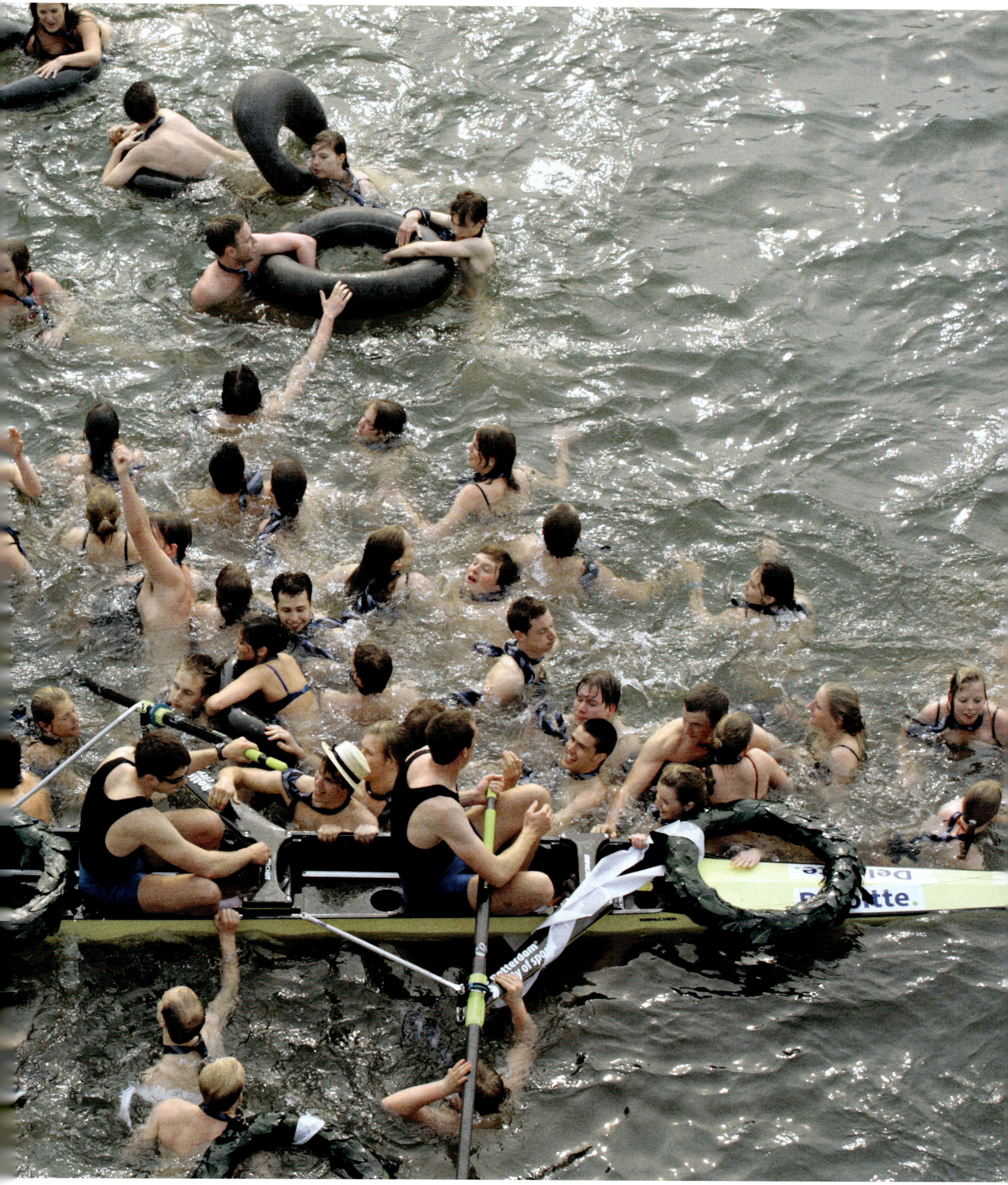

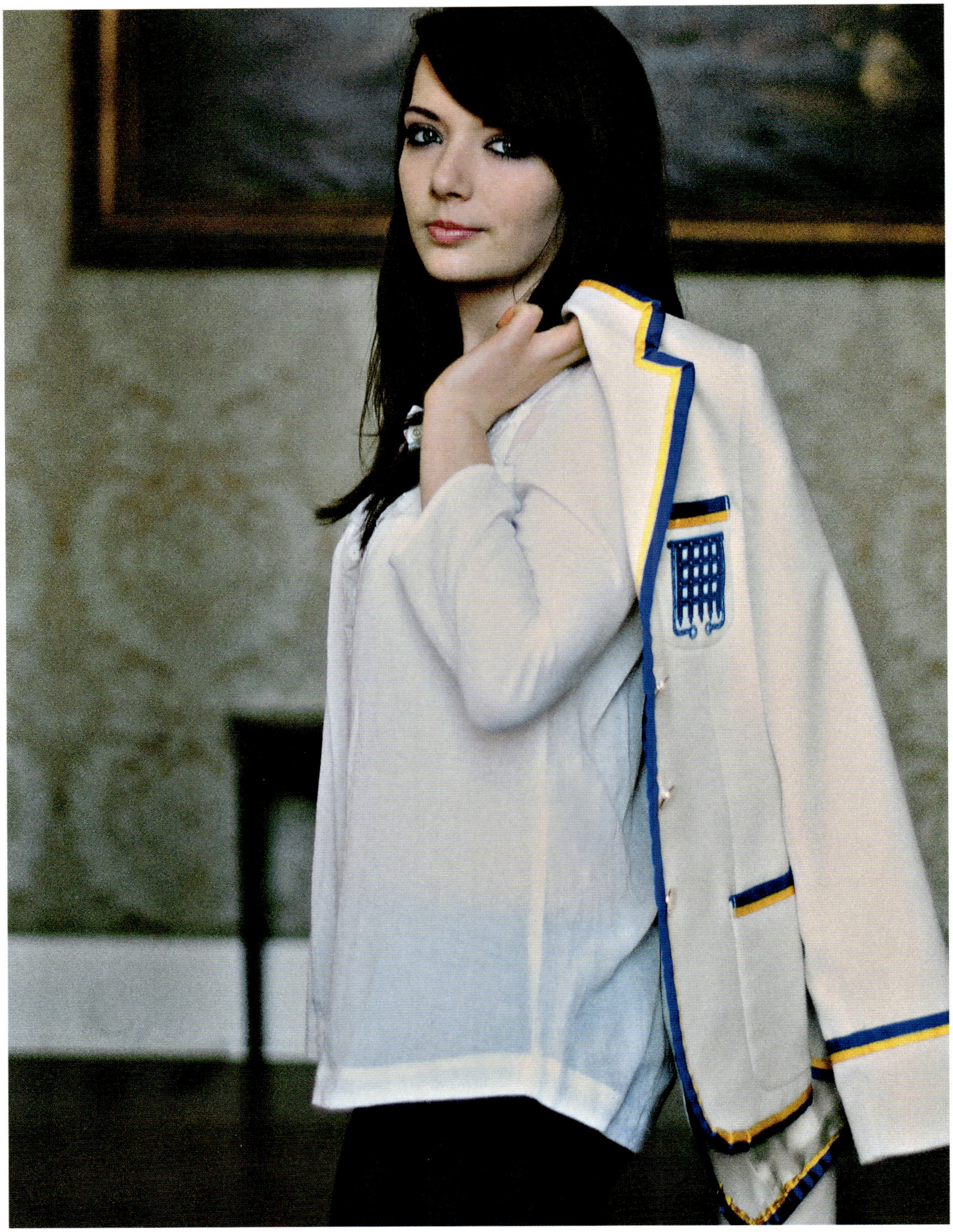

Oxford, England

Lady Margaret Hall Boat Club, Oxford

RACHEL YORK

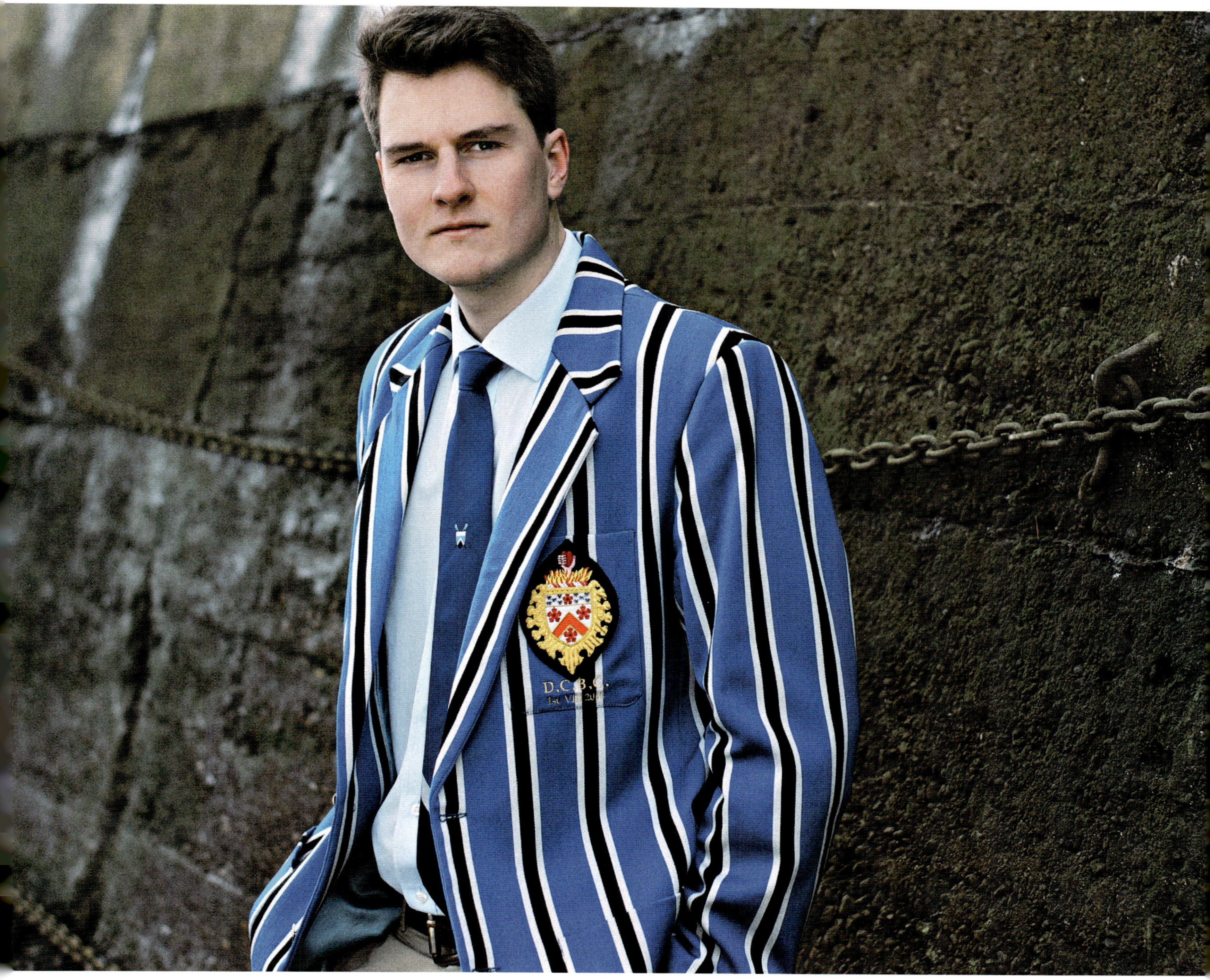

London, England

Dulwich College Boat Club

TOM MOUNTAIN

When Edward Alleyn founded Dulwich College as a school for "poor scholars" in 1619, he wrote that the students were to wear "a white calico surplice, a long coat . . . of sad colour . . . , a girdle and a black cap."

For the last two hundred years, Dulwich students could not have dressed more differently from Alleyn's vision. Brightly colored blazers and other accoutrements have proliferated: boarding house blazers in psychedelic house colors; blue-striped rugby and cricket blazers; the boater hat and special maroon-and-white-striped blazer for the school's croquet captain; and the coveted "white blazer," awarded only to boys who make the first team for both cricket and rugby and excel in one additional sport.

The rowing blazer is a very new addition to this variety (the boat club was established only in 1991) and is strictly regatta wear; it may not be worn with the school uniform.

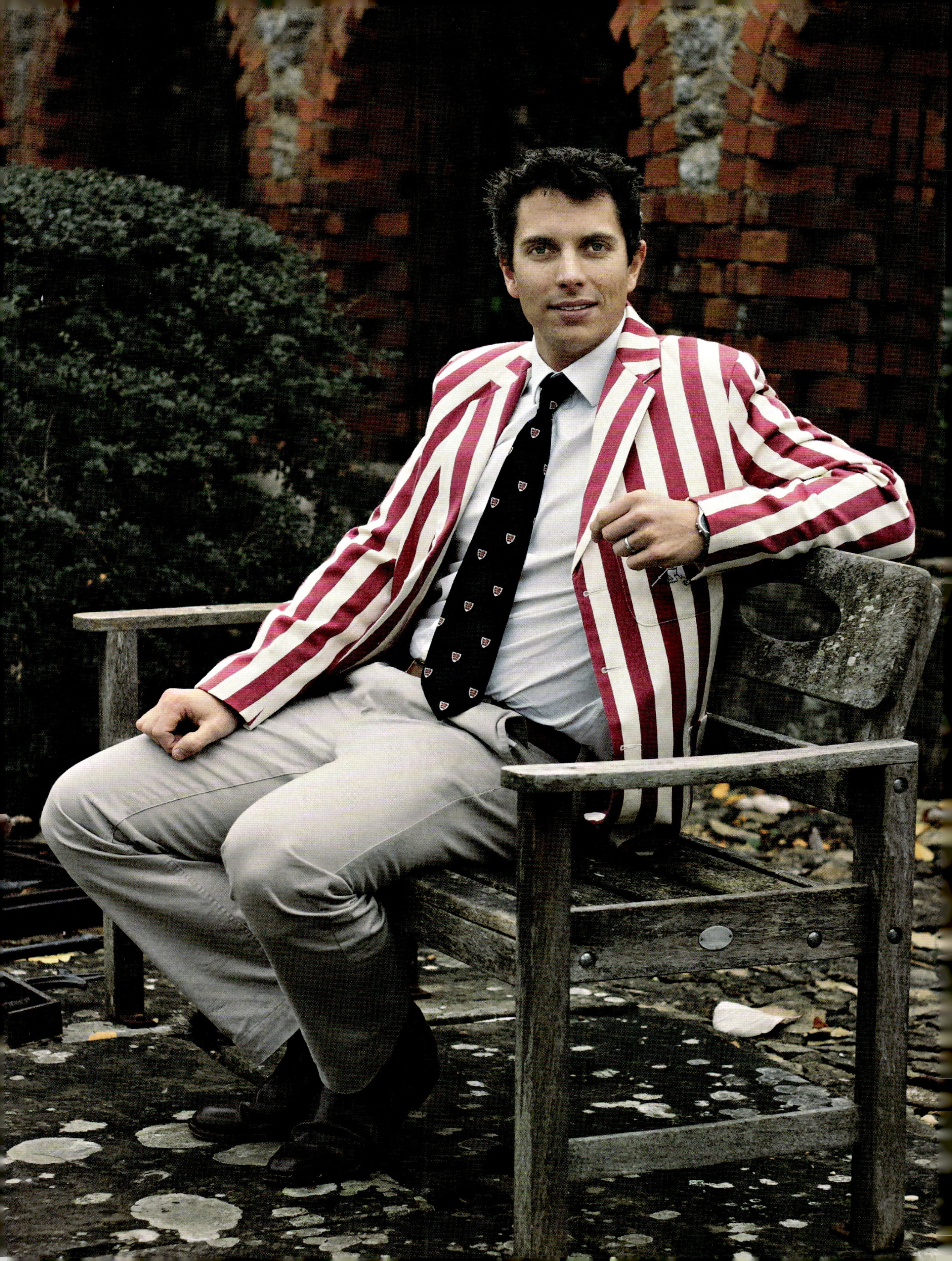

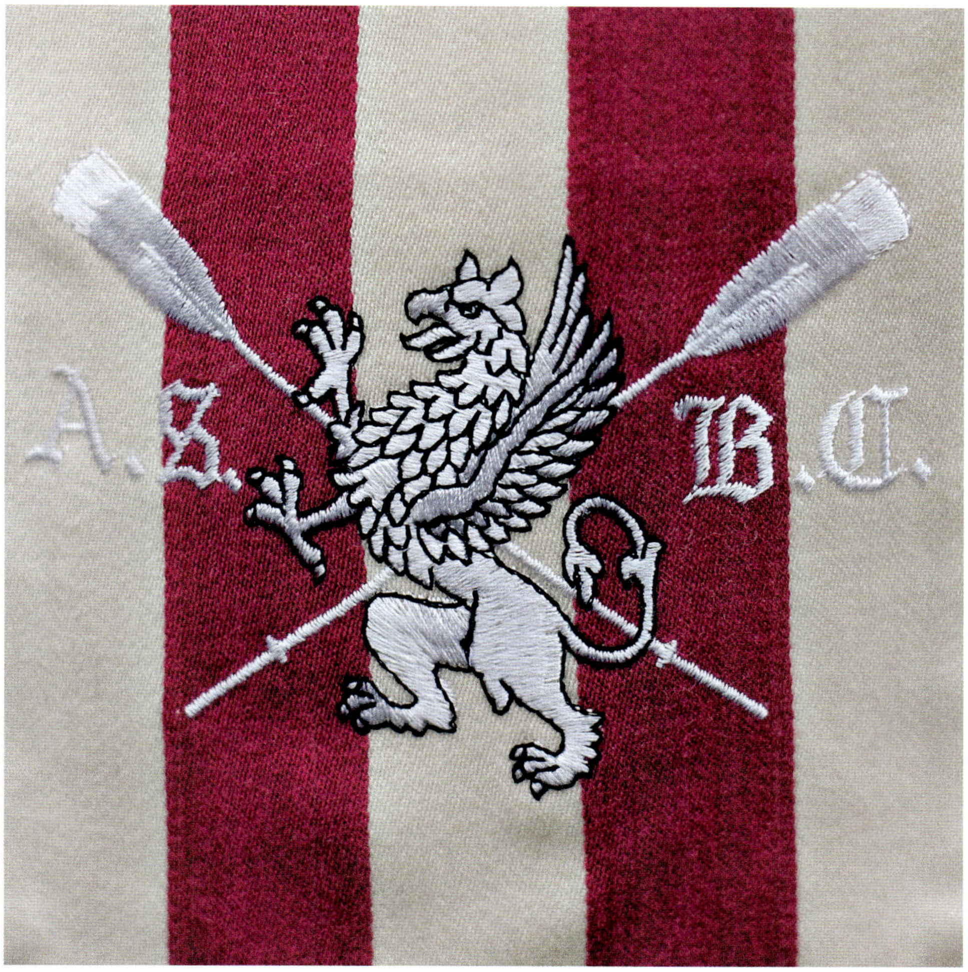

Abingdon, England

Abingdon School Boat Club

GEORGE WHITTAKER

The straitlaced serenity of the Henley Stewards' Enclosure erupts in temporary pandemonium whenever Abingdon races in the final because the Abingdon crew is invariably accompanied on the bank by a raucous pink-and-white blur of stampeding alumni. Abingdon boys in their garish blazers regularly grace the sports (and novelty) pages of British newspapers during Henley week and have come to personify the regatta in the public imagination.

After Eton and Westminster, Abingdon can claim to be the third-oldest school boat club in the world, with evidence of rowing there dating to 1830. But its oarsmen have not always worn the cerise (dark pink) and white; blue and gold was the color of choice in the early years. As one rower recalled years later, they wore "dark blue velvet caps with pendant gold tassels, which, however artistic in the eyes of the few who might behold them, were most trying to the rower as the tassel would provokingly 'bob' into his eyes."

Over the next several decades (and after discarding its impractical hat tassels), the club began using blue-and-white-striped uniforms before switching, for reasons that are not entirely clear, to its now-famous cerise-and-white-striped blazers and matching caps. It is possible that Abingdon's pink was adopted from Pembroke College, Oxford, which has historic links with the school and from which Abingdon borrowed boats in the early years. (Pembroke has used various shades of pink in its rowing uniform intermittently since the mid-nineteenth century.)

The griffen blazer badge ("griffen" is the Abingdon spelling) is adopted from the school's coat of arms and the arms of the school's sixteenth-century benefactor, John Roysse.

George Whittaker began his career in the sport as a coxswain at Abingdon before making the unusual transition to rowing. As an oarsman, George has won two Henley titles and an Oxford-Cambridge Boat Race.

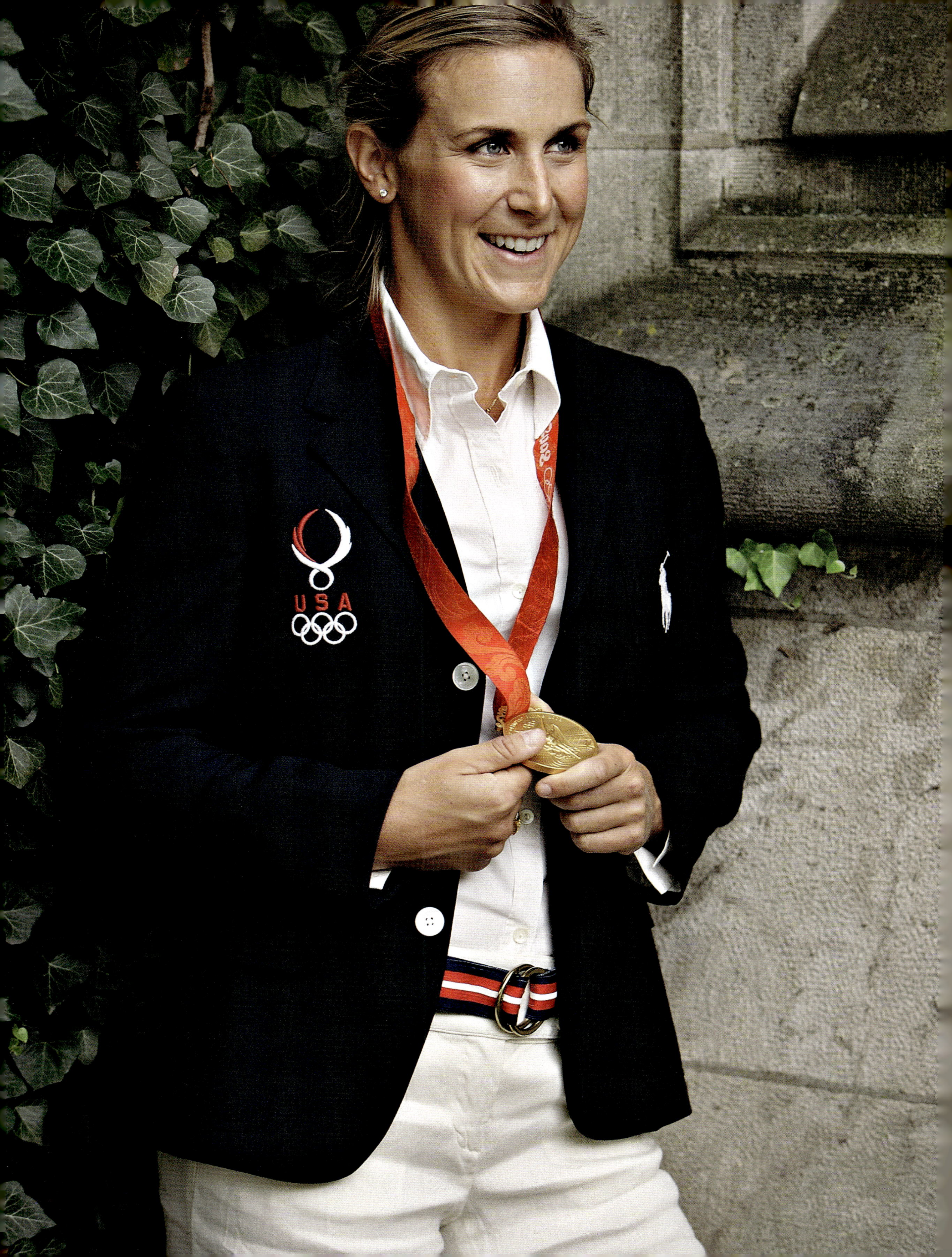
USA

United States Olympic Team

2004, 2008, and 2012

JASON READ, ERIN CAFARO, ZSUZSANNA FRANCIA

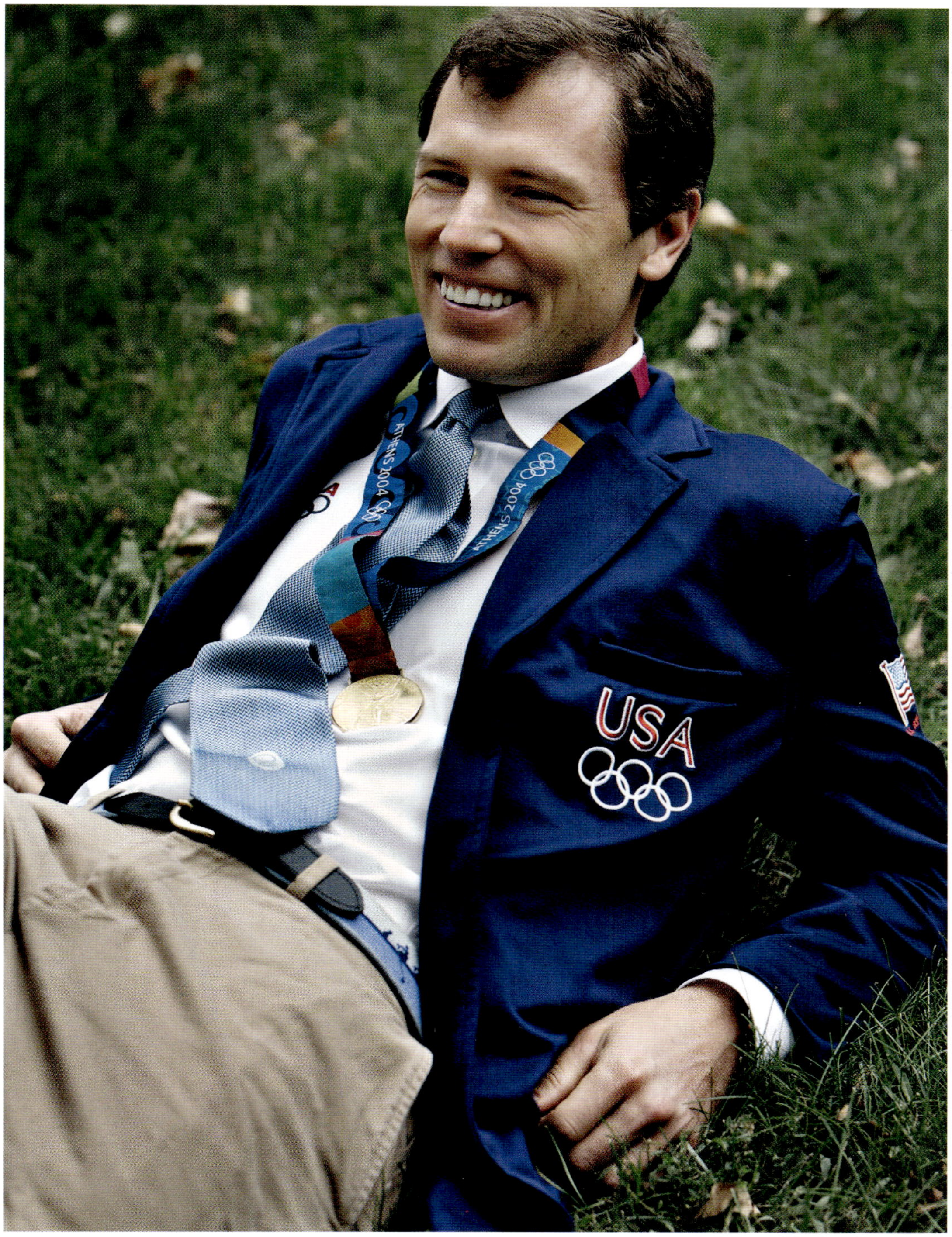

OPPOSITE: Erin Cafaro wears the 2008 U.S. Olympic blazer.
ABOVE: Jason Read is wearing the 2004 U.S. Olympic blazer and a needlepoint rowing belt handmade by his mother to commemorate the U.S.'s gold medal performance.

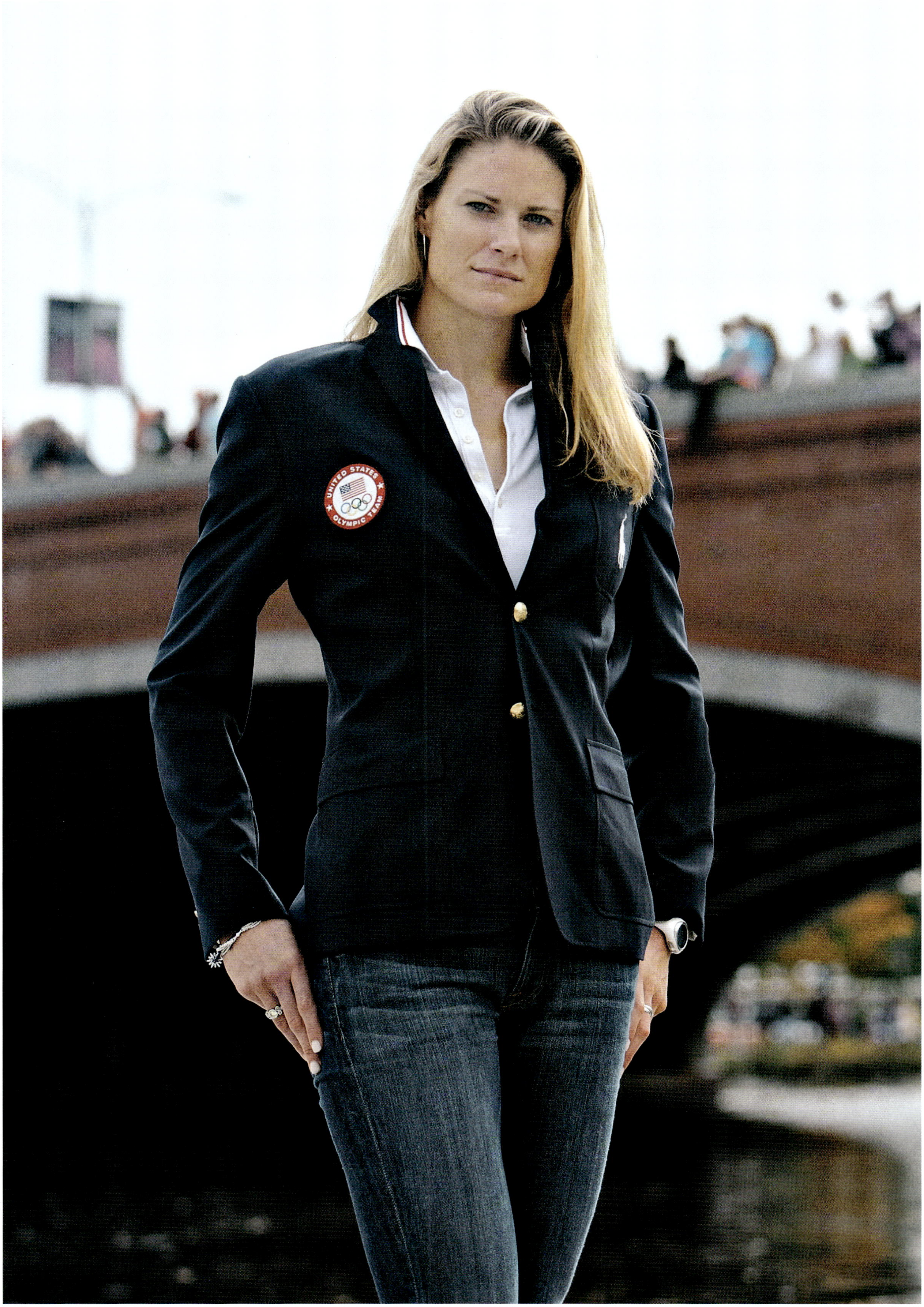
UNITED STATES
OLYMPIC TEAM

The design of the modern U.S. Olympic blazer changes with each Olympic cycle, depending on sponsorship. The 2004 blazer was created by Roots; the 2008 and 2012 versions were designed by Ralph Lauren, who drew inspiration from the Jesse Owens era and the film *Chariots of Fire*.

Jason Read rowed at bow in the U.S. men's eight that won gold and set the world record at the 2004 Athens Olympics. He is also a volunteer fire chief and the only man to be named USRowing Man of the Year twice: once after participating in rescue operations at Ground Zero on September 11, 2001, and once after winning the Olympics and setting a new world record in 2004.

Erin Cafaro and Zsuzsanna Francia won gold medals in the U.S. women's eight at both the 2008 and 2012 Olympics. In 2009, they rowed together in the first U.S. women's pair to win a world championship (doubling into the eight and winning gold there too). Both have been USRowing athletes of the year.

OPPOSITE:
Zsuzsanna Francia wears the 2012 U.S. Olympic blazer.

BELOW:
The United States men's eight celebrates after winning gold and setting a world record at the 2004 Olympic Games in Athens.

OVERLEAF:
The United States women's eight on the podium in Beijing, 2008. From left to right: Erin Cafaro, Lindsay Shoop, Anna Goodale, Elle Logan, Anna Cummins, Zsuzsanna Francia, Caroline Lind, Caryn Davies, and Mary Whipple.

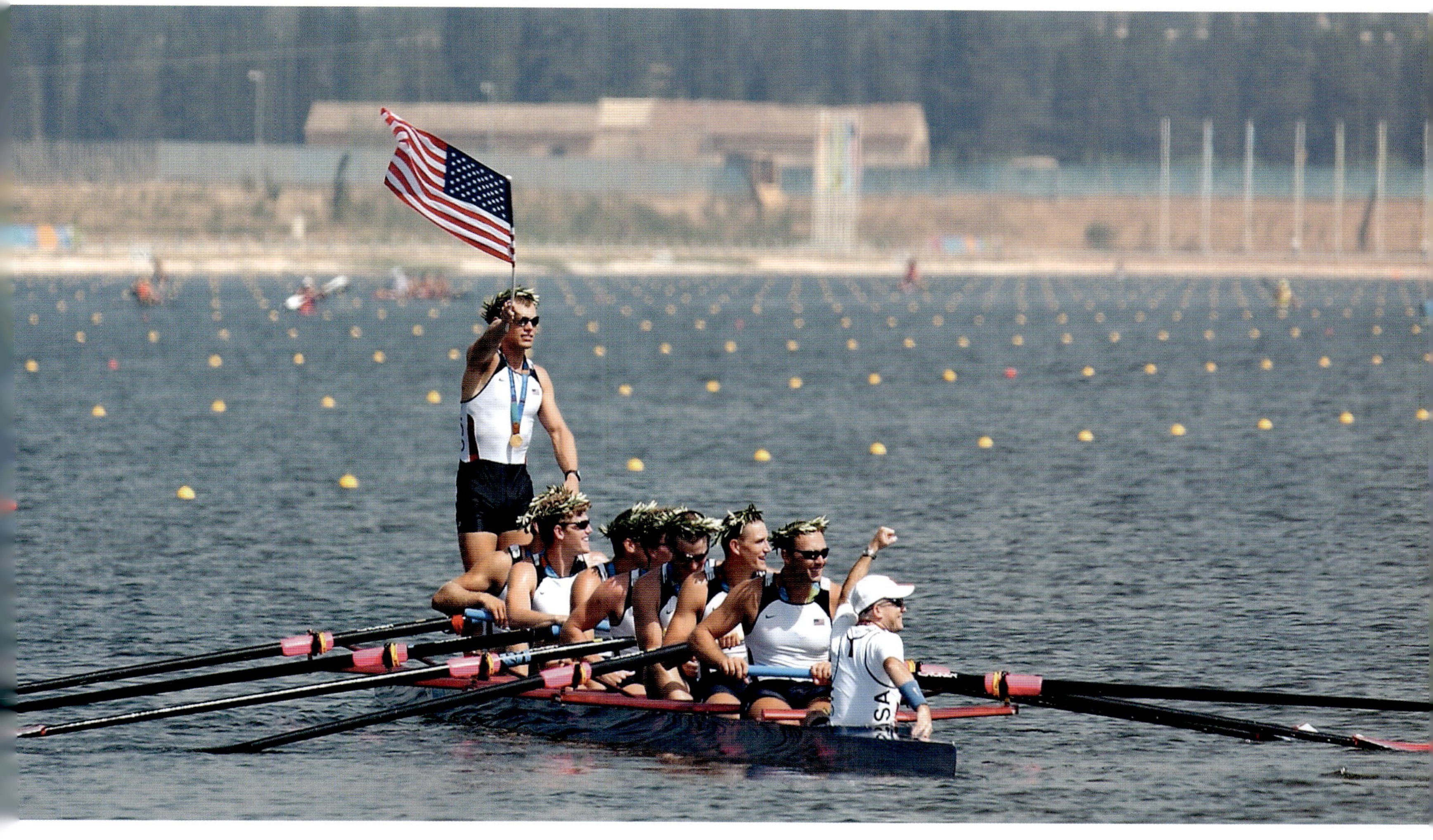

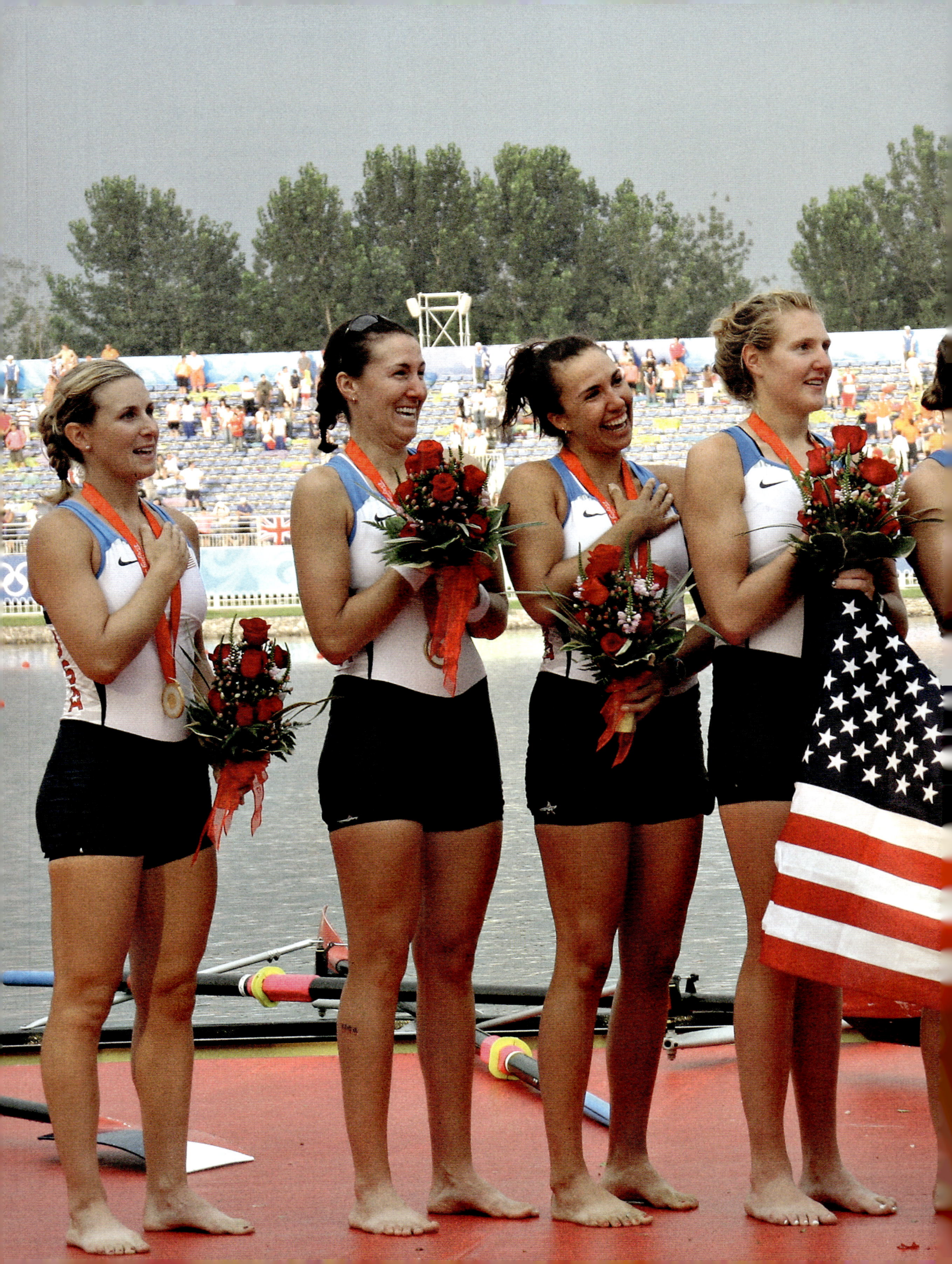

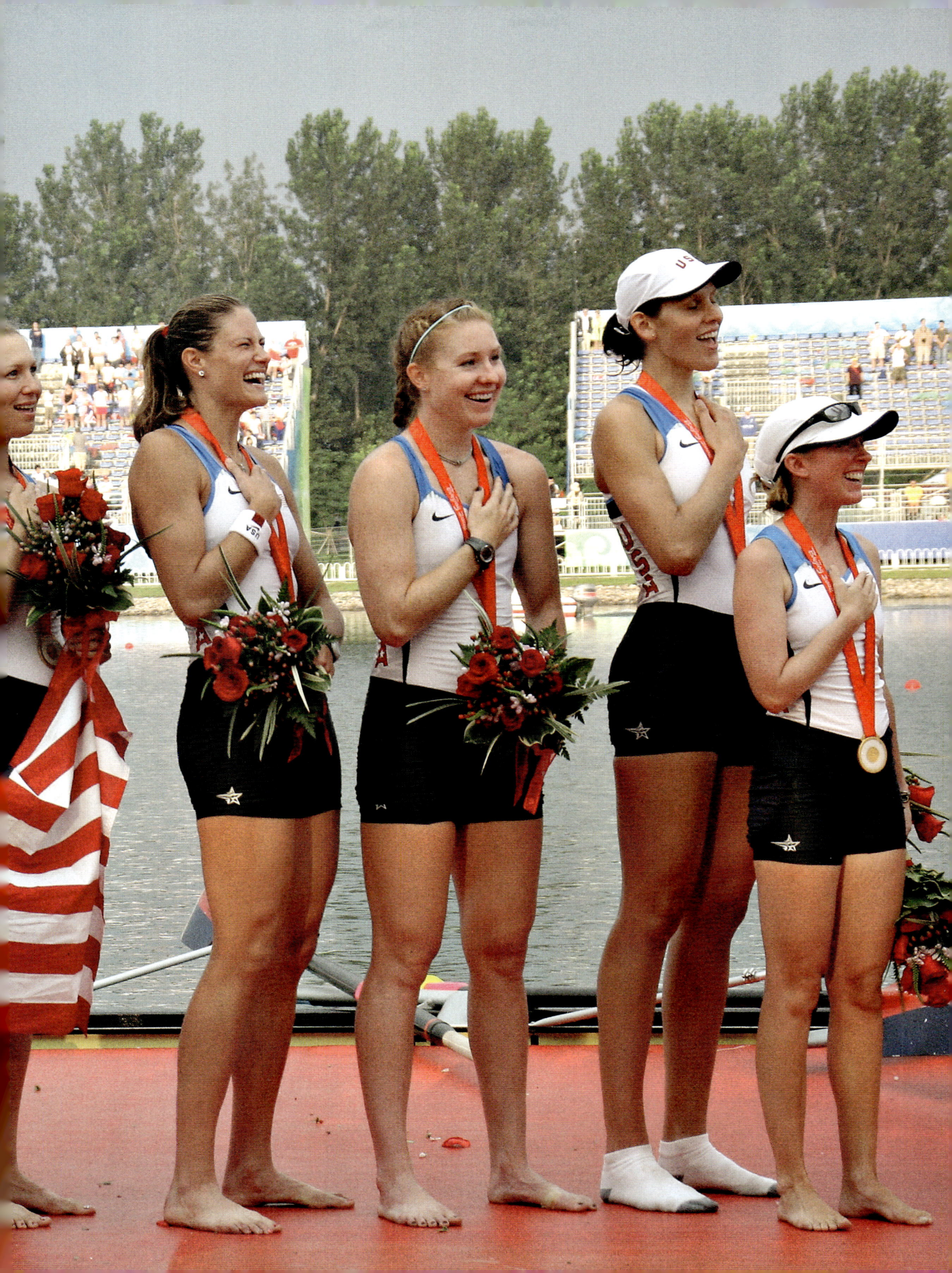

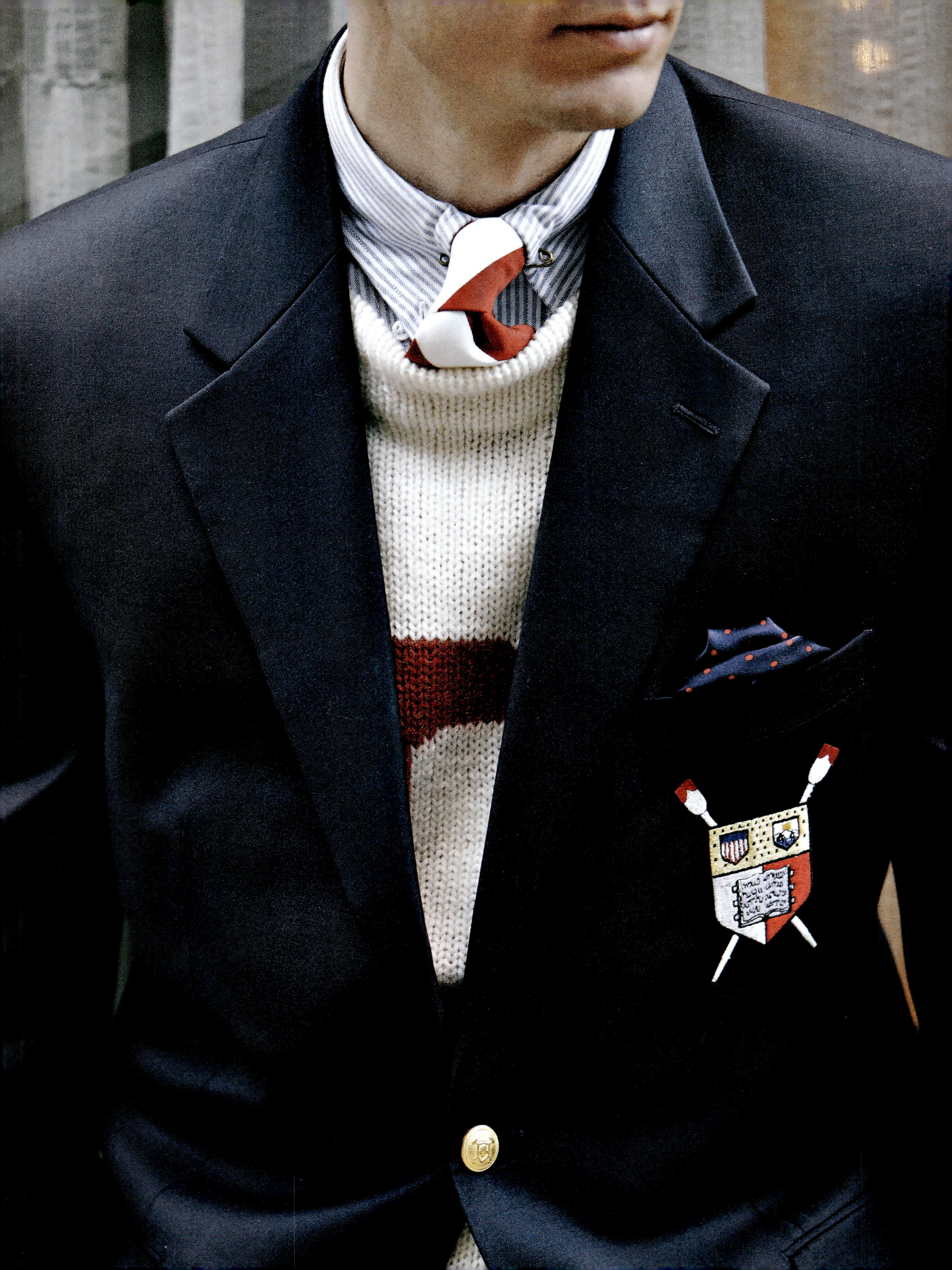

Ithaca, New York

Cornell University

MATT KOCHEM

"I looked at them as they jetted past, and then I quickly looked again. This boat appeared to be manned by skeletons. . . . Every leg and arm muscle showed as taut as steel cabling. . . . Pairs of deep-set eyes peered at us, conveying 'the look.' The men who were rowing that shell were a special breed of oarsmen known as 'lightweights.'" —Brad Alan Lewis, *Assault on Lake Casitas*, 1990

Cornell University co-founder A. D. White rowed for Yale in the very first Harvard-Yale race. In 1873, White hired a rowing coach and procured a boat for the young university, initiating in earnest what has proven to be one of the nation's strongest and most enduring collegiate rowing programs.

In 2006, 2007, and 2008 Cornell won three consecutive national titles in lightweight rowing. Matt Kochem was in all three championship crews. He has gone on to row in the United States lightweight eight three times, earning a silver medal at the 2009 world championships.

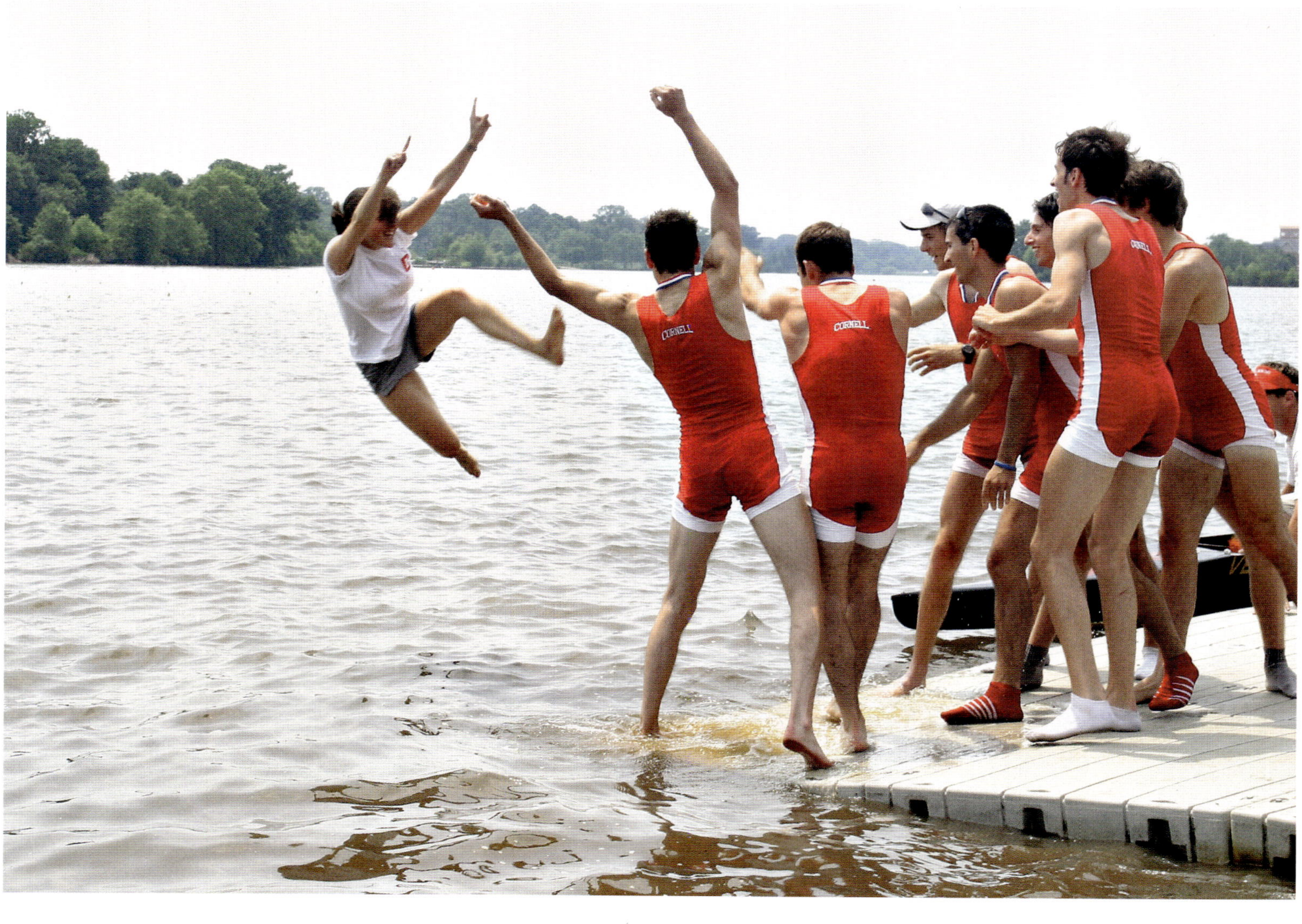

ABOVE: Per tradition, the Cornell lightweights throw their coxswain in the river after winning the national championship.

Oxford, England

Christ Church Boat Club, Oxford

MAGNUS STEINSVOLL PRØSCH

"Faith thought she had never seen him look so handsome as he looked just then in his bright Christ Church boating-jacket. . . . A manly man seldom looks manlier than in boating costume."

—Grant Allen, *The Scallywag*, 1895

In the very first Oxford-Cambridge race, the Oxford stroke and de facto captain, Thomas Staniforth, and four other members of the Oxford crew—including Charles Wordsworth, who founded both the University Boat Race and the University Cricket Match—were all in the same Oxford college: Christ Church. The crew decided, therefore, to row in the Christ Church color, dark blue. Oxford won and has continued to race in dark blue to this day.

Christ Church Boat Club itself had used dark blue since its establishment in 1817, and the earliest Christ Church crews rowed in long white trousers, striped jerseys, dark blue neckerchiefs, and—like naval midshipmen of the period—top hats.

In 1819, inspired, perhaps, by an influx of Scots aristocrats, the club replaced the top hat with traditional Caledonian headgear: a Tam O'Shanter bonnet trimmed with a white-and-dark-blue-checkered band. The check pattern, known in Christ Church as the "Duster," eventually found its way onto club neckties, shorts, and other accoutrements. Today, any oarsman who has represented the college in a major race is eligible to wear the Duster tie.

The blazer itself was originally solid dark blue with a red cardinal's-hat motif embroidered on the breast pocket. The Christ Church cardinal's hat, which commemorates the college's founder—the infamous Cardinal Wolsey—is probably among the first blazer badges ever created.

In 1904, the current design was adopted: a white jacket with dark blue Petersham trim, gilt buttons, and the cardinal's-hat badge on the pocket. Today this blazer may be worn by anyone who has rowed in the college's top crew in Oxford's principal bumping race, the Summer Eights. Members of the second eight wear the same blazer but without blue trim, while the third eight's blazer is identical to the second eight's, but with white, rather than gilt, buttons. This way, as an oarsman is promoted during his time at Christ Church, he has only to make minor changes to his jacket.

The rowers and cox for the first Torpid—the top crew for Oxford's less important, wintertime bumping race—may wear a different blazer entirely, one that bears the cardinal's-hat motif in silver thread and is solid dark blue, like the early Christ Church boating jackets.

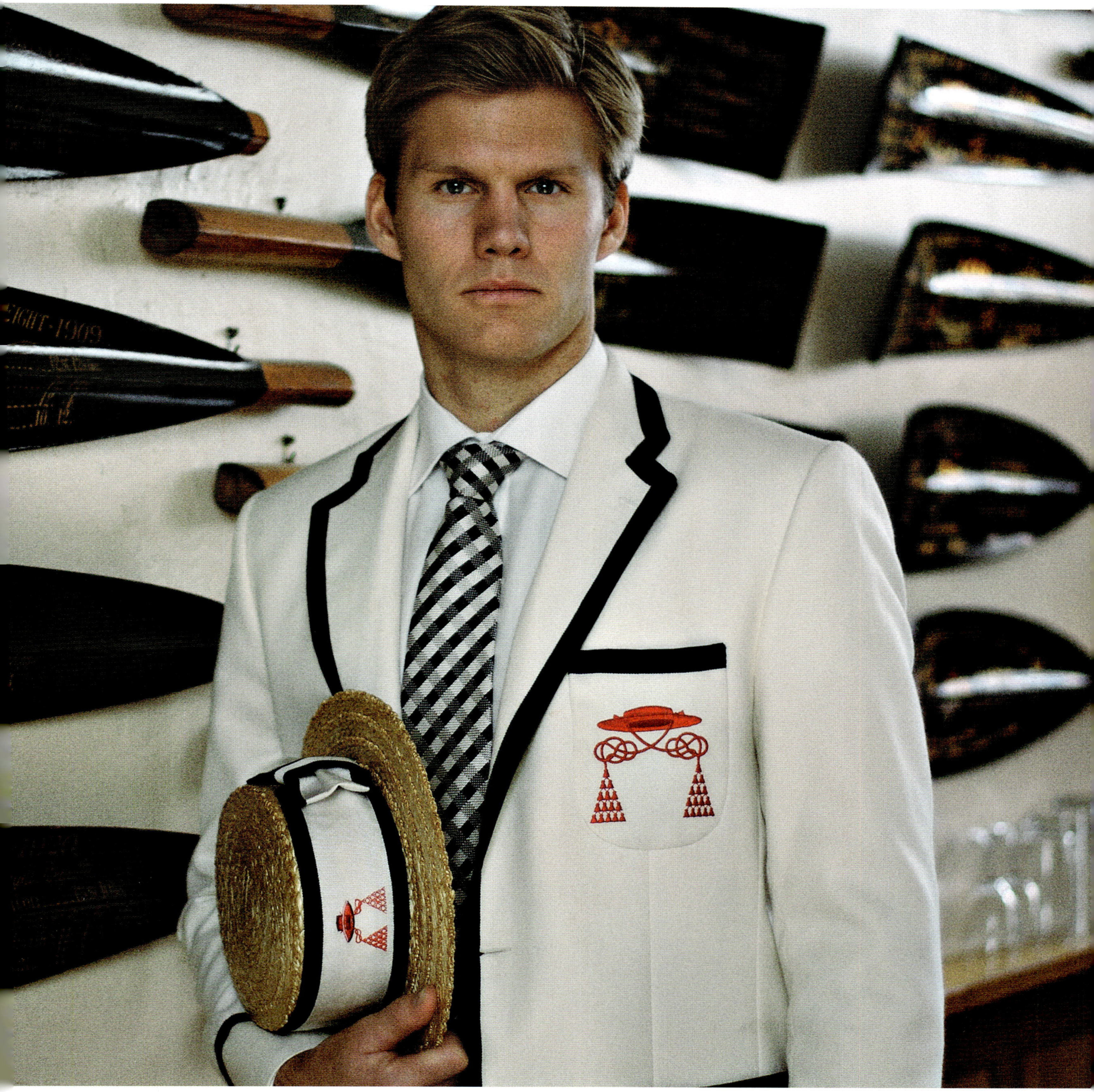

ABOVE: Magnus Prøsch won the Headship in both Torpids and Summer Eights with Christ Church in 2010.
OVERLEAF: Each year, the victorious crew at Oxford's Summer Eights race carries a wooden racing shell from the river back to its college quad, where the boat is set alight. The winning oarsmen and their friends—in bacchanalian revelry—take turns jumping over the burning hull, often singeing their feet and trousers.

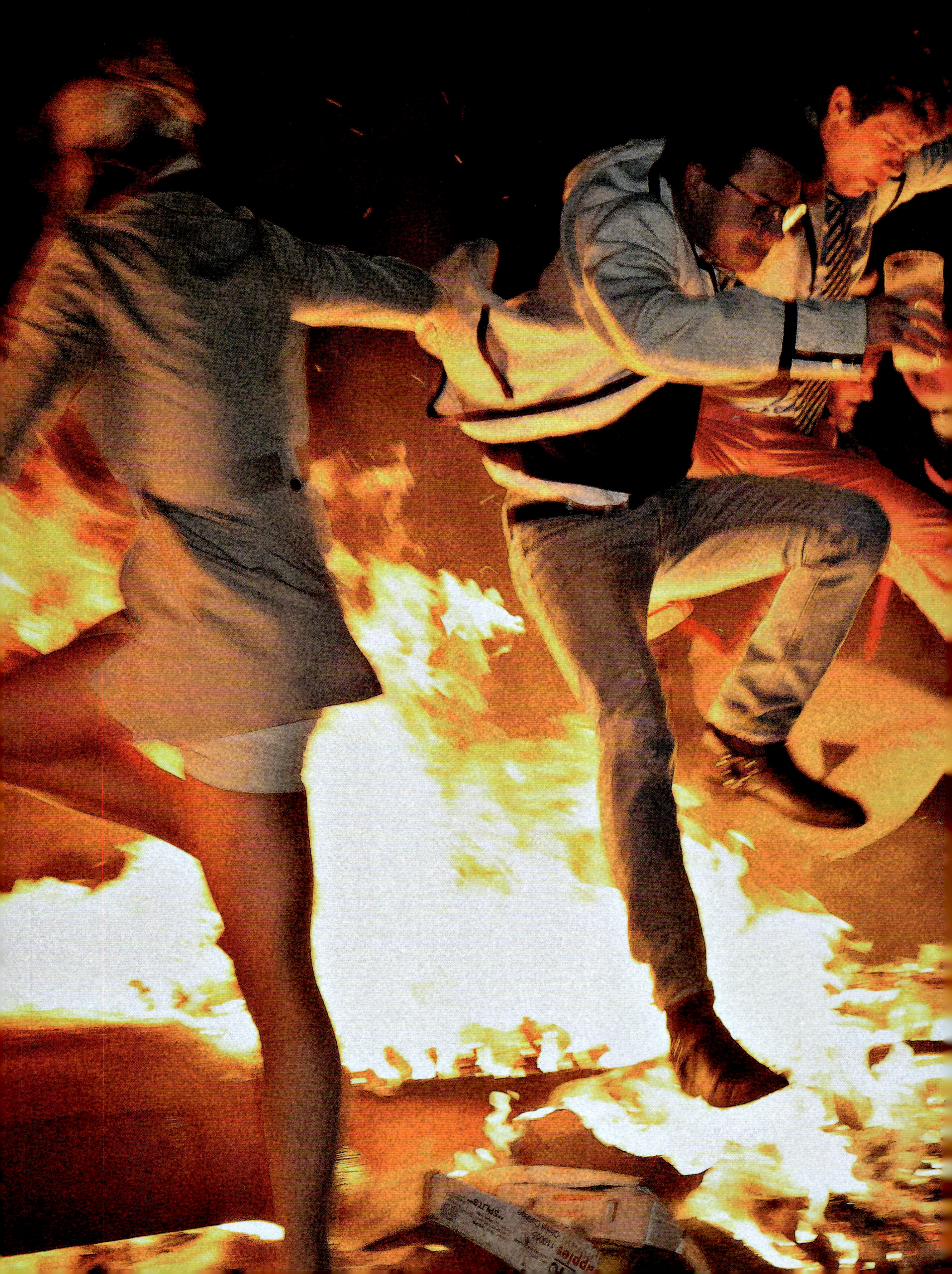

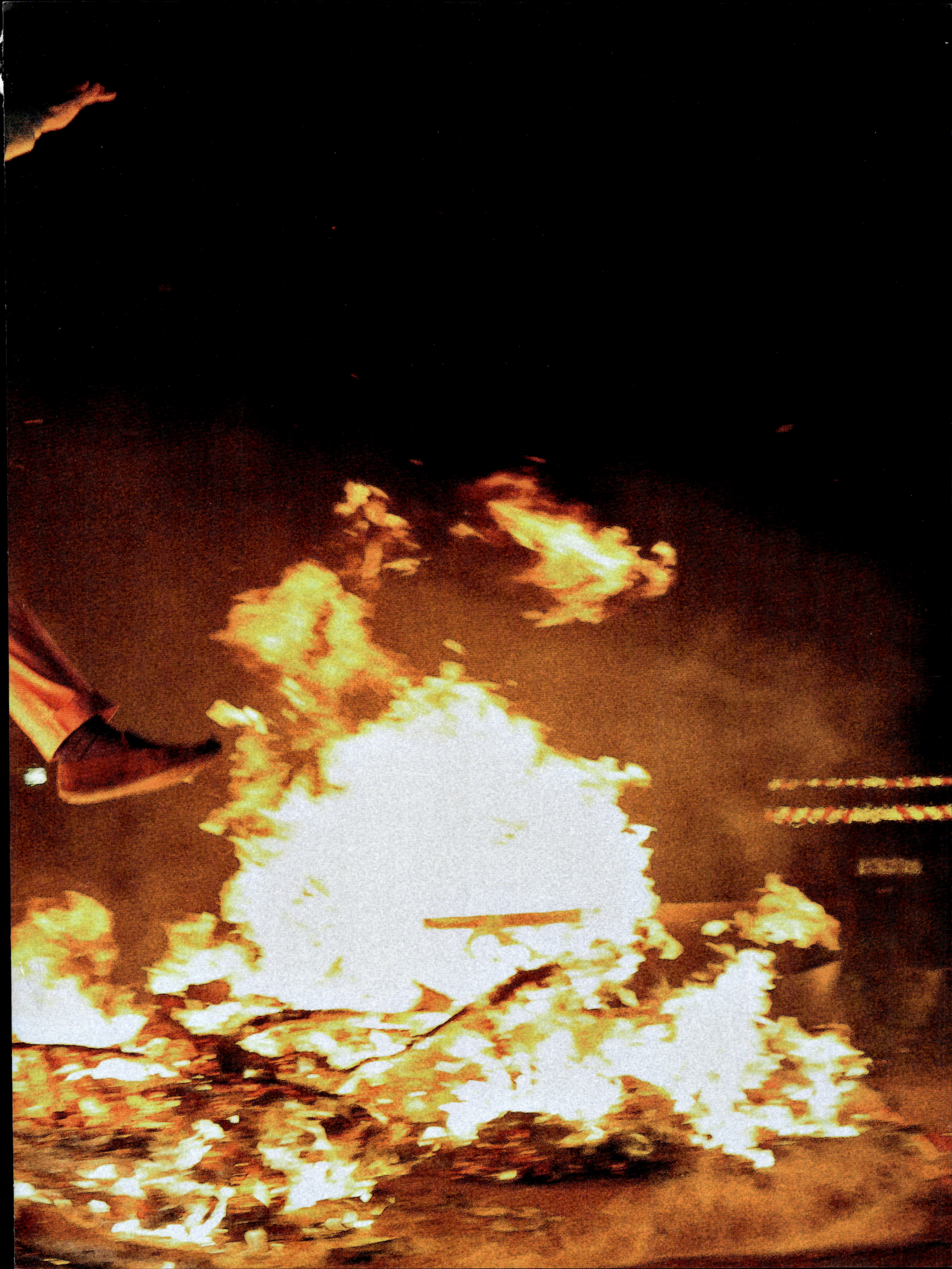

Glossary

blade: A rowing oar; also the wide, flat part of a rowing oar.

Blue (or Full Blue): The sporting award given to sportsmen and -women competing at the varsity level in a major sport at Oxford and Cambridge; equivalent to a varsity letter in the United States. The recipient of such an award may also be called a "Blue." The equivalent for minor sports is a Half-Blue. Other universities, especially in Commonwealth nations, also award Blues and Half-Blues, while the University of London awards Purples and Half Purples. Blazers are the primary manifestations of all of these awards.

Boat Race: The annual match race between the top men's crews from Oxford University and Cambridge University, first contested in 1829 at Henley-on-Thames, now held on the 7.2-kilometer (4¼-mile) championship course on the Thames Tideway in London during the Easter holiday.

bow: The forward section of a boat.

Britannia Challenge Cup: The event (and prize) for club coxed fours at Henley Royal Regatta.

bumping: A racing format (practiced principally by the college boat clubs at Oxford and Cambridge) in which the crews start in single file and each crew attempts to crash, or "bump," into the crew ahead.

coxswain (or cox): A crew member who does not row but is responsible for steering and directing the rest of the crew. The coxswain, usually very light in weight, sits facing forward, either in the stern or the bow of the boat.

crew: The collective members of a given rowing boat. The word is sometimes used incorrectly to refer to the sport of rowing, especially in North America.

Diamond Challenge Sculls: The event (and prize) for men's single sculls at Henley Royal Regatta.

double: A two-person sculling boat; also the crew of such a boat.

Double Sculls Challenge Cup: The event (and prize) for men's double sculls at Henley Royal Regatta.

Eastern Sprints: The annual championship for major university rowing programs in the Eastern and Midwestern United States, contested over 2 kilometers (approximately 1¼ miles) on Lake Quinsigamond in Worcester, Massachusetts, each May.

eight: A sweep rowing boat that is propelled by eight rowers and steered and commanded by one coxswain; the largest boat class. Also the crew of such a boat.

Fawley Challenge Cup: The event (and prize) for junior quads at Henley Royal Regatta.

four: A sweep rowing boat that is propelled by four rowers. Coxed fours are steered and commanded by a coxswain; coxless fours, like other coxless boat classes, are navigated by the rowers themselves. Also the crew of such a boat.

Grand Challenge Cup: The premier event (and prize) at Henley Royal Regatta, for elite men's eights.

Half-Blue: *See* Blue.

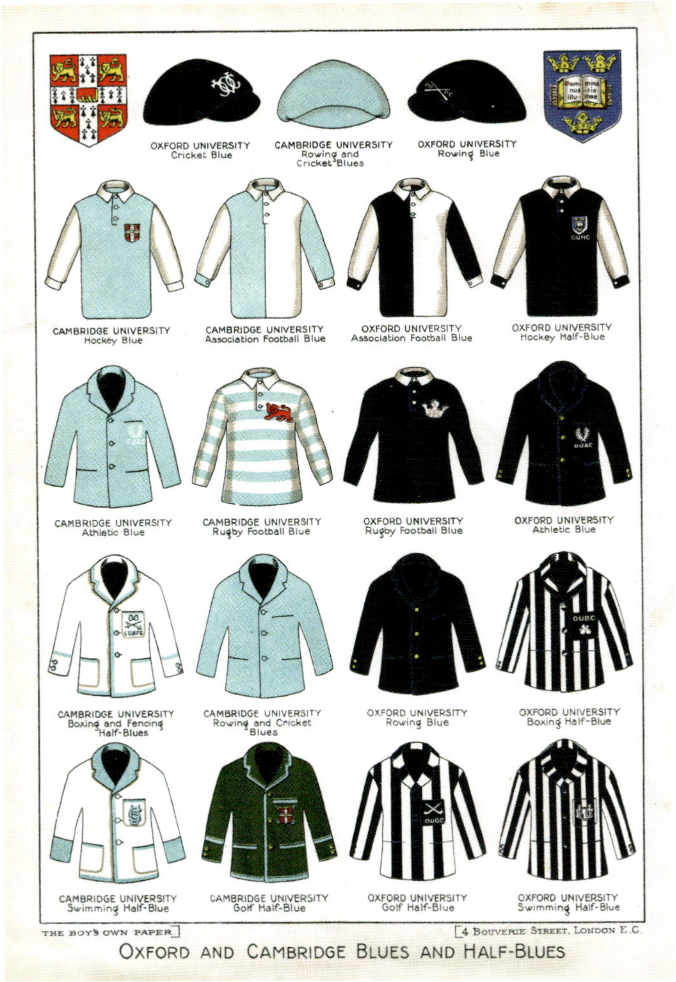

Chart of Oxford and Cambridge Blues and Half-Blues blazers, jerseys, and caps, drawn by V. Wheeler-Holohan for *The Boy's Own Paper*, December 1921.

Head of the Charles Regatta: The two-day series of 4.8-kilometer (3-mile) head races held each October on the Charles River in Massachusetts, first organized in 1964; the largest two-day rowing event in the world.

Head of the River Race: The annual head race for men's eights held each March on the 7.2-kilometer (4¼-mile) Thames Tideway championship course in London, first organized in 1925. More than four hundred eights now compete each year.

head race: A processional racing format in which crews start one after another rather than side by side and compete for time.

Headship: A championship or first-place finish in any of the Oxford and Cambridge bumping races.

heavyweight (or openweight): A crew with no restrictions on the individual or average weight of its members.

Henley Boat Races: The annual Oxford-Cambridge rowing regatta held at Henley-on-Thames during the Easter holiday, in which the principal events are races for the varsity lightweight men's and women's (and, until 2015, openweight women's) crews.

Henley Royal Regatta: The rowing regatta held each summer in Henley-on-Thames on a 2,112-meter (2,310-yard) course. It is run by a self-electing board of Stewards. First organized in 1829, the regatta received royal patronage in 1851. Many oarsmen consider the regatta to be surpassed in prestige only by the World Championships and the Olympic Games. The regatta is also an important part of the English summer social season, along with Wimbledon and Royal Ascot. In the principal viewing area, the Stewards' Enclosure, male spectators are required to wear jackets and ties, and ladies are "encouraged" to wear hats.

Ladies' Challenge Plate: The event (and prize) for intermediate men's eights at Henley Royal Regatta.

Lent Bumps: The secondary intercollegiate bumping race at Cambridge University, held annually in late winter.

lightweight: A crew with restrictions on the individual and/or average weights of its members. In international racing, men's lightweight crews must average 70 kg (154½ lbs.) with no individual weighing more than 72.5 kg (160 lbs.), while women's lightweight crews must average 57 kg (125½ lbs.) with no individual weighing more than 59 kg (130 lbs.).

May Bumps: The principal intercollegiate bumping race at Cambridge University, held annually in late spring.

openweight: *See* heavyweight.

pair: A two-person sweep rowing boat; also the crew of such a boat.

Prince Albert Challenge Cup: The event (and prize) for student coxed fours at Henley Royal Regatta.

Prince of Wales Challenge Cup: The event (and prize) for intermediate quadruple sculls at Henley Royal Regatta.

Princess Elizabeth Challenge Cup: The event (and prize) for school eights at Henley Royal Regatta.

quad: A four-person sculling boat; also the crew of such a boat.

Remenham Challenge Cup: The event (and prize) for women's eights at Henley Royal Regatta.

Ally Brooks and Bethan Walters,
Reading University Boat Club, Reading, England.

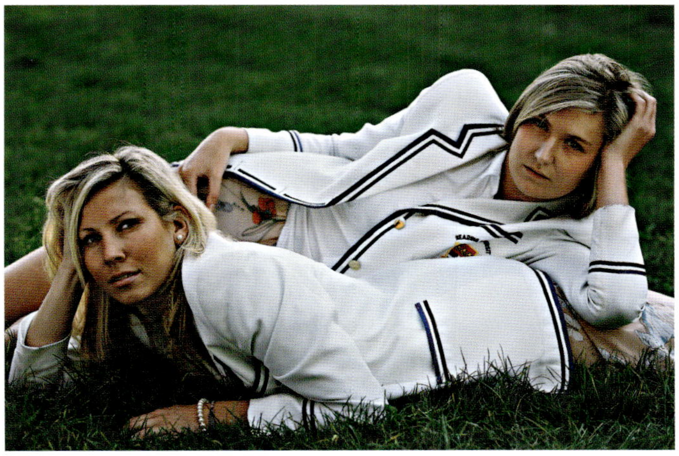

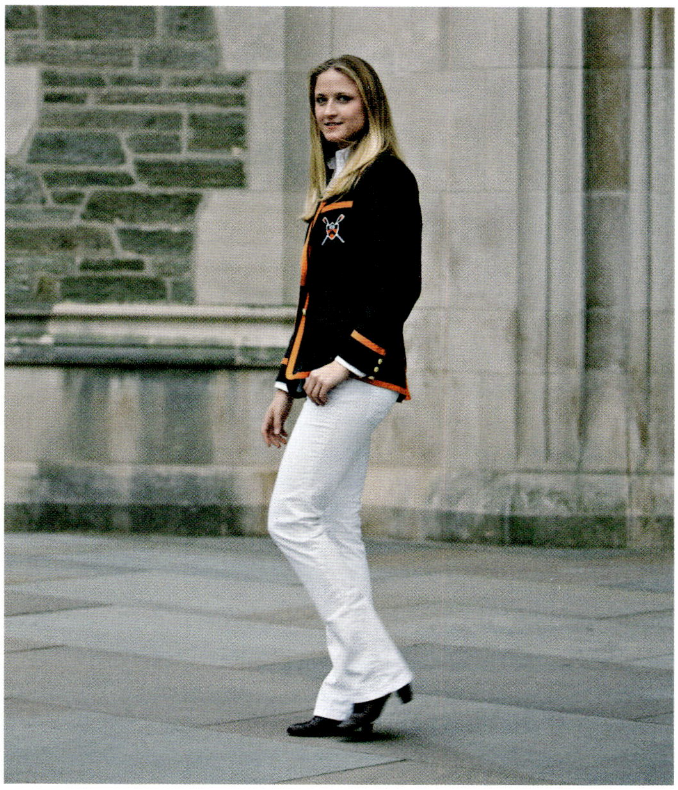

Phoebe White, Princeton University, Princeton, New Jersey.

sculling: The discipline in which each oarsman or -woman uses two rowing blades, one in each hand. The single, double, and quad are sculling boat classes.

shell: Another word for a rowing boat.

single: A one-person sculling boat; the smallest boat class.

stern: The rear section of a boat.

Steward: *See* Henley Royal Regatta.

Stewards' Enclosure: *See* Henley Royal Regatta.

stroke: The rower sitting farthest toward the stern in a rowing boat. Because rowers face backward (toward the stern) in racing shells, the stroke of a crew is responsible for setting the crew's rhythm.

Summer Eights: The principal intercollegiate bumping race at Oxford University, held annually in late spring.

sweep rowing: The discipline in which each oarsman or -woman uses one rowing blade and moves asymmetrically in the boat. The pair, the four, and the eight are sweep rowing boat classes.

Temple Challenge Cup: The event (and prize) for student eights at Henley Royal Regatta.

Thames Challenge Cup: The event (and prize) for club eights at Henley Royal Regatta.

Torpids: The secondary intercollegiate bumping race at Oxford University, held annually in late winter.

Varsity: The major annual regatta for Dutch student rowing clubs, contested over 3 kilometers (approximately 1⅞ miles) on the Amsterdam-Rhine Canal in Houten, first organized in 1883. The principal event is the Senior Four *(Oude Vier)*.

Wyfold Challenge Cup: The event (and prize) for club coxless fours at Henley Royal Regatta.

Selected Bibliography

Allen, G. *The Scallywag*. London: Chatto and Windus, 1895.

Anderson, A. "Doctor Rowing." *Rowing News*, September 2011: 61.

"Argonaut." *The Arts of Rowing and Training*. London: Horace Cox, 1866.

Ashby-Sterry, J. "Henley in July." *Punch*, July 1884: 86–87.

Atchison, G. T., and G. C. Brown. *The History of the Christ's College Boat Club*. Cambridge: Spalding, 1922.

Ball, W.W.R. *A History of the First Trinity Boat Club*. Cambridge: Bowse & Bowse, 1908.

Barr, A., and P. York. *The Official Sloane Ranger Handbook*. London: Ebury Press, 1982.

Birnbach, L. *The Official Preppy Handbook*. New York: Workman, 1980.

———. *True Prep*. New York: Alfred A. Knopf, 2010.

Blandford-Baker, M. *Upon the Elysian Stream: 150 Years of Magdalen College Boat Club*. Oxford: Magdalen College, 2008.

Blake, R. *In Black and White: A History of Rowing at Trinity College, Dublin*. Dublin: Dublin University Boat Club, 1991.

Boyer, G. B. "The Perfect Blazer." *The Rake*, October–November, 2010: 102–15.

Brittain, F., and H. Playford. *The Jesus College Cambridge Boat Club 1827–1962*. Cambridge: Heffer and Sons, 1962.

Buckrich, J. *Well Rowed University: Melbourne University Boat Club, the First 150 Years*. Melbourne: Melbourne University Boat Club, 2009.

Bundgaard, A. *Muscle and Manliness: The Rise of Sport in American Boarding Schools*. Syracuse, NY: Syracuse University Press, 2005.

Burnell, R. *One Hundred and Fifty Years of the Oxford and Cambridge Boat Race*. Marlow, Buckinghamshire, UK: Precision Press, 1979.

Burnell, R., and G. Page. *The Brilliants: A History of the Leander Club*. Henley-on-Thames: Leander Club, 1997.

Cambridge Boat Club: A Centennial History 1909–2009. Cambridge, MA: Cambridge Boat Club, 2009.

Cambridge University General Almanack & Register. Cambridge: Henry Wallis, 1853–1880.

Campbell, L. *Eton Colours*. London: Essential Works, 2008.

Coit, J. H., and G. C. Shattuck. *Memorials of St. Paul's School*. New York: D. Appleton, 1891.

Cook, E. *Eliza Cook's Journal*, vol. 9. London: J. O. Clarke, 1853.

Cook, T. A., and G. Nickalls. *Thomas Doggett Deceased*. London: A. Constable, 1908.

Crook, J. M. *Brasenose: The Biography of an Oxford College*. Oxford: Oxford University Press, 2008.

Crouch, R. G. *The Coat*. Victoria, British Columbia: Trafford, 2005.

Dalton, C., and A. Reford. "Olympic Games Medal 1912." In *New College Record 2001*. Edited by P. Williams. Oxford: New College, 2001, 44–45.

Dodd, C. *The Oxford & Cambridge Boat Race*. London: Stanley Paul, 1983.

Dodd, C., and J. Marks. *Battle of the Blues*. London: P to M, 2004.

Douglas, J. *Rowing on the Cam*. Barton, Cambridgeshire, UK: Bird's Farm Publications, 1977.

Dowd, M. "Always an England." *New York Times*, July 4, 1993.

Durack, J., G. Gilbert, and J. Marks. *The Bumps: An Account of the Cambridge University Bumping Races 1827–1999*. London: Butler and Tanner, 2000.

Eliot, T. H. *Two Schools in Cambridge: The Story of Browne & Nichols and Buckingham*. Cambridge, MA: Windflower Press, 1982.

Farmer, J. S. *The Public School Word-Book*. London: Hirschfeld Brothers, 1900.

Foster, R. H., et al. *The History of the Lady Margaret Boat Club*. Cambridge: Johnian Society, 1926.

Frost, R. *Christ Church Boat Club*. N.p., n.d.

Garran, D. K. *A History of Collegiate Rowing in America*. Atglen, PA.: Schiffer, 2012.

Glyn, A. *I Can Take It All*. London: Hutchinson, 1959.

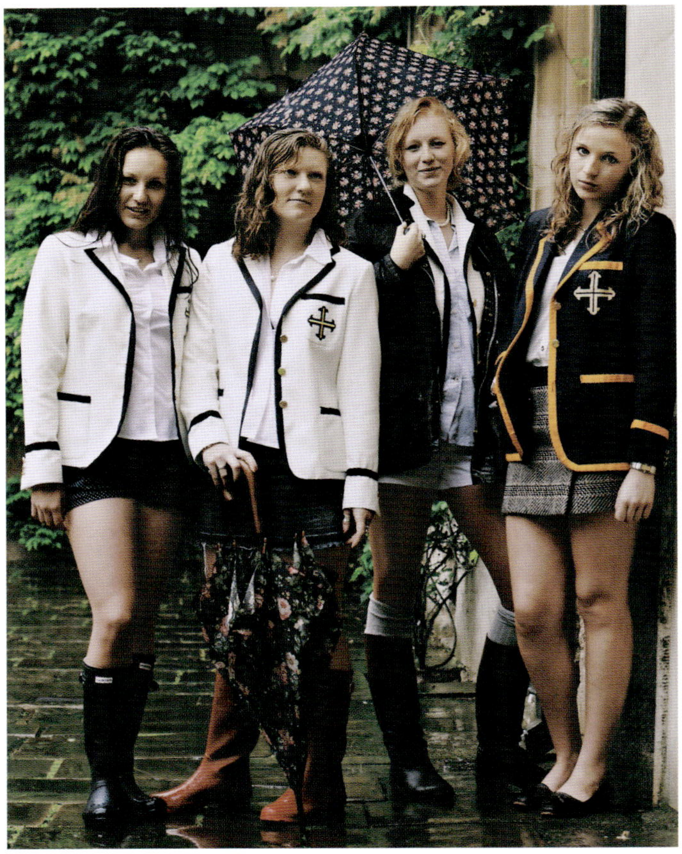

Laura Oakley, Aimee Campbell, Poppy Smith, and Hannah Roberts, Oxford, England, University College Boat Club, Oxford.

Goldstein, R. "Joe Burk, 93, Won Honors on Thames and in Pacific, Is Dead." *New York Times*, January 22, 2008.

Gregory, K., ed. *The Second Cuckoo: A Further Selection of Witty, Amusing and Memorable Letters to "The Times."* London: Allen & Unwin, 1983.

Hamilton, F. *Vanished Pomps of Yesterday*. New York: George H. Doran, 1921.

Harding Davis, R. *Adventures and Letters of Richard Harding Davis*. New York: Charles Scribner's Sons, 1917.

Hopkins, C., and B. Ward-Perkins. "The Trinity/Balliol Feud." *Trinity College Oxford Report 1989–90*: 45–66.

Hutchins, R. *"Well Rowed Magdalen!": A History of Magdalen College Boat Club, 1859–1993*. Oxford: Magdalen College, 1993.

Jeaffreson, J. C. *Crewe-Rise*, vol. 3. London: Hurst and Blackett, 1854.

Jerome, J. K. *Three Men in a Boat (To Say Nothing of the Dog)*. New York: H. Holt and Company, 1890.

Jones, J. *Balliol College: A History*. Oxford: Oxford University Press, 1997.

Joukowsky, A., H. Ambler, D. Philips, C. Albert, and M. Hooper. *Ever True: The History of Brown Crew*. Providence: Brown University Sports Foundation, 2010.

Korda, M. *Hero: The Life and Legend of Lawrence of Arabia*. New York: HarperCollins, 2010.

Lee, J. J. *The Measure of a Man: The Story of a Father, a Son, and a Suit*. Toronto: McClelland & Stewart, 2011.

Livingston, D., and J. Livingston. *Blood Over Water*. London: Bloomsbury, 2009.

Maglaty, J. "When Did Girls Start Wearing Pink?" *Smithsonian*, April 8, 2011.

Mallory, P. *The Sport of Rowing: Two Centuries of Competition*. 4 vols. Henley-on-Thames: River and Rowing Museum, 2011.

Mangan, J. A., and H. Fan. *Sport in Asian Society Past and Present*. London: Frank Cass, 2003.

Mansfield, A. "Blazers." *Costume* 5, no. 1, 1971: 25–28.

McFarland, M. "A Study of the Friends of Dartmouth Rowing Boathouse." 2013. http://friendsofdartmouthrowing.blogspot.co.uk/2013/03/part-1-introducing-study-of-friends-of.html

Mendenhall, T. C. *A Short History of American Rowing*. Boston: Charles River Books, 1981.

———. *The Harvard-Yale Boat Race, 1852–1924: And the Coming of Sport to the American College*. Mystic, CT: Mystic Seaport Museum, 1993.

Merton, T. *My Argument with the Gestapo: A Macaronic Journal*. New York: Doubleday, 1969.

Morison, S. E. *Three Centuries of Harvard, 1636–1936*. Cambridge, MA: Harvard University Press, 1936.

Mortimer, R. G. *A History of Rowing at Abingdon School*. London: Coombe, 1990.

Muggeridge, M. *Chronicles of Wasted Time*. London: Collins, 1972.

Nelson, I. "Introduction." *Queen's Rowing*. http://www.queensrowing.org/Resources/Documents/History/Queens-Rowing-History-1-1864.pdf

The Oxford University Almanack and Register. Oxford: J. Vincent, 1857–1909.

"Paulinus." "Oxford Snobs." *Magdalen College School Journal* 1, no. 8, March 1871.

Piggott, J., et al. *Dulwich College: A History, 1616–2008*. London: Dulwich College, 2008.

Reford, A. "N. C. Boat Club and the 1911 Olympics." In *New College Record 1986*. Edited by P. Williams. Oxford: New College, 15–21.

Rinehart, R. *Men of Kent: Ten Boys, a Fast Boat, and the Coach Who Made Them Champions*. Guilford, CT: Lyons Press, 2010.

Roberts, E. S. "The Boat Club." In *Biographical History of Gonville and Caius College, 1349–1897*, vol. 3. Edited by J. Venn. Cambridge: Cambridge University Press, 1901, 306–10.

Rosenbladt, O. "Badgers, Big Red Win National Titles." *Row2k*, June 2008. http://row2k.com/ira/features.cfm?ID=280#.UiUfHGRASnY

Royal Hong Kong Yacht Club. "History." 2014. http://www.rhkyc.org.hk/History.aspx

Saint Sing, S. *The Wonder Crew: The Untold Story of a Coach, Navy Rowing, and Olympic Immortality*. New York: St. Martin's Press, 2008.

Scott, H. C. *A History of the Caius College Boat Club 1827–1927*. Cambridge: Cambridge University Press, 1927.

Sherwood, W. E. *Oxford Rowing: A History of Boat-Racing at Oxford from the Earliest Times*. Oxford: Henry Frowde, 1900.

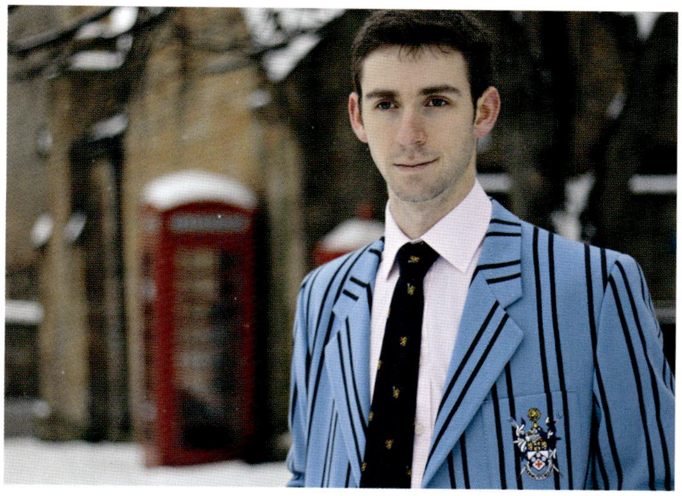

William Moreland, Hild Bede Boat Club, Durham, Durham, England.

Shoumatoff, A. "A Private School Affair." *Vanity Fair*, January 2006: 136ff.

Smith, G. *The English Companion*. London: Pavilion Books, 1984.

Smith, L. C., F. T. Prior, W. T. Lord, L. E. Reay, J. M. Sing, W. E. Sherwood, M. T. Perks, et al. *Annals of Public School Rowing*. Oxford: Blackwell, 1919.

Southworth, R., and G. Tanis. "The Impossible Dream: Crew at Dartmouth." 1986. http://friendsofdartmouthrowing.blogspot.co.uk/2012/12/the-impossible-dream-crew-at-dartmouth.html

Stewart, H. M. "Notes on the Word Blazer." *The Cambridge Review*, June 3, 1950: 582–83.

Storey, N. *History of Men's Fashion: What the Well Dressed Man Is Wearing*. Barnsley, South Yorkshire, UK: Pen and Sword Books, 2008.

Swanson, R. N. *A History of Christ's College Boat Club 1830–1980*. Cambridge: Christ's College, 1982.

Taylor, B. F. *Wisconsin Where They Row*. Madison: University of Wisconsin Press, 2005.

Topolski, D. *Boat Race: The Oxford Revival*. London: Collins Willow, 1985.

Travis, A. "Clare Boat Club." In *Clare through the Twentieth Century: Portrait of a Cambridge College*. Edited by L. Shaw-Miller. Lingfield, Surrey, UK: Third Millennium, 2001.

Wells, H. B. *Vesta Rowing Club: A Centenary History*. London: Vesta Rowing Club, 1969.

Wells, J. *Wadham College*. London: Robinson, 1898.

Whiting, C. E. *The University of Durham 1832–1932*. London: Sheldon Press 1932.

Wulf, S. "Title Waves." *ESPN The Magazine*. June 11, 2012.

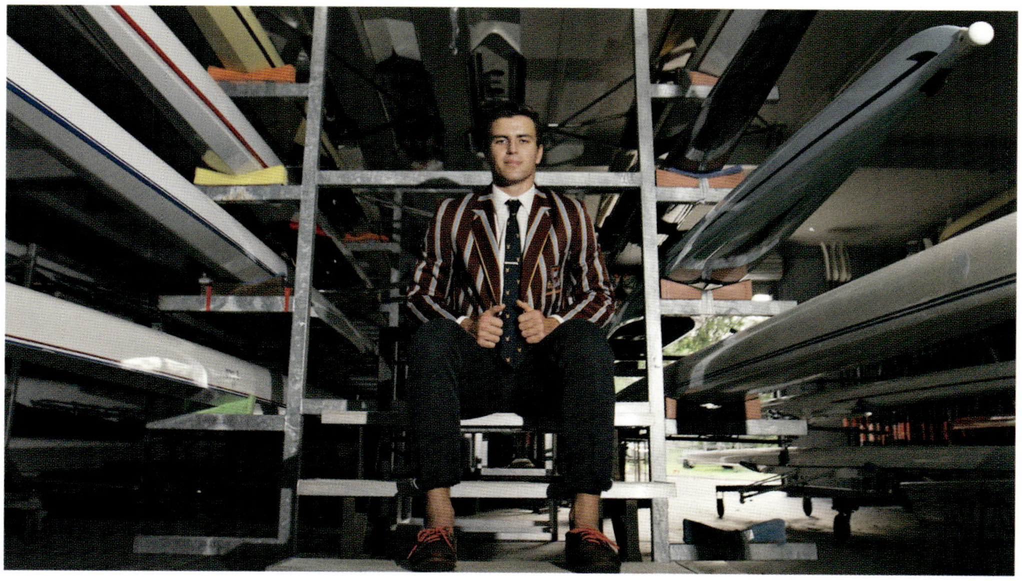

Harry Baxter, University of Queensland Boat Club, Brisbane, Australia.

Acknowledgments

To my parents

There are very many people—too many to list, in fact—without whom this book would not have been possible. First and foremost, thank you to all of the rowers and coxswains who were photographed for the book, including those whose pictures regrettably didn't end up in the final cut of the book. Thank you also to all of the captains, coaches, secretaries, committees, managers, and staff at the clubs featured in the book for all of your help. Thank you to all of the photographers whose beautiful images appear in the book and have made it a work of art. Very special thanks to George Carr, Victoria Stulgis, Carly Heitlinger, Jill Carlson, Alan Kaufman, Denise Seegal, Mark Magowan, Jamie Camplin, Rebecca Preece, Bodo Schulenburg, Boris Le Feber, Carole Sargent, Andy Craig, Ben Duggan, Graham Benton, Ross Hunter, Cameron and Tyler Winklevoss, Jackie Decter, Mark Melnick, Meghan Phillips, Irene Convey, Laura Willis, Rowena Stanyer, Natalie Evans, Sir Steve Redgrave, Jim Davis, Jason Read, Jason Nickel, Michiel Jonkman, Melissa Noucas, Rory Copus, Timo Völker, Eric Wind, Kenny McMahon, Tim Koch, Tom Gunter, Oli Williams, Suzie Tilbury, Peter Fiore, Tom Weil, Chris Dodd, Larry Mahoney, Charlie Davidson, Kristie Shemilt, John Calcagno, Oxford University Lightweight Rowing Club, Oxford Brookes University Boat Club, and Taurus Boat Club, as well as all of the following: Max Lau, Tex Holden-Smith, Andrew Glenn, Till Wirth, Leslie Noteboom, Jonathan Lewis, Jonny Pearson-Stuttard, Alex Woods, Scott Armstrong, Hardy Cubasch, Mia van Manen, Ben Mansfield, Jeremy Howick, Eric Houston, Stacy Thompson, Molly Somers, Emma Twigg, Amy Chuckrow, Jonathan Stulgis, Jay Alsing, Nathan O'Reilly, Karl Hudspith, Jim Glavin, Henry Goodier, Freddy Foks, Al Heathcote, Leander Club, Ellie Piggott, Robert Treharne Jones, Robin Ejsmond-Frey, Robin Bourne-Taylor CGC, Andy Triggs-Hodge, Jasper Warner, Mr. and Mrs. Hudspith, the Martons, Olivia Carnegie-Brown, Oli Cooke, Sophie Hosking, Ollie Holt, Callum Arnold, Jon Carley, Jonny Waite, Tilly King, Andy Anderson, Henry Hoffstot, Sean Redmond, Carlos Schuster, Gabriel Doran, Natalie Redgrave, George Blessley, Federico Casper, Fred Schoch, Anthony Petrillose, Jerry Lauren, Helen Thorne, Richard Thorne Classic Cars, Ben Reed, Hannah Patterson, Brianna Stubbs, Tom Smith, Lottie Stables, Jonny Ranstrand, Cheryl Vyvan, Toby Ryan, Richard Brown, Lindsey Barrington, Matt Stoller, Lizzie Quinn Brown, Tommy Hilfiger, Suzanne Cole, Fiona Godber, Adam White, Anna Heimbichner, Tom George, Charles Elwes, Alex Macintosh, Nick Zdrzalka, Imro Dawson, Dirk-Jan Fokkens, Pjotr Kerssens, Gevvie Stone, Zack Kurland, Danny Longman, Mike Guerrieri, Peter Nordberg, Sylvia Lassam, Andrew Cusack, Jennifer Thorp, Mark Blandford-Baker, Paul Guest, Ed Matthews, Paul Budd OBE, Olly Cox, Ryan Patton, Sandy Paul, Paul Garberson, Ray Del Bianco, Martin Copus, Rebecca Scown, Clive Cheesman, Richard Spratley, Lindsay Moreton, Paul Mainds, Oli Staite, Henry Bailhache-Webb, Eloise Chapman, Erwin Cardol, Rob Petre, Peter Haining, Juliette Drysdale, Alan Marron, Amber Morley, Allison Phua, Henry Edgar, Joe Ghory, Peter Fraser, Paul Crewe, Aimee Campbell, Ian Wilson, Peter Spurrier, Jory Cordy, Talia Lehmann, Erik Dresser, Rob Milam, Nick LaCava, Matt Burrard-Lucas, Tom Kay, Christine Cornege, Eric Murray, Ben Myers, Bill Manning, Harry Parker, Marc Mandel, Auriol Kensington Rowing Club, Father Tom King SJ, Colin McAllister, Ken Weinstein, Dan Roock, Paul Tong, Erika Pergel, Rob von Mesdag, Terry Morahan, Peter Mallory, Professor Boris Rankov, Mary Murray, Natalie Mastracci, Sam Albanie, Zsofi Novak, Roland Symons, John Gearing, John Glavin, Ed Hewitt, Scott Smith, Bruno Nicolis, Fabio Ferrandini, Zeno Ferrandini, Jim Kloiber, Phyllis Roback London, Jeff Trosch, Marisa Drew, Andrew Stanley, and many others who have lent a helping hand along the way.

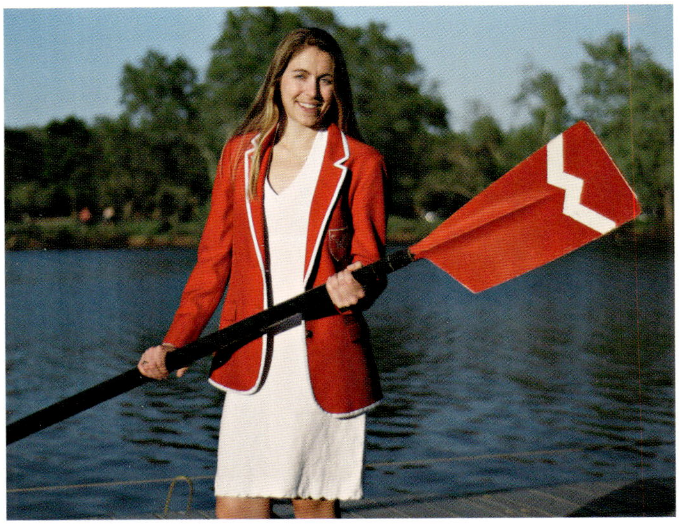

Gevvie Stone, Winsor School, Boston, Massachusetts.

Index

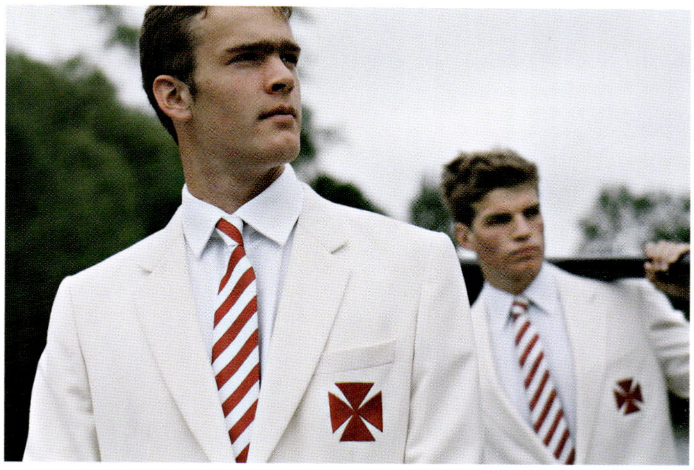

Charlie Elwes and Tom George, Radley College Boat Club, Radley, England.

Except for the following, all photos by F.E. Castleberry / © Carlson Media Inc. Carlson Media Inc. reserves all rights to these images.

The Collection of Thomas E. Weil: 1; Urša Mali / © Carlson Media Inc.: 4, 15, 36 bottom, 37, 44, 52–53, 54, 56–57, 68, 75, 88, 100, 122, 126, 127, 132, 145, 158 left, 159, 166 top, 167 bottom, 170, 184 bottom, 199, 201, 209, 212 top, 214, 215 226, 236, 237, 238, 252, 253 top; Adrian Krajewski / © Carlson Media Inc.: 6, 20, 21, 30–31, 36 top, 51, 55, 66–67, 70, 72, 73, 74, 97, 101, 118, 141, 148, 149, 158 right, 166 bottom, 167 top, 175 right, 184 top right, 194–95, 198 bottom, 205, 206, 212 bottom, 213, 217, 224, 234, 235, 246–47, 255, endpapers; © River & Rowing Museum: 8–9, 10 bottom, 14; Gift of the British American Arts Association from the Collection of Thomas E Weil: 10 top; Courtesy of Sabrina Club / Nick Randall: 11; Courtesy of the Master and Fellows of Trinity College Cambridge: 12; The Collection of Peter Andrew Henry: 13, 163 top, 250; The Collection of Tim Koch: 16; Courtesy of Oriel College Archives and Gillman & Soame: 17; Christopher Furlong / © Getty Images: 22–23; A.R.V. Westfalen / © Carlson Media Inc.: 32, 33; © row2k Media: 46–47, 106, 156–57, 172–73, 222–23, 242–43, 245; © Peter Spurrier / Intersport Images: 58–59, 138–39, 177, 241; Michal Plotkowiak: 69; Matthew Burrard-Lucas / © Carlson Media Inc.: 71, 182–83; Mark Kelsey / © Carlson Media Inc.: 77, 108, 178 left, 254; Joseph Lee / © Carlson Media Inc.: 80 bottom; © Gerard Brown: 84; Jory Cordy / © Carlson Media Inc.: 102, 103, 112, 113; Chris Bien / © Carlson Media Inc.: 109; Suzanne Gell / © Carlson Media Inc.: 110 left, 110–11, 228–29; Jack Carlson: 123; Nick Morris / © Carlson Media Inc.: 124, 125; Christine Cornege / © Carlson Media Inc.: 146, 147, 225; Ruth Cook / © Carlson Media Inc.: 150, 151; Alex Hutchinson / © Carlson Media Inc.: 160, 162; Dublin University Ladies Boat Club: 163 bottom; Steffan Hill / © Carlson Media Inc.: 168, 169; Karl Bratby: 192; Lisa Mininni / © Carlson Media Inc.: 208; Erwin Cardol / NLRoei: 232–33; Richer Sea Photography: 248–49; Thiago Theophilo / © Carlson Media Inc.: 253 (bottom)

All image licensing inquiries should be directed to Carlson Media Inc.: CarlsonMediaInc@gmail.com

Page 1: Walter Erskine "Crumbo" Crum, caricatured in his Oxford University Boat Club blazer by "Spy" in *Vanity Fair,* March 19, 1896.

Page 2: Ellie Piggott and Brianna Stubbs, Wallingford Rowing Club, gold medalists in the lightweight women's double sculls at the under-23 world championship in 2013 (see pages 170–71).

Page 4: Two-time Olympic gold medalist Tom James MBE in his Cambridge Archetypals blazer.

First published in the United Kingdom in 2014 by
THAMES & HUDSON LTD
181A High Holborn, London WC1V 7QX

Thank you to Collier & Robinson, Henley-on-Thames, for permission to photograph their badges for the endpapers.

Editor: Jacqueline Decter · *Production Editor:* Irene Convey · *Designer:* Mark Melnick

BRITISH LIBRARY CATALOGUING-IN-PUBLICATION DATA
A catalogue record for this book is available from the British Library

ISBN 978-0-500-51755-0

Printed in China by OGI

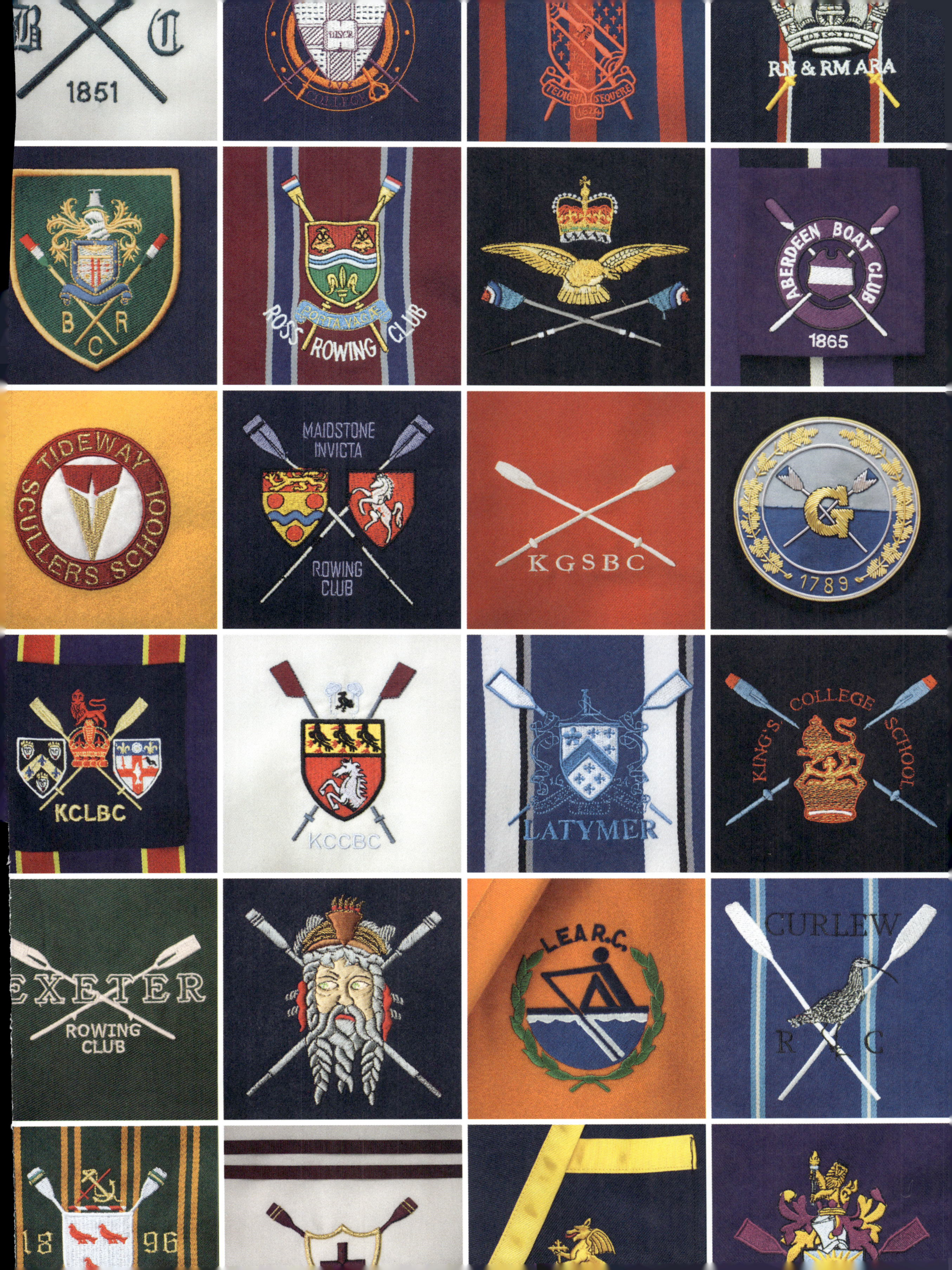
1851
RN & RM ARA
ROSS ROWING CLUB
ABERDEEN BOAT CLUB
1865
TIDEWAY SCULLERS SCHOOL
MAIDSTONE INVICTA
ROWING CLUB
KGSBC
1789
KCLBC
KCCBC
LATYMER
KING'S COLLEGE SCHOOL
EXETER
ROWING CLUB
L.E.A.R.C.
CURLEW
R C
18 96

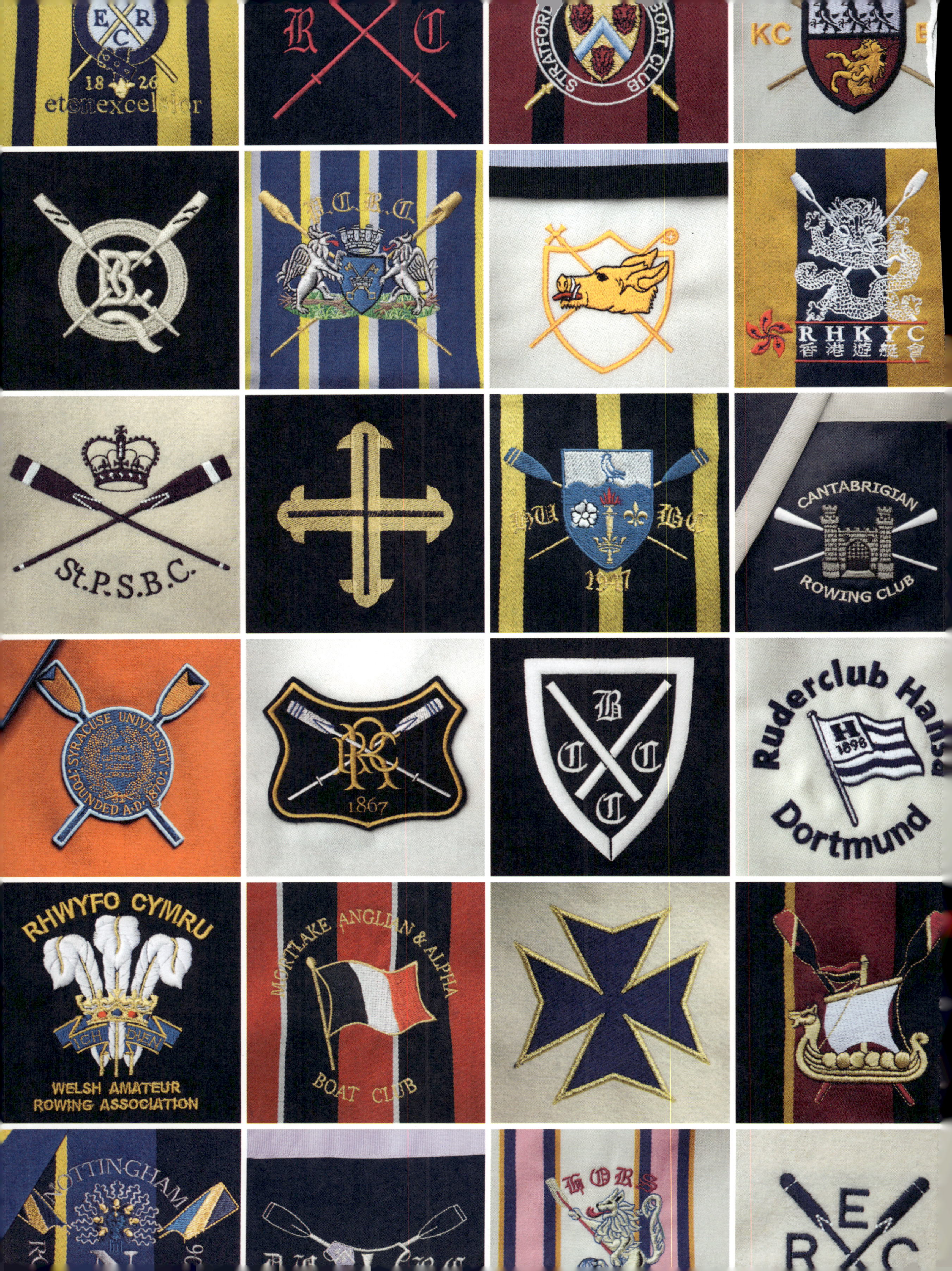
E R C
18 26
R C
BOAT CLUB
KC
RHKYC
香港遊艇會
St.P.S.B.C.
CANTABRIGIAN
ROWING CLUB
SYRACUSE UNIVERSITY
FOUNDED A.D. 1870
1867
B C C C
Ruderclub
H 1898
Dortmund
RHWYFO CYMRU
ICH DIEN
WELSH AMATEUR
ROWING ASSOCIATION
MORTLAKE ANGLIAN & ALPHA
BOAT CLUB
NOTTINGHAM
E R C